The
CONVICT
THEATRES
of
EARLY
AUSTRALIA
1788-1840

The
CONVICT
THEATRES
of
EARLY
AUSTRALIA
1788-1840

ROBERT JORDAN

UNIVERSITY OF HERTFORDSHIRE PRESS

First published in Great Britain in 2003 by
University of Hertfordshire Press
Learning and Information Services
University of Hertfordshire
College Lane
Hatfield
Hertfordshire ALIO 9AB

First published in Australia by
Currency House 2002

British Library Cataloguing-in-Publication-Data.
A catalogue record for this book is available from the British Library.

ISBN 1 902806 25 5

Book and cover design by Kate Florance
Set in Garamond 11/13.2
Endpapers: British Settlements at Port Jackson, &c. Inset on J. Aspin: A Chart of
New South Wales, Van Diemen's Land, &c. Surveys in the Interior of New South
Wales. J. Aspin del. Hewitt sculp. Buckingham Place, 1821.
Printed in Australia by Ligare Pty Ltd, Sydney

Contents

List of Illustrations

Acknowledgments

My heartfelt thanks must go to Kathy Arnold, who prepared the manuscript of this book for the publishers. I shall be forever grateful to her for her tolerance in the face of my obsessive tinkering with the text, and for the reassurance she provided by being interested in the contents.

My friend and colleague John Golder made a major contribution to this book by undertaking a complete and meticulous check of the text and apparatus for inconsistencies, infelicities and any form of slovenliness – all of this while engaged on research projects of his own. No doubt some of my inaccuracies will have escaped even his eagle eye, but his extraordinary helpfulness and enthusiasm are things I shall always value.

At Currency Press I was faced with the need to cut the text by 30,000 words. In this situation the publisher, Katharine Brisbane, came to my assistance and devoted what must have amounted to weeks of her time to making preliminary cuts and then responding to my adjustments to those cuts. It was a remarkable act of generosity, carried through with unwavering good humour. Currency's Claire Grady and Kate Florance also deserve my thanks for coping so cheerfully with a perfectionist author and his impatient assistant, and so does Margaret Leask, whose generous backstage assistance has not gone unnoticed. Alan Walker, as one would expect, has provided the book with a meticulous and comprehensive index.

This book is a product of my time at the University of New South Wales. I owe a great debt of gratitude to that institution. While engaged on it, all other research projects went by the board, and my publication output withered away – this at a time when maximising the number of publications was of critical importance to the University, the Faculty and the School. I was never made to feel uncomfortable at devoting so much time to such a long-term project, and all levels of the University gave me support, in funds or in kind, to pursue the project.

At the very beginning of this research I also received a two-year grant from the ARGC, as it then was. The organisation has had to wait a long time to see the results of its benificence. I can only hope those results justify its commitment.

In 1996 I was invited to deliver a report on my still embryonic research, at James Cook University, in the form of the Colin Roderick Lectures for that year. Considering Professor Roderick's own contributions to the study of convict theatre, through his work on the convict novelist and playwright James Tucker, there was a particular appropriateness to the occasion. I am extremely grateful for the honour the University extended to me, and for the friendliness and hospitality I experienced during my visit.

I have never had anything but helpfulness and courtesy from the vast range of librarians and archivists who have been called upon for assistance. Major debts are owed to the Mitchell Library, State Library of New South Wales; the British Library; the State Records of New South Wales and the Public Record Office, London; but brief visits to institutions such as the Archives of Tasmania and the State Library of Tasmania; the Tyne and Wear Archives; the Genealogical Society, London; and many others were not only fruitful but also pleasant. Selecting individuals to thank for their professional services in these institutions may be invidious, but at the risk of this I would like to express my gratitude to David Pollock of the Mitchell Library and Fabian Lo Schiavo of the State Records of New South Wales.

A great many friends and fellow scholars contributed either through general support or through valuable advice on specific points. Among these are Margaret Williams, Janis Balodis, John McCallum, Jim Davis, Richard Waterhouse, Grace Karskens, Veronica Kelly, Richard Fotheringham, Helen Tiffin, Paul Ranger, Hilary Golder, Harold Love, Brian Siversen, Gillian Winter, and, in the last days of the enterprise, Kalman Burnim and Warwick Gould.

I would like to think of my late friend and colleague, Philip Parsons, as a benign presence hovering over this book. Philip was the unwitting instrument of my partial conversion from English Restoration comedy to convict theatre. While preparing the ground-breaking *Companion to Theatre in Australia*, he asked me to write an entry on the first European theatrical production in Australia, which happened to be of a Restoration comedy. I declined, on the grounds that there was nothing that I could find out about the production that went beyond the readily available. My curiosity, however, had been aroused, and received a further prodding from Thomas Keneally's *The Playmaker*. As will be obvious, I never did find out a great deal about that first production of 1789, but from there I was led into more fruitful fields, from Sidaway's playhouse of 1796 to Maconochie's provocative gesture of 1840. So, thank you, Philip (and thanks, Tom Keneally).

Finally, but not least (as should be obvious), my thanks to Doctors Ronald Watts, Stephen Mulligan, James Isbister and Chris Ward, as well as the staff of the Concord and Royal North Shore Hospitals, for keeping me alive to finish this work and, hopefully, future projects to which I am now turning.

RJ
June 2002

Preliminary Notes

Australia in the Convict Era

On 13 May 1787 a fleet of 11 ships sailed from Portsmouth with over 1400 convicts, sailors, soldiers and officials to set up a penal colony at Botany Bay, on the east coast of Australia. It was to be the first European settlement in the continent.

The location was chosen on a casual impression of the area's fertility gained by Captain James Cook and Sir Joseph Banks in 1770. There was no further investigation of the site and no clear directive how the convicts were to be organised, though the assumption was that they would be employed chiefly in agriculture and would rapidly become self-sufficient, radically reducing the costs of penal servitude to the British government.

As it happened, Botany Bay, and the area nearby, to which the settlement was rapidly transferred, were particularly infertile. The convict establishment never became self-sufficient and the early years were marked by periods of famine, while the first really fertile area to be discovered, along the Hawkesbury River, proved subject to disastrous floods. Problems were exacerbated by friction between a succession of governors and the officers, particularly because of the latters' attempts to secure land and convict workers for themselves and to monopolise trade.

The end of the Napoleonic Wars saw a major rise in crime in Britain as demobilised soldiers and sailors were left without employment. An economic depression added to the crisis. The number of convicts sent to Australia rose significantly, as did the number of emigrants – tradesmen looking for work and decommissioned officers and others hoping to set up as gentlemen-farmers. Gradually the colony began to change from a penal settlement to an agricultural community in which convicts were assigned to labour for individuals or employed by the government in public works.

The continuing high cost of maintaining the system was a constant worry to the British authorities, as was a growing fear that the colony was ceasing to have much deterrent value for Britain's criminals. From the 1820s onwards, these concerns were met by increasing dispersal of convicts to private masters (who were responsible for feeding and clothing them) and by intensifying the severity with which convicts were treated, particularly those under direct government control, and most notably those recalcitrants who were sent to the new penal stations as places of secondary punishment.

Gradually opposition to the system built up in Britain, based on a humanitarian concern at its savagery, a belief in its inefficiency, and a misguided faith that a penitentiary system, set up in Britain itself, would provide better outcomes. In 1840 transportation was phased out in the oldest colony, New South Wales, with other penal colonies following suit in later decades.

Terminology of Botany Bay

[Names referred to in this book are highlighted in bold.]
Botany Bay was intended to be the site of the first British settlement in Australia, but proved so unpromising that within days the camp was moved to **Sydney Cove**, an inlet on **Sydney Harbour** (which itself was called **Port Jackson**). In time, the camp received the name of **Sydney**. The entire area under the governor's control was officially designated **New South Wales**, but **Botany Bay** remained a popular, faintly jocular name for the colony, while **Sydney**, **Sydney Town**, **Port Jackson** and **Sydney Cove** were used interchangeably to refer to the main area of settlement – a usage retained by this book. Readers may also find the maps, of Sydney (Fig. 8) and of New South Wales (endpapers), useful references.

Administrative terms

Assignment Commonly refers to the system of allocating convicts to work for private masters who, in return, undertook to provide them with food, clothing and other necessaries. Convicts remaining in government service could also be said to be assigned to a particular place or group (e.g. a road party).

Conditional / absolute pardon A conditional pardon, granted by the governor, entitled a recipient to live as a free person in the colony, but not to leave it; whereas an absolute pardon remitted the remainder of a convict's sentence, thus enabling the recipient to leave the colony or to live there as a free person.

Convict transports A numeral following the name of a vessel (e.g. *Tory* 3) indicates which voyage of a vessel of that name, carrying convicts, is the subject of the reference.

Indent   Ships carrying convicts from England normally brought with them an indent, or list of the convicts on board, which included some details of their sentence and, in later years, of their crime, occupation and physical appearance.

Musters Annual gatherings of inhabitants for census purposes. They normally excluded the troops serving in the colony, and sometimes the landholders also, the latter being recorded in the land and stock muster, which often accompanied the muster of inhabitants.

On/off stores Musters and other lists often included these words to indicate whether a person was provided with a government ration of food and clothing (i.e. on stores) or was not (i.e. off stores).

Secondary punishment In Britain the phrase usually meant any punishment other than death. In the colony it normally referred to an additional punishment for further offences committed in the colony. Notable among these punishments was transfer to a penal settlement, a 'place of secondary punishment'.

Specials Convicts of superior birth, breeding or education. They might receive favoured treatment by being appointed overseers or government clerks, but were also seen as a threat to orderly administration and in later years were often sent to remote establishments to keep them out of the way.

Ticket-of-leave A convict granted a ticket-of-leave was entitled to live and work as a free person, but was restricted to a particular district and obliged to report at regular intervals to the magistrates. A ticket-of-leave could be withdrawn for even a minor offence.

Chronology

26 January 1788	Arrival of First Fleet at Sydney Cove, with Captain Arthur Phillip, RN, as governor of the colony.
15 February 1788	Small detachment sent to establish settlement on Norfolk Island.
4 June 1789	Performance of *The Recruiting Officer*.
3–29 June 1790	First detachment of New South Wales Corps replaces Royal Marines as colony's garrison.
2 November 1791	Lieutenant Philip Gidley King, RN, arrives on Norfolk Island as lieutenant-governor.
11 December 1792	Governor Phillip leaves for England. Is replaced by Major Francis Grose, commander of NSW Corps, as lieutenant-governor.
1793?–1794	Brickfields theatre in operation.
1793–18 January 1794	Norfolk Island theatre active.
17 December 1794	Major Grose departs, leaving Captain William Paterson as lieutenant-governor.
7 September 1795	Captain John Hunter, RN, arrives as governor. Confronted by entrenched power of officer corps, by now heavily involved in trade and landholding.
16 January 1796	Sidaway's theatre opens in Sydney.
25 October 1796	Lieutenant-Governor King leaves Norfolk Island for England.
28 September 1800	Lieutenant, now Captain, King returns to replace Hunter as governor. Tension between governor and officers continues.
1804–1807	Sidaway's theatre closes at some point during this period.
1805–1806	Occasional play performances on Norfolk Island.
13 August 1806	King replaced by Captain William Bligh, RN, as governor.
1807	Bligh grants permission for new theatre, not realised because of rebellion.

26 January 1808	NSW Corps leads successful insurrection against Bligh.
28 December 1809	Colonel Lachlan Macquarie arrives with regiment to replace Bligh and NSW Corps.
1810–1821	Brickfield Hill theatre in operation for part of this period.
27 February 1814	Norfolk Island settlement abandoned.
11 September 1819	Plans to establish Emu Plains agricultural settlement announced.
26 September 1819	Commissioner John Bigge arrives, with a brief, *inter alia*, to propose ways of increasing colony's severity as a deterrent to crime.
1820	Occasional play performances in a Sydney salt works.
17 April 1821	Advance party lands at Port Macquarie to establish place of secondary punishment.
1 December 1821	Macquarie hands over governorship to Brigadier-General Sir Thomas Brisbane, who begins implementing Bigge's recommendations.
1822–1823	First performances at Emu Plains.
14 September 1824	Moreton Bay penal settlement established.
6 June 1825	Resettlement of Norfolk Island as penal station.
3 December 1825	Van Diemen's Land becomes separate colony.
17 December 1825	Major-General Sir Ralph Darling arrives in Sydney as governor. Policy of increasing severity towards prisoners continues.
22 November 1830	Orders sent to close Emu Plains theatre.
1830-1831	Lesser penal settlements such as Wellington Valley, Port Macquarie and Emu Plains closed to make way for free settlement, though core establishments remain at some.
3 December 1831	Darling replaced by Major-General Sir Richard Bourke, who begins liberalising treatment of convicts.
7 April 1837	Molesworth Committee, dominated by reformers who favour the penitentiary system over transportation, set up by British Parliament.
24 February 1838	Bourke replaced as governor by Major Sir George Gipps, who pursues further reforms of convict system.
3 August 1838	Molesworth Committee submits report, urging immediate cessation of assignment, improved regulations for convicts in government service and ultimate abandonment of transportation.
6 March 1840	Captain Alexander Maconochie, RN, arrives on Norfolk Island as reformist superintendent.
May 1840	Captain Charles Hyndman arranges convict performance at Port Macquarie.

22 May 1840	British government orders cessation of transportation to NSW, effective from 1 August. Van Diemen's Land remains penal colony.
25 May 1840	Maconochie organises convict performances on Norfolk Island for Queen's birthday.
7 February 1844	Maconochie leaves Norfolk Island.
29 September 1844	Norfolk Island transferred to jurisdiction of Van Diemen's Land.

Measurements

Length

1 inch	2.5 centimetres
1 foot (= 12 inches)	30.5 centimetres
1 yard (= 3 feet)	91.4 centimetres
1 rod (= 5½ yards)	502.7 centimetres
1 mile (= 1760 yards)	1.6 kilometres

Volume

1 pint	0.57 litres
1 gallon (= 8 pints)	4.55 litres
1 bushel (= 8 gallons)	36.4 litres

Area

1 acre (= 4849 square yards)	0.4 hectare
1 rood (=¼ acre)	0.1 hectare

Weight

1 pound (1lb)	0.4 kilograms

Currency

1 penny (1d.)	
1 shilling (1s.) 12 pennies/pence	
1 pound (£1)	20 shillings
1 guinea	21 shillings

Author's Note

Except where it might cause confusion, the original spelling and punctuation of quotations from eighteenth- and nineteenth-century documents have been retained.

To my wife Amanda,
for her unswerving support during
these last difficult years.

John Kemble remarked, when he heard of the brilliant success of the Botany Bay Company, that he was not at all surprised, for they had been sent there by excellent judges! We hope ere long these stars will revisit our hemisphere; for the stage is sadly in want of talented recruits, and we shall be happy to ship a fresh cargo in return.

Introduction to W.T. Moncrieff, *Van Diemen's Land*,
Cumberland's Minor Theatre, no. 91, London [n.d.], p. [5].

Introduction

The writing up of this research was completed in what may prove to have been the last phases of a losing battle with leukemia. I imagine that no author ever thinks a book is truly finished. While conscious of that, I would still have welcomed a little more time and energy to devote to the work – to polish the style, to follow up some haunting loose ends and, above all, to undertake further random searches through the newspapers and manuscripts of the half-century with which the book is concerned.

My subject, convict theatre from 1788 to 1840, falls into two phases; 1788–1830, when theatre associated with convicts was the only recorded theatre in the colony, and a further ten years during which that theatre became marginalised, as more conventional forms took its place. Strictly speaking, the book deals with convict theatre in New South Wales, the name given to the entire colony up to 1825, at which point Van Diemen's Land became a separate entity. The choice of 'Australia' for the title reflects the fact that I could find no evidence of convict theatre in other colonies between 1825 and 1840. It is also a concession to foreign readers, who may have found New South Wales as unidentifiable and mysterious a concept as Tibooburra, Yantabulla or Bong Bong. Contrary to expectation, this first phase of forty-two years, the origins of European theatre in Australia, has never been the subject of sustained and systematic inquiry. Barnett Levey's heroic efforts to launch a professional theatre in Sydney in the late 1820s have received due attention in the work of Eric Irvin and Helene Oppenheim, and, thanks to its appearance in the novel *Ralph Rashleigh*, some research has been done on the Emu Plains convict playhouse. For the most part, however, the history of theatre in this period has remained a matter of recycling a handful of brief and well-known primary references and retailing, with various degrees of scepticism, a number of tall stories of obscure origin and doubtful authenticity. The officer's dog that was skinned and sold as kangaroo meat to pay for a theatre ticket, and the chance meeting between an ebullient Robert Sidaway and the Scottish Martyrs on the morning Sidaway was to open his theatre, are both fabrications which continue to surface in the literature. If they have a value, it is not as fact, but as evidence of the desire to build a mythology around these events – to turn the early making of theatre in Australia into part of the national legend, to find it a place in the nation's folk history and popular culture.

What drives the urge to mythologise this early theatre, and what gives it a peculiar fascination as a subject of scholarly research, is not the ultimately pedestrian fact that it is the first phase of European theatre in Australia. Primacy, in itself, is no guarantee of excitement. The fascination of this early theatre is its exotic nature, the fact that, to an overwhelming extent, it was the product, not of free men but of convicts, not of a normal civil society but of a penal colony. To be sure, in some of the examples to be considered there were a few soldiers involved – even the occasional free settler – but the driving force seems to have been the serving convicts, or those with the equivocal freedom provided by a conditional pardon and those who, though time-expired, 'free by servitude', remained convicts in the eyes of their betters. The stain of past crime, the suspicion of a continued proclivity to it, and the social disadvantage arising from it, could never be expunged. The two phrases, 'the first half-century of European theatre in Australia' and 'convict theatre in New South Wales', do not coalesce seamlessly, but there is only the narrowest of fissures between them. It is the second of these phrases to which I have given prominence, not only because of its greater curiosity value, but also because it draws attention to what are ultimately the more interesting social issues – of power, control and the functions of theatre in an abnormal situation.

What I have been given, then, is the opportunity most scholars dream of, that of working in almost virgin territory and of finding avenues of approach which continue to fascinate me even as the end of the project approaches.

The negative side of the experience comes from the very reason that this opportunity has been available: the apparent hopelessness of the task. Pride of place in this book has been given to the most evocative of these theatres, the one associated with the name of Robert Sidaway. This theatre epitomises the major problem – the absence of a substantial and readily identifiable body of primary material on which to found an analysis. For this theatre there is no coherent body of information on which to draw. It has been a matter of combing through unindexed London, provincial and colonial newspapers, through official correspondence, private letters, legal records, statistical returns, account books, logbooks and the like in the hopes of finding a paragraph, or even a phrase, that might be relevant. Months of reading often left little that could find its way into the final manuscript. As a scholarly method this has its drawbacks, particularly since I cannot claim to have read every document that has survived from the period under survey. Small gold mines may remain undiscovered in places I have neglected, but the assumption that I have been there may discourage others from attempting another search through such unpromising terrain.

Since this is the first book to attempt a coverage of the earliest phase of European theatre in Australia, it carries with it the obligation to provide some sort of narrative line – a sequential account of what took place and when. That account necessarily contains much that is inferential or provisional, and is marked by large gaps where no information is available. Since I am also a theatre historian, the book may seem to carry the burden of an inordinate interest in theatre spaces, their dimensions and arrangement. The broader concern of this study, however, is theatre in its social relations. One aspect of this involves slippery concepts of social classification. What was the social background of those who made this theatre and of those who witnessed it? What cultural capital did they bring to these activities? How did the social composition of the audience colour the experience of performance for the players and, to a lesser extent, how did the composition of the player group influence the perceptions of the audience? A related issue is the transference of cultural forms from one world to another. Granted that the convict theatres set up in Australia would have been, almost unthinkingly, efforts to replicate British models, which models were most influential and what modifications did these undergo in the process of adaptation to a new country and a freakish social structure?

Beyond this there are the direct issues of power involved in the making of these theatres. Almost all of them are emanations from below, products of the initiative and the desires of those very groups the colony was set up to control and restrict. How did they make their way in the face of the would-be authoritarian systems of rule that confronted them? How did they accommodate themselves to the complexities of power and factionalism within the ruling elites? How did the forces of authority view these unlikely growths, and how did they choose to relate to them?

As we shall see, the answers to many of these questions are tantalisingly beyond the reach of detailed analysis, but, insofar as they can be sketched in or guessed at, they vary from instance to instance. The changing demographics of the colony and the emergence of new centres of power such as the Church and a large landholding class; shifting ideas on the purpose of the colony, on the treatment of prisoners and on the function of penal servitude; the degrees of isolation from the centre of rule; the temperaments and ideologies of powerful individuals – these are among the factors that played their part. Rather than treat these as the basic units of discussion, I have chosen to let them emerge and re-emerge in the course of the narrative, assuming that this recurrence of themes, and the variations on them in the different social contexts, require only the slightest pointing up to remind the reader of their structural significance to the book. The work's formal conclusion is devoted to a drawing together of some of these strands.

To some extent the decision to structure the work in this way is part of a concern to balance academic interests against an openness of form that will make the work more appealing to the interested lay reader. While scholarship is my first concern, this book is also driven by the romantic urge to celebrate the emergence of theatre in the most unpromising of situations, and those small triumphs of human ingenuity and enthusiasm that made the realisation of that theatre possible. Along with these goes the equally romantic urge to rescue from oblivion some of those individuals who were involved in these projects and who normally fall below the level of vision of political, economic or national histories. (This urge finds expression in the biographical sketches that constitute Appendix A.) While partly engaged in the business of exploding myths, this means that I am also complicit in their preservation, in a modified and hopefully enriched form. It is an aspiration that involves some risks to the dream of scholarly objectivity, notably in the difficult area of identifying the social backgrounds of those involved in the early theatre projects. Since the evidence denies me the possibility of classifying the bulk of these early playmakers as humble labourers, I may be unduly concerned to save most of them, at least, from the stigma of gentility, and to locate them among the middling sorts of people. No doubt there are other sources of potential bias of which I remain completely unconscious and so must leave the reader to detect.

Chapter ℑ

BRITONS ABROAD: THE EARLY CONVICTS AND THEIR THEATRICAL BACKGROUND

*T*he craze for amateur theatricals among the higher orders in late Georgian Britain is well documented. It was a passion given vent not only in the motherland itself but throughout the Empire, where military officers and civilian gentlefolk trod the boards in centres as far apart as Jamaica and Calcutta, Montreal and Cape Town. Even the diminutive island of St Helena boasted a theatre, though most of its activity no doubt occurred during the stay of the homeward-bound East India Company fleets.[1]

In striking contrast to all this activity is the situation in New South Wales. There the fever for performance seems to have found no place among the officers, the administrators and the handful of genteel settlers. The rigours of the posting, the minute numbers constituting the social elite, their geographic dispersal and the bitter factionalism of their community effectively killed off the possibility of such theatre for the first twenty-five years of the outpost's existence. For the next fifteen years the positive influence of a growing population was negated by the continuing factionalism, the caution of governors and the growing influence of the clergy, many of whom were bitterly hostile to theatre of any kind.[2]

Where theatre did flourish, however, was among that most unlikely of groups, the convicts and ex-convicts. Time and again during the colony's first decades we find convict theatre emerging as an isolated event or as a sustained, semi-professional activity. Moreover, this activity was probably much more widespread than the surviving records indicate. What the convicts did in their spare time was of no interest to officialdom unless it involved breaking the law, and between 1790 and the 1820s there is little in the way of gossipy diaries and correspondence which might have recorded such activities as a curiosity. Even where there is evidence for a theatre, it is often of the most fleeting and tangential kind. The proof that Sydney had a theatre as early as 1793 consists of ten words in parenthesis in a long report about something entirely different, and a series of convict performances in 1820 is known only through four brief and sour sentences in the spiritual journal of a hostile Methodist. There

5

are over 300 pages of official documents that throw light on the Norfolk Island theatre of 1793–94, but they all relate to one incident, a riot which took place in and near the playhouse on 18 January 1794. What they reveal about the theatre is limited, fragmentary and haphazard, and yet without this riot we would not even know that this playhouse had existed. In the light of this, can we be sure that there was no activity of a similar kind in Hobart, Parramatta, or even in the hell-hole that was Newcastle, simply because there is no reference to it in the archives? Was there a string of one-off productions in Sydney, both before and after Sidaway's theatre, of which only random instances have been recorded?

The idea of convicts and ex-convicts avidly pursuing theatre in these desolate outposts at the farthest extremity of the British Empire is made all the more extraordinary by common assumptions about the origins of those convicts. Britain's felons have been popularly thought of as drawn overwhelmingly from the lowest levels of society – uncouth, unskilled and usually illiterate. But while a thriving popular theatre was accepted as a feature of British society from the 1820s or 1830s onwards, there is still a tendency to think of the Georgian theatre that preceded it as a much more refined affair, dominated by audience-members with claims to education, cultivation and gentility. Accordingly, when F.C. Brewer wrote the first survey of theatre in New South Wales we find him asserting (rather than demonstrating) that the early presentations were created by 'men of education' among the convicts, men who were not professional actors, but had 'mixed a good deal with the professionals of England' and had seen 'all the great actors and actresses of the Augustan era'. In a similar vein Thomas Keneally's novel *The Playmaker*, of 1987/88, is based on the premise that it required one of the marine officers to initiate Australia's first recorded European theatrical production, in 1789, and to train the convict actors. The only performer in the novel with extensive playgoing experience is Robert Sidaway, and his acting is marked by an exaggeration of style which points to a distinctly vulgar understanding of the art he loved so well. On the other hand, Mary Brenham, the most sensitive of Keneally's convict actresses, is revealed as the daughter of a man brought up as companion to a baronet's son. Her sensibility and her background isolate her from the other women convicts. Timberlake Wertenbaker's 1988 play, *Our Country's Good*, based on the novel, reinforces this sense of a cultured elite and a culturally unsophisticated felonry.[3]

To note these premises on which Keneally and Wertenbaker build is not, of course, to criticise what are avowedly works of fiction. It is merely to take them as reflecting a popular assumption about the cultural patterns of early New South Wales. What is perhaps more significant is that one of the most incisive modern analyses of the social world of convict theatre seems to be coloured by the same assumptions. This is Harold Love's introduction to the relevant section of *The Australian Stage: A Documentary History*.[4] Its main points can be summarised as follows:

(i)   The overwhelming bulk of the early European population of New South Wales came from the lower orders and they had no significant tradition of theatregoing.

(ii) Theatre was essentially an activity of genteel society and that group was very thinly represented in New South Wales.

(iii) Therefore, the early convict theatre was an essentially fragile and marginal activity, with no firm cultural basis and with no prospect of development. It was a false start.

One objection can be raised immediately. There is simply no evidence that convict theatres failed for lack of an audience to support them. In fact, where we have evidence on the collapse of a convict theatre the reason for the closure was not audience indifference but government fiat. The Norfolk Island theatre of 1793–94, Sidaway's Sydney theatre and the Emu Plains theatre were all suppressed by the authorities because of their perceived danger to law and order.

Clearly, a series of related issues needs to be addressed here. What was the social composition of the early convict population, and to what extent was this population, prior to transportation, familiar with the world of Georgian theatre and participant in it? Was the social background of the performers significantly different from that of the audiences in the convict theatres?

II

The belief that the convicts were overwhelmingly drawn from the unskilled, the illiterate, the ignorant and the brutish is not simply popular opinion: it is the judgment of the last generation of scholars reacting against the romanticising of convicts by an earlier generation. That judgment is now being questioned, largely on the basis of statistical analysis. Working on crime in England, Peter Linebaugh has pointed out that some forty per cent of those hanged at Tyburn in the first half of the eighteenth century had been apprenticed to a trade.[5] There is no reason to believe that the proportion would have been lower in the latter part of the century or among those who were transported, rather than hanged.

It is only from 1817 that the convict records relating to Australia make a practice of including the transportee's occupation as well as his or her sentence and other details, but the information drawn from these and other sources gives a similar picture. Thus Stephen Nicholas and Peter Shergold, on the basis of their exhaustive analysis of the backgrounds of about one third (19,711) of the convicts transported to New South Wales from 1817 onwards, are able to declare that 'even the most generous overestimate of the proportion of low skilled among the [male] convicts transported, including labourers, porters, messengers, military and domestic servants, brings the total to less than half'. While a similar analysis is not possible for the earlier phase of transportation, Nicholas and Shergold note that 'over the sample period, there was a tendency for the semi-skilled and unskilled English and Irish intake to rise ... By the end of transportation, the convict arrivals were less skilled than at the beginning.'[6] This provides a useful warning against the assumption that the numbers of the skilled would have been lower in the first two or three decades of settlement. On the First-Fleet transport *Friendship* about 36 of the 76 male convicts fall into the skilled category, with another seven in occupations which could, perhaps, have been included in the statistic.[7] The *Morning Chronicle*, 22 November 1797, even made a joke of the matter: 'Among the convicts going to Botany Bay on board the *Barwell*, we observe only *two* gentlemen and *one* attorney – all the rest are creditable tradesmen!'

What is not clear from the evidence is where these skilled workers stood in the hierarchy of their occupations. Though most of them may have been apprenticed, how many of them had actually completed their apprenticeships before slipping into crime and convictism? How many of the remainder lived relatively precarious lives as journeymen, skilled artisans employed by others? How many of them ran starveling businesses as the lowest level of independent shoemakers, tailors and grocers? The probability is that the vast majority of the 'skilled' convicts came from these lowly categories, and relatively few from the world of prosperous businessmen, though we shall come across a few of the latter.

III

The assumption that there was a close relationship in the eighteenth century between high social status, 'civility', and education on the one hand, and theatregoing on the other, is not without foundation. Both the self-imaging of much of this theatre and some of the statistics and economic evidence relating to it point in this direction, notably in the case of London, from which a large proportion of convicts was drawn.

The self-imaging is at its most obvious in the type of phrase that was used to describe the audience at a successful performance. Time and again, in both London and the provinces, this description takes the form of a doublet, one half of which is 'crowded' and the other half 'brilliant', 'fashionable', 'genteel' or some equally pointed word. However, this is not the whole picture. The model eighteenth-century auditorium was divided into boxes, pit, lower gallery and upper gallery, with a hierarchy of prices to match. In the major London theatres, Covent Garden and Drury Lane, a box seat cost 5s. up to the early 1790s, and 6s. thereafter, and a pit seat 2s. 6d. (rising to 3s. 6d.), while the two galleries remained unchanged at 2s. and 1s. respectively. In the idealised view this price differentiation, and accompanying social pressures,[8] defined the composition of the group in each part of the house. The side boxes were for aristocrats, affluent gentry, rich merchants and their families; the front boxes for less affluent gentry and merchants. The pit was a little more heterogeneous, though particularly associated with slightly marginal groups who could still claim social standing by virtue of profession, cultural capital or birth, i.e. lower-ranking military officers, inns-of-court men, the litterati, the lesser gentry and moderately affluent merchants. This left the two galleries. The lower of these was usually generalised as the habitation of tradesmen and their wives, while the upper gallery was seen as the haunt of a diverse group of lesser mortals, such as apprentices, sailors, labourers, domestic servants.[9] The *Daily Universal Register*, 3 April 1786, even refers to the presence there of 'some untutored boys, vulgarly called blackguards'. In such an analysis, then, not everybody in the house warrants the terms 'fashionable' or 'genteel'.

Moreover, as is apparent from modern scholarly analysis, and from much of the incidental commentary in the period itself, this idealised picture of the audience is not the whole truth. In all parts of the house, even the boxes, the company was a little more mixed. This was particularly so in the latter half of the evening, when many theatres allowed vacant places to be taken at something approaching half price, bringing the pit within the reach of some members of society's lower echelons.

It is a common assumption that by the second decade of the nineteenth century the playhouses were well on the way to being dominated by the lower orders, an assumption that involves a large-scale penetration of the pit as well as control of the galleries. Some critics have accordingly argued that the period from about 1790 to 1810 was a transitional one, with the pit gradually succumbing to the inroads of the workers.[10] However, there seem to be no contemporary comments on this taking place, and other forms of evidence are not entirely clear. Mark Baer is able to demonstrate that over half the skilled workers arrested at Covent Garden during the 1809 riots over increased ticket prices were taken in the pit, as were two thirds of the clerks and tradesmen.[11] But a premeditated riot is an abnormal situation, which is likely to lure troublemakers into the pit, as the place from which they can present the maximum threat to the stage. In 1805 the opening at Covent Garden of Samuel Foote's *The Tailors* (an old play which had not previously given offence) was preceded by days of hysteria involving threatening letters and claims that a thousand tailors would descend upon the house to riot during the performance. The riot duly took place, with *The Times* describing both the pit and the galleries as crowded with tailors of the lower sort.[12] More than a quarter of a century before, the *Daily Universal Register*, 31 January 1787, had declared that at a planned riot at John O'Keeffe's *The Man Milliner* 'the whole tribe of *Men Milliners*, *Men Stay-makers*, *Men Mantua-makers*, &c. &c. with their despicable train of womanish attendants, were seen in the pit and galleries'. Earlier on the page it described them as gaining admission to every part of the house. However, when an unplanned disturbance took place among Jewish spectators at Covent Garden in 1802, at the singing of an anti-Semitic song, the same newspaper firmly located the rioters in the gallery, noted a few rich and non-rioting Jews in the boxes and made no mention of the pit.[13] The poor Jews of East London were noted for their passion for the theatre but were still, apparently, keeping to the galleries. Even more significant is the evidence from the Haymarket Theatre disaster of 1794, when fifteen people died attempting to get into the pit. The journalist James Boaden, who was on the scene before the bodies were moved, emphatically declared that 'eight of the sufferers were females of great respectability in life', an impression confirmed by the newspaper reports and obituaries. The men who died were even more substantial – two heralds, a naval officer, the captain of a merchant vessel, the son of a Gray's Inn attorney, the nephew of an industrialist and a successful farrier who had recently inherited his business.[14]

The evidence for a large-scale presence of London's skilled workers and tradesmen in the pit on a regular basis, then, is not as clear as one might like. The point has been laboured because a substantial restriction of these social groups and their inferiors to the galleries poses special problems in the capital. The system of royal patents and licences which controlled the operation of theatres meant that London, with a population of almost a million by 1800, was officially limited to two playhouses and an opera house which chose to operate an extended winter season, and to one small playhouse whose patent was for the summer months only. Beyond these were three or four 'irregular' theatres presenting musical pieces, dance, animal acts, equestrian performances, pantomimes, feats of skill and spectacular displays. In the 'legitimate' theatres, moreover, the galleries constituted only a small percentage of the seating available, even though they were notionally catering to the overwhelming mass of London's population. By 1800 Drury Lane, with a capacity of 3,611, had only 27.2% of its places in the galleries, with less than 12% in the upper gallery. Covent Garden had a capacity of 3,013, of whom 39.2% were in the two galleries. The summer theatre, the Haymarket, had a capacity of only 1,727, but 42.4% of these were in the galleries. Indeed, its shilling gallery was larger than that at Drury Lane, and only slightly smaller than that at Covent Garden.[15] Harry M. Pedicord investigated the implications of this for the slightly earlier period, the age of Garrick, taking into account the high proportion of a worker's income that even a gallery seat would require, and the fact that most would have been still at work when the curtain rose. His evidence seems to point to a limited presence of these social groups in the theatres.[16] Nor was the situation improving in the last quarter of the eighteenth century or the first decade of the nineteenth. While the winter theatres were constantly being rebuilt in this period to expand their capacity, the expansion was almost entirely in the area of the most expensive seats, the boxes, with the cheap gallery seats declining in proportion. Indeed, in the rebuilt Covent Garden theatre of 1792 it was originally intended to do away with the one-shilling gallery entirely, and only threats of a riot led to its hasty reinstatement, reduced in size.[17] A similar philosophy can be seen behind the plans of Sheridan and Harris in 1777 to open a third winter playhouse, designed exclusively for the upper levels of society, with an auditorium consisting entirely of box seats.[18]

Nor were there significant alternative venues providing the spoken drama at prices more attractive to the workers. Small professional companies, such as Oliver Carr's, systematically worked the villages around the capital, so that some of their venues were within walking distance of suburbs of London or Westminster. However, it is difficult to see these having a major impact on the London scene. Equally marginal were the companies which tried to set up illegally in Southwark, Tower Hamlets and other poor areas of London.[19] The evidence suggests that these were few and short-lived. There was nothing similar to the vast number of low-class penny gaffs which were a feature of the capital in the early years of Queen Victoria, and seem to have arrived on the scene no earlier than 1830.[20] Amateur theatre, which may have been more significant, will be considered later.

One way of addressing the problem is to assume that theatregoing for individuals in the lower orders of London was an occasional rather than a regular and frequent occurrence, thanks to the high prices, social pressures and inconveniences involved. Speaking of the situation in 1809, the playwright Frederick Reynolds suggested that the average pittite attended a London patent theatre only four times in the season.[21] If the frequency among galleryites was similar, or lower, then a correspondingly high proportion of London's humbler citizens would have been acquainted with theatre, but only as a special event. They might have been in much the same position as the village folk, but restricted by cost rather than by the infrequency of the performances.

IV

One further question about this humbler section of the audience remains. Was it a representative cross-section of the lower orders and of the lesser middle orders, or were certain groups disproportionately represented in it? In particular, did London's humbler theatregoers include a high percentage of lawbreakers, who would carry their enthusiasm to Botany Bay and give a particular dynamic to theatre there? Was the rowdiness of English gallery audiences characteristic of workers in general, or did it point to the large-scale presence of the exceptionally delinquent? Looking back at the end of the eighteenth century, Charles Macklin remembered Sadler's Wells theatre, decades before, as having 'a mixture of very odd company, (for I believe it was a good deal the baiting-place of thieves and highwaymen)'.[22] Was this true, to any degree, of the legitimate theatres later in the century? And were these offenders necessarily confined to the gallery?

Certain groups had good professional reasons for attending the theatre. Pickpockets habitually operated in places where crowds gathered, and the theatres were prominent among such places. Their presence there excited frequent and outraged comment in the press: 'The crowd of pickpockets which infest the Haymarket Theatre is a disgrace', thundered *The Times*, 28 June 1789, attacking both the magistrates and the management. The winter theatres were no better. At the beginning of the winter season of the same year *The Times*, 17 September, advised playgoers to leave their watches and all but the minimum of money at home, since 'the gangs of pickpockets are now become so formidable that they set all law at defiance'.

Needless to say, it was the more expensive parts of the house that most attracted these predators, since the pickings there were greatest. Some box areas were particularly infested. *The Times*, 13 November 1789, reported that the front and green boxes of the Playhouses, are certainly less reputably filled than heretofore; pick-pockets, pimps, and punks, now find their way to these places with ease, which some years ago were occupied by persons of the first consequence.

The last quotation also draws attention to a second group who were there in force, the punks, or prostitutes, who are described as infecting all parts of the house. One reporter went so far as to claim that the front boxes were almost entirely filled with them. Another article in *The Times*, 14 December 1789, inveighs against 'the admission of such numbers of notorious prostitutes into the upper and front boxes where such shamefaced scenes are exhibited as are a disgrace to the Theatre' and 'virtuous people ... become liable to the insults of the most abandoned and dissolute of both sexes'. Prostitution was not a transportable offence, but the theft of pocket-books, watches and the like that often accompanied prostitution brought many of that trade to Botany Bay, among them the turbulent and impulsive Sarah McCann, who was an actor with the Sydney theatre for a year or so.

Pickpockets and prostitutes were notionally present in the theatre for reasons of business, but it is difficult to avoid the impression that for many there was also excitement in the theatrical experience itself. The most famous pickpockets to make the voyage to Australia, George Barrington and James Hardy Vaux, both claimed a great love of theatre for its own sake. Barrington was a by-word for his literary accomplishments, and John Bernard bears testimony to his sophisticated knowledge of the stage.[23] Vaux claimed that from an early age he had a 'violent passion for the drama, which at once improved my understanding and amused my mind'. Later he declared:

In the evenings I generally attended one of the theatres, where I mixed with the best company in the boxes, and at the same time that I enjoyed the amusements of the place, I frequently conveyed pocket-books, snuff-boxes, and other portable articles, from the pockets of their proprietors into my own.[24]

Neither Barrington nor Vaux had any known connection with convict theatre in New South Wales, but two others seem to have involved themselves, if only obliquely, in the colony's thespian activities. David Greville, who was caught attempting a pocket in the pit passage at Drury Lane, took as his *de facto* in Sydney a woman who became one of the colony's earliest actresses. He also seems to have been on good terms with the company's first manager, John Sparrow. The J. Mackie who sold tickets for performances from the house next to the Sydney theatre in 1800, and who may have been a later manager of the company, or the box-office keeper, cannot be identified with certainty, but he is probably the James Mackie transported after picking a pocket in the lower gallery at Covent Garden.[25]

Some of these offenders undoubtedly had genteel connections. For others, however, the affectation of the externals of refinement seems to have become a feature of their life-style. Theirs was a sub-culture which operated, in part, as a simulacrum of high society, sometimes in full seriousness, sometimes mockingly.

Honorific military titles, such as 'captain', were adopted. Highwaymen were 'gentlemen of the road'. The pickpockets 'Gentleman' Harry Sterne and James Ackerman, alias My Lord, were among those who could claim something in birth and upbringing to justify their sobriquets, but when the above-mentioned James Mackie had a brush with the law in the purlieus of the Haymarket Theatre, the *Star*, 21 June 1793, referred to him with evident sarcasm as 'a notorious *gentleman* pickpocket'. The title is clearly suspect. John Nicol, a crew-member of the convict transport *Lady Juliana*, reports a family that had lived by crime for several generations, one of whose current members was a highwayman 'as well dressed and genteel in his appearance as any gentleman'.[26] In the light of this, it may be no accident that the adjective 'flash', the cant word applied to professional criminals (as in 'flash-cove', 'flash-ken') had a secondary meaning of foppish, ostentatiously dressed, as well as its primary meaning of sly or cunning.

The suggestion being made here is that, for certain types of delinquent, attendance at the theatres was as much part of their self-imaging as it was for the gentry they parodied. But there may have been other, deeper, psychological pressures that drew rogues to the theatre, irrespective of whether they indulged in affectations of gentility or not. The analogy is with sailors, who were a conspicuous and disproportionate presence in British theatres. Seamen worked under conditions of danger, deprivation and harsh discipline. After a voyage, which could last for a year or more, they were given their wages as a lump-sum payment and discharged. The money was then thrown away in a wild round of whores, drink and theatre, followed by a sheepish return to the sea.[27] Was a similar emotional necessity to be found among some of those who lived partly by crime? Here also life was a matter of great hazards, of high tension, and possibly of periods of desperate want, followed by the sudden release that came with a successful crime. Would this pattern of experience have led to a similar pattern of conduct as was found among sailors?

There is one connection between lawbreaking and theatregoing that the moralists of the eighteenth century had no hesitancy in arguing. Expenditure on a theatre ticket by a member of the working class implied a recklessness with money that could not be sustained on a small income. A continued pursuit of this pleasure, therefore, placed one in an economic situation where the temptation to crime became difficult to resist, particularly since such an addiction to pleasure suggested a weakness of the will. As the Act of Parliament 25 Geo.2.c.36 proclaimed of other forms of pleasure-seeking, 'the lower Sort of People … are thereby tempted to spend their small Substance in riotous Pleasures, and in consequence are put on unlawful Methods of supplying their Wants, and renewing their Pleasures'. In 1760 a magazine attacked theatres such as Sadler's Wells, claiming:

> Most of the unhappy wretches who pay their lives as forfeit to the law, are such as frequent these ill-conducted places of recreation, where their imaginations are enflamed to a degree of madness, that makes them run on any crime and danger for the gratification.[28]

If there is any truth in this view of things, it has the advantage of encompassing not only habitual criminals but those whose journey to Botany Bay was precipitated by a single impulsive crime arising out of an immediate financial pressure.

V

Many of the more successful playhouses in country towns, spas and major agricultural centres present the same picture as London, that of theatre as an entertainment for the refined. The brief visit of a company to a provincial town readily became the focus for social activity, drawing in the gentry from the surrounding countryside as well as those from the town itself and the officers of any militia or regular army unit that happened to be in the vicinity. Little information about these provincial theatres has survived, but the Margate theatre of 1787 allocated less than 32% of its places to the gallery and the Bristol theatre of 1764 fewer than 34%. These figures accord with the practice in London's legitimate theatres.[29] On the other hand, the prices of the better seats in these provincial playhouses were significantly lower than those of London's legitimate theatres, opening them to a more diverse audience, particularly at half-price time.

The theatres at Margate and Cheltenham, however, are not the full measure of provincial activity. Theatrical memoirs of the time are full of accounts of minor companies working the smaller towns and even the larger villages. Allowing for the exaggeration necessary to turn a lively tale, these give an unmistakable picture of decidedly plebeian audiences – a local squire, perhaps, but predominantly shopkeepers, tradesmen, milliners and farm people. John Edwin, performing at Bewdley, in Worcestershire, had 'the sublime satisfaction of administering pleasure to a matchless concourse of some sixty persons in a large barn and the singular honor to receive the compliments of Mr. Look, a master baker'. Later the audience is spoken of as 'those drama-loving bumkins, among whom, discernment was not eminently notorious'.[30]

Nor do these companies necessarily represent the lowest levels of thespian activity. That rung consisted of the so-called village hoppers or village hunters, small tatterdemalion troupes, usually talentless and little more than the rogues and vagabonds of the legislation, who wandered from village to village, living under circumstances of the utmost poverty. Charles Dibdin describes one such company in his *Tour Through England and Scotland*. 'Hawkie', toy-maker, china-mender, fraudulent field preacher, wanderer and petty thief, had two attempts at village hopping, rapidly abandoning them both because of the rigours of the trade and preferring to settle in Edinburgh as a professional beggar. Troupes of this kind might receive the occasional charity of a local squire, but it is difficult to imagine their audiences comprising anything but the most unsophisticated.[31]

There remains another group of theatres to be considered, those in the large provincial seaports and burgeoning industrial cities. The most notable feature here was the large size of the galleries, even after a rebuilding. The 1785 playhouse at Newcastle-upon-Tyne seems to have been based on the plans for a Birmingham theatre and boasted more than half its seats in the gallery, 840 out of 1,500.[32] At Liverpool, in the rebuilt theatre of 1803, the one-shilling gallery held 1,200 people and, according to the lessees in 1810, usually contained half the audience.[33] Edward Cape Everard provides similar evidence from the beginning of the nineteenth century. Having remarked that in Buxton, a genteel spa town, 'we never had, or expected gallery-people', he goes on to describe Bolton as 'a very different place from Buxton, This theatre was built and calculated for the gallery people, and, accordingly, it was very large, We frequently began a play to ten shillings and have had ten pounds in the shilling-gallery at half-price'.[34] Moreover, these houses boasted a significant presence of the lower orders in areas other than the galleries. When Thomas Snagg played in Sheffield in the late eighteenth century he reported:

> In this diabolical smoky dirty Town there is a very large and commodious theatre. There were stage and side boxes appropriated for the gentry of the neighbourhood, the prices of which were two shillings and sixpence; the pit, larger than any in England, one shilling and sixpence; the first gallery, one shilling, and the upper (parted off by a rail with spikes at the top) only sixpence. It was very whimsical on full nights to see the quantity of striped pudding caps in the pit and galleries, a covering for the head that the Cyclops of Sheffield were very much attached to then. The town is generally profitable for players, as it is very numerous, the receipts thus arising from twenty to eighty pounds per night.[35]

Similarly the *Memoirs of Charles Mathews* describes the Leeds theatre in 1799 as one where both pit and gallery were 'generally occupied with what were called 'croppers', and their wives and sweethearts, (namely, the working people in the cloth manufactories of the town)'.[36]

Liverpool, a major trading port, showed a similar large-scale invasion of the pit by the lower orders, and in particular by sailors. Writing of the 1759 reconstruction of this theatre, Charles Lee Lewes remarked: 'Here it was for the first time [in Liverpool] boxes were erected as a just partition for the better sort to withdraw from the near contact of drunken sailors and their female associates, who ... could and would afford [two shillings] for the honour of mixing with their employers and their families.' The situation was unchanged in 1799, when it was noted of the pit that 'those honest people who come to see and hear the play, are forced to sit intermingled with Jack Tars'.[37] A similar pattern can be found in the great naval depots, such as Portsmouth and Plymouth, which boasted a major concentration of dockyard labourers and tradesmen, as well as of sailors, though it is the latter who bulk largest in the anecdotes. In Portsmouth, as described by John Bernard, 'blue uniforms [that is, naval officers] thronged the boxes, and there was a strong muster nightly, in pit and gallery, of tarpaulin toppers, and pigtails'.[38]

What we have, then, is limited access by the lower orders to the professional 'regular' theatres of London, and probably to many of the provincial theatres in the county towns. This forces us to question whether those at high risk of transportation to Botany Bay were disproportionately represented in this small group. There is plausible anecdotal evidence for farm hands and petty shopkeepers being a major presence at performances in small towns and villages, even if we have to concede that the opportunities for this were infrequent. Moreover, there are clear indications that theatres in many industrial towns and seaports were in large part given over to sailors, mechanics and the like. The antecedents of the Victorian popular theatre were already becoming visible.

Put together, this evidence suggests that the humbler members of society were only too happy to go to the theatre in significant numbers when they were given the chance. If they were not a major presence in the picture their betters had of theatre, and not a major presence in many actual theatres, this was because of the barriers placed upon their attendance.

VI

What is at issue, however, is not only the degree of access to the theatres by the common people, but also the nature of their response to what they saw and heard. The popular view of late eighteenth-century theatre asserts both a limited presence of the lower orders and serious depravity of taste among those who came. There is a perceived division of society into the uncultured and the cultured that reflects the division between the lesser folk and their betters. In the more extreme pictures of the galleryites the image is of a brutish mob, often the worse for alcohol, whose greatest pleasure seems to lie in disrupting the evening's entertainment. The account of the German visitor Moritz in 1782 can stand for many:

> It is the tenants in this upper gallery who, for their shilling, make all that noise and uproar for which the English play-houses are so famous, I was in the pit … Often and often while I sat there, did a rotten orange, or piece of the peel of an orange, fly past me, or past some of my neighbours, and once one of them actually hit my hat, without my daring to look round, for fear another might then hit me on my face … Besides this perpetual pelting from the gallery, which renders an English play house so uncomfortable, there is no end to their calling out and knocking with their sticks, till the curtain is drawn up. … I sometimes heard too the people in the lower or middle gallery quarrelling with those of the upper one … Poor Edwin [the actor] was obliged … to sing himself almost hoarse, as he sometimes was called on to repeat his … songs, two or three times, only because it pleased the upper gallery … to roar out encore.

Nine years later another German, Schütz, provides an even more damning description, with liquids, as well as orange peel raining down.[39] The English newspapers of the time did much to support this picture with frequent accounts of disturbances, usually (though not always) emanating from the gallery, and a scattering of reports in which the missiles were much more dangerous than orange peel or liquids. To give a few random examples, a pewter quart bottle was hurled from the upper gallery at Covent Garden (*Star*, 3 January 1791) and a piece of a glass bottle from the gallery at Drury Lane (*Star*, 2 January 1800). *Bell's Weekly Messenger*, 10 February 1805, reported a 'groom to a nobleman of distinction' hurling a quart bottle from the two-shilling gallery at Drury Lane, injuring two people.

If London was difficult, the industrial towns and seaports seem at times to have been quite nightmarish. Writing of the year 1799, Charles Mathews declared that 'Leeds was at this period considered little better than the Botany Bay for actors. Their dread of the season was in proportion to the inconveniences and disagreeables they experienced during its course.' The working people who dominated in pit and galleries, it had earlier been explained,

> were at this time semi-barbarous in their manners and habits, and ... moreover held in the most supreme contempt, if not abhorrence, the professors of the art they willingly paid to be amused by. The men would not hesitate, like the Irish, to make their comments audibly, though *un*like the Irish, they were destitute of humour to compensate for their interruptions. It was very painful to the admirers of Mrs. Siddons to witness her involuntary submission to such brutal treatment. It was not surprising that the majestic and refined style of her performances should not be appreciated by such people.[40]

The vernacular poetry of Sheffield boasts a piece, 'The Cutlin Heroes', which contains the following verse:

> To ger reit into't gallera, whear we can rant an'roar,
>   Throw flat-backs, stooans, an'sticks,
>   Red herrins, booans, an'bricks.
> If they dooant play Nanca's fanca, or onna tune we fix,
> We'll do the best at e'er we can to braik sum o'ther necks.

While no doubt a gross exaggeration, it is not clear whether the song is a biting satire or an exultant celebration of the behaviour it describes.[41] Bristol seems to have been no better. The *Bristol Gazette*, 4 October 1792, reported a practice in that city of throwing 'apples, stones, &c. at the Performers'.

There are several ways of reading the behaviour patterns of the galleryites. Thus, for politically and economically disempowered labourers, petty tradesmen, and small shopkeepers, the theatre seems to have become an outlet for the frustrations of powerlessness. Somehow it had developed into a liberty, a place of misrule, where the lower orders were free to give some vent to their resentment by unruly behaviour at the expense of their betters. In Oliver Goldsmith's words,

> the rich in general were placed in the lowest seats, and the poor rose above them in degrees proportioned to their poverty. The order of precedence seemed here inverted; those who were undermost all the day now enjoyed a temporary eminence, and became masters of the

> ceremonies. It was they who called for the music, indulging every noisy
> freedom, and testifying all the insolence of beggary in exaltation.[42]

This is to treat it lightly. Though it was rarely resorted to, there always lurked behind this rowdyism the possibility of a full-scale riot, wrecking the theatre building itself and terrorising the gentry in pit and boxes. Occasionally these disturbances took on a radical political flavour, as in riots over the singing of 'God Save the King' at Manchester and at Nottingham.[43]

If carnival misrule with a dangerous edge to it is one way of interpreting the behaviour of the galleryites, another is to see all but the more extreme outbursts of hooliganism simply as the reflection of a different code of playhouse manners from that of their superiors. While pit and boxes could be unruly, the claims of gentility were already nudging the better sort of people towards the decorums of respectable Victorian theatregoers. The galleries, on the other hand, could be seen as preserving a much more warmly boisterous and interactive view of the theatrical experience, one involving a greater readiness to express approval or disapproval of what was offered, a taste for badinage between actors and audience and a pleasure in intra-audience activities – conversation, shared drinking and eating. It was the active audience that could still be found in the music-halls of the early twentieth century, and was to excite the admiration of the avant-garde polemicist, Filippo Tommaso Marinetti, in his assault on the passivity of the bourgeois theatre in 1913.[44]

This sympathetic reading of gallery audiences is not one that found support in the period itself. What was more likely to appeal was a view of their turbulence as a product of low taste and general brutishness. Their inclination was for crude entertainment rather than high art and, if gallery audiences were restless in the theatre, it was partly because their interests were not being met by what they saw there.

This distinction between the tastes of the crowd and those of their superiors is implicit in the law itself. Theatres for opera and the spoken drama were controlled by Prime Minister Robert Walpole's 1737 Licensing Act (10 Geo.2.c.28), which limited their number to the three London patent houses; by a series of acts from 1767 onwards extending the right to a patent theatre to individual provincial cities; and by an Act of 1788 (28 Geo.3.c.30) setting out the regulations for permitting a visiting company to operate for a limited period in other parts of the country. But there was a separate law of 1752 (25 Geo.2.c.36) for controlling 'any House, Room, Garden or other Place kept for publick Dancing, Musick or other publick Entertainment of the like Kind, in the Cities of *London* and *Westminster*, or within twenty Miles thereof'; and it specifically identified these as the 'Multitude of Places of Entertainment for the lower Sort of People', places in which they could pursue their 'riotous Pleasures'.

The Act of 1752 required venues to be licensed annually, and while it might have had in mind chiefly houses, rooms and gardens, it quickly became the means of providing legal protection for a number of 'irregular' theatres, of which London's Sadler's Wells and Astley's Amphitheatre were the most famous. As was mentioned earlier, these, while obliged to avoid the spoken drama, brought together all sorts of entertainment built around music, spectacle, acrobatic skills and the like. In this way a distinction was enshrined between the legitimate theatres, as places of cultured entertainment and rational pleasures for the better sort of people, and irregular theatres, providing mindless entertainment for the mob.

By the late eighteenth century, however, what presented itself as a clear distinction in theory bore little relation to the muddle and compromise of everyday practice. As the century wore on, the legitimate theatres increasingly larded their programs with songs, dances and spectacles as interludes in the mainpiece, and afterpieces that were sometimes farces but were just as likely to be burlettas, pantomimes, acrobatic displays, animal acts, pugilistic bouts or demonstrations of swordsmanship. On the other hand, the illegitimate theatres, banned from presenting the spoken drama, used their own subterfuges to avoid the letter of the law. The legendary chord of music struck at intervals during a spoken drama to convert it, notionally, into a burletta, is an example.[45] Beyond this, these theatres sought to establish their credentials as venues suited to the more refined and not simply the domain of the swinish multitude. The newspaper accounts of Astley's circus (paid advertisements thinly disguised as news reports) constantly emphasise the large numbers of the 'quality' attending the performance, the comfort of the house and the value of the productions as rational entertainments. Much the same is true of the Royal Circus.[46] At the doyen of the illegitimate theatres, Sadler's Wells, the successive renovations of 1778, 1782, 1792 and 1802 were aimed at increasing the number and attractiveness of box seats, sometimes at the expense of the gallery. Carriage access to this theatre was also improved, patrols were established along the access roads as protection against footpads, and box-tickets became available through an agent in St Martin's Lane. Half-price was abolished in 1803.[47]

In spite of this evident blurring of the lines, however, there remains a mass of evidence to indicate the hold that the equation between status and taste had on people's imagination. The structure of the normal evening at a patent house, with the legitimate drama (a tragedy or comedy) placed first, followed by a frequently 'illegitimate' afterpiece, might itself have reflected the assumed tastes of the half-price audience. Certainly, *The Times* occasionally suggests that the more genteel folk largely vacated the theatre before the afterpiece or -pieces, leaving the house to lesser mortals.[48] Actors' records frequently comment on the vulgar taste of galleryites or members of the lower orders. Edward Everard describes the theatre at Cowes, on the Isle of Wight, as a 'bear-garden', where, 'as in Portsmouth and Gosport, they were attentive only to song, dance and pantomime'. All three of these theatres catered largely to common sailors and soldiers. Thomas Dibdin similarly remarks that 'a good song, in a village, is thought more of by the audience than all the acting on the stage'. John Bernard, for his part, records two occasions on which small strolling companies, specialising in the legitimate drama, were badly mauled in country towns when they found themselves in opposition to an illegitimate troupe. By the later years of the Napoleonic wars at least one manager was learning to cope. John Brown records a company working in the environs of London which, in the week before a country fair, performed the legitimate drama in a well-appointed barn theatre before a crowded house containing 'many persons of unmistakable respectability', and for the fair week itself

> set up in a canvas booth in the fair-ground where the business was entirely changed. We enacted such 'raw-head-and-bloody-bones' work as I had never witnessed; nothing went down with the poor ignorant country people, but some tale of blood and murder, involving always a ghost in blue flames.[49]

Presumably there is some truth in the picture of a low audience which could appreciate only rough clowning, juggling and pyrotechnics; but one is left to wonder whether the alleged distinction between the taste of the upper and lower orders was to any extent a biased picture, created as part of the hegemonic apparatus of a particular social structure. Was it important for those with some status to belittle their inferiors by depicting them as not only poorer and less educated but also brutish in their sensibilities? Is the small size of the London galleries a reflection of the limited interest among labourers, artisans and petty shopkeepers, or part of a need to keep them in their place?

Thus it should be noted that while the tastelessness of this audience is much emphasised, qualifications are sometimes made. James Peller Malcolm provides a scarifying picture of the behaviour of the 'Londoner of the lowest class' in streets and other public places, and then, having declared, 'This class is fond of Theatrical amusements', continues:

> If we enter the One-shilling Gallery, we witness constant disputes often terminating in blows, and observe heated bodies stripped of the outward garments, furious faces, with others grinning horribly, hear loud and incessant talking and laughter, beating the floor with sticks, hissing, clapping the hands, and the piercing whistle, with exclamations for 'Musick'.

Having drawn this conventional picture, however, Malcolm goes on to declare:

> This motley collection are, however, generally attentive spectators and patient auditors during the representations; and I have remarked that any generous sentiment from the characters on the stage never fails to receive the loudest tokens of applause from the One-shilling Gallery.[50]

Similar qualifications to the generally negative picture were made by Everard in his account of the sailors in the Portsmouth theatre and other naval depots. Having remarked that 'a good hornpipe is sometimes more thought of than a good play in a sea-port town', he draws a similar picture of a noisy and sometimes dangerous audience, but goes on to note: 'We could not, however, but observe that in general our tragedies, such as *Macbeth*, *Richard*, and *Hamlet*, brought us much better houses than our comedies, and still more remarkable, they were not so clamorous.'[51]

Most accounts of boorish and outrageous behaviour in the theatres focus on the upper-gallery crowd and its kind. This group no doubt encompasses most of the theatre-loving unskilled labourers, apprentices, journeymen, and many of the poorer tradesmen and shopkeepers who found their unwilling way to New South Wales. But what of the lower gallery, traditionally the home of the more comfortably-situated small tradesmen and shopkeepers, some of whom were also dispatched to the antipodes?

The very fact that it is rarely mentioned in the same breath as the upper gallery in accounts of offensive behaviour suggests that its behaviour was thought of as more restrained. Thus, Goldsmith's citizen of the world, having described the upper gallery in the passage quoted above, goes on:

> They who hold the middle region seemed not so riotous as those above
> them, nor yet so tame as those below; to judge by their looks, many of
> them seem'd strangers there ... They were chiefly employed during this
> period of expectation [that is, before the show began] in eating oranges,
> reading the story of the play, or making assignations.[52]

The *Daily Universal Register*, 28 July 1786, declared: 'This gallery is frequently alarmed by fracas from drunken ruffians and abandoned prostitutes, but these disturbances, it must be allowed, are less frequent than heretofore.' The differences, it would appear, are of degree rather than kind.

VII

So far I have been concerned to demonstrate that, in spite of the difficulties they may have encountered in London, the countryside and some provincial towns, there was a strong taste for theatre among the lower orders and the lower levels of 'the middling sort of people', those who made up the bulk of the transportees to New South Wales. But what of the making of convict theatre, as opposed to its witnessing? What opportunities did members of these lower social groups have of acquiring practical experience of performance before arriving in the colony?

London, and possibly a few lesser towns, provided opportunities for obtaining a training in acting, though they were of the most dubious kind. On 16 June 1785 the *Daily Universal Register* lashed out at

> those impostors who pretend to teach and qualify *young gentlemen and*
> *ladies* for the *stage*; whereby apprentices, male and female, are enticed
> from their honest employments, defrauded of their property, and forced
> into strolling companies. These pretenders to dramatic art have no
> inconsiderate [*sic*] share in furnishing the road with highwaymen, and
> the stews with prostitutes.

Access, even to a provincial theatre company of some standing, however, did not require any formal training or significant prior experience. Managers were on the lookout for ways of saving money, and a standard one was to accept a stage-struck performer into the company on a miniscule salary or none at all, but with the hope of an appointment at the end of a trial period. In many cases not even a trial period was required. George Suttor provides an example. On the strength of an amateur performance or two and an interview with the Bath manager, he made his way into companies at Worthing and Exeter, finally receiving the offer of a properly paid position with the Cheltenham company. It was only the love of a good woman, and the consequent need for a secure income, that induced him to abandon his dreams and accept an appointment as plant-collector for Sir Joseph Banks in New South Wales. Suttor was the son of a market gardener, experienced in that line himself, and a person of no social standing, though the land holdings he gradually built up in the antipodes were later to transmogrify him into a colonial gentleman. He arrived in Sydney in 1800, a free man, and thereafter seems to have shown no interest whatever in theatre or in acting. He contributed nothing to the activities that are the subject of this book.[53]

If companies as established as those at Exeter and Cheltenham were this open to raw talent, the opportunities further down the line must have seemed limitless. John Brown was an army deserter on the run from the garrison at Chatham, and not yet seventeen, when he stumbled across a small touring group working its way around the southern perimeter of London. Short of a juvenile lead it took him on immediately.[54] This, moreover, was still a reasonably solid group, with a manager who knew his business. But by the time one reached the level of the village hoppers, talent, experience, appearance, even literacy seemed irrelevant. Indeed, at these levels the financial precariousness meant that the dividing line between art and crime had become remarkably tenuous. Many an actor must have been forced into occasional theft through sheer deprivation and, conversely, many a petty criminal may have found acting one of the unskilled occupations into which he or she could drift. Indeed, it is something of a trope in rogue literature for the wandering criminal to spend a period in the acting trade.[55] If his biography is to be believed, that most famous of early transportees, George Barrington, had done just that, joining a company run by a criminal named Page (later hanged) which wandered Ireland, combining theft with the muse.[56]

If taking on a career as a player seemed much too hazardous, there was always the possibility of a one-night stand as a guest performer in a visiting theatre company. Even leading roles were there for the taking. These were usually reserved for members of the local gentry, in the expectation that they would attract their circle of acquaintance to fill the boxes, but humbler folk were sometimes accorded the privilege. Mr Foote, the thespian butcher of Exeter, 'who absolutely sold steaks and beef in the morning at his stall and cut up Richard and Macbeth at night on the stage', no doubt gained his entrée by being part-owner of the local theatre; but in Bath, noted for its gentility, talent seems to have been the appeal. There 'a plain uneducated carpenter, performed with such feeling and judgment as to excite the warmest applause from the whole audience'. In these situations an unpleasant element of snobbery sometimes emerged. A tailor and his wife who starred in a charity performance at Cheltenham were the subject of venomous comment, and Tate Wilkinson reports the objections raised at Hull to a barber appearing in the role of Lothario, even though he was 'a master-barber of renown ... and now transplanted to London'.[57]

For those who did not tread the boards with the professionals, other avenues were available. There is abundant evidence that the enthusiasm for amateur acting had percolated down to the lesser orders, often to the dismay of observers:

> The prevalent phrenzy for spouting and acting ... has not only shown itself in the parlours of private houses, but even descended into the kitchen and stables, the very footmen and grooms becoming Romeos and Alexanders, while cooks and skullions have left their fire-sides and their dripping pans to love like Juliet and die like Statira.[58]

Nor was the countryside immune. The nobility and gentry

> support themselves for a month or two by giving their *rural retreat* some resemblance of a public place; and collecting a croud of half-civilised savages from the surrounding neighbourhood, to see the raree-show and applaud their performances. Hence the humour has spread itself among their tenants' sons and daughters; who, in imitation of their right honourable or right worshipful neighbours, spout heroics in their barns, with as much vehemence, though not always so much correctness of elocution, as their landlords 'have done in *hall* or *bower*'.[59]

George Frederick Cooke, as a Berwick-on-Tweed printer's apprentice, organised enthusiastic fellow apprentices into a performance that was raided by an irate master and the constable. It was the end of an amateur career going back several years. John Bernard describes a similar company in Portsmouth which was disrupted by the players' mothers, who concealed themselves behind an audience of 'cow-boys and town-boys' before storming the stage.[60] Not all authority figures were this hostile. The *English Chronicle*, 29 August 1789, possibly tongue-in-cheek, reported:

> Such is the rage for private theatricals, that *The West Indian* was performed last Saturday in the neighbourhood of Portland-street, by a celebrated mantua-maker, her journey-women, and apprentices only; the lady played the *Hibernian Major* herself, and in such a style as to prove to the audience that she had long *worn the breeches*.

In London one result of this passion was the emergence of a series of playhouses specifically devoted to amateur theatricals. The most famous of these, the Tottenham-court Road playhouse of the Pic-nic Society, projected itself as amateur theatre by and for the gentry, but there are references to at least four other such playhouses further down the social scale. While the performers are sometimes characterised as apprentices, these four nonetheless seem to have had a degree of respectability, one source describing the participants as possessing 'a comfortable subsistence'.[61] Could there have been another level of private playhouses below even these, too humble to be mentioned in the same breath as the Pic-nic Society? By 1808 the *European Magazine* could speak of private theatres 'scattered through every part of this town', and some of the amateur theatres in the country towns were associated with relatively lowly tradespeople. To give only two examples: Billy Purvis (a journeyman carpenter later to become a legend in the north as a clown) ran a company in the long room of a public house in Gateshead at the beginning of the nineteenth century; and slightly later we find Christopher Thomson (a shipwright turned sawyer) laboriously converting a loft at York for his amateur group.[62]

In the light of their enthusiasm for playgoing, one group whose involvement in amateur theatricals should cause no surprise is seamen. The crews of merchant vessels were too small and overworked to manage much in this line, but heavily manned men-of-war were a different proposition. Tate Wilkinson has a vivid picture of the ordinary seamen aboard the warship *Bedford* running their own amateur company, led by their more senior colleagues, the bosuns, carpenters and the like. Nelson's flagship, HMS *Victory*, had similar activities among the lower ranks, while HMS *Britannia* boasted both a seamen's company and an officers' company, each performing on separate occasions in different parts of the ship. Similarly, army theatricals were not entirely the prerogative of the officers. David Love records a performance of Allen Ramsay's *The Gentle Shepherd*, which took place in 1792 or 1793. This was arranged at the initiative of a sergeant who had been an actor and got up entirely by the common soldiers. They played both male and female roles, performing before the officers and local gentry and netting £2 apiece.[63]

In the countryside another form of lower-class amateur theatricals was also to be found. The lack of work in winter led villagers in some places to turn to playmaking, the audience usually paying by donation. The commonest form of this was no doubt the mummers' play, but even that, as in the case of Samuel Tilke and Harvey Teasdale, could be the first step towards more conventional types of theatre. In some places, moreover, there seems to have been a tradition of village companies presenting plays from the popular repertoire in the halls of local squires, as part of the Christmas festivities. The exact dates at which the locals ran winter seasons in a barn at Grassington has not been determined, but in 1827 it was spoken of as within living memory.[64]

There was, then, a significant amount of amateur theatre among the humbler social groups. However, the eighteenth century also boasted a phenomenon which greatly expanded the opportunities for theatrical performance, and which was particularly associated, in the public mind, with mechanics and apprentices. This was the spouting club.[65] There were probably scores of them in London, and untold numbers of them scattered across the British Isles during the second half of the eighteenth century. They were sufficiently conspicuous to become the subject of satire, most notably in Arthur Murphy's farce, *The Apprentice*, but also in Henry Dell's *The Spouter* and Andrew Franklin's musical entertainment, *The Hypocondriac*, as well as in short stories, novels, journalistic pieces and in the allegedly factual reports in memoirs and autobiographies.[66]

The common method of organising such a club was for a group of enthusiasts to pool their funds and hire a large room for an assembly once a week or once a month. The room was usually in an inn. A simple stage was set up at one end, complete with a curtain and candles and, in some cases, an all-purpose set of wings and a backscene. A chairman was appointed who called on members of the club to do their turns. What resulted was a random sequence of monologues or duologues drawn from the high points of established plays: Scrub and Archer from George Farquhar's *The Beaux Stratagem*, Jaffeir and Pierre from Thomas Otway's *Venice Preserv'd*, a sequence from the end of Shakespeare's *Richard III* and so on. Since most of these clubs had an all-male membership, the scenes displayed rarely involved women characters, but many clubs, once or twice a year, staged complete plays. Because of the improprieties associated with play-acting this often meant that any women co-opted were likely to be of a humble background, such as milliners and mantua makers.[67] Thomas Snagg's autobiography provides an example where they seem to have been little better than women of the streets. Indeed, one of London's better-known actresses, Mrs Farmer, had been a prostitute with a passion for spouting, whose talents had been recognised and promoted by one of her clients.[68]

The audience at a spouting club's evening comprised club members, friends, and in many cases the general public. Admission needed to be free if the performance was not to violate the law, but some clubs took the risk and charged sixpence or a shilling, occasionally bringing down the constables upon them.[69] Theatrical managers sometimes visited the better-known clubs in search of new talent for the profession, undoubtedly adding to the frisson of the evening. In this way William Farren, apprentice tinsmith, was recruited from the club at the One Tun in the Strand, John Edwin from the Falcon in Fetter Lane and John Bernard from a club in Bristol.[70]

A lively and detailed picture of one of these clubs in operation is provided in Anthony Pasquin's life of Edwin. Among its features is a visit to one of the more sophisticated city clubs by members of a suburban group from Norton Folgate. Despite reservations,

> the stage-struck Heroes from Norton Falgate [*sic*] were permitted to dash away; but their recital of the first scene of the *Fair Penitent*, evinced the insufficiency of two novitiates not practiced in a regular spouting club, and Mr Altamont's unhappy pronunciation of the first speech ruined him for ever as an actor in the opinion of the critics in Fetter Lane. With much solemnity of mien, and a tone of utterance not inaptly compared to the roaring of a Bull he began the following imperative declaration:
>
>> 'Let this auspicious day be ever sacred,
>> 'No mourning, no misfortunes *appen* on it,
>> 'Let it be mark'd for triumphs and rejoicings.
>> 'Let *appy* lovers *hever* make it *oly*,
>> 'Chuse it to bless their *opes* and crown their wishes;
>> 'This *appy* day that gives me my *Kalista*.'
>
> The gentle Altamont had scarcely finished when the laugh became loud and general, excepting two or three friends to the young Tyro, who, by clenching their fists and frowning indignant, seemed disposed to contest the prevailing opinion of the audience.[71]

What gives this scene its piquancy is the fact that the two men who could best claim to be the founders of Australia's most important convict theatre, Robert Sidaway and John Sparrow, had both been baptised in St Leonard's, Shoreditch, and had spent their early lives within a few hundred yards of the diminutive enclave that was Norton Folgate. It is possible that one or both had been members of this club, or had witnessed its performances. At the very least Pasquin's account may give some feeling of the cultural world from which these men emerged.

Spouting, however, was not a phenomenon limited to spouting clubs. While the self-generated entertainment in the tavern free-and-easies was predominantly musical, it could extend to brief dramatic presentations, so that the evening took on the characteristics of a variety show.[72] Nor was the term spouting limited to two-handed scenes from the theatrical repertoire: it could also cover monologues or a highly dramatic reading of verse. Such things, after all, were common as interludes in the evening's bill of fare at a playhouse, and many actors created complete evening entertainments out of medleys of song, recitation and dance, among them Charles Dibdin, George Alexander Stevens and Edward Cape Everard. At the humbler level with which we are concerned were the near beggars who made a living by 'spouting Billy', which a slightly later dictionary defined as earning a living by reciting Shakespeare in tap-rooms.[73] It is not surprising, therefore, that such eminently flexible activities also became a form of domestic amusement. Samuel Tilke was one who entertained his family in this way until religious scruples overwhelmed him.[74]

In all these ways, then, people not of high social standing could have witnessed theatre in London, as well as elsewhere, or could have honed their skills as performers. The fact that not one of the eighteenth-century Sydney or Norfolk Island actors has any recorded theatrical experience before departing for Botany Bay may say more about the paucity of the records than the backgrounds of those involved. In 1822 a group of would-be Sydney performers claimed to have been 'bred to the Stage, in London and other parts of England', but the records of those who can be identified are almost as blank. George Suttor and George Barrington might stand as the only people to arrive in the colony in its first thirty years for whom evidence of prior theatrical activity exists, but the odds are that many others had occasional or long-term involvement in the world of amateur theatre or spouting clubs, or on the margins of professionalism, and brought this experience and its accompanying passions with them to help vivify their bleak lives in the antipodes.

Chapter 2

THEATRE IN SYDNEY TO 1809:
A CHRONOLOGICAL ACCOUNT

n 15 November 1788 Botany Bay's only clergyman, the Rev. Richard Johnson, wrote home in deep depression. The people of the colony, it appeared,

> prefer their Lust before their Souls, yea, most of them will sell their souls for a Glass of Grog, so blind, so foolish, so hardened are they … No Church is yet begun of, & I am afraid scarcely thought of. Other things seem to be of greater Notice & Concern & most wd rather see a Tavern, a Play House, a Brothel – anything sooner than a place for publick worship.[1]

In fact the convict taste for theatre had been in evidence even before the First Fleet anchored at Botany Bay. On 2 January 1788, as the transport *Scarborough* drove through the Roaring Forties, some 650 miles south of where Adelaide now stands, a marine, John Easty, made the terse note in his diary, 'this Night the Convicts Made a play & Sang many Songs'.[2]

Does the Rev. Johnson's statement, then, indicate that theatre was an active presence in the colony in its very first year, or are his words merely a rhetorical flourish? Was the production of Farquhar's *The Recruiting Officer* on the King's birthday, 4 June 1789, the first European theatrical performance in Australia, as has long been accepted, or was it simply the first performance that caught the imagination of the officer class because it was directed to them? Was this why it found its way into their records and so into history?

Since the prologue specially written for that production spoke of the 'novelty' of the occasion,[3] there can be little doubt that it actually was Australia's first full-scale theatrical event. However, even before that the convicts would have had little difficulty in undertaking some of the simpler forms of theatre. For its first decades New South Wales operated, in effect, as a vast open-air prison. While the convicts were supposed not to stray too far from their settlement, they had a significant degree of freedom. Outside regulation working hours most of them came and went as they pleased, finding their own accommodation and mixing with the non-convict population – the sailors, the soldiers, the trickle of free settlers and (increasingly over the years) the emancipists. To cater for this leisure time alehouses quickly sprang up, and in Britain, as the last chapter indicated, establishments of that kind frequently became venues for organised singing, recitations and the performance of dramatic excerpts, through the institution of spouting clubs and free-and-easies. If no full-scale production was attempted before *The Recruiting Officer*, it may still have been preceded by a host of these miniature shows, building up the expectation of a playhouse sufficient to generate Johnson's sour comment. The convicts making a play and singing many songs on the *Scarborough* could well have been indulging in a tavern medley; and some of the disturbances broken up by the watch in convict huts in early Sydney may have been organised entertainments of one kind or another.[4]

Certainly there were nineteenth-century commentators who believed that this sort of pastime was an embryonic form of theatre first practised in the colony. In 1839 James Maclehose claimed:

> In looking over some old papers entrusted to us, and reverentially preserved by 'an old hand', we find, that as far back as when the now flourishing town of Sydney was a mere wild *bush*, that a few wretched exiles from their native land, cherished the remembrance of 'Home, sweet Home', by assembling in a *wooden gunyah*, and reciting various passages from Shakespeare's plays.[5]

The sentence that follows makes it clear that the author is referring to the period of the naval governors and sees this activity as preceding any full-scale theatre. In 1848 Joseph Fowles made similar claims,[6] but he is even less precise, does not mention Sydney, gives no hint of a date, and may be simply plagiarising Maclehose. One is left to hope that Maclehose's 'old papers' are not simply a fabrication to give credibility to what is otherwise a plausible guess concerning the origins of European theatre in Australia.

However early the first appearance of such entertainments, there are a few scattered hints to suggest that they remained an ongoing part of convict life well into the nineteenth century. On 9 December 1826 the *Sydney Gazette* reported the trial of Robert Newsham at Windsor for sheltering a runaway female convict. The paper describes Newsham as 'the spouting Government servant of a gentleman at Windsor, but who resides at a Curry-jong farm', and follows it with a mock-heroic speech for the defence, in verse, as if delivered by Newsham at his trial. The poem is presumably a *jeu d'esprit* by the journalist and the report itself has all the obscurity of an in-joke. Presumably Newsham was an occasional performer in the Windsor tap-rooms or had earned a local notoriety for entertaining himself and the cows of Kurrajong with declamatory outpourings in the fields. Even later in the century F.C. Brewer provides an account which, like Fowles, seems to draw on Maclehose, but replaces the latter's '*wooden gunyah*' in Sydney with open-air performances in the bush, and offers a concrete and suitably racy example of such a performance in progress. The details given point to a presentation in the Port Macquarie area (see Appendix B, Note 1). For the moment what is important is that activities of this kind may have been common and should be kept in mind as a shadowy background to the more formal theatrical productions that are the subject of this study.

II

Of all the official celebrations scattered through the year, the King's birthday was the one that seemed of most significance to the ruling elite of New South Wales. The ceremonies are described in elaborate detail in many accounts of the colony's early days and are more or less standardised. The event normally involved a holiday for the convicts and pardons for some of those in prison or awaiting execution for local crimes. The troops, and sometimes the convicts, received a celebratory issue of rum and there was a great deal in the way of twenty-one-gun salutes, flag-flying and parades, with bonfires in the evening. One finds the same pattern, as far as it could be achieved, in outposts such as Norfolk Island and later at Hobart.[7]

Another convention of the day was that in the afternoon, and stretching into the evening, members of the ruling elite gathered, by invitation, at Government House for a formal dinner, with toasts and music. In 1788, and apparently until the numbers became too great, the invitation extended to 'all the officers not on duty, both of the garrison and his Majesty's ships'.[8]

For the birthday celebrations on 4 June 1789, however, there was a variation. David Collins speaks of the day being 'observed with every distinction in our power' and, after describing the usual volleys and salutes, continues:

> The governor received the compliments due to the day in his new house, of which he had lately taken possession as the government-house of the colony, where his excellency afterwards entertained the officers at dinner, and in the evening some of the convicts were permitted to perform Farquhar's comedy of the Recruiting Officer, in a hut fitted up for the occasion. They professed no higher aim than 'humbly to excite a smile', and their efforts to please were not unattended with applause.[9]

But it is Watkin Tench who, with his carefully cultivated sensibility, provides a more extended and lyrical description of that occasion:

> The anniversary of his majesty's birth-day was celebrated, as heretofore, at the government-house, with loyal festivity. In the evening, the play of the Recruiting Officer was performed by a party of convicts, and honoured by the presence of his excellency, and the officers of the garrison. That every opportunity of escape from the dreariness and dejection of our situation should be eagerly embraced, will not be wondered at. The exhilarating effect of a splendid theatre is well known: and I am not ashamed to confess, that the proper distribution of three or four yards of stained paper, and a dozen farthing candles stuck around the mud walls of a convict-hut, failed not to diffuse general complacency on the countenances of sixty persons, of various descriptions, who were assembled to applaud the representation. Some of the actors acquitted themselves with great spirit, and received the praises of the audience: a prologue and an epilogue, written by one of the performers,

were also spoken on the occasion; which, although not worth inserting here, contained some tolerable allusions to the situation of the parties, and the novelty of a stage-representation in New South Wales.[10]

These are the only two accounts of this key moment in Australian theatre history to survive. What can be deduced from them?

As I indicated in the previous chapter, modern mythmaking, in the form of *The Playmaker* and *Our Country's Good*, has tended to assume that such an endeavour would have required the leadership of a gentleman officer. In this case Lieutenant Ralph Clark is singled out as an appealing possibility for the role, both because he is known to have read the occasional play and enjoyed playgoing,[11] and because of his interestingly convoluted and somewhat repellent personality. Certainly, there was at least one occasion many years later when an officer provided just this sort of leadership,[12] though the result was far from satisfactory and the officer himself was soon assigned to a lunatic asylum. In fact, the humbler sections of British society contained plenty of men and women with the cultural capital and the self-confidence to undertake such a project, and the form of words used by Collins – 'some of the convicts were permitted to perform Farquhar's comedy' – suggests a convict initiative, and not something conceived and guided from above.

The names of those who provided this entertainment are lost to history. What is interesting is that few, if any, of them went on to become participants in the later convict theatres of which we have a record. Most of those who are known to have been associated with the Norfolk Island theatre of 1793, or the Sydney theatre of 1796, had not arrived in the colony by June 1789. Henry Lavell (or Lavall or Lovell) and Edward Flynn were there, but Lavell was only a bit player in Sydney in 1796 and Flynn may have been merely a stage hand on Norfolk Island. If the redoubtable First Fleeter, Fanny Davis, was the Mrs Davis of 1796, she also could have participated in *The Recruiting Officer*. Sidaway was a First Fleeter but he was a theatrical entrepreneur, not an actor. However, he could have been the organisational force behind the 1789 production. This leaves William Hogg. Robert Irving makes a strong plea for his involvement with *The Recruiting Officer* on the grounds of his later reputation as a comic performer.[13] It is worth noting that he was involved in some capacity with the Norfolk Island theatre and that he had been shipped out on the *Scarborough*, the vessel whose convicts had been engaged in singing and playmaking off the coast of South Australia.

All of this, of course, remains speculation; but the lack of significant connection between this first performance and later convict theatres makes the point that the love of theatre among the convicts was so widespread that new performers were always available for new enterprises.

Though written in 1706, *The Recruiting Officer* would have been performed, as in England, in modern dress. The handful of military costumes required could have been begged from the officers and men of the marine garrison, a process made easier because of the patriotic nature of the event. As for the costumes of the ladies and civilian gentlemen, these could have been supplied by the convicts themselves.

Most had brought chests with them on the voyage, containing clothes, tools and other possessions. Some of them had been modish dressers in Britain, and renewed the habit on their free days in the colony. Convict women parading in their finery were a subject of early comment,[14] and when Ann Davis became the first woman to be hanged in Australia in November 1789 it was because of the theft of clothes from the convict baker, that same Robert Sidaway. Included among the stolen goods were four expensive linen shirts, two cambrick handkerchiefs, a silk waistcoat and a dimity waistcoat.[15] This is far from the normal image of convict dress, but Sidaway would not have been unique in his access to such things, even at this early stage in the colony's history. The venue may have been a rough convict hut, but there could have been a splash of finery on stage, particularly when viewed under the pale light of candles.

As for the hut itself, we are reduced to speculation, and that has been removed to Appendix B, Note 2. This leaves for consideration the question of the audience. Tench writes of it as comprising 'sixty persons of various descriptions', which suggests a socially-mixed group. However, we are also told that the performance was 'honoured by the presence of his excellency, and the officers of the garrison', while the implication in Collins' account is that the officers came there after the Government House dinner.

Detailed calculations of the number of officers in or near Sydney on 4 June 1789, and of the number of those who might have been at the dinner, are provided in Appendix B, Note 3. On the most plausible definition of the word 'officer' there were 55 or 56 individuals who were eligible to attend. What is unclear is the number of those not present at the dinner because they were on duty or for some other reason. In 1802, as Matthew Flinders noted, there were 40 at the dinner, at a time when there was a smaller naval presence in the port, and the number of military officers had diminished. In 1803 the number was 46, though six months later 59 people assembled for the Queen's birthday dinner, the greater number being due to the presence in port of HMS *Calcutta*.[16]

Not all of the dinner guests of 1789 would have gone to the play. It is difficult to imagine the Rev. Johnson, with all his prejudices, choosing to attend a theatre, with or without his wife. On the other hand, simple courtesy, the loyal nature of the occasion, the rarity of entertainments in the hard-pressed colony and the curiosity value would probably have induced the bulk of his guests to accompany the governor. Hypothetically, over forty of the sixty audience-members could have been drawn from the ruling elite. Although the actual number may have been below that, there still remain those immediate adjuncts of the ruling order, the storekeepers and superintendents, the marine sergeants (some of whom had brought their wives to the colony) and their naval equivalents, such as the bosuns and master-gunners. Tench's reference to an audience of 'various descriptions' suggests some common folk were present; but the few places remaining would not have gone far among the theatre-loving sailors and soldiers. There may well have been no convicts whatsoever in the audience, only convicts performing for the delectation of their betters. Though *The Recruiting Officer* was sufficiently popular to justify its selection on that ground alone, it was also a play that had a special appeal to the military. Its choice may have been a calculated attempt to flatter those who were expected to dominate not only the audience but also the lives of the players.

III

Hitherto, the theatrical record for Sydney has been completely blank between this performance of 4 June 1789 and 16 January 1796, when the township's first regular theatre burst, fully-formed, on the colony. In this view of things Norfolk Island had beaten the colony's major centre in opening a playhouse, since one was operational there by late 1793, though it was short-lived.

In fact, a tiny fragment of evidence exists which may point to a somewhat different situation. On 10 April 1794 the Rev. Johnson wrote an intensely bitter and lengthy report to England. Johnson was engaged in a savage feud with Governor Arthur Phillip's successor, Lieutenant-Governor Francis Grose, the commander of the New South Wales Corps. The letter is largely about the slights inflicted on him by Grose, the contempt with which he was treated by the other godless officers, and the extraordinary difficulties he was experiencing in carrying out his pastoral duties because of this lack of support. A central problem for Johnson was the absence of any designated space for divine service, and he tells a tale of services interrupted, of congregations assembling without the slightest idea of where the service was to be held and of his dissatisfaction with the places allocated. To make his point he gives a rapid list of these places, and it is here that evidence can be found, tucked into a parenthesis:

> Sometimes we have assembled in an Hospital full of Bugs & other vermin & nauseous smells – the next Sunday perhaps in a Barrack amongst the soldiers – the next in an old store House – in a granary (wh^ch it has been said was originally intended for a Church) – at another time, under a Tile shade (which has since been fitted up, & converted into a play House) – then under the shade of a saw pit.[17]

There can be little doubt that what is being described here is a venue for ongoing theatrical activity and not for a one-night stand, as was the case with the convict hut used for *The Recruiting Officer*.

We can deduce further information about this theatre from Johnson's comment. What he refers to as a 'Tile shade' was usually called a 'tile shed', but his description really captures the essence of the building. A tile shed was simply a roof supported on posts, without walls or flooring. It had tables along one side for moulding tiles and the bulk of the space was given up to tiered racks for storing the completed tiles while they waited for firing. A nineteenth-century authority gives the width of such sheds as some 21 feet, and the height to the eaves as about 8 feet. The length was variable, depending on the number of moulding tables. Three tables, for example, would apparently have required a shed some 36 feet in length.[18]

The width causes no great problems. The Sydney theatre of 1796 was probably itself only 21–22 feet across, and even a length of 36 feet, though tight, could have accommodated a theatre. It is the height that causes the heartburn, and yet for a tile shed anything beyond 8 feet would have been impractical for stacking. What this height means is that the stage could have been raised only a foot or so, that there was no scope for an elevated gallery, and very little for any raking of the auditorium. Walls were obviously a necessity. They could have been made of weatherboard nailed to the uprights, but equally they could have been of canvas or bagging, like those of an English tent show of the period. The bare earth or discarded bricks probably constituted the floor. Theatre boxes, for the dignitaries, in the English fashion, are highly unlikely. If people of any status attended this humble little establishment they were probably seated in the front two rows, as they were in Thomas Crowder's Norfolk Island theatre, discussed in Chapter 5.

The fact that the building was originally a tile shed makes it reasonably certain that it was not even situated in Sydney itself, but a mile out of town along the road to Parramatta. It was at this point that good quality clay for brick and tilemaking was discovered in the first days of the colony, and a tiny village had sprung up there as a centre for the industry. With an eye for the obvious, it was simply called Brickfields.[19] It lay east of the present Chinatown and it was a distinctly unruly place, controlled only by a local constable and watchmen. The convict brickmakers themselves were a notoriously tough bunch, suspected of much of the ongoing lawless activity in the town.[20] The insalubrious environment is enough to suggest that in this case we are dealing with performances chiefly for the lower orders.

A theatre group looking for a building to convert would surely have wished to be close to the centre of population. If it turned to the suburbs it might have been because the forces of legal control were weaker there but, given the desperate shortage of building stock in the colony, it is more likely that it was only there it could find a home. How the company managed to secure a tile shed for their purposes is unclear. It is possible that we are looking at one of those calculatedly temporary buildings that were thrown up in the first days of the colony, with a life expectancy of about four years.[21] By 1793 or thereabouts it may have been abandoned by the government, something that adds to the sense of this theatre's roughness. Alternatively, it could be that there was a lay-off period for brickmaking in the colony, similar to that operating in England, so that the Brickfields theatre was a seasonal affair. The brief but convoluted investigation of this possibility, which I am inclined not to favour, has been relegated to Appendix B, Note 4.

Since the Rev. Johnson was writing in April 1794, it is clear that the theatre existed by that time. There is no firm evidence, however, of its date of opening. Johnson had been confronted with similar difficulties during Phillip's tenure,[22] but since the letter is largely an attack on Grose the church service in the tile shed probably took place under that officer. Grose had succeeded Phillip on 11 December 1792, so that the theatre is unlikely to have been opened before mid-1793. This chapter opened with Johnson's bitter complaint that 'most wd rather see a Tavern, a Play House, a Brothel – anything sooner than a place for publick worship'. There is an awful possibility that his lament was prescient, and that Sydney had its theatre before it had its church, which Johnson finally opened on 25 August 1793.

IV

The existence of a rough theatre in 1793 or early 1794 slightly tarnishes the aura surrounding 16 January 1796, which has always been accepted as the opening date for Sydney's first playhouse. However, in view of the primitive nature of the tile-shed theatre, the uncertainty about its duration and the total lack of information about its activities, January 1796 retains most of its significance. Even though the company that opened the theatre on that night may have been the one which had earlier operated in the tile shed, 16 January is the date on which it firmly established itself. Thereafter it went on to become the most dynamic of all the convict theatres, as well as being the one which attracted the greatest attention, and for which we have the most diverse range of contemporary sources of information. The 1796 date justifies its place both in history and in legend.

The Sydney which greeted this theatre was little more than a large straggling village incongruously combined with the buildings of a government depot – army barracks, storehouses, forts, the governor's residence. While the forest pressed in all around, the area in which building had taken place was largely stripped of trees, so that it had a bare and desolate appearance. The streets were potholed dirt tracks, along which pigs, goats and dogs wandered and foraged, in spite of the governor's efforts to control them, particularly the pigs. Most of the houses were only one- or two-roomed constructions of lath and plaster, with a skillion or lean-to attached to the back and high paling fences. The bulk of them still had thatched roofs. The rear of the allotment sometimes contained a pig-sty, and often a fowl-yard, so that Sydney's dawn chorus was as much a matter of crowing roosters and yapping dogs as it was of kookaburras and parakeets. The older government buildings by this time were in a hopelessly dilapidated state and were being replaced by brick buildings with tiled or shingled roofs; but the lack of resources meant that progress was painfully slow. While the place may have looked passably pretty when the houses had fresh coats of lime wash, for much of the time, and especially in the heat of summer, it must have appeared as it did to the jaundiced Captain Colnett, of HMS *Glatton*. Sydney in 1803, he wrote, resembled nothing so much as some forlorn and miserable outpost of the Portuguese Empire.[23]

Though the colony had only been established for eight years at this time, a convict and emancipist business class was already emerging. At its top were men like Isaac Nicholls, Robert Sidaway, Matt. Kearns, William Miller, Henry Kable, David Bevan and the redoubtable Simeon Lord; but below these was a host of dealers, innkeepers and the like, including women such as Mary Mullett and Ann Marsh. Some had begun as agents for the officers, whose status prevented them from openly dabbling in trade; but by now they were entrepreneurs on their own account. Most invested in a bewildering array of activities. One individual could be involved in running an inn, conducting a general-goods shop, working at a trade, money-lending, farming and (for the most successful) owning or contracting small ships engaged in the coastal trade to the Hawkesbury, sealing in Bass Strait, or sandalwood-gathering and other traffic in the Pacific Islands. Some of these entrepreneurs had advantages of birth or education, but many of them were ruthlessly self-made. In 1796 much of this activity was still in an infant state, but by the beginning of the new century it was well established.[24]

Despite this enterprise, Sydney in this period must still have been a place of stupefying boredom, dominated by its work routine. The regiment's drums beat the reveille at 6.00 am and tapto at 8.00 or 9.00 pm, and the bells of the dockyard and lumber yard rang out the work sessions. Here a suffocatingly small elite, locked into one another's company, sat in power over an aggressive assembly of convict and emancipist entrepreneurs, a larger community of seemingly feckless and incorrigible felonry, and a growing number of political prisoners who added an edge of insecurity to the prevailing torpor and frustration. Drink, gambling, sexual license and the arrival of a new convict ship from England were projected as the major sources of excitement. So desperate for entertainment were many of the people that the dissection of an executed prisoner by the settlement's doctors attracted a large crowd, many of whose members, in other circumstances, could themselves have been the cadaver on the slab.[25]

Such a community might have seemed ripe for the excitements of theatre, but there was one significant drawback. Sydney and its environs in 1796 boasted a European population of only 2,400 or so. The Parramatta–Toongabbie area had another thousand, but convicts were forbidden to travel from one settlement to another without a pass. While the more daredevil of them, such as James Hardy (better known as 'Flash' Jim) Vaux a few years later, might have been prepared to walk the six hours from Toongabbie in the depths of night to spend an illicit weekend in the fleshpots of Sydney,[26] the number of convicts coming from this outpost must have been small. Even smaller would have been the number from the Hawkesbury, a three-day boat-trip away, down the river and along the coast.

On the other hand, Sydney was not only the centre of administration but also the colony's seaport. The arrival of a ship, particularly a warship, could unleash a swarm of sailors on the town. On the night that the Sydney theatre opened there were four ships in port – the colonial schooner *Francis*, the East India trader *Arthur*, and two naval vessels, HMS *Supply* and HMS *Reliance*.[27] Among them they could possibly have filled a small theatre by themselves.

Since Governor John Hunter took control of the colony on 11 September 1795 and the new Sydney theatre was opened on 16 January 1796, it is likely that Hunter's predecessor had granted permission for its development. Captain William

Paterson of the New South Wales Corps had held the position of lieutenant-governor since 17 December 1794, by virtue of being the senior military officer in the colony after Grose's departure. This is all the more likely since Collins actually notes that the company had obtained permission to prepare a playhouse 'some time since'.[28]

Whether Hunter or Paterson was responsible, it is slightly surprising that permission was given at all, in spite of the amiability of both men. It was, after all, only two years since the theatre riot at Norfolk Island that had generated a near mutiny among the soldiery. Though permission was granted, the authorities were clearly mindful of the risks. Judge-Advocate David Collins' account of the launching of the theatre puts significant emphasis on law and order: 'At the licensing of this exhibition they were informed, that the slightest impropriety would be noticed, and a repetition punished by the banishment of their company to the other settlements.' If the company in the tile shed was still operating in 1795 and had caused no trouble, this might have been one reason why permission was granted. This would have been all the more likely if the two enterprises had been related. It was common English practice to test a new town by beginning in a rough *ad hoc* space and only investing in a more substantial theatre where the market proved its viability. In spite of the impression given by Collins that the 1796 theatre came out of nowhere, it might well have been the product of this gradual approach.

V

The process whereby the company went about creating its 1796 playhouse, and the details of its construction, will be considered in Chapter 3; but the evidence suggests that the resulting building was a thoroughly respectable version of a small provincial English playhouse of the time. There were a few oddities in the layout, such as the large size of the gallery, which Collins noted, but the auditorium observed the tripartite division into pit, boxes and gallery, and there are hints that it attempted some of the refinements associated with the better sort of playhouse. Even the sardonic Collins admitted that it had 'more theatrical propriety than could have been expected'.

In a town as starved of variety as Sydney the opening of the playhouse must have been an occasion of high expectation. By late afternoon on 16 January a crowd would have gathered around the entrance well before the doors opened, waiting to secure the best seats. Since places were unnumbered and the seating was merely long benches, this huddle of people before the closed entrances was a common feature, even of long-established theatres in England, where playbills often announced the time at which the doors opened, as well as the time the performance began. The surviving Sydney playbills follow the convention, with a 5.30 opening for a 6.30 pm start. Avid Sydney theatregoers would thus spend fifty minutes or more kicking their heels against the wooden benches – and this after a lengthy wait outside.

Once the doors opened the admission began, a process in which David Collins found an oddity worthy of comment: the use of payment in kind by the galleryites: 'One evil was observable, which in fact could not well be prevented; in lieu of a shilling, as much flour, or as much meat or spirits, as the manager would take for that sum, was often paid at the gallery door.' Collins' anecdote greatly amused sophisticates on the other side of the world and jests on the subject began to appear soon after his account was published: 'According to a French journalist, admissions to the Theatre at Botany Bay are paid for either in money or eatables. For a leg of mutton you have free access to any place before the curtain, and if you add Caper Sauce you may take in a friend.'[29] Amusing it might have been, but some of the smaller country theatres in England practised a similar system of exchange. John Bernard gives the example of the manager, James Whitely:

> Jemmy was not particular, in poor communities, as to whether he received the public support in money or in 'kind'. He would take meat, fowl, vegetables, &c. value them by scales, &c. and pass in the owner and friends for as many admissions as they amounted to. Thus his treasury very often, on a Saturday, resembled a butcher's warehouse rather than a banker's. At a village on the coast, the inhabitants brought him nothing but fish.[30]

The custom may have been quaint, but in New South Wales it had justification. There was such a shortage of coinage in the colony that the entire community operated on a barter economy, with promissory notes as the only significant alternative.

If, as Collins suggests, the manager was supervising the gallery sales, there may have been another exotic touch to the process. John Sparrow, the manager, was also a lead actor in the company, which probably meant that this bartering had to be conducted in full theatrical costume. Samuel Ryley describes such a situation in a small English company's production of *Hamlet*, in which the manager 'presided at the receipt of custom' in the full armour of the Royal Dane, so that he could go direct from front of house to stage and not cause an awkward delay.[31]

Once inside the theatre, the audience faced a new set of problems. On that opening night the playhouse was probably packed to near capacity, and eighteenth-century ideas of capacity, from a modern point of view, are profoundly alarming. Many English theatres calculated as little as 15 inches of bench space per person as the standard allowance. In view of its background a Sydney crowd was likely to be more aggressive than one at home, so that the pushing, shoving and squeezing to secure a space can readily be imagined. In addition, the distance between the back of one bench and the back of the next in England was 2 feet at best. This was tight for the average-sized male and must have bordered on the painful for anyone much beyond 5 feet 6 inches in height. If the crowd spilled over and stood in the aisles (in English fashion), these could have become as close-packed as the benches. Though the Sydney Theatre may have had a notional capacity of 180, up to 220 bodies could have crowded into it on that first night.[32]

That night, moreover, was at the height of a Sydney summer. Theatres had no windows and in most cases that meant no ventilation. Crowded human bodies radiated heat and odour, and dozens of candles spluttered away, through the auditorium as well as on the stage, giving off more heat and their own fatty smells – for theatrical economy demanded tallow tapers, not expensive beeswax. Even the summer theatres of Britain were the subject of frequent comment because of their stifling heat. Since hot air rises, the problem was at its most extreme in the gallery. An extravagantly-coloured account of a summer performance in Aylesbury, by the time the fifth act of the mainpiece had been reached, gives some idea of the consequences:

> The heat, the reeking heat of the upper part of the gallery was almost unbearable. A cat – not even a cat – (notwithstanding its nine lives!) could not have lived long in such an exhausted atmosphere. I say exhausted, because there was no vital air, no *oxygen*, left unconsumed within it. As to the crowd at the top of the stairs, life was sustained in them only by the occasional whiffs of pure air that came up from the gallery door-way. But the poor devils puffing and panting for a time, were soon seen widely gasping for breath as fish do when they are first drawn out of the water.[33]

The heat in London's summer theatres, on occasion, became so intolerable that they had to be closed.[34]

If this was the effect of an English summer, the consequences of an Australian one can easily be imagined. The temperature in Sydney on 16 January 1796 has not been recorded, but by reading the logs of the ships in port a reasonably clear picture of the weather emerges. Four days before the performance there had been a violent storm with thunder and lightning. By the sixteenth the clouds were building up again and over the next few days the lightning returned, then squalls, developing into another violent storm. It was a classic semi-cyclonic Sydney January, with the rain or threat of rain keeping down the temperatures a little, but probably causing the most appalling humidity.[35]

Clearly, the eighteenth century had lower standards of comfort than the twenty-first; but what may be at issue here is not only levels of tolerance but also an attitude to playgoing. The large size of the gallery in Sydney suggests this was a predominantly plebeian theatre, and the plebeian audience, as Chapter 1 indicated, was regarded as particularly noisy and demonstrative. Its dynamic was very different from that of the modern mainstream. The comparison with a rock concert may be a little threadbare but it is still useful – an excitement born of densely-packed bodies, extravagant audience responses and a high level of squalor.

The program offered on that opening night was of the kind one would expect to find in any legitimate English theatre of the time. It comprised a mainpiece, drawn from the standard repertoire, followed by an afterpiece, on this occasion a farce. There would also have been the usual preliminaries, an extended musical introduction from a small orchestra, followed by an actor advancing in front of the curtain to deliver a prologue.

This prologue would almost certainly have been written locally for the occasion. It was commonplace in England for companies touring the provincial towns, as part of the process of ingratiation, to offer such pieces, normally replete with local references. Similarly, special events, such as the opening of a new theatre, were accorded the same treatment. A prologue of this kind had adorned that first Australian production of *The Recruiting Officer* and, in far off Leicester, Henry Carter had no difficulty imagining a similar effusion gracing the opening of the 1796 playhouse. The result was his 'Prologue, supposed to have been spoken at the Opening of the Theatre at Botany Bay', which he envisaged as 'spoken by the celebrated Mr. B-rr-ngt-n',[36] and which has come down to us as the 'Barrington Prologue', long thought to have been actually delivered on that night. This was not the case, but Carter's English squib has gone on to become the most famous poetic evocation of early convict Australia, and has helped to give that first Sydney theatre its faintly legendary quality:

> From distant climes, o'er wide-spread seas we come,
> Though not with much *éclat* or beat of drum,
> True patriots all – for be it understood,
> We left our Country, for our Country's good:
> No private views disgrac'd our generous zeal,
> What urg'd our travels was our Country's weal:
> And none will doubt but that our emigration
> Has prov'd most useful to the British Nation.[37]

And so it continues. The prologue that actually was spoken on that night could conceivably have been written, if not spoken, by Barrington, who had a reputation as a belletrist, but his posting to Parramatta, and his sense of dignity, would have been enough to exclude him. There were, no doubt, plenty of others to aspire, such as Laurence Davoren,[38] and it would not be surprising to find that the company manager, John Sparrow, or its best actor, Henry Green, could turn a couplet.

With the prologue over, the speaker retired and the curtain rose on the first image ever to adorn a regular theatre in mainland Australia – a solitary figure, outlandishly dressed in the stage-exotic style, his face blackened with burnt cork. It was Zanga, the Moorish villain, who promptly launched into a ranting soliloquy:

> Whether first nature, or long want of peace,
> Has wrought my mind to this, I cannot tell;
> But horrors now are not displeasing to me!
> I like this rocking of the battlements.
> Rage on, ye winds, burst clouds, and waters roar!
> You bear a just resemblance of my fortune,
> And suit the gloomy habit of my soul.

Edward Young's *The Revenge* was under way. It is an overblown and remorseless verse tragedy written in 1720. While the critics of the late eighteenth century were lukewarm about the play,[39] it still held a firm, though declining, place in the English theatrical repertory. Perhaps its melodramatic quality made it more appealing to a gallery audience than to refined critical taste, but nevertheless it represents a safe choice, a play sanctioned by decades of respectable theatregoers.

The afterpiece is somewhat more surprising. Thomas Vaughan's *The Hotel* had first appeared at Drury Lane on 21 November 1776. It had been savaged by many of the critics, even after a rapid rewriting for its second presentation on 23 November. It appeared only another six times before disappearing after the performance on 1 February 1777.[40] It managed publication in both London and Dublin at the time of its presentation, but never found a place in any of the collections of plays and afterpieces that were a feature of the age. The work is a wooden adaptation of Goldoni's *The Servant of Two Masters* and, in however mangled a form, represents the first appearance of a continental European classic on the Australian stage. What made the company choose this unlikely piece is a mystery, but they could have been sorely strapped for texts of any kind.

We have only Collins' assessment of the quality of the performance and, given his generally low opinion of convicts, his words probably amount to grudging praise. 'Their performance', he declares, 'was far above contempt', and then, in a somewhat more biting footnote, 'Of the men, Green best deserved to be called an actor.' Green, a prisoner older than the others, probably played the meaty role of Zanga.

One comment by Collins remains to be explored: 'Of their dresses the greater part was made by themselves; but we understood that some veteran articles from the York theatre were among the best that made their appearance.' The idea of costumes from the York theatre being transported around the world to adorn a convict performance borders on the fantastic; but it also shows some taste. The York company took an inordinate pride in the quality of its wardrobe and regarded it as one of the best in England.[41] One explanation is that the manager, or a vainglorious performer, had written to England to secure a few pieces of theatrical dress. If this was the case then it suggests that either the company had been in preparation for a long time indeed, or that the earlier Brickfields company had made the order. It would have taken at least five months for an order to reach England, followed by the delay awaiting for a returning vessel, and then the outward voyage itself – a year to 18 months or more.

There is, however, another possibility, one for which the word fantastic is entirely appropriate. At the beginning of 1790 William Richards, a one-eyed caster of ornaments for plastering work, took the road from Manchester to Yorkshire. *En route* he used a variety of aliases and gave varied accounts of his background, among them that he was a Covent Garden actor going to join some of his colleagues in the North. He was, in fact, a petty thief, but his claims to an involvement with theatre were true up to a point, for in his wanderings he made a specialty of robbing playhouses, chiefly by stealing costumes from the dressing rooms. Manchester itself had fallen prey, as had Derby, Margate and York, before he was captured hiding in the Newcastle theatre after the performance, presumably waiting to attack the dressing rooms there. He was returned to York, where various theatrical items were alleged to have been stolen by him, including a pair of red morocco leather buskins, a pair of linen ruffles, three black feathers, a pair of paste knee buckles, and a broad silk sash.

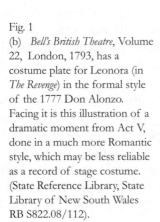

Fig. 1

(a) Stage costume for Don Alonzo in *The Revenge*, from *Bell's British Theatre*, London, 1777. The 'veteran articles from the York theatre', which graced Sydney's opening night, would have been in this style. Breeches, stockings and waistcoat are contemporary dress: ruff, ribbons and feathered cap are conventional theatrical adornment.

Fig. 1

(b) *Bell's British Theatre*, Volume 22, London, 1793, has a costume plate for Leonora (in *The Revenge*) in the formal style of the 1777 Don Alonzo. Facing it is this illustration of a dramatic moment from Act V, done in a much more Romantic style, which may be less reliable as a record of stage costume. (State Reference Library, State Library of New South Wales RB S822.08/112).

He was convicted, but apparently not on all counts, which may have left him with some York items, together with the loot from the other theatres.

Stealing stage costumes might have been profitable, but it is difficult to see how. The whole operation suggests someone partly driven by fantasies and obsessions. In any case, Richards could well have brought a range of these items with him when he sailed, a convict, on the *William and Ann*, arriving in Port Jackson on 28 August 1791. In 1797 a William Richards appears as a member of the Sydney theatre company, possibly as a house servant, and in 1800 he appears in the playbills as a performer. This may well have been the means whereby those venerable items from York arrived in Sydney.[42]

VI

While Collins describes the first performance in some detail, the date of the second remains a mystery. There is a remote possibility that it could have been as early as 18 January, two days after the first, since that was a major holiday, the Queen's birthday, and public holidays were an attractive time for performances, as the evidence from Norfolk Island indicates. Two shows in such rapid succession seems unlikely, but in the surviving playbill for Shakespeare's *Henry the Fourth*, of April 1800, there is clear evidence of presentations scheduled with four days between them and initially, perhaps, with three.

If the second performance was so soon after the first, then the more unreconstructed of Sydney's inhabitants learned swiftly, for, as Collins reports,

> some of the worst of the convicts, ever on the watch for opportunities, looked on the playhouse as a certain harvest for them, not by picking the pockets of the audience of their purses or their watches, but by breaking into their houses while the whole family might be enjoying themselves in the gallery. This actually happened on the second night of their playing.

By the late nineteenth century another colourful tale of criminal ingenuity relating to the theatre was current. According to this, a theatre-loving convict, desperate to obtain the money for a ticket, killed an officer's greyhound and passed off the meat as kangaroo flesh, selling it at ninepence a pound. The story, unfortunately, is apocryphal (see Appendix B, Note 5).

The only other performance which Collins mentions was a presentation on 4 February 1796 of Nicholas Rowe's tragedy *The Fair Penitent* and an unnamed farce. It was a rainy night, which should have dampened the ardour of playgoers, but instead it produced a full house, since it was a charity benefit for the recently widowed Mrs Eades.[43] This performance may have represented a very close shave for the new company. Two years before, the Norfolk Island theatre had been abruptly closed after a riot erupted between soldiers and civilians. The very day of the Eades benefit a spark had been struck that could have led to a similar explosion. A soldier who was on bad terms with the convict head of the carpenters' gang, John Baughan, was on guard duty. He left his musket at his post, went to the building in which the carpenter was working, and in the street outside began to make loud and abusive comments about Baughan. The carpenter's response was to steal out of the building unperceived, collect the abandoned musket, and report the soldier to the duty sergeant for deserting his post. This was a flogging matter, so that Baughan had exacted a most ingenious revenge on his persecutor.

Since Mrs Eades was the widow of a recently-drowned soldier, much of the audience would have been military. As word of the incident was passed around, the atmosphere must have been electric. Had Baughan and his family attended the theatre that night it could well have precipitated a riot similar to Norfolk Island. As it was, at 9.30 the following morning the whole of the off-duty corps assembled and 'in the most public and tumultuous manner' stormed Baughan's house. While some held Baughan to the ground with an axe at his neck, threatening to decapitate him, others demolished the house and all its contents. They then 'went off cheering, as if something meritorious had been effected, and marched in a body cross the parade before their commanding officer's house'.[44] It was probably the most violent and extraordinary outbreak of its kind in Port Jackson prior to the Rum Rebellion, and it gives some sense of the dangerously sensitive atmosphere in which this theatre had to work.

In July 1797 several British newspapers and journals published a copy of a Botany Bay playbill for the night of 23 July 1796, together with notes on some of the performers. The bill of fare consisted of Mrs Centlivre's *The Busy Body*, followed by John O'Keeffe's *The Poor Soldier* (see Fig. 2).[45] Whereas Collins, in describing the first production, gave only the names of the principal performers, the playbill gives a more extensive list. G.H. Hughes is unaccountably absent from this particular production, but all of the others named by Collins are still with the company.

After this playbill there is a gap of fifteen months before the next surviving reference to the theatre's existence. This occurs in the fragmentary court records of a robbery at the mill, the proceeds of which William Richards discovered while checking the security of the theatre and the house next door.[46] Since the discovery took place at about 11.00 pm on Saturday 11 November 1797, there can be little doubt that Richards, as a company member, was securing the buildings subsequent to a Saturday night performance. Evidently the house next to the playhouse was part of the theatre complex, as was common in England.

This fifteen-month gap probably represents nothing more than the fragmentary and chance nature of the sources. In all likelihood the company was in regular operation between January 1796 and November 1797. After the robbery at the mill, however, there is another fifteen months' silence, to mid-March 1799, and in view of one of the most widely-held beliefs about the theatre in Sydney this second break in the records needs to be considered more carefully.

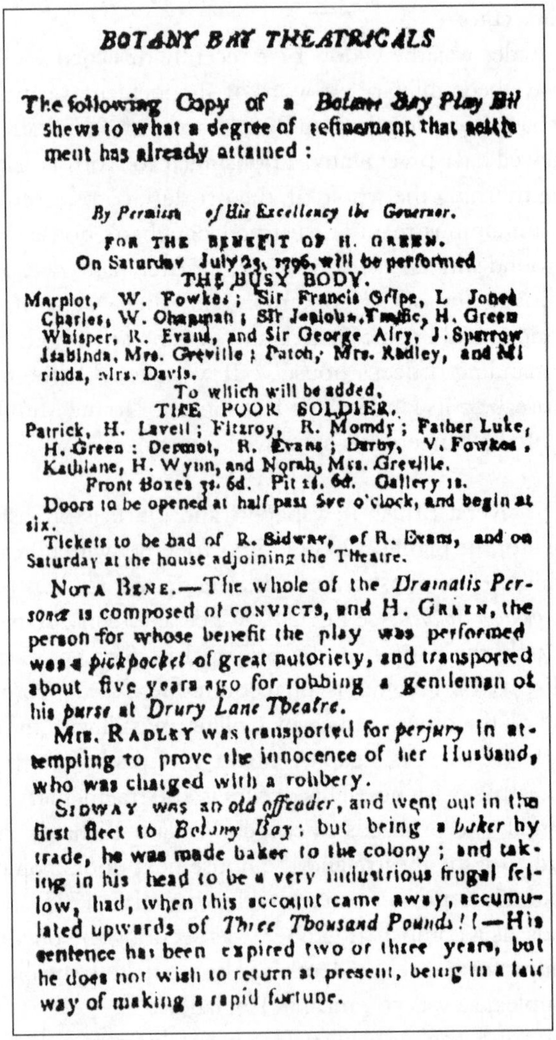

BOTANY BAY THEATRICALS

The following Copy of a *Botany Bay Play Bill*
shews to what a degree of refinement that settle
ment has already attained :

By Permission of His Excellency the Governor.

FOR THE BENEFIT OF H. GREEN.
On Saturday July 23, 1796, will be performed
THE BUSY BODY.
Marplot, W. Fowkes ; Sir Francis Gripe, L. Jones
Charles, W. Chapman ; Sir Jealous Traffic, H. Green
Whisper, R. Evans, and Sir George Airy, J. Sparrow
Isablinda, Mrs. Greville ; Patch, Mrs. Radley, and Mi
rinda, Mrs. Davis.
To which will be added,
THE POOR SOLDIER.
Patrick, H. Lavell ; Fitzroy, R. Momdy ; Father Luke,
H. Green : Dermot, R. Evans ; Darby, V. Fowkes ,
Kathlane, H. Wynn, and Norah, Mrs. Greville.
Front Boxes 3s. 6d.   Pit 2s. 6d.   Gallery 1s.
Doors to be opened at half past five o'clock, and begin at
six.
Tickets to be had of R. Sidway, of R. Evans, and on
Saturday at the house adjoining the Theatre.

NOTA BENE.—The whole of the *Dramatis Personæ* is composed of CONVICTS, and H. GREEN, the
person for whose benefit the play was performed
was a *pickpocket* of great notoriety, and transported
about five years ago for robbing a gentleman of
his *purse* at *Drury Lane Theatre*.

MRS. RADLEY was transported for *perjury* in attempting to prove the innocence of her Husband,
who was charged with a robbery.

SIDWAY was an *old offeader*, and went out in the
first fleet to *Botany Bay*; but being a *baker* by
trade, he was made baker to the colony ; and taking in his head to be a very industrious frugal fellow, had, when this account came away, accumulated upwards of *Three Thousand Pounds!!*—His
sentence has been expired two or three years, but
he does not wish to return at present, being in a fair
way of making a rapid fortune.

Fig. 2:   Playbill for the theatre, Sydney, 23 July 1796, as
printed in the *Oracle* of 13 July 1797, with accompanying
notes.

The commonest modern reading of the situation is that the theatre company opened on 16 January 1796, only to be very quickly suppressed, and that another company was opened in 1799 and lasted only until 1800 or so.[47] The genesis of this idea can easily be traced. David Collins' account of the theatre's opening in 1796 puts heavy emphasis on the threat that the participants would be removed from Sydney to one of the colony's outposts, if they caused trouble. The only other well-known account by a contemporary was that of D.D. Mann, published in 1811 (shortly after it was written). He declared that abuses which 'resulted from the establishment of the theatre … induced the governor to recall the permission which had been given for the performances, and the playhouse itself was soon afterwards levelled to the ground'.[48] Since his statement follows directly on three sentences adapted from Collins, in which the latter had described problems associated with the theatre's *opening*, the impression given is that the playhouse was closed almost immediately. Certainly, by the time of James Wallis, a decade later than Mann, the story had become that 'this theatre continued open only for a short time'. Later in the nineteenth century the ever-unreliable Roger Therry provided his own clearly spurious reasons for the closure, which implied it was almost instantaneous. J.H. Heaton (almost as doubtful an authority), stretched it out a little by roundly declaring the playhouse was suppressed in 1798, characteristically giving no sources for his claim.[49] The net effect of these statements was to build up a picture of a theatrical enterprise of extreme fragility, whose short life was one of its leading characteristics.

This consensus about the theatre's brief existence was disturbed in the early twentieth century by David Scott Mitchell's purchase of two newly discovered playbills from the Sydney theatre, both dated 1800.[50] However, so fixed had the commentators become on the idea of a theatre that was opened only to be swiftly closed, that most of them assumed there must have been two successive theatres, both rapidly shut down, even though D.D. Mann, the source of the closure story, mentioned only one. Even where the commentators did not commit themselves to two successive theatres, the idea of a short duration and a sudden termination was so ingrained that the theatre's closure was simply moved from shortly after its opening to shortly after the date of the newly-found playbills. Whichever option was taken, the image remained one of a fragile enterprise, an impression intensified by Harold Love's argument that such a theatre was doomed to insignificance because of the cultural backwardness of the only available audience.

As was suggested above, the gap in the records between November 1797 and March 1799 may reflect nothing more than the fragmentary nature of the evidence. There is, however, a small but significant body of evidence suggesting that during 1798 or early 1799 the playhouse in Sydney was rebuilt, or at least radically refurbished, something which could have involved an interruption to activities. The crucial statement comes from the convict William Noah, who arrived on the *Hillsborough* on 26 July 1799. At the end of his journal of the voyage is a brief account of the Sydney that greeted him and in this occurs the statement: 'Here is a Play House Done up very Neat this year.'[51] This statement is reinforced by the fact that the only reported playbill from before the beginning of 1799 shows the Sydney theatre at that stage to have been possessed only of front boxes, whereas all the playbills of 1799–1800 unequivocally present a theatre equipped with side boxes as well. One might also note that at some time between his release from Sydney gaol on 22 September 1798 and his re-arrest on 31 March 1799, the incorrigible convict artist John William Lancashire was employed in 'painting Scenery &c' for a theatre in the town.[52] This might indicate simply that he was touching up the existing scenery, but if it involves the preparation of new scenes the situation is somewhat different. British playhouses of the time worked off stock scenery, rarely adding greatly to the supply. (Tate Wilkinson, for example, reports that in 1795 Liverpool was still relying on the scenery painted for its opening in 1772.[53]) Since the Sydney theatre was only a little over two or three years old at the time of Lancashire's involvement, any extensive work on the scenery would probably indicate a major refurbishment or rebuilding.

While all this work on the theatre could have been a consequence of government closure, this seems inherently unlikely, since it would have involved the authorities not only in shutting the playhouse but in destroying all or part of its fabric and fittings. Displeasure of that magnitude would hardly be followed within fifteen months by renewed permission to operate. It seems more likely that the playhouse of 1796 was temporary in nature, and that the work undertaken in late 1798 represented an upgrading of theatrical facilities in the town. If this is the case, then, far from reflecting the theatre company's vulnerability, any closure that occurred was a reflection of its flourishing condition. Performances were suspended to permit the creation of a better, and slightly larger, playhouse, one that involved a significant increase in the number of expensive seats.

VII

Whatever interruptions may have taken place in 1798, the theatre was demonstrably active in early 1799. John William Lancashire was busily 'painting Scenery &c' in March or earlier and there is clear evidence of a performance in mid-April. This evidence can be found in the record of cases brought before the Bench of Magistrates on 20 April that year:

> Joseph Vasconcellis, Manager of the Theatre, Sydney, charged Cornelius Hennings with having obtained Admission into the said Theatre under false pretences by Means of three several Box Tickets which he had possessed himself of in the Name of Major Foveaux – the Major attending & declaring the same to have been without his Privity, Hennings was convicted of the Offence & Sentenced to receive 25 Lashes and to be discharged.[54]

Cases were normally brought before the courts in New South Wales on the Saturday following the apprehension of the offender. Given the frequency of Saturday performances in the colony, this makes Saturday 13 April the most likely date for the show. The fact that Hennings requested three tickets does not mean, as Robert Irving assumed, that each box contained that number of seats.[55] Places in a box were sold individually and it was not the usual situation for a single party to secure the entire box.

Hennings, who was frequently in trouble,[56] does not seem to have been particularly intelligent and, though he successfully passed himself off as a messenger from Major Foveaux in securing the tickets, he could hardly have expected to pass for Foveaux in the box itself. This might suggest that it was an accepted practice for senior officers to present tickets to underlings as small rewards, though whether these tickets were free, a form of *droit de seigneur*, or whether a playhouse servant confronted Foveaux with the bill after the event, is not documented.

In the middle of 1800 a second Botany Bay playbill was reproduced in an English paper, one for 1 June 1799 (see Fig. 3). On this occasion the plays performed were Frederick Reynolds' *Fortune's Fool* and David Garrick's *Bon Ton*. This performance will be discussed in detail in the Chapter 3.

A little over two months after that the theatre made another passing appearance in the legal records:

> Weekly Report 12th Augt 1799
> Mary Adams & others appeared to answer a Complaint of Sarah Macan for having violently assaulted her on Saturday Eveng after she had left the Theatre & was proceeding home – Evidence heard on both Sides from which it appeared that the said Sarah Macan spit in the face of Mary Adams, when she solicited payment of a Sum of Money said Macan was indebted to her, which induced and provoked her to strike said Macan. Complaint thereupon dismissed.[57]

The explosive Sarah McCann was an actress in the troupe, presumably returning home after a performance.

McCann was not the only turbulent spirit associated with the theatre, and on 18 September 1799 a violent dispute within the company found its way to the courts:

> George Hughes appeared and stated that he had been grossly assaulted & ill treated by Thomas Radley and Anne, otherwise Mary Anne Fowles (his Wife) – Informations taken, and confirmed by the Depositions of Mary Barnes and Henry Child – whereupon, the accused Parties were Committed for Trial – but afterwards produced Bail for their Appearance at the next Criml Court. Viz
>
> | Daniel Fane of Sydney in | £40 | |
> |---|---|---|
> | John Kenny of the same place in | £20 | each |
>
> Mary Barnes having also prayed Sureties of the Peace against the said Anne Radley otherwise Mary-Ann Fowles, who had threatened and otherwise put the Complainant in fear – Bail produced to keep the peace towards all His Majestys liege Subjects & especially towards Mary Barnes viz

We have our theatrical amusements here, and the following is a List of the Dramatis Personæ:—

MRS. PARRY'S NIGHT.

By Permission of his Excellency.

At the THEATRE, SYDNEY, on Saturday June 1, 1799, will be Presented, FORTUNE'S FOOL

Ap Hazard (for that night only) Mrs. Parry, Sir Charles Danvers, P Parry, * Tom Seymour, J. White; Orville, W. Smith; Samuel, H. Parsons, Sir Bambet Blackletter, G. H. Hughes; Mrs. Seymour, Mrs M'Can;† Miss Union, Mrs. Radley; Lady Danvers, (for that night only) Mrs. Miller.

After the Play, a New Occasional Address ‡ will be Spoken by Mrs. Parry.

To which will be added, BON TON

Sir John Trotley, G. H. Hughes ||, Colonel Tivy, W. Smith; Lord Minikin, W. Knight; Jessamy, H. Parsons; Davey, J. White; Lady Minikin, Mrs Radley; Gymp, Mrs Sparkes§. Miss Tittup, Mrs. Parry.

Boxes 5s—Front Boxes 8s 6d—Pit 2s 6d—Gallery 1s

Tickets to be had of Mrs. Parry, and of W. Miller.

Doors open at half past Five, begin at half past Six.

══════

* P. Parry, convict for life, late Grocer, in Oxford-street, London, highway robbery.

† Mrs M'Cann, convict by Britannia transport, for seven years, London; late in the service of a Royal Personage, and afterwards Brothel keeper, St. Mary-le bone.

‡ Written by Michael Massey Robinson, Clerk to Judge Advocate.

|| Hughes, a printer— prisoner

§ Sparkes, came out a free woman, lives with Vandercomb, who is a steady fellow.

Frances Grosvenor, alias Fey, convict by Britannia transport, for seven years, from London—Cyprian Corps. Pavey, a quondam Grocer, Oxford-street, Occasional Performers.

The women, altogether, are more drunken and infamous than possibly can be described

Fig. 3   Playbill for the theatre, Sydney, 1 June 1799, as printed in *Bell's Weekly Messenger* of 6 July 1800, with accompanying notes.

David Bevan of Sydney	...	£20
John Francis Molloy	...	£20
Mary Anne Fowles in	...	£40

Hughes, Fowles and Barnes were all actors with the company and Radley (who had probably already acquired his financial interest in the theatre) was the husband of Mary Ann Fowles. Infuriatingly enough, a marginal note appears against this entry:

> On the 13th December the Complainant George Hughes appeared at the Judge Advocates Office & prayed to withdraw his Recognizances. Leave granted accordingly.[58]

Regrettably, no further details of the dispute have survived.

It is for the early months of 1800 that we come closest to this theatre, through the survival, in the Mitchell Library, State Library of New South Wales, of two original playbills (see Figs 4 and 5). The first, for Saturday 8 March, announces performances of Farquhar's *The Recruiting Officer*, followed by Henry Fielding's 'Musical Entertainment', *The Virgin Unmask'd*. The second announces the postponement of the performance scheduled for Saturday 5 April to the following Saturday, and then goes on to detail a presentation of Shakespeare's *Henry the Fourth* and Garrick's *The Irish Widow* on Tuesday 8 April. These are followed by what appears to be the last of the playbills sent to England and published in papers and magazines there. It is for Monday 23 June 1800, and offers a full program – Oliver Goldsmith's *She Stoops to Conquer*, followed by Garrick's *Miss in Her Teens* and Charles Coffey's *The Devil to Pay* (see Fig. 6). Perhaps the subject was wearing thin by this time: I have found this playbill reproduced in only one magazine.[59]

Apart from the fact that it provides us with the earliest record of a Goldsmith production in Australia, the most interesting feature of this playbill is the statement that occurs towards its close: 'No person will be admitted without a Ticket; and it is requested that no person will attempt to smoak; or bring spirits into the Theatre. – No Money will be returned.' It is not clear whether the request to the audience not to smoke, or to bring spirits into the theatre, points to a newly emerging evil which the company is attempting to nip in the bud or to a long-standing practice which the organisation is finally challenging. Nor is there any indication whether the move is being made on the management's own initiative, or is a response to direct or anticipated pressure from the authorities. Was the company beginning to feel the threat of immediate closure if conduct in the theatre became too unruly?

If the company did manage to suppress drinking in the playhouse, this would have represented a significant advance on the situation in England. There, at various times, alcohol had been freely sold in the theatres, while some of those bottles and glasses dropped or thrown from the gallery and elsewhere are examples of patrons bringing their own alcohol with them as a matter of course and without impediment.[60]

Smoking seems not to have been a characteristic of British theatres, but it certainly was of American ones. This, and the fact that American theatres often had bars, enabled the English to indulge their feelings of superiority over their Yankee cousins. Thus at the Philadelphia theatre, the *True Briton*, 24 January 1791, assures us:

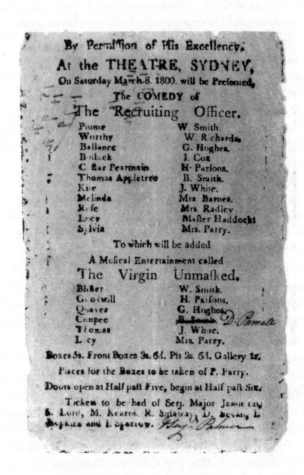

Fig. 4   Surviving playbill for *The Recruiting Officer* at the
theatre, Sydney, 8 March 1800 (Mitchell Library, State
Library of New South Wales, Z Safe 1/107:R246).

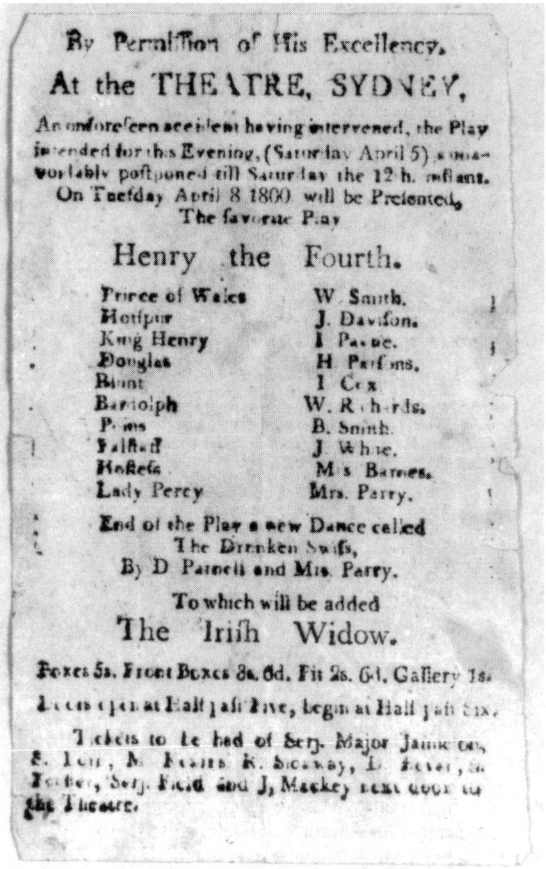

By Permission of His Excellency,

At the THEATRE, SYDNEY,

An unforeseen accident having intervened, the Play intended for this Evening, (Saturday April 5) is unavoidably postponed till Saturday the 12 h. instant. On Tuesday April 8 1800 will be Presented, The favorite Play

Henry the Fourth.

Prince of Wales	W Smith.
Hotspur	J. Davison.
King Henry	I Pauoe.
Douglas	H Parsons.
Blunt	I Cox
Bardolph	W. Richards.
Poins	B. Smith.
Falstaff	J White.
Hostess	Mis Barnes.
Lady Percy	Mrs. Parry.

End of the Play a new Dance called The Drunken Swifs, By D Parnell and Mis. Parry.

To which will be added

The Irish Widow.

Boxes 5s. Front Boxes 8s. 6d. Pit 2s. 6d. Gallery 1s.

Doors open at Half past Five, begin at Half past Six.

Tickets to be had of Serj. Major Jamieson, S. Lett, M Rains R. Sidaway, D Bever, &c ... Serj. Field and J, Mackey next door to the Theatre.

Fig. 5 Surviving playbill for *Henry the Fourth* at the theatre, Sydney, 8 April 1800 (Mitchell Library, State Library of New South Wales, Z Safe 1/107: R246).

PRECISE FORM OF A BOTANY-
BAY PLAY-BILL,

As there published June 23, 1800.

For the BENEFIT of Mrs. PARRY.

By permission of his Excellency,
At the THEATRE, SYDNEY,

This Evening will be presented the Favourite Comedy of,

She Stoops to Conquer; or, The
Mistakes of a Night,

Hardcastle	-	G. Hughes
Young Marlow	-	W. Smith
Hastings	-	W. Knight
Sir Cha. Marlow	-	H. Parsons
Diggory	-	J. Cox
Tony Lumpkin	-	J. White
Miss Neville	-	Mrs. Radley
Mrs. Hardcastle	-	Mrs. Barnes
Pimple	-	Mrs. Charlton; and
Miss Hardcastle	-	Mrs. Parry.

End of the Play, the Interlude of
Miss in her Teens.

To which will be added, a Musical Entertainment, called,

The Devil to Pay; or, The Wives
Metamorphosed.

Sir John Loverule	G. Hughes
Magician	- J. White
Jobson	- D. Parnell
Lady Loverule	- Mrs. Radley
Lucy	- Mrs. Barnes
Lettice	- Mrs. Charlton; and
Nell	- Mrs. Parry.

Boxes, 5s. Front Boxes, 3s. 6d. Pit 2s. 6d.
Gallery, 1s.

Doors open at Half past Five, begin at
Half past Six.

No person will be admitted without a
Ticket; and it is requested that no person
will attempt to smoak; or bring spirits into the Theatre.—No Money will be returned.

Tickets to be had of Serj.-Major Jamieson, D. Bevan, S. Lord, M. Kearns, Mrs.
Parry, Serj. Field, S. Forster, and J. Mackey, next door to the Theatre.

More recent advices from that
Settlement say, that a smart altercation had just taken place in the
Green-room of their Theatre, in
consequence of the *Beggar's Opera*
having been given out by the Manager. It was agreed, on all hands,
that the play was very *strongly*
cast.—Mackheath observed, that
as he had *acted*, on all occasions,
like a *Gentleman* in his profession,
he should have no objection to the
performance of the character.
Polly and *Lucy* remained passive—
Bagshot expressed some *scruples*—
the rest of the gang were divided
in opinion. At length, from a suggestion of *Filch*, how far the repre-
sentation of the piece might tend
to *wound the feelings* of both *au-*
dience and *performers*, the matter
was postponed for further consideration.

Fig. 6   Playbill for the theatre, Sydney,
23 June 1800, as printed in the *Sporting*
Magazine, 20 (1802), 225-6.

'Byrne and Madame Rossi trip it to the *jingling of glasses*, and the *puffs* of *tobacco* smoke in the Pit. The *Theatrical Performers* in *America*, unlike our Dramatic Heroes and Heroines here, are absolutely *choaked* with *puffs* of *tobacco*.' Similar jibes can be found in the *Star*, 26 March 1796, 10 January 1797 and elsewhere. In 1807 Charles William Janson took up the matter on a more serious note, echoing an earlier comment by Anthony Pasquin on 'the custom of smoking segars, and drinking':

> The lobbies of all American theatres are provided with bar-rooms, to which the men resort between each act to drink, and from which the ladies are regaled in their seats with glasses of their favourite beverage. Thus, on the fall of the curtain, the *dashing* fellows are in a state of intoxication. Smoaking is a still greater evil in a crouded house, to prevent which, the managers are constantly making unavailing remonstrances.[61]

With practices such as these in English-speaking countries, it is likely that the Sydney theatre had been confronted with similar problems for some time before 1800. Earlier in this chapter I noted the intolerably suffocating atmosphere that would have existed in a crowded Sydney theatre in the height of an antipodean summer. The addition, from that very first night, of the reek of alcohol and the fumes of tobacco to the stench of tallow candles, the sweat and odours of close-packed bodies, and the heat and humidity in a windowless room, makes the picture of Sydney's theatre all the more lurid.

The other curiosity in the footnote to the playbill of June 1800 is the statement that 'No person will be admitted without a Ticket'. Pre-purchased tickets for pit and boxes seem to have been a common feature of provincial English theatre, and the list of venues from which tickets could be bought which appears on most of the Sydney playbills indicates the importance of the practice in the colony. But is the implication in the playbill that there were to be no door-sales for pit and boxes, and, if so, is this yet another sign of the efforts being made to impose some order and control on clients? Does it also suggest that the theatre had no half-price system? Since an advance booking system apparently did not exist for galleries in English theatres (door sales being the only means of access), the assumption must be that the statement on the playbill has no reference to the gallery. If it does, then the efforts to impose order and crowd control were taking on major proportions.

VIII

After the relative rush of information regarding the theatre in 1799 and the first half of 1800, the near silence that follows is striking. There is, however, a reference in a civil law case to a conversation that took place in the playhouse sometime around Christmas 1800.[62] More tangible is the judge-advocate's Register of Assignments, against the date 17 September 1801, which has the entry 'Thomas Radley to Edwd Turley Smith. Assignment of 6 shares in the Theatre at Sydney to secure £17 payable the 20th Febr[y] 1802'.[63] In other words, six shares in the theatre, which are owned by Radley, are being accepted as security for a debt, indicating that the theatre was still in existence and looking financially secure.

Thereafter there is another gap in the records of over two years, followed by an eyewitness account in which the theatre still appears to be in a flourishing condition. Robert Eastwick made his only visit to New South Wales as master of the trading vessel *Betsy*. The port records list the ship's arrival on 24 December 1803, and its departure on 20 April 1804.[64] In his memoirs Eastwick provides a lively description of the colony, which includes the following:

> The colonists, in general, appeared to be well reconciled to their situation, and a proof that their minds were not very ill at ease is afforded by the fact that they had a theatre, and, under the patronage of Governor King, gave several representations during the time I was there, all very tolerably acted. Amongst other plays I remember witnessing Farquhar's comedy of *The Recruiting Officer*, and the entertainment of *The Virgin Unmasked*, both affording very excellent amusement.[65]

There is little reason to distrust Eastwick. His picture of Sydney is otherwise accurate, and his memory for play titles can be confirmed by his account of a visit made to Calcutta in 1816. A newspaper of that time reports the staging of the plays he claims to have seen there, as well as his arrival and departure.[66] The only reason for any disquiet is that the play and afterpiece he mentions comprise the program that was advertised for 8 March 1800. That popular pieces such as these should be repeated is no great surprise. It is the repetition of the pair that causes a slight discomfort, though not enough to raise a serious challenge to Eastwick's veracity.

The fragmentary nature of these sources makes it foolhardy to assume that there was no theatre between September 1801 and December 1803 simply because we have no evidence of it. The real question is what happened after April 1804, for there is no further reference to the theatre's activity. The one thing of which we can be reasonably confident is that it was no longer operating in January 1808. In a letter written in about 1810 Daniel Parnell, a performer with the company in 1799–1800, claimed that Governor Bligh had given permission for a theatre to be erected, but that the plan had been aborted by the governor's overthrow at the beginning of 1808.[67] It is difficult to imagine Bligh giving such an approval while the old theatre was still in operation.

There remains, however, a possibility that the theatre might have survived into Bligh's regime. A major factor leading to the mutiny that overthrew Bligh was his plan to repossess land and buildings he felt intruded on government and public activities. Thus Robert Sidaway's house and inn was threatened because it was too close to the granary, and a block of land owned by Captain John Macarthur because it was too close to the church.[68] In every case a new site, plus help with reconstruction, was promised. Might the theatre have fallen to Bligh's zeal for town planning? According to D.D. Mann, the playhouse, having been closed, 'was soon afterwards levelled to the ground'.[69] In view of the shortage of building stock, and the ease with which theatres in England were converted into storehouses, this rapid destruction is surprising, but it accords with Bligh's policy.

There are, however, major problems with this hypothesis and though, individually, they could be argued away, together they constitute a significant barrier to such an argument.

Thus D.D. Mann not only reports the closure of the theatre, but also gives a reason for it that has nothing to do with Bligh's reclamation projects. According to him it was the abuses that resulted from the establishment of the theatre that led an unnamed governor to suppress it. However, Mann's account is curiously dependent on Collins and gives the impression that the closure took place early in the theatre's history. In addition, he himself was one of the targets of Bligh's reclamation projects. His own house had been built on the governor's domain and was a particularly irksome presence for Bligh, high on his demolition list.[70] In the tense political climate of 1811, with nobody certain how vengeful the home government would be on those who had overthrown the governor, it might have been in Mann's interest to be a little evasive about the timing and circumstances of the theatre's closure. His book is heavily sanitised and does not refer to the rebellion.

On 5 March 1803 the *Sydney Gazette* made its first appearance and continued to be issued on a weekly basis throughout the relevant period, with one crucial gap from September 1807 to mid-May 1808. It is notable that this newspaper makes no mention of the theatre. The simplest explanation is that there was no theatre for most of this period. The paper, however, is also resolutely silent on later theatres, such as that on Brickfield Hill and that in the salt works at Cockle Bay, and it makes no mention of theatre over the period December 1803 to April 1804, when Eastwick records several performances. The editor of the *Sydney Gazette*, George Howe, seems to have been something of a puritan (albeit a convict) and may have censored the theatre out of his publication.

Much more difficult to account for is the silence of 'Flash' Jim Vaux, whose racy biography was first published in England in 1819. Vaux early speaks of his 'violent passion for the drama',[71] and there are frequent references to his theatregoing during his periods in England, before and between his compulsory voyages to New South Wales.[72] But though he talks occasionally of his pursuit of pleasures in Australia,[73] theatre receives no mention in that context. Given the strength of Vaux's feelings, his silence carries weight. It should, however, be noticed that though he arrived in the colony on the *Minorca* on 14 December 1801, he was immediately sent to the Hawkesbury as clerk to the storekeeper. He remained there for about three years, that is until late 1804 or early 1805, so that his silence would only be of significance from that time forward.

While it might be possible, therefore, to sustain an argument for the theatre's continued existence into Bligh's regime, it would be safer to assume an earlier date of closure. The most likely time would be between Eastwick's departure from Port Jackson and Vaux's arrival there from the Hawkesbury, that is, between 20 April 1804 and early 1805. It could well be that the jitteriness of the authorities after the Irish uprising at Castle Hill led them to close the theatre. On the other hand, gout, alcohol and a mounting sense of failure had made Governor King increasingly erratic. By 1804 even a minor infringement of good behaviour could have provoked him into a burst of resentment against the theatre and into its arbitrary closure. Certainly, the Bench records of that period contain nothing that involves the playhouse or any of its actors. The disappearance of Sidaway's theatre remains cloaked in mystery.

Chapter 3

THE SYDNEY THEATRE, 1796–1804/07: THE PLAYHOUSE AND COMPANY ORGANISATION

t was suggested in the previous chapter that the theatre that opened in 1796 was, in most respects, a faithful reproduction of a small provincial English playhouse of the time. The late eighteenth century had a preferred model for these theatres, and there is little doubt that any Britons setting out to establish a playhouse would have had this standard form powerfully present in their minds. The fact that the Britons in question were half a world away from home would have made no difference. If anything, it would have intensified the appeal of the model, out of sheer nostalgia.

The reconstructed theatre at Richmond in Yorkshire,[1] and the imaginary provincial theatre in Pierce Egan's *Life of an Actor*, provide clear examples of this model (see Fig. 7). The basic components were a scenic stage behind a proscenium arch, a forestage in front of the arch with a door on either side for actors' entrances, a small orchestra pit in front of that, and an auditorium. The scenery consisted of sets of wings, parallel to the footlights, painted in perspective and receding up the stage, with the rear of the stage concealed behind painted drops or behind shutters which slid from each side of the stage to meet in the middle. The auditorium consisted of the pit, stepped upwards from the orchestra, front boxes raised slightly behind the pit, side boxes extending from those front boxes down the full length of the side walls of the auditorium, and a gallery directly over both the front and side boxes.

In spite of the pervasiveness of this design, however, it was not universal. The commonest deviation was the small theatre which dispensed entirely with boxes and consisted only of pit and gallery, often with the gallery simply the rear section of the pit, marked off by a low wooden barrier or set of spikes. The Brickfields theatre, described in Chapter 2, was almost certainly of this kind. Though common, it was an arrangement not much approved by the purists: 'This necessary part of uniformity was added only ten years ago' is how the theatregoer James Winston described the addition of boxes to the Grantham theatre, which had hitherto been of the pit-and-gallery variety.[2]

Direct information about the Sydney theatre of 1796 is extremely limited.

Fig. 7   'A Beggarly Account of Empty Boxes'. Though dating from 1824/25, this illustration depicts
an old-fashioned provincial English theatre of a kind common in the late eighteenth-century (Pierce
Egan, *The Life of an Actor*, London, 1825).

Most of it comes from David Collins, who declared, in a passage to which reference has already been made:

> They had fitted up the house with more theatrical propriety than could have been expected ... A seat in their gallery, which was by far the largest place in the house, as likely to be the most resorted to, was to be procured for one shilling.

A footnote adds the fact that 'the building cost upwards of one hundred pounds', and the later reference to a charity performance for the Widow Eades mentions that the proceeds from the full house were 'upwards of twelve pounds'. The only other piece of information comes from the reprint in the English newspapers of the playbill of 23 July 1796, which includes the list of seat prices: 'Front Boxes, 3s. 6d. – Pit, 2s. 6d. – Gallery, 1s.'.

The size of the gallery, remarked upon by Collins, had precedents in provincial Britain. What is more striking is the indication from the playbill that this theatre had no side boxes, only front boxes. In Britain, this was a rarity. The immediate question is whether such an arrangement involved further departures from the norm. Hypothetically it was possible for such a theatre to consist of a pit with the gallery as a rearward extension of it, and the boxes raised behind the rear of this gallery or situated over the last gallery benches. An alternative would be a theatre with pew-style boxes at the front, with the pit behind them and the gallery behind or over the pit. I know of only one example of this from England, Charles Mate's 1779 theatre at Margate.[3] However, these unorthodox arrangements are difficult to reconcile with David Collins' praise for the 'theatrical propriety' of the establishment. A theatre with a gallery at the rear, immediately over the front boxes, and with neither gallery slips nor side boxes, remains the most likely model.

The reference to the size of the gallery, the playbill's list of seat prices and the £12 charity benefit are the only records from which to calculate the audience capacity of this playhouse. That calculation, in turn, becomes the basis for estimating the size of the building.[4] There are uncertainties at every point. How does one interpret the 'upwards of twelve pounds' the Widow Eades secured from the full house at her benefit? Was there a free list? Probably not. Was a half-price system operating that night? I have assumed that since it was a charity event this was not the case. Once again, does the £12 represent the gross or the net proceeds of the evening? Charity benefits in England could be based on either. In this case a net figure is the more likely; but if so, what were the gross takings? A study of English models suggests a figure approximating £17, but wide variations are observable in the house charges in English theatres. Then again, what does Collins mean by a full house, given the flexibility of bench seating and the readiness of managers to cram the aisles with standing patrons for an exceptionally popular show? Many theatres had a notional figure for a full house, but this could be exceeded by 10% or more for a famous visiting actor, a spectacular new entertainment or a royal command performance, such as that before the King of Denmark, described in alarming and vivid detail by John Harriott.[5]

One fact is immediately evident from the amount received by the Widow Eades: whether net or gross, it is a particularly small return by English standards. Only one playhouse in James Winston's *The Theatric Tourist*, for which the takings are given, comes in at under £30 for an actor's benefit. Other sources reveal that Mansfield, Kingsford (Herefordshire) and Ludlow were £20 houses, but the occupying actors scorned them. On the other hand, the large size of Sydney's one-shilling gallery and the absence of the highly remunerative side boxes meant that a disproportionately large audience was needed to achieve even this figure. My guess is an audience capacity of 180.

The same degree of uncertainty is apparent in any attempt to use the estimated audience capacity to calculate the dimensions of the theatre. The size and disposition of aisles in the auditorium, the width of benches, the distance between rows, the height of risers and the width of the orchestra pit were all close to standard in English theatres. It is therefore possible to make a plausible estimate of the size of a 180-seat auditorium – always assuming that pit, boxes and gallery were arranged in the usual fashion. However, the depth of the stage and foyer area and the location of dressing rooms are less standardised. Taking this into account, the building was probably about 50 feet long and 22–25 feet wide. If the dressing rooms were behind the stage, this could add another eight to 12 feet to the length. The height would be in the vicinity of 22 feet.

II

Size obviously had a bearing on the cost of the building; but even so Collins' figure of 'upwards of one hundred pounds' must give pause, when one considers the expense of building a provincial theatre in England. James Winston gives the cost of the 1798 Maidstone theatre as £1,300, excluding the land; the Tunbridge Wells theatre of 1803 as £1,500–£1,600; and the 'neat and commodious' theatre at Winchester as £1,000 in 1785. All three of these held audiences of £60, but it is difficult to imagine a house with approximately one quarter of that capacity costing only one tenth of the amount to build.

There are two ways of accounting for this discrepancy: either the Sydney theatre was not a new building or it was less substantial than these English examples. In fact, the conversion of an existing building or the construction of a 'temporary' one were strategies in common use in England when a company was first establishing itself in a town. Of the two approaches the conversion of an existing building was the commoner. Tennis courts, barns, stables, malt-houses, and granaries were among the buildings so converted. Many of these adaptations were regular in their layout of pit, box and gallery, but it is also notable that it was in converted buildings that many of the variations described above were to be found. Some small theatres may have done without boxes, or run pit into gallery, for reasons of economy, but the more usual reason was that the pre-existing building lacked the dimensions required for the normal layout.

For the cost of such conversions we can turn to the theatre at Margate, though there were oddities in its layout which may have kept its expenses unnaturally low. In 1779 the manager, Charles Mate,

> rented to Mr. Cobb, then banker and magistrate at Margate, upon lease, at twenty pounds per season (expending about two hundred pounds in the fitting up) a large stable behind the Fountain Inn. The building was 65 feet in length, 25 feet of which he converted into a raised stage, and the remainder into box, pit and gallery.

The house, we are told, held £33.[6]

Here we have a figure much closer to that given by Collins. There were, moreover, a number of buildings in Sydney of greater length, if not much broader, than has been so far estimated for the theatre. Many of the barns and storehouses built there up to that time had widths of 22–25 feet, and lengths of 80–100 feet were common.

The question is whether any of the buildings of this size would have been available for conversion. The colony, after all, had been in existence only eight years, and resources were desperately short. The year in which the theatre opened was one of particular crisis in this respect. Governor Hunter raised the matter in one of his first dispatches, on 21 December 1795, and elaborated his concern in later reports of 3 March and 20 August 1796, specifying storehouses, granaries and barns as the serious deficiencies. David Collins also wrote:

> Toward the latter end of the month [June] two men from each officer were ordered to join the public gangs, it being found wholly impracticable to erect without more assistance any of the buildings which had now become indispensably necessary. Storehouses were much wanted; the barracks were yet unfinished; houses were to be built for the assistant-surgeons, those which had been erected soon after our arrival being now no longer tenable.[7]

This, to be sure, refers only to government buildings, but there is no evidence that private enterprise had yet produced much in Sydney beyond the dimensions of a house. Moreover, if any buildings were prime candidates for conversion to a theatre, it was precisely those storehouses, granaries and barns that Hunter stressed were in such short supply. In addition, much of the building done in the early years of the settlement was calculatedly temporary in nature and was presumably by now in an advanced state of decay. Would building stock of that kind have been suitable for conversion, even if it were to be made available?

The mention of short-term structures, however, raises the second possibility. By 1796 the governor may have been housed in stone and most of the officers in brick (a material which had also been used for a number of storehouses), but the tradition of temporary, and hence inexpensive, building, was still alive and well in the colony, even for major structures. The Rev. Johnson's church, built two years before the theatre, is a case in point. It was avowedly temporary. Six months after the theatre's opening, 'the bricklayers' gang was employed … in erecting a temporary court-house of lath and plaster; as it was uncertain when one to be built of bricks could be begun'.[8] A few years later Governor Hunter went so far as to erect a temporary gaol. In such a context an English-style temporary theatre would have been perfectly at home. The redoubtable Mrs Baker had built one at Margate and, when she was worsted there by Charles Mate's company, had had it dismantled and shipped to Faversham for reassembly, opening it there in 1787. Theatres of a similar kind existed in Hythe, Tenterden and Yarmouth. At Tewkesbury two such theatres were built at different ends of the town, where competing companies battled it out over a period of several months. One of these may have cost as little as £63.

Such theatres were more substantial than the canvas booths that followed the fairs. In most cases they were of timber, and unseasoned hardwood was one material in ready supply around Sydney – there were thousands of square miles of it, expensive to transport and difficult to work, but available for the taking. Hunter's gaol was built of solid logs. Johnson's church had strong upright posts, linked by lath and plaster. It was much larger than the theatre, but of a simpler construction and it cost, as we know, £67 12s. 11½d.. The original estimate had been even lower, £30.[9] A number of factors may have distorted the figures, but clearly we are looking at a scale of expenditure which would admit of a temporary theatre being built for a little over £100.

The building techniques used on the church and the gaol were not the only ones available. Another option was weatherboard, which in some parts of England was used not only for temporary buildings and outhouses, but houses, shops and even a few of the more fashionable theatres, such as Brighton and Tunbridge Wells.[10] This may have been the solution to which the theatre builders turned. Large government weatherboard structures became a feature of Hunter's period as governor. Working painfully slowly, because of the lack of government artificers, a 'weatherboarded store-house with two wings' was completed in Sydney shortly before 1 October 1798. A shingle and weatherboard barn, 80 feet by 20 feet, had been built at Toongabbie during 1797 and at some unspecified date between October 1796 and September 1800 a granary of similar construction, 140 feet long, was constructed at Parramatta, to say nothing of smaller edifices such as barracks.[11]

Part of the appeal of weatherboard construction was its economy. Some forty years later a columnist in the Hobart *Colonial Times*, 4 November 1834, declared: 'We are surprised that Mr. Mackay does not select a more capacious building [as a theatre], more especially so, as a weatherboard one might be erected at a very trifling expense.'[12] Weatherboarding also had the virtue that it lent itself to greater wall heights than did lath and plaster or brickwork. Brick constructions in particular were limited by the poor quality of the local mortar and, though a granary with a wall height of 23 feet is recorded by 1803,[13] a height of 22 feet suggested for Sidaway's theatre would have been a challenge at Port Jackson in any material other than weatherboard.

In making a choice between conversion of an existing building and the erection of a new one, Ross Thorne's succinct argument for conversion carries weight. Collins writes of the convicts being given permission 'to prepare a play-house' and in Thorne's understanding the word 'prepare' does not imply 'erect' or 'construct' a whole building.[14] He could also have pointed to Collins' later reference to the playhouse being 'fitted up', a phrase which often refers to the setting up of a theatre in an existing room. In spite of the strength of this argument, however, I am inclined, hesitantly, to the belief that Sidaway's theatre was a new, and probably weatherboard structure, simply because of the problems associated with the acquisition and repair of an existing building.

This talk of converting old and possibly decaying buildings, or the use of temporary structures, need not mean that the playhouse was rough or shabby in its appearance. What matters most, of course, is the interior: plastered walls and paint, coupled with the low but warm illumination provided by candles, could well have resulted in an attractive and atmospheric environment. Watkin Tench was undoubtedly romanticising a little when he described the 1789 performance of *The Recruiting Officer* in a rough convict hut; but his account bears witness to the transformative effect on a humble space of candlelight, coloured paper and enthusiasm.

There is, moreover, a little evidence that points to the care that was taken in the theatre of 1796 to create the right ambience. According to Collins' account, 'their motto was modest and well chosen – "We cannot command success, but will endeavour to deserve it."'. The normal location of a motto in those theatres that affected one was as a decorative feature over the proscenium arch. The 1750 Liverpool Theatre had its *Totus Mundus Agit Histrionem* painted there. Covent Garden had its *Veluti in Speculum* in the same position, its design altered in successive refurbishings. The 1771 Liverpool Theatre appropriated the same Latin tag, initially painting it on a wooden plaque and later on a sheet of glass. The slogan of Philadelphia's Chestnut Street Theatre was featured on an elaborately carved or painted panel, complete with an eagle, clouds and trailing ribands. Sydney was determined not to be behind-hand in the small refinements of theatre design.

It should also be noticed that Collins' account refers to payments in kind being made at 'the gallery door'. If this was not merely an inner door opening from a communal foyer, the theatre was following best English practice by providing those who paid the higher prices with their own entrance or entrances, and possibly even a lobby. Many of the smaller provincial playhouses of Georgian England could not boast such a feature.

Outside the larger cities, most Georgian theatres had remarkably unpretentious, and even austere, facades. Accordingly, there would have been little pressure on the Sydney company to provide a decorative exterior to their building. It might have had the slightly more fashionable shingle roof, rather than the thatching used on many buildings, but if so this would have been because of the fire risk posed by candles. The building itself was probably a plain, barn-like structure. If it had any decorative features at all, the most likely would have been a simple columned portico. A number of the English theatres were given a touch of elegance in this way, and verandas, an allied form, were beginning to appear in the colony. James Winston's illustration of the theatre at Edmonton shows how a shingled weatherboard barn, on brick foundations, could be given a little gracefulness at low cost.[15] The side of the building remains completely untouched, but the facade is tricked out with elegant window frames, and has a diminutive neo-classic porch (presumably of painted timber) in front of the only door. The wall, on this side of the building alone, is of brick up to a height of about 8 feet. Above that it appears to be of stone blocks, carefully squared and trimmed, but these are almost certainly nothing more than timber planking incised and painted to give the illusion of masonry, as was the case at Brighton.[16] Simple refinements of the Edmonton kind were well within the reach of James Bloodsworth, the colony's principal architect-builder. In the overall austerity and drabness of the township, moreover, this small display of trumpery could have given the building a touch of glamour, and possibly even of excitement. It would have added, satisfyingly, to the faintly defiant air that attaches to the building of a temple of Thespis in such an unpromising wilderness.

III

If little information is available about the 1796 theatre, there is even less about the theatre that emerged from the building activities of 1798. The playbills of 1799 and 1800 make it clear that the theatre had been equipped with side boxes as well as the earlier front boxes, but the two eyewitness accounts are extremely brief. In William Noah's terse 1799 comment, the theatre was 'Done up very Neat this year', while Dr Price described it as 'not large but … commodious'.[17] The word 'commodious', in the sense of spacious, and hence comfortable, is too conventional a term on which to put much weight. Price's only additional comment is that 'the scenery is good'. If the scenery was Lancashire's, then this comment is surprising. Lancashire was not an artist by profession, though between the bouts of petty theft and forgery that made him such a nuisance, he scratched a living painting shop signs, numbers on bags, labels on pharmacy bottles and street names on finger posts. His only surviving painting, a view of Sydney Cove,[18] is in a robust naif style that hardly conforms to the ideals of scenic design, but in the dim light of a Georgian stage it might have made a reasonable impression.

One thing that the limited evidence does not reveal, unfortunately, is whether we are dealing in 1798–99 with a major refurbishing, a complete rebuilding on the same site, or the construction of a new theatre on different ground. If the absence of any record of performance between 11 November 1797 and 13 April 1799 is evidence that the theatre was closed for much of this time, that would suggest a rebuilding on the same site. A refurbishment would hardly have required a cessation of activities for more than a month or two; a new building on another site would have involved no interruption at all.

Some inferences, however, can be drawn from the existing evidence. The addition of side boxes suggests a theatre significantly wider than the earlier one, which implies major rebuilding or a new construction. Moreover, while the first theatre was almost certainly built of some basic material such as weatherboard or lath and plaster, there is a slight possibility that by 1800 the building was at least partly of brick. Describing the township that year, Dr Price noted the paucity of public buildings, 'the cause of which is obvious as the publick buildings are built with lime, none of which can be found in the country except what they make of shells'. Lime was used for mortar, which implies a stone or brick building. Later Price gives a list of these major public buildings, 'the Governor's and Lieutenant-Governor's houses, the Barracks, Hospitals, Goal, Criminal Court, Publick stores, Theatre, Magazines, Forts, Windmills and a steeple'.[19] His power of observation, like his grammar, is questionable, since parts of the hospital, one of the windmills, and probably the Criminal Court, were of timber or lath construction. However, his evidence cannot be dismissed out of hand. Similarly, while new scenery could have been part of a general smartening up at this surprisingly early date in the theatre's career, it would have been essential in any reconstruction that affected the dimensions of the scenic stage. On the whole, the evidence seems to point to the building of a new theatre. If there was a break in activity in late 1798, then that new theatre was almost certainly on the same site as its predecessor.

IV

One other point needs to be considered about the theatre, namely its location. This is not simply a matter of antiquarian interest. The physical environment of performance is invariably culturally encoded, and scholars have become increasingly sensitive to the urban as well as architectural semiotics of theatre-buildings. The Sydney theatre offers a particularly fascinating illustration of this.

Two sites for the theatre have received popular support over the last century. One school of thought locates it in Bell Row, now Bligh Street, close to Johnson's church. The other locates it on Robert Sidaway's property, behind the large granary and the military stores that fronted George Street (see Fig. 8). The first of these sites places the theatre a little behind the street which linked the governor's and the military commander's dwellings and itself was lined on its southern side by the houses of the principal civil officials – the commissary, the judge-advocate, the chaplain and the surveyor. In other words, this location places the theatre close to both the dress circle of Sydney society and the church. The theatre in Bath might have aspired to such a fashionable situation, but it is an incongruous location for Sydney's convict theatre. Locating the theatre on Sidaway's property has equally significant implications, for Sidaway's inn and dwelling were in the heart of the military district of the township, immediately behind the commanding officer's (the lieutenant-governor's) house. It made perfect sense that Sidaway, as government baker, should live close to the granary. However, putting the theatre on the same site identifies it with the soldiery rather

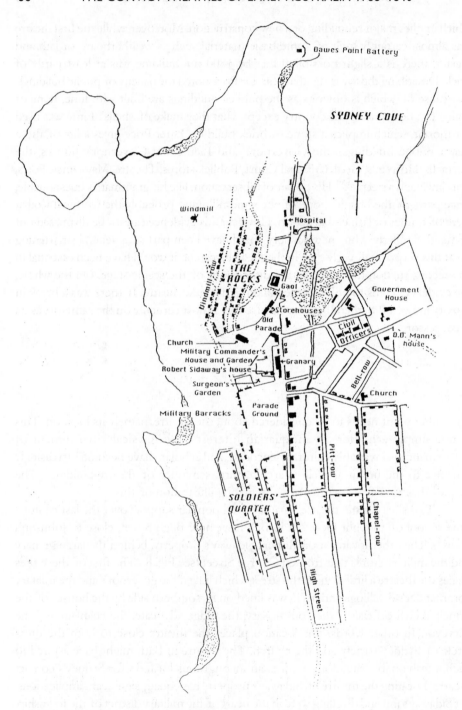

Fig. 8 Sydney, 1794-1806. This plan is a composite. The Bell-row church had gone by October
1798, and St Phillip's church, below Windmill-row, was built, for the most part, in 1803/04. A
clock tower, later incorporated into the church, had been completed in 1798 and is prominent in
Lesueur's view (see Fig. 9).

than with the convicts, and with the sources of military authority.

As it happens, both of these locations are wrong. The Bell Row site established itself in the 1940s on the authority of the writer Paul McGuire, who gives no evidence whatever for his claim. The only prior association of the theatre with this site with which I am familiar, an article in the *Triad*, also lacks evidence to back up its assertion.[20] Early illustrations suggest that the space behind the civil officers' dwellings was kept clear, as a *cordon sanitaire*, until some time after 1800. Prior to that the only building to appear in this space was the church and, when that burned down in 1798, Collins wrote that it 'stood entirely alone'. The church's bell-post survived the fire and in later illustrations it is still visible, and still isolated.[21]

The case against the Sidaway site is even stronger. Quite apart from the question of whether this small allotment could have contained the colony's leading inn, one of its larger bakeries and, presumably, a storage-shed as well as a theatre, there is the evidence of the playbills. On two of these, one prior to the 1798 rebuilding and one subsequent to it (23 July 1796 and 8 April 1800 respectively), the list of places from which tickets can be bought gives Sidaway's and the house next to the theatre as separate items. Since Sidaway's allotment lay between the gardens of the military commander and the military surgeon, any theatre on Sidaway's property would have been next to one house only, that of Sidaway. The playhouse must have been elsewhere.

Evidence has survived which appears to indicate the general area in which the theatre lay and it is neither near the church nor in the military district. A robbery of the mill in 1797 was carried out by a watchman on his rounds, who stole a bag of flour and concealed it in his room, which was in the house next to the theatre. Governor Hunter had recently divided Sydney into four districts and created a force of constables and watchmen. Since these were required to police the district in which they lived, the mill and the house next to the theatre must have been in the same district. In 1797 Sydney had only one windmill, which was on the ridge jutting out into the harbour on the western side of Sydney Cove. The administrative district, Maskelyne, probably included the streets on the level area beside the cove, but it consisted primarily of the ridge that even then was known as the Rocks. On the landward, southern side both Maskelyne and the Rocks terminated in the open space which contained the old parade ground and marked the beginning of the military district, a fifth area of the town which was controlled by the army itself.[22]

The Rocks area was an entirely different proposition from Bell Row or the military district. Consisting of a steep and irregular ridge, it was a difficult terrain on which, nevertheless, convicts had begun to throw up their primitive cottages from the early days of the settlement. Writing in 1792, an officer's wife described it as 'a gypsy encampment, with boggy tracks wending their way around rock and precipice'.[23] From this it gradually became an area of tortuous streets and cul-de-sacs, and in the theatre's heyday was on its way to becoming a liberty, where policing was ineffectual and the governor's writ did not fully run. In 1819 William Charles Wentworth described it as having been, in its earlier years, 'a chaos of building ... more like the abode of a horde of savages than the residence of a civilised community'. Governor Macquarie may have attempted to impose order on it after his arrival in 1810, but Commissioner Bigge could still present it in 1820 as an area of low taverns and dance halls, where out-of-bounds convicts and fully-fledged escapees could enjoy themselves with immunity.[24] Nor was the area below the Rocks and beside the Cove much more salubrious. While it contained the gaol, hospital, shipyards and market, it also boasted a high concentration of taverns, and its few side streets were nearly as tangled as those of the Rocks themselves. A theatre in Maskelyne, then, was a place on the margins of society, on the edge of respectability, perhaps even part of a counter-culture.

This idea, however, can be taken too far. If the theatre was in the Rocks, then the probability is that it was close to the perimeter. The very feature that made the Rocks such a retreat was the difficult terrain. Night-time forays into such an area, along rough and unlit pathways, would have been a deterrent to any audience. In 1796 the western slopes of the Rocks were still uninhabited. Settlement, which had begun at the southern end of the peninsular, was moving only gradually northwards along the east of the ridge and the foreshore of Sydney Cove. A site close to the southern extremity of the Rocks, where the open space separated it from the military district, is therefore an attractive possibility, as is the south-western margin of Sydney Cove, back from the waterfront and in one of the side streets.

The evidence drawn from the robbery at the windmill relates to the theatre prior to the refurbishment or rebuilding of 1798. Another source of information, however, is subsequent to that event. Dr Price had arrived as medical officer on the transport *Minerva* on 11 January 1800 and left in April. In his journal he describes the settlement, treating buildings, as far as possible, in a linear sequence beginning with those at the head of the cove from Government House in the east to the military commandant's house in the west. He then moves inland and southwards to the army barracks; and then northwards from the commandant's house along the western edge of the cove, where the gaol and the hospital were situated. After that, in sequence, he describes the Criminal Court, the public stores, the playhouse and Dawes' Point battery. The Criminal Court and the public stores were up the hill from the gaol, at the southern extremity of the Rocks, while the Dawes' Point battery was at its northern extremity. Logically then, the playhouse should have been somewhere on the slope of the Rocks overlooking Sydney Cove, between the Criminal Court and Dawes' Point. This location of both playhouses in Maskelyne may encourage the belief that they were built, successively, on the one site, but that remains unproven. Maskelyne ward was large: a second site for a theatre could easily have been found within its boundaries.

Assuming the suppositions made so far are correct, the analysis may be taken further. In the surviving playbills from 8 April and 23 June 1800 the list of ticket agencies ends with 'J. Mackey, next door to the Theatre'. If this building beside the playhouse was merely part of the theatre complex, as I have suggested it was with the 1796 theatre, then the information may be of limited use. However, if Mackie owned the property, the situation opens up slightly. Allowing for the interchangeable spelling of the name (Mackie, Mackey, McKoy, McKay, M'coy, McKee), there are several possible candidates in Sydney for the role of ticket-seller. In the *Sydney Gazette*, 12 April 1807, one of them, James M'coy/Mackie, who had married Frances Robinson on 26 January 1806 and signed the register with a strong clear hand, advertised the sale of his house at No. 1, Windmill Row. This is the earliest record of Mackie's residence in this house, but he might have been there for years. Was he, for example, the James Macoy of the Rocks, involved in a dispute over ownership of a small boat in 1803?[25]

If this is the Mackey in question, then a theatre next to Mackey's house perfectly fits the requirements outlined earlier. Windmill Row, later renamed Prince Street, was the uppermost street in the Rocks. By the early 1800s it boasted a few stone houses of distinction, such as that of Isaac Peyton, but most of the dwellings were still of lath and plaster, and some were little more than crude shanties.[26] As the advertisements for Mackey's house make clear, No. 1 was 'near the back of the New Church', which stood in the open ground between the Rocks and the military district and slightly down the hill from the southern end of Windmill Row. A theatre a few yards into Windmill Row would therefore have been on the margins of the Rocks. Indeed there is some evidence that the track running behind the church as a southwards extension of Windmill Row was regarded as part of that street even after it was officially named Church Street.[27] If this was the case, then the theatre may not even have been in the body of the Rocks, but on this offshoot of the area, located in a conspicuous position on the open ridge and symbolically placed between the main body of the Rocks and the soldiers' barracks.

Any effort to be more precise falls foul of the chaos and changeability of street-numbering systems in early Sydney[28] and the fact that most early views of the town do not portray the Rocks area with photographic accuracy. One reasonably careful painting of about 1799 shows a large building in Windmill Row, a short distance from its southern end; and the etching after Charles-Alexandre Lesueur's drawing of 1802 shows several large buildings at the end of Windmill Row or in the Church Street extension of it (see Fig. 9).[29]

If the theatre was indeed in Windmill Row, it had one other notable feature. Mrs Mackey was still trying to dispose of the house as late as January 1809 and, with a final round of advertisements launched in the *Sydney Gazette* on 27 November 1808, she raised her lyricism to a new pitch. It was 'that truly eligible House and Premises at the back of the Church ... the situation the most delightful in the Town of Sydney, from its vast command of prospect over the harbour'. Other property-sellers in Windmill Row were to pursue a similar tactic, with their references to a 'pleasant' or 'beautiful' situation.[30] The convicts, ex-convicts and ship's captains who squatted on allotments or bought into the area were evidently responsive to a romantic harbour view. Some of Sydney's playgoers of 1800 might have felt a similar emotion as they left the theatre's narrow passageways and looked down on the splendid vista at their feet: the dark and jagged foreshores, the silver water reaching away to the distant Heads and the opening beyond onto the vastness of the Pacific Ocean. By

Fig. 9   View across Sydney Cove towards the Rocks, by Charles-Alexandre Lesueur, 1802. This
engraving of Lesueur's drawing was published in François Péron & Louis-Claude D. de Freycinet's
Voyage de découvertes aux terres australes, [1807?] (Mitchell Library, State Library of New South Wales,
F980/P plate 38). Windmill-row is the topmost street, its southern extremity marked by the clock
tower and the second government windmill (see inset). The original windmill, scene of the robbery
mentioned on p.67, is to the right.

10.30 or 11.00 pm much of Sydney would have been deep in sleep, its silence broken only by the occasional gust of laughter, shouting, or music from the Rocks and the darkness pierced only by the distant glow of a campfire or the pale rectangle of a candle-lit window. For any playgoer with the sensibilities of a Watkin Tench or the maudlin dipsomania of Richard Atkins it must have been at once beautiful and haunting in its emptiness, so far removed from the ordered, busy and familiar world of Europe.

If the second Sydney theatre was anywhere in Windmill Row, the subsequent history of the area has denied us the possibility of ever turning it into a theatrical shrine. Prince Street stood in the direct path of the access road leading to the Sydney Harbour Bridge. When that monumental work was constructed in the 1930s, the street was levelled to the ground and then buried beneath tons of earth piled up to make the raised roadway. In the 1960s the southernmost end of this earthwork was re-excavated to provide a set of underpasses and a spaghetti junction linking bridge, city and the new Western Distributor. If Sidaway's theatre was located in this area its remains were swept away entirely by the bulldozers of the 1960s, or are now sleeping thirty feet under Sydney's most frenzied highway.

V

Just as the Botany Bay playhouse was constructed along British lines, so also its operations reflected British practice, though with interesting adjustments to local conditions. Thus, while the company may have addressed the problem of audience illiteracy through use of the town bellman, or a drummer wandering the town drumming up custom, their main method of advertising was probably the printed handbill, distributed about the town and displayed in alehouses and shops. Those that have survived are virtually identical in format to their English counterparts, but are notable for their small size, a mere 7½ by 4¾ inches. The chronic shortage of paper in the colony probably accounted for this, rather than the poverty of the company.

The playbills of which we have copies or transcripts list a whole range of people from whom tickets can be secured. Many of the names recur across several playbills, of which Robert Sidaway's is one. For the performance of *Henry the Fourth* on 8 April 1800, for example (see Fig. 5), the list reads:

> Tickets to be had of Serj. Major Jamieson, S. Lord, M. Kearns, R. Sidaway, D. Bevan, J.[or T.] Tober, Sarj. Field and J. Mackey next door to the Theatre.

As seems to have been the case in many provincial British theatres, the tickets referred to would have been for pit and boxes, the gallery being restricted to door sales. The number of vendors, however, is surprising. In British examples it rarely exceeded two or three.

With the possible exception of Mackey, all the civilians on this list were convicts or ex-convicts; even Jamieson had been sent out with the military equivalent of a criminal sentence, having taken a bayonet to a superior officer by whom his wife had been insulted. What is more to the point, however, is that most were flourishing businessmen who ran hotels as one of their activities. Jamieson held the licence for the Crown and Thistle, Simeon Lord for the Black Swan, Matt. Kearns for the Faithful Irishman, Robert Sidaway for the Chequers and David Bevan for the Union.[31] Public houses obviously made a good outlet for the sale of theatre tickets. While not recorded as an hotelier, Field probably followed the path of most sergeants in the New South Wales Corps and ran a shop on the side, and, if J. Mackey's house bore the title 'The Leaping Bar', it also must have been a trading outlet of some kind. Only T. Taber (if that is the name behind the badly mangled type) is an odd man out, since he is remembered as a schoolteacher and parish clerk, though it is possible that even he dabbled in business at this early stage in his Australian career.[32]

The prices of tickets for the Sydney theatre are also unexpected, since they are well out of line with British provincial practice. As noted earlier, there were no standard rates for respectable theatres outside London, but a common pattern was for the boxes to cost 3s., the pit 2s. and the gallery 1s.. In a few of the large cities and fashionable resorts a box seat might cost 4s., but rarely any more. In contrast, the Sydney theatre, once it had its full complement of boxes, charged prices close to those of the major London theatres, from 5s. for a side box to 1s. for the gallery. These had been the standard figures for Covent Garden and Drury Lane up to the early 1790s, and remained the prices for the Haymarket in subsequent years. Though the front boxes were less fashionable than the side boxes, London theatres, and most provincial companies, charged the same for both. The price differentiation that Sydney maintained between front and side had some precedents in Britain, but it might suggest that Sydney's front boxes were much less comfortable than those to the sides.

The reason for these relatively high costs can only be surmised. The expense in the colony of many of the goods and materials required for theatrical presentation could have gone some way to justifying such inflated figures. The small size of the theatre could have made it necessary to pitch pit and box prices as high as possible, if there was to be any hope of a margin of profit. However, what the prices are most likely to reflect is the dearth of entertainment in the township. With so little in the way of alternatives it was a seller's market.

Another anomaly about the Sydney theatre was the length of its seasons. The 1788 Act restricted English travelling companies to a stay of sixty days in any one town. Some Patents Royal had similar restrictions applied to the town for which the patent was issued, but even where they did not it was standard practice for the provincial patent companies to spend much of the year touring a more or less established circuit. In contrast, performances at Sydney are recorded over Christmas, in January, February, March, April, June, July, August and November. This suggests that the company ran on a year-round basis, giving the inhabitants of Sydney a much more sustained diet of theatre than was available anywhere in England outside London.

What cannot be determined, unfortunately, is the frequency of performances. On Norfolk Island in 1793, the outpost's lieutenant-governor, Philip Gidley King, had set out firm directions for his theatre. It was permitted to operate on one Saturday per month and on public holidays. It is tempting to assume that a similar pattern was imposed in Sydney when its theatre was established. Any such assumption falls foul of the fact that three of the recorded Sydney productions took place on days other than Saturday. On the other hand, two of these could be regarded as special cases, and it is notable that the bulk of the recorded Sydney performances took place on a Saturday. But no regular pattern is discernible: the Saturday performances did not fall on a uniform Saturday in the month, nor are the recorded performances at regular four-weekly intervals.

One explanation for the lack of a discernible monthly pattern might be that performances took place once a week. In the confusion of April 1800 we find the performance scheduled for Saturday 5 April postponed until Saturday 12, and a new play announced for Tuesday 8. This could be construed as an effort to preserve a pattern of weekly performances. One performance a week, however, seems more than such a small community could sustain. Nor is it easy to imagine a group of part-time actors having enough free hours or energy to get up a new play and afterpiece every seven days. (For an alternative explanation, see Appendix A: J. Davison.)

Another response to the evidence is to see the timetabling of plays at the Sydney theatre as random. Plays were staged when the cast was ready, or when some conjunction of events promised a bumper house. Actors not entirely dependent on the theatre for a living could have found this *ad hoc* approach convenient to their situation.

If performances were frequently given on Saturday nights in the Sydney theatre, it is a further, slight departure from customary English practice. Saturday night performances certainly took place in England, but most provincial companies offering three performances a week, and some of those offering four, actually avoided Saturday night. The appeal of that evening to the Botany Bay authorities is obvious: convicts finished work early on Saturday (if they worked on that day at all) and no labour was expected of them on Sunday. Saturday also seems to have been the designated market day for Sydney, so that the company might have had the advantage of a few visitors from outlying farms and settlements.[33]

Many provincial English theatres may not have programmed performances on Saturday nights in order to avoid violating the Sabbath, either because the show concluded after midnight or because the audience was obliged to travel home after that hour. In 1805 the Bishop of London caused a stir by threatening to have the capital's patent theatres closed for these very reasons.[34] In the event he was frustrated, but country theatres working under the 1788 Act were subject to close control by the local magistrates, many of whom were clergy or conservative laymen.

The risk of violating the Sabbath may never have been an issue in New South Wales. Control of the theatre seems to have been vested in the judge-advocate, and

David Collins and his successor, the worthless Richard Dore, were not men greatly exercised by matters of the spirit. The Rev. Johnson's correspondence is loud with complaint about the prevailing godlessness and the phlegmatic Samuel Marsden's response was just as appalled. Such feelings were not limited to the clergy or even to the pious. The down-to-earth government boat-builder, Daniel Paine, was cutting on the subject. Even the woeful Richard Atkins, through his alcoholic haze, found the attitude of his fellow gentlemen deplorable.[35]

One striking example of the administration's casual approach to religious niceties is the performance on 12 April 1800. An obligation that seems to have been respected throughout Britain was that of theatres being dark during Holy Week. Indeed, winter theatres often chose the beginning of this religious festival to terminate their season, while summer theatres opened on Easter Monday. But 12 April 1800 was Easter Saturday. This break with convention is in striking contrast to the situation twenty or thirty years later, when the power of the clergy was a major impediment to the development of Australian theatre.[36]

VI

The next consideration is what one might call the internal operations of the company. This includes the relationship between the theatre building and the performing company, the management of the company, and the financial arrangements between that management and the individual players, musicians, stage hands and scenic artists.

In the discussion up to this point one thing has been accepted without question, that Robert Sidaway, already a wealthy man, was responsible for erecting the playhouse. The proposition that the Sydney theatre was not built on the site of Sidaway's inn and bakery does not affect his claim to the theatre. Sidaway held leases on other properties in Sydney, and the theatre could just as readily have been on one of these. Indeed, in 1789 he was living in a house high in the Rocks and, if he was the builder of the theatre and still held this plot of land, it could well be a candidate for the site of the playhouse.

The questions that can be raised about the nature of Sidaway's involvement come from other directions. His close identification with the theatre building depends entirely on one brief newspaper article, which seems to have appeared first in the *London Chronicle*, 31 August–2 September 1797, and was thereafter reproduced verbatim elsewhere, in the *True Briton*, 7 September 1797, for example, and *Saunders' News-Letter*, 12 September 1797. The first of these offers it under the heading 'Remarkable Instance of the versatility of Fortune':

> Sidway, who was one of the first convicts landed at Botany Bay, whither
> he was transported for house-breaking, is now living there in a state,
> comparatively, of great respectability. He has a contract for serving the
> Colony with bread; has a perpetual grant from Government of several
> hundred acres of land which he cultivates; keeps the best house of

> public entertainment in the place; and, lastly, has erected a theatre, of
> which he is the manager.

Whether this article was adapted by a journalist from a letter, or reported by someone recently returned, is not recorded; but in either case it is information mediated by a London journalist. It is a second-hand report. The one first-hand account we have of the establishment of the theatre, however, by David Collins, makes no mention of Sidaway at all. Moreover, it claims that the performers built the theatre themselves:

> Some of the more decent class of prisoners, male and female, having
> some time since obtained permission to prepare a playhouse at Sydney,
> it was opened on Saturday 16th, under the management of John Sparrow
> … They had fitted up the house with more theatrical propriety than
> could have been expected … Of their dresses the greater part was
> made by themselves.

By 1808, in an anonymous and largely derivative account, this has become 'a playhouse had been erected at the expence of some persons who performed in it for their own emolument'. Furthermore, in Collins' account Sidaway is emphatically *not* the theatre's manager at the time of its opening. Nor is he in the list of performers appended in a footnote. Collins knew Sidaway and refers to him on several occasions in his history, so he was familiar with his doings.

One other significant piece of evidence may help to explain the situation. In the judge-advocate's Register of Assignments, as was noted in Chapter 2, the following entry appears against the date 17 September 1801: 'Thomas Radley to Edwd Turley Smith. Assignment of 6 Shares in the Theatre at Sydney to secure £17 payable the 20th Feby 1802.'[37] In other words, six shares in the theatre, owned by Radley, are being accepted as security for a debt. This suggests that the second theatre, at least, was financed in a way that was common in England. Under this system individuals would subscribe funds, usually in units of £25 or £50, to provide the capital for building the theatre, receiving in return the number of shares proportional to their investment. The completed theatre was then leased out to a manager to provide a regular season of performances. A committee of shareholders managed the leases, the maintenance of the building and the division of profits. In some cases they interfered significantly in the operations of the resident company.[38]

In the English model these subscribers were well-to-do businessmen, lawyers, doctors, and members of the lesser gentry. In the topsy-turvy world of Botany Bay it is entirely appropriate that the two proprietors we can identify, Sidaway and Radley, were an ex-convict and a serving convict respectively, the first a well-known housebreaker, the second a highwayman, and both of them Port Jackson entrepreneurs. They point to the probability that the group of thrusting convict and ex-convict businessmen and minor officials provided the subscribers to the building of the second theatre, and possibly the first, though each share in Sydney was clearly worth less than the £25 that was common in England. If the Sydney theatre shares were for £5 each, the face value of Radley's six shares would have been £30, sufficient to cover a £17 loan.

It was customary in the theatre for the shareholders to be quite distinct from the practitioners who used the playhouse, though some of the subscribers had a strong interest in the drama. However, it was not uncommon for a theatre manager to take the initiative in raising subscriptions and himself become one of the subscribers.[39] But I know of no case in the United Kingdom in which a company of actors went shares with local businessmen in erecting a theatre. Something like this, however, is a way of explaining the conflicting evidence about the creation of the Sydney theatre – on the one hand built by Sidaway, on the other by the players. Not all the performers in the original company are likely to have been shareholders, but a few of them, such as John Sparrow, were quite prosperous by 1800 and might have been well on the road to affluence by 1796. Henry Green had almost certainly brought funds with him from England. Others might have had oblique means of generating financial support. The shareholder Thomas Radley was not only a minor businessman but also the *de facto* husband of one of the actresses, Mrs Radley, *née* Mary Ann Fowles. It would not be at all surprising to find that Mrs Greville, another actress, had engaged her common-law husband, also a convict businessman, in a similar fashion.

In many of the British examples, however, one subscriber, by virtue of his energy, or the size of his shareholding, assumed a dominant position among the proprietors. Such a one was Henry Palmer, at Bath, and such, it may be, was Robert Sidaway at Port Jackson. What induced Sidaway to become involved will never be known. Certainly, in spite of the entertainingly foppish figure he cuts in *The Playmaker*, there is no evidence that he was ever an aspiring actor. It may be, as John West suggests, that he simply had an eye for a good business opportunity.[40] Perhaps he was driven by a spectator's love of theatre or had a desire to pose as a patron of the arts, like a gentleman or respectable bourgeois in provincial England. If it was the last of these, it was a pardonable vanity, shared with other upwardly-mobile convicts. Connections might also have had something to do with it. In its first year the performers included one of Sidaway's closest cronies, Henry Lavell, and Sidaway and John Sparrow could have had a family association, going back to their days in Shoreditch. In addition the pair might have had business dealings in the colony arising out of their earlier trades, Sparrow as a watchmaker and Sidaway as a maker of watch cases: certainly Sparrow maintained a watch-repairing business in Sydney along with his other enterprises. Whatever Sidaway's motive, it was this foray into theatre that earned this hardened criminal turned colonial baker, innkeeper and dealer his small niche in Australian history.

It should be noted that the evidence linking Sidaway to the theatre relates to the playhouse of 1796. Sidaway could have remained a dominant figure through to the theatre's closure in 1804–07 or he might have dropped out at an earlier date. If 1798 saw a major reconstruction or the building of a new theatre, this could have been accompanied by a significant change in the proprietorship of the playhouse and possibly the establishment of a completely new company of shareholders. So firmly is Sidaway's name associated with the Sydney theatre, however, that for convenience sake I shall continue to refer to it, throughout its life, as Sidaway's theatre.

VII

Nothing further seems discoverable about the size and operation of the group that built either the first or the second theatre. What, though, of the group that mounted the productions? How many people were involved, what were their functions and how were the returns of the enterprise allocated?

As was usual in England, the same players appeared in the mainpiece and the afterpiece, but there seems to have been no attempt at doubling within a play, a common device in the more impoverished companies. Occasionally a bit part of two or three lines, such as Bagatelle in *The Poor Soldier*, was not listed in the playbill and might have been cut from the performance as an economy. On most evenings for which we have details, 11–13 actors were involved in the enterprise. Beyond these there may have been one or two stage extras.

Next in importance to the actors were the musicians. Every self-respecting company needed a band, though the size of this was not standardised. There were frequent jokes about small companies trying to get by with a single fiddler. Sometimes it was one of the actors who leaped in and out of role as the exigencies of the evening required.[41] A group of six musicians would have been acceptable; decent minor companies such as Masterman's and Mrs Baker's seem to have been content with bands of three.[42] Since it did not have the burden of touring, the Sydney company may have inclined to the slightly larger figure of five or six.

The process of assembling a band could have been made easier by the fact that there was a body of trained musicians in the colony, in the form of the band of the New South Wales Corps. Evening duty calls other than on royal birthdays were probably rare and the men were almost certainly free to take on private commissions when not needed by their superiors. An eight-man 'Harmonie Musick' was the standard minimum for regimental purposes, but a larger band brought more prestige, and by 1802 François Péron could refer to that of the New South Wales Corps as 'numerous and well-composed'.[43] The only problem was that military bands consisted of woodwinds and brass, with the larger versions adding percussion. There was no place for strings, and the violin was a key instrument in theatre music. Since military bands were expected to perform at balls and feasts, as well as parades and public ceremonies, however, some members were usually multi-skilled.[44] There was also no shortage of street musicians and of amateurs in the colony, with fiddlers bulking large among their numbers. Their presence at humble social gatherings is well attested. On 27 October 1801, for example, a fiddler playing at John Sparrow's house late into the evening, on departure, severely intoxicated, stole four fowls. (The subsequent hearing of the case had to be held over when the fiddler turned out to be drunk on that occasion also.[45]) In one way or another the company would have had no difficulty in assembling its musicians.

The number of front-of-house and backstage staff is difficult to calculate, since in a small company, with limited box-office returns, many jobs could have been doubled, and some dispensed with, such as dressers. The geography of the playhouse could also have influenced staff numbers. A theatre with no green room and with dressing rooms removed from the stage (in an adjacent building, for example) would probably have needed a callboy. The prompter could have taken over many of the duties of the acting, or stage, manager, and have got by with two stagehands. The company would have required a clerk to keep the box-office records and manage advance sales, in all likelihood operating out of the house next to the theatre and doubling as one of the cash handlers on performance nights. Even if there were no dressers, someone must have been in charge of wardrobe. Similarly, there must have been a scene painter, preparing new scenes and touching up the old ones. Large numbers of candles had to be set and trimmed and the theatre cleaned. There were also playbills to be distributed and other advertising. In all, over 30 people could have been involved in the enterprise.

By 1800 the stronger British companies were moving towards a system of regular weekly salaries, but many of the smaller groups still operated on a system of profit-sharing. Usually each performer was allocated a single share, though an actor who had useful additional talents – song-writing, for example – might receive an additional half share, while actors on try-out, or of limited value, might receive less than a full share. Bit players, and all but a few key ancillary staff, were usually on a flat fee. The bugbear in this system was the manager, who was normally allocated four shares, or five if also an actor, since he or she bore the costs of supplying and maintaining the sets and much of the wardrobe, and of covering incidental expenses. The suspicion was widespread that managers rarely paid out in expenses sufficient to justify their shares; and, since they also kept the company records, they were open to accusations of falsifying the books. In consequence their profession had a bad name. Some memoirs, however, record the occasional honest, even generous, exception, while delivering a general blast at the tribe.[46]

Since the Botany Bay operation was such a small one, and the productions relatively infrequent, some kind of sharing system, performance by performance, was probably adopted. If this was the case the perquisites of management seem to have been insufficient to persuade anyone to cling to that post. The manager was usually the constant of any company. Not so in Botany Bay. Collins lists John Sparrow as the manager in January 1796. The *London Chronicle* of 31 August–2 September 1797 gives the post to Sidaway. Since the news might have taken up to a year to reach England, Sidaway could have taken over the position within a few months of the theatre's opening. In April 1799 Joseph Vasconcellis, a private in the New South Wales Corps, is recorded as company manager, but by January 1801 he was listed in the regimental musters as 'sick' and continued to be so recorded until his death on 25 May 1802. Additional managers may have intervened between Sidaway and Vasconcellis.

Because of the variables involved, it is impossible to make a firm estimate of an actor's income from a night's performance. However, if one had seven auxiliary staff and one stage extra, each on a flat fee of 2s. per night, two cash handlers and four musicians on 3s. each, and a clerk on a retainer of 10s. per show, this would absorb £2 4s. of the net income from a full house.[47] With four bit-players on half shares, the manager on four shares, and eight actors, the lead musician and the prompter each on a single share, those single shares would be worth 12s. apiece, if a full house netted the 'upwards of twelve pounds' suggested by Mrs Eades' benefit. Wages for cleaners, billposters, scenic artist, wardrobe keeper and others would have been borne by the manager as part of the house charges.

These figures, it should be noted, are based on the assumed net profit from a full house in the original theatre. The addition of side boxes in the second theatre would have added substantially to the takings, but, equally, a less-than-full house could have halved them. Eight shillings could well have been a good take-home pay for a leading actor. Thirty years later the convict theatre at Emu Plains is recorded as operating on a sharing basis, show by show, though the information given about this in James Tucker's novel *Ralph Rashleigh* is inconsistent. After the performance of Mathew Gregory ('Monk') Lewis's *Raymond and Agnes*, we are told, the manager distributed a 15-shilling share to each of the performers, and 10s. to each of the four musicians. At the performance in the innkeeper's barn the arrangement is given as a full share for the principal performers, a part-share for 'the lower rate of performers', and 'stipulated wages' for 'the supernumeraries – scene-shifters and others'. The share for the principal actors was allegedly 30s., while lesser performers were entitled to a figure below £1 2s. 6d..[48] In neither case is there any mention of a multiple share for the manager. The disappearance of that iniquitous system by the 1830s, the audience capacity of the innkeeper's 'large barn' – or even some poetic licence – could explain why the figures, especially those for the second performance, are so much higher than the hypothetical shares I have given for the Sydney theatre. Those Sydney figures, it must be emphasised, are merely illustrative; estimates using other suitable combinations of figures tend to result in a full share of 10s.–15s..

To gain some understanding of these figures we need to measure them against the wages prevailing in the colony. Governor Hunter tried to impose rates of 2s. 6d. per day for farm labourers without board and 1s. for those with board.[49] However, the shortage of workers was so great that much higher figures were paid. In mid-1800, for example, the Governor claimed that the wage being paid to a farm labourer with board was not 1s. but 5s..[50] For skilled tradesmen the figure was higher, 10s.–12s. per day.[51] In this context an occasional 10s. for a performance would have made an attractive supplement to an income derived by the men from other sources, though the disappearance of several from the stage into trade suggests the latter had more potential. For the actresses the money may have been of greater significance. The government at Botany Bay had more convict women on its hands than it could usefully employ, and this would suggest there was also a glut on the private market for occupations like washing, mending and repairing clothes, millinery and domestic service. Because of the disproportionate number of young males in the settlement, prostitution was probably the only trade with good opportunities. Since several of the actresses had stable family relationships, they were to some extent cushioned against hardship, though Mrs Charleton would have been grateful for the supplement to her husband's meagre wages, if she was indeed Mary Gatty, the convict wife of Private Charleton of the New South Wales Corps.

VIII

Independent of the regular income derived from their share or fee, actors had an additional financial inducement, the benefit. In a well-established British company every actor of significance was given the choice of a program in which to figure prominently and earn the net proceeds of the night. The manager, inevitably, was also given a night, whether or not he or she was an actor. Lesser actors would share an evening, and in many companies there would also be shared nights for the box-keepers and other staff. For most English actors the benefit was the glittering prize, the chance for a lump-sum reward after the often pitifully small scrapings returned by the sharing system.[52]

The benefit was yet another convention transported to New South Wales that may have undergone some modification in the process. Three playbills for actor's benefits have survived for Sydney, one for Henry Green on 23 July 1796 (see Fig. 2) and two for Mrs Parry – one on 1 June 1799 (see Fig. 3) and another on 23 June 1800 (see Fig. 6). In England benefits usually took place at the end of a theatre's season, after which the playhouse went dark until the following year. However, as we have seen, the Sydney theatre was a year-round affair. The choice of winter for their benefits may indicate the period at which this theatre was most popular, perhaps because European tradition made winter the high season socially, but also because the heat of summer made that a period to avoid.

The two actors with identified benefits were both leading players. It is unlikely that a theatre operating as infrequently as that in Sydney could afford to offer benefits to all, but for those offered benefits, the appeal would have been attractive, probably a figure of £8 or more at a blow. An actor offered a benefit had every incentive to maximise the box-office on that night and several procedures for achieving this were well established. One was the grubby business of solicitation, touting tickets to friends, acquaintances and total strangers. Another was to make the program as attractive as possible. Where the actor was a personality the solution was to fill the show with much-loved bravura pieces to display his or her skills. Other approaches were to pack the evening with variety in a program that went on well beyond the usual curtain time, or to go for novelty – unusual pieces and special guest performers.

Clearly, the modest resources of the Sydney company would have been strained by the effort of presenting anything too complex. Nevertheless efforts were made – nowhere more so than in the case of Mrs Parry's benefit of 1 June 1799. In the first place, there is the choice of a mainpiece. Frederick Reynolds' *Fortune's Fool* was not an established part of the English repertoire. It had the special appeal of being a new play. Indeed, it may have been one of the last new plays seen by Mrs Parry before her capture and imprisonment. It had opened at Covent Garden on Saturday 29 October 1796 and dropped out of the repertory on Wednesday 25 January 1797. Mrs Parry (who lived a stone's throw away from the theatre) was arrested on 10 March 1797.[53] *Fortune's Fool* was one of the more mechanical of Reynolds' pieces, damned with faint praise by most of the critics, but well received by the public. It had the advantage of being a work by one of the most popular dramatists of the age.

Secondly, there is Mrs Parry's choice of role. She chose not the heroine, but the comic male lead, Ap-hazard, the fortune's fool of the title, created at Covent Garden by the fashionable comic actor William Lewis. There is nothing in the text that requires cross-dressing. There was, however, a well-established tradition of actresses taking on the sprightlier male roles, with Dorothy Jordan the most famous example in this period.

The appeal of taking a male role is quite clear. In James Boaden's words, it 'calls upon females ... for a more complete display of the figure, than suits the decorum of a delicate mind'.[54] Scenes in which an actress in a play assumes male costume as a requirement of the plot date back to the Restoration, and from the outset the appeal had been the display of the female calf and, as breeches grew tighter, of the thigh. To judge from the fame of Peg Woffington as Sir Harry Wildair and Dorothy Jordan in a host of parts, the frisson increased exponentially when the actress took on a genuine male role, as did the outrage of the moralists.[55] It should be noticed, however, that the Botany Bay playbill has Mrs Parry performing the role 'for that night only'. Since more than one performance would have been unusual in a theatre of this kind, the comment probably gave the audience a further incentive by drawing attention to the fact that here would be their first chance to see Mrs Parry's legs in any role, or their only chance to see her in a complete male impersonation.

For a benefit an actor would normally choose a role which gave the best opportunities of exploiting his or her special talents. Ap-hazard, then, should give us some idea of Mrs Parry's style as an actor, or at least of what she thought was her special strength. The part was one of several Reynolds wrote for William Lewis, and some vivid accounts have survived of his characteristics as a performer. William Hazlitt remembered him as

> the gay, fluttering, hare-brained Lewis; he that was called 'Gentleman Lewis' – all life, and fashion, and volubility, and whim; the greatest comic *mannerist* that perhaps ever lived; whose head seemed to be in his heels, and his wit at his fingers' ends; who never let the stage stand still, and made your heart light and your head giddy with his infinite vivacity, and bustle, and hey-day animal spirits ... Nobody could break open a door, or jump over a table, or scale a ladder, or twirl a cocked hat, or dangle a cane, or play a jockey-nobleman, or a nobleman's jockey, like him.[56]

Leigh Hunt was more specific:

> Let the reader picture to himself a slight, youthful figure, of middle
> height, with sprightly eyes half shut with laughing, a mouth that showed
> its teeth a little when it smiled; restless, and yet gentlemanly manners; a
> pair of gloved hands that went through all the varieties of illustration
> that hands can insinuate, and thrust the point of a joke into your ribs
> with a finger, to the exclamation of 'you dog!' – light airy voice,
> harmonising with the look of the face, often out of breath with spirits,
> and reposing sometimes on long lower tones of ludicrous contrast; a
> head full of nods, and becks, and flutterings; and lastly, a habit of
> finishing his sentences with indescribable exclamations of *hoo!* And *phoo!*
> and a look of pouting astonishment, in order to be in the fashion. We
> have nothing like it nowadays: nothing so thin, so airy, so gentlemanly,
> so eternally young: for Lewis was the very same to the last.[57]

So well established was Lewis's style that the critics of *Fortune's Fool* had merely to allude to it. 'Lewis played *Aphazard* with his usual whim and animation; and he and the Author are reciprocally indebted to each other' was how the *Daily Universal Register* of 31 October 1796 reported it.

But Mrs Parry, as Ap-hazard, was not the only novelty in the piece. Mrs Parry's husband, Philip, was also performing, in the role of Sir Charles Danvers. His name appears in no other recorded production and a manuscript note on the transcription of the playbill identifies him as an 'occasional' performer. More interesting is Mrs Miller, who fills the role of Lady Danvers. Like Mrs Parry she also is listed 'for that night only', but in her case the phrase had a different significance. The lady was Mary Palmer, the *de facto* of William Miller, one of the more prominent emancipist businessmen – a baker, innkeeper, and owner of small vessels trading to the Hawkesbury. What we have here is the familiar stratagem of enlisting a local dignitary to make a once-only appearance, thereby drawing an extended circle of acquaintance – and the curious – to the theatre. No Mrs Miller or Mrs Palmer appears on any of the other surviving playbills. As befits Botany Bay, this dignitary gracing the boards was a petty thief from Covent Garden.

However, the support of the Millers went further than the corporeal presence of Mrs Miller and her crowd-appeal as a dignitary's wife. As part of the process of working for one's benefit, the actor involved is often named as one of those from whom tickets may be purchased – and sometimes as the only person. On this night it is announced that tickets are available not only from Mrs Parry herself, as one might expect, but also from William Miller. He is presumably adding his persuasive powers to Mrs Parry's, either out of friendship or the vanity of having his wife perform to the fullest possible house. Since he appears to have been involved in the murder of an Aborigine some time before the play, and violently assaulted the chief constable a few weeks after the performance, Miller was not a man to cross.[58] His persuasiveness as a ticket seller would have been considerable.

The lure of Mrs Parry's benefit did not stop with the mainpiece, for it was followed by the only recorded example of a locally-written interlude to grace Sidaway's stage. Probably there had been other interludes, but, whether or not this one was unique, it made a fine garnish to a lady's benefit. When locally-written, an interlude's pleasure usually lay in topical references. In this case all we learn is that, 'After the Play, a New Occasional Addres [*sic*] will be Spoken by Mrs. Parry'. The use of the word 'occasional' attests to its topicality, and, since its author is known to be Michael Massey Robinson, it was almost certainly in verse. This was his preferred medium, and the one that brought him to these shores after he attempted to blackmail a businessman by threatening to publish a defamatory poem about him.

This section has concerned itself primarily with the financial inducements to play-acting in Sidaway's theatre, but it must be remembered that then, as now, acting had an allure for many people quite apart from profit. For many the exhilaration of performance must have been the incentive. There can be little doubt that Mrs Radley and George Henry Hughes, who rarely, if ever, achieved a starring role, persisted with the company from 1796 to at least 1800 out of sheer love of the stage. They were probably not alone in this.

Chapter 4

THE SYDNEY THEATRE, 1796–1804/07: ACTORS, AUDIENCES AND OTHERS

The last chapter was preoccupied with the mechanics of Robert Sidaway's theatrical operation – the setting up and design of theatres, the organisation of performances, the structure and finances. The concern of the present chapter is with theatre as a social institution. What sort of people were the makers of this theatre? What was the composition of its audiences? What was its relation to the structures of power in New South Wales? How was the company perceived in England and elsewhere?

On 11 September 1797 the *Morning Chronicle* attempted a joke:

> The performers of Botany Bay theatre, we understand, have smaller salaries than those of our theatres, but more *permanent engagements*. Some are engaged for *seven years*, and some for *fourteen*!

Since most of the inhabitants of the colony *were* tied to the place by sentences of seven years, fourteen years or life, it is reasonable to expect a company with a relatively stable acting corps. In fact this was not the case. The *Morning Chronicle* was no more accurate than funny. Of the twelve performers known to be associated with the Sydney theatre in 1796 only two were still with it in 1799, George Henry Hughes and Mrs Radley. Several of the others had been replaced by recent convict arrivals, such as Frances Fox (Mrs Parry) and Sarah McCann, who had disembarked in July 1798, and Philip Parry, who had arrived in June 1797. It is a sign of the fluidity of the company that within a year of her arrival Mrs Parry was the group's leading lady. In a similar fashion Daniel Parnell, who was to arrive in July 1799, had worked his way into a significant position with the company by April 1800, presumably on the strength of his skills as a dancer. He is merely one of a further series of comings and goings revealed by the playbills of 1800.[1]

The reasons for the departures are varied. Death terminated the career of young William Fowkes in April 1797. There were others who left Sydney, possibly under compulsion, such as Daniel Parnell and William Richards, who had begun to cause trouble shortly after 1800 and found themselves on Norfolk Island in May 1803. John Sparrow probably gave up acting to concentrate on his more lucrative activities as a watchmaker and entrepreneur and Mrs Davis may have given up for similar reasons. However, the major source of instability was the expiration of sentences or the securing of absolute pardons, followed by a prompt departure for home. Henry Green had almost certainly brought enough money with him to buy his passage back to England as soon as he was freed. His pardon was granted on 6 August 1797, a year after his benefit performance. He does not appear in later productions and in a list of 1801 he is recorded as having left the colony. Mrs Parry and her husband also received absolute pardons, on 15 September and 4 June 1800 respectively. Parry sailed for England on 21 October 1800 and, since Mrs Parry is recorded as having left the colony by 1801, she no doubt accompanied him. George Henry Hughes may have departed shortly after. He disappears from the colonial records at about that time, and a 'George Hughs' is said to have left prior to September 1802.

A social analysis of the 34 actors, managers and other participants in Sidaway's theatre whose names have survived raises enormous difficulties. The first of these, obviously, is that of identifying them. Collins' list of the main performers in the opening production gives us both the first and surnames of five men, but the solitary woman is referred to as 'Mrs. Davis'. The playbills that have survived, or were reproduced in English newspapers, follow the English convention, that is, the adult males are listed by their surname preceded by an initial. Given the small size of the community this is often sufficient to make a firm identification possible. There was only one P. Parry in Sydney and one D. Parnell. As luck would have it, however, the male leads in 1799 and 1800 were W. Smith and J. White, names so common in the colony as to induce scholarly despair. There are also some players whose names do not occur anywhere else in the surviving records – R. Momdy is an example. Fortunately these were minor participants. Momdy appears only in a small role in the afterpiece at Green's benefit.

In the case of the women the situation is even more complex, for when Collins listed 'Mrs. Davis' he was himself following the convention of the playbills. The title itself simply designates an adult woman so that Mrs Davis could be a Davis by birth, or by marriage, or could simply have adopted the surname as an honorific because she was currently living with a Mr Davis. Such liaisons were common, sometimes changed rapidly, and were rarely picked up in official documents. Mrs Greville, one of the actresses in Green's benefit, is presumably the *de facto* of David Greville, but there are no records that give her real name and when he was transported for a second time, in 1806, a newly-arrived woman, Mary Davies, became his partner. In this way Mrs Greville, the actress, remains lost to history.

Where the individuals can be identified, one further piece of information is often recoverable with relative ease – at least in the case of the males. This is their notional occupation. We are thus able to say that the five men known to be associated with that original production of 1796 comprised a watchmaker, a hatter, a painter and glazier, another painter and, by the looks of it, a printer.[2] If one includes Robert Sidaway, as the putative entrepreneur, then a watchcase maker is added to the list. Two men who might have been there from the beginning, and were certainly in the company six months later, were an ivory turner, Henry Lavell, and a young man 'Educated for the accompting house', Richard Evans. In every case, that is, the occupation is one that would now be regarded as falling between upper working class and respectable bourgeois, depending on the individual's success in that trade. Among them there were no bargemen, carters or labourers. The identifiable male actors from the period 1799–1800 comprise a maker of plaster mouldings, a grocer, a bookbinder, a carpenter and a corporal who later became a highly-respected sergeant in the New South Wales Corps.[3] The only person of unmistakably genteel pretensions who can be associated with the theatre was the scandalous Michael Massey Robinson, an attorney and gentleman of Gray's Inn, who wrote the address included in Mrs Parry's 1799 benefit programme. This, however, may have been his only involvement with the company, and what is noticeable about this address is that it appears in the playbill anonymously, a gentlemanly affectation pointing the gap between an elegant versifier and a mere player.

In Chapter 1 social groupings in the theatre were discussed almost entirely in terms of occupation. Trade or profession was a major factor in determining status in the late eighteenth century and, for the broad generalisations required in Chapter 1, it provided a suitable approach. However, for the analysis of individuals or small groups a more detailed examination is needed.

Certain trades had greater inherent status than others: goldsmiths and watchmakers had an advantage over shoemakers and butchers. Beyond that, position within a trade could have a profound effect on social standing. Apprentices were traditionally held in low esteem. They were seen, if not quite in those words, as members of a youth sub-culture prone to frivolous behaviour, irresponsibility, riot and, in the worst cases, criminality. Hogarth's idle apprentice sums it up. In theory journeymen were fully-trained members of a trade working for others until such time as they could set up their own independent businesses. However, by the late eighteenth century it was obvious that changing industrial practices had doomed most of them to live out their lives as wage earners. Masters, qualified tradesmen running their own businesses, were the elite of a craft, but here the level of wealth and success became a major factor. An extremely successful entrepreneur could rise in social position to the point of taking on many of the characteristics of a gentleman. John Grant, acutely conscious of his own gentility, had no hesitation in describing the businessman Robert Campbell as 'by far the most worthy, opulent and really useful Gentleman in this Colony'. In contrast, Bligh's description of him was carefully nuanced: Campbell was a 'gentlemanlike merchant'.[4] But, whatever Bligh's qualifications, there was a world of difference between Robert Campbell and a master whose livelihood consisted of running a wretched corner store in the slums of St Giles or Wapping. The Norfolk Island theatre manager, Thomas Crowder, seems to have acquired no great status from his grocery and chandler's business at the notorious Seven Dials. On the other hand, the convict actor Henry Green, a hatter by trade, was referred to as a gentleman in a newspaper report of his trial. The word could have been empty of meaning, but was more likely to have been a courtesy title justified by Green's superior position as a successful businessman with a trading network that extended into the Home Counties.

If Sidaway and his actors are considered in these terms, a few discriminations can be made. Henry Green had been a respectable businessman; his conviction might actually have been a miscarriage of justice. Philip Parry was an Oxford Street grocer, but his wild foray as a highwayman suggests his trade might have been faltering. John Sparrow was convicted a little over three years after his apprenticeship was due for completion. There is no evidence that he completed it, but he was certainly active in the trade in New South Wales. Similar doubts may be held of Robert Sidaway and William Fowkes. Henry Lavell had moved around the country looking for work after completing his indentures, but had abandoned his trade to become a household servant. Richard Evans, a young clerk, was unemployed at the time of his arrest. In other words, while one or two may have been well established, others had been out of work or, at best, only casually employed at their trades, and some might have abandoned their training prematurely and been living by their wits. Writing on the state of the colony in 1803, George Caley declared:

> It [is] said in England that the people transported were the best of workmen; but I find this is a prejudiced error, for among the many that have been sent here there are very few of that description. They are chiefly runaway apprentices, and such as neither could nor would work for a living.

That this is not entirely fanciful is suggested by Governor King's comments on the low skills level of most of the Norfolk Island carpenters in 1794 and various remarks about tradesmen in 1803 and 1804.[5]

Whatever their status before they landed in the colony, several of those associated with the theatre went on to establish themselves as successful businessmen after their arrival. In this way Sparrow, Evans, Sidaway and William Chapman rose above the common run of convicts. Evidently they had flair. This may have been the rat cunning and ruthlessness of the socially disadvantaged fighting their way to the top, but it is more likely to have been a case of those bred to trade and commerce capitalising on their skills. In either case, the theatre company had more than its due share of the thrusting and the successful.

Along with occupation, the most significant factor in defining status was family. In particular the status of a father could become part of the inheritance of a son or daughter. But it was not simply a matter of one's immediate antecedents. A distant relative of exalted status could add lustre – even belonging to a family with a powerful or distinguished patron could be an asset. The picture becomes blurred, however, when birth and occupation did not readily coalesce. Thus, a gentleman's son was by definition a gentleman, but only certain occupations were compatible with gentility – living off an estate, an administrative or superior clerical position in government or an opulent household, a commission in the armed forces, qualification as a clergyman, a lawyer or a surgeon. However, the laws of primogeniture, coupled with limited funds, meant that many of the younger sons of the gentry were necessarily apprenticed to a trade. For the lower orders in the seventeenth century the premium normally required for an apprenticeship was a serious handicap. By the late eighteenth century, however, the demand for skilled workers was leading employers to reduce premiums or to waive them entirely. At the same time there were numerous charity apprenticeships whereby a bewildering range of organisations paid the premiums so that children of the poor could learn a trade.[6] It might well be that the majority of apprentices at that time were themselves the children of tradespeople, and that this was the case with the Botany Bay actors, but it is also possible that some had social pretensions above their occupation and others were of extremely humble origin.

In most cases the family backgrounds of the theatre-makers remain a mystery. A partial exception is John Sparrow. He was born in Shoreditch and, when his elder brother was apprenticed to a watchmaker in 1772, his father was described as a peruke maker. When John was apprenticed to the same watchmaker in 1779, his father had evidently retired from his trade, had moved to a slightly more refined part of the suburb and was described as 'gentleman'. This claim might have been an affectation, but was more likely to have been the reassertion of a status he had surrendered when he entered trade. The probability is that he was a younger son of the lesser gentry apprenticed in his youth for lack of better opportunity. What Sparrow seems to have had, before he compromised it, was a comfortable place in the middle ranks of society, with family connections into the gentry.

Robert Sidaway also came from Shoreditch, where several individuals of that name resided, one of them owning a three-quarter share in the Barking Dogs public house. His father's line of business is not known, but he was able to pay a small premium to a local tradesman so that his eldest son could train as a silver-buckle maker. Robert himself was likewise apprenticed as a watchcase maker, and another brother seems to have become a vintner in the adjacent Old Street parish. In other words, while the picture is less clear than in Sparrow's case, we have a reasonably solid family, though one lower down the middling ranks.

The evidence concerning Philip Parry's parentage is open to varying interpretations. At his trial it was reported that his father had held land in Wales, though this had been sold. The landholding could have been a substantial farm which Parry senior worked as a yeoman farmer, or a small estate run in such a way as to earn him the title of gentleman. When about to be captured, Parry had greeted his captor as a gentleman and appealed to his fellow feeling by proclaiming himself a gentleman also. The claim was clearly an attempt to avoid rough treatment. Parry had no knowledge of his pursuer's status and his own may have been as shadowy. On the other hand, if his father had been a gentleman landowner, Parry the grocer would have had a stronger claim to being on the margins of gentility than John Sparrow.

From what has been said so far it is clear that wealth could be a consideration in determining status, but its influence is sufficiently obvious not to require further comment. A person's moral standing could also be a factor, but, while excessive drunkenness, debauchery, violence or low practices might tarnish a reputation, they did not normally lead to loss of position. A gentleman's conduct might be 'ungentlemanly', but he remained a gentleman – though a criminal conviction would certainly have strained this convention to the extreme.

Apart from occupation, background, wealth and moral standing, one other complex of factors contributed to social positioning. This is the self-presentation of an individual.[7] Self-presentation was a matter of manners, deportment, dress and general care of the person, as well as style of speech, the use or absence of a dialect, the degree and type of education and the display of it. Finally, it was a matter of the degree of social ease in culturally-defining situations. When described in this way, self-presentation is the aspect of social classification that most immediately impinges on a person's engagement with theatre. Inasmuch as late eighteenth-century theatre concerned itself with the doings of gentlefolk and the nobility, a sophisticated mastery of it could be read as a sign of social superiority in a spectator or, to a degree, in a performer. Sensitivity to genteel behaviour and its codes, to the nuances of a literary text, and to the distinctions of dramatic genre were among the abilities that were required.

While the upper echelons of late eighteenth-century society may have regarded this cultural capital as their exclusive property, any such confidence was misplaced. Poorly-educated but alert body-servants to the upper orders such as valets, barbers and ladies' maids could acquire many of these social skills by osmosis, and because of their prestige they were sought after by many of those in the middling ranks of society. It was claimed that the box-lobby loungers who thronged the foyers of Drury Lane and Covent Garden, for all their air of gentility, were nothing more than shopkeepers and clerks. Similarly, the unjustifiably fashionable dress of a prisoner at the bar sometimes excited wry amusement.[8]

A significant tool in this building of a social image was formal education. In England and Scotland educational opportunities were more widely available than in much of Europe, but the type of education could vary from the basic skills of literacy, through a utilitarian training in writing, mathematics, bookkeeping and possibly geography, to a liberal education embracing French and the classics. Once literacy had been acquired, however, the possibility of self-education became available. A tradesman's son given a utilitarian education had access to the world of plays, novels, history and foreign works in translation, if his inclination drew him in that direction.

One type of concrete evidence which provides a clue to the cultural capital of the male players is their handwriting (often represented only by a signature) or the literary style of any surviving letters. The records, however, are unreliable: for example, a convict who signed with a cross on one document may be represented by a full signature on another, depending on what suited the convenience of the clerk. Even where there is a proven signature its full significance is debatable. The standard practice in British schools was to teach reading first, and then writing, so that the existence of a signature ought logically to indicate an ability to read and at least the beginnings of an ability to write. However, the need to be able to write one's name led many to learn that skill in isolation, while remaining otherwise illiterate. There is a further complication: some upwardly-mobile convicts learned to read or write in the colony, as Simeon Lord had done.[9] Literacy acquired in this way is no guide to the writer's social background in England. Equal caution is necessary in the evaluation of surviving correspondence. It could have been the work of a friend or professional letter writer, a common enough occurrence at this time.

In the case of signatures, the quality of the writing is nevertheless a useful indicator. Is the hand wavering or firm? Is the formation of the letters crude, plain or elegant? Using these criteria Sparrow, Evans, Jones, Chapman and Parry have signatures that vary from the strong to the elegant and indicate a significant level of literary competence. In the case of Evans, Chapman and Parnell letters or petitions have survived which seem to be written by the signatories and are fluent and reasonably grammatical. Parnell's could even be accused of being over-literary.

It may seem unnecessary to demonstrate that a group of actors can read, since it appears such a fundamental requirement for the profession. In fact, this was not necessarily the case in the late eighteenth century. There are suggestions that illiteracy was common in some of the more beggarly English strolling companies and there were even actors with a national reputation who were similarly afflicted. James Lackington said of the eminent low comic Ned Shuter that 'it was with difficulty he could read the parts he had to play, and could not write at all; he had attained to sign an order, but no more'.[10] Similarly there was a degree of illiteracy in most trades; even some apprentice printers were illiterate.[11] What these comments on handwriting and literary style suggest is that, as far as the evidence extends, the actors of Botany Bay were not a rag-tag and bob-tail collection of the ignorant. They were not at the bottom level of the acting fraternity, in this respect at least.

Another indicator of the social standing of the performers is the way they were viewed by others. Evidence of this can be garnered from reports of a convict's capture or trial, as was the case with Green. Comments made by others in the colony are sometimes available, the opinions of gentlefolk being particularly useful in matters of status.

Though the stigma of convictism could seriously affect a person's social relations, the military and civil officers of the colony often showed a marked sympathy for anyone of genteel demeanour who had fallen victim to the law. There is, for example, Governor Hunter's letter of 20 March 1800 concerning the newly-arrived Irish political prisoners:

> Many of those prisoners have been either bred up in genteel life, or to professions unaccustom'd to hard labor ... and really, my Lord, notwithstanding we cannot fail to have the most determin'd abhorrence of the crimes which sent many of them here, yet we can scarsely divest ourselves of the common feelings of humanity so far as to send a physician, a formerly respectable sheriff of a county, a Roman Catholic priest, or a Protestant clergyman and family to the grubbing hoe or timber carriage.[12]

The meteoric rise of George Barrington, Michael Massey Robinson, and John Stogdell owes much to such sentiments, as does John Macarthur's support for J.J. Grant.

Lieutenant-Governor Grose initially made much of the impeccably-connected attorney Laurence Davoren, before the latter's outrageous behaviour led to a severing of the connection. Similarly Governor King was remarkably considerate of the half-crazed gentleman John Grant, until his provocative behaviour proved too much for that severely-tried ruler.[13]

None of the theatre people seem to have excited this degree of empathy in the rulers of New South Wales, but there is evidence that they were regarded as a cut above the commonality. Collins speaks of the founders of the 1796 theatre as 'some of the more decent class of prisoners, male and female'. He refers to John Sparrow in another context as 'a young man of … good character' and to George Henry Hughes as 'a very decent young man'. What does Collins mean by phrases like these? Is he referring simply to the men's behaviour, as diligent and docile convicts, or to an air of moral rectitude still clinging to them? Or do some of his words imply recognition of a slightly superior social status, in terms of family background and education? The word 'decent', at least, may well carry any or all of these implications.

Not every foundation member of the theatre company attracted such respect. The responses to Robert Sidaway (who is not in Collins' list of founders) were anything but positive in his early days as a convict; Ralph Clark, Arthur Bowes Smyth and John White severally pictured him as a thoroughgoing villain. Some time later, however, Collins included him among those 'withdrawing from the society of vice and wretchedness, and forming such a character for themselves as to be thought deserving of emancipation'. As for William Chapman, Governor King, in 1803, described him as a 'bad character' and a 'miscreant'.[14] This might have been mere bad temper, but Chapman's antipodean career does have a faint touch of seediness to it.

Earlier I suggested that some of the actors' subsequent careers as dealers and entrepreneurs could indicate a background in the middling orders. There were, however, other paths to the entrepreneurial life. J.J. Grant was confident that the other gentlemen of New South Wales recognised his gentility and events seem to have reflected this, for he was set up in business by John Macarthur, ostensibly out of consideration for Grant's status.[15] No evidence of this kind survives for any of the actors, but one or more may have gained patronage in this way. On the other hand, officers sometimes set up convicts or ex-convicts in business as fronts for their own commercial activities, and in such cases entrepreneurial flair would have been the consideration rather than genteel connections. Similarly, the number of conditional or absolute pardons secured by people associated with the theatre company might indicate favoured treatment extended to those thought to be gentlefolk. Equally it might have been a form of patronage for valued servants of humbler origins, or even what it purported to be, a reward for good behaviour and useful service to the state, as Collins claimed it was in the case of Sidaway.

One other line of inquiry that leads to similarly ambiguous conclusions arises from the fact that several of the performers were employed in the colony, *inter alia*, as clerks and secretaries. Jones seems to have filled such a role for the Rev. Johnson, Evans for Simeon Lord and a number of them, notably Parry and Parnell, for the commissariat. James Hardy Vaux joined this world in 1804–05 and gives a lively picture of a lifestyle that had probably not changed much over the decade. He was withdrawn from the Hawkesbury establishment to become a clerk in the governor's office:

> By degrees … I began to degenerate. I increased my acquaintance among the Commissary's and some other clerks, most of whom lived an expensive and dissipated life. All I can say in my own favour, is that I continued to be regular in my attendance at the office, and was never found defective, or incapable of my duty; but no sooner was I at my own disposal than I eagerly sought my dissipated companions, and spent the rest of the day in drinking, and other irregularities, sometimes at public or disorderly houses, and frequently at my own, where I had often the expensive pleasure of entertaining a large party of my fellow-scribes at my own cost. … The expensive rate at which the Commissary's clerks constantly lived, had become matter of surprise to the Governor as well as the magistrates, and was the theme of much conjecture among the inhabitants of Sydney. Still, though it was palpable they had recourse to fraud, they managed matters so adroitly that no irregularity could be detected.[16]

Was this the world of Parry and Parnell, of Evans and Jones? The type of folly and affectation it suggests is eerily similar to that of the 'specials' of the 1820s and beyond. These were the well-educated convicts who, in those later years, were increasingly packed off to remote depots such as Wellington Valley and Port Macquarie and whose self-presentation irritated both their betters and their fellow convicts. Some of them were disgraced sons of the gentry and a few were even scions of noble houses, but most of them were nothing more than clerks of humble origin. As the convict Big Bill Delaforce wrote of those at Port Macquarie, they would

> talk about the fine wine that they drunk at those very places at home sush as the Angel of Islington … the most of these fellows wure counter jumpers and not one out of fifty ever drunk a glass … in any of those pubs for a counter jumper gets very low wages in London and they have to go a little bit respectubel or they would not get a billet in that part of the world.[17]

The same may well have been true of many of the young men who performed at the Sydney theatre.

So far the discussion has been limited largely to the male actors. The women are a much greater problem. Few of them had any recorded occupation before their conviction and they had limited opportunities for signing documents or achieving any sort of position in the colony that might offer a clue to their backgrounds or degree of refinement.

It is worth noting that Collins, in describing the performers in the first 1796 production, specifies that the women, as well as the men, were from 'the more decent class of prisoners', though the phrase is as problematic here as with the men. Undoubtedly some respectably brought up young women did fall victim to the law, the popular model being that of the innocent maiden seduced and abandoned by a callous lover.[18] There is no doubt that any young woman left without family protection was desperately vulnerable, and the press often made a point of the refinement, even the gentility, of some shoplifters active in the pilfering of expensive cloth and fashionable accessories.[19]

As with crime, so with transportation. In reporting the imminent departure of the *Lady Juliana*, *The Times*, 4 August 1789, noted that it had

> two hundred and sixty females on board; the youngest eleven, the oldest sixty eight. Five of them appear to have been blest with the favours of Providence, and a good education. — One of the latter class was about four years ago at Brighton, and, in the most gay and alluring style, drove her phæton.

The miss with her phæton was probably one of the high-flying prostitutes who were such a feature of the season at Brighton and Margate. But John Nicol, steward on the *Lady Juliana*, fills his account of the convicts on that vessel with pathetic pictures of young women such as Mary Rose, 'a timid modest girl' who was 'a wealthy farmer's daughter', and Sarah Dorset, the daughter of 'decent-looking people'.[20] If Collins is using the word 'decent' as Nicol uses it, the term has little in the way of class or educational implications and is primarily a matter of moral standing, something as available to a labourer as to a gentleman.

Collins names only one of his actresses, but the company does not seem to have changed greatly in its first six months, so that the other women in the July 1796 playbill, Mrs Radley and Mrs Greville, were probably part of the original group. Since they were both living in sin, their claims to decency would have been scorned in England, but in the looser atmosphere of New South Wales this was less of a consideration. If Mrs Davis is the sprightly Fanny Davis, she could act the demure young woman when called upon, even though she seems to have been a piece of Southwark low life who moved in criminal circles. There is, however, the possibility that in New South Wales she was mistress of an officer, something that would have given her an ersatz respectability in that part of the world. Needless to say, the convention that women took on the names of their *de facto* husbands did not extend to officers' concubines.

Whatever the position of the first actresses, the image had been tarnished by 1800. Sarah McCann had been one of the more successful prostitutes in London. Mrs Parry had allegedly been in the same profession at a humbler level. By 1799 both Mrs Radley and Sarah McCann were before the courts for turbulent and disruptive behaviour. The sardonic officer who reported the production of *Fortune's Fool* in *Bell's Weekly Messenger*, 6 July 1800, went on to note: 'The women, altogether, are more drunken and infamous than possibly can be described.' Years later, the *Sydney Gazette*, 25 June 1827, published an anecdote that conveys a similar impression, with the men no better than the women:

> Botany Bay Theatricals.— *Romeo and Juliet* was one of the earliest performances of the Thespian corps, in the land of 'Eminent

Personages'; and the Governor having announced his intention of honouring it with his presence, the police magistrate took the very necessary precaution of surrounding the house with a double row of constables, to secure the performance proceeding to a straightforward close, without that prolific garnishing of convulsive hiccupings, sentimental sighs, heigh-ho-, fainting fits, and other significant tokens of a *spiritual overpowering*, which had heretofore prolonged the performance to a very late hour. Things glided on most smoothly till the last scene, where the pensive *Romeo* was seen staggering towards the tomb of his dear *Juliet*, vociferating her name in a manner which too evidently showed *how* he was affected. To his repeated tender exclamations of *Juliet, Juliet*! not even a sigh was returned; the audience became impatient; but their murmurs of impatience were converted into one universal shudder of horror, on *Romeo* exclaiming, with a wild shriek, 'She is dead!' which was apparent to the whole auditory, on perceiving her heels sticking up out of the tomb. The fond *Romeo* passionately seized the protruding members, and dragged her feelingly forth from her place of rest, making, however, such a display of her charms in the chivalrous attempt, as forced the lady visitors to a hasty flight from this 'too theatric' sight. All eyes were now rivetted to this tragic spectacle of youth and beauty, and 'dead, dead!' burst in one unbroken exclamation from every part of the house. 'Yes', sighed the sentimental *Romeo* – '*dead drunk*'.

Taken in conjunction with the wild behaviour of Mrs Radley and Sarah McCann, this story has a degree of plausibility. Modern historians, however, have noted a tendency in the early colony to stereotype the women convicts as more depraved, drunken and degenerate than the men, and have questioned the accuracy of the picture, finding social, sexual and deeply psychological reasons for this depiction of them.[21] The *Romeo and Juliet* story calls for particular care. Drunkenness in performers on stage was a common motif and the story may be nothing more than a fabrication built around a popular theme (see Appendix B, Note 6). In addition, the narrator is sufficiently vague about the dating of the event to raise the possibility that its subject is not Sidaway's theatre but the tiny gaff that existed on the edge of the town in Governor Macquarie's period and was visited by him. Maclehose, who first mentions this gaff, appears completely unaware that a full-fledged theatre had preceded it.[22] Others may have been as ignorant, including the writer in the *Sydney Gazette*. The most interesting thing about the account may well be the incidental picture it gives of the formalities of a vice-regal visit to the theatre in early Sydney.

On the matter of the actresses' level of education as measured by literacy, the limited evidence is not encouraging. The most striking example is provided by the entry in St Phillip's register for the marriage of Mr and Mrs Parry. Philip Parry signs with a firm, confident, even elegant hand. Frances Fox, Mrs Parry, has a signature that is barely literate: the letters waver, are crabbed and ill-formed. Mary Barnes has a signature that is little better, and if Mrs Davis was Fanny Davis, she was apparently unable to sign her name. Sarah McCann's signature has not survived, but a letter her own counsel admitted was in her hand was a significant exhibit at her trial. Its style is fluent, if not elegant. While her career had its ups and downs – as brothel-keeper, kept women, mistress of a royal duke and casual prostitute – of all the actresses she was probably the one who had whatever polish came from mingling in the highest society, or at least the male part of it. The women of the time normally had less access to an education than the males, so that a faltering signature may be less significant than in the case of a man. It remains possible, if unlikely, that behind one of the names on a playbill lurks the fallen daughter of a country vicar or some other potent example of gentility in distress.

One final clue to the cultural competence of the actors, and hence perhaps to their social background, is the response by sophisticated observers to their performances. Enough has been said in Chapter 1 to indicate the disdain with which the cultivated looked down upon the theatrical efforts of their social inferiors. At best their attitude was one of condescension; more usually it was one of contempt. The *Romeo and Juliet* story, if it is genuine, and applies to Sidaway's company, would seem to place the group in this lowly category, but such stories were similarly told of leading theatres and illustrious performers.

There is little evidence relating to the standard of performance in Sidaway's theatre, but what there is confirms that the players were not a crowd of low-bred and ignorant shop-boys and apprentices. In 1796, David Collins' comment that 'their performance was far above contempt' was, for him, high praise. In 1800 Dr Price described the performers as 'not without merit'. The performances that Eastwick saw in 1803–04 were 'all very tolerably acted. Amongst other plays I remember witnessing Farquhar's comedy of *The Recruiting Officer*, and the entertainment of *The Virgin Unmask'd*, both affording very excellent amusement.'[23] This may seem almost as bland as Price, but it compares favourably with Eastwick's scathing dismissal of the amateurs of Calcutta, a company in a major colonial centre whose actors were drawn from the cultivated and genteel. It also compares favourably with the scorn heaped on the professional Sydney theatre in the early 1840s. Perhaps the commentators, expecting little of Sidaway's players, treated them gently, but it is at least possible that they were more competent than some of their professional successors.[24]

These, then, were the performers. Most of the men in the original company seem to have had a modicum of formal education, presumably of the type appropriate to clerks and tradesmen, though a few may have had more or have used what they were given as a basis for self-education of a liberal kind. The actresses appear to have come from a lower social stratum, with more limited educational opportunities, though some of them may have acquired an element of polish from contact with their betters.

The status of the male members of the 1799–1800 company is more problematic. Those who can be firmly identified, such as Parry, Parnell and Beckwith Smith, for the most part come from the same world as their predecessors, with Parry probably having some of the characteristics of a gentleman. Many members of the company at this later stage, however, are unidentifiable, and some of these could have had humbler backgrounds, particularly if they were drawn from the New South Wales Corps. While the army boasted a significant scattering of ex-tradesmen, and even the occasional fallen gentleman, a high proportion of the ranks were ex-labourers, or untrained men who had joined the forces in their adolescence. An influx from this source would have altered the social composition of the company and lowered its level of cultural sophistication. The question remains, of course, which kind of soldier chose to join the company and, even where the background was humble, did that necessarily mean uncouthness? Harry Parsons was a soldier from his youth and could well have been the son of a soldier, but he emerges from the records as an ardent, talented musician and a responsible administrator of charitable organisations.

II

If this was the composition of the company, what then was the make-up of its audience? David Collins' comment that the one-shilling gallery was by far the largest part of the house leaves little doubt as to whom the company assumed would comprise the bulk of its public. His comment dates from the opening of the theatre but D.D. Mann, who had arrived in the colony in 1799 and had seen out the theatre's career, could still picture a major part of its audience in these terms when writing in 1811: 'It was also a common practice to give provisions to obtain entrance, if money was scarce; and thus, by the frequent privations of their regular food, many of the convicts were unable to pursue their labour with proper energy and activity.'[25] Mann might focus on the convict component of the audience, but by 1800 Sydney's lower orders included many ex-convicts who were surviving as labourers and petty-tradesmen, as well as sailors and common soldiers. In an adult population of about 1,600 in early 1796 the Sydney garrison included some 270 privates, corporals, and drummers,[26] and, while their numbers occasionally rose towards 300, they became a diminishing proportion of the township's population. Nevertheless, they were a significant factor in the theatre's economy and wellbeing. Crowder's Norfolk Island theatre had drawn part of its audience from the soldiery and it is clear from the benefit for the widow of Private Eades that the Sydney theatre was also concerned to cultivate this group. By 1799, as we shall see, a few soldiers were active in the company or in the running of the theatre.

Since only one in four or five of the adult population of Sydney was female, for most of the theatre's life the audience would have been made up largely of single young men. Collins, however, specifically refers to family parties attending in the gallery, a comment which gives a pleasingly domestic touch to the whole affair.

So far the analysis has centred on the gallery, but what of the boxes, the most lucrative part of the house? As was pointed out above, the theatre began without side boxes. This may have been due to lack of space but may have reflected a belief that boxes of any kind would not be much in demand. However, the 1798 rebuilding saw side boxes installed: the experience of running a theatre for two years had demonstrated that there was a market. But who constituted it?

David Collins was there on opening night, and it is difficult to imagine him seated anywhere but in a front box. He may have been present in the line of duty, as the colony's chief law officer and the man ultimately responsible for the theatre's good governance, but the occasion was something of a gala event and many other officers, including the governor, might have attended, out of obligation or interest. Similarly, the Eades' benefit would have drawn officers of the New South Wales Corps. But if Sidaway's company pursued a policy of performing on royal birthdays, vice-regal attendance on such occasions did not harden into a custom. On most royal holidays the entertainment for the elite at Government House continued well into the evening, much too late to be followed by a visit to the theatre.

Respectable visitors to the town, such as Captain Eastwick and Dr Price, certainly visited the playhouse. But the latter, writing of the theatre between mid-January and April 1800, commented: 'I am sorry to say they [the theatre company] do not meet with encouragement either from the civil or military gentlemen or their ladies, many of whom prefer promoting scandal and debauchery, than a chearful & innocent recreation.'[27] It only takes a little reflection to see why the officers and gentlemen might have been less than comfortable in this theatre and so have avoided it. The building was diminutive and the members of the small ruling group might well have found the enforced intimacy with their charges unappealing. Since the boxes were not normally sold as units, but place by place, a visitor to the theatre could find himself or herself seated beside the most disagreeable of people – Cornelius Hennings, for example. Such intimacy could be tolerated in England, but in a penal colony things were otherwise.

However, the potential embarrassment was even greater than that. As was described in Chapter 1, British theatres were traditionally boisterous places and one of their most striking features was the way in which the higher orders, in pit and boxes, were obliged to tolerate the unruliness of the galleryites, as often as not becoming their target. What prevailed was a condition of carnival misrule, with the lower orders allowed their moment of self-assertion, of aggression towards their betters. This traditional right of the lowly in England was hardly something for an officer to expose himself to in New South Wales, where a convict's failure to doff his hat to a passing officer could result in a flogging.

There were other dimensions to the situation as well. English fashionable theatregoing, particularly for the box audience in the provinces, was very much a social and family affair. In Sydney, however, as Dr Price remarked, 'their society is very small and even that divided by party quarrels, which are formented by an incendary sett'. In the light of these bitter feuds in the Botany Bay elite, many of its members may have preferred not to meet an indiscriminate group of their social equals. Governor King, for example, seems to have been sent to Coventry by most of the military officers for much of his incumbency. Beyond that, few members of the ruling elite had their wives with them in the colony and (notoriously) the rest made up for this absence by taking convict women as mistresses. Here was an impossible social situation. Respectable married women simply could not be taken where they might have to mix socially with women living in sin, particularly since those women were also convicts or ex-convicts, and most of them decidedly low-class. To be sure, many of the officers seem to have had the decency not to make too much of a display of their *de facto*s. John Grant's salacious interest in meeting Esther Abrahams, the convict mistress of Major Johnston, was never satisfied. Even when he visited their house she was apparently kept out of sight.[28] However, one could never be sure when someone would break this unwritten code. There was scandal in Sydney when young Lieutenant Laycock appeared one Sunday on the parade ground dressed in full regimentals and with his father's doxy on his arm.[29] The same problems existed in Hobart, from where George Prideaux Harris wrote to his mother in 1805: 'There is no society – I cannot visit *with* my wife most of my brother Officers because they have female Companions – we seldom therefore visit except to Captn. Sladdens (Marines) who is married – or in her family, who are the only females she can associate with.' In Hobart the situation was exacerbated by the fact that David Collins, as lieutenant-governor of the new settlement, was publicly living with his convict mistress in Government House. The arrival of a new commandant, with his wife, after Collins' death made it 'very pleasant to the Married Officers of the Colony, whose Ladies in Govr. Collins's time never went to the entertainments at Government House'.[30] Governor Bligh had the same problem with Collins, giving as 'a very principal private reason' for not staying in Collins' house in Hobart his habit of 'walking with his kept woman (a poor low creature) arm-in-arm about Town, and bringing her almost daily to his Office adjoining the House, directly in view of my dear Mary [Bligh's daughter, Mrs Putland]'.[31] Collins seems to have been equally indiscreet in Sydney, though the comment there comes from an extremely hostile witness.[32] As these examples indicate, it was not only the theatre that suffered; all social life was drastically restricted. The *Observer*, 9 February 1800, summed it up as follows: 'Society here is very contracted; every man looks upon his neighbour with a jealous eye. In short, it is here divested of one of its greatest blessings and ornaments, the fair sex.' It was a complaint that was to remain current for decades.

If the elite of Sydney did not patronise the boxes, then who did? The most likely answer is a group which was described earlier, the convict and ex-convict entrepreneurs and the minor government officials who were themselves convicts or ex-convicts and usually managed some farming or trading on the side. Similar groups were probably dominant in the pit. A substantial amount of information has survived about audience composition in the Norfolk Island theatres and, as will be shown in Chapter 5, it was precisely these social groups that were found in the better seats there. What is true of Norfolk Island's audiences is almost certainly true of those in Sydney. The high-spending government clerks described by Vaux would also have graced the better seats in the Sydney theatre and to an extent not paralleled on Norfolk Island, where such functionaries were few in number.

There is only one brief glimpse of this convict elite at the Sydney theatre. The death of the ex-convict John Stogdell was followed by a protracted battle in the civil courts over the disbursement of his estate, and among the surviving papers is the evidence of D.D. Mann relating to the case. In the course of this he describes a conversation with Stogdell which he had in the theatre.[33] The pair might have been there for reasons other than attending a performance, but that seems unlikely. Stogdell and Mann were special cases, ex-convicts with cultivated tastes and, probably, genteel connections. Both revealed aspirations to live out the image of gentility in the colony. Mann's origins are unknown, but he had held responsible positions in the household staff of the Duke of Northumberland and then of Lord Somerset, who prosecuted him for fraud when he was twenty-two. In the colony he worked his way up through the bureaucracy, acquired land, and in 1804 was given the lease on the town block that was to cause him so much trouble under Governor Bligh. In Brian Fletcher's words:

> On this land he constructed a stable, carriage-house and a 'commodious' dwelling place costing over £400, where he resided with his wife … His employment in aristocratic houses had given him a taste for gracious living and in 1803 he sought a male cook and a waiter, stipulating that applicants 'must be very active and perfectly acquainted with waiting at table'. A later advertisement for a 'handsome sabre and sword belt' casts additional light on his pretensions.[34]

John Stogdell was cast in a similar mould. Again his origins are unclear, but, when he was taken before the Bow Street magistrate, a crowd had assembled, a not-uncommon event if the prisoner was well connected. The *Morning Post*, 17 September 1784, reporting on the committal, identified him as a barber, but in the Old Bailey Session Papers he is described as a person of genteel appearance who had been a valet and servant in the houses of influential people. He had a string of character witnesses who 'were very respectable, and were people of great consequence'.[35] Once in the colony he became an agent for the commissary, John Palmer, accumulating farms at a rapid rate and living in a conspicuously elegant style, with prints upon his walls, musical instruments, silverware and a small library. The witnesses at his marriage in Sydney were the commissary, Palmer, and the judge-advocate, David Collins, two of the colony's most senior officials. It was an unprecedented honour for a convict. The height of his ostentation was a curricle, in which he drove about the town, eliciting comment from the visiting Dr Price, and he is probably the anonymous convict described in 1806 by Henry Waterhouse:

> I knew a man myself who I have seen as a Convict at work at the hoe taken tied up & punishd by the common hang man for improper behavior who, when I left that place in 1800 have hardly went out but on horse back, & always a servant mounted (in livery) following, with his great Coat buckled round him – if wishing to go from Sydney to the Hawkesbury in one day & back again, had relays of Horses.[36]

On 2 March 1801 he was drowned in floodwaters when returning to his estates on the Hawkesbury. It was one of the few fatalities to be recorded in the 1806 almanac's chronicle of significant colonial events.

There were other convicts and emancipists in the town who would never have thrown off the rudeness of their origins; but that did not prevent them imitating the manners and style of their superiors. As early as 1793 the Rev. Johnson was inveighing against a convict couple who had built up their income through running a disreputable ale-house:

> This ... Family, having then turned Merchants, soon began to goe up in the world – Mr Waring appearing in his sattin Breeches, silk stockings, &c — his Lady dressing in silks, &c as fine as any Lady in the Colony – They are, as I am informed, now carrying on a capital Trade ... [but] I believe, that there are few of a more notorious, worthless, swindling Character than he, as many officers here will readily assert.

Waterhouse describes others in more restrained but similar terms.[37] Folks such as these could have found lolling in a box at the theatre irresistible. It is precisely such characters who were to dominate the boxes in the Norfolk Island theatre in 1805–06.

There are two other groups whose presence or otherwise in the theatre is worth speculating upon. By the time of the theatre's opening three convict ships had arrived from Ireland, and by 1800 another four had berthed. While some of these convicts were the petty criminals of Dublin, Cork, Belfast and Limerick, an increasing number were agrarian rioters and, after 1798, participants in the great rebellion of that year. The felons of Ireland's cities would have been as familiar with theatre as their London counterparts, but the riots and rebellion washed up on Australia's shores two notable groups. On the one hand there was a small but significant collection of cultivated gentlemen, leaders of the uprisings; on the other there was a much larger group of illiterate peasants, many from the more isolated counties, where theatre would have been a rarity.

Anne-Maree Whitaker has argued that the first group was large enough to outnumber the ruling elite in New South Wales. She pictures them as mingling with that elite; but it is also likely that they formed an independent and parallel society which embraced earlier radical arrivals such as Palmer, Margarot, Boston and Ellis, and maverick troublemakers such as Sir Henry Brown Hayes, who arrived in 1802.[38] This parallel society might well have been more ready than the ruling group to frequent the playhouse. Certainly the Irish rebel attorney, Matthew Sutton, after his secondary transportation to Norfolk Island, was to be found seated in the pit at that outpost's theatre, among the farmers and the ex-convict supervisors and constables.

A factor that needs to be taken into account in relation to the Irish peasant prisoners is that their native language would have been Irish. Patrick O'Farrell has explored this issue, but for lack of evidence has not been able to guess at the number of non-English speakers arriving from Ireland.[39] However, there is a rough estimate available for one vessel in the relevant period. This is the *Friendship*, which berthed on 16 May 1800 with 159 male convicts. The wife of its captain, Hugh Reid, wrote a long account of the voyage, in the course of which she remarked that 'there were about 30 of these poor men who could not speak English'. Many others were no doubt bilingual, with Irish the preferred tongue. As Charles Mathews noted, even Cork in the late eighteenth century was largely an Irish-speaking community.[40]

By May 1803 Governor King was estimating that over a quarter of the colony's convicts were Irish Catholics. This was probably an exaggeration reflecting his disquiet: a more recent estimate proposes that by 1803 some 1,600 male convicts had arrived from Ireland with a much-disputed proportion of them agrarian rioters or outright rebels.[41] Given the non-theatrical background of many of the humbler rebels, their preference for the Irish language and the dispatch of numbers of them to Toongabbie or Castle Hill, as a security measure, their influence upon Sydney theatre would have been limited. Nevertheless, one is left to wonder if the presence of plays such as *The Irish Widow* and O'Keeffe's *The Poor Soldier* in the company's repertoire owes anything to a desire to woo this group. *The Poor Soldier* had a broad appeal and was enormously popular at this time across Britain, Ireland and the United States, not least among soldiers, but many of its songs were based upon tunes by Carolan, the blind bard of Erin. A story is told of the convict priest, Father Harold, singing 'The Exile of Erin' at a dinner the evening after his arrival in Sydney Cove, and of a crowd of Irish prisoners gathering on the shore to listen.[42] Would the strains of Carolan have had a similar effect and have lured them to the theatre? Only two of the actors, it should be noted, were verifiably Irish, the Dublin Protestant Daniel Parnell and Sarah McCann, a Dublin Catholic who had moved to London and its *demi-monde*.

The other group whose contact with the theatre is worth speculation are the Aborigines. It is recorded that when Arthur Phillip's protégé, Bennelong, was sent to England he was taken to the theatre on several occasions and seated in the boxes. Years later Moowattye, brought to England by George Caley, was also taken to the theatre.[43] This was standard procedure when introducing 'savages' to the splendours of European civilisation, and had been so for well over a century. Was Bennelong, who returned with Governor Hunter in September 1795, also given the occasional ticket to Sydney's tiny convict theatre in later years? And what about the young Bungaree, 'King of the Broken Bay Tribe', so highly esteemed by Matthew Flinders and taken by him on his exploration of the south Queensland coast in July–August 1799, and on his circumnavigation of Australia, July 1802–June 1803?[44] At a humbler level there was John Bath, whose story is told in the *Sydney Gazette* of 2 December 1804, and who died at about the age of sixteen in November 1804. Rescued as an infant by a convict, James Bath, after his parents had been killed in an affray at Toongabbie,

> his protector, at leaving the colony, bequeathed his little charge to D.
> Greville, who likewise going away, left him to the care of J. Sparrow;
> but the boy expressing an inclination to reside with William Miller, at
> the Hospital Wharf, continued ever since in his service.

Since David Greville's *de facto* wife was an actress with the company in its early years, when John Sparrow was actor-manager, and since William Miller and his *de facto* bulk large in Mrs Parry's benefit of 1799, John Bath's attendance at the theatre would not have been at all surprising, particularly since he had been thoroughly deracinated:

> His origin he remembered with abhorrence, and never suffered to escape any occasion whereby he might testify a rooted and unconquerable aversion to all of his own colour ... he took much pride in cleanliness of dress, spoke none but our language.

Needless to say, he died in the odour of sanctity, giving 'undoubted proofs of Christian piety, fervently repeating the Lord's Prayer shortly before his dissolution'.

A playhouse with an exceptionally large gallery space, and with many of its boxes filled with poorly-educated *arrivistes*, might suggest that we are dealing with 'popular theatre' and that Sydney was further advanced towards this model than most of the playhouses of England. If that was the case, it is not revealed in the repertoire. The allegedly popular taste for fairground entertainment and irregular forms of theatre is little in evidence in the details of programming that have survived. They show no more bias towards the illegitimate, the irregular, the vulgar theatre forms than does any legitimate theatre in England, with mainpieces such as *The Revenge* and *She Stoops to Conquer* and standard afterpieces such as *Bon Ton* and *Miss in her Teens*. The nearest one comes to the 'popular' is probably the dance performed as an interlude by Mrs Parry and Daniel Parnell on 8 April 1800, 'The Drunken Swiss'. Drunken dances were popular in England,[45] and the piece performed by Parry and Parnell, for all the claims that it was 'a new Dance', was probably a version of one created by William West, for male and female performer, under the same name. West's 'The Drunken Swiss' was one of his mainstays throughout a long career. What is significant, however, is that his London appearances were shared indiscriminately between the legitimate theatres, Covent Garden and Drury Lane, and the illegitimate, the Royal Circus and Astley's Amphitheatre.[46] 'The Drunken Swiss' was at home in all cultural circles.

This general adherence of the Sydney theatre to the 'legitimate' model may mean that the defective taste attributed to the lower orders in Britain was nothing more than class prejudice. Alternatively, it may mean that this was the type of theatre that the performers themselves most valued, obliging the audiences to go along with them. Beyond that, many of the more irregular forms of entertainment required years of training in juggling, acrobatics or animal taming, for example. There was probably nobody in Botany Bay who could emulate performers such as Robinson, the 'Antipodean Whirligig' (to give an appropriate example) with his 'wonderful egg hornpipe, with 20 eggs on the floor, and he blindfolded, touching none' or his ability to 'whirl round on his head with crackers and other fireworks attached to his heels'.[47]

III

So far this chapter has dealt with those who had the most direct contact with the Sydney theatre, the people who built it, played in it and attended performances there. But how were its operations perceived by those less intimately involved? In particular, how did the local New South Wales representatives of imperial authority view it, and what impression of it was conveyed to the British public?

The authorities in Sydney nowhere made explicit their reasons for allowing Sidaway's venture (or its predecessor at Brickfields) to proceed. Lieutenant-Governor Philip Gidley King was more forthcoming about his reasons for permitting a theatre on Norfolk Island in 1793–94, although the statements he made on the subject were written after the theatre's closure and in a mood of self-justification. In some of these statements the decision to approve the theatre is presented as pure benevolence. He had agreed 'from the sole View of affording a little Amusement to every Description of People on the Island'. Others provide a slightly different perspective. He had sanctioned the theatre 'in hopes of it being a means of making every Person contented in their situation & pleased with each other'.[48] There is a distinct touch of political calculation here along with the benevolence. This is theatre as a social opiate, designed to serve the interests of the rulers by soothing away the discontent of the ruled. A similar calculation was probably in the minds of the authorities at Port Jackson when they permitted Sidaway's theatre to open. Captain Eastwick, for one, made a connection between that theatre and social harmony when he described its operations in 1803–04: 'The colonists, in general, appeared to be well reconciled to their situation, and a proof that their minds were not very ill at ease is afforded by the fact that they had a theatre … under the patronage of Governor King.'[49] Richard Waterhouse has suggested the theatres were permitted in order to draw convicts away from the more ruinous vices of drinking and gambling. The suggestion is attractive, but I am not aware of any statement to confirm this, though in the late 1820s the argument was used by advocates for a licensed theatre.[50]

The establishment of a theatre may have brought with it certain political advantages, but it also carried grave risks. The authorities in Britain were extremely nervous about any large-scale assembly because of the long tradition of popular disturbance, and playhouses were a particular source of worry because of the element of audience misrule which was a feature of English theatrical culture. In the late eighteenth century these fears intensified because of the Gordon Riots and, even more importantly, the French Revolution and the burgeoning of English Jacobinism. To the normal riots over unannounced program changes, imagined slights by actors or authors and attempts to alter prices, were added large-scale disturbances in a few Midlands theatres over the singing of 'God Save the King' and the shouting of inflammatory political sentiments from the anonymity of the auditorium.[51]

If the authorities in England had been worried about mob control, those in New South Wales would have felt an even graver concern. In their minds those they were guarding must have seemed like a distillation of that section of English society most prone to disorder. Similarly, the threat of rebellion, as opposed to mere riot, must have seemed much greater than in Britain. From the First Fleet onwards there were reports, some of them true, of convicts planning to seize their ships and sail them to freedom. If mutiny at sea, why not insurrection on land? Prior to 1804 this threat was seen as so slight that the only significant fortifications were directed seawards, against French invasion. Nonetheless, the signs of a simmering hostility were there, usually in the form of efforts to subvert the work regulations, but occasionally in symbolic acts such as the chopping down of the gallows the night before John Crow was hanged.[52] In 1794 the government's fears were refuelled when Botany Bay began its career as a dumping ground for political radicals, in the persons of the Scottish Martyrs – Muir, Palmer, Margarot, Gerrald and Skirving. Within a few years there followed the even more alarming arrival, *en masse*, of Irish rebels, breeding something close to paranoia in the authorities in the distant colony.[53] A spate of arson attacks destroyed Johnson's church and the gaols in Sydney and Parramatta,[54] and by 1800 real or imagined plans for Irish insurrections were being unearthed, precursors to the 1804 outbreak that led to the battle of Vinegar Hill and the consequent plans to build Fort Phillip.[55] Even though most of these events were in the future at the time Sidaway's theatre was built, it is easy to see why Collins, in his account of the event, puts so much emphasis on the authorities' threats of retaliation, if the theatre became a source of trouble.

In the light of this disquiet it would not be surprising to find the authorities had taken more practical measures than the issuing of threats. It was common for British theatres to have constables or other peace officers present in the house during performances, on an occasional or a regular basis. The authorities in Sydney may well have insisted on such a presence in their theatre, just as on Norfolk Island, by accident or design, the manager of the theatre company was also appointed constable.

What is notable about the warning issued by Collins and the governor, however, is that the threat of closure and dispersal of the actors is related to the behaviour of the company, not the audience. There is no indication of what behaviour the authorities had in mind, but an obvious issue would have been the choice of plays, and the question of censorship of those that were approved. In 1832 the British playwright Thomas Morton described the way audiences forced 'passages never meant by the author into political meanings … we all know that a theatre is a place of peculiar excitement'. The *Dramatic Censor*, an English journal which functioned from 1800 to 1801, bears out Morton's remarks for that earlier period with disapproving comments on political allusions in plays and prologues, while Frederick Reynolds provides an example from a production of 1795.[56] These comments are not confined to new works. They are also directed at established plays, where a speech takes on new meanings in a changed political climate. The possibility of actors creating a political meaning for innocuous lines through their performance is not mentioned but undoubtedly existed.

There is no question that the colonial government was in the business of censorship. Both governors King and Bligh exercised rigorous control over the contents of the local newspaper, the *Sydney Gazette*. In later years the editor, George Howe, provided a vivid picture of King personally checking the proofs of each issue and ruthlessly blue-pencilling entire items, leaving the rueful editor to fill the gaps at short notice. Similarly, there is a picture of Bligh poring over the text at a tense political moment. While local news items were the major concern, anything could fall victim to the system. John Grant was infuriated when King deleted a poem he had written.[57] Since Grant leant towards the mildly radical politics of the English Whigs and was totally incautious in his enthusiasms, King's act may have been based on political judgment rather than on the aesthetic principles he mockingly professed. Poetry could be dangerous.

In such an atmosphere it is difficult not to imagine the company manager being required to submit his plays for consideration to the governor, his secretary, or the judge-advocate. Pressure of business probably meant that for a work firmly established in the repertory, the title alone sufficed. But locally-written pieces, such as special prologues or Robinson's address, must have been subject to scrutiny. Considering Robinson's later career as a writer of fulsome odes to the establishment and as poet laureate to Governor Macquarie, he, at least, is unlikely to have caused too many difficulties.

At this early period there is no evidence of plays being forbidden, which is not to say that that never happened, but the little evidence available suggests a relatively relaxed attitude. While the journalistic wits of London made free play with fantasies of *The Beggar's Opera* being performed at Botany Bay, that is one play unlikely to have been offered, since it was widely seen in Britain as politically subversive and a dangerous celebration of the life of crime.[58] However, it is almost as surprising to find that nobody prevented the company from presenting Shakespeare's *Henry IV*, either *Part 1* or a conflation of both parts, in which Falstaff and the criminal sub-culture of London figure prominently. It is notable that when Henry Carter, in Leicester, wrote his fanciful comic prologue for the opening of Sidaway's playhouse, it is *Henry the Fourth* that is the subject of his allusions as much as *The Beggar's Opera*. There is, however, a remote chance that the performance of *Henry the Fourth* was an initiative of the military rather than the company, and hence not as subject to control (see Appendix A: J. Davison).

But if the company was at relative liberty to present the standard repertoire, individual plays may still have been subject to judicious pruning. The 1800 production of *The Recruiting Officer* is a perfect example. The playbill for this performance has survived, and a glance at the list of *dramatis personae* reveals a striking omission: the character of Captain Brazen has been excised. Such an excision is unprecedented, for Brazen is the leading comic figure in the work, the role chosen by Laurence Olivier, for example, in William Gaskill's famous 1963 production. The problem, obviously, was that Brazen, a loud-mouthed fop and an idiot, is also a military officer. The New South Wales Corps, and probably the governor, were unlikely to allow convicts to ridicule the officer class in this way.

Such censorship could have been the product of direct intervention by the authorities or self-censorship by the performers. A third possibility is the infiltration of government trusties within the company to influence its decisions. Joseph Vasconcellis had somehow emerged as company manager by April 1799. His claim to the office remains obscure, since he was never listed as an actor and never emerges as a Sydney entrepreneur. What may have secured him the post, probably at the instigation of his superiors, was the fact that he was a member of the New South

Wales Corps – a humble private who on two occasions rose to the status of corporal, only to fall back again into the ranks. Such a man would have been highly sensitive to the interests of his officers. Vasconcellis, moreover, had reinforcements. A constant in the four playbills from 1799 and 1800 is H. Parsons. This was the music-loving Henry (Harry) Parsons, one of the more attractive members of the Corps, who ended his career as a sergeant. The Master Haddocks who played a minor female role in *The Recruiting Officer* was either a drummer of that name or a soldier's child. Beyond these men identification becomes difficult. There were convicts, emancipists and soldiers named J. Cox, J. Davison, W. Knight and J. Payne, but while Payne the actor was probably the soldier, evidence in the other three cases is inconclusive. It may help that Privates Payne, Davison and Knight had arrived as convicts and the first two had only one recorded performance apiece, but unfortunately the two male leads, W. Smith and J. White, raise exactly the same problems. They are beyond identification. If they were soldiers, then the military hold on the company would have been exceptionally strong. However, it must be remembered that most of the performers who can be firmly identified in the period 1799–1800 were not soldiers, nor was the one known shareholder in the theatre building.

The plight of the unlovable John William Lancashire illustrates the influence of the military on the company. Lancashire, a convict on the *Barwell*, had been taken up by the ship's master, Captain Cameron, and employed as a clerk on the voyage. In return, he had given evidence before a Sydney court in the *Barwell* investigation which had offended the officers of the New South Wales Corps. He had followed this with evidence in favour of Isaac Nicholls in the latter's spectacular trial, in the face of the apparent determination of officers of the Corps to have Nicholls convicted. In Lancashire's own words,

> two Gentlemen … was preposess[d] against me – One of which positively
> declard Just after I came forward upon Capt[n]. Camerons Business that
> if he could he woud hang me before any Man upon the Ground … The
> second is inveterate against me – because I came forward & spoke the
> truth upon the trial of Isaac Nichols, thro which I was Obliged to leave
> the Theatre, And on Acc[t] of Attempt[g] to Obtain my Money for Work -
> painting Scenery &c – to the Comp[y] – I was called a Damnd Rascal –
> and many other Names of which I was not deserving.[59]

The two 'gentlemen' were probably George Bond, an ensign forced to leave the regiment over the troubles on the *Barwell*, and Captain John Macarthur, who had endeavoured to persuade Lancashire to change his evidence in the Nicholls' case in a way utterly damning to the defendant. Since Lancashire himself emphasised the military involvement in the theatre, referring to it as 'the Comp[y] of Comedians (Soldiers)' and claimed that his troubles arose, *inter alia*, because he was 'intermix[d] with Soldiers',[60] the implication is that he was persecuted by the company (most obviously Vasconcellis) for offending the officers.

The Nicholls' case had a further significance. It was one of the many foci for conflict between the governor and the officers of the Corps, the governor endeavouring to save Nicholls' life in the face of what he saw as the officers' determination to have him executed as a receiver of stolen goods. It was a determination driven by the factional politics of the place, Nicholls being a useful supporter of the governor, though an ex-convict. This factionalism within the ruling group could hardly have been comfortable for the theatre company members, since it could have put them in the position of having to satisfy two conflicting sources of authority at once. Indeed, there may even have been a third, since Vasconcellis and the other soldiery on occasion could have run agendas of their own. In mentioning the benefit for the widow of Private Eades, Collins describes it as an act of 'politic generosity' on the part of the players.[61] In this instance, with whom was the company trying to ingratiate itself – the common soldiers, the regiment as a unit (and hence its officers), or the regiment as an arm of government, and hence the governor himself?

IV

News of the 1789 performance of *The Recruiting Officer* first reached Britain in the form of Watkin Tench's account published in 1793. As an occasional event, apparently designed as an entertainment for the officers, it excited no comment in the newspapers of the time. Things were otherwise with Sidaway's theatre, news of which broke in the form of the playbill for Green's benefit, which first appeared in a newspaper and was reproduced in a string of others, up and down the country, as well as in journals of the time. The idea of a convict theatre at Botany Bay, imitating such niceties of the English model as benefits and boxes, was found to be irresistibly funny. The result was a string of jokes that peppered the papers for weeks, and briefly replaced wife-selling at Smithfields market as a source of amusement. The *Oracle* was the newspaper most swept away by the risibility of it all, probably because its editor was James Boaden, an afficionado of the theatre and later biographer of Kemble, Jordan and Siddons; but the jokes and puns were widespread, and were often recycled from paper to paper:

> The *Theatrical* accounts from *Botany Bay* are so flattering, that many *Heroes* of the *Road*, and *Heroines* of the *Night* are using their best endeavours to join that *Theatrical Corps* at the expense of Government.
>
> In Botany Bay the *fashionable circles* complain of the want of a good company of *dancers* to complete their amusements. If, however, they have no *light footed*, they have plenty of *light-fingered* gentry.
>
> It is said that the *Citizens of Botany Bay*, begin to *turn their hands* towards theatrical amusements. *The Beggar's Opera*, we hear, is the favourite Play, and *The Lock and Key* the most popular Farce.
>
> Of the Botany Bay Theatre, it was said whimsically, 'the *cast* consists of tried ACTORS, and the AUDIENCE must have been all transported'.
>
> Barrington and Major Semple have NO concern in the theatrical scheme

at *Botany Bay*. They, however, occasionally volunteer their service and *take the cash at the door*.[62]

These are only a few examples of the 20–30 jests about this antipodean event that can be found in the London press between 14 July and 14 September 1797, all of them making capital out of the eccentricity, the incongruity of the occurrence. In this period only one general newspaper in London adopted a different position. On 22–24 July the *Evening Mail* had run with the pack and included two witticisms of the standard kind, but in its issue for 25–28 July it adopted a much more severe tone:

> We rejoice in the prosperity of our Colony at *Botany Bay*, but cannot commend the *licence granted to the Theatre in that Province*. We repress the pleasantry that suggests itself on the occasion, nor shall we name the pieces we can imagine most likely to be well acted there. But it is impossible to forbear remarking, that whatever tends to diminish the fear or aversion to being sent *thither*, promotes vice and wickedness in England. Either we must find out a new place of exile, or we must preserve the morals and rigour of that which has cost us so much.

This fear that the colony was losing its impact as a deterrent was to be a growing concern over the next few decades. What is interesting is that none of these newspapers argues the corrupting influence of theatre on those prone to depravity, a note that was to be struck frequently in the colonial press and in the campaign against a Sydney theatre in the 1820s.

The publication in 1798 of Collins' account of the colony provided further stimulus for jokes about Sydney's convict playhouse, but it was not until 1800 that the most sustained and successful comic reading of the event appeared. This was Henry Carter's fictional prologue for the opening of the theatre, which was published in several journals and a slim volume of poetry, but which probably secured its widest audience when it was incorporated into the 1802 edition of *The History of New South Wales*, attributed to George Barrington.[63] From there it went on to become a minor classic of Australian cultural history, helped along by the longstanding belief that it was a genuine prologue from Sidaway's theatre.

Even as Carter's *jeu d'esprit* was being disseminated, however, an alternative way of viewing Sidaway's theatre was beginning to be formulated. At about the time the theatre opened various other developments were taking place. Collins notes these, but makes no connection between them. Later authors, appropriating his material, began to weave them together. In combination they became signs of a colony beginning to move towards maturity:

> Towards the close of 1796, the colony had acquired a degree of strength which seemed to ensure its future prosperity. Not only the necessary edifices were raised for the habitations of its people, but some for the purposes of religion, amusement, &c. A playhouse had been erected at the expence of some persons who performed in it for their own emolument, and who admitted auditors at one shilling each.
>
> A convenient church was built; a printing-press also was set up; the

civil court was open for the recovery of debts by action, and for proving wills; licences had been issued to regulate the sale of spirits; and passage-boats were established for the convenience of communication between the different settlements. In the houses of individuals were to be found most of the comforts and not a few of the luxuries of life; and, in a word, the former years of famine, toil, and difficulty, were now exchanged for those of plenty, ease, and pleasure.[64]

As a French historian expressed it a generation later,

> Dans cet état de progression, les arts, chers aux peuples civilisés, devaient commencer à paraître sur une terre promise à leur empire. Une presse, apportée d'Europe à l'époque de la fondation, était jusqu'alors restée inutile; les actes officiels n'avaient été publiés que par les ministres dans la chaire ou par des affiches à la main: un jeune *convict* fut chargé d'imprimer les ordonnances et les proclamations du gouverneur; tandis que l'inauguration d'un théâtre régulier promettait aux habitans de Sydney des jouissances de l'esprit qu'ils n'avaient goûtées jusqu'alors qu'à de longs intervalles.[65]

> *In this improving situation the arts, dear to civilised peoples, could be expected to appear in a land that was bound to come under their sway. A printing press, brought from Europe when the colony was first founded, had up until this time remained unused: official documents had only been published by clergymen from the pulpit or on handbills. A young convict was given the task of printing the governor's regulations and proclamations, while the opening of a regular theatre promised the inhabitants of Sydney intellectual pleasures that until then they had only enjoyed very intermittently.*

Sidaway's theatre, begun with dire warnings, to some extent spurned by the elite of Botany Bay, and greeted with laughter when the news reached England, had been reconfigured as part of a vision of the British Empire's civilising mission extending even to the blighted world of New South Wales.

Chapter 5

THE THEATRES OF NORFOLK ISLAND, 1793–1806

t was suggested in the previous chapter that Sydney might have launched its first regular theatre group as early as 1793. Given the uncertain dating of the Brickfields playhouse, however, there is a strong likelihood that Australia's first European-style theatre company was not in the colony's main settlement, Sydney, but on the most remote of its outposts, Norfolk Island.

If Botany Bay seemed like the end of the earth, then Norfolk Island contrived to be even beyond that absolute, a tiny speck lost in the Pacific Ocean, some 1,100 miles east-nor'-east of Port Jackson. In fact, it was little more than a low ridge jutting out of the ocean with a tangle of steep foothills and small valleys falling away to the south-east and with two rocky and waterless islets its only companions in a turbulent and dangerous sea. On Whitehall's orders a small party settled the island within two months of the landing at Port Jackson. In the words of one of the female convicts, this 'separation of several of us to an uninhabited island was like a second transportation'.[1]

The appeal of Norfolk Island to the British Government was its native flax and pines, which it was thought would become valuable raw materials for the Royal Navy. This was soon discovered to be a misjudgment, but in the meantime Governor Phillip, confronted with the wretchedly poor soil of Port Jackson, found a new attraction in the island's fertility. With famine facing the parent colony, large numbers of convicts were shipped off to the smaller settlement, so that by early 1794 its population stood at over 1,000, compared with 3,000 on the mainland, divided equally between Port Jackson and the Parramatta area. In spite of this, the viability of the outpost was soon being questioned:

> To what purpose retain a spot situated in the middle of the ocean, and at such a distance from England, when it is seldom possible for any vessel to approach it in safety from the dreadful surf which in general lashes its shore; where there is no kind of shelter even for a boat, nor any place of anchorage to be depended upon; and, in fine, whose utmost extent does not exceed five miles in length and three in breadth?[2]

By 1803 the British Government had decided to abandon the island. In spite of local resistance, the settlement was slowly run down and was finally evacuated in February 1814. Throughout its existence, however, it suffered from an isolation even more profound than Port Jackson itself. No ships were based on the island, and virtually the only vessels to approach its dangerous coasts were those sent on official business from the mainland. In mid-1793, while the Norfolk Island theatre was developing, six months passed without a single vessel touching at the island.[3]

Norfolk Island may not have been far behind Port Jackson in population, but its atmosphere was significantly different. Though little more than a village, Sydney was still the metropolis. Here were concentrated the instruments of government, and the ruling elite. Its eight civil and thirteen military officers may have made for an inordinately restricted society, but it was closer to a critical mass than Norfolk Island's six civil and four military officers, some of whom were not at the main settlement but at out-stations. The army was also a much more prominent component of Sydney society, with 271 privates and non-commissioned officers stationed there, compared with 73 on Norfolk Island.[4] Moreover, Sydney was the main point of contact with the outside world. Naval vessels, and ships under contract to the government, were directed to it and it became the port of call for whalers and traders. These vessels usually stayed for a month or more, adding significant numbers to the general community. In Collins' words, it 'possessed all the evils and allurements of a sea port of some standing'.[5] At Norfolk Island the dangers involved in getting ashore were such that ships hove to as much as fifteen miles off the coast and were usually away in a matter of days.[6] Furthermore, Sydney's inhabitants were more urban in their occupations than the residents of Norfolk Island. In the former were concentrated the bulk of the brick-makers, wheelwrights, cabinet-makers, boat-builders, government clerks and what specialist skills the colony could boast. Norfolk Island, on the other hand, remained overwhelmingly a farming community. In this respect it was much like the colony's other outpost, the Parramatta–Toongabbie settlement, with its 5 civil and military officers and 72 soldiers to control a population of almost 1,500, a significant difference being that Parramatta was only sixteen miles up river from Port Jackson.

There were other features, however, that distinguished Norfolk Island society. Where Norfolk Island by 19 March 1793 had a quarter of its population (252 of the 1,028) no longer victualled from government stores, Sydney, two months later, still reported an insignificant 20 individuals and Parramatta–Toongabbie a mere 5.[7] In part this difference reflects the efforts of Major Ross, while lieutenant-governor of the island, to reduce the drain on government stores by handing over land to convicts to farm in their own right, and allowing others to work as self-supporting labourers. In addition, the wreck of HMS *Sirius* had left the island with a number of stranded sailors who ultimately chose to settle there as farmers, while several marines, whose term of duty had expired, elected to do the same. The result was that Norfolk Island boasted a society that was not only geographically self-contained, but included a disproportionate number of free citizens and of convicts who lived virtually as free men – self-sufficient farmers, shopkeepers and labourers. One sign of this different social climate was the attempt by the farmer-settlers to establish a co-operative.[8] Another was the pressure put on successive lieutenant-governors to allow a group of citizens to build a small vessel to serve the island's needs more efficiently than the mainland government seemed concerned to do.[9] A further instance of this burgeoning civic life was the establishment of the Masonic Lodge of St John at some undetermined date. By 27 April 1800 it was flourishing enough to secure itself a half-acre town allotment for a Masonic hall.[10] The ease with which Lieutenant-Governor King was able to set up a militia force, when events at the theatre precipitated a crisis, also points in the same direction. On that occasion King may have been grateful for the existence of this group of independent citizens, though in other respects it constituted a problem in a system of government geared to the running of a penal establishment, as the flurry over the Fraternal Society and the boat-building indicates.

II

It takes little imagination to recognise that life on Norfolk Island must have been not only arduous but, even by the standards of New South Wales, exceptionally monotonous. Its isolation, and the narrowness of its concerns, can only have generated mind-numbing desolation. There is no better example of the effects of this than the extraordinary action of Lieutenant-Governor King, who in November 1793, with the flimsiest of excuses, escaped on a two-week jaunt to New Zealand. To achieve this he was forced to divert a vessel that was on an urgent mission, and he violently offended his second-in-charge in the process. It was an astonishing dereliction of duty and was seen as such not only by Lieutenant-Governor Grose in Port Jackson but also by the home government.[11]

No such invigorating holidays were available to the less-favoured members of the community, but steps had already been taken to provide some relief. As King reported to Whitehall on 10 March 1794, looking back at the disastrous consequences of his endorsement,

> A Soldier, several well behaved Settlers, Free-men, & Convicts, had as far back as May 1793, requested my permission to get up a Play; As an Officer had undertaken to see it conducted with regularity & Propriety, I granted their request; this amusement which only happened once a Month & on Publick days, I was rather inclined to sanction, In hopes of it being a means of making every Person contented in their situation & pleased with each other several Plays had been performed [by January 1794], & every Regulation was observed with much Respect, Propriety and Good Order.[12]

The way in which the request is said to go 'as far back as May', and the fact that 'several' rather than 'many' plays had been performed by January 1794, suggests that the scheme was not immediately put into execution. A second account of the theatre's genesis, in King's journal, confirms this impression. This journal was also written up well after the events of January and here, against a marginal annotation 'September [1793]', occurs the entry:

> A short time ago, one of the Magistrates informed me, that some of the Freemen, & Convicts, had applied to him to request my permitting them to get up a Play, & to allow them to perform it on Saturdays, when they were perfect in their respective parts, As indulging them in this request did not interfere with the Publick Work, & as such amusements (when unattended with licentious behaviour) tend to unbend & divert the mind; I very readily gave my consent, on condition, that the Magistrate who made the Application, would see it conducted with decency, & Propriety. With some little assistance, the Scenery, &c. was well arrang'd & Two Plays were performed during this Month, in which the Actors acquitted themselves with great Propriety, & the utmost regularity & decency was observed.[13]

The reason for the delay in launching the company is clear. The staging of plays on any regular basis required a theatre, and Norfolk Island was seriously lacking in buildings of any significant size. On his return to command of the island in November 1791, King had begun a vigorous building program, which included a series of granaries. The first of these was begun within a month of his arrival, and in May 1793 a larger stone granary to replace it was begun on the township's main street. This was substantially completed by August, with its floorings in place by September. As King recorded in his journal, 'During this Month, the whole of the Maize; & Wheat raised by the Convicts, & purchased from the Settlers & others, was removed from the Publick Granary, into the New Stone Granary'.[14] There is a mass of circumstantial evidence to prove that it was this vacated granary which was in use as a theatre in January 1794, and, if the company began operations in September 1793, the logical assumption is that its first production took place in this building immediately after it ceased to function as a granary. Admittedly, there is some confused evidence that could be used to argue for performances in August 1793, and the even wilder possibility that there was one in June (see Appendix B, Note 7). One or two performances could have taken place in temporary accommodation prior to September 1793, but it seems likely that the company only moved into sustained activity following the freeing up of King's first granary.

III

King claimed to have allowed the theatre to operate as 'a means of making every Person contented in their situation & pleased with each other'. But in such a constricted society petty jealousies and insignificant disputes had the potential to flare up into major outbursts and, as it happened, the theatre was to fall victim to the very tensions it was meant to ease. Much of the documentation of what took place at the theatre on 18 January 1794 comes from or through King, was written up after the event and was designed to put his actions in the best possible light. The sources, then, need to be approached cautiously, but the main features of the story are not in doubt. The affair takes up over 300 pages in the Colonial Office papers,[15] with supplementary references in King's journal, his official letter-book and his private correspondence with Sir Joseph Banks. What follows summarises these sources.

In King's view the trouble began in March 1793, when Johnston's company of the New South Wales Corps, unaccompanied by Captain Johnston himself, replaced Paterson's as the detachment on the island. King's concern at the lack of a senior officer was magnified by his low opinion of the junior officers who did arrive – the alcoholic Lieutenant Beckwith, the amiable but feckless Ensign Piper and, to lead them, the diminutive Lieutenant Abbott, who, as late as Governor Macquarie's time, was being viewed as a poor risk for a senior administrative post.[16] The problems were not long in arising: 'Soon after the arrival of this Detachment they were observed to be very intimate with the Convicts, living in their Huts, Eating, Drinking & Gambling with them.' The intimacy quickly turned sour. The soldiers were 'perpetually enticing the Women to leave the Men they were Married to, or those they lived with',[17] and this led to violence resulting in criminal charges or courts martial. King described the rapid increase of the latter as a sign of the officers' inability to control their men by less drastic means. The island community became polarised, soldiers against the rest and particularly against convicts and ex-convicts, epitomised in the person of William Dring, who had beaten up the soldier lover of his wife. The savage thrashing he himself had received from the military in a later incident did nothing to mollify the soldiery. By the time of the disturbance of 18 January, which was to close the theatre, it was alleged the soldiery had

> positively determined to murder ... [Dring, and] any of the others, if they had their Will, should share the same fate, ... [for] the Convicts were more indulged than the Soldiers, and ... they had taken an Oath to be true to one Another, and not to suffer any of their Comrades to be punished for an Offence against a Convict anymore.[18]

King had taken precautions to ensure that his theatre was well conducted. One of the magistrates, surgeon William Balmain, was given the responsibility of supervising it and the company manager, Thomas Restell Crowder, also held a position as a constable. Indeed, he may have been given that position precisely because of his role in the theatre company. The appointment was made on 25 August 1793.[19] In spite of this care, however, King's claim that all previous performances had been conducted with 'Propriety and Good Order' was not entirely true. The simmering tension between soldiers and civilians had resulted in dangerous moments in the theatre before 18 January. These seem to have arisen out of disputes over seating which had involved Sergeant Ikin and which Crowder had attempted to avoid at later performances by reserving the front bench for the soldiery.[20] Many of them promptly assumed this as their right.

King claimed that he attended this theatre only on special holiday performances and 18 January was such an occasion, celebrating the Queen's birthday. In addition to the normal *feu de joie*, loyal toasts and the dinner for the island's officials, arrangements were made for the vice-regal party to move on from the dinner to the theatre, accompanied by their servants – three or four of Mrs King's and three of surgeon Balmain's. Since Mrs King had asked that hers be placed near her person, Crowder decided that these servants were best placed in the first row, in front of the official party. This effectively halved the customary accommodation for soldiers. The soldiers' response, partly out of devilry, was to make a game out of occupying the reserved spaces whenever Crowder's back was turned, so that he was finally reduced to sitting there himself, with two assistants, arms and legs spread to secure the whole space. For a while the strategy worked and order was restored. Then Sergeants Whittle and Ikin entered.

In such a situation Crowder and Whittle were the last men to bring together. Both King and his predecessor, Ross, thought highly of Crowder, had secured him a conditional pardon and had given him positions of responsibility. Though he seems to have been an habitual criminal, his family were respectable tradesmen or shopkeepers and he was highly literate and something of a poet. However, he also emerges as thin-skinned, abrupt and abrasive. Whittle, on the other hand, was arguably the most pugnacious of the Corps' sergeants. He ran an aggressive business for much of his time at Port Jackson, indulged in 'threats and abusive language' towards the prickly Captain Colnett of the Royal Navy in 1803, and played a conspicuously rabble-rousing role in the insurrection against Governor Bligh.[21] In Crowder's version of what followed, Whittle made no effort to find a place elsewhere, but went straight to where Crowder was seated and demanded to sit there. When told that the places were being held for the lieutenant-governor's servants, his reply was that 'he would be damned if he cared. That he had as much right to sit there as they had, and that there he would sit'. After further argument Whittle seized Crowder and dragged him from the bench, tearing his shirt in the process. Crowder now found himself at the front of the auditorium surrounded by angry soldiers who threatened and struck him. His attempt to assert his authority as a constable inflamed Whittle even further. In the meantime the civilians in the audience began to respond: 'the other People jumped up from their Seats, and the whole House appeared a Scene of Confusion'.[22] With a full-scale riot threatening, John Fleming, a general overseer, took control. Fleming was a convict, but he was also about to be admitted to the New South Wales Corps and had the respect of both sides. He quickly restored order, while Whittle stormed off to complain to the duty officer, Lieutenant Abbott.

A string of civilian witnesses supported Crowder's story, several of them reporting on the inflammatory behaviour of Private Bannister, who attempted to stir the more docile soldiers into driving the civilians out of the theatre and even into taking over the island. Predictably, Whittle, Ikin and the soldiers drew an entirely different picture. They claimed that Whittle had innocently attempted to sit beside Crowder only to be pushed rudely away, and that Crowder had refused to say for whom the seats were held, declaring that he would not give him that satisfaction and that it was none of his business. After further attempts by Whittle to secure the seat,

Crowder had finally taken the fatal step of attempting to arrest the sergeant, shouting that as a peace officer 'he was his Superior, and commanded him, and called out for Assistance in the King's Name, to take him to Goal'. As soldiers and supporters of Crowder milled around, Ikin was allegedly struck a violent blow, and abuse and threats were showered upon the soldiers: 'A general tumult arose when the cry throughout the whole of the House, was kick out the bloody Villians, Kick out the bloody Soldiers.' As in the civilian version, it was Fleming who calmed the crowd and shortly afterwards came the whisper 'hist, the Governor is coming', which seems to have completed the temporary restoration of order.[23] The result was that King entered, entirely unaware of the fracas, though he had a mildly disagreeable experience of his own a few minutes later:

> Soon after I was seated I observed several Soldiers, with their Hats on, & very dirty, sitting near & incommoding the Officers; after the Play was began, a Soldier (whose Name is Bannister, & whose Name will be frequently mentioned) came into the House, in a dirty check shirt without any Coat, & keeping his hat on (whilst myself & every other Person was uncovered) placed himself in the most insolent Posture nearly opposite the seat I was sitting on; after he had remained some time in that position, I desired one of the Officers of the Detachment who sat next to me, to Order the Soldier to take his Hat off, which was done by the Soldier with a peculiar Insolence.[24]

King, incidentally, was not the only non-belligerent to suffer a few disagreeable moments. Sarah Gregg had the misfortune to be sitting somewhere in the house directly in front of Private Browngraver, who 'frequently spit upon her, and toss [?] her Gown & Handkerchief, & otherwise greatly incommoded her … she thinks the said Brown Graver was much the worse of Liquor at the same time'. For the honour of the army it must be said that several of the other soldiers attempted to restrain him, threatening that 'if he was not quiet, & did not let the People alone, they would pull him out of the House'. Browngraver's response to the warning that the lieutenant-governor was about to enter captures the attitude of many of the troops – a Pavlovian loyalty to their own officers and a disdain for civil authority: 'Damn the Governor, and all of you together, it's my own Officers only that I am to mind.'[25]

At the end of what seems otherwise to have been a trouble-free performance King and his party left, but, as the rest of the audience emerged, tempers flared again and the threatened riot erupted, becoming further inflamed when a fresh crowd of soldiers rushed from their barracks, with bayonets drawn, to join the fray. Somehow the dispute was once again contained and a soldier and a civilian arrested, but by the next day virtually the whole of the military detachment was on the verge of mutiny, furious at perceived insults, voicing their hostility to the civil administration, and close to threatening their own officers. In high alarm King managed, by a stratagem, to disarm many of the troops, hastily raised a militia from among the ex-seamen and ex-marines and arrested nineteen of the ringleaders. He then wrote a hasty letter about 'this unpleasant business' to his superior, Lieutenant-Governor Grose, and sent it, with ten of the mutineers, off to Port Jackson in the government schooner *Francis*, which fortuitously arrived at the island a few days after the disturbance.

Though the island's two magistrates, in investigating the matter, found themselves unable to reach a decision because the evidence was so contradictory, King had no doubt that the blame lay with the soldiery. As he wrote in his private journal, the whole affair was due to the 'determination of a Principal part of the Soldiers, (who were corrupted by Ten or Twelve Villains) to attempt the destruction of all Order, and regularity by Committing, and intending the Crimes of Mutiny & Cruelty'. Again, in a private letter to Sir Joseph Banks, he referred to the conflict as one between 'the Inhabitants & an undisciplinable Soldiery over whom their Officers had lost all Command'.[26] But if he expected to win the support of Grose for his actions he was sorely mistaken. Like many military officers Grose was fiercely sensitive to the honour of his regiment. The accusations made against some of his men; the low opinion of Abbott implicit in the report; the idea that the word of a convict might carry equal weight with that of a soldier in a court of inquiry; the action of disarming the troops and setting up a militia, all drove Grose to a fury. Within fifteen days of the *Francis'* arrival at Port Jackson it was on the way back with a savage instruction to the lieutenant-governor. The militia was to be disbanded immediately and the soldiers re-armed. No convict was permitted to lay charges against any soldier on any matter whatever. Thomas Restell Crowder and William Doran (a company member who allegedly attempted to incite the crowd to violence against the soldiers) were to be clapped in irons at once and sent to Port Jackson for trial. Crowder wrote an agonised letter to King, lamenting that his wife was seriously ill and his business affairs would be put at risk by his sudden removal from the island.[27] King secured Crowder's freedom to see to his affairs during the ship's stay, but he could do no more, and on 22 March the shackled Crowder and Doran sailed to an uncertain fate at headquarters. In the meantime King had peremptorily ordered the closure of the theatre that had been the immediate source of his troubles. As he noted briefly in his journal, the 'very improper use which was made of the indulgence of Acting Plays, on the 18th Compelled me to forbid any more amusements of that kind'. By July, at the latest, Crowder's theatre was once more a granary.[28]

IV

While the riot is reported in great detail, the information offered about the playhouse and its activities is fragmentary and often oblique. The one thing on which the documentation provides satisfactory evidence is the identification of the building itself, and that is discoverable only by the analysis of passing comments. Once that has been determined other sources come into play to provide information about the building's appearance, dimensions and layout. (The process of piecing this information together is set out in Appendix B, Note 8.) In summary, this granary-turned-playhouse

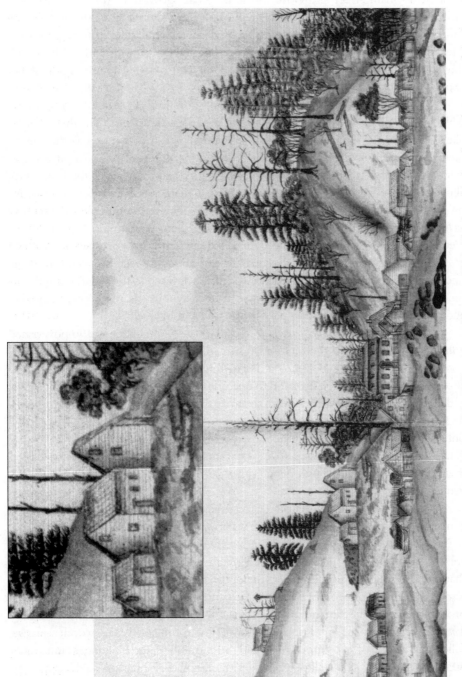

Fig. 10 View of the main settlement on Norfolk Island, by William Neate Chapman, 1796. The theatre is the tallest and rearmost of the three buildings on the hillside (see inset). Chapman's wash drawing has been stuck into Governor John Hunter's autographed copy of Arthur Phillip's *Voyage … to Botany Bay*, London, 1789 (Mitchell Library, State Library of New South Wales, C688/2).

was a weatherboard building conspicuously situated on a rise immediately behind the settlement's main street and close to the lieutenant-governor's house. It is clearly visible in William Neate Chapman's view of the township as the rearmost of the three buildings on the slope of Mount George (the two buildings in front of it were later additions)(see Fig. 10). It was 37–40 feet long and 24 feet wide and, if Chapman's drawing can be trusted, had a steeply-raked roof, whose ridge-cap was about 32 feet above ground level.

Internally the building consisted of two floors, with a small loft above them, which was probably tucked into the roof space at the seaward end. The theatre, in all likelihood, was on the upper of these two floors, with the loft used as the gallery. Since it had no boxes, the remainder of the auditorium consisted of a pit rising in steps towards this gallery. The wall height of 9 feet, and the void of the roof space above that, over pit and stage areas, meant that there was height for an effective proscenium arch, which was graced with a curtain. King himself described the scenery as 'well arranged'. The records make no reference to proscenium doors, but the 23-feet internal width would have allowed them and still permitted a proscenium opening of about 17 feet. The records are equally silent about an orchestra pit. Given the uncertainty as to how much of the floor space was devoted to the stage area and how much to the auditorium, the capacity of the playhouse is unknowable, but an auditorium accommodating 130 people was well within reach.

Talk of a granary converted into a playhouse in a small and impoverished community conjures up the picture of something crude and primitive. The well-known 1788 engraving, '*Macbeth* in a Barn', might seem the appropriate image.[29] It shows a stage at floor level, the band to one side of the auditorium in a small balcony, and what is probably a hayloft converted into a gallery. The building itself is ramshackle, with some dejected bunting across the front of the music box and the gallery as the only decoration in the auditorium. The stage setting appears to be just as sparse. While a few respectably dressed folk appear in the front row, the overall impression is one of a space tattered and dirty, with a performance probably as crude as the venue.

That is one way of visualising Crowder's theatre, but it might well have made a much braver appearance. The internal walls of a granary were often plastered and, if this were the case on Norfolk Island, a quick coat of white or coloured wash applied to the plaster would have helped greatly to enliven the space. King intimates that the authorities gave assistance in the refurbishing and this might have allowed of a more ambitious approach.[30] The best example of a rough space transformed is probably given in the illustration 'The UPPER REGIONS in disorder' in Pierce Egan's *The Life of an Actor* (see Fig. 11). The ceiling of the room consists of wooden planks, following the line of the hipped roof, and the end wall of the building is similarly of weatherboard. The side wall of the auditorium, however, presents itself as a set of elegant arches, with drapes of cloth behind them. The architecture of these archways is similar to that of the wings and there can be little doubt that what is visible is, in fact, a false wall, made on the same principles as the stage scenery, to conceal the

Fig. 11   'The Upper Regions in disorder: rapid descent of the Gods and Goddesses into the Pit.' A relatively elegant fit-up theatre in what appears to be a weatherboard barn (Pierce Egan, *The Life of an Actor*, London, 1825).

rough timber behind it. The floor of the pit is raked. The gallery is not simply an extension of it but a narrow balcony, which appears to have been erected along the back wall for the occasion and, because of its primitive workmanship, is collapsing under the weight of the spectators. It is unlikely that the Norfolk Island theatre would have gone this far in the pursuit of elegance, but it may have been closer to the Egan illustration than to the space in '*Macbeth* in a Barn'.

V

In a passage quoted earlier, King described the makers of this theatre as a soldier, several well-behaved settlers, freemen and convicts. His own papers, both official and private, provide us with the names of only two of those associated with the company; but the transcripts of the magistrates' investigation enable us to identify six people who were behind the scenes at the time of the Whittle incident. In addition there were Crowder and two assistants who were keeping order in the house itself and were presumably non-performers – certainly James Jordan was, since he specifically joined the audience after the row with Whittle.[31] As for those behind the scenes, the question is whether they were there as performers or simply as stagehands. Only one, Joseph Morrell, can definitely be identified as an actor, since he speaks of 'conning his part' at the time the dispute began.[32] Robert Higgins, because of his rank as senior NCO on the island, would hardly have been involved in any capacity less than that of a performer. Since Michael Lee appears to have been an actor in the 1805/06 company, he was probably one in 1793/94. The position of William Doran, Edward Flynn and Stephen Shore remains unclear.

William Hogg is not mentioned among those who were on the stage, but it is difficult to imagine him as absent, since he was the colony's leading comic performer. He is mentioned in the magistrates' examinations, but only as the person who had organised the attendance of Mrs King's servants at the theatre.[33] His participation remains a guess. It is noticeable that none of those known to be associated with the performance is a woman. The ladies of Botany Bay were as free with their tongues as the men and, since the dispute over seating was largely a slanging match, it is surprising that no woman is mentioned among those shouting from the stage. This raises the possibility that the company was an all-male affair, but this seems unlikely, since women were freely employed in Sidaway's troupe. Their absence from the Norfolk Island court records is probably nothing more than a matter of chance.

King's attribution of the company to a soldier and several well-behaved settlers may be an attempt to present the group in the best possible light. Of those who have been identified, only Higgins had come free to the colony. All the others had arrived as convicts, though by the time of the performance Crowder had a conditional pardon and Flynn was free by servitude. Only Crowder, moreover, fell into that elite group, the farmer-settlers.

The little that can be discovered about the backgrounds of most of these company members suggests they were from much the same social grouping as Sidaway's players. They are neither gentlefolk nor unskilled workers, but modestly-educated tradesmen and shopkeepers, with one or two possibly having connections with the lesser gentry. Something of Crowder's middle-class background has already been mentioned. At one stage he claimed to have been a chandler in London, though a Norfolk Island return lists his prior occupation as sailor, a vocation which his brother Edward pursued and returned to after leaving the island. William Hogg was of a similar status, trained as a silversmith, though on the island he declined into poverty, alcoholism and suicide. Nothing is known of Flynn's background. At the time of the riot he was superintendent of the hospital, which might imply a person of some abilities, but he was illiterate, the hospital was small and, apart from some slight signs of success around 1800, his later career was humble, some of it spent as a fisherman. Higgins' position as senior NCO in the military detachment gave him considerable status. Such an appointment could have gone to a man whose superior social background indicated leadership potential, but it could just as readily have been given to a dutiful thug and bully boy. William Doran, in spite of his trade as a brick-maker, was cook to the lieutenant-governor, a position of trust that suggests a degree of sophistication, at least in the culinary line. Stephen Shore later emerges as a respectable hairdresser in Parramatta and a member of the Parramatta Loyal Association. However, he seems to have been illiterate until long after his Norfolk Island years.

Morrell and Lee provide the most tantalising cases. Morrell had been a sailor, more than once in trouble with the law, and sometimes appears in the Norfolk Island documents working as a labourer, while Michael Lee was formally categorised in the musters and returns as a labourer. In both cases, however, the official evidence may be misleading. Lee seems to have held a significant post in the island's Masonic Lodge, and after his removal to Hobart he established himself as a hotelier. Morrell, after his departure for Port Jackson, soon rose to the position of master of a succession of colonial vessels, for a large part living a life of hardship, violence and high drama in the Bass Strait sealing trade. The refinements of theatre sit strangely with such an existence. Crowder, Morrell, and Lee have all left letters demonstrating a good command of written English, while Higgins has left a clear, firm signature, suggesting a comfortable level of literacy. (Further details of Crowder, Morell and Lee may be found in Appendix A.)

While Crowder's company members seem to come from much the same socio-economic background as Sidaway's, in other respects they are a little more heterogenous. The army penetrated Sidaway's company only in its later years: Sergeant Major Higgins was a member of Crowder's from the beginning. The ethnic background of Crowder's company was also a little more diverse, in that among the seven possible performers were Edward Flynn, an Irish Catholic, and Michael Lee, who was Jewish. James Jordan, Crowder's assistant in controlling the house, was also an Irish Catholic.

VI

King's firm statement that the playhouse was closed immediately after the riot, and the evidence that the building reverted to being a granary shortly afterwards, reads like the final pages in the story of theatre on the island during its first settlement. However, this impression may be misleading. Though King shut his playhouse in January 1794, David Collins, in his history of New South Wales, records the arrival of the *Fancy* from Norfolk Island on 3 September 1795, and summarises the reports it brought from the island to Port Jackson. Among these are

> William Hogg, a prisoner well known and approved at this place for his abilities as a silversmith, and an actor in the walk of low comedy, put an end to his existence in a very deliberate manner a few days before the *Fancy* sailed.[34]

The phrase 'at this place' is ambiguous, since it could mean Port Jackson, in which case Hogg's memory as a performer had been kept green since March 1790, when he left for Norfolk Island. What is more likely is that Collins is simply transcribing the contents of a letter received from the *Fancy*, in which case Hogg's reputation as a performer and silversmith relates to his life on the island. The question then arises: were 'his abilities as … an actor in the walk of low comedy' remembered from the performances that had taken place in Crowder's theatre some two years earlier, or had they been kept before the public eye over the intervening period? The latter seems the more likely explanation. It is not impossible that King may have relented once the scandal had died down and permitted the occasional performance under *ad hoc* conditions. Alternatively, the thespian art may have been kept alive in alehouses, with Hogg doing comic solo turns or performing scenes from well-known plays, in company with another actor or two and in the style of a spouting club.

What is certain is that there were performances taking place on Norfolk Island in 1805/06, under the benevolent reign of Lieutenant Piper. Piper had been an ensign there at the time of the earlier theatre. In his account of the highly eccentric gentleman convict, John Grant, who was on the island from 27 June 1805 to December 1807, W.S. Hill-Reid reports that he 'wrote a little play, a sort of masque which was performed with considerable skill in a rickety play-house improvised for the purpose'.[35] Hill-Reid's book is based entirely on the papers of Grant that had been discovered in a bank vault, and those papers were supposedly given in their entirety to the National Library of Australia. Unfortunately, the source of the above statement cannot be found in the Grant papers in the National Library of Australia; but there is no reason to disbelieve Hill-Reid, who is otherwise accurate and is not attempting to make any particular point here.

Luckily, there is another, somewhat unusual source, which confirms that costumed drama of some description was being staged on the island. Manuscript B437, in the Mitchell Library, State Library of New South Wales, is catalogued as 'Daybook of a Sydney Merchant, 1805–06'. The manuscript was discovered in a building in Sydney and the attribution is clearly based on this fact. However, a study of the names listed in the book, as well as the occasional, dated reports of ship arrivals and departures, makes it quite clear that the manuscript relates to Norfolk Island.[36]

The book is basically the day-by-day record of credit sales from a general store on the island, naming the goods sold and giving the surname of the customer involved, though there are also some records of produce taken into the public stores and occasional miscellaneous notes (see Fig. 12).[37] The manuscript covers the period 3 June 1805 to 27 September 1806. Most of the sales recorded in the book are of liquor, tea and sugar, but under the heading 'Die Lund 9 Dec[r] 1805' appears the entry:

> M[r] Robinson (Theatre D[r])
> 1 Piece Tape – 6.0

and under 'Die Martis 10th Dec[r] 1805' appears:

> Theatre
> 350 Shingle Nails
> 100 20[d] Nails
> 80 feet Battens

Thereafter items relating to the theatre begin to build up. A few of them relate to hardware ('To Copely for Nails – 1.8.-'), but the overwhelming bulk are for pieces of cloth and wearing apparel ('Theatre to making/a hat 15.-').[38] In many cases a name is associated with these purchases, as on 'Die Martis 17 Dec[r]':

> Theatre (pr Cox) D[r]
> 3 yards Hair Ribbon – 4.6
> 3 Skains Silk – 5.0

or on 'Die Saturni 8 Feb 1806':

> Theatre D[r] p[r] M[rs] Robley
> 4 yards B[*illegible*] Ribbon 8.-
> 2 yards fine Tape Mcqueen 1.-
> 1[*illegible*] Tape, Cox 2.6
> 1yd Hair Ribbon, waters 1.6
> D[o] Kearney's boy 3.0

One problem with entries for cloth, hats and the like is to determine whether the person named in conjunction with them is a servant collecting the items, or the costumier, or the performer who is to wear the resulting outfit. For example, the name of the Irish rebel, Francis Garty, occurs on several occasions. He may have been a performer, but it could be significant that he was by trade a tailor.[39] An additional problem is that there are no given names or initials, which would help identify these individuals. A final problem is that all entries of this kind cease on 4 April 1806. After that date there are many entries that could well be for playhouse costumes – the same types of material and the same individuals' names are listed – but they are not explicitly identified as purchases for the theatre, even though the playhouse continued to be active, at least until late June.

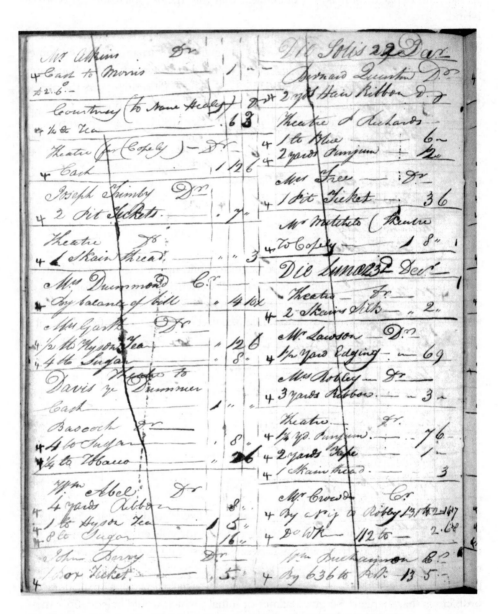

Fig. 12   Page from the Norfolk Island shopkeeper's daybook, 1805-06 (Mitchell Library, State Library of New South Wales, B437:CY2295, catalogued as 'Daybook of a Sydney Merchant, 1805–06). 'Davis the drummer' would have been hired, with his drum, to advertise the show around the island. 'Punjum' is an Indian cloth. Copley was the island's shingler.

Before the entries for purchases on behalf of the theatre are far advanced, a different type of entry, clear and unambiguous, begins to appear – records of sales of tickets to named individuals. A typical example, dated 17 December 1805, reads:

> Mʳ Kimberlay Dʳ
>
> Box Tickets 1.-.-

Many of the entries also include the given name of the purchaser. The prices are 5s. for box seats and 3s. 6d. for pit seats. One entry of 17 December 1805 specifies '3 Front Box Tickets' at 5s. each, while an entry of a different kind, on 26 June 1806, is for '2 Stage tickets', also at 5s. each. There are, of course, no entries for gallery places – assuming there *was* a gallery, which is virtually certain: these were customarily purchased at the door. Since these ticket sales are interspersed with sales of food, drink and other supplies, it is a simple matter to gain a sense of the relative value of tickets in this community. The 5s. it cost to secure a place in the boxes could have been used to buy ½ lb of tobacco or 2½ lb of sugar at the same shop. A pint of rum cost 7s. 6d. and 1 lb of tea £1 10s..

Beyond this point interpretation of the information proves surprisingly complicated, but in essence there is firm evidence for the sale of 24 box tickets to 10 named persons and 19 pit tickets to another 10 for a performance on 26 December 1805, which was a Saturday. In addition, the same vendor sold a much smaller number of tickets (15 box places to 10 purchasers, and a single pit seat) to a performance that appears to have taken place between 21 and 26 June 1806. There are a few ticket sales recorded at times well removed from these dates, and other entries which could relate to ticket sales, but many of these may be dismissed as lingering debts carried forward from one or another of these productions. Some consolidated lists also record the transfer of ticket monies from the vendor to an agent of the company. These are Thomas MacQueen on 26 June 1806, probably John Herbert on 6 January 1806 and Mrs Cox on 22 February 1806, but they do not match precisely the recorded figures for individual sales.

The evidence suggests that this was not a theatre in regular use but a building employed on a few festal occasions, once during the twelve days of Christmas and once close to the feast of St John, the northern hemisphere's summer solstice and a key date in the Masonic calendar. The daybook gives no hint of performances prior to Christmas 1805 or after mid-June 1806, but that could be a result of its own terminating dates. The two performances could have been isolated incidents or part of a pattern stretching over years.

The disparity between the number of ticket sales for the two performances has already been noted. What is also curious is that only two of those who bought tickets for December also bought tickets for the June presentation. Was one performance enough to satisfy that audience's curiosity, or were the actors so incompetent they lost public support? Neither suggestion seems plausible. Perhaps it was the ticket-selling procedures that made the difference. If pit and box tickets were available through a number of outlets, the decline in sales in June 1806 could simply reflect the desertion of one vendor for another or, more probably, an increase in the number of vendors. One consequence of having multiple sales points, of course, is that the number of tickets recorded in this particular daybook gives no indication of the maximum capacity of the house. Nevertheless, a shopkeeper who managed to sell 24 box tickets in December must have had a sizeable share of the market, since it is difficult to imagine a Norfolk Island theatre running to much more than fifty box places.

The theatre building of 1805 was a cut above Crowder's 1793 playhouse, in that it had front and side boxes. Prices for its box tickets matched those of Sidaway in Sydney, and its pit places cost even more than his. Nonetheless, if John Grant's biographer, William Hill-Reid, is reporting accurately, the 1805 theatre was a rickety old building adapted ('improvised') for the purpose of these shows, not a pre-existing theatre. Certainly the building needed repairs, but the only construction indicated in the shopkeeper's daybook was work on the roof. The tradesman mentioned, Copley, was the island's shingler and the purchases are primarily shingle nails and battens. There is no reference to materials that could be used to create risers in the pit or frames for the boxes. This leaves the possibility that the building was a dilapidated theatre set up at some time in the previous decade, currently in disrepair but requiring only renovations. While that may be the case, it is also possible that it was an abandoned barn and that the timbers for the internal construction work were purchased from a different dealer and so are unrecorded.

VII

A theatre that, on the most pessimistic estimate, offered only two performances, and those at a six-month interval, can hardly be seen as a major social phenomenon, but this Norfolk Island theatre has special interest in other ways. In the first place, it provides us with a strikingly different model of a convict theatre from those operated by Sidaway in Sydney and Jemmy King at Emu Plains. In the second place, those lists of ticket purchasers provide us with a remarkable insight into the audience composition in this theatre and, by extension and with some adjustments, into the likely audience that graced the Sydney theatre of a few years earlier.

The infrequency of its performances and their association with holiday occasions gives this second Norfolk Island theatre the flavour of English amateur theatricals of the time. With this in mind, some of the performers in the recorded productions make a fascinating contrast with the personnel in either Crowder's or Sidaway's playhouse. The name that crops up most frequently is Robinson, who is associated with the purchase of a fine hat, a sash, ribbon and cloth. There was only one Robinson on the island, and he had just arrived, Michael Massey Robinson, Gent., transported there from Port Jackson for corrupt financial practices in the colony. It is the same Michael Massey Robinson who had provided an address for Mrs Parry's benefit in Sydney in 1799, had been the colony's leading convict lawyer, and whose charm, sophistication, self-promotion and (limited) poetic flair was later to induce Governor Macquarie to become his patron.

A participant whose name appears against purchases of material, and who would certainly have been wearing the resulting costume, was 'Redfern'. The only person of that name on the island was William Redfern, who later became Sydney's leading doctor. Known as a well-educated, reserved, and somewhat haughty man, he was, in essence, a political prisoner. As surgeon's mate on board HMS *Standard* at the time of the mutiny at the Nore, he had shown some fellow feeling for the mutineers. In the campaign of government terror that followed, he was charged with mutiny and sent out to Botany Bay, along with others who had narrowly escaped the grisly ritual of a hanging at the yardarm.[40]

If the White who is also associated with costumes for the theatre is Richard White, then the same pattern is repeated, albeit with an exotic twist. 'Black Dick' White was a New York-born mulatto highwayman, who was referred to as a gentleman at his trial and signed himself as such in his will several decades later. Any romantic inclination to read him as a six-foot Afro-American matinee idol falls sadly flat in the face of the official description of this 'half american Black' as 5 feet 4 inches tall and of a dark yellow complexion. In later years he is also said to have been 'bandy or broken-legged', though this might have been due to an accident subsequent to the play. After leaving Norfolk Island he made money as an auctioneer and proprietor of a leading hotel in Launceston. Though he was regarded there as a faintly eccentric and even slightly comic figure, he might well have had some claims to gentility, presumably on his father's side. Certainly, in Launceston he worked hard to live the image of a gentleman. He raced horses, maintained one of the township's earliest carriages, built up substantial landholdings and was remembered for his smart Wellington boots, his white buckskin breeches, cutaway coat and top hat, as well as for his enthusiasm as a fiddle player.[41]

Another name frequently linked in the daybook to the purchase of materials is that of Thomas MacQueen (McQuin). MacQueen had been a schoolteacher in England and, after transportation, resumed that profession on Norfolk Island, and later at Sydney and Port Dalrymple. School teaching, other than in a major public school, was a lowly trade, and MacQueen seems to have been a somewhat contemptible figure, weak and improvident. The crime that brought him to Australia was pawning the furnishings of his rented room 'from motives of necessity'. By 1800 he was in the debtors' prison on the island and in 1807 was listed as penniless and owing £14 6s., an amount he contested. Nevertheless, his education gave him a seedy sort of gentility. At a time when the island lacked a clergyman he had conducted the Sunday prayer services and at one stage was acting surveyor, a government office of great respectability. He may have had a managerial role in the theatre company, as well as being a performer, since he is recorded as collecting the ticket money from the shopkeeper.[42]

John Grant's name appears nowhere in the daybook. His contribution was probably limited to the 'little play, a sort of masque' which he wrote for one of the performances, in all likelihood as an interlude. Grant was accepted as a gentleman in the colony and would have felt at home with those participants so far described, though whether the feeling was entirely reciprocated may be doubted, since Grant was obsessive, humourless and half-crazed. Samuel Marsden's ambivalent attitude to him can be seen in a letter of a few years later.[43]

Here, then, is a theatre whose schedules point to its amateur status, but whose affinities are not with the performances of city apprentices and journeymen or the rural amusements of farmers' sons and daughters. Instead, it appears more like the fashionable theatricals of the English gentry, despite the embarrassment that one of the participants was slightly unbalanced, the gentility of two is a little suspect, and all were convicts or ex-convicts. The whole is like some grotesque parody – Mansfield Park theatricals in an isolated, decaying, rum-sodden, sub-tropical, penal outpost at the farthest end of the world. The Mansfield Park play-acting in Jane Austen's novel, of course, was private entertainment, and required no entry fee. This was not the case on Norfolk Island, but the fact that the shows were occasional, and involved so many gentlefolk, might suggest charity benefits, the proceeds going to the orphanage, for example.

Those involved in these genteel amateur theatricals usually restricted their casts to members of their own class, but household servants were sometimes included, or neighbours of lesser rank. Even the well-known amateur theatricals of the Wynns of Wynstay reveal this pattern,[44] and there are light satiric works which poke fun at the practice, such as Isaac Jackman's 1777 farce, *All the World's a Stage*, and James Powell's *Private Theatricals* of a decade later. The Norfolk Island theatricals adopted this more inclusive approach. There was, for example, William Blunt. He had been a coachman to several respectable families and his own background seems to have been decent, but not elevated.[45] While he may have worked for the theatre as a servant of some kind, it is more than likely that he was a performer.

Unfortunately for the company, not all their lower-class support fell into this category of the humble but decent. The name Waters appears only once in connection with the purchase of materials, on 8 February 1806, and though it is virtually certain that this Waters wore the costume associated with the purchase, he may have been only a bit player. Some of the company may have wished he had no part at all, for the only Waters in the community was Patrick Waters, the island's flagellator.[46] In *The Playmaker* Thomas Keneally indulges the fiction of Port Jackson's hangman being one of the players in the 1789 production of *The Recruiting Officer*. Generally speaking, the flagellator was socially only one cut above the executioner. With such a creature we are far removed from the world of Jane Austen.

Two other possible male performers are worthy of note. The 'Lee' associated with theatrical entries in the shopkeeper's daybook is certain to be Michael Lee, who was mentioned earlier as a probable performer in Crowder's company, and is the only link with that earlier enterprise. Though Crowder himself appears frequently in the daybook, it is mainly as a purchaser of alcohol, and there is no reference to connect him with the theatre, either as a member of the company or of the audience. He was, however, familiar enough with John Grant for the latter to send Crowder's manuscript poems back to England. A second performer, who figures prominently in the daybook as 'Richards', is virtually certain to be the William Richards who was a notable figure in the Sydney theatre from 1797 to 1800. If so, he is the strongest identifiable link between the two companies. A Mr and Mrs Cox appear to be involved with the island playhouse, he as a performer, she perhaps in an administrative capacity, but the couple cannot be firmly identified, since that name was common to several of the inhabitants. It may be significant that Private Cox was in Sydney at the time J. Cox was a performer there and had been posted to Norfolk Island, with his wife, before the 1805 and 1806 productions.

It may be worthy of comment that two other players from the Sydney theatre of 1799–1800 spent short periods on Norfolk Island after 1800, though they had left by 1805. These were Beckwith Smith and Daniel Parnell. Three, or possibly four, Sydney players arriving in this way might suggest David Collins' original threat to disperse the company had been put into effect. This is probably not the case. While Richards and Parnell arrived on the same ship, the others arrived separately and the Sydney company seems to have continued after their departure. Other reasons can also be found for their transfers. It was Cox's company that was posted to Norfolk Island, not Cox alone. Beckwith Smith, a serving convict, might have been sent to answer a need for carpenters at the outpost. Richards and Parnell were both in trouble with the authorities for personal, not collective, misdemeanours, and could have been transferred as public nuisances. Both these men arrived as time-expired convicts. (Further details of Lee, Richards, Cox, Smith and Parnell may be found in Appendix A.)

Curiously, the shopkeeper's daybook contains little or no evidence of women performers. The name of Mrs Robley appears more frequently than any other in the entries relating to theatre, but the very frequency raises a question about her function, particularly as the items bought under her name often include a second name. She was probably the wardrobe mistress. One name that does occur in conjunction with hers is that of her daughter, Betty,[47] who at that stage was fourteen years old. Betty may well have been in the cast and if so, we could be dealing with that romantic phenomenon, a theatrical love affair. In May 1806, a few months after the first production, she married Michael Massey Robinson, a spectacular catch for the daughter of a well-to-do blacksmith and a woman who had been a grocer's house servant in east London and a notorious receiver of stolen goods in Sydney.[48] The only other jarring note in the romance was Robinson's age, since at this time he was 62.

VIII

The sources available for an analysis of the Norfolk Island theatres provide no information about the repertoire, a limited amount about the performers, and little about playhouse organisation and structure. What they do provide is information about the audience. The names of many of those present have been preserved, most of whom can be identified and a few facts about them gleaned from the records. The process of analysis is most productive when applied to the second theatre, for which it is possible to build up a profile of the pit and box audiences at the two known performances. It is precisely the sort of information that is so lacking for Robert Sidaway's Sydney theatre, though I have already assumed that what was true for Norfolk Island also held for Port Jackson.

The 1794 performance at which the riot took place was on a royal holiday and, as was the case with *The Recruiting Officer* in 1789, the event had been incorporated into the ceremonies of the ruling elite as a post-prandial entertainment. The lieutenant-governor 'went to the Play, with his Family, and the Officers who had dined with him on that day'.[49] But there are major differences between the two. *The Recruiting Officer* was a production especially created for the occasion, whereas the Norfolk Island presentation was one performance in the theatre's more-or-less regular program. To that extent it lacked the feeling of a special event. More importantly, there was no way in which the officer class on Norfolk Island could numerically dominate the house. There were only ten clearly identifiable members of that group in the community, together with the lieutenant-governor's wife. Nor did the soldiery contribute to the image of authority, being variously described as drunken, dirty, insolent, casually-dressed and consorting with the girls of the town.[50]

Excluding Crowder, his two assistants and those on stage, the magistrates' investigation of the dispute that took place before the play names nine soldiers, nine civilians and four members of the official party who were in the theatre. A series of affidavits 'voluntarily' lodged with the magistrates on 23 January 1794, dealing with mutinous or threatening utterances by soldiers, identifies another soldier and four civilian playgoers. Papers relating to the riot after the show name two other civilians who had been in the theatre, and another four civilians and two soldiers who may have been there or may simply have arrived later for the fight. Leaving aside this last group, we have the names of 29 people who witnessed, or intended to witness, the show. Depending on the size of the house they could have comprised between one third and one sixth of the entire audience. Additional to these are references to settlers' wives, to the seven officers' servants, and to the unspecified number of town girls sitting with the soldiers. With the exception of a servant of William Balmain, the island's surgeon, none of these is named.

As was indicated earlier, Norfolk Island, with its high proportion of free settlers and independent landholders, had a demographic composition different from that in the other settlements, one that gave it many of the social characteristics of an English farming community. Accordingly, it comes as no great surprise to find that five of the nine named civilians who can be identified as sitting in the pit were small-scale farmers, four of them ex-convicts and one an ex-marine.[51] In addition, there was another ex-convict, who seems to have attained the dignity of a constable, and three serving convicts. One of these was the government overseer, John Fleming. Of the other two convicts Edward Crowder apparently worked a small allotment (he was never classified as a settler, but sold some grain to the stores), while Thomas Petrie appears in the records as a casual labourer. However, since they seem to have been friends and, since Edward was Thomas Crowder's brother, they might have been there under special circumstances.[52] Also, a wife and child accompanied one of the small farmers, and there is a separate reference to the wives of two settlers who might or might not be among those named.

This picture of a pit audience largely composed of farmer-settlers and minor government functionaries, with most of them emancipists, may be a distortion of the facts. Though the magisterial inquiry into the dispute prior to the production served the function of a government investigation, it was actually set up as a case brought by Whittle against Crowder for grossly insulting him in the playhouse. All the civilians interrogated were therefore witnesses chosen by Crowder to speak on his behalf, and it was in his interest that they should be respectable citizens. Certainly, there were also significant numbers of serving convicts present somewhere in the house. King, writing of the audience response to the provocations of Whittle and Bannister, declared that 'on this the settlers and convicts rose up'.[53] The four civilians identified as theatregoers in the affidavits that dealt with other aspects of the troops' behaviour that weekend were convicts (one a woman), as were five of the six mentioned in the separate investigation into the post-performance riot.[54] There is no evidence of where these convicts sat but, given their limited finances, the gallery is the most likely place. In other words, in spite of the possibility of a bias in the sampling, I am inclined to envisage a theatre in which the bulk of the serving convicts were relegated to the gallery. This would also help to explain why they did not join the dispute at the beginning of the show, but held their peace until the end when, free of the building, they turned on the troops.

If this interpretation is accurate, it is possible to read this audience in the same terms as that of an English village performance. Here, the local equivalent of the squire and his family and retainers occupy a position to the front of the pit, surrounded by the small farmers of the district, with the antipodean version of agricultural labourers in the gallery. Shifting focus a little, we might see in a lieutenant-governor and his officials attending a royal birthday celebration, seated in the midst of soldiers and of farmers who had been soldiers, sailors or convicts, with convict labourers and others in the gallery, a picture of authority unbending a little and mixing with its inferiors. It was one of the more subtle strategies whereby an authoritarian power wins the consent of the dominated, by showing a human face and a touch of conviviality in carefully chosen situations. The fact that the occasion is not the Twelfth Day of Christmas, or a pre-Lenten carnival, but a royal occasion, makes the operation a little more overt. There sits the lieutenant-governor as a sort of *pater familias*, surrounded by his extended family, celebrating the birthday of the wife of King George III, 'Farmer George', whose own image had been reshaped as that of someone fatherly and homely, as well as the embodiment of state power.[55] It was unfortunate for Lieutenant-Governor King that his attempt to play on these familiar themes went so disastrously wrong.

The audience of the second theatre lends itself to a more detailed, and potentially more useful, analysis. This theatre had boxes as well as a pit and the tickets bought identify in which part of the house individuals sat. Since the price of pit and box seats is known, and was high, it becomes possible to investigate whether social differentiation existed between those two parts of the house. In addition, more can be discovered about the background and status of this later audience.

If the ticket sales recorded in the daybook for the Boxing Day and June performances are conflated, we have the names of 18 people who at various times bought box places in the theatre, and 11 who bought pit tickets. An unidentified Mr Tindall, who paid for a pit ticket to the first performance and a box ticket to the second, is the only person to be counted twice in this process. While there may be a hidden bias in this sample, because this shopkeeper attracted a specialised clientele, it seems unlikely. In most respects these purchasers are probably representative of the pit and box audiences in general.

Two of the 18 buyers of box tickets are at present untraced.[56] Of the remainder, only one had any evident claim to gentility: James Connellan, the island's doctor, who paid for a single place. Six were government overseers or constables of whom one was still a convict and the remainder ex-convicts. In addition to their government posts they also held plots of land.[57] Another six were farmer-settlers, one an ex-marine and the others ex-convicts. The ex-marine, James Beresford, had the third largest landholding on the island, 110 acres, and bought six box seats, presumably for himself, his wife and his four older children. This was the largest single sale.[58] Of the remaining three purchasers one was Thomas Self, a private in the New South Wales Corps, who bought one ticket, and two were women. Hannah Whittaker, born in the colony of convict parents, secured a single box ticket, while her father, George, bought two. Hannah may already have been living independently, for in December 1807, aged eighteen, she sailed for Hobart without her family.[59] The other woman ticket buyer was Kate Kearney, who secured three places. Kearney later became an astute businesswoman in Tasmania and something of a character, running a dairy in the heart of Hobart, and numbering Government House among her clients. On Norfolk Island she had a town lease, and may have been in business there also, though the only mention of her at this time is as 'a very seditious troublesome character'. Her presence in the theatre may have been a matter of family pride, since her eldest son was probably among the performers.[60]

What this analysis reveals, of course, is that while the gentlemen performed, ex-convicts who had made good in the colony dominated the boxes with their families. For many of them, moreover, 'making good' involved taking office under the government, becoming instruments to control and oppress their fellow convicts. A notorious example of this was the sinister figure of Edward Kimberley (or Kimberlay), the ruthless chief constable. Several of those whom I have described as farmer-settlers had, in the past, also held office as overseers or constables, and were part of the network, though not in the same dark mould as Kimberley.

The boxes, then, were occupied by an emancipist elite, the second tier in the island's hierarchy, with a few soldiers or ex-soldiers scattered among them. But it must be remembered that the private soldiers at the time were regarded as the dregs of society, not much better than convicts and nearly as badly treated.

The next question is whether these individuals came to the island already bearing marks of social and cultural superiority. Was their presence in the boxes a sign of cultural capital and social status acquired through education and breeding before their slide into felony? The criteria used earlier to analyse Sidaway's actors can again be brought into play – family background, their reputation among contemporaries (both rarely discoverable), their occupation prior to conviction, their level of literacy and their careers in the colony.

If the six farmer-settlers are analysed in these terms we find that every one was illiterate. In their earlier lives one was a farmer, two were seamen, one a leather-dresser, another a breeches-maker and one a blacksmith who had left that trade to spend ten years in a Guards regiment as a private, later becoming a London watchman.[61]

The six overseers and constables are a little harder to assess. Only two of them (Barry and Fisher) were illiterate and in neither case is their prior occupation known, though Fisher may have been a seaman since in his early years at Norfolk Island he was a member of the boat crew. The prior occupation of Joseph Symonds/Simmonds is also unknown, but he signed his name with a flourish. Of the other three, John Best had been a clerk while Robert Nash was also literate and the son of a well-to-do miller. Later, in Tasmania, he built and operated mills himself and owned a large and profitable wheat farm. He could well have ended his career as a gentleman. The last of these three overseers, Edward Kimberley, had been a farmer. He seems to have arrived in the colony illiterate and to have taught himself to read and write (or at least sign his name in a firm hand) while in New South Wales.[62] He and another constable were described as 'Infamous' and 'hardened old Villains, insensible to remorse, and callous to the stings of Conscience' and with two others as 'three hardened villains who from fear or promise of reward would swear a man's life away'.[63] The occasion, however, was an explosive incident in which Kimberley and other ex-convict constables were the principal witnesses against a gentleman official who had been charged with incest. The comments are heavily-coloured, since the first comes from the panic-stricken defendant and the second from an officer clearly driven by class interests. Neither comment would have been seen as plausible, however, had Kimberley shown any signs of gentility. An equally notorious overseer, Robert Buckey Jones (if his 'Recollections' are not a complete fabrication) remembered Kimberley as not only brutal, but as 'a bright and intelligent Irishman'.[64] Perhaps here we have an example of the autodidact who developed a taste for theatre.

Of the private soldier sitting alone in the boxes nothing whatever has survived beyond a laboured signature and the suggestion that he had trained as a cooper. He came and went without leaving a trace in the colony, dying on the passage back to England.[65]

Because of the high price of pit tickets it is not surprising to find that the patrons in that part of the house had much in common with those in the boxes. There is no clear social division between the two sections of the audience, though the pit contained one convict servant paying his own way and one convict gentleman, Matthew Sutton, an Irish attorney sent out for rebellion, and re-transported to Norfolk Island for his part in operating an illicit still.[66] The complete absence of soldiery among the ticket buyers for the pit is noteworthy, but perhaps this ticket agency was not convenient to the barracks. Thomas Self, the soldier sitting alone in the boxes, seems to have lived out-of-barracks in his own house.[67]

Obviously, this sort of analysis cannot tell the whole story. Those who had been farmers in England could have been anything from farmhands to well-to-do proprietors of what were virtually small estates. Similarly there were moderately wealthy blacksmiths, though one who gave up the trade to become a common soldier and then a watchman is unlikely to have been prospering. Among these sailors, blacksmiths, gardeners and the like who became convicts or soldiers, and then achieved a degree of status on Norfolk Island, may have been one or two from backgrounds that had provided some cultural capital before misfortune struck. These, however, are likely to be the exceptions. This second Norfolk Island theatre was largely the province of lesser mortals, often illiterate and low-skilled. If, in the exotic world of Norfolk Island, they had attained some status, it was still of a modest kind. The types of people who crowded the galleries of Drury Lane or the provincial Theatres Royal were here in the ascendant, as they were soon to become in the theatres of England.

Chapter 6

CONVICT THEATRE, 1807–1830

The history of convict theatre in New South Wales after the overthrow of Governor Bligh takes the form of a contrast between Sydney and the bush. For Sydney, up to 1833, that history is almost entirely one of isolated performances permitted under special circumstances by the governor, coupled with a steady refusal to countenance the establishment of anything resembling a permanent theatre. In 1832, when Barnett Levey finally broke through the barrier and obtained permission to open a regular playhouse, it was as a conventional commercial enterprise and convicts were excluded from the company. Thereafter there was little room in Sydney even for the occasional performance by convicts in an *ad hoc* performance space. Convict theatre was at an end in the capital.

Both governors Macquarie and Brisbane, if not Governor Darling, enjoyed play-going. This near-eclipse of convict theatre in Sydney, even before Levey delivered the *coup de grâce*, owed little to their personal preferences. Rather it reflected growing moral objections in powerful sections of the community, coupled with increasingly severe government policies on penal administration, particularly after the submission of the Bigge Report. To be sure it was only in such monstrous creations as the penal stations, mainly designed for secondary offenders, and in teams such as the road gangs, that the government was able to attempt policies of sustained dehumanisation; but the impulse to control was evident elsewhere. It can be seen in the erection of Macquarie's walled Hyde Park barracks: a half-hearted effort, since it could not contain all the convicts employed by the government around Sydney, and for those who were confined a system of leave passes existed. Under Governor Brisbane, however, a tightening of the ticket-of-leave system was begun, clearing parties were organised and Norfolk Island and Moreton Bay were established as penal stations, while under Darling a series of harsh new regulations for agricultural settlements and road gangs was instituted.

Although an increasingly efficient bureaucracy was working to implement these restrictive policies, progress was not uniform. Sydney and Parramatta may have been under some control, but in the outlying areas local conditions, distance from the centre and the quirks of local administrators could lead to wide variations in practice. So it was that the government establishments at Emu Plains in the 1820s, and Port Macquarie in the 1840s, became centres for an energetic convict theatre movement.

Once again the lack of evidence leaves it unclear whether similar activity was taking place in other convict out-stations. The composition of the convict workforce at Wellington Plains was such that it could have seen the occasional performance, but the problem here would have been that of assembling an audience rather than a company. Moreton Bay seems a less likely venue, given its reputation for brutality, but that does not close off the possibility entirely (see Appendix B, Note 1, footnote 3). Van Diemen's Land remains a mystery. The relatively open nature of this colony in its early years should have provided opportunities for some convict entertainment, but no evidence has been found. What does survive, from the late 1830s and 1840s, are tantalisingly brief references to theatrical or para-theatrical activities in the island's female factories, along with singing and dancing. Kay Daniels' summary of the evidence suggests these may have been brief improvised pieces, possibly in the form of mock trials (a long-established pastime in English prisons) or parodic skits on prison routine and authority figures. They warrant further investigation.[1]

Apart from government policy towards those convicts under its direct control, one other factor that restricted convict theatre was the increasing emphasis on the assignment of convicts to private masters, in order to reduce the costs of the system.[2] For the most part the full rigours of government control were restricted to a percentage of the newcomers and to recidivists. Assignment was obviously a lottery. There was a world of difference between falling into the hands of the amiable Captain Cox and those of the murderous Major Mudie. However, what is at issue here is not so much the nature of the control as the fact of dispersal. No doubt an increasing number of potential performers served their time on some isolated property, where nothing more than the occasional recitation was possible.

This chapter, then, commences as a study of the frustrations of convict theatre in Sydney and moves on to compare this with the relatively bustling theatrical life of Emu Plains. The following chapter touches briefly on convict theatre in Port Macquarie, but for the most part is concerned with a single event, Captain Maconochie's royal birthday celebration of 1840, which nicely focuses many of the concerns about convict theatre from the 1820s to the 1840s. The material in these two chapters is thus treated in a roughly chronological order, though its concern is not with any evolutionary process, but with examining an expanding range of ways in which convict theatre manifested itself.

II

The earliest surviving evidence of an attempt to launch a new theatrical enterprise after the disappearance of Sidaway's theatre and the Norfolk Island playhouse has already been mentioned. This is the petition from Daniel Parnell to Secretary Campbell, and through him to Governor Macquarie.[3] The letter is undated, but was found in a bundle of papers from 1810 and appears to relate to a period shortly after Macquarie's arrival on 28 December 1809. The petition is for permission to stage two or three charity performances to relieve the 'pecuniary difficulties' under which Parnell was labouring, as a result of 'successive misfortunes'. But what the petition reveals, almost in passing, is that 'Gov'r Bligh had given his permission for the erection of a permanent and spacious theatre for the performance of regular drama, and which, but for the circumstance of the change in the Government, had long since been carried into effect'. In other words, within a few years of the closure of Sidaway's playhouse, actors and entrepreneurs were pressing for a resumption of theatre. Clearly, they had confidence in the viability of the enterprise, and whatever had led to the closure of the earlier theatre was not of sufficient seriousness for Bligh to reject their application. Even if the earlier theatre had been shut down in late 1804, rather than in 1807, it would have seemed more like an effort to resume activities rather than a completely new venture, though there would have been changes in personnel. Radley and Vasconcellis had been dead for some years and Sparrow had recently returned to England. Sidaway was still in the colony, but he was a sick man and was shortly to die.

Parnell may have been involved in this project for a new theatre, but his petition of 1810 is concerned only with a few isolated performances to help pay his debts. Permission for these had been granted by Lieutenant-Governor Paterson during his period in office (10 January–27 December 1809) and an advertisement in the *Sydney Gazette*, 3 December 1809, may well indicate that preparations were under way:

> BOOKS – Any person who may have borrowed of a Gentleman a Volume of *Sharpe's British Theatre*, containing among other Pieces the Musical Entertainment of *Incle and Yaricho*, is requested to leave it at the Gazette Office.

Plays, of course, were standard reading matter and the advertisement may have nothing to do with Parnell; but George Colman the Younger's *Inkle and Yarico* was a popular theatre piece and could well have suited his purposes.

The impression left by Parnell's petition is that while he had secured Paterson's permission he had not had the opportunity to put his plan into execution and so was forced to re-apply to the new governor. Whether or not Macquarie granted permission or, if he did, whether Parnell was able to realise his productions is not recorded. Certainly, his financial problems were not solved, for in a list of outstanding debts to the crown is one for £12 8s. 5d., incurred by Parnell under Governor King, against which is the terse annotation, 'run' (that is, absconded). The list itself dates from the time of the Bigge inquiry.[4]

The most serious gap in our knowledge of early theatre in New South Wales, however, concerns the playhouse that operated on the outskirts of the town for an undetermined period during Macquarie's time. The best-known reference to this is a single sentence in Maclehose's *Picture of Sydney ... for 1839* that mistakenly represents it as Sydney's first regular theatre: 'The venerable Macquarie honoured "the heroes of an hour" with his presence, in a small loft, on the Brickfield-hill, now crumbled with its former owners into dust.'[5] Many years later Obed West provided additional information. Describing the western side of George Street, between Bathurst and Liverpool Streets, he wrote in his memoirs:

> Starting from Bathurst Street was another manufactory, though a small one – that of clay pipes by a Mr. Clewitt. Next to this and running about halfway to Liverpool Street was one block in which stood a small cottage surrounded by a fine fruit garden, and a painter's named Noble. At the back of his place was a large bakehouse and granary which served two purposes, being used both in connection with baking and as a theatre. Many were the blood and thunder tragedies enacted there with the price of admission only a dump cut from a 'holey dollar'. Just beyond this was Mr. Bowman's large wheelwright's establishment and on the corner, a blacksmith named Wilkinson.[6]

A Surveyor-General's Field Book of 1815 describes Noble's allotment as extending the full depth of the block, from George to Kent streets, so that access to the theatre could have been from the latter.[7] With some appropriateness this part of George Street is now the heartland of those successors of the nineteenth-century gaffs, the film theatres. Planted squarely over the site of Noble's holding are the Hoyts and Greater Union cinema complexes.

Noble had been a successful painter and glazier in London before his arrival in the colony as a convict in December 1808. He married fellow-convict Elizabeth Thompson in September 1809 and died in 1826.[8] Neither he nor his wife had any prior record of involvement with theatre and, while that is true of all the early performers in New South Wales, it is probable that Noble was nothing more than a proprietor, who had leased out his granary to the players. These remain unknown. Mrs Radley, Sarah McCann and a few of the other old hands from Sidaway's theatre were still in the town and in 1818 Daniel Parnell had reappeared under an alias, Charles Manning. It would be pleasing to think that one or two of them returned to the boards, but there is nothing to prove that convicts or ex-convicts of any kind were involved in this enterprise. Though highly unlikely, it remains a possibility that the company was run, and largely staffed, by free settlers. If the *Sydney Gazette* story about the production of *Romeo and Juliet* is not a fabrication, and relates to Noble's theatre, and not Sidaway's, that is as close as we are likely to get to this suburban playhouse. In its own time it was completely overshadowed by the proliferation of dance halls, which seem to have been the chief entertainment for the lower orders.[9]

Considering Governor Macquarie's ambitions for his colony, and his relative benevolence to convicts and emancipists, it is not surprising that he showed some support for theatre in New South Wales. This support extended beyond the Brickfield Hill theatre, though we have indisputable evidence in only one other case. In 1820 the King's birthday was celebrated on 5 July rather than the customary 4 July, which in that year was a Sunday. The event was recorded in the diary of the austere George Allen, who described not only the official celebrations but some less pleasing:

> A holiday was given to the prisoners on the occasion. This day a play was performed by some prisoners at Blaxland's Salt pans at Cockle Bay. This is the 3rd play that has been performed there this year, viz: – on Easter Monday, on Whit Monday and today. There are no respectable persons engaged in it, neither were there many – if any – there. (I was not present but know it to be a fact.)[10]

The *Sydney Gazette* dutifully recorded the official celebrations in detail but, following what seems to have been its policy, made no reference to the performance. Evidently, permission had been granted for presentations on festival days. Whether that permission was granted for festivals subsequent to the King's birthday is unknown. Cockle Bay (now Darling Harbour) was, like Brickfield Hill, on the margins of Sydney and there can have been little scope for adapting a saltworks to make anything but the crudest of occasional theatres.

The early efforts of Parnell and the work of the Brickfield Hill and saltworks playhouses are the full extent of our knowledge of theatrical life in Sydney under Macquarie. The record is as meagre as it was to be in the subsequent reigns of Brisbane and Darling, and it may justify the assumption that a full-scale theatrical blight had descended upon the city by 1810. The significant difference between the Macquarie era and the periods of Brisbane and Darling is that mysterious Brickfield Hill theatre. This would need to have run for at least a year or two to justify the terms in which it is described, and by its very nature as an ongoing theatrical enterprise it points to a more supportive attitude on Macquarie's part than either of his successors revealed.

That still leaves a puzzle. If Macquarie had patronised these performances, why was the Brickfield Hill playhouse not a building to match Sidaway's theatre or the playhouse that Bligh had promised in 1807? Why was it the humble suburban loft theatre it seems to have been? Sydney had grown significantly under Macquarie and it is difficult to believe that a theatre on a more ambitious scale than the Brickfield Hill gaff would not have been economically sustainable. The *Australian Dictionary of Biography* bears witness to Macquarie's fondness for theatre and there are some entertaining vignettes of the newly-appointed Judge-Advocate, Ellis Bent, reading plays to the dour governor and his wife *en route* to New South Wales.[11] More interesting is the reference to Mrs Macquarie's support for Henry McKeen's projects in the petition shortly to be discussed. In view of this evidence, the slightness of Macquarie's contribution to the performing arts calls for explanation.

The moral conservatism that was so potent a force in the late 1820 was already emerging and could have been a check on Macquarie's instincts. Throughout Macquarie's reign the Rev. William Cowper, an intense evangelical, headed the Anglican establishment. It was he who persuaded Macquarie to forbid Sunday performances by the military bands[12] and he and his kind could have applied similar pressure against theatres. Another possible source of constraint was Macquarie's own concern for law and order. The notorious dullness of Sydney life in this period owed at least something to the persistence of the 9 o'clock curfew. Even under Macquarie, implementation of this was well short of perfect, but, while small-scale violations in the dance halls of the Rocks or a theatre in suburban Brickfields might have been overlooked, a significant theatre in the town was likely to have been too great a risk.

Governor Macquarie handed over authority to his successor, Governor Brisbane, on 1 December 1821. Within six or seven weeks new moves were under way to secure permission for the opening of a theatre. The earliest evidence is a memorial, or petition, by 'Henry MacKeen and other Prisoners of ~ Crown out of yᵉ Barracks', addressed to 'D'arcy Wentworth Esq. And the Respectable magistrates of the Town of Sydney' and dated 22 January 1822:

> That Memorialists begs leave to acquaint your Worships their intention of Amusing the respectable part of the Inhabitants of Sydney and its Vicinity – in their small Theatre No 44 Castlereagh Street provided it meets the approbation of your Worships having recently obtained a considerable part of our dresses and Scenery from the Amiable Lady Macquarie …
>
> Memorialist therefore most humbly prays your Worships to take our case into your Kind consideration and Grant us permission to perform on Friday evening the 15th instant for which mark of Kindness Memorialists as in duty bound will ever Pray.
>
> Henry McKeen
& others[13]

The names of the other petitioners are unfortunately not included. The reverse side of the page has a set of signatures which are evidently the endorsements of respectable citizens supporting the memorial, including John Piper, many officers of the regiment in garrison and, among the others, a Robert Brown.

The immediately striking feature of the document is the statement that Mrs Macquarie had provided costumes and settings. The ex-governor and his wife were still in the colony, preparing for their departure on the *Surry* on 12 February. Perhaps they had engaged in Government House private theatricals and were disposing of the remnants. This would suggest that they knew McKeen as a performer or theatrical entrepreneur. Had he been associated with the Brickfield Hill theatre, or with occasional productions around the town?

Number 44, Castlereagh Street, the site of this 'small theatre', had been home to a succession of schools, run by Mrs Jones, Mr Vale, Mrs Speed and Mr Nott, the last of these vacating the premises in August 1821. Having been a school suggests that it had one or two rooms somewhat larger than usual – though the competition for students in Sydney was so strong even the bustling Mr Nott, complete with assistant, might have attracted only small numbers. The property was offered for sale on 18 January 1822, but whether the sale went through, or any tenant was threatened with eviction, is not noted.[14]

The Memorial of 22 January is not an isolated document. On 9 March 1822

'Henry McKean, William Tyson and others' submitted a petition to the new governor, Sir Thomas Brisbane which

> Respectfully Sheweth
>
> That Petitioners incouraged by Several Gentlemen and respectable inhabitants of Sydney have been at considerable expence for the performance of a Play. Some of them having been accustomed to the Stage and are flattered they would be able to keepe good Order and render their performance respectable and amusing to the public.
>
> That as such entertainments have been occasionally permitted they have been induced to contract some debts in the preparation in confidence that they would be enabled to exonerate themselves by their performance and they most humbly pray that your Excellency will in consideration of the annexed reputable recommendation be graciously pleased to grant your permission for them to perform on such day or days as your Excellency may deem Meet.[15]

The 'annexed reputable recommendation' was signed by some thirty citizens, including Michael Robinson and Joseph Underwood. They expressed their confidence that good order would be kept. A further note records that a petition on the same matter had been presented to the colonial secretary, signed by Captain Piper and twelve officers of the 48th Regiment.

One other related document survives. It is not dated but has been filed with documents of 1822, and evidently represents a further development. This is another petition addressed to Governor Brisbane, this time by Isaac Saunders and Robert Brown:

> Most Respectfully Sheweth, That your Excellency's Petitioners have at a considerable expence fitted up a Large Building, on the Brickfield hill Sydney, as a Theatre, for the Representation of Dramatic Pieces.
>
> That Petitioners have been solicited by many respectable Inhabitants of the Town of Sydney, and its Vicinity to undertake a concern of the kind, they considering that an establishment of this description, would meet with the encouragement of the Public at large.
>
> That Petitioners with the exception of 2 Only are Free Subjects, and the greater part of them have been bred to the Stage, in London and other parts of England.
>
> That Petitioners are determined (should they meet the sanction of your Excellency) to Perform no Piece of an Evil or Immoral tendency on any account whatever, and that good order shall be observed respecting Time and all other Matters.[16]

Appended to the petition as a postscript, and as a further sweetener, is the note:

> And Petitioners humbly beg leave to acquaint your Excellency that they are most willing to appropriate the proceeds of one Nights performance in a Quarter for the benefit of any Institution to which your Excellency may think proper to apply it.

A further note is yet another recommendation from John Piper that the petition be favoured.

At first sight this document appears to have no connection with the earlier ones, but to be the project of a different set of entrepreneurs eager to start their own playhouse. That would be powerful testimony to the strength of the theatrical urge in Sydney. However, the Constables' Notebooks for the 1822 muster, drawn up in the second half of that year, reveal that Robert Brown, Isaac Saunders and Henry McKeean [*sic*] were by then living in the same house in George Street. Brown's position as the first to be listed indicates he was the owner or tenant of the building, and the Assignment Registers reveal that McKeen was his assigned convict servant from 15 March until 19 July 1822, when he received his certificate of freedom. The muster, subsequent to that date, recorded him as Brown's lodger. Saunders was presumably also a lodger.[17] As for Robert Brown, he is probably the man of that name whose signature is lurking in the first document as one of the worthy citizens and officers supporting McKeen's original petition.

The three documents together do not tell the full story, but it is possible to make some inferences. The initial memorandum begins as if applying for a licence to operate a regular theatre. By the end it has become a request to present a single performance. Is the tone of the opening misleading, or was there a hidden agenda? The petition that follows is dated some three weeks after the performance proposed in the first. The wording is obscure, but it appears that a response to the first petition had not come through in time and the performers were renewing their petition, in some panic because of financial commitments already entered into. Whatever the situation, the petitioners took the opportunity of raising the bid by proposing performances on 'such day *or days* as your Excellency may deem Meet [my italics]'.

Neither of the first two documents has any official annotation upon it, but one or both of the requests must have been successful for the company to have submitted a third. Here at last we have a proposal for a licensed regular theatre (see Fig. 13). Perhaps the strategy had been to start with requests for single performances before trying for the main objective. But if this was the scheme, it failed. Written across the reverse side of the final petition over the initials of Frederick Goulburn, the colonial secretary, is the terse note 'Cannot be Granted'. Thereafter McKeen, Brown, Saunders and Tyson seem to have abandoned their plans for a theatre, though McKeen was later to realise his aspirations as a performer in less happy circumstances, as a prisoner at Emu Plains. Tyson may have had a similar pleasure.

Some shifting emphases between the documents are worthy of note. The participants in the January memorial are unequivocally described as 'Prisoners of ∼ Crown out of ye Barracks'. This meant they fell into the categories of trustworthy or married convicts allowed to live in their own accommodation.[18] But by the time of the third document all but two of the petitioners are described as 'Free Subjects'. The term applied both to those who had arrived as free settlers and those who had served their term or had been granted a conditional or absolute pardon. While one or two in the group at the time of the first petition could have obtained their freedom

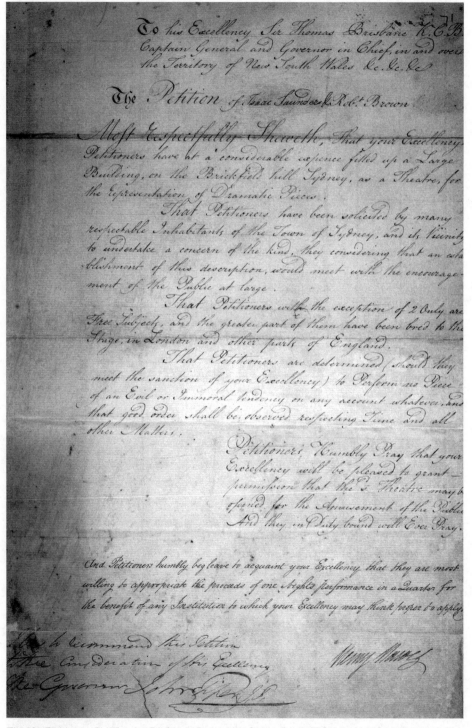

Fig. 13 Petition to Sir Thomas Brisbane, Governor of New South Wales, seeking permission to open
a regular licensed theatre, [1822?] (SRNSW, 4/1759, p.71).

at some time during 1822 (McKeen certainly did), the shift in phraseology suggests there may have been some winnowing of serving convicts from the group.

Of the four men whose names appear on this succession of documents Robert Brown was 25 at the time he earned himself a life sentence. He had arrived in 1797 and obtained a conditional pardon on 4 June 1802. Around 1822 he was running his own brick-making business and he may be the same Robert Brown recorded in the *Sydney Gazette*, 1 April 1815, as securing a publican's licence. Isaac Saunders, a fellow lifer, was described as a servant at the time of his conviction in 1814. In September 1821 the government was employing him as a boatman, but by the time of the September 1822 muster he had secured his ticket-of-leave and was listed as a dealer in Sydney. McKeen had arrived in the colony in 1818, appearing in the indent of the *Lady Castlereagh* as Henry Mackay. He had been sentenced to seven years at the Surrey Quarter Sessions on 17 July 1815. At the time of the two dated theatre petitions he was still in government service, employed as a tailor (a trade with which he is frequently identified in later documents) and could already have been living in Brown's house. William Tyson, the fourth of the group, had been sentenced in 1817 at the Old Bailey to seven years for shoplifting and like McKeen was still serving his sentence at the time of the 1822 theatre negotiations. The ship's indent for the *Almorah* describes him as a servant, a native of St Kitts in the West Indies, and a half-caste. By 1822 he had been a watchman at Hyde Park Barracks for about three years. Fragmentary records of 1820–21 show that his behaviour was not impeccable, but in an undated petition ascribed to 1822, fluently written and signed as William Nathaniel Tyson, he made a bid for a ticket-of-leave or a conditional pardon. His grounds were two-fold: good conduct and his success 'in apprehending absentees from the Derwent for which reason he is despised by his fellow prisoners and therefore he cannot enjoy that peace of mind among them which every individual wishes to obtain'. By the time of the September 1822 muster, however, he had been reduced to membership of a Sydney road gang, which would have meant a return to barracks and working in irons.[19] Earlier, as a Barracks watchman, he had probably enjoyed much greater freedom than the other prisoners and might have been allowed to live in the community.

As was noted, the final petition claimed that only two of those involved in the project at that stage were convicts. One of the two memorialists named in the document, Saunders, falls into this category. If McKeen and Tyson were still involved and the petition predates McKeen's certificate of freedom, it would have brought the number of serving convicts to three. Were the petitioners being less than honest?

There remains the assertion that the performers had a prior association with theatre. The subject is not raised in the memorial of 22 January, but the petition of 9 March refers to 'some of them having been accustomed to the Stage'; and in the final petition the claim is made that 'the greater part of them have been bred to the Stage, in London and other parts of England'. This may have been stretching the truth, or it may be evidence of professional strengthening of the troupe. As was the case with earlier companies, there is no evidence that Brown, McKeen or Tyson had ever been associated with the theatre. It is noteworthy that Brown had been in the colony for most of the life of Sidaway's company but had no recorded part in its activities. Moreover, McKeen was only 17 and Tyson 18 at the time of their conviction, which makes much in the way of professional theatre experience unlikely before their transportation.

In the case of Saunders there are tantalising hints at a possible connection with theatre, or at least an indication of where his theatrical talents, or aspirations, lay. On a list of those sailing for Port Macquarie on 26 November 1823 he appeared as serving a three-year colonial sentence and was listed, not as a servant or dealer, but as a dancing master. By July 1829, when sent to the *Phoenix* hulk to serve a further 12-month sentence for theft, he was being described as a music master.[20] Since he was only 17 at the time of his London conviction, the claims seem grandiose, but they could point to some activity as a singing, dancing juvenile.

Sir Thomas Brisbane survived as governor until November 1825, and was succeeded by Sir Ralph Darling, who landed on 17 December of that year. Under Darling sporadic performances probably continued but only one has been recorded, a production in the Sydney gaol within a year of the new governor's arrival:

> The next theatrical attempt, of which we have heard, took place in no less singular a theatre than Sydney Gaol, among 'confines to hard labour', &c. This occurred in 1826 … and one of the pieces produced on that occasion, was *Bombastes Furioso*. The scene was in the debtors' room, and the guard-bed of many an insolvent was converted into the stage. Persons of respectability in the town visited the Gaol, and witnessed the rude performance through the iron gratings of the window; their astonishment, no doubt, being excited at the cultivation of the *drama* being pursued in such a place, and by such persons.[21]

Commissioner Bigge described the debtors' wing of Sydney gaol as a building 'containing two rooms, one of which is twenty-eight feet by twelve, and divided into two bed rooms, and the other is twenty-eight by seventeen'.[22] The building did not change significantly over the succeeding five or six years so that it is probably the 28-by 17-foot room that was adapted as a theatre. Bigge was critical of the gaol's poor repair and by 1825 its condition had become a matter of attention for the press. The Grand Inquest of 9 February 1826, as reported in the *Sydney Gazette* of 15 February, spelled out the special problems of the debtors' wing:

> From the want of proper ventillation, and common sewers in the establishment, it is almost impossible to prevent the bad effects arising from the want of pure air in a place so generally crowded. The apartments allotted for the reception of the unfortunate debtors, are exceedingly damp and unhealthy, arising from the situation being against the back of the gaol, and under the influence of the water oozing out from the hill side against which they are placed in such quantities, as oblige them frequently to carry it out in vessels from a hole into which

> it runs open to these apartments; and, from their continued intercourse
> in the same yard with the common felons, their morals are exposed to
> contamination.

Repairs to the debtors' prison were undertaken in early 1827, but were presumably among those described in the *Sydney Gazette,* 20 July 1827, as 'trifling'.

The most curious feature of the whole business is that in June 1826, four months after the description of the debtors' wing as 'so generally crowded', there were only fifteen debtors in the entire gaol,[23] a figure much in line with those that have survived for 1825. Since the families and friends of debtors had free access to the gaol, it was probably they who created the sense of crowding; though some of the space might have been appropriated by the gaolers for money-making enterprises, as was alleged in the *Monitor,* 15 December 1826.

In considering the group who organised the performance, four possibilities suggest themselves. One is that the fifteen or so debtors clubbed together to put on a show and divided the proceeds among them. The second is that a few debtors combined with convicted prisoners to stage the plays. And a third is that the debtors' space was borrowed by some of the 250 convicts and remand prisoners to stage a performance of their own.[24] There remains a fourth possibility: that the production was organised by one debtor for his own benefit and that he drew on his friends and family to make up the cast.

The appeal of this fourth solution is that for part of 1826 the debtors' gaol contained the ideal person to conceive such a scheme. Laurence Hynes Halloran (or O'Halloran) was the colony's finest teacher. He was also a forger and claimed both a doctorate of divinity and Anglican orders to which he was almost certainly not entitled. Halloran had been sent out for seven years in 1819, immediately given a ticket-of-leave because of his abilities, and was only recently free of his original sentence. A minor poet, known to William Hazlitt and other Romantics, he was also violently abusive, litigious, financially improvident and said to be scandalous in his private behaviour. In May 1826 he had won a vigorously-contested libel suit against the editor E.S. Hall, who had published a blistering letter outlining some of his personal deficiencies, but he had received derisory damages of only one shilling and was left to pay the costs of the case. Even before this outcome he was in serious financial difficulties and during 1826 his long-maturing plans to establish the Sydney Grammar School, with himself as headmaster, had fallen apart after he alienated most of the trustees. In October they had resolved to suspend the school's activities from the end of term, depriving him of a major part of his income.[25] By November he was in the debtors' prison and in such desperate straits that he was forced to undergo the humiliation of making public appeals for charity through the pages of those newspapers whose editors had hitherto been outspoken about his failings or suffered his invective. In an advertisement which appeared in the *Australian* of 25 November 1826, as well as in other issues of that paper and in the *Sydney Gazette* and the *Monitor,* he declared that his family was now reduced to a state of absolute destitution by his protracted imprisonment for debt. The sense of his own worth would have prevented him making such an appeal, but 'when the *father* looks round on his numerous young family, those feelings, strong as they are, yield to the resistless impulse of "paternal affection"'.

A man prepared to face this degree of humiliation might well attempt other stratagems. Professional and amateur theatre companies in England occasionally staged charity benefits for imprisoned debtors, and it would not have been beyond so fertile a projector as Halloran to have taken the idea a step further and have staged his own benefit in gaol. His 'numerous young family' would have been an asset here. W.B. Rhodes' burlesque tragedy *Bombastes Furioso*, which was presumably the evening's afterpiece, lent itself to child performers. At this time Halloran had nine children in the colony, so that the family on its own was sufficient to form a small company. The eldest of these, the adult Laurence Henry Halloran, certainly attended his father in the gaol, since the *Sydney Gazette* of 6 January 1827 reported that he was taken to law by an underkeeper for his abusive language while within the prison precinct. Most of the others were minors, and the youngest an infant.

Halloran, moreover, had useful prior experience for an enterprise of this kind. He had written a patriotic naval play and had been a naval chaplain on board HMS *Britannia*, one of Nelson's warships on which amateur theatricals were a mania among both sailors and officers. His son, Laurence Boutcher O'Halloran, a marine lieutenant, had also been on board the vessel, and a performer on one occasion, speaking a prologue that was probably written by Halloran himself.[26] There is no conclusive proof here that the Halloran family was behind the performance in the debtors' prison, but it remains an attractive possibility. Even though Halloran had alienated many of Sydney's rich and famous, he still had connections in the upper echelons of colonial society, including that unlikely pair, John Macarthur, the leading exclusionist, and Simeon Lord, one of the richest emancipists in the town. He would certainly have been in a position to attract those 'persons of respectability' who, we are told, attended the performance.

III

Whatever the special arrangements in the gaol, by 1826 the prospects for convict-based theatre in Sydney were receding. The pressure was growing for a conventional playhouse appropriate to a small and flourishing city. The movement was reflected in a string of newspaper articles and letters on the morality, or otherwise, of theatre and its appropriateness, or otherwise, in a penal colony. The debate took on an added intensity as the merchant Barnett Levey commenced his campaign to open such a theatre in Sydney, a campaign in which he employed cajolery, self-promotion, bravado, harnessing public opinion and testing the limits of the law. Whether hostile or well disposed, the papers avidly reported his doings.[27]

Apart from general debates on the desirability of theatre, and specific reports on Levey's doings, there was a third strand to the newspapers' coverage. From 1825 they began to report the activities of a convict theatre at Emu Plains, some 36 miles west of the city. While the accounts of this theatre often appear as innocent reportage, they may also be seen as part of the campaign for a new Sydney theatre. On several occasions the link is made explicit, as in the *Sydney Gazette*, 21 July 1825:

> It must be rather mortifying, I should think, to the lovers of the drama, in this metropolis, where is to be found the concentration of our colonial respectability and gaiety, that in this species of fashionable entertainment, the amateurs of Emu Plains have taken the lead of them.

Similarly the *Australian*, 26 May 1825, had noted:

> It appears that there is a greater variety of pleasure and entertainment in the Bush than the Sydney residents dream of. The good people at Emu Plains contrive to amuse themselves in a way that deserves at least imitation, if it does not show that they leave us of the Town far behind in the powers of invention and in the art of pleasing.

It is in this context that Emu Plains becomes the only convict theatre to be given significant treatment in the Australian press, with the exception of Maconochie's disastrous experiment on Norfolk Island in 1840. Apart from this newspaper coverage, Emu Plains also has the advantage of being described at length in the novel, *Ralph Rashleigh*, written by James Tucker, a convict posted to the settlement in 1827 who seems to have been a player. A work of fiction, of course, is a source that needs to be used with even greater care than a newspaper. On the other hand, the Emu Plains sequence seems much closer to documentary than other parts of the novel, and so must constitute valuable, if shaky, evidence.[28]

IV

Emu Plains was a small pocket of land caught between a bend in the Nepean River and the foothills of the Blue Mountains (see endpapers). Its 2,000 or so acres of alluvial soil were accounted among the richest in the colony. For some years the plains were used for grazing the government's herds of cattle, but late in 1819, in the effort to find employment for the 'Vast Number of Male Convicts' who had arrived in the previous two years, Macquarie converted the area into an agricultural station (see Fig. 14). Initially he showed no great enthusiasm for this solution, since he had little faith in government farms, but within a year and a half he was reporting that the establishment 'exceeds even beyond my most sanguine hopes'. A year after that, in his final report to Lord Bathurst, he was urging that the area should never be alienated from the crown, because it was 'so extremely fertile, and so peculiarly well situated for a Government Agricultural Establishment'.[29]

In pursuance of the new policy approximately 140 convicts had been removed

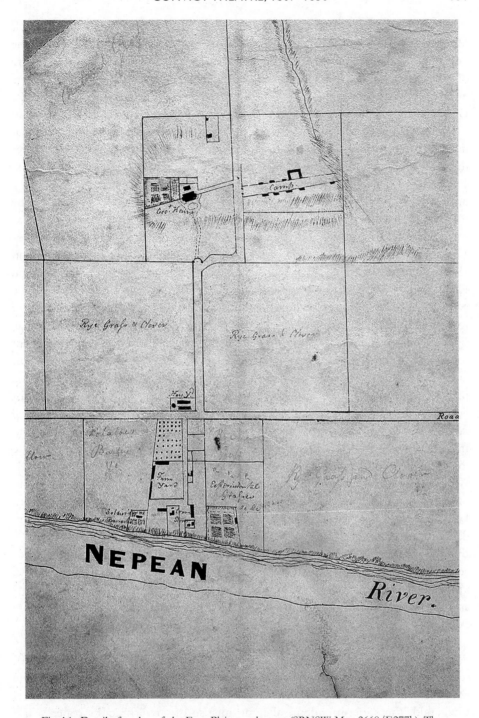

Fig. 14 Detail of a plan of the Emu Plains settlement (SRNSW, Map 2660/E277b). The superintendent's house and the convict camp stand on a low rise in the centre of the plain, now the site of an Anglican church and graveyard. The military (later, police) barracks are among the buildings beside the river.

to the settlement by the end of 1819, the number rising to 300 by November 1821. Macquarie's successor, Governor Brisbane, 'with an entire conviction of the importance of Agricultural establishments', enlarged the settlement to a peak figure of 500; but, under directions from Lord Bathurst to reduce the number of convicts in direct government employ, he had cut the figure back to 200 by March 1825. During 1828 the numbers averaged only 82 and in 1829 the average had declined to 61, figures that may have included a dozen men at the Mulgoa outstation.[30] By that time the pressure was building to close the agricultural establishments and to transfer their valuable land into private hands. Wellington Valley was shut down in late 1830 and Bathurst and Port Macquarie reduced to a few acres. Emu Plains held on for a little longer because of its value to the government, but in 1831 it was finally disestablished, leaving only a refurbished stockade to house convict road-workers.

Emu Plains' distance from Sydney was no doubt regarded as one of its virtues as a prison farm. This was certainly a consideration with Bathurst and Wellington Valley. Moreover, the authorities made some attempts to impose a cordon on Emu Plains, initially by regulating to prevent private settlement on the west bank of the Nepean River, where the agricultural station lay, and then by threatening punishment for anyone attempting to fraternise with the convicts. Such measures were ineffectual, since the only road across the Blue Mountains cut through the property and settlement had already reached the eastern bank of the river. Directly opposite the government farm was the estate of Sir John Jamison, the 'knight of Regentville', with his horde of house servants and farm labourers, mainly convicts, and his 40 or more tenant farmers, chiefly emancipists and ticket-of-leave men.[31] The same mixture of small farmers and large estate holders, such as the McHenrys and Coxes, spread downstream from Regentville, and only a few miles from the convict huts of Emu Plains was the township of Penrith, the local administrative centre. Writing of the area in 1831, William Edward Riley spoke of the fine view of the region from Jamison's house and of the numerous settlers' farms that were visible. However, the longer prospect from Lapstone Hill, which towered over Emu Plains, revealed that it was a ribbon development along the river, with the 'continuous mass of thick, lofty forest' beyond.[32] By 1826 any thought of keeping the west bank of the Nepean free of settlement was compromised when Chief Justice Forbes was granted a small estate, Edenglassie, immediately upstream of Emu Plains, as a country retreat. By then a few inns and labourers' cottages had probably appeared on the downstream side, opposite Penrith.

Of all Emu Plains' neighbours the most significant was Sir John, who took a deep interest in the government station, in part springing from his early dreams of securing the property for himself. At times this brought him into acrimonious dispute with the central authorities. In the early 1820s he made bitter attacks on Robert Fitzgerald, the superintendent, alleging misuse of government property and misappropriation of the farm produce. Since Fitzgerald was a trusted supporter of Governor Macquarie, and retained the confidence of Governor Brisbane, the attack was counterproductive. But in 1824 he was involved in an even more explosive affair, contributing to the claims that a group of female convicts transferred from Parramatta to Emu Plains were there to act as prostitutes to the prisoners. A committee of inquiry undertook a classic whitewash of the governor and the colonial secretary, and Jamison was made *persona non grata* and denied any government office. The women, however, were removed and the incident played its part in the recalling of Brisbane and the colonial secretary. Although banned from any government appointment, Jamison was able to maintain a significant presence at Emu Plains. He lived a lavish and ostentatious life, taking enormous pleasure in extending his hospitality to any passing gentleman and equally enjoying the role of patron to the less fortunate.

There is no direct evidence for the date at which performances first began at Emu Plains, but a series of clues (set out in Appendix B, Note 9) suggests that the theatre was in existence by mid-1822 or the beginning of 1823, an earlier date than is normally supposed. This is a little more than two years after the agricultural station had been established, which says a great deal for the energy and the enterprise of those involved, particularly since the evidence for this early date points, not to an isolated performance, but to a series of productions. One convict apparently involved in Emu Plains theatricals at this early date was James Lawrence, who claimed to have been a professional actor in England and North America. If this was so, he is the first identifiable professional to have appeared on the boards in Australia. Jemmy King, who was to be a mainstay of the Emu Plains theatre for several years, had arrived at the settlement on 3 October 1820 and William Tyson, who was associated with the 1822 theatre petitions, was there from an unspecified date in late 1822 or in 1823. On 3 October 1823 he was punished for absconding from the Plains and on 8 November was assigned to private service. He too could have been involved in the early work of the company.[33]

It was not until mid-1825 that the theatre began to attract the attention of the newspapers – that is, at the time when the demand for a theatre in Sydney was becoming an issue. These reports give the impression of a theatre already well-established, though one of them, *Howe's Weekly Commercial Express*, 25 July 1825, suggests that the company had only recently begun to attract a fashionable audience:

EMU THEATRE
[FROM A CORRESPONDENT.]

This is one of those novelties of recent importation. By the perseverance and industry of a few forlorn heroes of the *sock* and *buskin*, this place of entertainment has become rather attractive of late. The scenery, dresses, and decorations are becomingly appropriate, and ... considerable additions have been made to the scenic embellishments, and a tolerable fit-up of pit and boxes for the accommodation of a respectable audience has been recently effected.

The reports of 1825 deal with two productions, on Monday 16 May and Monday 18 July, the latter of which attracted the above comments.[34] At some time between 18 September 1823 and 14 July 1826 Henry McKeen found himself a prisoner at Emu Plains for an unrecorded colonial crime. The information comes from a report of the sessions at Windsor on the latter date, as printed in the *Sydney Gazette*, 22 July 1826:

> Henry M'Keen, late of the company of comedians at Emu Plains, appeared in a different character to either Harlequin or Jeremy Diddler; he was suspected to have appropriated a certain garment to his own use, but he adduced such satisfactory evidence to the Court, that an accident had caused the apparent impropriety, that the prosecution was withdrawn, and he withdrew also – all parties satisfied.

McKeen's imprisonment was probably a brief one, but without knowing the date and duration of the sentence the information is of little use in pinpointing periods during which productions took place.[35]

Thanks to the efforts of Marc Serge Rivière, an eyewitness account of a further performance, on Saturday 13 August 1825, has recently become available. The author is Captain Hyacinthe de Bougainville, who was in charge of a French expedition which put into Port Jackson in 1825. As was customary, he and his officers found time to visit outlying areas in pursuit of specimens and to gauge the development of the colony. In this way he became a recipient of the somewhat smothering hospitality of Sir John Jamison and, on 7 August 1825, was introduced to Emu Plains:

> Went with Sir John to visit the government agricultural establishments at Emu Plains. The director is Mr Kinghorn, a civil engineer. There are 200 convicts in the surrounding districts. We then made for the attractive residence of Mr Kinghorn; the convicts lined up in front of the door and a clerk read prayers aloud for quarter of an hour. The convicts listened bare-headed and with the most decorous attitude; they were quite well-dressed, seemed to be in good health but I did not see a single face that was remotely distinguished. We then visited their shacks, the bakery, a tobacco factory and the hospital. The hut in which it was housed, was quite small and only contained three men; this climate is quite healthy ... Mr Kinghorn then gave us a guided tour of a theatre recently built by the convicts; the theatre of Bobèche [the tiny Spectacle des Pygmées in Paris, run by the clown Mardelard, known as Bobèche] would seem like the Paris Opera compared to this one.

This visit was followed, on 10 August, by the arrival of

> a fine poster written in French and advertising a show. It was in effect an invitation from Mr Kinghorn, asking me to name a day for a gala performance in the theatre of Emu Plains. I asked Mr Ducamper to reply in English, which he can write correctly, and I chose next Saturday, when we ought to be back from our expedition.

Accordingly, at 6.30 pm on Saturday 13,

> we took our seats in the theatre of Emu Plains. We were alone in the one and only box in the front row of the stalls. Five soldiers (who with

a sentinel made up the entire garrison) and two ladies made up the audience. The prologue in verse was recited by a small man with a ghastly face and who, I think, was the director of the company. The play was called *The Lying Valet* [by David Garrick] and two convicts, dressed as women, made us laugh until we cried. The protagonist was not entirely lacking in talent. We also saw [Henry Fielding's] *The Village Doctor*, based on the *Médecin malgré lui* [by Molière], in which an English dance was performed to a tune played at a frenetic pace and with great gusto on a violin which formed the entire orchestra. The violinist was a one-eyed man (who had made his own violin in two days). The last play on the bill was *Bombasto Furioso* [*sic*], a gibberish farce that was completely baffling. At 9 o'clock after the performance, we returned to the house, but not before calling on the two daughters of Mr Kinghorn who are very pretty and must be fed up to the teeth with Emu Plains.[36]

The image of this command performance before an audience that may have been outnumbered by the cast is faintly disagreeable, giving an impression of the performers as trained monkeys going through their routines to satisfy the social aspirations of their superintendent. It is not clear whether the spectators were laughing at or with the two prisoners dressed as women, but it was probably the former as much as the latter.

The next reference to the theatre comes from the *Australian*, 30 March 1826, which briefly announced that 'the amateur performers at the Emu Theatre are getting up an entertainment for Saturday evening … something out of the common way is intended to be produced'. Nothing further is heard of this promise and it may be significant that the Saturday in question was April Fool's Day. Furthermore, when the *Monitor*, 19 June 1827, reported a recent production, it indicated that the theatre was re-opening after a long break, the preceding performance having been given before Governor Brisbane and Chief Justice Forbes. Since Brisbane had left the colony on 1 December 1825, this contradicts the story of any performance on 1 April 1826 and points to a break in operations of at least eighteen months. The most likely date for this previous production is late September 1825, when Brisbane and Forbes passed through the settlement together on a sight-seeing trip to the cascade, 27 miles beyond the camp.[37]

As it happened, there can be little doubt that the performance reported by the *Monitor* in June 1827 was the one described in loving detail in *Ralph Rashleigh*. The two guests of honour were the same (Forbes and Jamison), as was the program ('Monk' Lewis's *Raymond and Agnes; or, The Bleeding Nun* and Coffey's *The Devil to Pay*). If this is the case, the vivid picture brings with it a problem, for the novel makes no suggestion that this was an inaugural production: rather it gives the impression that it was one in a well-established series, probably preceded by an evening which included *Bombastes Furioso*. However, James Tucker, the author of *Ralph Rashleigh*, had only arrived at Emu Plains in late March 1827.[38] Perhaps Tucker reshaped his material to give the impression of a much more established theatre than was the case; or perhaps the

Monitor's reporter had been unaware of shows staged in the preceding months, and so misrepresented the length of the break in activities.

After the *Monitor's* account of the June 1827 production, the papers fall silent again. When the *Sydney Gazette*, 15 May 1830, finally reports another production, it is introduced with the possibly significant statement: 'On the evening of Saturday last, *His Majesty's servants* opened the theatre at Emu Plains.' The same paper, on 8 July 1830, heads an account of another production, on the previous Saturday, as 'EMU PLAINS, NEW THEATRE'. Whether we are looking at another cessation of activity or an interruption caused by the setting up of a new playhouse is not clarified. Between these two newspaper reports comes a private letter, written by Christiana Brooks on 18 June, which reports a production 'last week', presumably on Saturday 12.[39]

One more production is on record, though it never saw the light of day. On 6 and 10 November the *Sydney Monitor* (as it was by then called) announced a forthcoming presentation of John Home's *Douglas* and Isaac Bickerstaffe's *The Padlock*, scheduled for 30 November (see Fig. 15). The announcement was in the form of a playbill, as was usual in such cases, and listed the names of the players and their roles. This is the only occasion on which we have such detailed information for the Emu Plains theatre. Unfortunately, this announcement may have been a fabrication, though I shall be arguing against that possibility at a later point. Whether or not these advertisements referred to a genuine event, they had the immediate effect of calling down the wrath of the governor on the players. The performance was forbidden and the company closed down. The Emu Plains theatre was at an end.

A caveat must be issued concerning this record of productions. Most of the newspaper reports are preoccupied with performances attended by the gentry, but the *Sydney Gazette* of 21 July 1825 suggests that those performances were the exception rather than the rule. A comment in *Ralph Rashleigh* gives a similar impression, describing such performances as special events and claiming that 'the chiefest number of the audience consisted mainly of small farmers and their families from the locality'. If the novel can be trusted, there was at least one occasion in early 1829 on which the *corps dramatique* was allowed out of the camp to perform in a distant inn-yard barn 'to the small settlers round about'.[40] Since the press had overlooked several (or many) productions before the colony's notables, and been largely indifferent to performances before small farmers and artisans, the theatre may have had a much more dynamic existence than the records suggest. But it is unlikely to have been the weekly occurrence claimed by the unreliable James O'Connell. At the time of the November 1830 debacle the settlement's superintendent referred to productions as having been 'occasional' events,[41] though the evidence cited above for at least one production a month in early May, June and July of that year suggests something approaching regularity, for that period at least.

It should be noted that most of the confirmed performances took place in the winter months. Some of the breaks in production activity mentioned in the papers might have been the result of factors to be discussed later, but it may also be that this

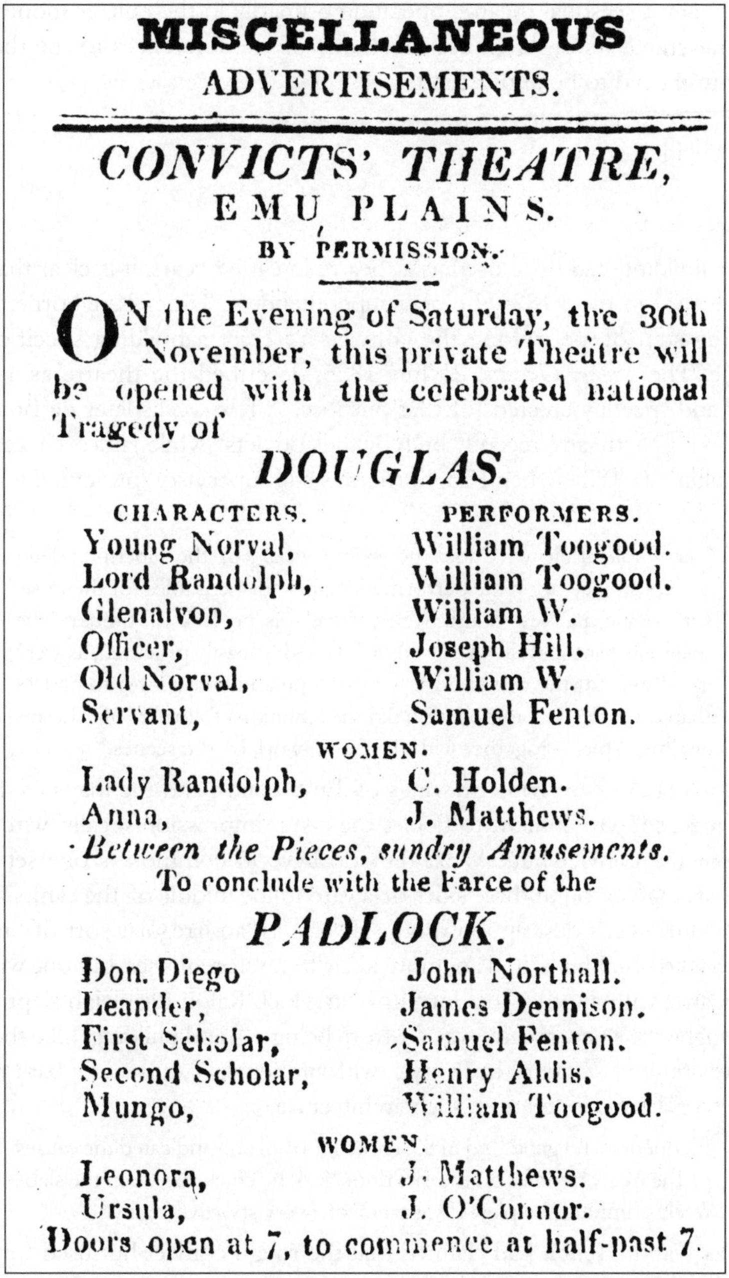

MISCELLANEOUS
ADVERTISEMENTS.

CONVICTS' THEATRE,
EMU PLAINS.
BY PERMISSION.

ON the Evening of Saturday, the 30th November, this private Theatre will be opened with the celebrated national Tragedy of

DOUGLAS.

CHARACTERS.	PERFORMERS.
Young Norval,	William Toogood.
Lord Randolph,	William Toogood.
Glenalvon,	William W.
Officer,	Joseph Hill.
Old Norval,	William W.
Servant,	Samuel Fenton.

WOMEN.

Lady Randolph,	C. Holden.
Anna,	J. Matthews.

Between the Pieces, sundry Amusements.
To conclude with the Farce of the

PADLOCK.

Don. Diego	John Northall.
Leander,	James Dennison.
First Scholar,	Samuel Fenton.
Second Scholar,	Henry Aldis.
Mungo,	William Toogood.

WOMEN.

Leonora,	J. Matthews.
Ursula,	J. O'Connor.

Doors open at 7, to commence at half-past 7.

Fig. 15 Advertisement for the proposed performance of *Douglas* and *The Padlock* at Emu Plains (State Reference Library, BN 348, State Library of New South Wales, *Sydney Monitor*, 6 November 1830).

was essentially a seasonal theatre, operating primarily in the quieter months of the agricultural year. It is in this sense that some of the references to the theatre 're-opening' may need to be understood.

V

Whatever building had been used as a theatre in earlier years, it is clear that shortly after his arrival in early 1825 the new superintendent, James Kinghorne, took the astonishing step of permitting the convicts to erect a building specifically as a playhouse. The *Sydney Gazette*, 21 July 1825, described the theatre as a building specially and speedily erected for that purpose. A few weeks later de Bougainville referred to it as 'a theatre recently built by the convicts', while James Tucker, writing of the building in 1827, when Kinghorne was still supervisor, presented it in similar terms:

> The whole affair was under the *benign patronage* of the superintendent, who bestowed upon the performers many indispensables for their use. Of course, in New South Wales, there was no lack of timber. The materials for the walls of the edifice were thus easily procured, as were also those for the very rude seats of the pit and boxes – for to no less than the latter accommodation did the ambitious followers of Thespis at Emu aspire – together with the frame-work of the scenes.[42]

There are no surviving drawings of Emu Plains, and the maps of 1826 (see Fig. 14) and 1831 are content to depict the camp impressionistically, with random squares for the convict huts. What they do have in common is one set of large buildings arranged around three sides of a yard in the middle of the camp. These do not quite fit Tucker's description of the theatre as 'an irregular sort of straggling-looking mass of buildings' and are more likely to be storehouses, but one wing could be the theatre, with another the dormitory in which Ralph Rashleigh slept.[43]

Kinghorne's new theatre was far from being a grand building. Like the convict huts, it was built in standard bush style, with timber slab walls and a bark roof, and had all the problems inherent in such architecture:

> Frequent awful gapes [*sic*] in the barken roof plainly indicated the causes of the many puddles on the dirt floor, and the cracks between the slabs freely admitted the playful vagrancy of every sportive zephyr.[44]

But just as Watkin Tench had claimed that the rough convict hut used for the first production of *The Recruiting Officer* in Australia had been transformed by candles and coloured paper into a place of magic, so Tucker describes the transformation of the Emu Plains theatre: 'The interstices of the walls being filled in with mud, and the whole of the interior whitewashed with pipeclay, of which there was abundance near, it produced no despicable effect by candlelight.'[45]

Tucker has a great deal of fun describing the ingenuity of the properties and costumes, and even more in relating the preposterousness of the results, particularly in the case of the costumes:

> But the wardrobe! Oh, the wardrobe! No powers of language can enable me to do justice to a description of the wardrobe.
>
> In the first place, to survey 'King Artexomines' in the solemn extravaganza of *Bumbastes Furioso*: his glittering crown was composed of odds and ends of tin and copper, brightly furbished, most of it garnished with pieces of window glass set on parti-coloured foils ... a flowing wig [was] fabricated of bits of sheepskin, the wool being powdered with bone ashes; [a gaudy fringe of fur bedecked a regal mantle that in the days of its] pristine freshness had been a purple stiff cloak with cape and hood, and belonging to 'Mother' Row, the wife of the camp constable, which splendid fur trimming had once covered a native cat ... and to complete the truly magnificent ensemble of this august monarch, his boots of russet hue had assumed their present form from the legs of an ancient pair of duck trowsers, whilom the property of Manager King, dyed to that colour by the juice of wattle-bark.

At the same time, however, Tucker stresses the effectiveness of the costumes on stage, describing the amazement of the gentry after the show, when they saw at close range 'the many shifts which it now became apparent had been resorted to in order to trick forth the male performers'.[46]

A subject on which Tucker says little is the company's use of scenery and machinery. However, when the group performed away from Emu Plains, it took a settler's dray to carry the 'scenery, machinery, dresses and decorations'. An early reference to the rough timber frames and canvas of the scenes points to what one would expect, a conventional 'wing-and-backscene' system, while later references indicate the use of footlights and of a drop curtain, or drop scene, at the front of the stage. But what of stage machinery? Among Jemmy King's skills are those of 'machinist' and 'mechanician', the manufacturer and operator of stage machines.[47] 'Stage machinery' is a term used to cover anything from brackets for candles and troughs for oil-lamps to the wherewithal for spectacular scenic effects – burning buildings, bridges across torrents and so on. Elaborate spectacle like this was a standard feature of much Romantic melodrama, one of the genres in which the company specialised.

The texts of two of their pieces, Isaac Pocock's *Rob Roy Macgregor* and Lewis's *Raymond and Agnes*, call for numerous scene-changes, while much of the latter play is set at night. Dimming mechanisms for the candles would have been no challenge for Jemmy King, but what of the play's closing moment of spectacle?

> [*RAYMOND and AGNES*] *kneel, [centre stage]. – a loud knock is heard – the back of the cavern falls to pieces, and discovers the* BLEEDING NUN, *in a blue ethereal flame, invoking a blessing on them – she slowly ascends, still blessing them – they form a tableau, and the curtain descends.* [48]

The simplest solution is that the company made do with a rumble on its tin drum, a puff of gunpowder and an exit through the wings. But this may be to underestimate the capabilities of men who contrived audience boxes, scenery 'painted with great taste',[49] a drop-curtain, oil- and wax lights and, even in their temporary theatre in the inn-yard barn, built a raised stage and a railed-off orchestra pit.[50]

While the newspapers over the period 1825–30 were certainly describing different performers, different costumes and possibly even different buildings in use as a theatre, they tend to bear out Tucker's description of the effects achieved. In most cases they even added a surprisingly high assessment of the quality of the performances. One of the cooler early appraisals of the company appears in *Howe's Weekly Commercial Express*, 25 July 1825, to which reference has already been made. Apart from praising the scenery, costumes and decorations as 'becomingly appropriate' and the fit-up as 'tolerable', it says of the actors:

> The little company certainly rises above mediocrity … [The pieces] were played, considering all things, in a very masterly manner; and in many points displaying a bold outline of character, originality, and humour, which met with loud and reiterated applause.

The *Sydney Gazette*, 21 July 1825, had fewer qualifications. Declaring that the pieces were 'played off in high style', it goes on to declare,

> The scenery, which is painted with great taste, the dresses, which were in part furnished by some of the ladies in the neighbourhood, together with the performances of the *dramatis personae*, won the admiration, and excited the joyful acclamations of the delighted spectators.

The *Australian*, 26 May 1825, had been content to note of an earlier performance that 'we are further informed that the performances are very respectable, very *toll-loll-ish*'. Christiana Brooks' letter of 18 June 1830 reports deficiencies in the costumes, but is even more positive about some of the actors:

> Have you heard of the Emu Theatricals – Charity was there with a large party of fashionables from Sir Johns last week and I am told the performance was infinitely superior to many Provincial Theatres in England. The Heroine to be sure had rather a *masculine* appearance – her petticoats were *too short* and her *trains too long*, but the male characters were very well supported particularly that of NJ [i.e. Bailie Nicol Jarvie] – and the whole was a very amusing representation of Rob Roy.[51]

By 15 May 1830 the *Sydney Gazette* was declaring that the pieces, 'our informant states, could not be better performed, in some of the parts, at Covent Garden or Drury Lane (!)'. The account goes on to report that 'the house was crowded to excess – there having been not less than two hundred persons present'. The same crowding is recorded at a performance in the following month, when the *Sydney Gazette*, 8 July 1830, provided a more detailed social analysis of the audience: 'The most liberal applause and satisfaction were manifested by a numerous and highly respectable audience, upwards of two hundred, among whom were noticed nearly forty ladies and gentlemen.'

Of all the newspaper reports only the *Australian*, 26 May 1825, makes a feature of the singing at the Emu Plains theatre, even though many of the pieces performed are ballad operas, or other plays with music. Later accounts, however, recall it as one of the delights of the place. Maclehose refers to 'several vocalists, some of whose melodious voices are now remembered by the surviving hearers, although the possessors have long been laid in the "narrow tomb"'. O'Connell claims that 'here I first heard Hunt sing ... He was an excellent ballad singer, and this accomplishment procured him the temporary alleviation of his sentence enjoyed while singing songs and ballads upon the stage'.[52] Hunt was a particularly infamous prisoner, having saved his life by informing on his fellow murderer in one of the most sensational criminal cases in early nineteenth-century England. His singing voice was much remarked upon, not least because it had a function in the murder plot, and its fame came with him to Australia. Hunt was stationed at Bathurst, but it is quite possible that he could have sung at Emu Plains in 1829 or 1830, when the Bathurst and Wellington Plains stations were administered from there, and there was some movement of convicts between the three centres. James Lawrence, who claimed to have performed at Emu Plains in 1822–23, is worth a mention in this context, since he was more of a singer-actor than a straight actor. On 26 May 1829 the *Sydney Gazette* published the words of a new song, 'The Exile of Erin, on the Plains of Emu', presumably a localisation of the Irish song with which Father Harold had allegedly delighted the Sydney croppies in 1800. There is nothing to connect the piece with performances at Emu Plains, but it remains a possibility that it was originally sung there.[53]

VI

In the period 1822–30 six successive superintendents or acting superintendents were in charge of Emu Plains. De Bougainville gives the impression that James Kinghorne, the incumbent in 1825, was an enthusiast for the theatre, but all of them seem to have supported, or at least tolerated, it. In spite of this general support they may also have been responsible for occasional breaks in its activities. In early May 1828, for example, Kinghorne misconstrued a government directive and ceased issuing passes to his men to undertake limited amounts of external work for remuneration. His misreading of his instructions could well have led him to suspend theatre productions also, though there is no evidence that this was the case. It was not until 21 July, in response to a prisoner's petition, that the colonial secretary wrote to Kinghorne removing his confusion and setting out some of the terms on which paid outside work was to be permitted.[54]

Even with a sympathetic superintendent the difficult working conditions of the convicts were sufficient to have caused some interruption to the theatre's output. Tucker was no doubt reporting the facts when he wrote that the company had to rehearse and to prepare their costumes and properties at night after an exhausting day in the fields.[55] This would have been particularly the case in summer, during the harvesting and haymaking, and might explain the near-absence of recorded productions at that time of the year.

Another possible reason for periods of darkness in the theatre was the instability of the convict population. The running down of numbers during the station's later years would have made inroads into any performing group, quite apart from the normal changes occasioned by individuals being assigned to private masters, securing tickets-of-leave or completing their sentences. The baker who was co-manager of the company in 1825 seems to have left by 1826.[56] After two and a half years or so James Lawrence was transferred to Port Macquarie for attempting to escape, while James Tucker's fictional *alter ego*, Ralph Rashleigh, was assigned after two years to a master in the Airds district.[57] Of the ten performers who were advertised to appear in the production of November 1830 only one, William Toogood, was on the establishment in August 1826: John A. Matthews, along with James Tucker, was not sent there until March 1827. There is no mention of James King, who looms so large in *Ralph Rashleigh*. He had received a ticket-of-leave as early as 22 March 1827, but probably remained at Emu Plains for a short period after that, waiting for the ticket to become effective. In the 1828 census he is recorded as living in Parramatta.[58]

The fact that the theatre survived this frequent dislocation may owe something to good fortune, in finding new arrivals with the talent and commitment to sustain or revive its operations. If Tucker is to be believed, James King was passionate about the stage and, since he was at Emu Plains from 3 October 1820 until late 1827, he provided the dynamic for much of its life. The trial records of John A. Matthews suggest that he shared this love of theatre; and he had the opportunity of working with King before taking on a leadership role in the last years of the company. William Toogood might have had the same level of commitment, in view of his subsequent involvement with free-and-easies. He also overlapped with King before becoming a central figure in the company's final phase.

Another force contributing to the theatre's capacity for revival was probably the influence of Sir John Jamison. Sir John's deep interest in the affairs of Emu Plains extended to its playhouse. He was its most consistent patron and may have had a strong involvement in its growth and maintenance. I have already referred to the *Monitor*'s description of him as 'the physician who nurses the illustrious little darling lately come into this mutable world'.

However, the major reason for the survival of the Emu Plains theatre was undoubtedly economic. Under Hunter and King most convicts lived in the community and were free to take whatever paid work they could find outside the hours of government labour. Emu Plains, in contrast, was notionally a closed prison farm. Inadequate facilities and inefficient staff (mainly convicts themselves) meant that the policy of enclosure was poorly implemented. Moreover, the government itself had already made compromises: though basic food and clothing were supplied, it was accepted that convicts should be given restricted opportunities to earn money for luxuries such as tea, coffee and tobacco. So it was, for example, that short-term passes were available for selected inmates to work on the local farms.

It is in this context that the operation of the Emu Plains theatre needs to be seen. There can be little doubt that from 1789 onwards the financial returns of acting had been an inducement to perform. At Emu Plains that inducement might well have been paramount. By 1830 there were only about 60 convicts remaining in the establishment and yet of this number 16 were occasional performers in its theatrical activities, to say nothing of the musicians and stage hands. The likelihood of finding 16 in a group of 60 convicts performing out of love of the art is remote indeed. No doubt some were driven by the joys of performance, but for others it was the money that counted.

The means of securing an income from the performances at Emu Plains differed substantially from those employed in Sidaway's theatre, the second Norfolk Island theatre and, no doubt, most of the other theatres so far discussed. While the *Sydney Gazette*, 21 July 1825, declared that the price of admission was a dump, or 1s. 3d. (referring presumably to the pit), this is the only surviving reference to a regular charge being made. The same article, referring to the better class of clients, put all its emphasis on donations made after the performance: 'Sir John, with his accustomed liberality, afterwards sent the managers a 10 dollar note.' *Howe's Weekly Commercial Express*, 25 July 1825, wrote of the 'magnificent donation' given collectively by the local gentry at the same performance.

If there was any entry fee in 1825, the practice seems to have changed by 1827. *Ralph Rashleigh* makes no mention of charges in any part of the house. Even the humbler spectators were apparently asked only to make a donation. The performances which took place away from Emu Plains, in the barn behind the inn, followed the same system, with the innkeeper working assiduously to boost the amount donated.[59] At Emu Plains itself, as in the earlier period, the donations of the gentry made the greatest impact. For the performance described in the novel Sir John had sent a gift of wine for the performers before the show and afterwards Judge Forbes slipped a £1 note to Rashleigh for his personal use, while

> the Knight of Regentville and all his party ... made such presents to
> the manager for the Company as, with gifts more suited to their humble
> circumstances made by other spectators, enabled that functionary to
> distribute a share amounting to no less than ten shillings to each of the
> musicians and fifteen shillings to the performers.[60]

Entry by donation suggests an attempt to distance the theatre from the normal commercial venture. There were good legal and political reasons for this that will be examined later. On the evidence of the novel, however, a reliance on donations was not financially ruinous. A 15s. reward for a performance must have been enormously satisfactory to most convict players. In the 1828 dispute over outside work at Emu Plains it was said that those granted the indulgence could make 5s.–6s. a week, out of hours, as haymakers. Such opportunities, of course, were only available for a limited period of the year and only to those approved by the superintendent.[61]

Since this theatre was a money-making enterprise, its focus was on an audience drawn from the outside world that could pay for the privilege. While, in its earlier years, with convict numbers approaching 500, prisoners may have been a part of the clientele, they were conspicuously absent from the small audience at de Bougainville's command performance of August 1825. In 1827 those who were present in Tucker's version were intruders, and unwelcome ones at that:

> the only drawback to the manager's satisfaction being that a number of the men belonging to the camp, as there was no gallery, had taken undisturbed possession of the roof, where they vented their criticisms in rather an obstreperous manner, deaf to the *dignified* remonstrances of the irritated Jemmy King, who ever and anon devoted them to the *Deis infernis* in 'curses, not loud, but deep'.[62]

As the numbers declined towards 60, those convicts not involved in the show became less and less a factor for consideration.

During the period in which 20–30 women prisoners were resident at Emu Plains they could have been drawn upon to fill the female roles. Thereafter there was no choice but to use young male convicts for these parts. Tucker speaks of 'a new and youthful recruit, whose beardless face well suited the female parts he sustained',[63] and in the questionable playbill of 30 November 1830 the young women's roles in both main- and afterpiece are allotted to John Matthews, who at that stage was 20 years old. Even while there were women on the prison farm, of course, it might have been easier to employ all-male casts. The young 'lad of some genius', who is identified in Appendix B, Note 9 as performing there in 1822 or early 1823, sounds like a prime candidate for female roles.

VII

What, then, was the social composition of the acting troupe at Emu Plains? The first mention of the theatre in *Ralph Rashleigh* occurs when the watchman Row sets about allocating Rashleigh to a hut, remarking, 'As you bees another of theasem dom'd quill drivers, I do zuppose you had better be put along with the rest; so you will stop in the pla'house there.'[64] The theatre, that is, is being identified with the specials.

When it comes to a detailed account of the playmaking, however, Tucker's story is dominated by the figure of Jemmy King, who gives a thoroughly different impression:

> Among the prisoners at Emu Plains a theatre was established under the auspices of one 'Jemmy King', a most eccentric genius, on a small scale, who was at once architect, manager, carpenter, scene-painter, decorator, machinist, mechanician, and to crown all, a very passable comic actor.

What rendered this combination of talents more extraordinary, Jemmy could neither read nor write, the only method he possessed of learning his parts being to listen while another read them; and though during these lessons the ever busy fingers of Manager King would still be at work, perhaps in the discordant avocation of a tinker, employed in making or mending the theatrical lamps, yet none of the *corps dramatique* were more perfect at rehearsal.[65]

It is easy to read this as the portrait of a humble labourer with a wild imagination and the energy to teach himself a range of mechanical skills of the kind associated with tinkers and odd-job men. Since the other members of the company are not described, we might assume, overlooking the watchman's association of the theatre with 'quill drivers', that most of these were of that same background, humble workmen. But is Jemmy King what he appears to be?

The list of convicts at Emu Plains in August 1826 includes 'James King, *per* ship *General Stewart*', and gives his employment as 'In care of Tools &c'. He had disembarked from the *General Stewart* in January 1819 and been sent to Windsor for allocation, moving to Emu Plains on 3 October 1820. In 1822 he applied for a ticket-of-leave:

> Memorialist has served as Overseer at Windsor and on the Establishment at Emu Plains … for 18 Months without any benefit or Emolument arising therefrom – in which situation he would have continued but that at the request of Mr Fitzgerald and under the promise of favour he gave it up, that he might make himself more usefull to the aforesaid Establishment by his Handicraft.[66]

There can be little doubt that this is the Jemmy King of Tucker's story. The petition, which is unsigned, must have been the work of a scribe, since later convict records agree with Tucker in describing King as able neither to read nor write (see Appendix B, Note 11). This is in spite of the fact that he had a respectable trade. The indent for the *General Stewart* lists him as a watch finisher. The crime for which he was convicted, at age 27, was larceny in a dwelling house, the chief items of plunder being two watches and a watchmaker's eyeglass.[67] Was this a journeyman robbing his master? After obtaining his ticket-of-leave in 1827, he appeared in the 1828 census as a watchmaker at Parramatta. The account of the Emu Plains theatricals in the *Sydney Gazette*, 21 July 1825, refers to two managers and describes them as 'degraded, one to the occupation of a baker, and the other to that of tinker'. The baker cannot be identified, but the tinker was surely King, and for a watch-repairer such an appointment would be a degradation, at least in the eyes of the public.

King, then, came from the same class of tradesmen as the majority of the performers in Sidaway's playhouse, but the specials were undoubtedly a force in the Emu Plains theatre. James Lawrence, who was Jewish, was the son of a London diamond broker and had wealthy relatives in the West Indies and New York.[68] The flash language and crudity of sentiment in his autobiography suggests that much of his polish had rubbed off, and his career as habitual thief and occasional actor cannot have helped his image; but he could probably make some claims to 'special' status. More useful, however, is the list of those who were to be dispersed from Emu Plains for being involved in the theatre, and the playbill that precipitated the order for this dispersal. Here we have a picture of the entire company at a particular point in time, though three of those on the playbill do not appear on the list.

The first thing of note is that, of the five actors who are allocated large to medium roles in the playbill, John A. Matthews had been appointed as clerk at the end of 1829 and thereafter promoted to principal overseer. William Watt, from the Wellington Valley outpost, was his replacement as clerk. John Northall was the overseer of invalids and lunatics, and William Toogood was the personal servant of the superintendent.[69] To a significant extent, then, those with position or influence at Emu Plains dominated the theatre in its final stage. Perhaps the same situation had prevailed when King and the baker were the company managers in the mid-1820s. This pattern was not without precedent. In Wilkinson's description of a performance by the ship's crew of HMS *Bedford* it is the ship's carpenter, one of the petty officers, who bulks largest as a performer. The carpenter's mate and the bosun also figure on the list. Did their positions of authority give the men a right to dominate proceedings (whatever their talent), or were the qualities required to obtain that authority also those useful for performance?

In the case of two of the principal performers in this last company at Emu Plains, the connection between their positions in the hierarchy, their social background and their cultural pretensions is clear. William Watt and John Alexander Matthews were specials. Watt had been a principal clerk in Scotland with a taste for high living. Discovered embezzling money, he fled to London, secured a similar appointment there and continued with his career of embezzlement and the high life: 'Although it was stipulated by Mr. Ellis, that he should board and lodge on the premises, he, in fact, passed his nights with a very dashing young woman at Greenwich, to whose place he rode every evening upon a beautiful horse he had purchased.'[70] Convicted and shipped to Australia, he was sent to the remote Wellington Valley, a repository popularly known as 'the swells' paradise'. Described by John Maxwell as 'a person of an irritable temper – a meddling disposition',[71] Watt found the place not to his taste and sent an anonymous letter to the *Sydney Monitor*, which nicely catches his snobbery and sense of his own social significance. Many of the prisoners there, he declares, are

> men, who have never been accustomed to hardship; who have moved in, or been educated for respectable Society, and their feelings are of course, more liable to be destroyed than those persons who have followed depravity as a regular profession …
>
> They are not kept apart from the other men, for huts have recently been built to keep them constantly mixing with the common laborers. A few who hold situations are however otherwise indulged, but all cannot act in this capacity; and therefore it follows, that they must effect here with the lowest characters in the Country, and that too, in a narrow space surrounded with walls …

> The dashing fashionable of Regent Street, may here be seen patiently
> handling the stubborn hoe or pitchfork ... They wash till their linen
> assumes a tawny color, and it would excite the commisseration of any
> feeling mind, to see a broken-down broken-hearted 'swell', baking a
> damper for his dinner, or going through the usual culinary operations.
> He must wash, bake and cook for himself, or go like a hog and starve.[72]

Needless to say, prisoners at Wellington Valley were strictly forbidden to write letters
to the press, and Watt's letter had the added provocation that it contained a sharp
attack on the governor. It was a characteristic piece of recklessness on Watt's part.
Nevertheless, so valuable was he as a clerk that when Maxwell was made superintendent
of Emu Plains, while still retaining control of Bathurst and Wellington Valley, he had
Watt transferred to his new base.

John A. Matthews appears in the convict indents as 'shopboy and clerk'. On
the death of his father he and his brother had been taken in and employed by a
wealthy uncle, who ran a large boot and shoe business in Blackfriars Road. The
uncle, who took his family responsibilities seriously, 'frequented the theatres at one
time, as he had been in the musical profession ... and as he did not wish the boys to
be slaves, he had sent them to the theatre, in order that they might be edified, and
obtain a proper pronunciation of the language'.[73] His good intentions were in vain.
The young John Matthews fell into the company of a couple of minor players from
the Coburg Theatre, William Jones and Frederick Stannard, who seem to have preyed
upon his inexperience (he was only 16 at the time) and persuaded him to steal from
his uncle's shop. This was no petty crime. Over time some £2,000-worth of shoes
and boots, as well as the occasional piece of jewellery, was stolen before Matthews
was apprehended, tried, and dispatched to Australia.

After the arrival of Watt at Emu Plains, he and Matthews seem to have teamed
up. They were most probably the 'two very mischevious Clerks' who were troubling
Maxwell on 10 November 1830 and they certainly provoked the local police magistrate,
the petulant, thuggish and unlovely Captain Wright. Wright's dark comment on 'the
ascendancy these subtle villains are attaining over Mr. Maxwell' was probably a
reference to the duo, and elsewhere he complained directly of the 'insolence of Watt
& Matthews'. His answer was to harass them in every way, even though he had
allegedly praised Matthews at an earlier stage as 'exceedingly clever at his duty'. In
spite of his reservations about Watt, and probably about Matthews, Maxwell sprang
to their defence, but the dispute was overtaken by the events surrounding the final
Emu Plains production.[74]

Although two of the participants in the last days of the Emu Plains theatre
were specials, literate and moderately cultured, that was the extent of that group's
contribution to the theatre. As performers they were edged aside by William Toogood
and Charles Holden, who came from a different world entirely. Toogood had secured
for himself the romantic lead, Young Norval, in *Douglas*, together with the major but
less glamorous role of Lord Randolph. In the afterpiece, *The Padlock*, he was assigned

the low comic part of Mungo, the principal attraction in the play. Holden had only one role in the mainpiece, but it was the plum part of Lady Randolph, a tragic heroine who had been brilliantly realised in London by Mrs Siddons. While Young Norval was a much-admired role, he is overshadowed by Lady Randolph. One can only wonder at the self-assurance of an all-male company choosing to stage a she-tragedy.

Of these two men Toogood has left the more substantial record. He was a little over 16, and apprenticed to that most vulnerable of trades, ribbon weaving, when he committed a street robbery in Newport Pagnell. For his pains he was sentenced to transportation for life. His father, a labourer of Coventry, was 'extremely poor and having a Wife and residing at such a distance from where his Son was tried and large Family he was unable to take … means for the defence of his Son'. After the event he desperately petitioned for a reduction of the sentence, pleading his son's hitherto blameless record, and the honest and industrious character of the parents. Twenty respectable citizens of Coventry supported the petition, but to no avail. Toogood arrived in Sydney in March 1823 and in July 1824 had the good fortune to be assigned to the Rev. Cowper. Three months later he wrecked his chances by being involved in the theft of tea, sugar and tobacco from a fellow convict's master. He received 25 lashes. Though returned to Cowper, he presumably committed a further offence and was sent to Emu Plains. In his early years there he was employed in stump-grinding and flax-dressing, according to the August 1826 return, and in February 1827 was one of a group refused assignment because they were 'of bad character and unworthy any indulgences'. Up to this point we have a portrait of a low-skilled worker of humble parentage, drifting downwards; but somehow he redeemed himself, gaining the regard of Superintendent Maxwell and a dominant position in the theatre company. Later, after securing his ticket-of-leave for Sydney (19 November 1831), he made a respectable career as a restauranteur and publican. It is gratifying to note that as a publican he also secured a theatre licence for his premises. Like his younger brother Alfred, a 'labouring boy' sent out for the much more romantic crime of machine wrecking, he went into the business of free-and-easies, professional and amateur saloon entertainments built around a succession of solo performers, mainly singers.[75]

Charles Holden, a tailor, was 22, with two previous convictions, when he was arrested as part of a gang involved in a housebreaking in his home town of Bath. Three of his four co-accused were found not guilty and the other received seven years, but Holden was concurrently being charged with a separate theft, and suffered the full weight of the law. He received the death sentence, which was later commuted to transportation for life. Arriving in November 1826, he spent a brief period assigned to a Sydney publican and was then transferred to a master in the Illawarra district from whom he ran in May 1828. It was this act, no doubt, which sent him to Emu Plains. From Emu Plains he was assigned to J. Smith of Newcastle, and remained there at least until the muster of 1837. As a potential tragic heroine his appearance was not promising. Long sleeves would have hidden the tattoo marks on his arms, and one can only hope that the 'scrophulous marks on the mouth' noted on the ship's indent, and in the surgeon's journal when he was transported, had vanished by the time he was called upon to perform Lady Randolph. He received his ticket-of-leave in 1842, for the Cassilis district, and obtained a conditional pardon in 1847. Cassilis, over the Great Dividing Range beyond the Upper Hunter Valley, was little more than a frontier village and can have had little use for interpreters of tragic heroines. Holden may have had respectable connections or an element of refinement, but it does not emerge from the surviving records.[76]

Two other performers warrant some mention, James Dennison, who was scheduled to play the juvenile lead, Leander, in *The Padlock*, and John Northall, who took on the heavy-father role of Don Diego. Dennison, a London plasterer with no previous convictions, was sentenced for picking a pocket of a handkerchief, valued at 6 shillings. He was 16 at the time. Apart from his casting in *The Padlock*, he seems to have left no traces in the colony. By 16 he would not have completed a plasterer's apprenticeship, so he probably belonged to the same world of lowly artisans as Toogood and Holden. On an Emu Plains list he appears as a 'plasterers boy'.[77]

John Northall, a seaman by trade, is a more ambiguous case. Imprisoned for an unspecified offence in 1813, he had escaped, and within a day was captured after attempting a violent street robbery. His death sentence was commuted to transportation for life. After arriving in New South Wales he had a chequered career. He ran from one master, but earned the approval of others as sober and industrious. In October 1818 he successfully petitioned for a ticket-of-leave, but lost it on 16 May 1820 for 'Riotous and Disorderly conduct in the Streets of Sydney, at a late hour, and wantonly abusing the Soldiers of the Guard, when in the execution of their duty'. Sent to work in the stores, he was convicted of stealing in November 1820, given a hundred lashes and shipped to Newcastle for a year. Thereafter he was posted to a work gang in the Airds district, but in late 1822 was convicted as a member of a group involved in a series of robberies in the area. For a second time in his career a death sentence was commuted to life. He was sent to Port Macquarie as his place of secondary punishment and after four years was able to establish that he was innocent of the Airds robberies. He was then transferred to Emu Plains, arriving in January 1827.[78] This move has a surprising twist, as he was sent there to act as medical officer. He must have been seriously underqualified for the position, since, on the arrival of Henry White, whose own medical qualifications were doubtful,[79] he was replaced by the newcomer and given the post of overseer of invalids and lunatics. Northall might have gained his medical experience from a period as an orderly to the doctor on a naval vessel; but the possibility remains that, lurking behind this portrait of a tough seaman, missing a finger and frequently in trouble for theft and drunkenness, lay someone who had started life in more exalted circumstances. Northall was removed from Emu Plains in 1831, as part of the order to disperse the actors, and was apparently assigned to a master in the Port Stephens area. He received a ticket-of-leave in May 1834 and had it transferred to Newcastle in August 1836.

He obtained a conditional pardon in 1842 and thereafter vanished from the records.[80]

This catalogue could be extended by exploring the background of the actors cast for minor roles in *Douglas* and *The Padlock*, such as Samuel Fenton, sailor, and Henry Aldis, blacksmith; or by investigating the other men listed as members of the company. There was William Bryant, blacksmith; Charles Chamberlain, labourer; Henry Daunt, sailor; Thomas Foster, a naïve and probably innocent groom and waggoner; and Joseph Stiles, a butcher. Some of these may have been only occasional performers. Charles Chamberlain, described as 'a supernumerary performer', was accidentally omitted from Maxwell's original list of performers because he had never seen him act.[81]

The picture, then, seems to be of an 1830 company which may have depended on two specials for managerial skills and the delicate task of negotiating with the authorities, but in which most of the actors, including the leading performers, came from the world of relatively lowly trades. They are further down the social scale than Sidaway's original group, though most are still above the level of labourers. It may be of significance that only the two specials, Matthews and Watt, together with the talented Toogood, made comfortable careers after leaving Emu Plains, whereas many of Sidaway's players found a place for themselves in the middle ranks of early colonial society. Matthews was assigned to Alexander Berry at Shoalhaven, where he acted as clerk and constable. He won the trust of Berry and, after obtaining his freedom in 1839, built a career as a successful Sydney commercial agent. In later years he also became a pillar of one of the Masonic orders in the city. Watt became a leading radical journalist and capped his career by marrying the well-to-do widow of Robert Howe, proprietor of the *Sydney Gazette*, before his enemies finally brought him low. Toogood died a pillar of society, he or his brother – or both – having a street in Newtown named after them.[82] All the other members of the company, including John Northall and Charles Holden, faded into obscurity. If William Watt had felt such discomfort at fraternising with the lowly of Wellington Valley, did these Emu Plains performers similarly discomfort him? This might explain an oddity in the playbill for *Douglas*, where Watt's identity is concealed behind a modest 'William W.'. Was it the shame of acting, or the shame of acting in such company, that led to this evasion?

VIII

The repertoire of the Emu Plains theatre reveals a cultural shift that had been under way in England since the early years of the century and was being reflected in Australia. While the afterpieces, *The Lying Valet*, *The Devil to Pay* and *The Padlock*, might as readily have found a place in Sidaway's theatre (*The Devil to Pay* actually did so), the mainpieces reveal a move towards Romantic melodrama: *Raymond and Agnes; or, the Bleeding Nun of Lindenberg; Rob Roy Macgregor; or, Auld Lang Syne* and Charles Dibdin Jnr's *Barsissa; or, The Hermit Robber* (see Appendix C). *Douglas* and *John Bull* would certainly have been acceptable in Sidaway's theatre, but the former never reached production at Emu Plains and the latter may have suffered a similar fate for different reasons.[83] The recurrence of certain plays is also worth noting. Play texts could readily have been obtained from Sir John Jamison, so the repetition probably indicates the difficulty of getting up new productions.

The shift to Romantic melodrama in England is often associated with large-scale changes in audience composition: the move away from the theatre of respectable society and the emergence of a popular theatre. In such a reading the choice of mainpieces at Emu Plains could be seen to reflect the taste of the playmakers of the settlement. It might even be possible to interpret their planned production of *Douglas* as Watt and Matthews making a last stand for quality theatre and the classic national repertoire. Such readings of the company's offerings, however, are difficult to sustain. In a few cases for which evidence is available it was gentlefolk who determined the choice of mainpieces. Tucker describes how Sir John, having notified the prisoners of his desire to see a show, was forwarded a list of the pieces they were ready to present. It was he who selected from the list *Raymond and Agnes*.[84] Similarly the *Sydney Gazette*, 8 July 1830, reports that the program intended for 3 July had been changed 'in compliance with the request of several ladies', who wished to see the recently-performed musical drama of *Rob Roy* instead of the advertised *Lying Valet*.

There are a few references to locally prepared material included in the programs. Usually this was in the form of an address, such as the 'respectful valedictory address … delivered by the manager' at the end of the performance before Sir John and Justice Forbes, described by Tucker, or the 'appropriate address', which was part of the performance in May 1830. Much more interesting, however, is the 'entire new performance entitled *The Welders Wedge-box, or Vulcan disappointed*', which was included as an afterpiece in July 1825.[85] There is no English work of this name: it appears to be a locally-written playlet. Since Jemmy King, tinker *extraordinaire*, was already at Emu Plains, it may well be a topical piece built around his eccentricities. If so, it probably stands as the earliest locally-written play known to have been performed in Australia – unless John Grant's 'masque' of 1805 had already earned that distinction.

IX

Early in this discussion I noted that the newspapers' interest in the Emu Plains theatre arose partly from the contrast with Sydney, which had no playhouse. The comparison was more than an innocent observation. Responsibility for the lack of a theatre in Sydney rested squarely with the governor. With the partial exception of Arthur Phillip, every governor since 1788 had found his position difficult, being required to rule as an autocrat, frequently without a strong executive, but opposed by a range of powerful interest groups bent on subverting his authority. Under Governor Darling the factionalism and the feuding were at fever pitch, aided by Darling's own taste for military-style authority, which confronted a newly emergent radical press and a liberal establishment arguing for the founding of English civil institutions and limitations on the governor's power. In such a context Governor Darling's refusal to permit a theatre in Sydney could take on a political significance out of proportion to the act itself. This was the more so as Darling was confronted, not by a vague desire for a Sydney theatre, but by the thoroughly focussed and provocative attempts of Barnett Levey to secure one.

With the climate in Sydney so charged, it is surprising that Darling did not move earlier against Emu Plains. This is all the more so since the theatre was, to a notable extent, the plaything of his liberal opponents. Sir John Jamison maintained a working relationship with Darling, but he had helped to destroy his predecessor, Governor Brisbane, by attacking him over the female convict issue at Emu Plains. Others of the Nepean gentry who frequented the theatre, such as Gregory Blaxland, William Cox and William Lawson, were also classifiable as members of a liberal opposition. Chief Justice Forbes was above these machinations but his defence of the rule of law made him a thorn in the governor's flesh. Commentators presented Brisbane as an active patron of this theatre, but there is no record that Darling ever visited it.

That the theatre was aware of its vulnerability is suggested by an increasing emphasis on its non-commercial basis. The *Sydney Gazette*, 15 May 1830, spells this out: 'The theatre is a place of private amusement only, no price being charged for admission: but presents are made and accepted, of, and for, dresses, decorations. &c. &c.' The point of the stratagem is clear. Under English law a theatre without a licence that charged for performances was subject to immediate closure and the players liable to punishment as rogues and vagabonds. Private theatres, in which no fee was charged, were not subject to this control. Reiterating that Emu Plains was a private theatre was a fragile attempt to protect the operation from attacks by authority. The *Sydney Gazette*, 8 July 1830, pointedly referred to it as 'this private theatre' and, when the forthcoming performances of *Douglas* and *The Padlock* were announced in November 1830, the advertisement again described it as 'this private theatre' and made no mention of a charge for entry.

Darling's tolerance must have been under strain for some time. In 1829 he had drawn up a new set of draconian regulations for convicts in agricultural establishments, which was followed by an equally vicious set for iron gangs in stockades.[86] While, in a separate ruling, the governor spelled out some limited rights to private work on the part of the prisoners at Emu Plains (Saturday afternoons, but *never* on Sunday),[87] the staging of plays sat uncomfortably with this new restrictiveness. Moreover, the comparison between Sydney with no theatre and Emu Plains with its playhouse was revived in a particularly barbed form in the radical newspaper, the *Sydney Monitor*, 10 July 1830:

> THEATRE AT LAST!
>
> Mr. Levey built a Theatre in Sydney, the non-licensing of which ruined him. His was a Theatre at which free and freed persons only were to perform and be present. Yet he, and the Colony through him, was refused the pleasures of the Drama on the score of their being irreligious and immoral. Not so with the convicts. They, worthy men, are allowed to have a Theatre, and at Emu Plains too, a demi-penal domestic settlement, where discipline in flogging, &c, has always existed to a comfortable degree.

What finally stung the governor into action, however, were those advertisements for the production of *Douglas* and *The Padlock*. It was one thing for a newspaper to report a production that had already taken place at Emu Plains; it was quite another for convicts to be advertising their own wares in the public press. The advertisements, moreover, appeared in the *Sydney Monitor*, which raised the possibility that they were part of a scheme to embarrass the government. No sooner had the first of these advertisements appeared (6 November) than Captain Wright, the police magistrate at Penrith, was sent post-haste to Emu Plains. He wrote promptly, on 9 November:

> Since my return to the plains I have ascertained from Maxwell that he not only never knew of the advertisement but that it was never projected to play on the 30 Nov. – His story is simply this –
>
> When he arrived at Emu to supply the vacancy of Mr. Kinghorne he found a theatre in which the Convicts amused themselves occasionally when he gave permission – but it was merely *private permission* – a settlement relaxation just on the principles on which he had found to exist on his arrival –
>
> Whatever may be the result it is certain that the Monitor has rec[d] it either through private vanity or spleen or uses it as an instrument for future malignity which we shall no doubt soon discover – I think Maxwell rather wishes to get rid of the theatre than continue it – but it is an affair with which I have never troubled myself in any way.[88]

The assertion in this report that the advertisements were spurious, and that no production was scheduled, is considered in detail in Appendix B, Note 10. Though I am inclined to believe that a performance was being planned, the suggestion that the whole affair was a fabrication can only have added to the governor's discomfiture.

This report from Emu Plains was received in Sydney on 22 November and on that same day the colonial secretary sent a peremptory instruction to Maxwell:

> I am directed by H. Ex. The Governor to inform you that any fur*ther Theatrical performance by the Convicts at Emu Plains is to be immediately discontinued*, and that the *Principal Superintendent of Convicts* has been instructed, to assign the performers to private Service, replacing them by other Prisoners – You will therefore be pleased to Communicate to Mr. Hely the Names of all the Men alluded to.[89]

Maxwell replied, just as promptly, on 26 November, acknowledging the order to discontinue performances immediately and announcing the dispatch to the principal superintendent of convicts of a list of performers. However, he requested that the four prisoners, Watt, Matthews, Northall and Toogood (or at least the first three), be retained at Emu Plains, since 'an immediate removal of them would put the establishment to very great inconvenience'.[90] The board assigned Aldis, Holden, Dennison, Daunt, Foster, Oakley, Bryant and Stiles to new masters on 2 and 8 December, and Chamberlain soon after. On 4 December the colonial secretary demanded of the superintendent of convicts how many performers remained at Emu Plains. He repeated the inquiry on 12 January 1831 after no reply had been received.[91] The letters indicate the concern of the colonial secretary to ensure the process of dispersal was going ahead. In fact, in spite of the bluntness of the order he had received, Maxwell coolly delayed the departure of the men until February. The first of them officially left on the seventh of that month and the last, Chamberlain, on the sixteenth. Maxwell subsequently claimed that the men were needed for this extra period at Emu Plains, and this was probably the case, since harvesting and haymaking were in progress when the order first came.[92]

With the bulk of the performers removed and with the principal superintendent of convicts tacitly approving Maxwell's retention of the four key theatre personnel, the matter might have rested. Watt, Matthews, Northall and Toogood might even have hoped for a renewal of activity when time had elapsed; after all, Governor Darling was approaching the end of his six-year term. Unfortunately for them, a new wave of troubles swept over Emu Plains, and one in which the theatre, though closed, played a prominent part.[93]

The relationship between the police magistrate, Captain Wright, and the superintendent of Emu Plains, John Maxwell, had never been an easy one. Temperamentally they were worlds apart – Wright an abusive and hysterical disciplinarian and Maxwell an amiable and relatively easy-going administrator, but one who reacted strongly to any challenge to his position. From Wright's point of view Maxwell was lax in his control of the convicts and dangerously under the influence of Watt and Matthews, whom he (Wright) had come to detest. From Maxwell's point of view his own mild approach led to contented and efficient workers, and Matthews and Watt were so skilled they had to be protected.

The feud between the two officials came to a head in a series of incidents in late February and early March 1831. On about 18 February Northall, who was scheduled to remain at the station, had been a prominent member of a small but wildly drunken farewell party for two of the performers who were being sent to their new assignment the following day. (Dennison is named. The other was probably Chamberlain.)[94] On the same evening the barracks of the mounted police were robbed. Wright, who reported that Northall was frequently drunk but rarely punished for it, suspected that he and his party were responsible, but got little support from Maxwell. On 23 February a group of prisoners complained to Wright of the violent and abusive behaviour of a police officer, but were driven off by the police magistrate with his own torrent of abuse. The next morning Wright announced to Maxwell he was setting up a picquet around the Emu Plains camp to put a halt to the night-time absences of the prisoners. Maxwell refused to co-operate. Later the same day there were more attacks by Wright on groups of prisoners, leaving the camp in turmoil. Matthews, later to be described by Wright as 'a little effeminate creature who played the part of a woman at the Theatre',[95] wrote a waspish letter of complaint to Maxwell. 'I beg respectfully to inform you, that I find it perfectly impossible, to continue to discharge the duty you have been pleased to entrust me with, if I am not protected by you', he complained, and so on. Watt's response was to organise a petition signed by 67 prisoners listing their complaints against Wright and asking Maxwell to forward the petition to the governor.[96] Wright explained the ill feeling between himself and the prisoners as follows:

> Some time since an order was received on the plains for suppressing the Theatre – a report was circulated amongst them that its suppression originated with me – and this has been corroborated by the result ... since then the prisoners have behaved with the falsehood & irregularity of which I complain.[97]

The next day (25 February) Maxwell departed for Sydney, leaving Matthews in charge at Emu Plains (he had no choice, since none of his staff were free men). Wright now had to deal with Matthews' unhelpfulness, which reached a peak when a prisoner, terrorised by a mounted policeman, failed to turn up for duty watering and feeding the police horses. Frustration at Matthews' lack of concern turned to fury when the returning Maxwell supported Matthews and the absentee. The result was a wild outpouring of letters from Wright to the colonial secretary – five of them over 1–2 March – in one of which Wright, probably out of malice, alerted the colonial secretary once again to the issue of the players. In the opening paragraph he pointedly referred to 'Watt Mr Maxwell's Clerk & a player Matthews the Overseer & a player'; and later, commenting on the order to disperse the actors, declared, 'Mr Maxwell suppressed the order near two months'. Against the first of these comments appeared the colonial secretary's astonished question: 'Why are these men retained so long? It is long since they were ordered to be assigned.' Against the second was another: 'It appears very extr[aordinar]y that the assignment of these men should have been so long delayed.'[98]

This was not the end of the fracas at Emu Plains. A further stream of letters from Wright was dispatched when he discovered that the absconded prisoner had been hiding for a week in the theatre and that Watt and Matthews were suspected of abetting him. Wright's hopes of securing the pair 150 lashes apiece for concealing a runaway were frustrated when the Penrith Bench threw out the charges.[99] Before this little drama had seen its course, however, the colonial secretary had begun to move. On 8 March he organised a committee of inquiry to investigate the dispute at Emu Plains, and on 12 March yet another letter was sent to the principal superintendent of convicts demanding to know what had happened to the players.[100] The reply, stating that all had been assigned but the four Maxwell had asked to retain – Watt, Matthews, Northall and Toogood – was, however, not sent until 30 March and by then the report of the investigating committee had been submitted. Accordingly, it was on this that the colonial secretary acted. Both Wright and Maxwell were roundly criticised for their behaviour, Maxwell for his 'undue and unnecessary indulgence' to the convicts. He was ordered to lock the prisoners in their barracks at night, to have regular nightly roll-calls and to grant passes less frequently. On the subject of the players the letter was at its most cutting, speaking of the governor's 'surprise and His displeasure that you should have considered yourself authorised to suppress for a time however short, His Commands for the distribution of the players'. Maxwell was ordered, immediately on the receipt of the letter, to send Watt to Hyde Park Barracks, and transmit the names of any remaining players so that they could be removed.[101] Watt had been singled out in this way because he seemed to be 'a most mischievous Character'. Wright's hostility may have been directed chiefly at Matthews, but for the colonial secretary a convict who organised petitions was a much greater danger than one who provoked a splenetic military officer. At the same time it was made clear that none of the four was to be assigned: instead they were to be 'sent away to distant stations', a phrase that recurred in several letters.[102] In no case was this intention carried out, though Watt came closest to it, and was later to suffer the indignity for subsequent offences.

By 1 April 1831 Watt was gone. Surprisingly, a return of 12 May 1831 shows Toogood, Matthews and Northall still remaining,[103] but with Emu Plains closing down they were soon to be dispersed. Maxwell himself had submitted his resignation as early as March, though it was some time before he was fully able to disengage himself.

Maxwell's delaying tactics, and his strenuous efforts to retain four key members of the company, could suggest that he was not as indifferent to his theatre as was implied. However, it is safer to see his primary concern as the efficient running of the establishment:

> The theatrical performers were detained for a short time after the Order on account of the Public Service – I also requested that Watt, Matthews, and Northall, might not be removed on account of the Service, the only private feeling I was influenced by was in asking permission to detain Toogood my servant.[104]

The sudden loss of two overseers and an efficient clerk would undoubtedly have been a blow to the administration. Whatever Maxwell's interests in the affair, however, this violent reaction from the governor was a sharp reminder of the vulnerability of any convict enterprise.

It remains to consider these final events in a broader perspective, to see what they tell us about the complex social interplay that lay behind the formal power structures of convictism and about the strategies of confrontation, manipulation, negotiation and ingratiation convicts used to achieve a space for themselves.[105] Captain Wright argued that resentment at the closure of the theatre, and his perceived part in it, were behind the obstructionism he experienced at the hands of the Emu Plains prisoners. If this was the case, it was a tactic of limited value – the revenge of the weak at plans frustrated. It had its satisfactions, but they were fewer, and the risks greater, than the classic forms of convict resistance, malingering and the go-slow.

Maxwell's approach to his men was the reverse of Wright's. He justified his alleged leniency by the work results it achieved.[106] Tolerance of the convict theatre would have been part of such a policy. Moreover, two of the key theatre personnel, Watt and Matthews, were of particular concern to him. Maxwell justified his defence of them, and particularly of Watt, on the grounds of their extreme value to the settlement. They were industrious and efficient workers. Watt's subsequent career lends plausibility to this. Sent down to Sydney for dispatch to Port Macquarie by the first available vessel, he made himself so useful on the *Phoenix* hulk that its superintendent begged his services as clerk to the vessel. Within a few months the colonial secretary was arranging for his transfer to his own office, which necessitated Watt living in the open community, and shortly after that he secured the further indulgence of a ticket-of-leave.[107] A punitive intent had been completely blunted by the man's usefulness – aided, no doubt, by some deft footwork on his part. If obstructionism had its satisfaction, willing compliance could sometimes achieve greater rewards.

That is not, of course, how Captain Wright saw the situation at Emu Plains. In his view Matthews was a 'tell tale rascal who poisoned his Masters ear', while Watt and Matthews together were 'subtle villains' who had obtained an ascendency over Maxwell 'by studied application to his weakness – vanity'. Maxwell, he added, was 'so precipitate and so credulous as he now is and ever notoriously has been to confidents'.[108] What Wright saw as vanity may have been nothing more than Maxwell's determination not to have his rights as superintendent usurped by the police magistrate, but there is certainly no subservience about the letter in which Matthews complained to Maxwell about Wright's behaviour. It is almost hectoring in its tone.[109] A few years later Major Mudie, with as little objectivity as Wright, described how Watt had 'duped' Maxwell, and attributed his success to the fact that Maxwell was 'an easy good-natured Scotchman, knowing nothing of the ways of the world, and having never, indeed, mixed in intelligent society'.[110] This presents a picture of a sophisticated Watt manipulating a provincial Maxwell; but it may contain a hint of something further – Maxwell vulnerable because of a sense of social inferiority to his refined and genteel assistant. There must often have been potential for a special to take advantage of a socially-insecure master, just as a master confident of his place in the world might have been seduced by fellow feeling for a gentleman prisoner. Whatever the nature of the association between Wright, Maxwell, Watt and Matthews, it provides a salutary reminder that the normal interplay of personalities, or the calculated exploitation of vulnerabilities, could undermine the best-laid plans of officialdom. Convict theatre may have made its opportunities by exploiting advantages such as these.

Chapter 7

'GALLANT CAPTAINS': HYNDMAN, MACONOCHIE AND THE FADING OF CONVICT THEATRE

Two years after the enforced closure of the Emu Plains theatre, Sydney finally obtained its commercial playhouse with the approval of a new governor. Its first licence, effective for six months from 26 December 1832, placed no limitations on those allowed to act, but subsequent licences included the provision that the licensee 'shall not nor will at any time during the term aforesaid employ permit or suffer any Convict whether under a temporary remission of sentence or otherwise to Act Perform or appear upon the stage of the said Theatre'.[1] It would appear that convicts had begun to infiltrate the new company, to the concern of the authorities. The unreliable O'Connell tells a story of a prisoner named Palmer from Hyde Park Barracks who obtained an evening leave pass, valid until nine o'clock, and used his time to perform for Levey as Richard III. He was recognised, and Police Superintendent Rossi had him arrested on stage, at the stroke of nine, as he was in the middle of Richard's death throes. Since Rossi's period as police superintendent effectively terminated in November 1833, the story could relate to the period of that first licence. It may be relevant that an actor named Palmer subsequently played with the company and was an enthusiastic Richard III.[2] Whether or not O'Connell's story is true is of less significance than the fact that, from the second licence onwards, convicts, including ticket-of-leave holders, were excluded from this new phase of Australian theatre-making.

The governor's regulation did not, of course, prevent emancipists from taking employment in Levey's theatre. The background of many of his players is obscure, but a number can be identified as transportees and some had prior theatrical experience, such as George Buckingham, Frederick White, Denis Fitzgerald and the irrepressible James Lawrence, who made an occasional appearance.[3] A few, like Buckingham and Mackay, were prominent in the company; but most were soon outshone by emigrants or those born in the colony, such as Conrad Knowles and Eliza Winstanley.

The position of these emancipists within the company was an uneasy one. On 25 March 1833 the *Sydney Monitor* reported that Levey was planning in future not to employ actors with a convict background. While presenting it as a rumour, the paper treated it as fact, predicting dire consequences. Levey was allowed a long response on 27 March 1833, but on 3 April 1835 the matter took a new turn with a further attack on Levey, in which he was accused of paying emancipist actors less than other performers of comparable talent. Thereafter the dispute seems to have fizzled out and with it any further discrimination against emancipists.

If serving prisoners were excluded from the company, they were not excluded from the audience. Levey conveniently overlooked, or was excused from, an earlier promise to ban such creatures from his auditorium.[4] From the beginning they were there in significant numbers, becoming a convenient target for journalists concerned at the unruliness of the house, as in the *Sydney Monitor* of 30 January 1833:

> A prisoner named Wood, who belongs to the Prisoners' Barracks … made himself very conspicuous at the Theatre on Monday night before half price commenced. He joined in expressions and gesticulations of the lowest and most insulting kind. When the half price mob entered, behaviour of the most disgusting description took place – too disgusting in short for us to describe. Prisoners of the crown were seen in all parts of the house, and the boxes were filled with the lowest of the low.

Poor behaviour, of course, was not the prerogative of convicts. On another occasion it was the theatre-going felons of Kent Street who attracted a diatribe, while in many instances it was evident that the conduct of the general public left much to be desired.

Sydney's Theatre Royal was not the only manifestation of the emerging new commercialism. The 'irregular' theatre was finally beginning to make its appearance as well. As early as 10 June 1804 the *Sydney Gazette* had announced the arrival of a galanty show for children in the colony, probably brought out by a convict on the *Coromandel*. He, or another children's entertainer, was active in early 1808, when a disgusted George Caley mentioned that, among the other highly improper carnivalesque celebrations of Bligh's overthrow, 'he was exposed by a showman to excite the laughter of children'. A galanty show was a magic lantern show operated by a narrator/actor and often supported by a musician, though there is later evidence of the term being applied to shadow puppets.[5] While the thought of a puppet Governor Bligh emerging from under a bed and covered with feathers is difficult to resist, the children of Sydney were probably entertained by a less substantial creation of moving shadows or projected images. Both these forms of theatre, by their nature, tended to be night-time activities and so could be carried out after a convict completed his regulation daytime tasks.

Another isolated manifestation of illegitimate or para-theatrical activity is provided by a criminal prosecution of 14 September 1816, in which an innkeeper was charged with using a back room for 'an Entertainment there of Slight of Hand upon Cards' at an entrance fee of one shilling per person.[6] In 1826 an entertainment in the style of the English fairgrounds was reported as if it were a novelty. It was probably inspired by the flurry of amateur concerts that year, arranged as part of Levey's attempt to launch a theatre:

A desire to entertain and to dispel the dull monotony that fills with *ennui* the minds of the good Sydney folks, (many of whom have not yet forgot the pleasureable moments passed on Tumble-down-Hill, and the purlieus of Brook Green, with the gaudy and astounding performances of Gyngell, Richardson, and Scowton) appears to influence both high and low. Like the more distinguished amateurs of the day; an humble individual, but of great name, even *Sydney Smith*, announced, in due form, *by printed circulars*, his intention of entertaining his *friends, 'by particular desire,'* with a display of his *'extraordinary abilities.'* There was first and foremost – 'The Wonders of the World' – and a very wonderful recitation it was, and as *wonderfully* delivered! Then there was 'imitations (inimitable) of London performers,' accompanied by *lots* of murders, not only of the heroes of the scene, but of Shakespeare, and the respective authors into the bargain! There were also comic songs, set comically to funny tunes, and sung in a style equally original and comic. And last, though not least in this extraordinary catalogue of wonders, *salamander-like* properties of this actor of-all-work, were exhibited, passing a red hot iron over his tongue, with divers resistencies of fire, &c.

In a neat set speech, the salamander then thanked his auditors for their patronage, promised better sport next time – all of which candour and good-humour, was answered by a liberal donation of *dollars, rupees, and dumps*. Mr. Kelly, of Pitt-street, accommodated the assemblage with the use of a capacious building, recently erected, which, for *the sort of thing*, was very passably fitted-up.[7]

From the mid-1830s onwards, the official record of licences granted by the government traces the growth of such activities not only in Sydney but also in the towns and hamlets across the colony. Rising above the smaller operators was Thomas Arnott who, in the latter part of the decade, was touring to townships as far apart as Kiama and Port Macquarie and as small as Freeman's Reach. At one stage his entertainment consisted of 'Illusions, dancing, Singing, Recitations on Logic – Imitations of the Principal Actors in England, Ventriloquism[,] balancing with various feats of Salamandering termed Fantoccini'. Almost as active was George Croft, who had appeared in Sydney as a tightrope dancer in 1833 and whose later touring shows focussed on 'Rope Dancing, Tumbling and Horsemanship'.[8] No doubt there were many unrecorded operators who ignored the requirement to secure a licence. Toby Ryan's recollection of 'the usual Punch and Judy, and Lollie Pop Joe; a big black American conjurer, and other attractions' in booths at a Penrith race meeting in 1824 is suspect for a variety of reasons. Greater plausibility attaches to his account of an 1833 Killarney race meeting at which, he claimed, 'Blind Loftus, a very ugly man, was dancing, and Black Simon playing the tambourine, at G. Freeman's booth. Every kind of amusement imaginable was going on, nine pins, poppet shows, the devil among the tailors'. He even made a passing reference to actors, though it is not clear what that word encompassed.[9]

Activities of this kind no doubt involved emancipists, but once again serving convicts were probably excluded, since even ticket-of-leave men were normally restricted to a district. At the same time these shows might have helped reduce the public interest in convict performances by providing a professional alternative, particularly in the larger towns such as Parramatta, Windsor and Maitland, which occasionally could support a legitimate theatre company from Sydney for a short season.[10]

If one cause of the decay of convict theatre was the challenge of a new professionalism, far more important were the changes in the convict system. Increasingly, attempts were made to isolate convicts from the community and, in the case of secondary offenders, to make their existence as joyless as possible by imposing on them a penitentiary-style discipline. When Baron von Hügel visited Emu Plains in 1834, the land had been sold off, but the convict depot remained as a base for the gangs labouring on the road through the Blue Mountains. The old stockade and the corrupt and inefficient convict supervisors were gone. Instead armed soldiers now policed a double-walled stockade equipped with night lights, and the station was on the way to earning the fearsome reputation that it has in the pages of Toby Ryan's memoirs. The Mount Victoria stockade, described by William Govett, is just as disturbing, with its floggings for those who so much as whistled or sang as the gang moved out to work.[11] Over all was that model of the new system, the *ne plus ultra* that was Norfolk Island.

In the light of this changing climate it is no surprise to find that the grass-roots theatre movement most conspicuous in the 1830s was not convict theatre, but forms of amateur theatre previously unrecorded in Australia. These were military theatre and, on a smaller scale, the amateur theatricals of respectable society. The first is best represented by the activities of the Windsor and Norfolk Island garrisons, and the second by the performances of the Melbourne company led by the Honourable J. Erskine Murray and a host of esquires.[12]

The evolution of the penal system was not as uniform as the last paragraphs might suggest. There were exceptions. After Port Macquarie was opened to free settlement, a nucleus of convicts, mainly specials or invalids, remained in the town under relatively relaxed rules, while others were assigned to private masters or given tickets-of-leave. In 1840 Captain Charles Hyndman made a doomed attempt to set up a convict theatre company in the settlement. As the *Australian*, 9 April 1840, commented: 'We fear the gallant captain will find that producing plays *sans* actors, *sans* orchestra, *sans* scenery, and indeed, *sans* theatre, will be rather a puzzling speculation.' In the event, it was the limitations of the actors that damned the inaugural production in the eyes of the *Australian*'s correspondent, on the 26 May:

> The principal cause of the non-success of the experiment is, we suspect, the unpliant material wherewithal the gallant captain essayed to form his company. They who require of the *bond* 'a song and melody in their heaviness' ought not to be surprised when they are told that their harps are hanged up; and we are somewhat amazed at the request having been made to any of this class. In other respects we do not disapprove

of the idea, and if some of the talent of the aristocracy of the district
could be engaged in the cause, we should augur rather favourably of
the attempt.

Even at this late date the assumption is being made that it takes gentlemen to produce
quality amateur theatre. It is possible that 'Nosey' Herring's unfortunate performance
as Shylock (Appendix B, Note 1) was part of this entertainment.

The impression given by the *Australian* is that the failure of that inaugural
production would have put an end to the scheme: certainly, the newspapers record
no further performances. Local oral history, however, as recorded by Colin Roderick,
speaks of an active theatre movement later in the decade, operating out of a disused
and dilapidated barn attached to the Government store. Port Macquarie boasted a
literary society, but it was the creation of the local gentry – men such as Nairn Grey
and Dr Fattorini – while the theatre company seems to have had a significant convict
and ex-convict component and might even have been an all-convict affair. The Port
Macquarie Literary Association could have acted as the company's patron, but it is
difficult to imagine the gentlefolk of the region sharing the stage with felons. On the
other hand, there can be little doubt that the audience reached down to the lower
echelons of society, since much of the surviving information about this theatre and
its plays seems to come from the recollections of the convict Big Bill Delaforce.

The most significant product of this obscure enterprise is the presence in its
repertoire of a number of plays from the pen of James Tucker, the chronicler of the
Emu Plains theatre, who was now a convict undergoing secondary punishment for
forgery. Tucker had arrived at Port Macquarie early in 1845 and secured a post as
storekeeper to the superintendent of convicts. He obtained a ticket-of-leave for the
district in January 1847 and left, without permission, in early 1849.[13] Oral tradition
has left us the names of three of his plays that were staged during his period at the
settlement – a skit, *Old Tumbledown* (whose title referred to the decaying theatre building
itself), *Makin' Money* and *Who Built that Cozy Cottage?*. These last two are described as
comedies, but were more likely to have been afterpieces. On internal evidence Tucker's
one surviving afterpiece, *Jemmy Green in Australia*, could have been written no earlier
than April 1844 and was probably also performed at this theatre. Whether his historical
verse drama with a Scottish setting, *The Grahame's Vengeance*, was presented here is
another question. There is a world of difference between mounting a topical afterpiece
and building the evening's entertainment around an untried drama; but Tucker might
have had enough influence to have prevailed.

Whether Tucker was writing for convicts or free men one claim seems doubtful,
namely that *Makin' Money* was a satire on the rum regime and that *Who Built that Cozy
Cottage?* poked fun at the activities of Major Archibald Innes, the local magnate,
whose house on Lake Innes was the grandest in the district. The involvement of an
earlier generation of the gentry in the rum trade was still a sensitive subject. Unless it
was treated with remarkable delicacy it is difficult to see any company, genteel or
convict, taking the risks involved. The same considerations could apply to convict
jesting at the expense of Major Innes, though in this case it is easier to imagine a type

of gentle humour that ultimately amounted to a form of flattery for its subject.

Activities at Port Macquarie extended into the late 1840s, but the spirit of the new age, and the end of convict theatre, are much better represented by the spectacular events at Norfolk Island in 1840. There is an added appropriateness to this in that 1840 saw the official termination of transportation to New South Wales. Those convicts who had already arrived remained in the colony, completing their sentences, but any theatrical activity subsequent to that year can be regarded as an afterglow.

II

In the grim history of the second settlement at Norfolk Island, with its policy of brutalisation and its succession of commandants who range from the frighteningly insensitive to the near sadistic, Captain Alexander Maconochie stands as an aberration, a quixotic idealist committed to the concept of convict reformation. His vision and his plan might have been impractical in many respects and tinged with an element of self-promotion, but they are a monument to decency in the middle of so much that was monstrous. Maconochie, however, was not a romantic who by some freak of maladministration found himself with a particularly distasteful posting. Many in the colony were horrified by the brutality of the convict system and the same feelings were abroad in influential circles in Britain. His appointment was the direct result of a change in policy on the part of the imperial government, though it was a change that was to be short-lived in the case of Norfolk Island.

In 1837 the Molesworth Committee on Transportation had made the latest of several parliamentary inquiries into the penal system. The government responded with a dispatch to Governor Sir George Gipps reiterating its intention to abandon assignment, outlining its plan to reduce the number of prisoners sent to the colony and instructing the governor to house on Norfolk Island as many as possible of those who were sent. It also declared 'that an essential alteration should be made in the system of punishment pursued there'. The instructions about this were sketchy, but central to them was the idea of remissions of sentence in the later years of imprisonment on grounds such as good behaviour. To implement such a change a new type of superintendent was required: 'He should feel a deep interest in the moral improvement of the Convicts, and be disposed to devote his whole energies to this important object.'[14] Maconochie's name was put forward in a separate note, with the acknowledgment that the final decision was Gipps'. A report by Maconochie on the convict system in Van Diemen's Land had influenced the Molesworth Committee, leading to this recommendation.

Maconochie's plans for Norfolk Island went well beyond the instructions to Gipps. His scheme had three main planks to it. One was a system whereby sentences were measured not in years but in thousands of marks. The convict was given credit points for good conduct and achievement, which could be accumulated until they equalled the mark value of the sentence, earning the prisoner his freedom. The aim was to develop habits of self-discipline and industry, which would remain with the convict after release, converting him into a useful member of society.

The second plank was a series of strategies to combat sociopathic tendencies. This involved treating the convicts with respect, minimising the use of violent punishment and demeaning petty regulations. It also obliged them to work in teams and encouraged patriotic and religious feelings, partly to build a sense of connectedness with others. As will be seen, patriotism was to play a significant part in Maconochie's plans for his theatricals.

It is the third plank of Maconochie's system that is most relevant to this study. Maconochie believed that the criminal sensibility could be transformed by exposure to education and the civilised arts. Shortly before his departure for Norfolk Island, he submitted to the governor, Sir George Gipps, a series of seven memoranda on key aspects of his scheme. Two of the seven relate to these matters, one dealing with the need for a library and another 'on the expediency of cultivating a taste for Music in Prisoners'. The proposed library shows some bias towards works that are morally improving or deal with farming and the mechanic arts, though even here the concern is not so much with the imparting of facts and orthodoxies as with the stimulation of the imagination. A case is also made for English history, 'the most popular *National Poetry*' and novels such as those of Sir Walter Scott, Maria Edgeworth, Jane Austen and Mary Mitford. Finally, Maconochie's ruling passion was reached:

> Few positions are more readily admitted in conversation than those which maintain the humanizing powers of Music; Yet in England Scarcely any practical results are founded on them. In dealing with Criminals especially, however, I am convinced that this is much to be regretted. Music is an eminently *Social* occupation. Including performers and listeners, it employs many Individuals together. Its acquisition is difficult, and it therefore cultivates patience and perseverance … It is of itself elevating and ennobling, and is, besides, combined frequently with high and elevating Poetry and Sentiment.

Interestingly, in view of what was to happen, theatre makes no direct appearance in Maconochie's policy documents, and in discussing the possibility of plays being included in his convict library, his discomfort is palpable:

> I am … doubtful of [including] … National Theatre; yet Shakespeare's Plays ought to be included; and I would not myself object to any, though I fear rather than hesitate to recommend many more. The English Drama is often Licentious; but substantially its tendency is moral; and I extremely doubt the value of any virtue founded on Ignorance, or the mere absence of licentious images. Besides, dramatic representation is a portion of the Natural Sequence in training the mind from complete ignorance up to knowledge, from the necessity of being read to to the power and pleasure of itself reading.[15]

If Maconochie did, in the end, endorse the performance of plays by Norfolk Island convicts, then his motive must be found in the half-hearted argument of his final sentence, or inferred from the fact that music, in the British culture from which he came, found one of its major outlets in the theatre – as opera, burletta, the play with music, and as incidental songs. As will be noted later, the playbill for the Kingston production reveals a heavy bias towards musical pieces.

III

Maconochie might have taken over Norfolk Island with the blessing of the central government, but the support for him in that quarter was quickly put to the test. His cavalier disregard for rules, regulations and direct orders, the overweening confidence with which he pursued his objectives, and the verbose reports he submitted in explanation or defence of them, exasperated Gipps, whose dispatches to the Colonial Office quite properly reflected this. Though sympathetic to reform, Gipps was sceptical of Maconochie's approach and irritated by his manner. Soon the home government was reflecting this concern, and as early as 10 September 1840 Lord Russell was authorising Gipps to dispose of Maconochie, if he saw fit. It says much for Gipps' fairness that he took no such step, and ultimately it was the central government which terminated Maconochie's appointment.[16]

The friction between Maconochie and his superiors, however, was mild in comparison to the hostility revealed by influential sections of colonial society. In these quarters self-interest merged with the view of prisons as places of terror, whose chief function was to act as a deterrent to crime. The result was outrage and fear, voiced often through the sarcasm and ridicule to which Maconochie's more utopian ideas lent themselves. This sarcasm and ridicule was evident before much in the way of reports had filtered back from Norfolk Island. On 22 February 1840, the *Australian* was relatively amiable in its joking reference to Maconochie's faith in music:

> A musical doctor of eminence has accompanied Captain M. to Norfolk Island, with a box of appropriate instruments. The prisoners will, we suppose, be made to march, like the Spartans of old, to the sound of Dorian flutes, and the lesson of future reformation will doubtless be most effectual, when it is recommended by the persuasive music of the tuneful *reed*.

Richard Jones, Esquire, a member of the Legislative Council, was much more acid, interjecting into a Council meeting on 2 June 1840 a reference to 'the tea drinking comforts of Captain Machonochie's absurd system of discipline at Norfolk Island'.[17]

However, these comments were minor tremors compared to the full earthquake that was to engulf Maconochie at the end of June, when the government supply vessel returned from the island with private letters describing recent activities in the settlement. As the *Colonist*, 1 July 1840, expressed it:

Since the arrival of the *Governor Phillip* from Norfolk Island, nothing has been so much the topic of conversation as the reports which have reached us of the working of Captain MACONHOCHIE's penal discipline in Norfolk Island.

Central to these reports were descriptions of the Queen's birthday celebrations, in which theatre figured prominently. They caused an immediate furore, and throughout his rule, and for years after, the playmaking, along with the lemon-juice laced with rum issued to the convicts to toast the Queen, were used remorselessly to exemplify the folly of Maconochie's policy. As Maconochie wrote, several years later, the rum punch and the plays were 'one of the wisest, and best-considered acts of my whole administration, and which has been the most pertinaciously censured'. He went on to describe the events wryly as 'this act of high treason against existing notions of prison discipline' and 'those unlucky plays ... which gave so much after offence'.[18]

The details of the festivities were revealed in the *Australian Chronicle* on 23 June 1840; and at even greater length on the following day in the *Sydney Herald* where, after an ominous introduction, a letter from Norfolk Island was reproduced:

> The Queen's birthday was celebrated here on Monday, the 25th ultimo, and Norfolk Island was on that day one universal scene of loyalty and merriment, a short sketch of which may not be uninteresting: – At daylight the whole of the new code of signal flags, upwards of twenty in number, were displayed on the rigging of the new signal staff, with the Royal George at the top; and the gates were thrown open to the whole eighteen hundred prisoners, who proceeded to the cricket ground, and commenced cricket and various other amusements, Captain Maconochie occasionally appearing among them; at twelve, a royal salute of twenty-one guns was fired from the top of the hill towards Longridge; the two guns from Government House and others from the vessel having been previously carried there. This salute was answered by three rounds from the military, after which the prisoners sat down to dinner in a line on the road, extending from the salt-house upwards almost as far as the lime-kiln. After dinner, with Captain Maconochie at their head, every prisoner was supplied with a glass of grog to drink the Queen's health, which was followed with shouts that almost rent the air – 'Three times three for Queen Victoria!' 'Three times three for Captain Maconochie!' &c. This being over, the men resumed their sports, and a play was performed in the large mess room with new scenery, dresses, music, songs, &c., the whole of which was witnessed by Captain M. In the evening a grand display of fireworks were let off by the prisoners, and all were permitted to be at large until 8 o'clock at night, at which hour another salute of 21 guns was fired, which terminated their day's amusement, and every man retired to the barracks, perhaps for the first time, with satisfaction. Not a single instance of theft, disorder, or accident occurred during the day, nor was there one solitary instance of a man being in the gaol that day or following morning for misconduct.

> In the evening government house was illuminated, and a ball and supper given to entertain the military and civil officers, &c. Capt. M. is an exceedingly clever man, with an unbounded share of humanity and kindness. But some persons here think he is carrying his benevolence *too far*. He is all mildness and indulgence, and the men do almost as they wish. The day is past for tyranny. Here is now no flogging, no irons, no oppressive labour, no shutting men up in gaol cells, &c. But I expect that some part of the Sydney press will soon begin to apply its lash upon the Captain. But reformation and contentment are far more likely to ensue from the present system, than from the heartless manner in which they were treated in times gone by.

The letter, in turn, was followed by Maconochie's proclamation, and then by the playbill for the 'Royal Victoria Theatre', an original of which was sent by Gipps to his superiors in London, where it is preserved in the Colonial Office papers[19] (see Fig. 16).

The account published in the *Australian Chronicle* is based on another letter from Norfolk Island, and provides further details, notably in relation to the theatrical performance. The convict population of Norfolk Island comprised over 1,200 hardened offenders shipped from Van Diemen's Land and the mainland for crimes committed there, and 600 new offenders from England, regarded as more docile and reclaimable than the others. The two groups were kept apart, the old lags in the main settlement at Kingston, and the new hands at Longridge. Maconochie's instructions were to maintain the separation and though, on his first arrival, he had grandly decided to ignore the rule, because of its near impracticability, a blunt letter from Gipps had quickly made him more cautious. On the occasion of the Queen's birthday, then, two separate celebrations were necessary, and two separate play performances. Maconochie himself is specific about this,[20] and the letter in the *Australian Chronicle* provides a few details about the Longridge presentation. According to this account, after inaugurating the celebrations at Kingston, Maconochie and his party had moved on to Longridge (renamed Queenstown for the event), where he again addressed the prisoners. Then,

> at the close of this exhortation the curtain rose on a temporary stage, erected in the open area, and a band of vocal and instrumental music commenced the national anthem of God save the Queen. A large placard was then exhibited, announcing in due form that the 'Exile's Return' would be then performed 'by permission' for the *first* time, at the Queen's Town Theatre Royal: this produced thunders of applause. A similar exhibition took place at the old settlement, and thus the evening passed on, with some good acting and some excellent songs and glees, which were closed with fireworks and another salute of twenty-one guns.

Kingston actually possessed a 'very comfortable' weatherboard theatre with dress boxes and pit, built several years earlier by Colonel Joseph Anderson; but it was intended for performances by the military. A few convicts were employed there in ancillary capacities: 'Excellent scenery of all kinds was painted by artists amongst the

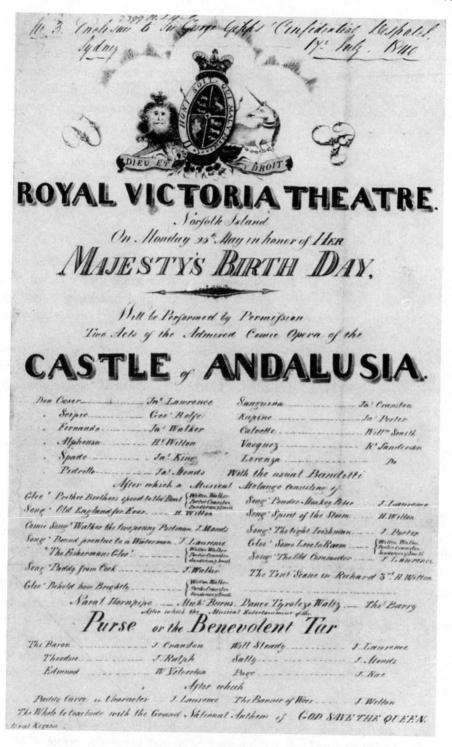

Fig.16 Playbill for *The Castle of Andalusia*, Norfolk Island, 25 May 1840 (Public Records Office, CO201/199, p.108).

prisoners, and the orchestra was composed of about half a dozen well-conducted convicts, who played the violin and clarions well.'[21] This military theatre would have been too small to accommodate the audience assembled on the Queen's birthday, and in any case the soldiery would almost certainly have resented its use by convicts. Accordingly, the Kingston performance took place in the 'large mess room', which, despite its title, could only accommodate two thirds of the prisoners.[22] A few years later an officer said of the mess-huts that

> worse accommodation for that purpose was certainly never beheld. Tables and forms black with dirt, out of repair, and insufficient in number, were scattered about without arrangement or uniformity. The sheds were open to the wind and clouds of dust, the roofs not watertight, the walls and rafters black and filthy … the floor of mud, full of holes and fissures, no facilities for cleaning or draining – a wretched, comfortless style.[23]

The writer was giving a composite picture of the large mess hall and the even more wretched second hut, which took the overflow of convicts at mealtime; but even with that allowance the image is dismal enough. The mess hall was also used for religious services, and one of the minor sources of outrage at Maconochie's behaviour was that this grubby house of God was being turned into a theatre.[24]

The Longridge performance, to judge from the *Australian Chronicle*, took place on an open-air stage. According to the *Australian Chronicle*'s account, an active building program had been under way at Longridge, which included 'several spacious buildings' for use as dormitories, but these would have been too small to accommodate the crowd.

IV

While there is only limited information about the Longridge performance, the Kingston entertainment is survived by its playbill. In this a central figure, as actor and singer, is the self-same James Lawrence or Laurent who claimed in his memoirs to have performed at Emu Plains seventeen years before. One of Maconochie's experiments was apparently to encourage the convicts to write their life narratives, and Lawrence's is one of a few that have survived. The text ends as Lawrence's sentence expires and he is about to leave the island. He makes some general comments on the impact of Maconochie's policies, but does not mention the Queen's birthday celebrations. The importance of Lawrence's contribution to these celebrations was noted in a letter to the *Sydney Gazette*, 25 June 1840, attacking Maconochie's innovations:

> A play has been allowed to be performed by the prisoners, to amuse their companions. A prisoner, I think of the name of Laurent, was the chief promoter and performer of this. Some of the colonists in all probability have heard of this hero of the Norfolk Island stage, before

to-day. Now, are the prisoners transported to be amused with this man and his companions absurdities on the stage?

This description of Lawrence as the 'chief promoter' of the performance may well be justified. In his General Order of 20 May, announcing the celebrations, Maconochie refers to the play being acted 'by Prisoners who have volunteered thus to amuse their companions'.[25] This could suggest that the idea originated with the convicts, in which case Lawrence was the obvious person to plant the idea in the superintendent's head. This is the more likely, since there is earlier evidence of his attempting to initiate a production at Norfolk Island, when Major Thomas Ryan was commandant. In his journal, under the date Tuesday 31 December 1839, the Rev. Thomas Sharpe, a stickler for Sunday observance, recorded:

> Last Sunday a Jew of the name of Laurent, had the audacity to write out on the Sunday a Play Bill, of some performance they wished to get up for New Years day, in case the Commandant gave them a Holiday. The Bill was taken from him, but he was not punished. In the list of performers I was sorry to find some of the Church singers whom I intend to remove, if they gave their consent to be put down as performers or singers in this absurd business. I rather think the Major will give them a half-holiday, but of course, will not allow them to perform their play.[26]

On the same page Sharpe described Lawrence/Laurent as 'the chief instigator of the play affair'. Since there is no mention of a performance in the following account of the half-day holiday itself, Sharpe's assumption that Ryan would forbid the play was probably justified.

This, moreover, may not have been Lawrence's only effort to achieve the near-impossible on Norfolk Island. Recording his experiences under Ryan's predecessor, Lawrence made the cryptic comment:

> In Major Bunburys time I was sentenced 50 lashes for singing, and caught out of my Hammock, after Six o clock in the Evening, but the Flogging omitted owing to my indisposition, the Major was a very strict man and no Lover of the Drama.[27]

Does the last phrase refer to his punishment for singing or does it point to some more ambitious project that was also thwarted by the Major?

Even if Lawrence had not originated the Queen's birthday event, he was almost certainly behind the choice of the mainpiece for the old lags of Kingston, John O'Keeffe's *The Castle of Andalusia*. The role of Don Caesar was Lawrence's *pièce de résistance*: in his autobiography he claims to have performed it on his first appearance in New York, and again in the Sydney theatre in the 1830s.[28] The play is an intrigue drama in which cardboard Mediterranean heroes and heroines pursue love, money and revenge in the castle and its surrounding forests. The ingredients might suggest Gothic melodrama, but in O'Keeffe's handling they become a pale comedy of confused identities, with the threats remote, the passions mild and the villains figures of fun. Presumably the heavy interspersing of songs attracted Lawrence, who was as much a dramatic singer as an actor. Maconochie was probably happy to accept Lawrence's urgings because, as a play with music, it also satisfied one of his strongest passions: the playbill, like the first edition, describes it as a comic opera.

The content of the piece, however, should have given the superintendent pause. The role that Lawrence had made his own was that of a brigand chief who, with his gang of banditti, dominates Act I, which opens and closes with rousing songs in celebration of the criminal life:

Air. IV. Don Caesar.
On by the spur of valour goaded,
Pistols prim'd and carbines loaded,
Courage strikes on hearts of steel;
While each spark
Through the dark
Gloom of night,
Lends a clear and cheering light,
Who, a fear or doubt can feel?

Like serpents now, through thickets creeping.
Then on our prey, like lions, leaping!
Calvette to the onset lead us,
Let the wand'ring trav'ler dread us!
Struck with terror and amaze,
While our swords with lightning blaze. (Thunder.)
Thunder to our carbines roaring,
Bursting clouds in torrents pouring,
Each a free and roving blade,
Ours a free and roving trade,
To the onset let's away,
Valour calls, and we obey.[29]

One wonders at the redemptive effect of such songs on a group of performers and an audience of hardened criminals. Though no such concern was voiced in the colonial press, an English journal of 1842 suggested contemporaries were sensitive to such matters. In a description of Sydney the writer claimed the actors in the local theatre were convicts, and lamented that

> so entirely lost are they to all sense of shame for their own situation in
> the colony, that men of notorious crimes have been heard to sing with
> perfect indifference such songs as 'The Wolf,' and the robber's song in
> the Castle of Andalusia, 'Some love to roam', &c.[30]

The account is in error, in that Sydney's Royal Victoria actors were not convicts, but the judgment does convey the rising moral concern of the time. There is even the possibility that the comment is a confused recollection of debates in Sydney about the Kingston performance, since that included not only the piece from O'Keeffe's play but one of the other songs mentioned, 'Some love to roam'. Two pages earlier the writer had made the curious comment that 'Sir George Gipps … shows himself humanely solicitous to improve the minds and benefit the conditions of the prisoners; with which view he has attempted to set on foot a love of the arts, and to excite a laudable spirit of emulation amongst the convicts'. It is difficult to see what this might refer to other than Maconochie's experiments at Norfolk Island.

The rest of the Kingston program was unexceptionable. *The Castle of Andalusia* had been cut back to the first two acts. This left ample room for a mass of solo songs and glees, a couple of dances, and that standby of the spouting fraternity, the tent scene from the last act of *Richard III*. The evening terminated not with a farce but with a short 'Musical Entertainment', as the playbill describes it, John Cross's *The Purse; or, The Benevolent Tar*. Maconochie's commitment to music clearly shaped the program, but, with the exception of *The Castle of Andalusia*, it served another end that was dear to his heart, a revival of feeling for the *patria*, which he saw as one of the major bonding forces in a community. The following day he emphasised this in an address to the convicts:

> No Man can be a good member of any Society who is indifferent to the ties which connect him with its other Members; – and no one can thus be a good Englishman to whom its national rejoicings are matter of indifference. Among the lesser virtues, – lesser because not directly commanded by God ... there is none, accordingly, which the Superintendent desires more anxiously to cultivate among those under his charge, than that of *Patriotism* – the love of the '*Old Country*'.[31]

The choice of Queen Victoria's birthday for his celebration was itself a calculated gesture. Recollecting the event in later years, he spoke of the hatred most convicts felt for their country and declared: 'The anniversary of the birth of a young female sovereign, who had only recently ascended the throne, appeared to me precisely the occasion to call out different emotions.'[32]

The choice of songs and afterpiece was clearly designed to further this love of country. *The Purse* is built around the English sailor, celebrating his conventional attributes of heroism, patriotism, simplicity, warmth of feeling and decency – in this case all embodied in the character of Will Steady, enacted, not surprisingly, by James Lawrence. In the period of the Napoleonic wars the English tar had been elevated into a nationalist icon, calculated to suffuse an audience with a patriotic glow. Similarly, the songs used as an interlude between the play and the afterpiece are stirring national tunes or ballads of English or Irish life. The performers had some choice (Lawrence, for example, sang a song he had earlier performed in the Sydney theatre), but the guiding hand was Maconochie's. Writing of the Thursday evening concerts he instituted on the island, he confided: 'I especially seek to encourage patriotic, national, naval and other Music, calculated to keep up affectionate Recollections of home; and I attribute much of the general softening of Manners among us to this.'[33]

No playbill survives for the Longridge performance and there is a hovering uncertainty about the activities there. The *Australian Chronicle*'s reference to the two presentations as 'similar' rather than 'the same', and its naming of the mainpiece at Longridge as *The Exile's Return* implies there were two distinct productions.

Maconochie's subsequent account is even clearer. He had 'two plays acted the same evening' and also describes them as 'those unlucky plays … one at each principal station'. In his General Order of 20 May 1840, however, he is more ambiguous ('a play will be acted at both Establishments by Prisoners'). The real problem here is that there is no English or American play with the title or subtitle, *The Exile's Return*, though there is a work by Frederick Reynolds, *The Exile; or, The Deserts of Siberia*, which had been performed at the Theatre Royal in Sydney on 2 May 1836. Once again it was a play with music. Assuming there were two 'similar' productions, the one at Longridge would have consisted of a short, or shortened, mainpiece, followed by a medley of songs and afterpieces, as the *Australian Chronicle* seems to imply.

James Lawrence, with his professional experience and his much-faded claim to a respectable background, might have been the leading actor and the driving force behind the performance, but another performer, Henry Whitton, was almost as significant. He had a prominent role as Don Alphonso in *The Castle of Andalusia*, had three solo songs, and was the bravura performer of the tent scene from *Richard III*. Whitton was a musical instrument-maker, with fraud and forgery his avocations. The former sent him to Van Diemen's Land in 1833 and the latter to Norfolk Island in 1839. On Norfolk Island he was highly regarded: an undated list of men recommended for transfer to Sydney described him as 'Chief Clerk in Engineer Office – Strongly recommended by Foreman of Works – educated – intelligent'. The claim is repeated in a list of twenty-five convicts especially recommended by Maconochie for transfer to Sydney and accepted on 23 February 1844. Once again the emphasis falls on his status as 'An educated man'. As an actor Whitton had one problem: he was seriously disfigured:

> Lost two front teeth left side of upper jaw, small scar under right eye, scar under right jaw, right cheek swollen from a fracture, lame of right leg, scar inside left wrist, scar on back of left hand, another on knuckle of third finger of same.[34]

Richard III might have been a favourite role among spouters, but it was one to which Whitton's disfigurements had a grisly appropriateness. Lawrence, incidentally, was not without his own disfigurements by this stage of his career. The Description Book of the hulk *Phoenix*, on which he had been held pending transfer to Norfolk Island, recorded him as 'pock pitted, large Roman Nose broken, squints with left eye, Scar on Breast and right Arm contracted'.[35]

Kingston, then, appears to have had a performance dominated by two specials, one of them particularly well-educated. Two of the remaining actor-singers, William Smith and James Walker, cannot be identified, but of the other seven only one seems to be a person of status comparable to that of Lawrence or Whitton. This is James Monds, who had indulged in the genteel crime of forgery while a clerk in the East India Office. However, his contribution as a performer is no more significant than that of the remainder, who included three labourers (one of whom was probably illiterate), two sailors (one semi-literate) and a boat builder. Three were English Protestants, one a Scottish nonconformist and two Irish Catholics.[36]

One man remains, James King. There were two prisoners of that name on the island, but of these one was the Jemmy King who had been such a force in the Emu Plains theatre (see Appendix B, Note 11). He is the more likely of the two to have taken part in the Norfolk Island entertainment. In *Ralph Rashleigh* King is said to have been particularly effective in comic roles, and it is such a role that 'Ja[s]. King' took on at Norfolk Island, where he appeared as Spado, the cowardly time-serving brigand in *The Castle of Andalusia*. While the role gave him great opportunities, it was his only part in the entertainment. The man who had been the life and soul of the Emu Plains theatre seems to have been overshadowed by his social superiors on Norfolk Island.

IV

In this way the Queen's birthday was celebrated on Norfolk Island. The writer of the original letter utilised in the *Sydney Herald* had prophesied that 'some part of the Sydney press will soon begin to apply its lash upon the Captain', and he was not wrong. On 25 June the *Sydney Gazette* carried a long letter attacking Maconochie's system, part of which is the account of the play and Lawrence's part in it. The full blast came in the *Sydney Herald* on 1 July in the form of three closely-packed columns headed 'Fete at Norfolk Island'. The writer used the Queen's birthday activities as a springboard for a broad attack on Maconochie's experiment and beyond that on the British government for a range of policies, some of them at a considerable remove from the immediate concerns of Norfolk Island. The article began with the announcement that, while the paper had a great deal of additional information about the 'Fete', it would defer publishing it until the governor's feelings on the matter were known. It then promptly suggests that a matter that should concern Gipps was

> this invasion of his prerogative, by a sub-superintendent of Convicts, defying the law, and setting at personal liberty 1800 convicts condemned to irons for life … Captain Maconochie, in the plenitude of his power, has done what Governor Gipps has never, we believe, authorised. He has done what Lord Normanby would not have ventured on without her Majesty's order. He has in fact set himself above law.

From this point forward any pretence of restraint disappears. The *Sydney Gazette*'s letter of 25 June had attacked the play on the grounds of theatre's tendency to deprave and corrupt, a feeling voiced on the island itself, according to the *Australian Chronicle* of 23 June, by one gentleman, probably the Anglican clergyman. The *Sydney Herald* had quite a different concern:

> We protest against such excitements to insubordination so long as there are convicts assigned to settlers in this colony. Had her Majesty's Secretary for the Colonies witnessed the gloom and depression that pervaded the minds of some of the most humane, liberal, and honorable men in the Colony when the proceedings of that day were published, he would

> have dismissed the perpetrator from the office he prostitutes to purposes
> detrimental to Colonial prosperity, loyalty, and peace. The employers
> of convicts … apprehend the worst consequences when information is
> communicated in the interior as to the altered state of Norfolk Island,
> the fear of which … 'was worse than death to delinquents'. Settlers
> apprehend that the small portion of subordination, restraint, and
> discipline now existing over incorrigible and irreclaimable men, is at an
> end. The festivities and allurements of Norfolk Island, by placing them
> in a better condition than in assigned service, will act as a *Bonus to crime*.

The diatribe continues in this vein, imagining the effects of the new order at Norfolk Island on other government prisoners in the colony and on 'the thousands of starving men in England restrained from crime, not by moral obligations, but by the fear of penal servitude'. The poor of England, it continues, 'will have no dread to join the revellers at Norfolk Island, indulging in plays and punch, who by crime have not incurred, but escaped from labour, sheep-farming and daily toil'.

For all this invective it is worth noting that only a few months earlier the *Australian* had reported, in an amused tone, the efforts of Captain Hyndman to set up a convict theatre at Port Macquarie. The event excited no comment in the *Sydney Herald* – no outrage, no protest. Port Macquarie was the declining product of an earlier system and the implication was that the production was intended to entertain not the convicts but the free population. In the case of Norfolk Island, moreover, the production was seen, not as an aberrant departure from the principles of harsh punishment, but as part of a wholesale attack on them.

The *Sydney Herald*'s declared readiness to wait for the governor's response did not involve it in any great delay. On 4 July 1840, the *Australian* reported the doings of the latest meeting of the Legislative Council:

> Mr Jones brought under the notice of His Excellency the proclamation
> of Captain Machonochie … to the convicts at Norfolk Island, directing
> the proceedings of the festivities on the Queen's Birth day, and
> concluding with the bill of the play, which he denounced as highly
> improper both in precept and example to the prison population in this
> Colony.
>
> The Governor expressed himself in the strongest terms of
> disapprobation of the theoretical experiments of Captain Machonochie,
> which he said, he would not suffer him to pursue to risque the security
> of this community.

The governor justified this public rebuke in a confidential dispatch to Lord John Russell on 17 July:

> The excitement in the Colony produced by Captn. Maconochie's
> proceedings has been very great, and would have been much greater,
> had I not avowed my disapproval of some of them. Play Bills from
> Norfolk Island, similar to the one which I enclose, are circulated in the
> Colony, and have given rise to loud expressions of dissatisfaction.

In his first report of the convict population being 'regaled with Punch, and entertained with the performance of a Play', he had referred to 'the very general alarm created in the Colony by Captn. Maconochie's proceedings'.[37]

If the amount of newsprint devoted to it is a measure of public interest in an issue, then there was a strong response to Maconochie's activities; but not all of the comment was negative. The Catholic newspaper, the *Australian Chronicle*, supported Maconochie, as did the *Commercial Journal*, though it paid little attention to the birthday festivities and the playmaking. In Van Diemen's Land the *Colonial Times* was similarly sympathetic. The *Australian* and the *Colonist* were equivocal, claiming respect for Maconochie's aspirations, but raising doubts about his policies. The *Sydney Gazette* was hostile, but its attacks were overshadowed by those in the *Sydney Herald* which, in their inflated rhetoric, their savage abuse, their hysteria and their misinformation, represented the reactionary press at its lowest. Nevertheless, it was the *Sydney Herald* that set the tone. That Gipps read the public response as one of alarm might reflect the narrow circle in which he moved, and the abusive power of the *Sydney Herald* which, as a *de facto* Tory journal, was determined to discomfort a Whig governor.

While Maconochie resolutely maintained his convict bands and continued to observe some national holidays on a much-reduced scale, the theatrical performances he permitted on the Queen's birthday were his first and last.[38] However, it is characteristic of Maconochie that, even though he abandoned theatricals in practice, he continued to ponder on a place for them in Norfolk Island's future. One of his ideas was that in the last phase of a convict's sentence he should be allowed to live a life as close as possible to that prevailing in outside society, as part of a process of acclimatisation. Accordingly, only two months after the Queen's birthday affair, he is to be found proposing that

> as they approach their Freedom, a well regulated Theatre, or public Readings of any other Kind, should be open to them on suitable Payment for Admission. In every Way their Minds should thus be stirred, and their Position raised up to the usual Privileges of Freedom before they are fully confided to them.[39]

Maconochie may have produced no more plays, but he was not allowed to forget that he had once done so. On 5 May 1842 the *Sydney Herald* referred to the island as the 'head quarters of fiddle and fun' and spoke of the 'senseless mummeries' the governor had rebuked. It even implied that such activities were continuing:

> The gallant Captain was despatched to Norfolk Island, some two years ago, with the appointment of Superintendent; and … there he has ever since remained, training up the convicts in the way they should go, and instructing them in the accomplishments of fiddling, dancing, drinking rum-punch, enacting plays, and greeting the name of Her Most Gracious MAJESTY with loyal and lusty huzzas.

Only three months before, in the *Free Press*, 20 January 1842, a correspondent from Norfolk Island had complained that from the observations that have appeared on this subject, it may be supposed ... that these performances are a daily or weekly occurrence. For the information of such parties ... I deem it necessary to state, that the play on the Queen's birthday, in 1840, was the only one that has taken place on the island in which the *prisoners have participated*.

The italicised words are there to preserve the distinction between convict theatre and military theatre, the latter of which continued unabated.

The isolation of Norfolk Island made it possible to sustain stories of frequent performances and to generate new rumours such as those in the *Australian*, 31 July 1841:

There are strange stories going about relative to Norfolk Island ... We have every desire to give Captain Maconochie's system a full trial. But with regard to Norfolk Island; there is, we are told, a Theatre (!) building; there are sixteen men employed as a Band (!) to discourse sweet music to the unfortunates on the island ... Of course but little can be positively known here, as correspondence with Norfolk Island is but limited; but we believe his Excellency Sir George Gipps has received some strange information before this, which will not enhance the system in his estimation.

There is no evidence that any theatre was being built, but by 1842 the rumours and the distortions had alienated most of the press, which was describing the experiment as a failure. When Gipps himself, in an effort to get at the truth, made an unannounced visit to the island, he was surprised how far the reality was from the lurid accounts being published, and impressed by many of the achievements of Maconochie's system. However, it was too late. Maconochie's dismissal was already on its way from England.

While the intention was to replace Maconochie with a firm disciplinarian, his departure was not followed by a reversion to systematic brutality. His successor, Major Joseph Childs, was a decent and honourable man, but in spite of his reputation as an efficient officer he proved unable to control either the staff or the convicts. The resultant disorder culminated in a particularly savage uprising in July 1846, a little over two years after Maconochie's departure, and after the governance of the island had been transferred from New South Wales to Van Diemen's Land. On that occasion a large group of convicts, maddened by petty provocations, broke out of the lumber yard and butchered four minor functionaries before being overwhelmed. Childs was dismissed, and thirteen of the convicts were hanged.

And yet, only six months after this uprising, and ten weeks after the hangings, there was one last flicker of convict theatre on the island, and this under the most infamous and feared of all the superintendents, John Price. Only one account survives, in the unemotional journal of Aaron Price, ex-convict and principal overseer of public works:

This day being Christmas Day each prisoner was served with 1 lb of Fresh Beef. There was DIVINE service held Twice as on Sundays. The men made themselves as comfortable as possible under the

circumstances they are placed in they got up a play amongst themselves
in the Lumber Yard and made themselves as merry as possible.[40]

Such a brief account necessarily leaves many questions unresolved. Had John Price granted approval for the play or was it an improvised affair, got up on the day without authority? The lumber yard was a dangerous place for prison officers, who might have chosen not to notice such a minor infringement of the rules, but given Price's elaborate spy systems, this is unlikely. Considering Lawrence's attempt to produce a Christmas day play in Ryan's period, there could have been a fitful tradition of such things on the island, which Price, astonishingly, chose to recognise on this occasion. But, whatever its aegis, whatever its quality, this act of theatre was still a memorial to civilisation and the joys of creation in a community constructed on the negation of such things. The same could be said, if to a lesser degree, of many of the theatres that have been the subject of this study.

Conclusion

rguably the most striking feature of convict theatre in early New South Wales is that so many attempts were made to launch and sustain it. These attempts were not the work of the one small group trying repeatedly to achieve its goal. A few names crop up on more than one occasion, but for the most part the urge to make theatre was widespread. The 1789 production of *The Recruiting Officer* and the 1796 production of *The Revenge*, though less than seven years apart, would have had few actors in common and may have had none. Robert Brown had no known involvement in the theatre of 1800, but emerges as a key figure in the efforts to launch a company in the early 1820s. Thomas Restell Crowder was the pivotal figure in the first Norfolk Island theatre, but was not drawn into the second. Only one actor, Michael Lee, seems to have been common to both those island undertakings.

It has been difficult to obtain a picture of the social and cultural background of the convicts who created these theatres. However, only the second Norfolk Island theatre company approximates Francis Brewer's image of convict theatre as essentially the product of well-educated criminals, and none of them quite fits Thomas Keneally's picture of an uncouth troupe dependent on an officer and gentleman for polish and understanding. In fact, the Sydney theatre of 1796 drew its male participants from the middling ranks of society, from tradespeople and shopkeepers, with a significant bias towards the more respectable trades – watchmaker, printer, watchcase maker, ivory turner, hatter. The Emu Plains theatre of 1829–30 also drew on the trades for many of its players, though in this case the trades are less elevated – butcher, blacksmith, tailor – and there is a significant number of semi-skilled in the group, men such as sailors and carters. The mix is not dissimilar to that in Maconochie's theatre of a decade later and possibly reflects a shift in the composition of the convict intake or a growing interest in theatre among the lower orders.

No member of Sidaway's original company of 1796 is identified, unequivocally, as a gentleman, but some of these tradesmen seem to have had family links with the gentry, or otherwise to have acquired something of the gentlemanly manner. Men of this kind could have enriched the group by giving it improved access to the social and cultural competencies of the elite, all the more so if they held positions of influence among the performers. It may be significant that the two players in the opening production of 18 January 1796 for whom some evidence of gentility can be found are John Sparrow and Henry Green. These were, respectively, the company manager and the leading actor.

201

By the time of Emu Plains the word 'special' had become well entrenched in the language to describe a convict who, because of family influence, a significant level of education, or other claims to status, was in a position to be a nuisance to the authorities. The term, then, normally points to a gentleman criminal, but it could just as easily be applied to a clerk from the middle ranks of society with the cheek and the affectation to play the swell. In the Emu Plains theatre of 1829–30 it is easy to picture the two specials, William Watt and John Matthews, as the prime movers, setting the standard for the group. In the face of any such reading it is salutary to recall that the leading actor seems to have been neither of these, but the humble weaver, William Toogood, and that all three (if James Tucker can be trusted) were heirs to the achievement of the illiterate James King. Gentlemen or pseudo-gentlemen may have been an asset, but were not the *sine qua non* of convict theatre.

A feature of convict theatre that is of particular interest is the composition of its audiences and its differing relationships with those audiences. In part, but in part only, this reflects the different penal situations that existed from time to time or place to place. The 1789 production of *The Recruiting Officer* was a case of convicts performing for those who oppressed them, their subservience as players reflecting their subservience as prisoners. In all probability the performance organised at Port Macquarie in 1840 by Captain Hyndman was of a similar kind, while a more extreme example is the production at Emu Plains in 1825 described by de Bougainville. Here we seem to have a command performance arranged by a superintendent anxious to show off his latest toy and impress a visiting dignitary. The performers probably outnumbered the spectators – the visiting Frenchmen, the superintendent and his daughters and a few soldiers. Consciously or unconsciously, de Bougainville manages to convey the impression of the actors as grimacing puppets jerking about at the whim of the gentry.

Very different from this were the theatres of Sidaway and Crowder. Here we have commercial enterprises working in a relatively open society that allowed them to draw on a mixed audience of the convict and the free. The same openness meant that the companies themselves were not restricted to serving convicts. Among the participants were many free by servitude or with some form of pardon. From its very beginning Crowder's company numbered a senior NCO of the New South Wales Corps among its members, and by 1800 the Sydney company included some soldiers and, briefly, one person who had come free to the colony. In spite of the strange performance staged for de Bougainville, the Emu Plains theatre was also a commercial enterprise, but one with a difference – a money-making activity inside a notionally enclosed agricultural station in which the performers were serving convicts but the audience came from outside. That audience was a mixture of the local gentry and of small farmers, many of the latter ex-convicts or ticket-of-leave men.

Most of the other companies or isolated performances mentioned in this book were variations on one or another of these models, though the variations, as with the second Norfolk Island theatre, can be intriguing in themselves. One example that may be unique, however, is provided by Maconochie's 1840 production on Norfolk Island. Here the performance was part of a program planned at the highest level of authority on the island, but, though it was organised in this way and the company was exclusively convict, it was not intended for the delectation of officials, but for the benefit of their fellows. It was an experiment in social engineering.

Behind these questions of who comprised the acting group and who the audience lurks the broader issue of the structures of power within which these theatres had to operate and how they accommodated themselves to those structures. The 1789 production of *The Recruiting Officer* might be an example of convicts performing for their betters, but that did not make it a straightforward case of power and subservience. If I am correct in my suggestion that the initiative for the performance came from the convicts, then the event might be read as convicts seizing an opportunity of turning the rituals of the powerful to their own purpose. The play might have been proposed to the authorities as a contribution to the royal birthday celebrations, but the chance to perform a play was probably of much greater significance to the players than the occasion or the composition of the audience. The evidence in this case is of the slightest, but a little more of this type of manoeuvre can be seen in the case of Maconochie's 1840 production on Norfolk Island. The plan to make the Queen's birthday into an island-wide celebration was clearly Maconochie's own, and no doubt many elements of the celebration were also conceived by him – the open-air lunch, the loyal toast, the village-green competitions. But the proposal for a play might well have come from the convicts, led by James Lawrence, who is recorded as the prime mover in a hostile report from the island. Here the interests – and even the taste – of the ruler and the ruled are happily joined: both favoured music, Maconochie looking for a strongly national flavour and Lawrence for a chance to repeat one of his bravura performance pieces. The medley of songs, and the performance of *The Purse; or, The Benevolent Tar*, probably satisfied both men. The tent scene from *Richard III* answered Maconochie's needs and for his part Lawrence secured two acts of *The Castle of Andalusia*, a musical piece but in most respects decidedly inappropriate to a penal colony.

With so little detail surviving about convict theatre, the opportunities for charting delicate subversions of the formal power structures are severely limited. The Port Macquarie theatre of 1840 is reported as conceived and controlled by yet another authority figure, Captain Hyndman. In this case it is impossible to produce evidence for any sort of power play behind the event; but a few years after Hyndman's failure, and his downward spiral into paranoia and the madhouse, a second convict theatre emerged in the settlement. Another authority figure, such as Dr Fattorini, may have taken up the reins where Hyndman had left off, but Port Macquarie was known for the number of cultivated (or affected) specials among its convicts. One of these could well have been behind the second project, in which case could an already erratic Hyndman have been simply a front man for a wily convict? Henry Herring, for one, was notoriously manipulative. Was his performance as Shylock part of Hyndman's production, and did the unfortunate loss of his silver nose contribute to the failure of the project?

Less speculative examples of convict players exploiting their superiors' weaknesses come from Emu Plains, though even these are based on slender evidence. James Kinghorne was evidently enamoured of his convict theatre and made the most of the social advantages it offered him; but the theatre clearly had its own momentum. Presumably, the convicts were able to negotiate special benefits for their project because it brought advantages to the superintendent. Governor Brisbane's partiality to this theatre, as well as Sir John Jamison's patronage, would have been useful levers with any superintendent who was less well disposed. John Maxwell was one later superintendent who professed little interest in the theatre. The claim might have been made to distance himself from an activity which had suddenly become an embarrassment, but even if he was indifferent there remains the tantalising suggestion that he was powerfully under the influence of the two convicts at the centre of the playmaking. They, presumably, were happy to use their influence to serve the interests of theatre. Maxwell himself admitted to a heavy dependence on the pair because of their high calibre as administrators, but their power over him could have been based on something as inappropriate as a sense of social inferiority generated by their apparent refinement and gentility.

The manoeuvres considered in the last few paragraphs could be described as politics in little. But politics in a larger sense was also a feature of convict theatre, with the difference that at this level the convicts were usually the pawns in the political game, rather than the masters of it. The authorities were undoubtedly aware of the capacity of theatres to become sites of civil disorder, and had an early example to remind them when Norfolk Island erupted at the performance on 18 January 1794. On the other hand, there was the value of theatre as a social sedative, a means of keeping people satisfied with their lot. Balancing the dangers and the profits was a delicate task, and the willingness of the authorities to risk the experiment in Sydney after its failure at Norfolk Island is surprising. In spite of the slightness of the evidence, it is clear that those in power kept a close eye on this theatre, through direct or indirect censorship or through its infiltration by men upon whom they felt they could rely, the soldiery.

For all the documentation on the Norfolk Island disturbance of 1794, it remains unclear whether the fact that the outbreak took place in a theatre was fortuitous or whether the theatre itself had somehow become a focus for conflict. The fact that there had been earlier disturbances over the seating of the military suggests the latter – that the troops, consciously or unconsciously, had turned it into a testing ground for their rights and status and ultimately into an oblique challenge to the lieutenant-governor and his civil administration.

It is at Emu Plains that we first find reasonably clear evidence of the theatre caught up in other people's politics. I have argued that from 1825 the existence of this theatre was used as an argument for the licensing of a professional theatre in

Sydney; and as an instrument in the campaign against Governor Darling's authoritarian administration – indeed, as a challenge to the whole system of rule from London. At least one of Darling's officials saw the announcement of the 30 November 1830 performance as a political manoeuvre on the part of somebody from within or beyond Emu Plains – probably the latter. But Darling's prompt closure of the playhouse was accomplished with no further howls of protest. It did not itself become the occasion of public challenge to him. From his point of view the operation was a complete success. The men of Emu Plains no doubt felt differently about it.

Maconochie's 1840 production also has a broad political framework to it. The decision to celebrate the Queen's birthday in the way he chose was itself a political act – an extreme example of the liberal reformist nailing his ideological colours to the mast. The response was both savage and multi-layered. At one level it represented a violent conservative reaction to Maconochie and his reform agenda. But the opportunity was also taken to use it as a means of attacking Governor Sir George Gipps, who was seen by the ultra Tory press of Sydney as an instrument of the Whig administration in Britain. A small-scale theatrical enterprise in a remote outpost of a distant colony had political ramifications which, in however faint a form, reached to the heart of empire.

Appendix A

DRAMATIS PERSONAE

1. PERFORMERS AND OTHERS ASSOCIATED WITH THE SYDNEY THEATRE, 1796–1800

This appendix honours the men and women who first brought European theatre to Australia. The research into their lives was undertaken in order to gauge their social background and cultural competence and also to measure the extent to which the military had penetrated the mainland company in 1799–1800. It thus constitutes the detailed evidence that underpins the discussion in Chapter 4 of theatre as a social institution and its relation to the structures of colonial authority.

The name headings are those by which the individuals are identified in primary documents.

MRS BARNES

RONSW, Marriages. 4.312.

The Mrs Barnes who in 1800 played the major roles of Melinda in *The Recruiting Officer*, the Hostess in *Henry the Fourth* and Mrs Hardcastle in *She Stoops to Conquer* is, on the evidence, the same woman who sought court injunctions against Thomas Radley and Mary Ann Fowles on 18 September 1799 in a playhouse squabble. Since she does not appear in Mrs Parry's benefit of 1 June 1799, she might well have joined the company between those two dates. The casting suggests that her perceived strength lay in comic character parts, to which Mary Ann Fowles herself might have had aspirations.

Since the record of the dispute is an official court document, Barnes was probably the actor's legal name. The same document records 'Mrs Radley' by *her* legal name, Mary Ann Fowles. The only Mary Barnes clearly recorded as arriving in the country under that name by 1800 was one of a group of four female shoplifters charged with stealing lengths of cloth from two Deptford mercers. Sentenced to seven years' transportation at Maidstone in March 1789, she arrived at Port Jackson on the *Lady Juliana* on 3 June 1790 and was sent on to Norfolk Island two months later. There she bore two children (father or fathers unknown), one of whom died in infancy. She disappears from the island records in 1794, and her two-year-old son in 1796, so that she either died or left the island in the poorly-documented period between then and 1800.[1] If this is the actress, as I believe, a return to the mainland late in 1799 best accounts for her absence from the company in earlier productions.

Mary Barnes is curiously absent from all the musters taken in the colony after 1800. However, as no other adult Mary Barnes is known to have been in the colony at that time, Mary Barnes of the *Lady Juliana* was almost certainly the witness to the marriage of John Lee and Catharine Riley at St Phillip's church on 25 December 1803. Her laboured and wavering signature on the register suggests that she was barely literate.[2]

The same Mary Barnes apparently owned a house at No.15, Chapel Row, which was used in September 1805 as security for a debt of £20 to Edward Wills, dealer, 'which I am at present unable to pay and satisfy'. If the debt was not paid within six months, the house was to be forfeited to Wills. The security for loans was usually well in excess of the debt: in 1812, for example, a property worth £150 was used to cover a debt of £43.[3] Mary Barnes' house, then, was probably worth significantly more than £20, a figure which would have bought only a modest dwelling. The outcome of the assignment is unknown, but by 1810 the house was in the possession of John James. By 1821, when its next owner, William Cluer, was attempting to sell it, the building on the site had become 'a capital HOUSE ... containing several good rooms, outhouses, garden, and a well of the purest water in the colony ... The premises are well adapted to the residence of two families.'[4]

Mary Barnes was in difficulties of a different kind in July 1806, when, along with several other women, she was sentenced to six months at Newcastle, for rowing out to meet an incoming vessel, the *Vulture*, before it had been cleared by the authorities. The *Vulture* was a southern whaler returning to port and one might guess at the women's interest in it. Two of Mrs Barnes' companions had been London prostitutes, one of whom was sent to Newcastle for a second visit in 1809, after being accused of robbing the boatswain of the *Admiral Gambier* while consoling him in his bunk. (The charge could not be substantiated, but the magistrate packed her off, nonetheless, as a disorderly person.)[5]

In the second and third decades of the nineteenth century the number of references to a Mary or Mary Ann Barnes increases. Only one seems to relate to the earlier Mary Barnes, though a difficulty is involved. In June 1827 Mary Barnes, aged 63, of Sussex Street, Sydney, died. She was buried from St James' Church, the register of which notes her as having arrived on the *Mary Ann* 1, which had berthed on 9 July 1791. However, no convict or soldier's wife of that name is known to have travelled on that ship, while Sara Barnes, who was on board, lived as a farmer's wife beyond Parramatta and died in 1853.[6] It seems likely that the attributed ship of arrival is an error, and that it was the erstwhile actress in the Sydney theatre who was buried on that day.

WILLIAM CHAPMAN

[signature: William Chapman]

SRNSW, 4/1821, no. 58.

Only one William Chapman seems to have arrived in New South Wales as a convict prior to 1802.[1] There was no-one of that name in the New South Wales Corps or recorded in any other capacity in the early colony, apart from the genteel official William Neate Chapman, who was posted to Norfolk Island in the relevant years (see Fig. 10).

Accordingly, the William Chapman whom Collins names as a performer in the inaugural production, and who also appeared in Henry Green's benefit on 23 July 1796, can only be the William Chapman who was convicted at the Old Bailey in April 1791. This remarkably cool young man, with a colleague, stripped 400 lb of lead from the roof of Stepney Church in broad daylight, after claiming they had been sent by the regular plumber to repair leaks. To achieve their ends the two had to talk their way past the female sexton, a pew-opener and the gravedigger. Finally, a plumber working on an adjacent building grew suspicious and had them brought down from the roof for interrogation. Their plausible speech was probably reinforced by their respectable appearance, since the sexton described them as 'dressed very smart, in long coats, clean shirts, and very tidy'. For all the smoothness of the operation, it was also thoroughly foolish, since the thieves were probably locals: the plumber recognised them, even if he did not know their names.[2]

Chapman made no speech in his defence and called no character witnesses. Aged 23 at the time, he was sentenced to seven years' transportation, and sailed on the *Pitt*, which arrived in Sydney in February 1792.

In a petition of 30 January 1810 Chapman claimed that

> General Grose was pleased to recommend the applicant to Governor Phillip, and from His Excellency to every successor; and his General good conduct has enabled him to refer with all respects to every Commander in chief, and many officers in the Colony.[3]

Grose had also sailed on the *Pitt*, so that Chapman might have won his approval during the voyage. The suggestion that Chapman gained the respect of later governors and officers is an exaggeration, but he did keep out of trouble throughout the 1790s: he was never before the courts and only appears in David Collins' history in connection with the theatre company.

By the end of 1796 Chapman's steadiness had earned him a position as a constable. Since that position could involve evening work, it may have terminated his acting career. Certainly, he is not listed in Mrs Parry's 1799 benefit, nor in the playbills of 1800. By February of the latter year he had ceased to be a constable,[4] but was already involved in other activities. In late 1798 or 1799 he had commenced living with the formidable Ann Marsh: their first child was born in March 1800. Ann Marsh (or Mash) had managed a liaison with the ship's surgeon on the voyage out, had wed a convict doctor after her arrival and on his death had married a wild Irishman. She had three children surviving from these relationships and was already an established businesswoman by the mid-1790s, owning a ferryboat service to Parramatta, for which Robert Sidaway at one stage was her guarantor.[5]

Chapman too might have expanded his activities beyond the plumbing and glazing trade into other lines of business, but it was only after the alliance with Ann Marsh that this becomes evident. At the centre of their activities was a general goods shop in lower George Street, close to the head of Sydney Cove, referred to indiscriminately as Marsh's or Chapman's. Whenever there was trouble, Marsh was usually at the forefront. One notable incident was over the sale of liquor without a licence – and on a Sunday – and a subsequent attempt to bribe the constable.[6] On another charge, in late 1802, Chapman himself was accused of illicit traffic in wine involving officers of the French naval vessel *Le Naturaliste*, then in port as part of the Baudin expedition. This became a case of his word against the officers' – a hopeless position made the more so by Governor King's determination to cultivate the visitors. The officers claimed that Chapman had negotiated to supply them with vegetables and other goods during their stay, but, because of his 'having conducted himself improperly', they had severed the connection. Governor King described him as a 'bad character' and a 'miscreant'.

Despite this, Chapman was accepted – albeit briefly – into the Sydney Loyal Association, a militia set up by King in 1800 and limited to respectable householders. He appears in the members' roll of November 1802, but in the next surviving list, 7 April 1804, his name is scored through with the marginal note, 'Dism'd', that is 'Dismissed'.

Against these intimations of a shaky reputation is an entertaining account of a magistrate's examination, as reported in the *Sydney Gazette*, 10 June 1804:

> Mr. *William Chapman*, painter and glazier, having some time since given notice of the sale of a cask of oil, was called upon by Mr. *William Stuart*, master of the sloop George, to declare from whom he had purchased the said oil, he having nearly about the same time entertained suspicion that a quantity had been brought on shore from the vessel without his knowledge.
>
> He assured the BENCH that it was very far from his intention by any such enquiry to asperse the character or wound the feelings of Mr. *Chapman*, as he was convinced that no illegality in the transaction would be found imputable to him; but the information he desired was barely for his own personal satisfaction, in clearing up his doubts respecting those who might have availed themselves of opportunities to take advantage of his necessary absence.
>
> The Respondent then addressing the BENCH, acknowledged that the motive by which he had been induced to refuse gratifying Mr. *Stuart* privately was, that in the very suggestion itself suspicion of his conduct had been evidently implied; and therefore he had conceived a duty to his character, upon which a family depended, to reserve the explanation for the public occasion that now presented itself.
>
> Here he gave that explanation, which was so thoroughly satisfactory as to induce the MAGISTRATES to give him the strongest assurances that they were in all respects satisfied with his conduct; and at the same time recommended that their opinion should be made public through the present channel.

Over the first decade of the nineteenth century the Chapman/Marsh enterprise gave all the signs of being a flourishing business, expanding to include a bakery, a butchery and a pie manufactory, while being maintained as a general store. In 1809 a wine and spirit licence was secured for the premises, as the King's Head Tavern, with William Chapman as the licensee. It was renewed in 1810. Throughout this period Chapman continued to be active as a plumber, painter and glazier, normally describing himself in those terms.

Chapman's financial position, however, may have been precarious, since the petition of 30 January 1810 is a request for land on the grounds of the large family he has to support. On 16 June of that year he died. He is presumably the William Chapman who is recorded in a later document as having passed away insolvent, leaving a debt to the government of £5 18s. incurred under Governor King. As his tombstone noted, he was 45, and left a widow and nine children.

Since Ann Marsh had never married Chapman, insolvency on his part did not strip her of any property held in her own name. She kept the ferryboat service until her death, and the King's Head public house in George Street until at least May 1813; there is no record of a licence after that year. In 1818 she is described as a baker of New Street. All, or most, of Chapman's children either became comfortably placed tradespeople or their wives.

Chapman's role in the theatre's first production is unrecorded. In Green's benefit of 23 July 1796 he played the part of Charles, one of the two rakish young men about town who are the heroes of Mrs Centlivre's *The Busy Body*. While Charles is slightly overshadowed by his more exuberant friend, Sir George Airy, the role is still a substantial one. It called for the elegance and urbanity of the polished gentleman, qualities that might have been well within the reach of the smooth-talking, smartly-dressed young man from Stepney Church.

Chapman's signature has survived in a number of places. In its extreme form it is assured and characterised by bold flourishes, suggesting a good basic education and a concern to present well. The petition of 1810 appears to be his composition and does not live up to the signature. It is plain and functional, with no signs of the literary skills (or pretensions) of a Daniel Parnell or a Thomas Crowder.

MRS CHARLETON

Mrs Charleton is recorded as a bit player in the production of 23 June 1800, performing Pimple in *She Stoops to Conquer* and Lettice in the afterpiece, *The Devil to Pay*. Two women have been identified with a claim to the name Charleton. The second is the more likely to have been the actress, though neither is a strong candidate.

Mary Gittos, or Gatehouse, arrived in Port Jackson on the *Lady Juliana* on 3 June 1790. She had received a seven-year sentence at the Old Bailey in September 1788 for stealing clothes and 24 halfpence. Gittos had been given shelter for the night in a room and had robbed the resident of the next room. The modest value of the stolen clothes, the 24 halfpence, the tenement-like accommodation and Gittos' apparent homelessness suggest she was one of London's poor. She was 19 at the time.[1]

Within two months of her arrival Mary Gittos was sent to Norfolk Island, where she formed a relationship with Private William Charleton of the New South Wales Corps. Charleton was in the audience on the night of the Norfolk Island theatre riot, but there is no mention of Gittos. Since no female actors are named in the records, there is no way of knowing whether she was of their number.[2]

The couple returned to Sydney in November 1795 and seem to have remained until 1802, the period covered by all the playbills.[3] The presence of a Mrs Charleton in only the last of these may weaken the case for Mary Gittos being the performer.

By 1802 the Charletons were back on Norfolk Island. They returned to Sydney in March 1805, thus missing the performances at that outpost recorded in the shopkeeper's day-book. The couple finally married, in Sydney, on 16 April 1810, Mary marking the register with a cross. In the same year, when the New South Wales Corps was withdrawn, Charleton transferred to the Veteran Company, serving with it until its disbandment in 1823. Thereafter the family lived at Windsor, and later near Bathurst, where William Charleton died in 1839. No record of Mary's death has been found.[4]

The other candidate for acting honours is Hannah/Ann Charlton/Carleton, sentenced in December 1789 at the Old Bailey to seven years for shoplifting a 14-yard piece of calico from a Newgate Street linen draper's, in company with another woman. The pair made no defence, had no witnesses, and at the time of their arrest had 'no property about them, nor any money, except a few bad halfpence', suggesting that they were destitute. Hannah sailed on the *Mary Anne*, arriving in July 1791. In a list of people off stores, thought to date from 1801, she appears as Anna Carlton, a resident of Sydney.[5] In the *Sydney Gazette*, 6 February 1813, and a year later, 19 March 1814, an Ann Charlton announced her intention of leaving the colony, as did a Mrs Hannah Charlton on 7 October 1824, but whether these intentions were realised, or whether either woman was the actress, is unknown.

I. OR J. COX

An I. Cox appears in the playbill as a performer in *The Recruiting Officer* and *Henry the Fourth* in 1800, while a J. Cox is a participant in *She Stoops to Conquer*, later in that year. No I. Cox is on record in the colony and, since the printer occasionally substituted an upper-case I for J, the probability is that one man played all three roles and that his initial was J. This J. Cox was a bit player, who performed as Bullock in *The Recruiting Officer*, Blunt in *Henry the Fourth* and Diggory in *She Stoops to Conquer*.

Two convicts named J. Cox are recorded on the mainland in 1800.[1] The first, Joseph Cox, arrived on the *Ganges* in June 1797, with a life sentence imposed at Southampton, 3 March 1795, for killing a sheep, preparatory to stealing it. By early 1800 he had almost certainly moved to Kissing Point, where he was listed in the service of Captain William Kent in a document dating from the middle of that year. He spent the rest of his working life in the district as a small-scale farmer and labourer before being admitted to the Benevolent Asylum, where he died in November 1839.[2] The *Ganges* indent and the records of the *Lion* hulk give his age at conviction as 25, though his marriage and death certificates, and the 1828 census, present him as six to nine years older. The record of his conditional pardon gives his native place as Market Drayton and his trade as weaver. Cox signed his name in the marriage register on 17 October 1815 in a slightly awkward hand. His petition of 1819 is fluent in both writing and expression, but it might have been the work of a professional scribe.[3]

Though not the most convenient of addresses, Kissing Point was only a few miles up the harbour from Sydney and within easy reach for rehearsals and performances. Cox would have required the permission of Captain Kent or his farm manager to make the trip to town, but he could well have been there on most Saturdays with a boat-load of vegetables for the market. He remains a remote possibility as the actor.

The second J. Cox is James Cox, who arrived on the *Barwell* in May 1798. He spent much of his life in the colony as a sawyer and small-scale farmer in areas south of Sydney, before dying in the Benevolent Asylum in January 1851. He may, however, have been in Sydney up to 1806, since the muster records him as indented to Joseph Taylor, a painter of dubious reputation.[4] Cox had been convicted at the Hereford Assizes, March 1797, for burglary in a dwelling house, the theft consisting mainly of lengths of cloth. His age at the time was given in the ship's indent as 19, which accords with the 73 given in the record of his death. He would therefore have been 22 in 1800. When he married at St Phillip's Church in April 1812, he signed the register with a cross.[5] Since the parts Cox the actor played were small ones, illiteracy would not have been a great impediment, though it weighs a little against him.

Two other men remain, James Cox and John Cox, who were members of the New South Wales Corps. Of these James is the more immediately attractive as a possible actor. At his marriage in Sydney (26 July 1796) he signed the register in a neat hand. His petition of 8 January 1810 seems to be his own work and, while its literary style is clumsy, the handwriting is assured.[6] His social positioning also brings him closer than any of the others to Sidaway's known actors. James Cox was a career soldier who had joined the New South Wales Corps as a 16-year-old in July 1790. By early 1800 he had been a corporal for several years, and in November was to become a sergeant, later rising to colour sergeant (1808) and sergeant major (1813). The Corps' pay lists suggest he was stationed at headquarters at the relevant time and the evidence in a court case firmly locates him on duty there in January 1800, a few months before the recorded productions.[7]

Cox was born in Gloucestershire in June 1774, so would have been 26 in early 1800. Military records of 1808 describe him as 5 feet 9 inches tall, of fair complexion, with light brown hair and a round visage.[8] He makes few appearances in civil records, which might give an insight into his personality or private life.

The military records are even less forthcoming about John Cox. They reveal only that he enlisted in England in May 1791, was a member of Joseph Foveaux' company and never rose above the rank of private. He had arrived on the *Pitt* in 1792, as did Ann Brooks. The pair began a liaison that produced a long line of children. The Corps' pay lists indicate his presence in Sydney throughout the relevant period, and his son Samuel was baptised there on 2 February 1800, only a month before *The Recruiting Officer* was performed.[9] On 27 June 1800 Foveaux sailed for Norfolk Island, with Cox among his troops. There he turned himself energetically to farming, selling produce to the commissariat within a year of his arrival. He was, however, illiterate, signing his receipts with a cross. In 1810 he left the Corps to become a full-time farmer on the island, and in 1813 was relocated to Van Diemen's Land, where, by 1820, he held 220 acres, owned 37 cattle and 500 sheep, and was a district constable. He died in 1848, aged about 84.[10]

There is one slight piece of evidence suggesting the apparently colourless Private John Cox could have been the Sydney actor. He left Sydney after the productions in which an I. or J. Cox performed and was on Norfolk Island at the time of the Christmas 1805 production there. In the shopkeeper's daybook both a Cox and a Mrs Cox appear to be participants in that undertaking, he as an actor and she possibly in an administrative role.[11] There were three other men named Cox on the island at the time (one of whom, John Massey Cox, was living alone), but John Cox and his wife seem likely candidates. If the performer was indeed Private John Cox (or, for that matter, Corporal James Cox), this reinforces the case for a partial military takeover of the theatre company in 1799 and 1800.

MRS DAVIS

Since at least 11 women and 31 men named Davis or Davies had arrived in the first three fleets, and a proportional number in vessels thereafter, the possibility of identifying the actress is remote. The case made here is by far the most speculative in this appendix. It turns on the intimate friendship that existed between Frances Davis and Robert Sidaway's *de facto*, Mary Marshall, and is weakly supported by the dangerously seductive theatricality of Mrs Davis' life. On the other hand, it has to confront the fact that Frances Davis was illiterate, and firm evidence would normally be required before nominating as the leading actress in Sidaway's founding company a person unable even to sign her name.

Frances, or Fanny, Davis (see Fig. 17) lived in Southwark and moved in criminal circles. She was said to have been a member of a gang which had long been active in Essex, but the exploit which earned her a few months of fame was a solo operation, of a kind she had allegedly carried out several times before. On the evening of 2 September 1785 a grazier spent the night at an Essex inn *en route* for Smithfield market, with a canvas bag containing over £1,200 in cash, drafts and banknotes. At the inn a 'genteelly dressed' young man who passed himself off as a horse dealer struck up an acquaintance with the grazier, sat smoking with him, and allegedly became aware of the money he was carrying – though it is more likely the victim had been targeted in advance. During the night the young man, who was Fanny Davis in disguise, stole the bag from the sleeping grazier (with whom she was sharing a room) and disappeared from the inn.

Fanny would have escaped undetected, had it not been for her indiscretion. Immediately after the theft she visited a friend in Newgate gaol and revealed the exploit to her. Unfortunately for Fanny, her friend was having an affair with the hangman, who passed the information to the authorities. Fanny was arrested at her 'obscure lodging in the Mint, Southwark'. 'With great composure' she denied any knowledge of the affair, even though her male costume and £900 of the booty were found with her. Returned to Essex she was sentenced to death at the Chelmsford Assizes in March 1786, but refused to reveal the whereabouts of the missing £350. The court records gave her age as 20 and, according to one account, she was 'extremely handsome'. [1]

Cross-dressing was a subject of intense fascination for the late eighteenth-century public, particularly where it involved women serving as soldiers or sailors, or criminals such as Margaret Catchpole or Mary Reiby assuming male dress for an immediate need. Fanny Davis became the subject of several lengthy newspaper articles, two utterly fanciful biographies (the second plagiarised from the first), a chapbook and several prints. [2] Most of these accounts end with Fanny sentenced without hope of reprieve, or actually hanged – a fate which in real life she escaped. This outcome may have owed a little to her adaptability. The *Daily Universal Register*, 26 April 1786, reporting on her behaviour in prison, declared:

> The celebrated Miss Davies, who committed a late capital robbery in man's apparel, and who was respited by the Judge at Chelmsford, conducts herself with the utmost prudence in the prison of that town, and works assiduously at her needle. The gaudy portrait of her in the print-shops by no means resembles her present appearance, which is all modesty and neatness.

By the time the article was printed Fanny's respited sentence had been converted into fourteen years' transportation. She sailed for Botany Bay on the first-fleet vessel *Lady Penrhyn*, where Bowes Smyth noted her as having been in service and aged 22. [3] Languishing on the same vessel was the convict Mary Marshall.

The first mention of Fanny in the colony occurred on 24 October 1789, when a new-born child whose mother had died giving birth was put into her care: 'Davis was informed she would be allowed to keep the Child as long as she did Justice to it.' Whether Fanny knew the dead woman, Susannah Allen, is not recorded. Her obvious function would have been as wet nurse for the child, implying that she had lost an infant of her own; but there is no record of this. In any case, her obligation to Susannah Allen's daughter was of short duration, since the little girl was buried on 1 February 1790. [4]

On 4 March 1790 Frances was one of a large party that sailed for Norfolk Island on HMS *Sirius*. The voyage ended in high drama, with the vessel forced onto the reef and totally wrecked after the passengers had made a difficult landing at Cascade Bay and the women had spent the night in the forest, part way between there and the main settlement. Over the next few years Davis was one of the few women on the island recorded as living alone, most of the convict women having formed liaisons. Her stay on the island was unremarkable, and in March 1793 she returned to the mainland. [5] Here again few records of her life have survived – unless, as I am assuming, she is Mrs Davis the actress. This Mrs Davis is the only woman in Collins' list of the more important performers on the theatre's opening night. While the afterpiece, *The Hotel*, has three roles for women, the mainpiece, *The Revenge*, has only two, one a colourless supporting part. Mrs Davis undoubtedly played Leonora, the emotion-charged tragic heroine in this reworking of the *Othello* plot. In Henry Green's benefit, six months later, she played the madcap female lead, Miranda, in Mrs Centlivre's comedy *The Busy Body*. If she could manage that range effectively, she was an actress of some talent.

The performance of 23 July 1796 is Mrs Davis' last on record. On 13 September 1796 Frances Davis received an absolute pardon. [6] The reasons for the favour are unknown, but it

Fig. 17   Fanny Davis/Davies as depicted in the frontispiece to *An Authentic Narrative … of Miss Fanny Davies*, London, 1786. Thompson's *The Female Amazon*, [London, 1786], has a different frontispiece. The *Daily Universal Register*, 26 April 1786, also mentions a 'gaudy portrait of her in the print shops'. (By permission of the British Library, T. 4065).

is more likely to have been for services to an amorous officer than for any contribution to the performing arts. Though free to leave the colony for good, however, Fanny did not do so. This was not because she lacked the means: indeed, her tombstone boasted both that she was a First-Fleeter and that she had visited England three times. [7] This suggests a degree of wealth, as well as hardiness.

The first of these round trips probably took place shortly after the absolute pardon was granted, for she is said to be 'gone to England' on a list of 1800–01. [8] She appears as a returning passenger on the *Minerva*, whose doctor, John Price, said of her: 'This woman was formerly sent to the colony a convict but in time was emancipated, and returned to England, but is now going out again having got some property in the country.' [9] The *Minerva* arrived in Sydney on 1 January 1800. If she is Mrs Davis the actor, her absence from the playbills for 1800 suggests that, like John Sparrow and William Chapman, she now had priorities other than performing. Her return was marred by an unpleasant dispute in the Civil Court and the Court of Appeal over her house, which James Bloodsworth had contracted to repair in her absence and for which he submitted a bill for the exorbitant sum of £88 13s.11d.. On the Appeal Court papers Governor King wrote a cranky note, giving his opinion that Bloodworth had clearly exploited her, but had acted within the law and therefore had to be awarded the judgment, a feeling shared by the judges. [10] However extravagant the fee, the house itself must have been a substantial one to justify work of even half the value that Bloodsworth had placed upon it. Once again the evidence suggests Fanny Davis was very comfortably placed.

On 9 January 1811 Frances Davis, described as a widow, married Martin Mintz, widower and farmer on the Nepean River. The wedding took place at St Phillip's Church, Sydney. She signed the register with a cross, and Mary Marshall was one of her witnesses. [11] Mintz, whose wife had died on 9 October 1810, had been a soldier in the New South Wales Corps and had been demobilised in 1803, receiving a land grant of eighty acres on the Hawkesbury (Nepean) River in June of that year. He was evidently no farmer, for he disposed of thirty acres in August 1806 and was preparing to sell the remaining acres and the farmhouse in September 1810. The sale was left in suspension for some time, due to the death of the purchaser, Anthony L'Andre (Landrin), on 11 August 1811, but a few months after the marriage this property was finally disposed of to L'Andre's widow. At the same time, thirty acres of farmland at the foot of Prospect Hill were sold by 'Martin Mintz & Frances Mintz his Wife'. [12] The inclusion of Frances in the transfer documents implies she had brought this property to the marriage.

In all likelihood the couple lived in Sydney from the time of the wedding, but the first evidence of their whereabouts comes from an item in the *Sydney Gazette*, 5 June 1813. Martin Mintz, of No. 4, Clarence Street, was advertising for a 'Man Servant of Good Character, whose Work will be to attend about a House, and keep a small Garden in order'. In February 1810 Mintz had been granted a wine and spirit licence for the Hawkesbury, and by July 1813 he had applied for a similar licence for his residence at Clarence Street. But, in spite of the sale of the two farms, his financial position was serious. On 12 July 1813 he assigned the Clarence Street property to Samuel Terry as surety for a loan of £80, repayable by 14 November, describing himself, in the process, as a baker and dealer. Ten days later he disappeared from his house and a week after that his body was found 'in a mutilated state' in Sydney Harbour. The coroner's verdict was *felo de se*, the victim having drowned himself 'in consequence of some pecuniary embarrassments'.

Martin Mintz died intestate, and on 25 September 1813 Thomas Rushton, who had been witness for the sale of the Prospect Hill property, announced in the *Sydney Gazette* his intention to apply for letters of administration for Mintz's estate and effects. Rushton claimed to be Mintz's principal creditor, the debt being £70, and was moving to protect himself, with Frances' consent. Her note of approval is signed, not marked with a cross, but the handwriting is that of the clerk who prepared the document of which it is a part. Both she and Rushton seem to have been unaware of the mortgage to Terry, since on 6 January 1814 Rushton announced in the *Sydney Gazette* that he was selling Mintz's residence, described as 'a Capital Dwelling House and Bakehouse, situate in Clarence street … with a good Piece of Land'. Frances must already have vacated the premises, since Terry's response was to claim the property in a petition of that same day and install a tenant. Ironically, Mintz's wine and spirit licence had come through shortly after his death. It was valued at £25, and became part of the dispute. In the *Sydney Gazette*, 5 February 1814, Rushton, as administrator, readvertised the sale of the property, this time by auction. Presumably an accommodation had been reached with Terry.

How closely Frances was involved in these dealings is not clear, but the end result may have been devastating for her. Since she was legally married to Mintz, everything she held in her own name before the marriage was subject to seizure for his debts. There is no indication whether everything was lost, but the probability is that she came out of the marriage much poorer than she entered into it.

From this point onwards Fanny largely disappears from the records. On 10 September 1823 she submitted an affidavit concerning the loss of her certificate of freedom, signed with a cross, and in the 1825 muster she appears simply as a housekeeper (not a householder) of Sydney. 'Housekeeper' was often a euphemism for a *de facto* wife, but, whatever its implications here, it suggests a sad decline for an independent lady who had once owned her own substantial dwelling and funded three voyages to England.

Fanny Davis died on 11 November 1828. Her tombstone described her as 'much respected by all who knew her' and gave her age as 64, which would make her 22 at the time of her trial and 32 in 1796, when Mrs Davis was the leading lady in Robert Sidaway's company. Mary Marshall, her close friend, lived on until 1849. On her death she was buried in the same grave as Fanny.

J. DAVISON

J. Davison has only one recorded appearance with the company, as Hotspur in *Henry the Fourth*, on 8 April 1800.

The spelling Davison or Davidson is used erratically in the records, but by 1800 at least 5 John and 2 James Davisons (or Davidsons) are known to have arrived in the colony, all of them as convicts. Of the five John Davisons, four had completed their sentences by 1798, and the fifth, *per Marquis Cornwallis*, is identified by Barbara Hall as the 'rough and uncouth' millwright who built Sydney's first windmill and was seriously incapacitated in an accident there in April 1797. He, however, was consistently referred to in the colony as John Davis, and is an unlikely candidate for the role of Hotspur, both because of his incapacity and because the ship's indent (as Davison) gives his age as 40 at the time of trial. This would have made him 45 when the performance took place. It is difficult to envisage a minor member of the company being given the role at that age.[1]

No clear reference to any of the other John Davisons has been found subsequent to 1793, though a list of 1800–01 includes the name, but with no identifying details.[2] Two of the candidates would have been about 30 in 1800, while another, John Davisere or Davison, age unknown, was sentenced for an interesting crime – stealing forty-six yards of gold lace from one person and 'one gold Epaulet and other Goods' from another.[3] The victims, however, were probably military outfitters rather than theatrical costumiers. Of the two who were 30 or so in 1800, one, the leader of a three-member juvenile gang which broke into a London house, was sent to Norfolk Island, where he became a farmer. Once free, he sold his property and left the island, presumably to make his way back to England. The other, arrested while picking a pocket at Alnwick market, Northumberland, arrived on the *Matilda* in August 1791 and, like 'Davisere', is not heard of thereafter.[4] There is no information about the trade, social background, personality or literacy of any of these men, so that, even if we could identify one of them as the actor, we would still lack any real picture.

Of the two James Davisons, one was buried on 14 November 1791. Michael Flynn makes a good circumstantial case for the survivor being the man who was sentenced to seven years at the Old Bailey for stealing lead from a government building, and who arrived on the *Neptune* on 28 June 1790.[5] This man, however, raises the same difficulties as John Davis the millwright, since he was aged 30 when convicted in December 1787 and would have been a 43-year-old Hotspur in 1800.[6]

The James Davison who survived enlisted in the New South Wales Corps on 28 February 1792 and received the customary conditional pardon on 4 October 1793. Though assigned to Captain George Johnston's company, he did not join it on Norfolk Island until October 1794, too late to be involved in the theatre there, or in the military riot that led to its suppression. After November 1795, when he left the island, he probably spent most of his time in Sydney: the Corps' pay lists show him there at the time *Henry the Fourth* was staged.[7]

Davison never rose above the rank of private, made no recorded impact on the community and left with the Corps on its return to England, where he was transferred to the Fifth Veterans' Battalion on 7 September 1811. In the regimental muster of September 1808 he is given as 46 years and 11 months of age, 5 feet 6½ inches tall, with a fair complexion and a 'Long Visage', a native of Edinburgh and a silk dyer by trade.[8] The age discrepancy between the hulk records of 1789 and the army record of 1808 (about four years) is not unusual. However, the identification of the soldier with the actor is by default. The one thing of which we can be confident is that he was in Sydney at the time *Henry the Fourth* was staged.

The inability to identify the performer with any certainty is frustrating, not so much because his role was important, but because we are left uncertain whether the actor was a convict, an ex-convict or a soldier. The choice is between the John Davison on the 1800–01 list, about whom nothing can be discovered, but who is likely to be a convict or ex-convict, and James Davison the convict-turned-soldier. If Private Davison was the actor, this could assist the case for the military being a dominant force in the second phase of the theatre. However, *Henry the Fourth* is the only recorded production in which Davison and Payne appeared. If they were both soldiers, it is possible the production was a special event got up by the military, drawing on the theatre company, but utilising some soldier-performers who were not normal company members. The dislocation of normal scheduling suggested by the playbill may also point in this direction.

R. EVANS

RONSW, Marriages.4.312.

The Evans who appeared in Henry Green's benefit on 23 July 1796 was probably the Richard Evans who arrived on the *Active* on 20 September 1791. He was the only convict of this name in the colony before 1800. A Richard Evans of the New South Wales Corps arrived on the *Admiral Barrington* in October 1791, rose to the rank of sergeant, and was in Sydney in June 1796; but he was illiterate and therefore less likely to be the actor.[1] In 1796 the military man would have been 37–40 years old.

    Richard Evans the convict was tried at the Old Bailey in September 1790 on a succession of charges involving theft of glassware from various merchants. His approach was to claim fraudulently to be a servant of Mr Spode and to tender an order for glasses on which the signature of Spode's clerk had been forged. At his trial Evans protested that he was the dupe of his fellow prisoner, Lockett, who had devised the scheme. He escaped one charge on a technicality, but was convicted on two others and sentenced to seven years' transportation.[2] While his age was not given, he was evidently a young man, probably still in his teens.

    Evans' conviction was followed by a petition, in which he claimed never to have been in trouble before, to have an aged mother, to have been 'Educated for the accompting house' and, though currently unemployed, to have earned his living by honest industry. He claimed to have friends in sufficient circumstances to assist him. Somewhat implausibly, he also claimed that the 'evil designing' Lockett had paid him to carry out the fraud, that he was to have no share in the loot and that 'neither did your Petitioner know he was committing a Fraud untill he was apprehended for it'.[3] The appeal was futile.

    Evans' first appearance in the records of the colony is in the playbill for Green's benefit, 23 July 1796, when he played bit parts in both main and afterpiece – Whisper and Dermot respectively. Though not in Collins' list of principal players on the opening night, he could well have been playing minor parts on that occasion as well, but he does not appear in any of the later playbills. For the Green benefit he is also listed as one of those from whom tickets could be obtained, along with 'R. Sidway' and 'the house adjoining the Theatre'. When sergeants of the Corps were advertised as ticket vendors, their rank was always included – a further indication that this was the convict, not the soldier. Since the vendors were almost always businessmen, the likelihood is that Evans was already active as a shopkeeper, a calling for which there is firm evidence by 1798. He appears on several occasions taking action to recover small debts through the legal process, one for 18s. owed by Ann Radley and another for £2 10s. owed by William Chapman. A deposition in his own well-formed hand has survived, in which he describes himself as a 'Dealer' of Sydney and claims nearly £50 from a debtor, part of it for 'various Articles of Calico, Dungaree Chuk and other Goods'. This was in September 1798, when he also acted as surety for John Prosser on Prosser's receipt of a wine and spirit licence. In a criminal trial of October 1799 Richard Evans is referred to as 'clerk and book-keeper to Simeon Lord'.[4] In the absence of another candidate, this could well be Evans the dealer. Such an appointment was not incompatible with his private business.

There is evidence that Richard Evans was still active in Sydney in 1800. On 15 February of that year he was a witness to the marriage of William Green and Mary Rose, signing in a near-copperplate hand similar to that on the deposition mentioned above. On 7 July 1800 a Richard Evans took action through the courts for the recovery of a debt of £10.[5] Thereafter the record is silent. Richard Evans the soldier was demobilised in 1803 and granted a farm, which he worked till his murder in 1812. The Richard Evans who appears after 1803 in the court records as a debtor, not a creditor, would have been the ex-soldier, as was the Evans appearing in the Bigge list of debtors to the Crown. In this he is reported to have died prior to 1820, leaving a debt of £16 8s. incurred under Governor King.[6] Evans the convict actor would have been free by servitude in late 1797 and probably left the colony in late 1800 or in 1801.

W. FOWKES

The only W. Fowkes, or Foulkes, transported to Botany Bay prior to the nineteenth century was William Foulkes. On 8 September 1791 he was transferred from New Prison, where he had been held since early July, to Newgate where he was described as 20 years of age, 5 feet 8½ inches tall, with brown hair, light eyes and a fair complexion. He was said to be a painter by trade and born in London.[1] He was captured coming out of a room with a trunk on his shoulder, the contents of which the owner valued at £2 7s. 6d.. Breaking and entering, with the theft of goods beyond 40s., was a capital offence, entitling the prosecutor to a reward. Foulkes bitterly accused the prosecutor of pursuing him for this reward, claiming: 'A man offered me a pot of beer to carry it to Kingsgate-street; the man ran away; I told Franklin [the first witness] it was none of mine.' The story was weak and the jury convicted, but valued the goods at 39s., saving him from the death penalty.[2] He was sentenced to seven years' transportation, delivered to the *Stanislaus* hulk at Woolwich and sailed on the *Royal Admiral*, which arrived on 7 October 1792.

Apart from his involvement with Sidaway's theatre, Foulkes left no mark on the colony. Collins lists him as one of the principal performers in the inaugural production of 16 January 1796, and in the playbill of Green's benefit on 23 July 1796 he plays the title role of Marplot in *The Busy Body* and the part of Darby in *The Poor Soldier*. While Darby offers few opportunities, Marplot is the plum role of an extravagant who repeatedly blunders into the intrigues of others and accidentally exposes them. He is a less elegant version of Ben Jonson's Truewit in *The Silent Woman* and Wilmot in Aphra Behn's *The Rover*.

On 30 April 1797 William Foulkes was buried in Sydney. He was only 26 years old.[3]

H. GREEN

Henry Green was described in the *Star*, 17 February 1791, as 'a Gentleman in a considerable line of business, as a Town Agent for hatters, and who had acquired a decent competency'. He was accused by a visiting Frenchman of attempting to pick his pocket while they were part of a crowd in the courtyard of St James' Palace. The trial took place at the Old Bailey on 16 February 1791. The Frenchman claimed he had seized the hand of his assailant as it was coming out of his pocket and then secured him by the collar. At this point the alleged pickpocket threw money against a wall and, while the victim was searching for it, a second man left holding him claimed that more had fallen from him. At his trial Green was allowed a written defence, in which he said: 'The situation I am in, and the troubles of a distressed mind, has rendered me incapable of addressing you.' Green claimed that another man, seen behaving suspiciously, had picked the pocket. Not speaking English, the Frenchman had not understood Green's denials or his instructions to seize the other man, who had thrown the money and made his escape. Green then made an appeal in more personal terms:

> I have a wife much opressed with grief and trouble at this unfortunate affair: I have a son at the age of sixteen, which I have put apprentice to a respectable gentleman in the city of London … Gentlemen, my circumstances in business has rendered me capable of living happy and comfortable, therefore I could not think of committing an act of this kind, when I was not in distress. Gentlemen of the jury, I am now at the age of forty-seven years, and from my earliest days down to this unhappy time, that my character was never brought into question before.[1]

The *Star*, 17 February 1791, best describes what followed:

> [Green] called a Mr. West, a hatter in Brentford, with whom he was about to enter into partnership, and more than twenty other persons of very respectable lines of business, all of whom gave him the best of characters, and were sure that it was impossible for him to have been guilty of the offence, as he was in good circumstances and no way distressed … the jury entertaining a doubt under all circumstances of the case, retired for a very long time to consider of their verdict; but at their return into Court found him *Guilty*.

> The prisoner bowed very respectfully on the verdict being pronounced, and without seeming to feel his situation, calmly enquired whether the conviction was for a *single felony* or for a *capital offence!*

He was sentenced to transportation for seven years.

Once convicted, Green petitioned the Home Office for a reconsideration of his sentence:

> Henry Green on board the Fortune Hulk. Tried at the Old Bailey in Feb[y] 1791 & sentenced to be Transported for 7 years.

> Prays a Pardon on condition of Transporting himself

> Trade. a Hatmaker.[2]

D'Arcy Wentworth, the highwayman with aristocratic connections, and a few gentlemen political prisoners were sufficiently influential to secure the status of exile rather than transportee, but the privilege was not extended to Green. He sailed, a convict, on the *Royal Admiral*, arriving in the colony in October 1792.

Once in Sydney, Green largely disappears from sight. Because of his age and background he may have secured a position as a clerk in the commissariat or with the governor, but there is no evidence of this. He was not active as a businessman, since he is only once recorded as pursuing a debt through the Court of Civil Jurisdiction, on 13 February 1797.[3] In fact, it is only as an actor that he attracts attention. David Collins claimed he was the best of the performers in the opening production, and within six months was receiving a benefit, a privilege usually restricted to leading performers in Sydney. In that benefit he played Sir Jealous Traffic in *The Busy Body* and Father Luke in *The Poor Soldier*. Both are secondary roles, old-men parts, chosen either because Green preferred them, or because in a young company he was forced towards them. He might have had more opportunity in *The Revenge*, where the heavy role of the villainous Moor, Zanga, might have been within his grasp, despite his age.

On 6 August 1797 Green was given an absolute pardon, six months before his sentence was to expire. In a list of 1801 he is recorded as having returned to England.[4]

MRS GREVILLE

David Greville was the only person with that family name officially recorded in the colony prior to 1800. He had been transported for seven years for picking a pocket in Drury Lane theatre and arrived in New South Wales on the *Active* in September 1791.[1] He could have been accompanied by his wife, travelling as a free woman, but it is more likely that the Mrs Greville of the 1796 playbill was Greville's *de facto* at the time. Since it is only on the playbill that the name appears, she remains untraceable.

To judge by a string of debtors he was pursuing in August 1798, Greville was probably a shopkeeper or dealer (one of his debtors, incidentally, was the actor Henry Lavell). He was also a constable, applying to be relieved of the post in December 1798.[2] His sentence would have expired in 1797 or 1798. The resignation of his post, the calling-in of debts and a dispute over a house ownership in 1798[3] suggest a man preparing to return to England. Certainly, the *Sydney Gazette*, 2 December 1804, records him as having left the colony some time before, and suggests he had been a friend of John Sparrow. If the actress's sentence had expired before his, she could have accompanied him, though it was common for men to desert both *de facto* and legal wives on leaving the colony.

Greville was to return to Sydney to serve another seven years for picking a pocket outside a chapel.[4] He arrived on the *Fortune* in July 1806 and was soon co-habiting with a Mary Davis, but this was a new relationship: Davis had arrived as a convict in 1806, on the *William Pitt*. The couple married in March 1810, Greville being identified as a baker (he later became a schoolteacher).[5]

The elusive Mrs Greville might have had a role in the opening production of Sidaway's company. Collins includes only one woman, Mrs Davis, in his list of principal actors, but the mainpiece on that occasion required two women and the afterpiece three. In Green's benefit of July 1796 Mrs Greville appears in major roles, but is subordinate to Mrs Davis. She has the leading female role in the afterpiece, *The Poor Soldier*, but the playlet is slight and the character colourless. In *The Busy Body*, it is Mrs Davis who secures the most attractive female role of Miranda, leaving Mrs Greville with Isabinda, the demure secondary heroine.

MASTER HADDOCKS

The Master Haddocks who played the small part of Lucy, the maid, in the 1800 production of *The Recruiting Officer* was probably 9–14 years of age at the time. Since he could not have been born later than 1791, he must have been a child convict, a child born in the colony, or one brought to the colony by a parent or parents. No male convict, of any age, with the name Haddock, Haddick or Haydock arrived in the colony before the production, and the only female convict, Mary Haddock, is better known as the energetic colonial businesswoman, Mary Reibey. Mary was only 15 at the time of her arrival, on the *Royal Admiral* in October 1792, and no researcher has discovered any offspring prior to 1796, after her marriage to Thomas Reibey.[1]

There were, however, three soldiers named Haddock, Haddicks or Haddick with the New South Wales Corps in 1800, one of whom, Sergeant Armourer John Haddick, had been accompanied by his wife Diana, when he arrived on the *Neptune* in July 1790. No children appear in the records; and in Samuel Marsden's 1806 list of the colony's women, which includes their offspring, none appear against the name of Diana Haddick.[2] The number of wives allowed to each company was limited and there is no evidence that John Haddocks, who arrived in November 1796, was allowed the privilege, while Thomas Haddick was too young to be considered. There remains the remote possibility that the performer was Thomas Haddick himself. He was a drummer, born on 7 September 1781, who joined the corps on 6 March 1790, in his eighth year.[3] He would, however, have been 18 by early 1800, too old for the title of 'Master'. Whoever he was, it is likely Master Haddocks had military connections as a soldier or the unrecorded son of a soldier, probably Sergeant Haddick. In either case he becomes further evidence of the soldiers' infiltration of the company in 1799–1800.

G. H. HUGHES

George Henry Hughes is an elusive figure. Writing of November 1795, David Collins reported:

> A small printing-press, which had been brought into the settlement by Mr. Phillip, and had remained from that time unemployed, was now found very useful; a very decent young man, one George Hughes, of some abilities in the printing line, having been found equal to conducting the whole business of the press. All orders were now printed, and a number thrown off sufficient to ensure a more general publication of them than had hitherto been accomplished.

Shortly afterwards Collins lists 'G.H. Hughes' among the principal performers in the opening production at Sidaway's theatre,[1] while an annotation on the playbill for Mrs Parry's night, 1 June 1799, identifies the G.H. Hughes in the cast as 'Hughes, a printer, prisoner'. His control of the printing press, of course, meant that he was able to run off the company's playbills.

Thus far the evidence seems clear. The difficulty is to connect this Hughes with any convict who arrived prior to 1796. In an 1801 list of emancipated and free people off stores, a George Hughes appears. He is described as arriving by the *Pitt*, and a resident of Sydney whose sentence had expired.[2] However, the convict indents of the *Pitt*, which arrived on 14 February 1792, do not list any George or George Henry Hughes, though they do contain a John Hughes.

Hughes was involved in the opening production at Sidaway's new theatre, but did not participate in Green's benefit, or in *Henry the Fourth* on 8 April 1800. He and Mrs Radley, however, were the only performers from 1796 who were still with the company in 1800. Though relatively young, he seems to have been cast in older roles, mainly of a secondary nature – Sir Bamber Blackletter in *The Busy Body*, Sir John Trotley in *Bon Ton*, Balance in *The Recruiting Officer*, Hardcastle in *She Stoops to Conquer* and Sir John Loverule in *The Devil to Pay*.

On 1 December 1798 Hughes made a court appearance:

> Hughes, a Printer preferred a Complaint ag.[st] Anne Franklin for Abuse & Defamation – but as it appeared that both parties were culpable

> The matter was dismissed & the woman cautioned how she made use of unbecoming Language in the future.

On 18 November 1799 he appeared again, in the matter of the playhouse dispute, claiming that the Radleys had 'grossly assaulted & ill treated' him, a charge supported by witnesses, though he later withdrew the action.[3] It is difficult to make much of these two events. Do they suggest an aggressive litigant or someone querulous and insecure, who fled to the law for protection?

Hughes had probably completed his sentence as early as 1797. During 1801 or 1802 he was succeeded as printer by the newly-arrived George Howe, and in a court case of 10 September 1802 William Wilson, ex-purser of HMS *Reliance*, claimed to have bought a quantity of cloth from 'George Hughs who has left the Country'.[4] This was probably Hughes the ex-printer and actor.

L. JONES

Luke Jones (signature)

ML, FM4/3700, p.17.

Though L. Jones has only one recorded appearance, in Henry Green's benefit on 23 July 1796, he was by no means a bit player. His role of Sir Francis Gripe, the mean and vicious father in *The Busy Body*, is central to the play, with excellent opportunities for comedy. In fact, it is a more substantial part than the companion role of Sir Jealous Traffic, played by Green himself. Both are old-man's roles. The number of older convicts in the colony was limited, so the role could have fallen to a younger man by default; but there is appeal in the idea that Jones was a man in his late 40s or 50s, as was Green.

The only L. Jones recorded as entering the colony prior to 1802 is Luke Jones, who had been sentenced to seven years at the Old Bailey in April 1788 for the attempted theft of clothes from a dwelling place. After being seen entering the house with a companion, he was captured hiding in the garret chimney: 'We pulled him down directly; he said, do not use me ill; and he laughed at us.'[1] As Michael Flynn has suggested, the laughter was probably hysterical. A Luke Jones had already been confined to Newgate for a year from January 1787 'for a certain Trespass and Assault'.[2] If this is the same person, he could barely have been released before committing the offence that was to send him to Australia.

After his conviction for theft, Jones was sent to the hulk *Dunkirk*, where his age at the time of sentencing was given as 19. From here he was embarked on the *Neptune*, part of the Second Fleet infamous for its mortality rate. The *Neptune* arrived in Sydney on 28 June 1790, and in the list of burials that followed, most of them Second-Fleet prisoners, appears 'Lewis Jones, c', the 'c' indicating convict. In spite of the difference of first name, Flynn assumes, understandably, that this is the Luke Jones of the *Neptune*, and so brings his account of the Second-Fleet convict to an end.[3] A nineteenth-century index of convicts, however, includes the annotation that Luke Jones of the *Neptune* died in Hobart on 11 April 1811. In fact, the Luke Jones of Hobart (also known as Luke Bryan Jones, Luke O'Brien and Luke O'Bryan Jones) had arrived in Sydney on the *Duke of Portland* on 10 November 1807. The annotation on the index is probably an error, but the convict of 1807 could be the earlier man re-transported, since his age at conviction in 1805 was 36. He was a native of London, a waterman by trade, sentenced to seven years at the Middlesex Court of Petty Sessions for stealing a handkerchief.[4]

One thing certain is that a Luke Jones was active in the colony from 24 June 1792 to 13 July 1794. He appears as a witness to a large number of weddings at Parramatta between those dates, signing the register in a clear, if inelegant, hand. Evidently, he was a servant of the Rev. Johnson, carrying out one of the duties of a vestry clerk, just as Thomas Taber would do in later years. An unnamed convict is on record as stationed at Parramatta to serve the clergyman and the judge-advocate on their visits. This man was removed by Lieutenant-Governor Grose on 25 July 1794, twelve days after the last Jones signature in the Register.[5] Alternatively, and even more tantalisingly, one of Johnson's two male convict servants in Sydney, from at least November 1793 until early July 1794, was named Jones and, though the clergyman on one occasion gives his first name as James, he was an older man:

> I … do pity Jones on account of his age. He appears to be a Man of good Understanding, & who once lived in Credit & has left a family living in Reputation & have treated him rather as a Father than as a Convict.

By mid-1794, however, Jones' behaviour had deteriorated: 'his Conduct for some Time has been very indifferent – he has been intoxicated very often, & withal very insolent'. Jones repeatedly promised to reform, but at the beginning of July it was discovered that he had stolen several pairs of shoes. He was punished, and on 9 July Johnson wrote to Grose asking for a replacement. Four days later Luke Jones' signature makes its last appearance in the marriage register.[6]

Johnson only identifies Jones by the first name, James, in his letter to Grose. The questions that then arise are, which James Jones was employed by Johnson, and is there any evidence that he was also known as Luke? By 1793 two middle-aged convicts named James Jones had arrived in the colony, one on the *Neptune* (aged 38 in March 1787) and the other on the *Surprise* (aged 35 in May 1788). Of these, the second is the more interesting, as his crime centred on an attempt to buy a flute at a Haymarket musical instrument shop. His flustered behaviour aroused suspicion and suggests he was not an experienced criminal. Michael Flynn, however, argues that he was the James Jones who was buried at Sydney Cove a few days after the *Surprise* arrived. The other James Jones was a worker in a Manchester cotton warehouse who, in an assertion of the moral economy, had taken the loose sweepings of cotton wool on the grounds that he had a right to them. Pamela Statham identifies him as enlisting in the New South Wales Corps on 2 June 1794, a month before the Jones in Johnson's service was handed back to Grose for re-assignment. If the cotton worker did enlist, the dating prevents Jones of the *Neptune* from being Johnson's servant.[7] This soldier, moreover, was on detachment from 1796. There is no evidence that either of these men was ever known as Luke.

We are left, then, with uncertainty – Luke Jones, *per Neptune*, who might have been buried as Lewis Jones in 1790 or might have survived and re-emerged as Luke Bryan Jones in 1807 – though a London waterman makes an implausible vestry clerk. The vestry clerk himself might have been an otherwise-unknown convict Luke Jones, assigned as hut-keeper for Collins and Johnson at Parramatta and removed from Johnson's service when the hut was repossessed. Or he might have been James Jones, Johnson's aged convict servant at Sydney, who matches with none of the convicts of that name in the colony.

W. KNIGHT

W. Knight played Lord Minikin in the afterpiece *Bon Ton* at Mrs Parry's benefit in June 1799. He also performed Hastings in *She Stoops to Conquer* on 23 June 1800, but does not appear in either of the playbills for earlier in that year. Hastings, as the hero's friend, is an important but undemanding role and, while Lord Minikin gives an actor scope for comic extravagance, he can be overshadowed by other figures in the play. Knight could have been a useful second-string actor of gentlemen roles who was called upon for occasional performances. He may have been only intermittently in Sydney.

Apart from the ship's carpenter to HMS *Sirius*, who departed in 1791, there were three convicts, all named William Knight, recorded as sailing for the colony. One was a runaway who lived intermittently with the Aborigines. At the time of the performances he was either labouring on the provost-marshal's farm as punishment for his first sojourn in the bush, or had already fled to rejoin the natives. Flynn makes a strong case for identifying him with the convict of unknown background who arrived on the *Atlantic*, but there is one inconsistency: Collins writes that the runaway's sentence was expired by 1795, which was not the case with this man.[1]

The remaining William Knights were both Second-Fleet convicts. One, a coachman who claimed to have driven for the Sheriff of Bristol, was convicted at the Old Bailey in January 1787 for stealing a horse. His death sentence was commuted to seven years and he was sent to the *Lion* hulk, where his age at conviction was said to be 26. He sailed for Botany Bay on the *Neptune*, arriving on 28 June 1790. Within a few weeks he was transferred to Norfolk Island, where he worked as a casual labourer and small farmer, leasing twelve acres on 21 July 1792. In May 1792 he had sold a sow to the government, signing the receipt with a cross.[2] It is this cross which points to the convict from the *Neptune*, since the other Second-Fleet convict was literate.

While he was on the island, Knight formed an alliance with the explosive Amelia Levy, a Jewish arrival on the First Fleet. On 26 July 1794, with their sentences expired, the couple left for the mainland.[3] On 7 November 1795 Amelia, a witness at a criminal trial, was described as living with an unnamed settler on the road to Prospect Hill, about a mile from Parramatta. A little over a year later (15 December 1796), a grant of fifty acres was made to William Knight in the Parramatta district. In one record of the transaction he was described as a 'Convict whose Sentence is Expired'.[4] As a settler at Parramatta a William Knight put his name to a petition to Governor Hunter in February 1798, but, since the surviving document is a transcript, there is no indication whether this was by signature or cross. By 1800 the property had been purchased by D'Arcy Wentworth. The sale may have followed Wentworth's transfer from Sydney to Parramatta in May 1799,[5] but Knight could have moved to Sydney much earlier.

Amelia Levy disappears from the records with the 1795 court case and there are no references to William Knight of the *Neptune* after 1800. In the *Sydney Gazette*, 26 May 1806, a William Knight announced his impending departure for England. This could have been the ex-coachman.[6]

The William Knight who is easiest to trace was sentenced to seven years at the Old Bailey on 12 September 1787, aged 24. He was said to have run a sale-shop in Hounsditch and was convicted for stealing 22 yards of shalloon from a draper's shop in Drury Lane. After a protracted stay at Newgate, and then on the *Stanislaus* hulk (where his age at conviction was given as 24), he sailed for New South Wales on the Second-Fleet ship *Surprise*, arriving on June 1790.[7] He is almost certainly the convict who enrolled in the New South Wales Corps on 11 February 1793, in consequence gaining a conditional pardon on 14 October. In March 1803 the Corps was required to reduce its numbers, and Knight was discharged.[8] In June 1804 a William Knight was granted 80 acres at Bostons Reach, on the Hawkesbury, subsequent references making it clear that the grantee was the man who had arrived on the *Surprise*. In a list of October 1820 the land-holder is described as holding a conditional pardon, a privilege that only the soldier of that name received.[9]

Knight's subsequent career as a farmer was a troubled one. In June 1805 his farmhouse was raided and stripped by a group of Aborigines, who were said to have taken over £100 of goods. On at least three occasions between 1809 and 1814 his property was threatened with sale by the provost-marshal to cover debts, and on several occasions he was forced to use it as surety for loans.[10] On the other hand, he seems to have been a responsible citizen, serving as a juror on coronial inquests and providing references for convicts, job applicants and the like. By 1806 he was living with Mary Lawrence (*per Experiment*, arrived June 1804), whom he married in May 1814, giving his age as 40, over ten years less than seems the case. He died in December 1816. On this occasion his age was overestimated by nearly ten years, being given as 62.[11]

If Knight the ex-coachman was the man who left the colony in 1806, he could well be the actor, though his apparent illiteracy is an inconvenience. The erstwhile shopkeeper who became a soldier and then a farmer seems the more likely candidate, except for one fact: the Corps' pay lists show him as on detachment in June 1799 and June 1800, the dates of the two recorded performances. For a later detachment (November–December 1801) it is known that he was assigned to South Head,[12] the small outpost at the mouth of the harbour. If this was his posting in the earlier years, it would involve a stiff walk to Sydney for rehearsals and performances. One is thus left with two doubtful candidates for the position of actor, unless, of course, a third and completely unrecorded William Knight was at large in the colony.

JOHN WILLIAM LANCASHIRE

PRO, CO201/15, fol.104.

The career of John William Lancashire is one of the less edifying of those to come out of early New South Wales. At the Old Bailey in April 1796 he was accused of stealing £25 of cambric from a Fleet Street drapers, in company with another man who had since disappeared. A specious story was used to gain access to an inner room where the valuable cloths were stored and, when Lancashire was arrested a week later, stolen material was found in his apartment at Cold Bath Fields.

Lancashire had no money for a lawyer, but in court defended himself vigorously. He claimed that the stolen goods had been left by his comrade at his house a few days after the pair had visited the drapers; and argued that his friend must have returned to the shop and stolen the goods. He then ended with an eloquent address, in which he stressed his innocent and co-operative behaviour on being accosted by the law officers. Eloquent or not, Lancashire was found guilty, but an accommodating jury valued the cloth at 39s., not the £25 estimate put on it by the draper. In this way he escaped the death penalty and was sentenced to transportation for seven years.[1] In the course of the trial it emerged that Lancashire had persuaded the prosecuting draper to give him 5s. per week during the pre-trial imprisonment to support his young wife. Two weeks later the arrangement had collapsed, when the draper discovered Lancashire was not married to the recipient, but to another. Lancashire promptly counter-claimed that the money was offered as an inducement to plead guilty. The whole incident was a striking example of his manipulative skills, effrontery and readiness to defame others to save his own skin.

When Lancashire was committed to Newgate, on 19 February 1796, he was recorded as aged 22, 5 feet 4 inches tall, with a fair complexion, brown hair, and dark eyes, a native of Bath and a heraldic painter by trade. No record of his birth has been found in Bath, but a Lancashire family was prominent in the city as marble masons and carvers.[2] In the colony he was to claim, in a petition to Governor Hunter, that he was

> a youth of honest respectable and worthy parents who ever lived in affluence
> and whose Character was never Blemished untill that unfortunate period of my

Life I made the Breach. That your Excellencys Petitioner Lived with M[r]. Rob[t] Williams Banker in Birchin Lane – London – (an Uncle to your petitioner) for some considerable time as Cash Clerk – and prior to that Captains Clerk on Board the Mars 74 Sir Ch[s] Cotton Comdr, but owing to an ill state of health was necessitated to quit the service.[3]

After his conviction Lancashire lingered in Newgate for the greater part of a year, before an order of 11 November had him sent to the hulks at Woolwich. From there he was embarked on the convict transport *Barwell*. Also on board was another plausible rogue, Michael Massey Robinson. While Robinson was successfully cultivating the eminent passenger, Judge-Advocate Dore, Lancashire was winning the confidence of Captain Cameron, the ship's commanding officer, and was employed to keep the ship's journals during the voyage.[4] Towards the end of the passage, however, the relationship soured and on arrival (18 May 1798) Cameron had Lancashire thrown into Sydney's gaol for insolence. He was still in prison on 11 August, when the magistrates extended his sentence by three months. From gaol he was brought forward on 24 August as a witness in the investigation into Cameron's charges that Ensign Bond and others had conspired to seize the ship.[5]

The magistrates ordered Lancashire's release on 22 September 1798, only to put him on trial on the same day for stealing a £3 bill and some silver from that same Ensign Bond. He escaped conviction because of lack of evidence. On 24 October came the charge of stealing a cake of government soap. While allowing the case 'was not sufficiently established in Law', the magistrates consoled themselves by ordering him 50 lashes and a 'return to his Duty as a Servant of Government', presumably as a clerk or storeman in the depot from which he had stolen the soap.[6]

Lancashire next emerges in late January 1799. While using his free time on a Sunday to mark bags for Isaac Nicholls, he was witness to events leading to Nicholls' trial for receiving stolen goods. On 14 March Lancashire gave evidence in support of Nicholls, whose enemies were not above suggesting that this had been secured with a £20 bribe.[7] Two weeks later it was Lancashire's turn to be on trial, this time for attempting to pass a promissory note forged in the name of John Stogdell. Again Lancashire defended himself with great flair and again to no avail, but this time there was no considerate jury, merely a panel of officers and Judge-Advocate Dore, who sentenced him to death.[8]

In London, Lancashire had sought, in his defence, to suggest dubious practice on the part of the prosecuting draper. He now made a similar attempt on a grander scale. In petitions to both Governor Hunter and Lieutenant Kent, RN, he claimed that the officers of the New South Wales Corps (who made up the majority of the bench) had determined to punish him for his defence of Captain Cameron against Ensign Bond, and even more so for his support of Nicholls. He had already felt the hostility of the Corps, he claimed, in the way the 'Comp[y] of Comedians (Soldiers)' had abused him and refused to pay him for his scene painting and other work in the theatre. These were extreme allegations, but they might have contained some truth. In the *Barwell* case it is not clear how his evidence favoured Cameron, but Governor Hunter certainly believed that the Corps' officers were determined to destroy Nicholls as part of their vendetta against Hunter himself. Nicholls, an ex-convict, was Hunter's chief overseer of the convict gangs, as well as a trader. Lancashire even claimed that Bond and the great perturbator himself, Captain John Macarthur, had attempted to persuade him to change his evidence in the Nicholls' case on the promise of securing him a pardon. Certainly, the pair had visited him in prison.[9]

In the event Lancashire was saved by a legal technicality: the majority on the bench voting for a conviction was less than legally required in the colony to secure a death penalty. The execution was held over until advice was received from England; Lancashire in the meantime remained in gaol.[10] Even in prison he was irrepressible. While there he gained possession of a letter from Deputy Commissary Williamson and, by moistening the paper, was able to erase everything but Williamson's signature. The document was subsequently rewritten as a promissory note for £23. Lancashire's partner in the conspiracy, who had passed the note, received a death sentence. Lancashire was not put to the bar, since he was already awaiting execution. In view of the company of players' alleged hostility to Lancashire, it is interesting that Philip Parry, commissary clerk and occasional actor, gave evidence favourable to the suspects, though none related directly to Lancashire. Early in 1800 he escaped from gaol, but was soon recaptured and was still there when Governor King assumed office.[11]

Because of the time he had already spent in gaol King allowed Lancashire out on bail, pending the arrival of instructions from England. These came in June 1802, recommending a pardon on grounds of the mental suffering brought about by living so long under sentence of death. King accordingly granted him a conditional pardon, even though he had once more disgraced himself in the interval. On 21 October 1801, while living in the Rocks, he had been gaoled for stealing the fowl of a poor neighbour and sent to an outlying settlement.[12] By mid-1802 he was back in Sydney, preparing labels for bottles from the hospital pharmacy. On 17 July he was charged with stealing some of the bottles, with a charge of stealing pork thrown in. He was sentenced to 100 lashes and three months at Castle Hill. At the end of September came a close shave at Parramatta, where William Richards, probably the actor of that name, turned evidence against him on a charge of forging mess tickets. Lancashire tried to turn the evidence against Richards, failed, but still managed to secure his own acquittal.[13]

Crimes (and occasional punishments) continued unabated: on 16 July 1803 a charge of issuing promissory notes forged in the name of Michael Massey Robinson (acquitted), on 28 September 1805 one of running an illicit still (judgment held over) and in January 1806 one of forging a bill in the name of Commissary John Palmer. This last was a classic case of Lancashire escaping conviction by deft cross-examination of witnesses. He also impugned the integrity of Magistrate John Harris with several 'gross, impudent and malevolent calumnies', and, as a final touch, claimed he had been 'treated with inhumanity by the county gaoler while in custody'. This was later investigated, but dismissed because of Lancashire's 'notorious bad character'. In the meantime, Lancashire had so manipulated the proceedings that he was acquitted.[14] By this time Governor King's patience had snapped. What followed was an extraordinarily vituperative account from the governor, the longest he was ever to write about any convict. Lancashire was an 'artful delinquent ... constantly in some trouble or other': he was 'possessed of every art & cunning that human invention could turn to the worst of purposes': his claims about magistrate John Harris were 'infamous & vilifying falsehoods'.[15]

Most of the bills Lancashire was suspected of forging were for petty amounts and yet, once granted his conditional pardon, he appears to have done quite nicely in the colony by legitimate means – unless, of course, his illicit still was more successful and long-lived than is assumed. In the *Sydney Gazette*, 3 July and 7 August 1803, he advertised his Parramatta house for sale: 'Three boarded and ceiled Rooms, Skillings, &c.', a bakehouse, ovens and the beginnings of a new stone dwelling. The sale was in preparation for a move to Sydney, at first to Chapel Row and later to No. 1, Back Row. On 23 January 1805 he finalised the purchase of a property at Brickfield Hill that had once belonged to Lieutenant Patullo of the New South Wales Corps.[16] He obtained it for only £16, even though the *Sydney Gazette*, 23 March 1806, described it as 2½ acres of garden with upwards of 100 fruit trees, with a cottage and the frame of a new building; and facilities for rearing stock, 'upwards of 500 head of poultry having been reared on the premises within 10 months'. Lancashire, incidentally, changed his *de facto* almost as often as his house: Jane Crombie was his partner at the time of the fowl stealing, Elizabeth Fielder in July 1803 and Margaret Silk in late 1805 and early 1806. All of them were drawn into his criminal activities, Fielder being gaoled for her part in the Robinson forgeries.

In his last years before transportation Lancashire seems to have been employed as a clerk, but in the colony he turned to activities loosely related to his original trade – painting theatrical scenery, numbers on bags, labels on bottles. This move is confirmed by the small advertising blitz he conducted in the *Sydney Gazette*, beginning 11 September 1803. In it he announced himself as a draftsman and as a ship, house, sign and ornament painter and glazier. He solicited a continuance of public patronage and declared his hopes of developing a new product to replace linseed oil, a scarce commodity in the colony. The faint air of the snake oil salesman that pervades this advertisement is even more pronounced in the last of the series, 25 December 1803, which announced that

> he continues to carry on Painting in all its various Branches as usual; and he having procured a supply of fine Varnishes and Colours, so as to enable him to execute the Coach and Herald Painting, further hopes for a continuance of the favour he has already received, trusting at the same time that his experience and knowledge of the whole profession, together with his expedition in the performance, and moderate rates of charge will tend to recommend him, and furnish a preventative against the gross impositions made by those that have but little pretension to the profession, and are whereby only remarkable for an extravagant use of Oil and Colour, which turns out in the end to have been thrown away. He recommends and undertakes to use the Elephant Oil, prepared, for all outside work.

The advertisement ends with a call for one or two experienced house painters, to be employed on good wages.

Like most colonial businessmen, however, Lancashire pursued a range of activities. The fruit trees and chickens at Patullo Gardens point to activity as a primary producer, while one feature of his Parramatta house was its riverside location 'with a convenience of Boats coming to the Premises from Sydney' and its space for holding stock. In the *Sydney Gazette*, 11 August and 22 September 1805, he advertised the sale at Parramatta of a recently-built eight-to-ten ton schooner, the *Margaret*, capable of carrying nearly 300 bushels of wheat, a vessel later recorded on the Sydney–Hawkesbury run.[17] By this time Lancashire was living at Brickfields and it is not clear whether Rowland Hassall, whose name is also mentioned in the advertisement, was a co-owner or Lancashire's Parramatta agent. The eminently respectable and religious Hassall makes an unlikely business partner for the irredeemable Lancashire.

In the advertisement of 11 September 1803, Lancashire had also announced that his stay in the colony would 'not be of long continuance' and asked for all creditors to render their accounts by 30 November. It is doubtful, however, that he was entitled to leave: his original sentence had expired, but he was tied to the colony by the conditional pardon for his colonial crimes granted by Governor King. His advertisements of 18 and 25 December make no mention of any departure. Less than 18 months later, however, Patullo Gardens was advertised for sale in the *Sydney Gazette*, 23 March 1806. This might have been part of a precipitate plan to leave the colony, but if so it unravelled. Only two weeks later, well before any sale could be completed, the *Sydney Gazette*, 6 April 1806, announced his capture as he lay concealed aboard the outward bound *Tellicherry*. He was ordered 100 lashes and three years' labour for the Crown. Governor King sent him to Port Dalrymple to serve this sentence, stressing that he was 'to be kept at work for that period'. By this time the man who ten years before had been of fair complexion, with brown hair and dark eyes, was being described as sallow, a little marked with the small pox and of an emaciated appearance. His trade was recorded as painter.[18]

With his departure for Port Dalrymple on the *Venus*, the last and most spectacular phase of Lancashire's colonial career was about to begin. Some of the ship's crew, led by the mate, Benjamin Kelly, were mutinous and pilfering the goods on board. When the captain went ashore at their destination, the mate and his allies seized the ship, forcibly landed five sailors unwilling to participate and sailed off. Lancashire, though one of only two male convicts on board, was not named among the mutineers by the *Sydney Gazette*, 13 July 1806, but he did not come ashore with the five sailors. On 12 April 1807 the paper reported that in the intervening December Captain Eben Bunker of the *Elizabeth* had learned that the *Venus* had recently sailed from the Bay of Islands, New Zealand, leaving the mate and Lancashire ashore. Those on board planned to return the vessel to Port Jackson. Kelly and Lancashire, who were living in huts they had constructed, and subsisting on stores that had been left with them, were both captured. An account from another source, published in the same paper, added that Lancashire was now a prisoner on the Sydney-bound sealer *Brothers*. Unfortunately, that vessel arrived in Port Jackson at a time when the *Sydney Gazette* was not being published and no evidence has been found elsewhere to indicate he ever returned to the colony. Like the *Venus* itself, which never reached Sydney, he disappeared off the face of the earth.

Lancashire's scene painting – if, as he claimed, the dispute with the 'Comp^y of Comedians (Soldiers)' was partly over his role in the Nicholls' case – probably took place between September 1798 and 14 March 1799. He was in prison until 22 September 1798, appeared for Nicholls on 14 March 1799 and was back in gaol on Sunday 31 March. It seems improbable that the soldiers would have been disposed to employ him during or after the hearing. He was still a convict working for government and his painting for the theatre, like his work for Nicholls, would have been undertaken in his free time, chiefly on Sundays and part of Saturday afternoon.

It is virtually certain that the scenery Dr Price admired in late 1800 was that prepared by Lancashire.[19] Given the mercurial shifts in allegiances that were part of factional politics in the colony, it is quite conceivable that he was re-employed as a scenic painter once he set up as a draftsman, ship and sign painter in Sydney – that is, in 1803 and beyond. This is all the more likely if his work was of high quality, but in spite of Dr Price there must be some doubt about this. His only surviving painting, a view of Sydney, has been described in Joan Kerr's *Dictionary of Australian Artists* as

> rather crudely executed for such an experienced ornamental and heraldic painter
> as Lancashire claimed to be. In true primitive style every detail is of equal value,
> while the whole, rendered with earnest fidelity to nature, shows as little respect
> for the laws of perspective as he personally showed for the laws of colonial
> society. Because of this the landscape has a rather static quality, highlighted by
> the artist's inability to convey any sense of depth. The sharp focus and bright
> colours, however, give it an almost hypnotic intensity.[20]

Lancashire's signature is reassuringly elegant.[21] His petitions to Hunter and Kent reveal him to be highly literate and well able to manipulate the language to achieve a maximum of pathos, when that became a matter of life and death.

H. LAVELL

Henry Lavell [signature]

PRO, T1/613, *Dunkirk*, 11 December 1784.

On 16 August 1782 Henry Lavell (or Lavall, or Lovell), a servant in a house in the fashionable Portland Place area, absconded with his master's gold watch and chain, which he pawned the next day. He then forged two orders on his master's bank account, using a porter to deliver them and return with the money. By the time the porter arrived on 26 August with a third order, for 10 guineas, the bank had been alerted and Lavell was arrested at the Covent Garden Coffee House, from which the porter had been sent. At the ensuing trial Lavell had no defence. Instead he offered a vague account of his recent history:

> I lived with my father till I went down to Birmingham to work; I went to Jersey, I was there a little while before this gentleman took me, he promised me my discharge; afterwards he would not let me have it: I received nothing of him; I had but a little money when I came to town.[1]

The sentence was a foregone conclusion, death. The case was held over until 4 December because of a possible flaw in the indictment, but the challenge was swept aside and Lavell was left awaiting his punishment in Newgate. In the prison was Robert Sidaway, who had been convicted at the same sitting and was also under a death sentence. The two may have become acquainted at this time.

After a year in Newgate, Lavell's sentence was commuted to transportation for life. On 26 March 1784 he boarded the convict transport *Mercury*, which was sailing for North America. Also on board was Robert Sidaway. Shortly after its departure the *Mercury* was seized by the convicts, who sailed it into Torbay, in an attempt to escape. Lavell was one of those who did not make it to land, being recaptured by the crew of HMS *Helena* while still on the vessel. After a brief period in Exeter gaol, he was transferred to the *Dunkirk* hulk in late June, his age given as 22, presumably his age at conviction. On 1 December 1784 he signed for an issue of slop clothing in a confident hand, and in October 1786 was described as 'in general tolerably well behaved, but troublesome at times'. On 11 March 1787, 4½ years after his first imprisonment, he was embarked on the *Friendship* in the first fleet to Botany Bay. His age was given as 23 and his trade as ivory-turner. On board once again was Robert Sidaway.[2]

On the voyage Lavell was initially regarded as one of the trustier convicts, used in tasks about the ship such as manning the pumps. Ralph Clark also records him as reading the burial service over a dead child. On 23 December his credibility was destroyed, when he and another trusty were found using their freedom to raid the fore-hold and steal large amounts of wood and beef, which they passed to the other prisoners.[3]

At Botany Bay his career began on an even worse note. Within a month of landing he was tried as a member of a gang that had robbed the public stores. Once again he received the death sentence. With two others he was led out to what was to be the first execution in the colony's history. The convict hangman was both nervous and inexperienced, leading to confusion and delay. One man was hanged, but Lavell and his fellow prisoner were respited. The next day they were once again led out, but at the foot of the gallows received a reprieve. They were exiled to Pinchgut, a barren rock in the harbour. In Surgeon White's version of the story, Sidaway was also sent to the rock. The outcasts remained there until freed on the King's birthday, 4 June 1788. White considered this pardoning of Lavell and Sidaway as misguided, 'because they seem so truly abandoned and incorrigible'.[4]

Between January 1790 and March 1793 Lavell was on Norfolk Island, where he was punished in February 1791 'for telling a palpable lye', but given a pig to help him achieve independence. By July he was reported as having cleared eighty roods of land and by 13 December was reported as independent of the store as far as meat was concerned. He was also supporting an unnamed companion, presumably female.[5]

After his return to Port Jackson Lavell seems to have kept out of trouble. On 30 January 1794, however, he received a bad fright, when a friend of his lodger left a bundle of stolen clothes in the house. In panic, the lodger and Mary Carroll, Lavell's mistress, threw the bundle into the backyard. On his return from work, Lavell's solution was to take the goods to Sidaway's house as a safe place from which they could be returned to the owner.[6] Apparently he felt he could rely on Sidaway's help.

In August 1798 Lavell was proceeded against by David Greville and John Sparrow for recovery of debts of 17s. and £3 5s. respectively, which he fought hard not to pay. In September of the same year he was involved in a curious dispute with Shadrach Shaw, as a result of which he was ordered to supply Shaw 'with 2 Bedsteads one in one month & the other in 2 Months equal in Value to £4 each'. This suggests that Lavell was earning his living from cabinet making.[7]

On 7 November 1798 Lavell received an absolute pardon, on what grounds is not clear. In a list of 1801 he is recorded as having 'Gone to England'.[8]

Lavell is not mentioned by Collins among the 'principal performers' on the opening night of Sidaway's theatre, but he could have been a bit player. His only recorded performance is in the afterpiece at Green's benefit, where he played Patrick, the 'poor soldier' of the title. Though the play was extremely popular, its plot is little more than a frame on which to hang a series of songs. Ability as a singer probably earned Lavell the role which, incidentally, was normally taken by a woman. (Mrs Kennedy, who first performed it, was said to have 'one of the finest counter-tenor voices ever heard'.[9]) Lavell's absence from the playbill for Mrs Parry's benefit on 1 June 1799 suggests he might have been an occasional performer, but it is just as likely he had already left the country.

One witness at his trial referred to Lavell as a 'gentleman' and there is a hint of style about his manner in the coffee-house. Since his master appears to have been a wealthy man, Lavell could have been a servant of a superior kind. On the other hand, no highborn persons offered character references at his trial and, though he was given special status on the *Friendship*, it was still as a labourer. He was not the recipient of that unmistakable sign of grace extended to some gentlemen convicts, the freedom of the vessel.[10] The absolute pardon could suggest influential English connections, but by 1798 he had spent sixteen years as a convict. Genteel manners (however acquired), together with good behaviour after his unpromising beginnings, could have been sufficient to obtain the release.

MRS McCANN

Sarah McCann, alias Lloyd, alias Bevan, was committed to Newgate on 19 September 1796, where she was listed as a single woman, aged 27 and a native of Dublin. She was described as of fair complexion with brown hair and grey eyes, and was 5 feet 6 inches tall. She was fine-looking, and could put on a show of refinement. A witness spoke of her as 'a lusty woman' and a newspaper account of her trial described her as 'a genteel woman, well dressed in black silk'.[1] The 1828 census of New South Wales reveals that she was a Roman Catholic.

Sarah McCann was already in trouble when she committed the crime which brought her into Newgate. She had been indicted at the General Quarter Sessions of the Peace for the County of Middlesex on 25 April for keeping 'a certain common ill governed and disorderly house', but had not yet appeared to plead her case.[2] The disorderly house was in Marylebone, whose high street was notorious for its concentration of brothels. Sarah was a daughter of the game, and in many respects a successful one. Not only had she risen to controlling her own brothel, but she also claimed to have been kept by a wealthy businessman, who took her to Margate for the summer and planned to marry her. Beyond that was the story reported in the colony that she had been the mistress of a royal duke, one of the profligate sons of George III.[3] Her aliases, Lloyd and Bevan, were probably the names of successive pimps, though her current bully-boy was one Lloyd McCulloch.

McCann emerges from the records as a tempestuous creature. She had possessed large sums of money, but at the time of her offence many of her goods were in pawn and she was indebted to a baker for £15.. She had apparently returned to working the streets, in the Charing Cross area, when she accosted a businessman, John Milne, late at night, enticed him into a nearby house of accommodation, and ended the adventure in possession of his pocket-book. It contained £79 in banknotes and a mass of bills of exchange. What followed was a flurry of activity, as she set about paying off her debts, attempting to redeem the pawned goods and exchange the notes for coinage. Her behaviour was characteristically reckless. On the evening of the crime she awoke the baker shortly before midnight to clear her debt; and displayed the money to others with wild incaution: 'She took out of her pocket a parcel of Bank-notes in a careless manner, as you would waste paper', said one witness.

The bubble burst when she discovered her victim had advertised for her capture and that the runners were after her. In panic, she abandoned her house in Westminster Road and went to earth in Finsbury. Then, when McCulloch was arrested, she took the desperate step of trying to save him, and herself, by returning the pocket-book and the bills of exchange to the victim's wife, accompanied by a letter written in her own hand:

> Madam,
> I met your husband sometime ago, whom I did not know, nor would I know if
> I were to see him; there was another company in the room that went out when
> we went in; along-side of the sofa I saw a pocket-book; I did not know who it
> belonged to; but I kept it from Thursday until the Monday; you shall hear
> more; and I mean to make Mr. Trotter acquainted with the whole transaction,
> as he is well acquainted with the innocent man Mr. Milne has imprisoned; I am
> very sorry to hurt you by making you acquainted with this affair.

Instead of helping her cause, the letter became evidence for the prosecution. Nor was her alleged attempt to buy off Milne by selling her furniture and giving him the proceeds any more successful. She claimed that he had actually gone to her house to estimate the value of the moveables, but the agreement could not be finalised before she was arrested.

The trial attracted a great deal of attention, largely because of its salacious nature and the discomfiture of the well-to-do and faintly reptilian Mr Milne. The judge raised the nice issue of whether it could be proved that the pocket-book had been stolen in the house rather than the street, since street robbery carried a milder sentence than robbery in a house. The jury opted for the latter, and Mrs McCann was sentenced to seven years' transportation. At this point, according to the *Oracle*, 26 September 1797, she made one last throw:

> Mrs. McCann was, as is usual on conviction, asked her age? After consulting
> M'Culloch, she replied forty-five. It was obvious to all in Court that she could

not be more than thirty. Her persisting in the assertion is attributed to a notion, that women on the wrong side of forty, not being proper objects for the purposes of colonization, would not be transported to Botany Bay.

However, she could not avoid her fate. She was packed off to New South Wales on the *Britannia*, and arrived on 18 July 1798.

Less than a year after her arrival Sarah McCann was recorded as a player with the Sydney company, performing the role of Mrs Seymour in *Fortune's Fool* at Mrs Parry's benefit on 1 June 1798. She was almost certainly in another performance on Saturday 10 August, when she was accosted by a creditor 'after she had left the Theatre & was proceeding home', but she makes no appearance in the playbills of 1800. Her fiery temper might have been part of the problem. The creditor who accosted her in August 1799 was spat in the face for her trouble and charged with assault by Sarah, when she struck back in response. Sarah lost the case. On 16 January 1802 she attempted to lay charges against Mary Donovan for assaulting her in Daniel Cubit's inn, only to have the accusation once again rebound on her: 'From ye Testemony of Fenwick it appeared to ye Bench that McCann had thrown a pot of water & some vinegar into Donovan's face, excited thereto by some Impulse.'[4]

In a list of about 1800 McCann is shown as off stores and living with John Redman, a constable who was a seaman by trade and had arrived as a convict. Redman was to have a prosperous career as chief constable, keeper of Sydney Gaol, publican, landholder and trader, but Sarah was not to share it with him. In the general muster of 1806 she is shown as free by servitude and living in Sydney with a William Smith. In the general muster of 1814 she is described as single, with one child, and in the muster of 1822 as the 'Wife of J. Chambers Sydney'.[5] The child mentioned has left no further trace, its age, sex and paternity unknown.

In the 1825 muster she is recorded simply as a 'Housekeeper' of Pitt Street, Sydney.[6] This probably points forward to the relationship which appears in the 1828 census, where she is described as aged 60, free by servitude, a Catholic and housekeeper to William Smith of Pitt Street, Sydney. Smith himself is listed as a Protestant and a labourer, aged 68, who had arrived a freeman on the *Matilda*. This is William Smith senior, who came to the colony as a private in the New South Wales Corps in August 1791 and was discharged from the Corps on 24 April 1795.[7] Given the closeness in date of the 1825 muster and the 1828 census, this Sarah is unlikely to be the Sarah Macan who, at an inquest on 29 January 1827, said she had been living with the deceased James Elgin for about a year and a half at Sydney Road.[8]

One question remains. Could either of the William Smiths who occur in McCann's later life (in 1806 and 1828), and who may be the same man, be the William Smith who was a leading actor with the company when Sarah joined it? (This issue is considered later, in the entry on Smith.)

The 1828 census provides the last evidence of Sarah McCann. Her career was one of sad decline, from the glittering world of the London and Margate *demi monde* to life as the *de facto* wife of a labourer at the end of the world. She was probably too old and too poor to return to Britain and died in unrecorded poverty in Sydney.

MRS MILLER

In all likelihood Mrs Miller lived up to her promise and acted only once on the Sydney stage, as a guest player in Mrs Parry's benefit on 1 June 1799. She performed in the mainpiece, *Fortune's Fool*, as Lady Danvers opposite Philip Parry's Sir Charles Danvers. The two open the play in a bravura scene that is probably the wittiest in the piece, and thereafter only have to put in an occasional appearance – an eminently satisfactory arrangement for guest artists.

Mary Palmer, who was to assume the name Mrs Miller in the colony, was tried in September 1795 for stealing a pair of leather slippers, value 2s., from a shop in Maiden Lane, Covent Garden. She was seen pocketing the goods, while a male accomplice attempted to distract the staff by pretending to buy shoes. Palmer put up a spirited defence at her trial, but to no effect.[1] She was sentenced to seven years' transportation and arrived in Sydney on the *Indispensable* on 30 April 1796. The ship's indent gave her age at the time of conviction as 22.

The man with whom she was to cohabit was tried in December 1789 as John Williams, alias William Miller, but in the colony was always known by the latter name. He and a companion were charged on two separate counts of highway robbery. During the trial they both claimed to have been servants to gentlemen and great play was made of their respectable backgrounds, though no details were given. The jury and prosecutor were sufficiently impressed to recommend them to mercy because of their reputable upbringing. In consequence, the 19-year-old Miller's death sentence was reduced to transportation for life at the sessions for December 1790.[2]

Miller arrived in Sydney on board the *Albemarle* on 13 October 1791, and quickly established himself. Collins described him in 1796 as 'a young man who, on account of his good behaviour, had been allowed to exercise the trade of a baker'. By 1798 he was proprietor of licensed premises, The Barley Mow, close to Hospital Wharf in George Street.[3]

In 1796 Miller was living with Ann Martin; indeed, the couple had baptised their child on 17 April.[4] At what point Mary Palmer replaced Ann Martin in his affections is not known. The earliest evidence of the connection postdates the playbill by a few days: on 11 June 1799 Palmer appeared in lieu of Miller before the Civil Court in pursuit of a debt owing to him. She is probably the Mary Palmer who in February of that year had secured the imprisonment of a sailor and obtained legal possession of his sea chest, evidently a dispute over a debt. Similarly, she is probably the Mary Palmer pursuing Mary Mullett through the court on 22 May 1799 over £17 owing to her.[5] These cases could indicate that she too was an entrepreneur.

On 15 August 1799 the couple were involved in a riot that gives some sense of their temperaments:

> Henry Kable appeared & charged William Miller, Mary Miller, o'wise Mary
> Palmer, and Daniel Cubitt (all in Custody) with having violently assaulted him
> the preceding Evening in the Execution of his Duty, when he went, aided by
> other peace Officers, to quell a Riot, of which said Kable had Information &
> found was existing, at the time of entering said Miller's House. – The Fact
> being established ... the Magistrates ordered William Miller and Mary Palmer
> to stand Committed for Trial ... for the Assault ... and as this Affray had
> happened in the House of Will[m] Miller who had been licenced to keep a Public-
> house ... the said Licence became forfeit.[6]

In the fashion of the colony Kable soon after appeared before the court to withdraw the charge and the licence was restored, though Mary lost it for them again in October 1802, when she was convicted of obtaining spirits by fraud.[7]

By 1800 the pair had become one of those formidable convict business couples that were a feature of early New South Wales – people such as Elisabeth Needham and John Driver, William Chapman and Ann Marsh. When Miller was absent on 7 July 1801, Mary acted as his attorney in the Civil Court, and, when he bought his first vessel in 1800, a twelve-ton sloop to be used mainly to bring grain from the Hawkesbury, it was named the *William and Mary*.[8] Miller seems also to have had interests at Kissing Point and throughout 1803, when the

Sydney Gazette advertised the weekly arrival of the Kissing Point market boats, the news item was often accompanied by a note that between markets the produce could be obtained direct from Mary. In October 1807, when she was accused of receiving stolen goods, she described herself as keeping 'a public Warehouse for the reception of all Kinds of Goods'.[9] This is evidently the warehouse referred to as 'William Miller's Store-Rooms, near the Hospital Wharf' in the *Sydney Gazette*, 22 April 1804.

On 18 January 1802 William Miller, baker of Sydney, was granted an absolute pardon by Governor King. The lease on his George Street property was confirmed by Lieutenant-Colonel William Paterson during the interregnum and endorsed by Governor Macquarie on his arrival.[10] However, in the *Sydney Gazette*, 15 February 1812, the property was advertised for sale. It was offered again on 7 November 1812 'near the Wharf, with good Bakehouse and other Conveniencies, and a clear intercourse to the water side'. This is the last record of the Millers. A Mrs Mary Miller, who could well be the actress, announced her impending departure from the colony in the *Sydney Gazette*, 4 December 1813, but there is no mention of William accompanying her, and nothing to identify him with any of the William Millers who appear as farmers thereafter.[11]

R. MOMDY

R. Momdy, who played the insignificant role of Fitzroy in *The Poor Soldier*, the afterpiece at Green's benefit on 23 July 1796, is untraceable. No person with that family name appears in the records. Since the name is derived from one newspaper's transcription of another newspaper's transcription of the worn and damaged typeface of the original playbill, Momdy may well be a misreading or typographical error.

J. PAINE OR PAYNE

An I. Paine is recorded in only one of the surviving playbills, performing the small but significant title role in *Henry the Fourth* on 8 April 1800. No I. Paine or Payne is recorded in the colony, but, as the printer had elsewhere substituted an I for a J in proper names, the actor is evidently J. Paine.

Two individuals named James Payne had reached the colony by April 1800. Both were convicts, one sentenced to seven years at the Stafford assizes in July 1790 for robbing a shop,[1] and the other, similarly sentenced at Chelmsford, also in July 1790, for stealing clothing and money from a house in the village of Thundersley. The court records gave his age as 30, making him 40 at the time of the performance.[2] Both men sailed in the Third Fleet, the former on the *Britannia* and the latter on the *William and Ann*, which arrived on 14 October 1791 and 28 August 1791 respectively.

Though both convicts seem to have arrived safely, one of them disappears from the records from that time forward. Perhaps he managed to escape from the colony or was an unrecorded burial. The other was granted a conditional pardon provisional upon his enlisting in the New South Wales Corps. He was admitted to the Corps on 6 February 1793 and the pardon was granted on 14 October. Pamela Statham identifies him as the convict who arrived on the *William and Ann*, though the reason for this is not clear.[3] The eight-year discrepancy between this man's alleged age at conviction and the soldier's age as given in 1808 is worrying, but not without precedent.

Whichever James Payne it was who joined the New South Wales Corps, he was described in a muster of 1808 as born in Berkshire, 5 feet 7 inches tall, with a sallow complexion, hazel eyes, dark brown hair and a round face. His age was given as 56 years and his profession as upholsterer. Though he received a share in a fifty-acre land grant in 1797, he nowhere appears in subsequent lists as a holder of that property.[4] As with many soldiers' grants, it was probably sold for cash almost immediately.

One difficulty in identifying the soldier with the actor is that the pay lists show Payne on detachment in the month in which *Henry the Fourth* was staged.[5] The place of posting is not named, but if it was, for example, South Head or the battery under construction at George's Head, it is possible to imagine him slipping into town for rehearsals and performance. Further afield it would have required leave within the month to visit Sydney. Payne was frequently on detachment, which might account for his being involved in only one recorded production. The hypothesis of an out-of-town actor, however, remains sustainable only because no other identifiable J. Payne can be found in the colony.

With the reduction in the size of the British army after the short-lived peace of 1803, Payne was one of the Corps' members chosen for demobilisation and sent back to England. By the time he arrived there the fragile peace had already broken down, and on 30 June 1804 he was enlisted into the Second Guards Battalion, serving there until 18 January 1807, and transferring back into the New South Wales Corps (the 102nd Regiment) on the following day. On the *Admiral Gambier* he once again sailed for Australia, reaching Port Jackson on 21 December 1808. On 24 April 1810, with the regiment preparing to return to England, he was transferred to the Royal Veterans' Company. Thereafter he appears as a witness at an inquest in the Sydney area on 10 October 1814 and in company musters as on duty at Parramatta, Windsor and other centres.[6]

By 1823 the Veterans' Company had been disbanded, and on 28 October of that year Payne was authorised to receive a grant of 100 acres of land in any part of the colony already surveyed. By that time he had been thirty years in the army without ever having risen above the rank of private and would have been 63, if the figure given in the Chelmsford records is correct, or 71, if the 1808 muster can be trusted. In either case it was an implausible age at which to become a farmer – all the more so since from 25 December 1819 to August 1823 Payne is consistently recorded as sick and in quarters. No record of a grant being made has survived, and it is more likely he moved to the Benevolent Asylum and was the James Payne who died there on 23 June 1840, his age noted as 87 years.[7] That figure is a near match for the soldier's age as given in 1808.

D. PARNELL

On 8 April 1797 Daniel Parnell was sentenced to death at the Bristol assizes for stealing a gold watchcase from Edward Bird, 'privately in his shop'. He was promptly reprieved, but ten months later his punishment had not been finalised, when, on 22 November, the recorder of Bristol wrote that 'severable favourable circumstances' led the court to reprieve him and it was now recommending he be transported for fourteen years.[1] 'Favourable circumstances' was a formulaic phrase common in such documents, but King George accepted the recommendation and Parnell was placed on board the convict transport *Hillsborough*, reaching Sydney on 26 July 1799. Within seven months he had joined the theatre company. His name appears in the earliest of the surviving playbills of that period, for *The Recruiting Officer* on 8 March 1800. The name of B. Smith has been crossed out as the performer of Coppee in the afterpiece, *The Virgin Unmask'd*, and replaced with D. Parnell. It may be significant that Coppee is a dancing master, for in the playbill for *Henry the Fourth* (8 April 1800) the interlude 'The

Drunken Swiss' is danced by Parnell and Mrs Parry. On neither occasion does he appear in the mainpiece. Similarly, when *She Stoops to Conquer* was presented on 23 July 1800, he was confined to the afterpiece, *The Devil to Pay*, where, admittedly, he had a major role as Jobson, the clownish country tailor. Jobson is one of the key singers in the piece, so perhaps he was employed chiefly for his singing and dancing. But it may be that he was too busy a man to accept larger parts.

Parnell appears in William Noah's list of *Hillsborough* transportees as a bookbinder, and it was in this capacity that the government employed him. On an 1800 list of officers' servants he is shown as convict bookbinder to the commissary's office, as he was on an 1801 list. He must have been doing moderately well, since in 1800, with the permission of Governor Hunter, he had built a house for himself in Bell Street. On 4 June 1801 he was one of several men granted conditional pardons 'to enable them to become Settlers'.[2]

In late May 1802 things began to go wrong for Parnell. On 28th he received 50 lashes for buying goods from the government store, allegedly for his own use, and then selling them on at a profit.[3] Parnell was punished as a warning to others, since King was determined to suppress this 'extortionate traffic'. As the commissariat ran the store and Parnell was, or had been, a member of its staff, his offence might have seemed the more unforgivable. The next day he appeared in court to give information against William and Ursula Field for receiving stolen goods; but a few minutes later found himself on a charge, being accused by D.D. Mann of spreading rumours that Mann was guilty of forgery. 'Parnell acknowledged his fault and begged Pardon of Mann who was satisfied with the Confession'.[4] There may have been further problems, since in May 1803 he went (or was sent) to Norfolk Island, returning to the mainland before February 1804.[5]

By the time of his return to Sydney, Parnell had lost his house in Bell Street and was striking out in a new direction. On 9 September 1804 an advertisement appeared in the *Sydney Gazette*:

> The Public are most Respectfully informed, that an ACADEMY will be opened
> To-morrow, near the Lower End of South Row, for the Instruction of Youth,
> in the Principles of the English Language, Writing, and Arithmetic; in which
> every attention will be paid by
>
> D. PARNELL
> Late Schoolmaster at Norfolk Island:
>
> Such of the Inhabitants as think proper to commit the Education of their
> Children to his Charge, may place every Confidence in his unremitting assiduity
> in promoting the object of his undertaking. To Reading, Writing, and speaking
> the Mother Tongue with purity and propriety, and to render easy and familiar
> those essential Branches that form the basis of Literary Science, shall be his
> constant Care; in this alone he founds his prospect of Support, and his Claim
> upon the Patronage of a liberal and discerning Public.

The Norfolk Island records do not list him as a teacher, but he might have stood in for Thomas MacQueen, whose financial incompetence and poor behaviour saw him sometimes in the debtors' prison and sometimes suspended from his duties.

School teaching was a precarious occupation in New South Wales, and Parnell proved no more successful than MacQueen. In 1805 and 1806 he was being pursued through the Court of Civil Jurisdiction for unpaid debts owed to private individuals,[6] and had accumulated a debt to the government of £12 8s. 5d.. In 1809 he approached Acting Governor Paterson, and in 1810 Governor Macquarie's secretary, for permission to stage one or more plays to help relieve his financial embarrassment. The petition to Macquarie has survived in a modern transcript and is interesting for its strained literary qualities and for its glimpses of Sydney's theatrical scene:

> Sir,
>
> I beg respectfully to apologise for the liberty I take in this address. As the subject I am to trouble you with embraces a case of personal distress, I am induced to hope your humanity will kindly induce you to second the means whereby its abatement may be effected, to explain which, I am, sir, under the necessity of troubling you with a more detailed statement than I could otherwise have wished. A short time previous to the arrival of His Excellency Gov'r Macquarie, I was induced to make a representation of the embarrassment I laboured under (from successive misfortunes) to Mrs. Paterson, who was pleased to lay my case before Colonel Paterson, who favoured me with his sanction for a few nights' theatrical representation, as well with a view to extricate me from my pecuniary difficulties, as to gratify the public with a theatrical temporary display, which would have taken place but for the causes above assigned. Altho', sir, I am far from imagining that His Excellency will be biassed by anything like precedent in cases of this nature, I cannot refuse myself the favourable opportunity of here informing you that Gov'r Bligh had given his permission for the erection of a permanent and spacious theatre for the performance of regular drama, and which, but for the circumstance of the change in the Government, had long since been carried into effect. How far His Excellency, our honored Governor, may consider the drama capable of producing a moral end, when properly conducted, I very submissively submit to your better knowledge; yet I flatter myself with the hope at the same time that His Excell'y will see no impropriety in granting his permission to my entertaining a select company for two or three nights, whose contributions might release me from pecuniary claims, and render this flattering imagination. I feel some assurance that your acquaintance with the Muses will befriend me at so critical a juncture, by a representation to His Excellency favourable to my application, confident as you may be in the assurance that regularity and good order shall be premier objects of attention, with,
>
> Sir, &c.,
> DAN'L
> PARNELL.[7]

It is not known whether permission was granted, but in the *Sydney Gazette*, 14 September 1811, a Daniel Parnell was listed as about to leave for England on the ship *New Zealander*, and required all claims against him to be presented for payment immediately. Since his sentence had expired earlier that year, he was entitled to depart, but in spite of the advertisement he managed to do so without clearing some of his debts. The money owing to government during King's administration was still unpaid at the time of the Bigge inquiry, the explanation being that Parnell had 'run'.[8]

This, however, was not the end of Parnell's colonial experience. On 8 December 1817 a Charles Manning was sentenced to seven years at Northampton assizes. He arrived in Sydney on 14 September 1818 on the *Isabella*, the indent describing him as a native of Dublin, a 52-year-old printer and bookbinder, 5 feet 4½ inches tall with grey hair and grey eyes. On 12 March 1822 he appeared before the Sydney bench on an unrecorded charge and was sentenced to serve out the rest of his time at a penal station. The indent of the vessel carrying him to Newcastle later that month named him 'Dan¹ Parnell as Charles Manning'. The 1822 muster listed him as Daniel Parnell, at Newcastle, but the *Sydney Gazette*, 13 January 1825, reverted to the name Charles Manning in reporting that he had secured his certificate of freedom.[9]

Thereafter he was known only as Daniel Parnell.

The muster completed in 1825 listed Parnell as employed by Robert Howe, in Sydney.[10] Since Howe was the publisher of the *Sydney Gazette*, Parnell would have been working as a printer. But from here onwards his path led inexorably downwards. On 5 April 1827 the *Sydney Gazette* reported that

> Daniel Parnell, an elderly man, upwards of thirty years an inhabitant in the Colony, was indicted for stealing two pewter pint pots from a public house, the property of Henry Spencer. The prosecutor refusing to swear to the property, and respectable evidence being offered, who gave the prisoner a good character, he was acquitted.

It was reported that Parnell was drunk when, later on the same day, he was apprehended trying to sell the pewter pots, valued at 10d., in bars of various ale-houses.

A little over two months later, Parnell, 'a man between sixty and seventy years of age, and resident of the Colony nearly thirty years' was in trouble again, for stealing a brass candlestick valued at 5s., which he pawned for a dump. He readily admitted to the crime when challenged and was sentenced to the House of Correction for six months.[11] The erstwhile actor and teacher seems to have dwindled away to a drunken pilferer, possibly even a derelict. He appears in the 1828 census as Daniel Charles Parnell, *per Hillsborough*, and is given as aged 55, a Protestant labourer employed by John Pyke at Prospect. If the age is correct, he would have been about 27 at the time of his appearance on the Sydney stage. On the other hand, if he was 52 in 1818, as the *Isabella* indent stated, or between 60 and 70 in 1827, as the newspaper reported, he would have been a dancer in his mid-30s in 1800.

In 1835 Parnell appeared once again, in a replay of his 1827 brushes with the law. On 2 February, while living at Parramatta, he was charged with stealing a flat iron, value 1s., which he then sold for 6d. to a man who spoke of him as 'in a very distressed state'. The theft was clumsy and again Parnell wilted when challenged, taking a constable to recover the iron. Remarkably, he was acquitted, presumably because the owners could not identify the iron with certainty. In October 1837 he was in further trouble in Sydney, bailed to appear before the Quarter Sessions on 3 January 1838 for an unspecified offence.[12]

This was to be Parnell's last appearance. In view of his age and poverty he is unlikely to have left the colony, but there is no record of his death or burial. It is probable he went to an unremarked pauper's grave, without the ministrations of a clergyman.

P. PARRY AND MRS PARRY

RONSW, Marriages.4.274.

Frances Ferguson, alias Grosvenor, alias Fox, was said in the colony to have been a prostitute, or member of the 'London Cyprian corps', as a footnote to one of the playbills published in England puts it. For 18 months before her arrest she had been living with Charles Herbert

Fox at No. 4, Harcourt Place, Drury Lane, in a two-room apartment up one flight of stairs. Fox had worked for the customs and then had been a sheriff's officer, and witnesses claimed he was 'a sober, honest man'. Mrs Ibbetson, who owned the house, had known Frances Ferguson/Fox for nine or ten years, so she was presumably well established in the locality. Several witnesses, including Ibbetson, 'gave her the Character of an honest Woman – Tho she cohabited with Fox without the least Pretence of their being married: and in an House which seemed to be a Receptacle for Whores & Rogues'.

There can be little doubt that technically Ferguson and Fox were innocent of the crime of which they were convicted on 20 March 1797. A house in Bermondsey had been broken into on 4 March and a wide range of goods stolen, including a black petticoat. The prime suspect was Henry Potter, who had been a servant in the house. Charles Fox claimed the couple had met Potter during their period at Harcourt Place and that shortly after the robbery he had asked Ferguson, in Fox's absence, if he could leave a parcel in their rooms for an hour or so. During that hour the police arrived and found some of the stolen goods in the parcel. Fox and Ferguson claimed no knowledge of the parcel's content, but their argument was undermined by the fact that Ferguson was wearing the stolen black petticoat and attempted to conceal it. Both were convicted and sentenced to seven years' transportation. They lodged a petition, to which the original judge, with a taste for rough justice, responded that they had probably not committed the robbery, but deserved no mercy since the evidence suggested they had knowingly received the stolen goods. Charles Fox was never sent to Australia, but Frances made the voyage on the *Britannia*, arriving on 18 July 1798. Her age was given as 26 in the trial records.[1]

A little over a year before Frances Ferguson was convicted at Kingston-upon-Thames, Philip Parry was facing the judge at the Old Bailey. Parry was a grocer in Oxford Street, 28 years old, by which age he should have been well established in his trade. However, his business may have been faltering, since on 16 December 1795 he had turned his hand to highway robbery, holding up a one-horse chaise containing a brewer's clerk and his wife. Parry and his partner, Thomas Thompson, accosted the vehicle at about 1.00 pm in a country lane near Twickenham, with none of the refinement shown by that other highwayman-transportee, Thomas Radley:

> Parry came upon the left side of the chaise, and presented a pistol immediately, and swore most terribly; he demanded my money; I immediately cut the horse, and he cou'd not lay hold of the reins. I got on a little distance, and he laid hold of them again; while he did that, Thompson came up upon the right-hand side, and Parry called him a buggar, and made use of very bad language to Thompson.

For all Parry's bluster, the clerk was resolute, offering only the loose change in his pockets and denying he had any more, despite his wife's hysterics. However, it soon became the turn of the highwaymen to panic, as several foot passengers and a solitary horseman approached. The pair galloped off pursued by the horseman, who was unarmed, and later by a mounted servant. The chase continued through Twickenham and onto the Hampton Court road, where Thompson was thrown from his horse at a parish gate and was secured. Parry finally abandoned his horse and was found hiding in some bushes. As his original pursuer approached, Parry, in considerable fear, said

> he hoped I should not use him ill … he begged I would use him as a gentleman; he said, he believed I was a gentleman, and he would be no other to me; he begged me to search him, and said, he had not taken the advantage of me that he might have done.

Parry was convicted in April 1796 and arrived in the colony on the *Ganges* on 2 June 1797, sentenced to transportation for life. At his trial a character witness declared:

> I live at Brecknock, in South Wales: I have known the prisoner, Parry, and his family, upwards of twenty years; they were people of respectability and property; the prisoner bore a very good character; I had a transaction with him of a recent date, I bought an estate of him, eight or nine months ago; there was a circumstance happened, in which he could have taken an advantage of me, and he came forward in the most honourable manner.[2]

Parry's claims to gentility might have been exaggerated. Parents of 'respectability and property' could have been wealthy yeoman farmers rather than petty gentry. His comfortable passage through New South Wales, however, argues that he was recognised there as a person of breeding.

Within four months of disembarkation Frances Ferguson had found her replacement for Charles Fox. On 7 November 1798 a 'List of women convicts in the households of Officers or Householders' was issued. In it her name appears against that of Parry, who is described as clerk to the commissary. At some stage the couple occupied a house at the northern end of what is now O'Connell Street, directly behind the houses of the civil officers, including that of the commissary.[3]

The first record of Mrs Parry's involvement with the Sydney theatre, the playbill of 1 June 1799, is less than a year after her arrival. By that time she was already the company's leading actress and receiving a benefit. It was a meteoric rise, suggesting either that she was exceptionally talented by the standards of Botany Bay, or that she was lucky enough to fill a sudden gap in the company. Philip Parry also acted on this occasion, playing an undemanding role opposite Mrs Miller, who was making a guest appearance. Parry himself was described in the London report of the event as an 'Occasional Performer' and this is his only recorded appearance. The main role Mrs Parry performed on that night has been described in detail in Chapter 3. It points to her belief in herself as an effervescent and dashing comedienne, in the style of Dorothy Jordan. The role of Lady Percy in *Henry the Fourth*, on 8 April 1800, would have given her few opportunities to display her strengths, but on the same evening she partnered Daniel Parnell in a lively comic dance. On 23 June 1800 she performed one of the classic roles for comic actresses of her type, Nell, in the afterpiece *The Devil to Pay*. Other parts in her repertoire also lent themselves to this approach – Miss Tittup in *Bon Ton*, Miss Hardcastle in *She Stoops to Conquer*, Lucy in *The Virgin Unmask'd*, and Sylvia in *The Recruiting Officer*. The playbills of 1800 continue to show her as the dominant female player in the company.

On 1 September 1799 Frances Ferguson and Philip Parry were married in Sydney. He signed the register in a firm, polished hand. Her signature bore the marks of semi-literacy.[4]

Philip Parry makes no appearance pursuing debts through the courts, so he was probably not active in the business world of Sydney.[5] He seems to have concentrated on his work at the commissariat and to have kept out of trouble. The only unpleasantness recorded is a court action by Simeon Lord to recover the watch of a Captain Hingston that had been left with Parry shortly before Hingston sailed for Norfolk Island.[6]

On 4 June 1800 Philip Parry, after serving three years of his sentence, was granted an absolute pardon on the grounds of his 'Extreme Diligence and Assiduity' as chief clerk in the commissary's office. Frances Parry received a similar pardon on 15 September 1800 'in Consequence of the Solicitation of [her] husband … for Permission to Accompany Her said Husband to England'. The records of HMS *Buffalo* reveal that Philip Parry was a supernumerary on that vessel, which departed for England on 21 October 1800, and received rations as a servant, presumably to James Williamson, deputy commissary, who also sailed on the *Buffalo* and had recommended him for the absolute pardon. Mrs Parry was no doubt also on board, as a paying passenger. In a list of 1801 both are noted as having gone to England.[7]

The fact that Parry was able to secure an absolute pardon, not only for himself but for his wife, and in such a short time, points to a considerable degree of influence. Perhaps the consideration shown to him was due to his good and faithful service, but on the whole I suspect that in spite of his trade, and his bad language and lack of bravado as a highwayman, Parry's admission to the commissariat and his ultimate freedom were primarily the consequences of social status and family connections. What the family made of Mrs Parry, when the couple arrived back in England, is another issue entirely.

H. PARSONS

Harry Parsons

RONSW, Marriages.4.228.

Henry (Harry) Parsons was born in the parish of Stoke Demeral, Plymouth Dock, Devon, on 29 August 1768, and joined the Plymouth division of marines on 17 November 1776.[1] This would have been as a drummer, since he was only 8 years old at the time. At 19 he sailed on HMS *Sirius* as part of the initial garrison for the Botany Bay colony and on 4 March 1790 he was posted to Norfolk Island. There, on 9 April 1791, he seems to have been one of the marines who went close to mutiny over a reduction in their rations and a complaint that the convicts were better treated.[2] Parsons was not a leading figure in the disturbance. His career, on the whole, is the record of a good soldier rewarded.

On 6 April 1792 Parsons transferred to the incoming New South Wales Corps and returned to Sydney on 27 April, becoming a corporal on 20 October 1794. For the most part, thereafter, he remained in Sydney. On 6 September 1796 he married Mary Swain, a convict, who was to bear him nine children, five of whom survived infancy. He signed the register in a clear hand. In April 1797 he left the regiment, but re-enlisted in October, reaching the rank of sergeant in March 1801 and obtaining a grant of 250 acres at Bankstown in July 1804. In September 1808 he was described as 5 feet 7 inches tall, fair, with light brown hair, hazel eyes and a round face. In 1809 he was involved in a dispute with Edward Lamb which went from the Court of Civil Judicature to the Court of Appeal.[3] No details of this can be found in the records of either court.

On 14 April 1810, with the Corps about to be returned to England, Henry Parsons transferred to the Veterans' Company, which was to remain in the colony. Initially he was listed as a sergeant, and by 1817 as barrack sergeant, a position which he held until his death. In the same year, 1817, he was appointed as a collector and distributor for the Auxiliary Bible Society and in the following year as Collector and Storekeeper for the Benevolent Society. He died in Sydney on 1 May 1819.[4] A delayed obituary in the *Sydney Gazette*, 22 May 1819, declared that 'he was a much respected man; and at his funeral received the parting honours of his military profession, accompanied by the deepest regret from all who knew him'. In his case the conventional funeral pieties may have been justified.

Harry Parsons was a performer in each of the four productions, 1799–1800, for which a playbill has survived. In Mrs Parry's benefit of 1 June 1799 he played Samuel in *Fortune's Fool* and Jessamy in *Bon Ton*, on 8 March 1800 he played Costar Pearmain in *The Recruiting Officer* and Goodwill in *The Virgin Unmask'd*, on 8 April 1800 he was Douglas in *Henry the Fourth* and on 23 June 1800 Sir Charles Marlow in *She Stoops to Conquer*. These are all small or straightforward roles, so that Parsons emerges as a keen but minor player. Other evidence suggests that his real talent was for music. A balance sheet for the orphan fund shows him as receiving 3 guineas on 1 June 1802 as singing master to the orphans.[5] It was a commitment he must have maintained for many years, since his obituary referred to his 'great utility to the Colony as Instructor of Sacred Music to the little female Orphans, and their constant leader at divine worship'. In the sketchy records of the New South Wales Corps he is listed as a member of the band in 1809,[6] and his obituary describes him as master of the band. Once again, it is a position he must have held for some time to warrant its mention. On 15 August 1818 he was paid from the Police Fund for the performance of sacred music at St Phillip's Church.[7] With this background he may have been, not only an actor, but an instructor and occasional player in the theatre band.

MR AND MRS RADLEY

Mary Ann Fowles (Mrs Radley) was transferred from New Prison to Newgate on 18 October 1792. The Newgate Register described her as a 26-year-old spinster, 5 feet tall, with light brown hair, blue eyes and a fair complexion. She was committed for receiving stolen goods from Thomas Radley, who was entered at Newgate on the same day, aged 25, a striking 5 feet 11 inches tall, with dark hair and grey eyes. He was born in Ireland and she in Exeter. The Register listed him as a hairdresser, but the Old Bailey Session Papers refer to him as a 'hackney writer'. The couple had apparently been together for five years and Mary Ann claimed she had made a trip to Ireland 18 months before. At the time of their arrest they seem to have been living in the Drury Lane area.[1]

Whatever occupation Radley professed, he also had another, that of highwayman. The law was already searching for him when he held up a female member of the Thellusson family, robbing her 'with the utmost politeness' of a jewelled watch and a red leather purse. His behaviour throughout was that of the idealised gentleman of the road: 'I desired him to take away his pistol, he did so … he desired me not to be frightened, and put the pistol in his pocket when I desired him.'[2]

Returning from the robbery, Radley sent Mary Ann to pawn a diamond from Mrs Thellusson's watch. In the meantime another man had been arrested for some of Radley's earlier crimes and was being held at a Bow Street inn for identification by his victims. Driven by a suicidal curiosity, Radley went to the inn, was recognised as being himself the highwayman, and was promptly arrested. No better luck attended Mary Ann. A suspicious pawnbroker, unimpressed by her story that she had found the jewel in Broad Street, St Giles, fetched a Bow Street runner. Initially the connection between the two crimes was not recognised, but, once the relationship between the prisoners was discovered, Mary Ann was bullied into incriminating Radley.

Radley was brought to trial on 31 October 1792, with Mary Ann denying everything she had said that incriminated him. His character references were merely landlords from whom he had rented rooms over the last few years – in other words, if he had any influential friends they were in Ireland, out of reach. He was found guilty and sentenced to death. For her attempt to save Radley, Fowles was committed to stand trial for perjury, the earlier charges of receiving being 'discharged by Proclamation'. She was tried on 12 December 1792 (her age given as 25) and sentenced to seven years' transportation. Radley was scheduled to hang on 26 December 1792.

On 26 December an event took place which shocked even the hardened journalists of the time:

> Yesterday morning, at the usual hour, the following convicts, pursuant to their sentence, were brought forth for execution, opposite the debtor's door, Newgate: Thomas Radley, Thomas Folkes, John Brown, William Graham, John Bonus, and Philip Davis. As these unfortunate men were on the immediate point of being turned off, there came down for one of them (Thomas Radley) a reprieve. This circumstance threw the awful ceremony into confusion, to the great agitation of all the unhappy wretches, each of whom upon the verge of eternity, no doubt, at the moment, caught the *ignus fatus* gleam of hope! – These delays of office are surely censurable.[3]

Radley was respited for a week pending a decision about his future. At some time during the proceedings a petition had been submitted to the authorities by Radley or on his behalf. This has not survived, but a response to it has, dated 31 December 1792:

> Doubts certainly may fairly be entertained of his having even countenanced any Perjury in his Case on the part of the woman with whom he cohabited and viewing what has been stated by Governor Franklin and Dr. O Leary of the Conduct of the Prisoner previous to his Tryal in resisting the Attempt proposed to be set up by means of Perjury for procuring an Alibi I do not hesitate after the Reprieve w[ch] has been granted to give my Opinion, that public Justice will not suffer, by transporting Thomas Radley for Life.[4]

Accordingly, on 9 January 1793, Radley was brought back to court and accepted the new sentence. He was sent to the *Prudentia* hulk at Woolwich to wait for a passage to New South Wales.[5]

Either through good fortune or compassion Radley and Fowles were both assigned to the *Surprise* for the voyage to Australia. The vessel was carrying four of the Scottish Martyrs and the ship's captain was so fearful they might cause mutiny that the journey became a nightmare of spying, violence and abuse. One of the martyrs, Thomas Fyshe Palmer, published a detailed account of the voyage and there was also a government investigation upon the ship's arrival in New South Wales, in October 1794. The Radleys make no appearance in these accounts.[6]

Once in Sydney, the couple resumed cohabitation (they never married). Radley was assigned to the commissariat as an assistant in the provision store and, on 4 June 1800 (with Mary Ann's sentence already expired), received a conditional pardon for his six years' 'honest, faithful and diligent' service there. Subsequently he seems to have moved into business. His name appears in the court records pursuing relatively small debtors, but he seems never to have achieved the status of Sparrow, Sidaway and their peers. In 1800 Governor King raised a small militia among respectable householders and Radley was accepted into the organisation, his name appearing on the earliest surviving roll of 9 November 1802.[7]

In the light of her appearance in every surviving playbill, except that for *Henry the Fourth*, Mrs Radley would seem to have been with the company from the beginning. Her later roles suggest she was in the second rank of performers with no very clear line of her own. Her known parts are Patch in *The Busy Body*, Miss Union in *Fortune's Fool*, Lady Minikin in *Bon Ton*, Rose in *The Recruiting Officer*, Miss Neville in *She Stoops to Conquer* and Lady Loverule in *The*

Devil to Pay. Lady Minikin, the scatter-brained lady about town and Lady Loverule, the vile-tempered and haughty foil to the kind-hearted Nell, would have given her the best opportunities for a bravura performance, but those were in afterpieces. While there is no suggestion that Radley himself performed, he was certainly involved in the enterprise: he owned six shares in the theatre and supported his wife in a violent backstage squabble in which they were the aggressors.[8]

In 1803 Thomas Radley died, and was buried on 4 February.[9] He was only 37. Mary Ann Fowles had another 45 years to live.

In the general muster of 1806 Mary Ann is given as free by servitude and living with Laurence Butler, a convict in government service as a carpenter at the Sydney lumber-yard. He had been transported on *Atlas* 2, which had arrived on 30 October 1802. From 1806 the Rev. Marsden's record of female convicts lists Mary Ann as a concubine with one illegitimate male child.[10] No father is named, nor is there any subsequent mention of the boy. Relations between Radley and Butler had had their fiery moments. On 19 October 1808 Butler and 'Mary Ann Bradley' [*sic*] were

> bro' before the Bench charged with having disturbed the peace of the Neighbourhood, and altho' required by the Constables to be quiet still continued to quarrel, & beat and abused Ann Johnston who was turned into the Streets at 12 o'Clock at Night – Butler reprimanded – & Mary Ann Bradley ordered a Weeks imprisonment.[11]

Ann Johnston is probably Ann Johnson *per Britannia* who, in a list of persons off stores *circa* 1800, is shown as living in Sydney with J. Kenny, one of the men who had gone surety for the Radleys after the playhouse fracas.[12]

By 1812 Butler seems to have left Mary Ann, since in that year he had a child by Ann Roberts, who had arrived on the *Speke* on 15 November 1808. Another child followed in 1815 and in 1817 Butler and Roberts were married.[13] Mary Ann Fowles/Radley does not appear in the 1811 or 1814 musters, but in an appendix to the Bigge report, listing those owning property in Sydney and dated 29 May 1820, she appears as an unmarried woman with a residence in Kent Street. In the 1822 muster she is listed as a householder of Sydney, while the Constables' Notebooks for that muster show her as the sole occupant of the Kent Street house. The 1825 muster lists her once again as a Sydney householder and in the 1828 census she appears as a Protestant, aged 56, still living in Kent Street and working as a mantua maker, one of the humbler professions for women.[14]

Seventeen years later, on 26 September 1848, Mary Ann Fowles was buried from a Catholic, not a Protestant, church. Her age was registered as 100, a guess that presumably reflected her physical decay, since she was, in fact, only 79 or 80.[15] Her passing went unremarked in the press.

W. RICHARDS

Six W. Richards are known to have sailed for New South Wales before mid-1800, all of them convicts and all named William. Of the first two, who sailed on the *Neptune,* one died on the passage and the other a week after landing. Of the two who sailed on the *Admiral Barrington* and the *Britannia,* one was buried on 15 November 1791 and the other left no trace in the colony.

Two men remain. One arrived on the *Salamander* on 21 August 1791, sentenced to seven years at Exeter Assizes in March 1790 for stealing two linen shirts and other goods to a total value of 7s. 11d.. The hulk registers gave his age as 21.[1] He was transferred to Norfolk Island in September 1791, recorded as undertaking casual labouring work there, and returned to the mainland on 9 March 1793. He is next recorded living in the Sydney area, and probably in Sydney itself, in the fragmentary muster of 1800–01.[2]

On 23 October 1801 a William Richards enlisted as a private in Lieutenant-Colonel Paterson's company of the New South Wales Corps, initially remaining in Sydney and later posted to Parramatta. Pamela Statham identifies this person as the son of Private Laurence Richards, but that currency lad was only 11 at the time – old enough to be a drummer, but an unlikely recruit as a private. Laurence's son was evidently the young man who enlisted on 25 June 1808 and whose age a few months later was given as 18 years 9 months. The person who enlisted in 1801 would have been Richards of the *Salamander*, whom Statham identifies as the recruit of 1808. If so, he stayed with the Corps until he was demobilised on 25 March 1810.[3] In the 1811 muster the transportee from the *Salamander* reappears in the civilian records and in 1814 is recorded as a labourer at Liverpool.[4]

While this Richards could well be the performer (he was in the right place at the right time), the other Richards is a more plausible candidate. His claim is based on a curious earlier involvement with theatre and his later association with John Sparrow.

On 27 February 1790 the 'General Hue and Cry' column of the *Newcastle Courant* announced:

> WILLIAM RICHARDS, who appears to be about 20 years of age, five feet two inches and a quarter high, blind of the left eye, has brown hair … says he belongs to Manchester, gets his bread by casting ornaments for plaistering work, and came from thence hither to seek employment, tho' he owns he was in no want of work at Manchester, nor had any acquaintance here … is suspected of having robbed the Manchester, the Margate, the Derby, and York Theatres, of sundry articles … and was detected in the Theatre here, under suspicious circumstances.

On 6 March 1790 the paper provided more details, among them that Richards had given wildly different accounts of his background in different towns. At various times he claimed to be the natural son of Whitbread· the famous brewer, or the child of a dealer in muslins in High Street, Manchester, while at one place 'he said he belonged to Covent Garden Theatre, and was going to join some of the London players, who had gone into the north'.

Since he had not actually stolen anything in the Newcastle theatre, Richards was sent back to York, where he was tried for theft from his landlord and for robbing the theatre of various costume accessories. He was convicted and sentenced to seven years' transportation. After the event the *York Herald*, 27 March 1790, gave further details of his capture, which suggested that his habit of pilfering from theatres was not new. Hearing several of the York players complaining of the thefts from their boxes in the dressing-room,

> Mr. Grist observed, that there had been a man with *only one eye*, who had been notorious for pilfering from several playhouses to which Mr. G. had formerly belonged. Mr. Wilkinson recollected he had seen a few nights before, in the gallery here, a man answering the description given by Mr. Grist, and therefore concluded he would write to the Managers of other Theatres, to caution them against similar depredations. His first letter was addressed to Mr. Whitlock of Newcastle. On the receipt of it, Mr. Whitlock thought it necessary that search should immediately be made in his Theatre, to be certain that all was safe; when, to his astonishment, he found the very man (Richards) locked up there, and concealed beyond a violin case. The various articles lost from the York

Theatre were in his possession, and no less than five bills of indictment were found against him at our Assizes.[5]

Richards arrived at Port Jackson aboard the *William and Ann* on 28 August 1791 and for some time disappears from sight. In view of his trade as a maker of plaster ornaments, he is probably the William Richards sent to Toongabbie to work as a plasterer on 31 December 1796. On 13 March 1797, still at Toongabbie, he and Peter Lillis were accused of stealing various items from the farmhouse of Daniel Kelly, including newspapers and books. Richards was able to convince the court that the items were given as a gratuity by Kelly's wife for his work in taking parcels to Kelly, who was in Parramatta gaol.[6] Eight months later, on the evening of Saturday 11 November, a William Richards was on duty at the theatre in Sydney, checking its security, almost certainly after a performance.

On 13 July 1799 an unspecified William Richards appears in a list of vagrants who had been taken up in a general search of Sydney. An annotation records that on a recognisance of £20 he had been discharged on John Sparrow for six months. That this is the York playhouse robber is strongly suggested by a list of expired or emancipated convicts and free people off stores in 1801. Many names are grouped in households and William Richards, *per William and Ann*, is entered between John Sparrow and M. Hughes, that is Mary Hughes, Sparrow's housekeeper.[7] Sparrow's interest in helping Richards is best explained as support for the theatre company, with which he might still have been involved. It is in this period that a William Richards appears on the two surviving playbills, playing the roles of Worthy in *The Recruiting Officer* and Bardolph in *Henry the Fourth*. These parts are very different in character, and argue either versatility on Richards' part or his use as a general-purpose actor. He was not listed for the production of *She Stoops to Conquer* a few months later.

In 1802 a William Richards was in trouble again. On 22 July he was convicted of stealing a blanket and rug, the property of William Noah and Charles Williams of Sydney. The result, for Richards, was removal for three months to Castle Hill to work for the government. Before that sentence was completed, a William Richards was brought before the Parramatta bench, which serviced Castle Hill. He was charged as a vagrant with obtaining wheat under false pretences and sentenced to 100 lashes and three years' hard labour. For the serving of this three-year sentence he might well have been sent to Toongabbie, for in August 1802 a William Richards was to be found there in the company of none other than the theatre's erstwhile scenic artist, John William Lancashire. On 30 September he gave evidence against Lancashire for forging mess tickets and so drawing extra rations.[8] The records of the case do not tell the whole story, but it could well be that both were forging the tickets and that Richards escaped by turning King's evidence.

If only one William Richards was involved in all these post-1800 escapades, it still remains unproven that he was the convict from the *William and Ann*, but he could not have been the soldier. The guesswork continues when one turns to the records of Norfolk Island, where a William Richards appears on the victualling registers from 14 May 1803, apparently as one of those newly arrived from Port Jackson on the *Buffalo*. Since he is recorded consistently among the 'Free Men from Sentence Expired', he could be the man sentenced to three years in mid-1802 only if that sentence was waived for the evidence given against Lancashire. The 1805 Norfolk Island muster records him as working as a sawyer, which does not rule out the convict from the *William and Ann*, since plasterers were not employed on Norfolk Island and some other source of income had to be found. During his stay Richards moved on and off stores, reflecting moves between government and private employment, and finally, on 14 November 1807, is listed as 'gone off to England'.[9] This statement rules out the transportee from the *Salamander* and leaves the one-eyed pilferer of theatrical costumes as the man on Norfolk Island.

What is virtually certain is that the Norfolk Islander was also the man associated with the Sydney theatre. He was the only Richards on the island in 1805 and his name is linked in the shopkeeper's daybook with a stream of purchases on behalf of the theatre – skeins of silk, blue mode, stockings, ribbon, thread and papers of pins.[10] It looks as if he was one of the more prominent of the actors in the island company.

On 19 April 1819 a William Richards, plasterer and house painter, was sentenced to seven years at the Bristol Quarter Sessions for stealing 70lb of iron and sent to New South Wales on the *Eliza*, arriving on 21 January 1820. The age given on the ship's indent, 45, is close to that of the actor, and his height is similar, but there is no mention of a blind eye. It is an outside possibility that this is the theatromane again transported. If so, he made no further recorded contribution to the cultural life of the colony. In a list of 8 September 1821 he appears as a plasterer in government service, but between March 1822 and May 1823 was assigned to a master at Liverpool and then, by April 1824, to the convict depot at Bathurst. There, crossing a river, he drowned on 6 March 1825.[11]

ROBERT SIDAWAY

ML, A1892.

Robert Sidaway (or Sidway) was born on 14 January and baptised on 5 February 1758 at St Leonard's, Shoreditch. His parents were John and Elizabeth Sidaway, of Horse Shoe Alley in that parish.[1]

John Sidaway's occupation or background has not been discovered, but several Sidaways were living in the St Leonard's and Old Street parishes. They included an Amos Sidaway, a William Sidaway and a Thomas Sidaway, the last of whom paid land tax on a substantial block of land and a three-quarter share in The Barking Dogs ale-house. John Sidaway himself paid 2 guineas land tax in 1756–57 on his Horse Shoe Alley residence – a solid amount for the area, and high for Horse Shoe Alley.[2] He was also in a position to set up his sons in respectable trades. Robert's elder brother, John, was apprenticed to Edward Higgs, a buckle-maker of St Leonard's, Shoreditch, in 1762, on a modest premium of £7 10s., and is recorded as a London silversmith in 1777 and in 1790–93. A younger brother, James, could have been the victualler who died in 1796. Robert himself was later recorded as a watchcase maker,[3] a trade related to that of his elder brother, though there is no record of him ever practising it.

In later years Sidaway was remembered in England as 'the notorious *Robert Sidaway*, who was several times tried for housebreaking, highway robberies, &c, when in this country'.[4] He seems to have been an habitual criminal and one of some daring. His earliest recorded brush with the law was in 1778, when he was 20 and was sent to the hulks as one of a trio caught trying to rob a house. He had barely been released when he was pursued as a member of another gang accused of stealing a large trunk containing 600 guineas and a quantity of clothing from a dwelling house. He and another were tried at the Old Bailey in the April 1782 sessions, but acquitted because of unreliable evidence. In the September sessions he was not so lucky. He was seen trying to steal a box from a coach at the gate of an inn, made a desperate effort to escape, but was captured. At his trial he gave his address as Old Street, in the parish adjacent to Shoreditch. He was sentenced to seven years' transportation, but, while being returned to prison, escaped with several other prisoners. He was quickly recaptured, still in irons, and sentenced to death. This was later reduced to transportation for life.[5] Accordingly, he was shipped aboard the *Mercury* for North America, but the ship had barely left port when it was seized by the prisoners and driven into Torbay. Most of the convicts were recaptured, but Sidaway, even though he had been badly wounded in the arm by the ship's doctor, managed to get ashore with fellow convict Charles Frame and reached Totnes before being recaptured. He was brought back to Exeter by chaise and detained in hospital for some months. Thereafter he was removed to the *Dunkirk* hulk, where he was said to have behaved 'remarkably well'.[6] He sailed on the first fleet for New South Wales in the *Friendship*, spending the last month of the voyage in irons for impertinence to an officer. Lieutenant Ralph Clark, who was on the same vessel, described him as 'a darring Valinous fellow I should have flogg him if I had being Commanding officer for his behaviour'.

Within a month of the fleet's arrival in Port Jackson, other officers were echoing this low opinion of Sidaway. Though not charged in the theft of stores that resulted in Sydney's first hanging, he was an associate of the gang responsible, and was the last man Thomas Barrett asked to speak to before he was hanged for the crime. Bowes Smyth described Sidaway on that occasion as 'a very bad kind of man', and when Barrett's fellow conspirators were reprieved and exiled to Pinchgut, Surgeon White reported that Sidaway was sent off a prisoner with them. The group was pardoned on the King's birthday, 4 June 1788, though White thought the effort wasted on Sidaway and Henry Lavell, since 'they seem so truly abandoned and incorrigible'.[7]

From these beginnings Sidaway managed to turn his fortunes around. In about March 1789 he was appointed to the commissariat as baker, and for his efforts was rewarded with a percentage of the flour given to him for baking.[8] News of his transformation reached England with the arrival of Mary Bryant and the other convicts who had made a daring escape to Timor in an open boat. Sidaway, it transpired, had sold them 100lb of flour before their departure.[9] This transaction does not seem to have damaged his credibility in New South Wales, although there, also, a few aspersions were cast upon him. On 2 May 1791 a drunken convict, Mary Whiting, was charged with shouting out claims that Sidaway and his superior, Under Commissary Zachariah Clark, were robbing the store.[10] The claim might have referred to the legal case of December 1789, when Sidaway gave evidence in defence of Clark, accused of misappropriating government wine under his control. Whatever the truth of Whiting's claim, it was not supported by Sidaway's exemplary behaviour a year later, when he was offered flour he suspected of being stolen. Six months after that came a curious incident in which we find him, apparently out of public spirit, setting a trap to catch a suspected thief. His behaviour is strange, since it would have been simpler to call a constable and leave the matter to him. There may be levels to this affair not revealed in the court minutes.[11]

A glimpse of Sidaway's life at this early stage occurs in records of the trial of Ann Davis on 21 November 1789. Davis had stolen clothing from his residence and was destined to become the first woman hanged in New South Wales. Sidaway was by this time cohabiting with Mary Marshall in a two-room house high in the Rocks, with a convict servant accommodated in a skillion. The bakery was on the edge of Sydney Cove, below the house, and the couple evidently worked long hours.[12] On 29 November 1792 Sidaway received a conditional pardon, and on 27 September 1794 an absolute pardon 'in consideration of his diligence, unremitting good conduct, and strict integrity in his employment for several years as the public baker of the settlement'.[13] Shortly afterwards (6 November) he secured a plot of land in the military district, between the commanding officer's residence and the military surgeon's gardens, and on the opposite side of the road from the granary. Here he re-situated his bakery and house. The house appears on the earliest surviving list of licensed premises, as the Chequers Inn. The list dates from 19 September 1798, but there is evidence it was a drinking place by January 1797. It remained his base of operations for the rest of his life, though he also held other town properties and, in later years at least, various farms by purchase or lease.[14]

In 1796 came the act that was to entitle him to a place in this book, his contribution to the building and management of the Sydney theatre. By that time he was living in relative affluence, exaggerated reports of which were sent to England:

> *Remarkable Instance of the versatility of Fortune* – Sidway, who was one of the first convicts landed at Botany Bay, whither he was transported for house-breaking, is now living there in a state, comparatively, of great respectability. He has a contract for serving the Colony with bread; has a perpetual grant from Government of several hundred acres of land which he cultivates; keeps the best house of public entertainment in the place; and, lastly, has erected a theatre, of which he is the Manager.[15]

A brief note on him, attached to the newspaper transcript of the playbill for Green's benefit, provides a few more details:

> He was one of the first that went out to Botany Bay, transported for a burglary, and was appointed baker to the Colony, in which situation he has realized upwards of three thousand pounds. His time of transportation has been long expired, but he does not choose to leave the settlement, where he has a great prospect of increasing his wealth.[16]

In 1799 he became marginally involved in the sensational criminal proceedings against Isaac Nicholls, who was accused of receiving stolen goods. It transpired that the thieves had first approached Sidaway, who had been curiously casual in reporting this fact to the authorities and in otherwise giving information that might have helped Nicholls in his defence. The questions thrown at Sidaway, and the comments of Henry Waterhouse, suggest that some people were not convinced of his probity.[17]

A year later he was to have another uncomfortable experience. He led a group of businessmen in securing from Governor Hunter permission to buy part of the cargo of the *Minerva* at moderate prices, allegedly with the aim of reducing the cost of imported goods. In the group was John Sparrow. The transaction ended in an acrimonious civil court case in February 1800, in which a group of fellow-speculators charged him with deception in his method of levying commission for his services. Sparrow was not among the complainants, who seem to have won their case.[18]

The *Minerva* affair would appear to be a concerted effort to weaken the monopoly hold of the military and civil officers on the import trade. If it was, at least one of the senior officers involved in that trade bore him no ill will, since in November 1805 Lieutenant-Colonel Foveaux was reported as having forgiven Sidaway a debt. The context suggests the sum was significant. The time and circumstances are obscure, but the linking of James Bloodsworth with the affair implies a date prior to the latter's death in March 1804.[19]

There were other financial embarrassments. On 6 July 1801 James Larra took civil action against Sidaway and a business partner, Thomas Abbott, over a debt of £624 6s. 6d. and against Sidaway alone for £64 19s. 9d.. The debts were settled shortly after, but on 5 March 1802 Sidaway was obliged to assign one of his Sydney houses to John Palmer as security for a debt of £202 owing to the estate of John Stogdell. On 11 October 1802 he sublet part of his own residence to Edward Meads, on condition that it should not compete with the Chequers in selling spirits. It became the base for Mrs Mead's millinery and mantua business. Signs of financial difficulty continued. The land and stock muster of 1806 shows him as possessed of 130 acres by purchase or lease; but in September 1805, August 1808 and May 1809 farms apparently owned by him were offered for sale, the first complete with contents, including the works of Shakespeare and other books. In 1807 Governor Bligh's town planning threatened to force him to relocate his business premises – which no doubt contributed to his support for the Rum Rebellion. He signed both the request to Captain Johnston for the arrest of Bligh, and the address thanking him once the deed was done.[20]

Sidaway's problems might have been exacerbated by ill health. On 4 December 1803 the *Sydney Gazette* reported that he had broken his arm in a fall, and on 4 December 1808 that he was dangerously ill. Finally, on 15 October 1809, following his death two days earlier, the paper reported he had suffered a 'long and painful illness'. The death notice also characterised Sidaway as a 'true philanthropist'. In earlier years the *Sydney Gazette* had twice referred to one example of his compassion, the way he and Mary Marshall, who had no children of their own, had brought up a mentally and physically afflicted young woman.[21]

Sidaway seems never to have been an actor. His involvement was as owner, or part-owner, of the 1796 theatre building, and later, for what may have been only a brief period, as manager of the acting company. There is no evidence of any involvement with the second phase of the theatre's activity, from 1799 onwards, apart from his role as a ticket agent, but he could have remained a shareholder in the building. The volume of Shakespeare and other books in the farmhouse might argue genuine theatrical and literary interests, and his friendship with Lavell and Sparrow might also have contributed to his involvement with the company.

B. SMITH

RONSW, Marriages.4.281.

B. Smith appears in the playbills of 8 March 1800 and 8 April 1800, playing Thomas Appletree in *The Recruiting Officer* and Poins in *Henry the Fourth*. He was also scheduled to play Coppee in *The Virgin Unmask'd*, the afterpiece to *The Recruiting Officer*, but after the playbill had been printed he was replaced in the role by Daniel Parnell, necessitating a hand-written correction in the surviving copy.

There is only one B. Smith recorded in the colony in the relevant period. He arrived as George Curtis, alias Beckwith Smith, on the *Ganges*, on 2 June 1797, but in the colony he was always referred to as Beckwith Smith or George Beckwith Smith. He had been sentenced to seven years' transportation in Kent, on 10 March 1795, for stealing a bay gelding, and thereafter sent to the hulk *Fortune*, where his age was given as 20.[1]

Initially Smith was located in Sydney, where, in December 1798, he was ordered 100 lashes for stealing fowls from the poultry house of the merchant, John Black. The suspicion was that he had been responsible for 'divers Misdemeanors & Felonies', to which the premises had been subjected. On 12 May 1800, a month after the production of *Henry the Fourth*, he was a witness to the marriage of Thomas Rose and Jane Jones in St Phillip's Church, signing the register in a firm, clear hand. By 1801 he had been recorded as no longer dependent on government rations, and living at the Northern Boundary, an area a short distance north of Parramatta.[2]

On 9 January 1802 Smith was landed on Norfolk Island from the *Harrington*. He remained there until 28 February 1805, appearing, among the convict labourers on stores, as George Beckwith Smith or George B. Smith. The category 'labourers' in this context includes tradesmen, and Smith may have been sent to the island as a skilled worker, since in the 1806 muster he is recorded as free by servitude and working as a carpenter, presumably in Sydney.[3]

No further reference to Smith has been discovered. As a carpenter he would have had no difficulty in gaining employment on a vessel bound for England.

W. SMITH

W. Smith was the male romantic lead in the Sydney company in 1799–1800, playing Orville in *Fortune's Fool*, Plume in *The Recruiting Officer*, Prince Hal in *Henry the Fourth* and Young Marlow in *She Stoops to Conquer*. The problem is to identify him.

Of the 20 or so convicts named W. Smith who had arrived in the colony by 1799, at least four had died, and at least one had left the colony by that year. The number of deaths and departures was undoubtedly greater than this, but ten or a dozen could still have been in New South Wales at the time Smith the actor was performing. All had the given name of William. In addition, there was at least one William Smith who had arrived free, a refugee missionary from the Pacific Islands. Like a number of his fellow refugees, this ex-missionary lapsed from his earlier piety, becoming agent to Robert Campbell, the merchant. But his autobiography and other references make no mention of him descending to play-acting.[1] There are also four men associated with the New South Wales Corps who must be considered.

With the probable exception of Mary Barnes, those convicts who can be identified as joining the theatre company in 1799 and 1800 (Parnell, the Parrys, Beckwith Smith, McCann) were all recent arrivals. If Smith the actor was a convict, it is most likely he was also a recent arrival. Four men fall into this category, all of them capital respites. One, aged 21 and apparently a sailor, stole a watch with some violence in a Holborn street in 1792. He arrived on the *Ganges* in June 1797, with a life sentence. Three others came on the *Barwell*, landing in May 1798. One was a soldier, aged 18, also on a life sentence for a robbery with violence, this time in Salisbury. A second was a private in the Nottinghamshire militia, who escaped with seven years for a robbery in Cambridgeshire. The third, a fisherman, used William Smith merely as one of several aliases, and was known in the colony as John Bingham. This makes him unlikely to be the actor, though his crime has some interest. He had received a life sentence for breaking into a dwelling-house in Alverstoke, Hampshire, and stealing three books valued at £10.[2]

The difficulty is that only John Bingham can be traced in later records. The others do not appear in any of the musters that name the ship of arrival and they cannot be identified among the many William Smiths who are mentioned in the records by name alone. The same is true of most of the earlier arrivals. What little can be discovered about John Bingham tends to locate him in Parramatta rather than Sydney.

The pay lists of 1799 show two William Smiths in the New South Wales Corps, both in Grose's company and numbered 1 and 2 respectively. In 1800 a third William Smith was recruited into Paterson's company. The first William Smith was on detachment throughout the period and will have been the Private Smith who was occasionally recorded at Parramatta, which makes it unlikely he was the actor. Another document identifies him with the soldier who had enlisted on 21 December 1791 (apparently in Sydney) and was discharged on 24 April 1803.[3] The other member of Grose's company was in Sydney throughout the relevant period. He was a peruke-maker by trade, born in Marylebone in 1768 and described in 1808 as 5 feet 7 inches tall, of a swarthy complexion, with grey eyes, dark brown hair and a long visage. The soldier in Paterson's company also seems to have been stationed in Sydney. He had been recruited in Sydney in November 1793 and discharged in November 1794, re-enlisting on 6 January 1800. He also was born in 1768 and was 5 feet 7 inches tall. He was a native of Swanton Abbey, Norfolk, and was of dark complexion, with grey eyes, light brown hair, and a round visage. According to Statham, he was a weaver by trade. Both men left New South Wales with the Corps in May 1810. The peruke-maker died in Guernsey on 21 October 1811 and the weaver was discharged on 25 December of that year.[4]

One other tenuous line of thought can be followed. In the 1806 muster and the 1828 census the ex-actress Sarah McCann was recorded as living with a William Smith, on the latter occasion described as having come free to the colony on the *Matilda*. This is clearly another soldier, who had arrived in August 1791, the month in which the *Matilda* berthed, and who had been discharged in 1795.[5] It is tempting to postulate that the liaison was between Smith the actor and McCann, but if so it was an intermittent one, since she is recorded as living with other men in 1801 and 1822. Weakening the case further is the fact that, though the census records the Smith of 1828 as a Sydney labourer (aged 68), the 1825 muster describes him as a mariner. In a petition of 23 November 1823 he had applied for, and been granted, a waterman's licence to work on the harbour. In this he noted that he had spent the previous three years as a seaman on the *Haweis*, a brig trading along the coast and to the Pacific Islands. This makes it possible that he was one of the two W. Smiths recorded in the *Sydney Gazette* in the first decade of the century as employed on colonial vessels engaged in sealing.[6] If he was of this trade in 1799–1800, the chance that he could also be the actor is remote.

It is noteworthy that the newly-arrived convicts described above are all of humble occupation and none, apart from the ex-missionary, seems to have achieved prominence in Sydney, though one became a successful farmer at Parramatta.[7] Similarly, none of the soldiers rose above the rank of private or provided any other indication of special qualities, unless being a peruke-maker implies some degree of gentility. Smith the actor, then, might have been from a lower social order than other players, but his success in the leading young gentleman roles must raise doubts about this.[8]

In weighing the balance between Smith as a convict and Smith as a soldier, one aspect of the two playbills of 1799–1800 that were published in England is significant. While their publication included sardonic notes on the criminal backgrounds of some of the performers, there are no comments whatever on Smith, even though he was the leading actor. Since the aim of the annotations was to exploit for comic effect the contrast between the real life of these convicts and their pretensions as performers, the silence on Smith may mean that he was not a convict, but a soldier.

The search for William Smith the leading actor, then, is sadly inconclusive. If he had been a soldier, this would powerfully strengthen the case for military control of the company in its later years. If he was a convict of lower rank than other company members, this in turn could influence the socio-cultural composition of the performing group, at least in its second phase.

MRS SPARKS

Mrs Sparks appears in only one of the surviving playbills, that for Mrs Parry's benefit on 1 June 1799, where she had the minor part of Gymp in the afterpiece, *Bon Ton*. This playbill survives only in the version published in the English press, where it has the annotation 'Sparks came out a free woman, and lives with Vandercomb who is a steady fellow'. (Vandercomb, a convict bricklayer and plasterer, in later years owned an inn in Windmill Row.) Completing the triangle was Samuel Sparks, the man whose name Mrs Sparks bore. There is no record of him arriving as a convict or a soldier, so that he came either as an immigrant or as a convict whose name is missing from the registers.[1] In either case Mrs Sparks might have accompanied him from England, or else come independently under another name.

Samuel Sparks was a dangerous man. On 31 October 1798 he was before the courts for stabbing Mary Anderson in the throat with a case knife, 'by reason whereof she underwent great pain and anguish and her life was for some time greatly despaired of'.[2] Sparks pleaded guilty and was sentenced to seven years on Norfolk Island 'and to be secured in the Common Gaol until the time of his Embarkation'. Sparks was still waiting for transportation to Norfolk Island when, in early January 1799, he escaped from the Sydney gaol and went in search of his wife's lover:

> [He] violently entered the Dwelling House of James Vandercom & whilst the said Vandercom was asleep on his Bed, wickedly & Maliciously stabbed the said Vandercom with a Case-Knife under his left Eye in a dangerous Manner, having first attempted to stab him in the left Side.[3]

Sparks was recaptured and returned to gaol, this time with instructions that he be kept in irons and chained to the floor. With unbelievable incompetence, however, the gaol officials allowed him to escape yet again, on 1 April. This time 'he Committed another violent and dreadful assault on his Wife by cutting her Head open with a Tomahawk and otherwise so mangled and maimed her that her Life is almost despaired of'.[4] The reference to this as 'another' attack on his wife points to an earlier, otherwise unrecorded, act of violence, unless the Mary Anderson stabbed seven months earlier was, in fact, Mrs Sparks. The only Mary Anderson recorded, however, had come as a convict.[5]

As a result of this trial Sparks was 'to be chained down to the Floor until further notice'. There is, however, no record of that 'further notice', or of the original sentence of seven years on Norfolk Island being carried out, but he was in Sydney on 22 February 1800, when he was ordered 50 lashes for stealing hats.[6] The crime seems to have been committed in the gaol, so that Sparks was still a prisoner there, though not, one assumes, chained to the floor.[7] Thereafter he disappears from the record.

Mrs Sparks recovered from the hatchet attack with amazing rapidity. Two months later she was appearing on the Sydney stage as Gymp, without, it is too be hoped, too much of the mangling and maiming in evidence. Thereafter she, also, disappears from the records. By 1806 Vandercomb was living with Elizabeth Jones, who had arrived as a convict.[8]

J. SPARROW

John Sparrow [signature]

RONSW, Marriages.4.330.

The only J. Sparrow known in the colony at this time is John Sparrow.

In Peter Chassereau's 1745 survey map of Shoreditch a small open field, owned by the City of London, is marked as occupied by 'Sparrow'.[1] This evidently was Anthony Sparrow who paid land tax at about that time on properties in Holywell Lane and Black Horse Yard, the former close to the leased land and the latter immediately adjacent to it.[2] The register of St Leonard's, Shoreditch, along with the churches in adjacent parishes, includes many individuals named Sparrow; and the late eighteenth- and early nineteenth-century London trade directories list several respectable businessmen of that name. There was James Sparrow, hot-presser of Cox's Square, Spitalfields; Jonathan Sparrow, ironmonger of West Smithfield; and Henry Sparrow, a turner of Charterhouse Lane. On 19 January 1802 the marriage of Jonathan Sparrow's daughter was of sufficient importance to rate a mention in the *Observer*.

Whether we are dealing with an extended family of London businessmen is not clear, but what is demonstrable is that John was the son of Henry and Mary Sparrow, was born on 9 July 1766 and was baptised in St Leonard's, Shoreditch, on 31 July. The couple probably lived in Mulberry Court, in a heavily built-up area at the southernmost extremity of the parish, since a Henry Sparrow had paid a significant amount of land tax on a property there a few years earlier.[3]

On 5 February 1772 John's elder brother, Thomas, was apprenticed to Robert Mills, a member of the Worshipful Company of Clockmakers of the City of London. He is given as the son of Henry, of Moorfields, a peruke-maker. The premium was 15 guineas, the term the usual seven years. On 3 September 1787 Thomas took out the Freedom of the Company.

Thomas Sparrow's apprenticeship was almost complete when his brother John was contracted to the same clockmaker on 9 December 1779. By this time the premium had risen to £21 and John's father described himself as a gentleman of Hackney Road – still in the same parish, but in the main thoroughfare.[4] The choice of a member of the guild as a master indicates a concern with social standing, since, though the guilds had no power outside the old city limits and dwindling powers within them, they still had considerable prestige. Henry's claim to the title 'gentleman', as was suggested in Chapter 4, could be something he arrogated to himself on his retirement, or it could mean he was the son of a gentleman who surrendered that title while he worked as a peruke-maker.

John Sparrow probably completed his apprenticeship but, unlike his brother, never took out the Freedom of the Company. Instead, in April 1791 he was convicted at the Old Bailey of feloniously stealing, and was sentenced to seven years' transportation. The trial is dealt with only briefly in the Old Bailey Session Papers. Sparrow had gone into St George's Coffee House with a cheap plated spoon concealed about his person. He ordered a basin of mutton broth and, before he left, switched his own spoon for the silver one, value 10s., which the waiter had supplied. It was a form of theft that had been familiar for some years and was, of course, premeditated.[5]

Sparrow was dispatched to Australia in the *Pitt*, which arrived on 14 February 1792. Thereafter the first reference to him is in David Collins, who reports that during the night of 26 October 1793:

a box belonging to John Sparrow (a convict) was broke open, and three watches stolen out, one of which with the seals had cost thirty-two guineas, and belonged to an officer. This theft was committed at the hospital, where Sparrow was at the time a patient, although able to work occasionally at his business; and being a young man of abilities as a watchmaker, and of good character, was employed by most of the gentlemen of the settlement.[6]

Though other watchmakers assumed greater prominence in later years, Sparrow kept at his trade until his departure from the colony. In the 1806 general muster he is listed as a self-employed watchmaker, and on 18 July 1807 Gregory Blaxland records, 'paid Sparrow the Watchmaker's Bill £1 17s.'.[7] On the eve of his departure the Sydney Gazette, 30 August 1807, included in a list of his goods for sale 'about eight hundred watch glasses'.

Watch-repairing, however, was only one source of income. While not at the level of Simeon Lord, Sparrow was prominent as a dealer and moneylender. He was frequently before the Court of Civil Jurisdiction pursuing his debtors, and in the register of assignments he can be found lending money to several farmers, with their farms or crops as security. He acquired land himself and sold grain to the public store.[8] He was a bidder at the sale of John Stogdell's assets, and joined Sidaway's scheme to secure the right to purchase the goods on the Minerva. Not all of his dealings seem to have been scrupulous. In a list of land and stock held by officers in 1800 a substantial grant to the ailing surveyor-general, Augustus Alt, is recorded. A marginal comment reads: 'In possession of John Sparrow this an infamous transaction'.[9] On another occasion, Sparrow and his de facto purchased a suspiciously large amount of spirits for somebody without a spirit licence and, according to the vendor, Ann Thompson, had then attempted to defraud her by understating the amount they had received. Nor were all his dealings successful, particularly in the earlier years. In August 1796, a month after his performance at Green's benefit, he was sent to the debtors' prison for £41 owed to Simeon Lord and £52 to Shadrach Shaw.[10] Debt and dubious dealings made no great impact on his reputation in the freebooting business world of New South Wales. He was judged to be a respectable householder and was admitted to Governor King's militia, the Sydney Loyal Association, where his name appears on membership lists of 9 November 1802 and 7 April 1804.[11]

The general muster of 1806 lists him as living with Mary Hughes, alias Mary Johnson, who arrived as a convict on the First-Fleet vessel, The Prince of Wales. Her name is juxtaposed with Sparrow's in lists dating from 1801, and in the dispute with Ann Thompson over spirits, in 1804, she is described as his housekeeper.[12]

In December 1806 the burial of a Mary Hughes took place in Sydney. The deceased was almost certainly John Sparrow's wife.[13] Shortly afterwards, in a Sydney Gazette notice of 4 January 1807, Sparrow called on all his creditors to present their demands 'for immediate liquidation' and his debtors to pay their bills. Another advertisement, in the Sydney Gazette, 1 February 1807, announced that since so few debtors had come forward he was under the necessity, 'being about to quit the Colony', of using coercion, which he would resort to in a fortnight's time. The same threat appeared in the Sydney Gazette on 15 February.

After this flurry of activity it is surprising to find Sparrow still 'about to quit the Colony' on 23 August 1807, when his 'truly valuable and eligible Dwelling house and premises, out houses, &c' were offered for sale. By 19 June 1808 the house was in the ownership of William Hutchinson who, in offering it for sale in the Sydney Gazette on that date, gave a more vivid picture of the premises. It was

a truly eligible and convenient Dwelling house, centrally and desirably situate on the best part of the Rocks, being formerly the residence of John Sparrow

> ... to which is an excellent bakehouse with inclosed oven, and all necessary
> utensils; two tenements detached, which can be separately let, good stock
> inclosures, a capital cultivated garden, two wells constantly supplied.

But it is the list of household contents which Sparrow offered for sale by auction in the *Sydney Gazette*, 23 August 1807, that permits an evocative glimpse of his lifestyle:

> tent and other bedsteads with furniture, feather beds, bolsters and mattrasses,
> dining, card, and tea tables, mahogany chairs, a capital bureau, cedar chests,
> looking glasses and pictures, decanters, water bottles, goblets, tumblers and
> wine glasses, japanned tea trays, bread baskets, tea caddies ... a small quantity
> of jewellery, spy glasses and quadrant ... English prints, and fine muslins, wearing
> apparel.

Evidently, the colony had been good to John Sparrow. After these sale notices he disappears, possibly sailing for England in October 1807 on the *Sydney Cove*, in the company of another convict entrepreneur, James Underwood.

In Collins' account of the establishment of the theatre in 1796, John Sparrow is described as the actor-manager. This provides an indication of his entrepreneurial flair, but also suggests that he would have a claim on a major role in any production. This assumption is confirmed by the only surviving playbill from the theatre's early period (23 July 1796), where he is listed as the juvenile lead in Mrs Centlivre's *The Busy Body*, the witty young gentleman-lover. This is precisely the type of role William Smith was to perform in 1799 and 1800. The likelihood, therefore, is that in the inaugural production of Young's *The Revenge*, Sparrow played the heroic lover, Don Alonzo, a white-faced and youthful version of Othello.

It is not certain at what date Sparrow gave up the management of the company. The English press of early September 1797 gives Sidaway this function in a news item that must have been at least six months old. Nor does Sparrow appear as a performer in any of the four surviving playbills of 1799–1800, though he appears as a ticket agent for one of these productions. The support he gave to the actor William Richards in 1800, however, points to a continuing association with the playhouse. He could have been a share-holder in the second theatre building, just as he almost certainly was in the first.

JOSEPH VASCONCELLIS

Soldiers of the New South Wales Corps rarely appeared in the civil records of the colony except as witnesses in the criminal court, while the surviving military records, particularly of men who died or left the Corps before 1808, are mostly musters, which reveal little about the men behind the names. In consequence, Vasconcellis is not alone among the soldiery in coming down to us as only a shadowy presence. The name is probably Portuguese, so that he was one of that scattering of continentals who were recruited to the Corps. If he was as foreign as his name suggests, his familiarity with the English theatrical repertoire and performance conventions could have been quite limited.

Vasconcellis joined the Corps at its formation, recruited in England by Captain Paterson with the rank of private on 2 July 1789. On 22 June 1790 he was promoted to corporal, but six months later he deserted. The departure of the fleet for New South Wales was approaching and Vasconcellis was evidently having second thoughts about a voyage to the end of the world. He was captured a month later, on 20 January 1791, demoted to private, and sent off with the fleet, arriving in Port Jackson in September 1791. In 1793 he was once more promoted to corporal, but in December 1794 was again reduced to private.[1] In 1795 he was one of the troops to receive a 25-acre grant at Mulgrave Place, though he does not appear in any later list of land-holders. It is difficult to see what a soldier based in Sydney or Parramatta could do with land on the Hawkesbury. Like others, he probably sold the property almost immediately. In April 1799, still a private, he was described as manager of the company, but in the regimental pay records, 25 January–24 February 1800, he was listed as sick. It was to be a lingering illness. From that time onwards he continued to be recorded as ill until his death on 25 May 1802.[2]

The fact that Vasconcellis was twice promoted to corporal suggests he was thought to have some special qualities, such as exceptional toughness, diligence or education. His failure to progress further, or even to maintain that position, indicates that his promise was not fulfilled. Perhaps he was better suited to running a theatre company than to the brutalities of the British army, though he must have had a major part in the thuggish tactics allegedly used on John William Lancashire, the scene-painter, after he became a witness against the officers in the Nicholls case.

It is only the court case of 20 April 1799 that identifies Vasconcellis as the theatre's manager, and there is no telling how long he held the post. How he achieved the position as manager is undiscoverable, but it is tempting to suspect he was imposed on the company by the officers or the governor as a means of controlling the theatre.

J. WHITE

J. White appears in all the surviving playbills of 1799–1800 as one of the leading actors, along with W. Smith. Whereas Smith was the company's juvenile lead, White specialised in the major comic character roles – Tom Seymour in *Fortune's Fool*, Kite in *The Recruiting Officer*, Falstaff in *Henry the Fourth* and Tony Lumpkin in *She Stoops to Conquer*.

The name J. White brings with it the same problems as W. Smith. Leaving out of account the surgeon of that name, at least 11 J. Whites had arrived in the colony by mid-1799. None is recorded as having left by then, but some had undoubtedly done so, while an unidentifiable James White was registered as buried in February 1795. As with Smith, the two relevant playbills reproduced in the English newspapers provide no accompanying information about White, even though they do so about less important performers. It is a silence that can be construed as meaning that White was not a convict; but that is mere supposition. The reprinted playbills, after all, are equally silent about other significant performers.

One or more of the J. Whites, however, were moderately significant members of the Sydney community. A John White arrived with a life sentence on the *Barwell*, on 18 May 1798. This is the last convict transport to dock before White begins to appear in the surviving playbills in June 1799, and the conjunction may be important, since most of the identifiable convicts who first appear in the 1799–1800 playbills were also recent arrivals. This John White had been a wheelwright and worked for the government in that capacity until 1806. By 12 November 1809 he had set up on his own, apparently in a house on the corner of Bell Street and Bell Row (renamed Hunter and Bligh Streets, 6 October 1810). The premises included a wheelwright's workshop and also a well-equipped bakehouse, so that he is probably the John White who was fined for selling underweight bread on 25 August 1804 and on 2 December 1809. He was granted a beer licence 21 July 1810, but on 8 September the *Sydney Gazette* announced that his 'former premises' in Bell Street were for sale or letting by Samuel Terry.[1] White might have been able to stall this sale, but on 27 October the newspaper advertised White's premises, apparently the same ones, as scheduled for auction by the provost-marshal for unpaid debts. On 23 March 1811 the paper published an advertisement for E. Lamb at what was 'late the Residence of John White'. On 14 July 1810 White the wheelwright had applied to Governor Macquarie for confirmation of the absolute pardon granted to him in the interregnum following Bligh's overthrow. The application was presumably successful since, unlike some others, the pardon is not marked in the register as cancelled. White of the *Barwell* is listed for the last time in the 1811 muster.[2] A John White, who might have been this man, announced he was about to leave the colony in the *Sydney Gazette*, 4 January 1812. There is nothing to indicate whether or not the wheelwright was the John White whose wife, Catherine Mellon, absconded with his promissory notes in June 1808, though a man possessed of a bundle of promissory notes was probably a trader. An unidentifiable John White, who could have been the same man, had already been in trouble over a woman, when an irate husband took him to court for the return of his wife.[3] The court instructed the woman to return to her spouse.

While there is an argument by analogy for identifying White the actor with White the businessman, there is no firm evidence to justify it. Indeed, the wheelwright may not be the only businessman of that name in Sydney, unless he was also the J. White of South Row who advertised the sale of firewood and of salt in the *Sydney Gazette*, 2 December 1804 and 16 February 1806 respectively.

Apart from John White the shipwright, who had come with the Second Fleet, and whose details are recorded by Michael Flynn,[4] most of the other convicts named J. White had either disappeared entirely or were living outside the Sydney region. However, two soldiers named J. White must remain as candidates for the position of actor, since the pay lists indicate that both were stationed in Sydney during the relevant period. Neither ever rose above private or made any recorded impact on colonial society, and both returned to England with the Corps in 1810, being discharged there in 1811. Joseph White was an ex-cordwainer born at Portsmouth and about 32 years old in 1800. In 1808 he was described as 5 feet 6 inches tall, of a dark complexion, hazel eyes, dark brown hair and a long visage. The other soldier, James White, was born in Glasgow, 5 feet 10 inches tall, with a dark complexion and, in 1808, a round face. Since he was 59 in that year, it is not surprising that his hair was grey. No trade is given, but at that stage he had nearly 32 years of military service, in a foot regiment, the marines, and the New South Wales Corps.[5] He would have been 50–51 years old at the time of the productions, which makes him a highly unlikely Tony Lumpkin or Tom Seymour, but a plausible Falstaff.

H. WYNN

H. Wynn's only recorded performance is as Kathlane, the female lead in *The Poor Soldier*, presented as the afterpiece at Henry Green's benefit on 23 July 1796.

The only H. Wynn known to have arrived in the colony by that date was Hannah Wynn, who was sentenced to seven years at the Old Bailey in April 1790 for stealing two small remnants of ribbon, value 1s., from a Holborn-bridge haberdashery. The ribbon was concealed in the frock of a young child she was carrying. Hannah arrived in the colony on the *Mary Ann* in July 1791 and in November was transferred to Norfolk Island, where she was employed as washerwoman to the deputy commissary. She sailed for Port Jackson on 19 February 1796 and thereafter vanishes from the records.[1] Her sentence would not have expired until April 1797.

In a petition subsequent to her conviction Hannah was presented as an innocent seduced by 'the Art, evil Persuasion and Subtlety of this vile woman', her co-accused, though she was also said, incongruously enough, to have been 'almost a Stranger' to the woman. The petition claims Hannah was 'virtuously brought up and educated by her dear honest Parents', but, since the petition is unsigned, there is no indication of whether the education was a formal one, extending to literacy. An attached character reference describes her as a 'prudent industrious and honest young woman', the nearest we come to gaining a sense of her age.[2]

There is one obvious problem about identifying Hannah as the person acting Kathlane. Identification of the performer as H. Wynn, not Mrs Wynn, implies the character had been played by a man. From the play's first production, Patrick, the leading male role, had often been taken by a woman, but there seems no tradition of men performing Kathlane.[3] Either the playbill broke with convention, or an otherwise unrecorded male performed the role. Since *The Poor Soldier* is primarily a musical piece, and Kathlane is as much a singing as an acting role, this male could well have been a boy soprano. Did Mrs Wynn have a son? The child she held during the robbery was of unspecified sex and still in skirts – that is an infant, so unlikely to be ready for performance six years later. On Norfolk Island, moreover, she was recorded as having no dependent children.[4] The only other prisoner named Wynn known to have arrived in the colony was Lawrence Wynn, sentenced to seven years for stealing a loaf of sugar, value 5s..[5] A desperate solution would be to propose a compositor's error – L. Wynn mistakenly set as H. Wynn, or a badly battered H. misread as L by the English typesetter reproducing the playbill. Such speculation, however, leads nowhere, since the court proceedings tell us nothing about Lawrence, who arrived on the *Admiral Barrington* and promptly disappeared from the records.

2. PERFORMERS AND OTHERS ASSOCIATED WITH THE NORFOLK ISLAND THEATRE, 1793–1794

THOMAS RESTELL CROWDER

Thos Restell Crowder

PRO, CO201/9, fol.137.

Thomas Restell Crowder was sometimes referred to as Thomas Restil, alias Crowder, and his names were variously spelled Restill, Restol or Risdale, and Crouther or Crowther. He was born on 26 December 1757 and baptised at St Martin-in-the-Fields, Westminster, on 20 January 1758. He was the son of Nathaniel Crowder and his wife Susannah (*née* Ward), who themselves had been married at St George, Mayfair, on 28 September 1751. An elder son died young, leaving Thomas as the heir. Nathaniel was buried on 2 January 1784, leaving a will that had been made out on 24 December 1783.[1] At that time he was living in Scotland Yard, St Martin-in-the-Fields, which was largely given up to the residences, stables and coach-houses of gentlefolk, many of whom seem to have been court officials. His own residence there, however, had one of the lowest tax ratings in the Yard,[2] and his will does not identify him or either of his witnesses as a gentleman (indeed, one of the latter is a stationer). The probability is that Nathaniel was a shopkeeper or tradesman serving the neighbourhood, though his trade cannot be discovered. Prominent in the stationery and card-making business in the city of London was another family of Crowders, one of whom, John, an enthusiastic amateur actor, rose to be Lord Mayor of London.[3] In view of the contrasting career paths of John and Thomas, both theatre-lovers, a family relationship would be ironic.

In Nathaniel's will, Thomas was cut off with a shilling 'for certain Reasons', while younger sons Edward and Mark received £50 and £80 respectively and the bulk of the estate, both real and personal, went to his widow. The reason for the severance was, no doubt, Thomas's conviction in the Old Bailey Sessions twelve months earlier for burgling a gentleman's house in Rathbone Place, off the eastern end of Oxford Street. Crowder was the only member of the gang to be captured and this after he had escaped into the public street and briefly been lost to sight by the watchmen. The trial records reveal that he was married and claimed to be the proprietor of a grocery and chandlery business in the insalubrious area of Seven Dials. On Norfolk Island, however, he was listed as a seaman, as was his younger brother, Edward, who followed him down the path to crime and to Botany Bay.[4] At the Old Bailey, Crowder insisted he was an innocent passer-by in Rathbone Place, but the witnesses supporting this claim read suspiciously like perjurers. The jury was unimpressed and Crowder was sentenced to death, a sentence commuted to transportation to the East Indies on 17 January 1783. The destination was altered to America on 12 September 1783.[5]

What happened next is not clear. On 22 April 1785, the recorder of Bristol reported that Crowder was accused of being an escapee from the convict transport *Mercury*, which had been seized by the prisoners *en route* to America and run into Torbay on 13 April of the previous year.[6] His name, however, does not appear in the documents relating to the vessel or the mutiny. What is clear is that he was free and in Bristol in late April and May 1784, allegedly as a member of a gang that had been active 'in and about this city for a considerable time past'.[7] In April and May it had conducted a series of highly successful raids on warehouses and shops. In mid-May, however, the gang's leader, a butcher named James Paul, was captured and turned King's evidence, incriminating Crowder, who was arrested on about 20 May. Evidently he had only recently joined the gang for, in reporting his capture, the *Western Flying Post*, 31 May 1784, associated him with most of the robberies that had been 'lately' committed. The earliest offence with which he was charged, the robbery of James Cunning's sale room, had taken place on 20 April.

Crowder was one of four men implicated by Paul who were taken to the city's Bridewell. On 25 May three escaped, but were recaptured on the same day and transferred to Bristol's Newgate gaol to await trial. There Crowder and at least one of his co-accused, Aaron Davis, languished for almost a year. The trial might have been delayed while the authorities pursued other members of the gang, since by that time the number held on Paul's evidence had reportedly risen to six or seven.

Crowder and Davis were brought to trial at the assizes beginning 29 March 1785, Crowder receiving a death sentence and Davis (who was also to become a prominent figure on Norfolk Island) transportation for seven years. Before leaving the city, the recorder respited three of the five death sentences passed: Crowder was one of the two left to hang, the execution being scheduled for Friday 22 April. On 19 April, however, a respite arrived, and on 22 April the recorder, in the letter mentioned above, recommended transportation for life. He claimed to have been troubled by a death sentence based on the word of a reprobate such as Paul, but had consoled himself with the thought that he had 'good reason to be satisfyd that he has been guilty of other Robberys, (whether guilty or innocent of this)'. Crowder was removed to the *Justitia* hulk, his age given as 30, and on 6 January 1787 was transferred to the First-Fleet vessel *Alexander* for transportation to Australia.[8] Although he had allegedly been married in

England, Crowder married fellow First-Fleeter Sarah Davis within six months of their arrival (7 June 1788). His evidence in a criminal case of 7 November 1788 gives the impression that they had a house high in the Rocks. On the night of 15 November Sarah got herself noisily drunk and, in attempting to restrain her, Crowder struck her a blow. Their stories agreeing, the magistrates on the next day reprimanded him and set her to labour for a month.[9]

In 1789 Crowder and his wife were transferred to Norfolk Island, and arrived on 2 March. There an initial allocation of two acres had been expanded to fourteen by December 1791, and through purchase a further sixty acres was added in October 1794. At that time he was a prominent figure in the setting up of the Norfolk Island Settlers' Society, designed to further the interests of the land-holders.[10]

Concurrently with these activities he was proving himself useful to the authorities. On 10 January 1792 the island's lieutenant-governor, Philip Gidley King, wrote to Governor Phillip proposing that Crowder be emancipated. King spoke of Crowder's honesty, activity and good behaviour, and indicated that his predecessor, Lieutenant-Governor Ross, had shared his high opinion of the convict. Crowder, it appeared, had been employed as a general inspector of convicts since King's earlier period on the island and had been 'of the greatest Service to the Publick'. Phillip responded by granting Crowder a conditional pardon on 3 November 1792. It was to become an absolute pardon on 13 September 1796. As of 22 February 1793 Crowder was classified as a 'settler'.[11]

By January 1794, at the latest, Crowder had added the management of the island's theatre company to his busy round of activities. While it is reasonable to assume he was a leader of the group from the beginning, his position as manager may owe something to the fact that he was also a constable, and so had both a special obligation and official powers to maintain law and order in the playhouse. By 19 December 1791 he had been made responsible for the night watch in the island's leading settlement, and on 25 August 1793 was appointed constable for that settlement and adjacent areas.[12]

The riot in the theatre on 18 January 1794, described in detail in Chapter 5, was a serious blow to Crowder. He was a key figure in the preliminary stages of the dispute, and Lieutenant-Governor Grose, furious at King over the affair, vented some of his spleen on Crowder. King had packed ten of the soldiers off to Sydney after the affair, but had sent none of the opposing party. Grose immediately wrote back ordering King to send Crowder and William Doran to him as prisoners and to keep both of them in chains until their departure.[13] Crowder wrote a plaintive letter to King:

> Sir,
> The very Distressing situation in which I now stand I hope will plead in my behalf & be admitted as a sufficient excuse for troubling you at this busy moment.
> Lieut' Towson has informed me that he has received Major Groses Orders to put me in Irons & send me to Port Jackson, but says he is not authorized to tell me, with what Crime I am charged. I therefore cannot request your Honour for any witness's to defend a Charge I am totally unacquainted with, of which I have no doubt could I make it appear to you Sir that they was Needfull you wou'd readily Grant.
> I have therefore only to request, Sir, that you would order me the Copy of the warrant, by which I was sworn in a Constable & likewise beg leave to state the heavy losses I am likely to sustain.
> I am in possession of two Farms one of Thirty Acres the other of Fourteen, the first acquired by my own Industry the other as a lease from the Crown: my Wife in a Languishing state for ten Weeks past as the Surgeon can testify, the

rent of the larger Farm coming due, to be paid in Corn amounting to Eighty Bushells which I am likely to lose without strict looking after – various other Debts, to a considerable amount due from different Persons, my own credit at stake, if my own bills when they come due are not taken up which I have always hitherto carefully attended to, near 200 Bushels of Corn on the Farm where I reside which must be gathered & housed before cropping time, which will arrive, before I can possible return besides Two & Twenty Hogs to attend & look after: I have likewise other engagements to the amount of Seventy or Eighty Pounds.

I therefore cannot help thinking my case very hard when I consider that, from my Wife & all my concerns I am torn away fettered like a criminal, carried to a distant prison without being made acquainted with the Crime I am Charged with, or the Consequences that may attend it & the whole of my affairs left in the hands of a weak helpless Woman.

I therefore hope you will be so good to acquaint Major Grose, who is a stranger to my Person, Character, & affairs, of the heavy losses I am likely to suffer by my detention at Port Jackson.

I flatter myself from your known probity, & Justice to individuals of every description, you will comply with a request which I hope you will not think unreasonable from him who is Sir

> With the utmost
> submission &
> Respect your dutiful and
> Obedient
> Servant to
> Command
> Tho Restil Crowder[14]

As a result of the letter, Crowder was allowed a week, free of chains, to settle his affairs, though King, in reporting this to Grose, was careful to spell out that the decision on this was made by the newly arrived senior military officer on the island, Lieutenant Townson. Crowder and Doran sailed, under guard, on 22 May 1794. No record of Crowder's interrogation at Sydney has been located, but Reg Wright states that he received 100 lashes for his behaviour. Richard Atkins, later to become judge-advocate, reported that the soldiers involved received that punishment, and it was the penalty Grose insisted King should impose in future on any convict striking a soldier.[15] On 4 June, while Crowder was still at Port Jackson, his ailing wife died, a fact pointedly noted by King in his journal. Doran is recorded as returning on 19 July, presumably accompanied by Crowder.[16]

If his absence from the island caused Crowder any economic problems, they had been overcome by 1796, when he held 100 acres, located in four lots. It was the third largest holding on the island.[17] Thereafter he continued to buy and sell land, to appear occasionally in the records as a constable, and to sell produce to the government store.[18] In his last years on the island he was recorded as living in a substantial two-storey house, boarded and shingled, with a small thatched, boarded and floored barn and two thatched log outhouses. The government valued the buildings at £90, a significant amount for Norfolk Island.[19]

At some point after the death of his first wife, Crowder met Mary Christmas, alias Cowcher, a household servant who had been transported in 1789 on the *Lady Juliana*. They were married on 22 December 1799.[20] She had arrived on Norfolk Island on 7 August 1790, and lost her first antipodean husband, Charles Smith, in February 1793. The Crowders appear frequently in the shopkeeper's daybook of 1805–06 that includes entries for the theatre, but

Crowder's name is not linked with any of these entries. He seems not to have been involved in the production and, if he attended the show, it was on tickets purchased elsewhere. He appears, however, to have struck up an association with the eccentric gentleman convict John Grant, who sent a collection of Crowder's poems back to England along with a volume of his own rambling memoirs and poetic effusions.[21] It is the only evidence of Crowder's artistic leanings apart from his management of the 1793 theatre – where he seems not to have been an actor, but purely an administrator.

With the Norfolk Island settlement scheduled for abandonment, Crowder, his wife and two daughters left in one of the earliest vessels, the *Porpoise*, which sailed for the Derwent on 26 December 1807. On 21 May 1809 he earned the ire of Lieutenant-Governor Collins, when he became the leading signatory of an address to the deposed Governor Bligh, in spite of Collins' proclamation forbidding such addresses. Five months later Collins still remembered the affront, expressing the desire to have Crowder flogged.[22] Collins' death in March 1810 doubtless eased Crowder's situation. In 1813 he was appointed superintendent of convicts at Hobart and was employed in other government activities, such as making a survey of land to be resumed in Hobart. Mollie Gillen states that he had also received a grant of 120 acres as compensation for the loss of his Norfolk Island holdings. Though the 1819 muster shows him with only a thirty-acre grant, he was, by that time, making substantial sales of swines' flesh to the commissariat.[23]

In 1820 Crowder appeared before the Bigge inquiry in his capacity as superintendent, but by this time he was about 62 and clearly in decline. In his final report Bigge notes the inadequacy of Crowder's record keeping. He also declares that, 'by reason of the advanced age and incompetence of the officer who holds the situation of superintendent at Hobart Town', many of his tasks had been taken over by the magistrate of police, the acting engineer and, in one case, by Lieutenant-Governor Sorell himself.[24] Sorell had written to Governor Macquarie in August 1820 to advise him that, needing 'a more active person', he had replaced Crowder as superintendent and put him in charge of the new church (St David's) on a retirement allowance of £25 per annum. This was half the sum he had received in his earlier position. Macquarie wrote on 13 October approving Sorell's action. Initially the appointment to St David's involved supervision of the materials used for erecting the church, but thereafter he is described as verger.[25]

Crowder died on 28 November 1824 at his house in Elizabeth Street, Hobart, 'much lamented and regretted by his numerous family and friends'. The newspaper and the burial register at St David's gave his age as 67. The family included his ex-convict brother Edward, who ran a ferry service on the Derwent; his wife Mary; a stepdaughter and at least one of his daughters by Mary, as well as a son, Thomas Restil Crowder Jnr, born to the couple in October 1810, after their arrival in Hobart. Descendants of this son still live in Hobart.[26]

Crowder seems to have been a somewhat prickly character. At his Old Bailey trial he intervened heatedly to challenge witnesses, and the flare-up in the theatre at Norfolk Island seems to have been as much a provoked by his standing upon his dignity, and his brusqueness, as by Sergeant Whittle's thuggishness. His answers to Commissioner Bigge's inquiries in 1820 are often terse, and his open defiance of Collins in the Bligh affair indicates his readiness to challenge authority. The loss of the volume of poems which Grant sent back to England is regrettable, not only because it might have contained prologues and epilogues to some of the Norfolk Island plays, but because it might have brought us closer to the man himself and given us some sense of his literary sophistication.

WILLIAM DORAN

William Doran, described as a brick-maker, was tried at the Lancashire Quarter Sessions of 3 March 1788. He was sentenced to seven years' transportation and moved to the *Dunkirk* hulk at Plymouth a month later, his age given as 20. He reached Botany Bay, on the Second-Fleet *Neptune*, on 28 June 1790.[1]

On 27 April 1792 Doran arrived at Norfolk Island. Norfolk Island bricks were of poor quality and little used, so he was probably not sent there for his trade skills. Instead he emerges as cook to Lieutenant-Governor King.[2] Doran was backstage at the time of the playhouse fracas between Crowder and Whittle, but in what capacity is not known. However, he had the misfortune to be the only one identified by name in the subsequent proceedings. He was accused of having 'looked out from behind the Curtain' and initiated the cry to 'Kick the bloody Soldiers out of the House', thus inflaming the audience.[3] In the tense exchange of letters that followed between King and the furious Lieutenant-Governor Grose, the latter ordered King to throw Doran and Crowder into gaol, in irons, until they could be sent to Sydney. The pair sailed on the *Francis* on 22 March 1794, Doran in all probability to receive a flogging for his actions. He returned to the island, again on the *Francis*, on 19 July 1794, probably to his earlier post with King, since the latter blamed the soldiers for the whole affray and was mortified by Grose's response.[4]

By early 1795 Doran's sentence had expired. On 6 November of that year he left the island on HMS *Supply* for Port Jackson.[5] It is his last appearance in the records. He could easily have paid or worked his passage home shortly afterwards.

EDWARD FLYNN

Edward Flynn was tried in January 1784 for snatching eleven pairs of breeches from a slopseller's shop in Cock Hill, probably the street of that name in the dockyards area of Shadwell. He had sprinted off down the street, dropping a bundle of goods as he ran, but was soon caught. His anxiety to recover his hat, which was under the bundle of dropped breeches, merely confirmed that he was the thief. Flynn's immediate concern was the prospect of hanging, and the slopseller seemed eager to pursue that outcome, but when it came to the trial he valued the goods at 39s., one shilling short of a hanging offence. Flynn was sentenced to transportation for seven years and sailed for America on the *Mercury*, but, after the convicts seized the ship and sailed into Torbay, he was one of those captured on board by the crew of the *Helena*. He was sent to the *Dunkirk* hulk in June, where his age was recorded as 30. He signed for an issue of clothing with a cross, as he was subsequently to do on the wedding register, an affidavit and a document in support of Judge-Advocate Dore.[1]

In March 1787 Flynn was transferred to the First-Fleet vessel *Friendship*, where Ralph Clark gave his age as 27 and recorded him as having no trade. Thereafter there is no mention of him until 28 September 1789, when (his name spelled Phlyn) he married Sarah Ault or Alt in Sydney. The couple were soon transferred to Norfolk Island, arriving on 13 March 1790. In the first half of 1791 each of them was recorded as receiving a piglet as part of the plan to encourage self-sufficiency.[2]

In the magistrates' minutes regarding the playhouse disturbance Flyn [*sic*] was referred to as superintendent of the hospital, and free by servitude. Before giving his evidence he was 'sworn on the Holy Cross', and later directly identified as a Catholic. He described himself as coming 'from behind the Scenes' in time to see Whittle's first approach to Crowder and everything that followed. His evidence strongly favoured Crowder, but tells us little about

Flynn, except that he was prepared to confront the violently aggressive Private Bannister. In the aftermath of the affair King was obliged to eject several overseers from their small plots of land adjacent to the settlement, so that they could be handed over to the military. Flynn was one of those ejected on 19 March 1794, though he would have received a replacement at some less convenient spot. There is no record of him ever expanding his holdings or selling produce to the commissariat.[3]

Flynn and Sarah Ault left the island for Port Jackson in August 1795, by which time her sentence also had expired. In the list of those off government stores in 1801 she is noted as living in Sydney, but is not recorded thereafter (the Sarah Ault who received an absolute pardon and left for England was Sarah Ault, or Hunt, *per Britannia*). In this period a few references to an Edward Flynn occur in the records which almost certainly relate to the First-Fleeter, since no other person of that name is known in the colony. Thus, in late 1798 or early 1799, his mark had appeared on a document praising Judge-Advocate Dore's expeditious system of issuing writs in cases of debt. The document explicitly identifies itself with those who have property to protect and represents 'the Interest of the better part of the Community'. This, and the fact that many of the appended names are readily identifiable as business people (Shadrach Shaw, Elizabeth Needham, Henry Kable, Simeon Lord, John Sparrow, Matt. Kearns, Robert Sidaway etc.), argues that Flynn had become a member of this entrepreneurial group. He certainly appears in the Civil Court records in pursuit of debtors, some owing amounts from £10 to £35 (in one case an affidavit signed with a cross has also survived), but the number of occasions is not large and most activity is concentrated in late 1798. His period as a businessman may have been brief.[4]

On 28 August 1803 the *Sydney Gazette* reported a case of breach of agreement brought by an Edward Flynn, who charged the contractors with delaying repairs on a boat he owned, to the point at which it was virtually beyond saving. It is not clear whether the boat was important to Flynn's livelihood, but it must have been in poor condition initially to have deteriorated so badly in the intervening six or seven months.

In the 1806 list of landholdings Edward Flynn and John Rossiter are shown as co-lessees of ten acres at Cattai on the Hawkesbury. It is not clear what a share in ten acres at that outpost could achieve – hardly subsistence, one would think. Perhaps poverty sent him back to crime, for in May 1810 he and two others were convicted of the robbery of John Cox at the Hawkesbury. The death sentence was commuted, but he was given a life term. In the 1814 muster he appears as a convict, off stores, at Sydney and assigned to D'Arcy Wentworth. Wentworth was assistant surgeon at Norfolk Island when Flynn was overseer of the hospital, so Flynn might have assisted Wentworth in some medical capacity. By 1822, however, he was employed in the Sydney area by R. Henderson. His master was presumably Robert Henderson, a farmer at Brisbane Water, which fell within the Sydney region. The 1825 muster records Flynn as a Sydney labourer on a ticket-of-leave,[5] while the 1828 census describes him as still on a ticket, aged 74, a Catholic and a fisherman at Pitt Water. Had this been his employment at Sydney in 1803, when he was so concerned at the decay of his boat?

According to Mollie Gillen, an Edward Flynn, age given as 78, was buried in 1837. The age, though out of line with that in the census, accords with that given by Clark in 1787.[6]

It is difficult to obtain a clear sense of Flynn's social position. The hospital at Norfolk Island was a small affair. In May 1793 it was recorded as having only ten inmates and one attendant, while in October it had one attendant but no patients.[7] Being its superintendent, then, might not have been a particularly exalted position, unless that superintendent had significant medical knowledge, which might not have been necessary. If it was, Flynn's last years represent a sad decline. It seems more likely that he was a fisherman or sailor by trade, whose moments of prominence at the hospital and as a Sydney businessman were the aberration. As with Stephen Shore, his illiteracy would have been a barrier to him being an actor, but not an insuperable one.

ROBERT HIGGINS

[signature: Robert Higgins]

RONSW, Marriages.4.61.

Robert Higgins was born about 1762 in Wiltshire and enlisted in the New South Wales Corps in England on 3 February 1791 as a private. By then he was 29. It was his first military appointment, and his prior occupation is unknown. In September 1808 he was described as 5 feet 7 inches tall, with a dark complexion, hazel eyes, dark brown hair and a thin visage. He arrived in New South Wales on board the *Queen* in September 1791.[1]

On 14 March 1792 Higgins was promoted to corporal and, as a member of Captain Johnston's company, was transferred to Norfolk Island, arriving on 11 February 1793. By 15 August 1793 he had been promoted to acting sergeant major, a position he still held at the time of the theatre riot.[2]

As with most of the lower ranks of the Corps, information about Higgins' social background is lacking. He is presumably the soldier whom King mentions among those involved in the setting up of the theatre. As the senior non-commissioned officer on the island (even though he was a corporal acting in that position), he would have been a person of some influence in the playhouse. His status alone would have guaranteed him a significant role as an actor. What little reference there is to him in the records of the riot suggests he was a sensible and moderating influence during that difficult time.[3]

Higgins left the island on the *Daedalus*, 6 November 1794, and was confirmed in the rank of sergeant on 3 April 1795. For most of the nine years that followed, the period in which the Sydney playhouse flourished, he was based in that town,[4] but there is no evidence that he ever joined the company, even after other soldiers began to appear on the boards. After a period in Parramatta, Higgins was once again back in Sydney in 1809. On 30 July he secured a lease on a thirty-rod allotment in High Street. Otherwise, however, it was not a good year for him. On 26 January he was reduced from sergeant to private, and on 15 September he was gaoled for debt. Able to take advantage of the English act for the relief of insolvent debtors, however, he was released on 19 January 1810.[5]

On 3 April 1810 Robert Higgins transferred to the incoming 73rd Regiment, apparently with the rank of sergeant, though in all later returns he was listed as a private. On 25 March 1811 he was discharged. On 9 July 1810, he had married Lydia Farrell, an ex-convict. He signed the register in a competent hand, describing himself as a corporal in the 73rd Regiment.[6]

On 30 July 1811 Higgins was listed as a discharged soldier who was to receive fifty acres of land in the new districts of Airds or Appin. In the 1814 muster Robert Higgins, *per Queen*, was recorded as a landholder at Liverpool, off stores and with a convict servant, Thomas Seymour. He is presumably the same Robert Higgins who, on 1 July 1813, subscribed £2 to the building of the Sydney Court House and on 1 August 1814 was a juror on a coroner's inquest at Camden, where he and the others are described as 'Men of Minto'. Higgins signs the report of the inquest with a firm hand and a few flourishes.[7]

In the 1822 and 1824 musters Higgins was recorded as employed by John Macarthur, in the first at Parramatta and in the second at Cawdor. However, he seems to have retained his farm, which later passed to his family. Though he does not appear in the 1828 census, his death is recorded as taking place 8 March 1843. He was buried at Camden three days later and described in the register as 'Settler and formerly serjeant of the 102nd Reg.'. His age was stated as 81, matching the earlier figure given in the Corps' records.[8]

WILLIAM HOGG

RONSW, Marriages.5.153.

In late March 1784 two men tried to recruit a known criminal to supply them with cheap metal buckles. Since it was obvious from their behaviour that they were in the business of plating such objects with silver and passing them off as sterling, he reported them to Bow Street and agreed to act as a decoy. Accordingly, on 9 April, a party of law officers burst in on the three men in lodgings near Red Lion Square, and discovered them coating buckles and a spoon and stamping them with false marks. At his trial in late April 1784 William Hogg called four unidentified witnesses to vouch for his good character, but both men were sentenced to fourteen years' transportation and Hogg was sent to the *Censor* hulk at Woolwich prior to 11 July. There is confusion about his age, the *Censor* records describing him sometimes as 36 and sometimes as 20.[1]

Hogg was no self-taught counterfeiter. Collins declares that he was highly regarded in the colony as a silversmith, so he was evidently fully trained, though not a member of the Livery Company. (There was an Andrew Hogg trading as a goldsmith in the Strand in the 1760s and 1770s, but no relationship can be established.) Collins also remembered Hogg for his abilities as 'an actor in the Walk of low comedy'. It might be relevant that he was dispatched to Australia on the First-Fleet vessel *Scarborough*, on which the convicts got up a theatrical entertainment *en route* to Botany Bay.[2]

At 11.00 pm on Saturday 13 June 1789 the patrol in Sydney broke up a wild party at the convict hut of Barney Dennison, who cheekily claimed to be 'Landlord' of the premises. A sailor and seven convicts were arrested, including Hogg. He was one of the first escorted to the guard house, so avoiding the worst of the confrontation that followed, and at his trial five days later acknowledged that 'he was culpable in being out an improper Hour'. He escaped with a reprimand. This was only nine days after the production of *The Recruiting Officer*, in which Hogg could well have been a performer. On 31 August 1788 he had signed his name, a little roughly but with decorative flourishes, as witness to the marriage of Christopher Magee and Eleanor McCane.[3]

On 13 March 1790 Hogg was among those landed at Norfolk Island from HMS *Supply*. By 1 July 1791 he was partially subsisting on an allotment at Queensborough, with thirty-four roods cleared and with a one-third share in a pig. He never, however, made the transition to settler and farmer. He is mentioned in the magistrates' hearings on the playhouse riot, where

Crowder claimed 'he had received an Order by Wm Hogg from the Lieut. Governor's Lady to reserve three or four Seats for her Servants'.[4] Perhaps Hogg had a position in the administration of the theatre or, like Doran, in the household of the lieutenant-governor. The latter is marginally the more likely. Though he is not among those identified as behind the scenes at the beginning of the Crowder/Whittle confrontation, it is difficult not to see him as one of the performers on that night, in view of his reputation as low comic actor. On the evidence we have, this could only have been gained from acting in *The Recruiting Officer* of 1789 or in theatricals on Norfolk Island.

The last mention of Hogg is Collins' account of his miserable death. On 8 August 1795, he

> put an end to his existence in a very deliberate manner a few days before the *Fancy* sailed. Spirits being in circulation after her arrival, he went to the 'Grog-shop' as long as he had money; but, finding that he had no credit, he could no longer endure the loss of character which he thought attached to it; and though he did not 'make his quietus with a bare bodkin', yet he found a convenient rope that put him out of the world.[5]

MICHAEL LEE

Michael Lee

SRNSW, 4/1168A, p.57.

Michael Lee was sentenced to seven years' transportation at the Old Bailey on 25 February 1789 for stealing a gentleman's trunk full of clothes. The robbery involved the hazardous business of securing a hold under a moving chaise and cutting away the straps that held the travelling trunk to the front of the vehicle. For all its riskiness this was a common form of theft, though one which required considerable skill. Lee, moreover, seems to have had an accomplice in the operation, acting as lookout, reinforcing the suggestion of an organised crime. The whole affair took place in the Seven Dials area of London and one of the witnesses claimed to have known Lee by sight, implying he was a local. On 22 July 1790, after 'Confinement for near two Years in a crowded Prison whereby your Petitioners health is much affected', Lee asked to be allowed to serve out his remaining sentence by joining the Royal Navy. Officials reported that he had conducted himself 'orderly and quietly' in prison, and the recorder of London recommended that his request be granted, but the petition was ignored. Early in the third year of his sentence Lee sailed for Australia. Though he appears on the indent of the *Active*, that indent is annotated 'gone to the Gorgon' and in the 1811 and 1818 musters he is listed as arriving on the latter vessel.[1]

Lee landed at Port Jackson in September 1791 and was immediately transferred to Norfolk Island on board the *Queen*, arriving on 11 November. In a list of 7 May 1792 he was among those selling sows to the store and later (January–May 1794), as a 'Convict on ground allotted him by the Lt. Gov.', was selling grain to the government. This land grant seems to have been more substantial than the single acre he held as an overseer on a hill overlooking the main settlement and which was taken over on 10 March 1794 for military use. The 'wounds' he was recorded as suffering in a sick list of January – June 1794 could have come from his work as an overseer.[2]

Lee's early success suggests his abilities were quickly recognised, but thereafter his career does not follow the usual pattern of a rise to prominence as a farmer and government functionary. His land grant was never officially registered and he does not appear as a land-holder in the 1796 list. He was not a member of the 1793 Settlers' Society and for several years his name disappears as a seller of farm produce to the commissariat. Nor is he ever again mentioned as a government official on Norfolk Island.

It is not until after the turn of the century that Lee reappears in the official records. On 31 March 1801 he obtained a government lease on an allotment of unspecified size 'on the east side of Cascade Road' at a rent of 2s. 6d. per year. On 20 July 1801 he purchased the remainder of a lease on twelve acres from Thomas MacQueen and James Ormond.[3] During 1801 and 1802 he emerges frequently as a seller of large amounts of swine's flesh and lesser amounts of wheat and maize to the government store, signing the receipts in an awkward hand. In these records of sale he is described sometimes as a settler and sometimes as a free man, suggesting a slight uncertainty about his status.[4] The lack of civil and criminal court records, and of a local newspaper, as well as the shortage of visitors' accounts, leaves the business life of the island obscure; but, in view of his later activity in Van Diemen's Land, Lee may have achieved some success as a dealer or inn-keeper.

At the end of 1802 Lee's name disappears from the lists of suppliers to the commissariat, and in the 1805 muster he is simply a labourer, with his sentence expired and off stores. Although a solitary sale of swine's flesh is recorded in early 1807, the shipping list for the *Estramuria*, in which he departed for Van Diemen's Land on 15 May 1808, records him as holding only half an acre of land. This appears to refer to land held by grant, not purchase or lease.[5] The circumstances surrounding it point to him as a person of some significance on the island, since the shipping list notes that it actually 'belonged to the Society of Freemasons of which he is a member'. This was the half-acre bought from Aaron Davis for £55 by the Masonic Order of St John No. 1 on 17 April 1800. Lee is not one of the three leading Freemasons who signed a letter of appreciation to Lieutenant Piper on 18 December 1807 for his support of their institution, but his position as titular owner of the order's land indicates his importance in the group.[6] In an 1805 list of what appears to be houses on town allotments Lee is shown as holding one of the more valuable, though the £25 estimate put upon it would have bought only a modest dwelling at Port Jackson.[7]

The evidence of the magistrates' hearings of January 1794 places Lee behind the scenes during the altercation and he was called upon to testify. He took the oaths upon the Old Testament only, indicating that he was Jewish. In his version of events he claimed that

> he heard a Disturbance without the Curtain and going to the Place saw Serjeant Whittle and Crowder, having hold of each other. That he placed himself between them, and desired Whittle to let Crowder loose, when Whittle replied go about your Business. That this Witness then said he had a right to assist in quelling any Disturbance, and that Whittle replied he had no right so to do, as he was a Convict. That Whittle then pushed this Witness aside, and again running up to Crowder, called him an Animal, and a Dog, at the same time putting his fist to his Face but that no Blows passed on either Side. That this Witness then desired Serjeant Ikin to use his Influence in restoring Peace in the House, in doing which some Words rose between him [Ikin] and Crowder. That Bannister, who was then present, said, he would fight any Man in the House, and, no Answer being made to this, further said, now Soldiers, let's clear the House. That upon hearing this, a general Murmur arose which was quieted by the Interposition of John Fleming. That this Witness then called Serjeant Higgins behind the Scenes,

and begged of him to use his Influence in restoring Peace, which he believes he
did.[8]

It is not clear whether Lee's intervention arose out of social conscience or his position as
overseer. When the situation was at its most threatening, he seems to have sought the security
of backstage. Like the other civilian witnesses, he presents Whittle and Bannister as the
aggressors.

Unfortunately, Lee's evidence does not reveal whether he was as an actor or a stagehand.
He was probably an actor, as he almost certainly was in the later company of 1805–06, though
the references to him in the shopkeeper's daybook are few and brief. On 26 December 1805
a list of materials purchased for the theatre has the name of a different individual against each
item, presumably the actor on whose behalf that item was bought. In Lee's case it is two yards
of white ribbon. On 23 June 1806, as an individual entry, appears 'Mr Lee Dr./1 Skein Silk 1/
–'. The item is not specifically identified as needed for the theatre, but it probably was. By that
time purchases for the theatre in the daybook were only rarely classified as such. Lee may have
been no more than a bit player, but his love of the stage remained undimmed for over a
decade.

Lee arrived at Hobart Town on 5 June 1808. Almost a year later, on 21 May 1809, he
was one of those who followed the lead of Crowder, Belbin and Dodding in signing an
address to Bligh, after the latter's flight to Van Diemen's Land. The consequences of this
defiance of the island's lieutenant-governor, David Collins, who had turned against the irascible
governor-in-exile, were still being felt seven months later. It may have been because of this act
that at some time before October Lee was stripped of a position as constable and locked in
the guard-house.[9]

Once settled in Hobart, Lee was granted a half-acre allotment on behalf of the
Freemasons' Lodge on the New Town Road. As the lodge of St John it was still in existence
in June 1819, when twelve members donated 5s. apiece to the Bible Society. Lee's name was
first in the list. However, the organisation did not flourish. Stone foundations for a building
were laid but work progressed no further and the site was left abandoned. In 1827 it became
the subject of a dispute between Lee and Henry Chapman, by which time Lee was referring
to himself as 'now advanced in Years and one of the oldest Residents in the Island'.[10]

The documents relating to this dispute reveal that Lee had received a grant of thirty
acres at Clarence Plains in recompense for the loss of his Norfolk Island house and allotment.
However, in the *Hobart Town Gazette*, 16 October 1819, he was described as the proprietor of
the appropriately named Hobart hotel, the Freemasons' Arms. This would have been the
weatherboard house in Liverpool Street, near Wellington Bridge, which the same paper gave
as his address on 15 November 1817 and 1 May 1819. On 6 October 1827 it described him as
host of the Crown and Sceptre in Murray Street, while the *Tasmanian*, 3 October 1828, identified
him as proprietor of the Castle Inn, Harrington Street. We are left to wonder whether, as an
hotelier, he did what Toogood was to do a decade or two later, and made his inns the venues
for free-and-easies, or even for spouting clubs. He seems to have had no connection with the
Freemason's Tavern, built on a different site from the Freemasons' Arms, which became the
venue for Hobart's first theatrical season in 1833.

Lee seems to have been active in the Hobart Jewish community. John Simon Levi
records him as a spokesman for the group in a government enquiry in 1829 and also records
his burial in the Hobart Jewish cemetery in 1845.[11]

JOSEPH MORRELL

Joseph Morrell

SRNSW, 2/8148, p.705.

Joseph Morrell (or Murrell) was the one person recorded as 'behind the scenes' during the Crowder/Whittle affray, who was unquestionably there as an actor. He was 'conning his part' when the noise of the dispute reached him.

Morrell had first appeared at the Old Bailey in May 1784, accused, with William Cady, of two separate thefts of large copper washing-kettles. The pair were apprehended within a matter of minutes of the second theft, each carrying one of the kettles and with Morrell wearing a pair of worsted stockings that had also been stolen. The chief witness used the phrase 'that gentleman' in separate references to both Morrell and Cady, but the term was also thrown around by Cady in reference to the four men who apprehended them. Morrell called three character witnesses, but they were not identified in the court report. The pair was sentenced to be transported for seven years to America.[1]

A petition seeking clemency was evidently submitted by Morrell or on his behalf. Unfortunately it has not survived, but the recorder of London's response to it has. Dated 5 October 1784, it says of Morrell:

> Whatever he may have formerly been he appears, from his connexion with the
> other prisoner, who is a common thief, and having two separate crimes proved
> against him, to have formed such habits and connexions as would render him
> dangerous to the public, if permitted to remain in the kingdom, and whenever
> his sentence of transportation can be carried into effect, it seems to me, the
> best way of disposing of him.[2]

The first clause in this statement implies that the plea for clemency turned on Morrell's background, but whether it refers to family background or, for example, meritorious naval service is open to speculation. The petition was rejected, but like so many transportees Morrell was sent no further than the hulks at Woolwich. He was placed on board the *Censor* and his age was given as 24.[3] He escaped in February 1786 and fled to sea, but on 24 October, during a return visit of his ship to London, he was apprehended in the dockside suburb of Shadwell. At his subsequent Old Bailey trial, in December 1786, he declared:

> I do not deny that I made my escape; I did it with an intent to go to sea; I led
> but a bad life with the people down there; I have been at sea ever since, and the
> ship I was taken from is gone to sea, which was the Roman Emperor, Captain
> Armstrong; I was going to the Streights with her again; I was on board her
> better I believe than six months and a fortnight.

Morrell was sentenced to death, but 'humbly recommended to mercy by the Jury'.[4] Thereafter he rotted in Newgate until September 1789, when he was called again to the bar and his death sentence commuted to transportation for life. Accepting the reprieve, he declared:

> I wish to speak a few words; I have been here six years for transportation, since
> I was sent to gaol; and I went to Woolwich; I suffered such hardships, that I
> made my escape; since that, I have been three years in this gaol; I hope I shall
> not go on board any more hulks; I accept my sentence very freely, only not to
> send me on board the hulks.

This last wish was granted. He remained in Newgate until transferred to the *Scarborough* on 10 November, due to sail to Botany Bay as part of the Second Fleet.[5]

Morrell reached Sydney on 28 June 1790 and in a little over a month was transferred to Norfolk Island on board the *Surprise*. He landed on 7 August and was posted to Charlotte Field, a new farming area towards the western side of the island. The commandant, Major Ross, was already planning to make the island self-sufficient by giving small allocations of land and livestock to the convicts and releasing them from public labour on Fridays and Saturdays. From 28 February 1791 Lieutenant Clark was employed in measuring up the cleared convict land at Charlotte Field. At that time Morrell was issued with a sow and was recorded as cultivating a small piece of land in the area.[6]

In March 1791, with near famine conditions on the island, Morrell and a companion stole away from Charlotte Field to Mount Pitt, where they discovered the migratory mutton birds had returned. They captured twenty-three, but were seized and taken before Lieutenant Clark, who noted: 'I order them to work and tooke the Birds from them.' The offence had no long-term consequences for Morrell, who on 1 July was recorded as living alone on his land allocation at Charlotte Field, with eighty roods cleared.[7]

Many convicts, Thomas Crowder amongst them, later received more substantial land grants and became farmer settlers. Morrell never achieved this. From 5 May 1792 he was off stores for an indeterminate period, working for John Welch, another of these farmer-settlers, who held a grant at Queensborough, as Charlotte Field had been renamed.[8]

The next reference to Morrell is his evidence at the inquiry into the theatre disturbance on 18 January 1794. Like the other non-military witnesses, Morrell emphasised Whittle's aggressive demeanour and Private Bannister's attempts to incite a riot. Morrell claimed he had attempted to urge calm, with the result that Sergeant Ikin and Bannister

> abused him in very gross terms calling him a Scoudrel & a Villain, & asking him how he dared speak to him [Ikin]. That this Witness replied it was of no use to hold any Argument with him, and that it was better to inform the Governor and Lieut' Abbott of his Conduct, & that Ikin replied he might be damned, and the Governor too, for that he was a Soldier, and cared for nobody.[9]

At this point Morrell's evidence ceased. As with Michael Lee, discretion prevailed. Nevertheless, aggression does seem to have been in his nature. Less than two months later, on 1 March, he was charged with 'infamous abuse to J. Owens', for which he received 25 lashes and was ordered to ask Owens' pardon.[10]

Morrell then disappears from the records until December 1800, when he was granted a conditional pardon. He was still on the island at that stage, the document itself referring to his 'exemplary good Conduct ... and the recommendation of all the Officers Civil and Military on Norfolk Island where the said Joseph Morrell has been for the last Ten Years'. The pardon once secured, Morrell left the island almost immediately. In a list made slightly later his current employment (like that of others pardoned about the same time) was given as seaman, and that occupation could only be carried out from Sydney.[11] He soon emerges from the pages of the *Sydney Gazette* as master of a series of small privately-owned vessels, engaged chiefly in the violent, hazardous and exhausting business of sealing, in Bass Strait and beyond. On 30 March 1803 he sailed as commander of Kable and Underwood's *Surprise* and did not return until 26 August. The sloop was caught in a violent gale and driven upwards of 140 miles off course in 14 hours, with a wrecked bowsprit and a lost anchor. Even more dramatic was a sealing voyage begun on 16 December. The *Surprise* left port so suddenly that a party of 'three FAIR visitors' on board did not have time to disembark. They were unceremoniously dumped on the beach at South Head as night fell and left to walk back to Sydney.[12] Out to sea the ship hit a violent storm that shredded the sails and forced the vessel into Broken Bay for repairs. Morrell and his men then established a camp on Cape Barren Island and set about the grisly business of clubbing the seals to death, skinning them and boiling up their fat in cauldrons. They soon found themselves menaced by a group of escaped convicts, but Morrell went in pursuit, burnt their skin boat and captured their leader, who subsequently escaped.[13] This danger was soon overshadowed by the rivalries between the *Surprise* and two American sealing vessels captained by the Delano brothers. Amaso Delano's autobiography represents Morrell as the villain, luring the Delanos' sailors away, stealing their property and finally attacking them. It vividly describes Morrell seizing the American camp while most of the men were absent:

> Morril, the head man of the gang, ground his cutlass on our grindstone, and loaded two or three old muskets. He told a lad who was left to take care of their houses on the point, 'that he should make his sweet lips do its duty on the present occasion', kissing his old cutlass repeatedly.[14]

The Port Jackson men then mounted an attack on the American sealing party only to be routed (according to Delano), leaving several seriously injured. Shortly afterwards a group of Americans, bent on further revenge, seized Morrell and others, tied them to a tree and flogged them with a cat o' nine tails. Morrell, in escaping, also received a number of violent blows, one of which, 'falling lengthwise on the part of the arm between the elbow and the wrist, was so heavy as to cause the flesh to burst open'. Delano denied complicity in this last outrage, but gave in defence that 'every one of the people so punished was a convict'.

Morrell's own version of events also survives, in a long and vivid letter of 21 October 1804, sent to Kable and Underwood and through them to the governor. It is notable for its fluency (which shows him a man of some education), its faintly posturing heroics and its tone of outraged innocence. The Americans were guilty of 'bloody Cruelties … exercised upon Men without Humanity Law or Justice'; the captured Morrell 'answered that they could only take my Life, and desired them to do it immediately as I was in their power'. There is also much play with the savagery of the beatings and the desperate condition in which he was left: 'I … have ever since undergone the most excruciating pains … and was for three Hours this Night given over – some Times for ten Minutes together deprived of Speech.' Unfortunately for Morrell, the master of another Kable and Underwood vessel, Benjamin Higgins, also wrote a brief note to the owners, in Delano's favour. It emphasised the Americans' distress at what had happened and suggested that the crisis had been precipitated by alcohol brought from Port Jackson.[15]

In spite of these events the proprietors put Morrell in charge of the *Endeavour* and sent him back to the sealing grounds. A second voyage as master of the *Endeavour* began on 10 February 1805, but did not conclude until 16 May. The delay was attributed to Morrell and his men illegally procuring spirits from a passing vessel and devoting themselves to inebriation rather than seal killing.[16] Kable confronted Morrell on his return, dismissed him, and in a heated exchange struck the ship's master. Morrell promptly sued Kable for assault, claiming £250 damages in a florid deposition before the Court of Civil Jurisdiction on 27 May 1805: 'In this Instance I appear before you more reluctant than the most fertile Genius could point out – My Complaint – my Action, is for an Assault, personal abuse, maltreatment, and every other species of wrong that blows could direct.'[17] The outcome of the case is not recorded, but Morrell almost certainly lost.

Morrell next appears setting out for King Island once again, this time in a whale boat, with a crew of six. Once again there was a bad beginning. Aborigines attacked the party at

Twofold Bay and Morrell was speared through the side. He then lost all his provisions in a second attack on a nearby island to which the sailors had retreated. Within a week of their return to Sydney, Morrell was 'almost perfectly recovered' and sailed off again. This time he disappeared for almost three years, ending up wrecked on Kangaroo Island, well beyond Bass Strait, with only three months' supplies. In April 1809 the castaways were sighted by the sloop *Eliza*, which returned to Sydney with Morrell and two companions, the others being left, one assumes, to continue sealing.[18]

A few weeks after his return Morrell was made master of a new vessel, also called the *Endeavour*, and busied himself on round trips to Norfolk Island and a successful expedition to salvage the *Governor Hunter*, wrecked in Bass Strait. He took advantage of this expedition to sail on to Kangaroo Island to recover his whaleboat crew and a store of skins. Thereafter the records are fewer, though he is noted as a ship's master in 1812 and 1814.[19]

In February 1815, in what was to be his last voyage, he sailed once again for Kangaroo Island, in charge of the *Governor Hunter*. In July 1816, on his return voyage, he signalled a passing vessel three days out of Sydney, but he never reached the port, being driven past the entrance by strong winds which developed into a full gale. Two years later the wreck of his vessel was discovered, some forty miles north of Port Stephens, almost buried in the sand of a coastal lagoon, with its mast cut away and its sails missing. Morrell and his crew were never found.[20]

Morrell provides little comfort to believers in the morally improving effects of the drama. Histrionic he undoubtedly was, and his tinge of self-pity might be taken as a form of sensitivity, but the dominant impression is of a hard man living a violent life. He had a reasonable education and, in all probability, a respectable background in the middle ranks of society, though Delano, for one, failed to discern any refinement in him. His career on Norfolk Island was undistinguished, apart from his involvement in the theatre. It was only as a seaman that he became a force with which to be reckoned.

STEPHEN SHORE

Stephen Shore was sentenced to seven years' transportation at the Hertford assizes in March 1787. He was convicted of Grand Larceny for having stolen four silk handerkerchiefs in Welwyn parish on 7 March. In 1789 he was transferred to the *Lion* hulk at Portsmouth. He was listed as 34 years old, a figure representing his age at the time of conviction.[1]

Shore was held in England until the departure of the Third Fleet, sailed on the *Matilda* on 27 March 1791, and reached Port Jackson on 1 August. He was immediately transferred to Norfolk Island on the *Mary Ann*. No record of his presence there has been discovered apart from his participation in the play. He makes only a brief appearance in the magistrate's hearings following the riot, where he appears a little less warm in his defence of Crowder than the other civilians. While he was among those behind the scenes, there is no mention of his function either in the theatre or in the broader community.[2]

On 14 August 1795, with his sentence expired, Shore left for Port Jackson. There, at St Phillip's, he married Sara Eldridge on 28 May 1797. She signed the register, while he marked it with a cross. In the Settlers' Muster Book of 1800 he is recorded as a resident of Sydney and off stores, while she appears as a resident of Parramatta in the house of T. White. In a list apparently dated 1802 he is shown as having rented 160 acres at Bankstown. Though only five acres of the forty cleared were under grain and the livestock consisted of only fourteen pigs, the holding itself was one of the largest in the area, suggesting that he had significant financial resources. He himself was off stores, as was an unnamed woman companion. On 4 June 1804 he received a grant of thirty acres at Bankstown, which the 1806 muster indicates as mainly pasture, though the livestock consisted of only three pigs. In December 1809 he received a further grant. As this was awarded during the last days of the interregnum between Governors Bligh and Macquarie, it is presumably the thirty acres later recorded as granted by Governor Macquarie on 1 January 1810.[3]

By 1810 Shore seems to have moved to Parramatta, since in June of that year he was listed as a member of the Parramatta Loyal Association, a militia which, at least in theory, was confined to men who were 'housekeepers who are free men, possessing property and good characters'. On 19 June 1811, again with a cross, he witnessed the marriage of Robert Richardson and Elizabeth Rogers, also at Parramatta. The 1814 muster lists him as a resident of that town and as a barber, as does the 1822 muster. In January 1816 he had been a member of a coroner's jury there, and in July 1817 was again recorded as a resident of Parramatta, when he assigned the thirty acres received from Governor Macquarie to John Hodges. In April 1823 his address was given as No. 5, Macquarie Street, Parramatta. None of these references, apart from the two musters, firmly identifies this man as the convict who had arrived on the *Matilda*, but no other Stephen Shore (or Shaw) was known in the colony, apart from a Stephen Shaw who arrived in January 1819 and was still a member of a road gang in the 1822 muster.[4]

Shore was not exclusively a barber. The 1814 muster, which lists him in that trade, also lists Sara Eldridge as 'Wife to the Gardener Parramatta' and, when he was buried at St John's Church in that town on 22 April 1826, age given as 86, his occupation was recorded as gardener. To confuse matters further, the 1823–25 muster lists him as employed by Charles Walker, a publican of that town.[5] In view of his advanced years he might have been reduced to working for a living in whatever way he could.

Shore never appears as an overseer, constable or landholder on Norfolk Island, so his social position there remains unclear. However, his later emergence in the middle ranks of Parramatta society makes it likely that he was born into that world and preserved something of his status while on the island. While a neat signature appears on the inquest papers of 1816, it may not be authentic, since he appears to have been illiterate at the time of his involvement with Crowder's theatre.

Appendix B

LONGER NOTES TO CHAPTERS 1–7

NOTE 1: THE MAN WITH THE SILVER NOSE

Francis Brewer's account of a performance by 'involuntary residents' of the colony is as follows:

> One incident in connection with a bush performance may be related. It took place in a settlement to the north of Sydney, on a Saturday afternoon. The judgment scene in the 4th act of 'The Merchant of Venice' was chosen for representation, the character of Portia having been entrusted to a young man. The Shylock of the occasion was a really good amateur, but he had lost his nasal organ and wore a false nose made of silver, most artistically coloured in harmony with the hues of his face. The lack of this organ interfered but slightly with his enunciation, and all went well until the Jew stooped to whet his knife, and, jerking up his head to answer Bassanio's inquiry, 'Why dost thou whet thy knife so earnestly?' the false nose fell off, and behold the Israelite without that most distinctive appendage. The performance abruptly terminated amid shouts of laughter from the audience and all the actors, except Shylock, who was more completely 'dished' by a freak of force than he could have been by all the arguments of the learned Bellario and the decision of the Duke to boot.[1]

Since silver-nosed convicts were something of a rarity in New South Wales, and the number of settlements north of Sydney was itself limited, this Shylock was almost certainly the outrageous Henry 'Nosey' Herring, the Flying Fish, the instability of whose artificial nose was the subject of several stories.[2]

On his third transportation Herring had been sent to Wellington Valley, where his bad conduct earned him a colonial sentence, to be served at Moreton Bay. He was at Moreton Bay from 15 January 1830 to 8 July 1831, after which he was returned to Sydney, only to be ordered to Port Macquarie on 23 August 1831. Apart from brief absences on business, he lived at Port Macquarie and in the vicinity until his death in November 1856. Moreton Bay and Port Macquarie are both, of course, 'north of Sydney'. While Moreton Bay was not quite the cultural desert its fearsome reputation suggests,[3] Port Macquarie was the more likely location for his performance, in part because of the length of his stay there and in part because of the shadowy record of theatrical activities associated with the town in the 1840s.

NOTE 2: THE VENUE FOR *THE RECRUITING OFFICER*, 4 JUNE 1789

In Collins' account the *ad hoc* theatre is a 'hut fitted up for the occasion'. Tench refers to 'the mud walls of a convict hut'. Probably what he had in mind was the form of construction described by Collins as being under way in March 1788:

> The long boats … were employed in bringing up cabbage-tree from the lower
> part of the harbour, where it grew in great abundance, and was found, when
> cut into proper lengths, very fit for the purpose of erecting temporary huts, the
> posts and plates of which being made of the pine of this country, and the sides
> and ends filled with lengths of the cabbage-tree, plastered over with clay, formed
> a very good hovel. The roofs were generally thatched with the grass of the
> gum-rush.[1]

The problem is that the records of 1788 and 1789 make no clear mention of barracks or dormitories being built for the convicts. Instead, the emphasis is on the prisoners arranging their own accommodation, in the form of tiny shacks: 'Nor were the convicts forgotten; and as leisure was frequently afforded them for the purpose, little edifices quickly multiplied on the ground.'[2]

An audience of 60 or so, as given by Tench, would require 150 square feet to accommodate them, on the commonly-assumed ratio of 2½ square feet per person. The stage would probably have been diminutive. A hundred square feet is about as small as can be imagined, resulting in a total area of some 250 square feet. This leaves whatever orchestra there was to shift for itself and makes no allowance for wing space.

Such a floor area, which represents an absolute minimum, seems large for a small convict hut, and there is only one early reference that could point to the existence of something larger. In April 1788 'a range of huts' for women prisoners was begun west of the stream. These sound more like barracks than individual dwellings, but no dimensions are given. However, by November 1790 Parramatta boasted 32 convict barracks, apparently built as part of the expansion of the town in that year and housing 10 to 14 men each. These were 'of 24 feet by 12 each, on a ground floor only, built of wattles plaistered with clay, and thatched'. They were distinguished from the 'small huts' where convict families of good character were permitted to reside and were divided into two rooms.[3] In April 1792 the work in progress included 'building brick huts at Sydney for convicts, consisting of two apartments, each hut being twenty-six feet in front, and fourteen feet in width, and intended to contain ten people'.[4] Despite the paucity of the records the probability is that Sydney had been building cabbage-palm or wattle-and-daub convict barracks from April 1788, using the model then taken up by Parramatta; and that the brick barracks of 1792 were replacements for the earlier structures that were calculated to last only a few years.[5] These earlier structures, then, could have had a floor space of 288–364 square feet, sufficient (if unencumbered) to accommodate the production.

The obvious problem is that the Parramatta huts, and the later brick huts in Sydney, were divided into two rooms. If this were the case with the hypothetical cabbage-tree huts in Sydney, one room would need to have been exceptionally small if the other were to accommodate both stage and auditorium. At most it could have been 8 feet deep and running the width of the building, with a little of that depth sacrificed to the partitioning. If this small room had a chimney, as at Parramatta, it could have been a cooking and eating area. For theatrical purposes it would have been particularly handy as a dressing room. With even that small section of the hut set aside, however, the space remaining for the stage in the other room would have been a mere 7 feet deep and 14 wide. At 14 feet there is little prospect of setting up proscenium doors or practicable wing space. If such a hut had been appropriated for the theatre, the performance would have taken place on an almost bare and shallow end-stage. It may be significant that Tench seems to be attributing the magic of the space to decorations in the auditorium, not on the stage, unless the 'three or four yards of stained paper' to which he refers were used to make scenery. Paper scenery was a common feature of performances by the more beggarly of strolling players and the humbler amateur groups.[6]

NOTE 3: DINERS AND PLAYGOERS, 4 JUNE 1789

Calculating the number of military (marine) officers in or near Sydney on 4 June 1789 is relatively straightforward. There were 18 of them, including the subaltern in charge of the small detachment at Parramatta. The only uncertainty relates to the status of James Duncan Campbell, a youth who was a relative and protégé of the senior marine captain, James Campbell. He was one of two young gentlemen who had accompanied the unit as volunteers, but were clearly awaiting the opportunity to secure a second lieutenancy. Major Ross' son had already made the transition, in February 1789.[1]

The lines of demarcation are much less clear in the case of civil officers. I have included the governor, the judge-advocate, the commissary and his three variously-titled assistant commissaries (Clark, Freeman, Smith), the four surgeons (White, Balmain, Considen, Arndell), the surveyor-general, the clergyman and the provost marshal.[2] I have excluded from consideration the storekeepers, though this may be a mistake. William Broughton, at Parramatta, could possibly mount a case. Similarly, a superintendent of convicts such as Henry Dodd, though he was held in high esteem, has been excluded, in spite of providing the 27-pound cabbage which was a feature of the dinner itself.[3] Since Mrs Johnson was the only respectable woman in the colony, her modesty alone could have kept her from such an occasion, which in any case was probably conceived as an all male-affair. The result is a list of 13 civil officers.

On naval vessels the officers comprised captains, lieutenants and midshipmen, but also masters and surgeons and their respective mates, as well as pursers and the captain's clerk.[4] The position of some as invitees may have been slightly equivocal. Masters and masters' mates stood a little aside from the main naval hierarchy – captains, lieutenants, midshipmen – but midshipmen were commonly promoted to master's mate and masters to lieutenant or captain.[5] It is difficult to see them excluded from the list. Doctors, as professional men, should have been similarly assured of a place.

Pursers and captains' clerks might seem a more marginal group. In 1801 a duel between Captain John Macarthur and Lieutenant Marshall, RN, was aborted on the grounds that Maxwell's second, the purser of the *Earl Cornwallis*, was not of sufficient status. On the other hand, as Governor King sharply pointed out, Macarthur was happy to invite the purser to his house, in company with his own second, Captain Abbott.[6] Nor should it be forgotten that John Palmer, purser of HMS *Sirius*, was soon to be catapulted into one of the colony's most senior positions, that of commissary.

Accordingly, I have felt free to include in my list of potential dinner guests all naval officers from captain to clerk, with the exception of those seconded to roles in the colonial administration. These were Lieutenant King, two surgeons and a midshipman, all on Norfolk Island,[7] and men such as Midshipman Henry Brewer and ship's clerk Thomas Freeman, who were serving the colony in Sydney as provost-marshal and under-commissary respectively. This results in a raw figure of 18 officers on board HMS *Sirius* and the 6 on HMS *Supply*.[8]

While these calculations result in a total of 55 officers plus young Campbell in the mainland colony, it can be safely assumed that rather less than this number actually attended. Would any of the three officers at Parramatta have come to Sydney for the event? I suspect the answer is yes, but probably the marine subaltern was constrained to remain there as a duty officer.

Since the captain of the guard dined with the governor in the normal course of events, he would have done so on this occasion, though the two subalterns on duty with him might not have been so lucky, and all three might have been obliged to miss the play.[9] It is difficult to imagine HMS *Sirius* and *Supply* being left without a significant complement of officers on board – perhaps 6 in the case of HMS *Sirius* and 2 on board HMS *Supply*.[10] In this way the number of potential dinner guests dwindles to 45 or so.

NOTE 4: SEASONAL BRICK-MAKING AND THE BRICKFIELDS THEATRE

The law operating in England at the time specifically interdicted the making of bricks and tiles between 30 September and the end of February. During that period the brick-makers were restricted to the digging and turning of the clay in preparation for the actual manufacturing process. This law reinforced common practice, since it prevented the making of bricks and tiles in the damp season of the year. The careful drying of bricks and tiles was a crucial part of the process before they were placed in the kilns, since those that had dried out irregularly, or were too damp on firing, would be weakened and defective.[1] The fact that a law was in place in England was no guarantee that it was observed in Australia, but the colonists had found the torrential rains of the Sydney winter a major problem in many ways. In the colony's first winter, before the situation was fully understood, the attempt had been made to continue brick-making through this period, with calamitous results:

> All public labour was suspended for many days in the beginning of the month of August by heavy rain; and the work of much time was also rendered fruitless by its effects; the brick-kiln fell in more than once, and bricks to a large amount were destroyed.[2]

It remains possible that after 1788 brick and tile making were suspended during July and August, leaving the sheds empty. If this were the case then the tile-shed theatre may have operated on a seasonal basis. Of these two options, the takeover of an abandoned tile shed, and the intermittent leasing of a functioning one, the former is the simpler arrangement. Quite apart from anything else, brick-making in Sydney would have been confronted with the problem that, while winter was notionally the wet season, summer was also prone to violent storms and torrential rains.

NOTE 5: THE STORY OF THE OFFICER'S DOG

David Collins tells the story of a convict who, in the middle of one of the recurrent food shortages

> played off a trick that he thought would go down with the hungry; he stole a very fine greyhound, and instead of secretly employing him in procuring occasionally a fresh meal, he actually killed the dog, and sold it to different people in the town for kangaroo at nine-pence per pound. Being detected in this villainous traffic, he was severely punished.[1]

This was in July 1795, before Sidaway's theatre had opened (though possibly during the time of the Brickfields theatre). It contains no suggestion that the crime was committed for anything but money, but the facts that the victim was a greyhound, and was sold as kangaroo meat at 9d. a pound, mirror precisely the features of the story about the theatre ticket. While a second greyhound killing might have taken place in 1796 or later to support a theatre-going habit, it is more likely that a nineteenth-century raconteur picked up the reference in Collins and embroidered it. The greyhound killing and the theatre's opening are only 26 pages apart in the first edition of Collins' history. The earliest version of the legend I have noticed dates from 1865, but its origin is probably earlier.[2]

NOTE 6: DRUNKEN ACTORS

For some typical drunken-actor jokes, see *The Times*, 24 October 1786 and 10 May 1788, Oxberry's *Dramatic Biography* and Parke's *Musical Memoirs*.[1] Another Oxberry volume, *The Theatrical Banquet* of 1809, contains a tantalising fiction in the form of a friendly correspondence between 'two theatres in the Antipodes'. One of the letters ends with the postscript: 'The lady you sent me to play Juliet, from some cause or other, fell off the bier at the mouth of the tomb, and nearly rolled into the orchestra.'[2] Most readers would have had no trouble in guessing at the 'some cause or other'. *The Theatrical Banquet* was a well-known collection. Was this reference the trigger for the story in the *Sydney Gazette*?

NOTE 7: THE OPENING DATE OF THE NORFOLK ISLAND THEATRE

There are two discordant elements in the evidence, which could be used to suggest that Crowder's theatre opened in August 1793 rather than September. The difference of a month has some awkward consequences.

Part of the time scheme set out in Chapter 5 turns on a marginal annotation in the copy of King's journal that he sent as an appendix to his letter to Henry Dundas on 6 November 1794. This annotation identifies September as the month of the theatre's opening. However, a second version of King's journal was preserved among the family papers and is now in the National Library of Australia. This varies in many small details from the official version, and in it, crucially, the marginal annotation reads 'August', not 'September'.[1] King, moreover, in both versions of the journal, writes of the company performing twice in its first month of operations. Quite possibly King permitted the opening month to be graced by a gala presentation and a regular Saturday performance, so that a September opening could have admitted of two shows. However, if King adhered to the policy, outlined in his letter to Dundas of 19 March 1794, of only allowing one Saturday performance a month and an additional performance on public holidays,[2] then the evidence could point to an August opening. The Prince of Wales' birthday, one such holiday, fell on the twelfth of that month and there was no public holiday in September. An August opening, however, raises the problem of gaining access to the granary on the terrace. If King's dating of the completion of the stone granary and the clearing of the old granary is accurate, then one is forced to hypothesise an August opening in temporary premises or the terrace granary sufficiently cleared by 12 August to permit its adaptation as a theatre. It is difficult to imagine the company so impatient to begin work that it went to the bother of setting up a temporary theatre. One is then forced back on an August opening in a half-cleared granary, an error in King's dating of the opening of the new granary or a September opening with a second performance permitted by King as a special gesture. In this confusion of possibilities a September opening, with two performances in that month, is the simplest option, but an August opening cannot be ruled out entirely.

There is one other complicating factor, which weighs against an August opening but raises another spectre. In his second reference to the playhouse in his journal, King writes of performances 'Once a Month, & on the King & Queen's Birth days'.[3] This rules out a second August performance for the Prince of Wales' birthday, strengthening the case for a September opening. The problem is the mention of the King's birthday, which fell on 4 June and is well before any possible opening of the granary theatre. Is it simply a date never utilised, because the theatre was closed before that birthday arrived, or does it hint at a performance taking place on 4 June 1793? One remembers that the permission to perform a play was initially sought 'as far back as May 1793' and that Governor King asserted that 'on all Publick Days I generally went to the Play'.[4] This suggests that there had been several performances on such days prior to 18 January. One of these could have been on Christmas or Boxing Day, but one or two others would have been necessary to justify King's generalisation. Perhaps there was an isolated performance, in an *ad hoc* theatre, on the King's birthday, 1793, in the style of the 1789 production of *The Recruiting Officer*, out of which sprang plans for further productions realised with the opening of the granary playhouse. An alternative is a grand opening on the King's birthday with monthly and holiday performances thereafter, in a temporary space up to August or September.

NOTE 8: THOMAS CROWDER'S NORFOLK ISLAND PLAYHOUSE, 1793/94

The plan of the main settlement on Norfolk Island was a simple one. A short main street, which had almost the dimensions of a town square, led up from the landing place to the lieutenant-governor's house, which terminated the street and looked down it and out to sea. Immediately next to Government House, on its eastern side and facing onto a side street running off the main thoroughfare, were the military barracks, handily placed to provide protection for the civil authorities. Along both sides of the main street were public buildings and houses for some of the officials, with the rest of the township straggling along the water's edge to the east. The buildings along the western side of the main street marked the edge of the settlement, since behind them rose Mount George, left largely unoccupied apart from a flagpole and lookout half-way to its crown and a granary set up on a terrace a short way up the rise. This granary was on the seaward side of a road that began at the lieutenant-governor's house and led to the settlement at Longridge, beyond Mount George. Circumstantial evidence points to that granary being the building used as a playhouse.

While Crowder's building was described almost invariably as a theatre, even by Lieutenant-Governor King, Crowder himself makes a passing reference to it as a granary.[1] This makes the building on the terrace a likely candidate, but there was also the stone granary in the main street and a granary in nearby Arthur's Vale, as well as other buildings that might occasionally have been used for this purpose. However, Crowder's comment is not necessary to make the identification: other evidence in the voluminous papers relating to the riot pinpoints the building. First, when the civilians were calling out during the confrontation between Crowder and Whittle, one of the shouts was 'Throw the vagabond soldiers down the Hill'.[2] The theatre, then, was in a raised position. Secondly, as the soldiers from the barracks raced to assist their comrades after the play, King saw them 'run along the Front Paling of my House from the Barracks toward the place where the fray was',[3] a line of movement which would have taken them into the Longridge road. Thirdly, when he himself became fully aware of the tumult, it was 'only Fifteen Yards from the spot where I was standing'.[4] The terrace granary is the only building that satisfies all these requirements.

One of the civil authorities at Norfolk Island, who was to wear the plume of an officer in King's short-lived militia, was his young friend and protégé, William Neate Chapman, the deputy commissary. In 1796 Chapman whiled away some of his time by executing a detailed and quite elegant pen and pencil view of the township from the seaward side (see Fig. 10). The terrace on Mount George can be seen to the left of this. By that time it boasted three granaries, one behind the other, the second having been built in March 1794 and the third later in the year to accommodate the bumper harvest and permit the transformation of the much larger stone granary in the main street into a storehouse.[5] In addition to Chapman's drawing, two plans of the town in this era have survived: one showing only the one granary and the other all three.[6] Comparison of these makes it plain that the first granary was the one farthest from the sea and that the road to Longridge passed immediately behind it. That granary can be seen in Chapman's drawing, much the largest of the three and rising above the other two.

King's correspondence provides us with further information about this granary. On his arrival he found that his predecessor, Major Ross, had erected the frame for a wooden building '80 feet long, 24 feet wide and 17 feet high, the upper part of which was designed for a granary and the lower part for a storehouse'.[7] King rightly felt that this double function was ill-advised, since it compounded the threat of weevil infestation. He also felt (wrongly) that it was inappropriately situated on the main street and too large for either function alone. All of this, as he said in a report to Governor Phillip on 29 December 1791,

> made me resolve on taking the Frame down, & building a Granary of 40 Feet long by 24 Feet wide, on the Terrace which Major Ross had ordered to be cut in the side of Mount George, where it will be in a cool Place & contiguous to the different Grounds in cultivation, & from its situation will not require an additional Centinel.[8]

Looking at the dimensions it is clear that he had simply taken half the existing frame and transferred it up the hill, which presumably meant preserving not only the breadth of the earlier building but also its height, 17 feet. King tended to give his heights to the upper wall plate, as was customary, rather than to the ridge cap. The proportions in Chapman's drawing suggest that the height of the side walls was indeed a little more than two-thirds of the 24-foot width of the building – the 17 feet, approximately, that one would expect. Also notable in Chapman's drawing is the steep pitch of the building's roof, and the great additional height that results from this. If his proportions are accurate the ridge-cap was some 32–33 feet above ground level, almost doubling the overall height of the structure. Later views of the town by John Eyre, Edward Dayes and P.P. King give the building similar proportions, but since they seem to be derived from Chapman they probably have no independent authority.[9]

Since the building whose frame King had appropriated to make his granary was of two storeys, one would expect this feature to be preserved in the new structure. In a list of his building activities on the island King includes this structure as 'a Framed & Weather Boarded Granary … 37 Feet long, by 23 feet wide, with a large Loft'.[10] Two reports on the government's grain holdings in 1794 provide further, if ambiguous, information about the space. The first, of 19 July, reads:

> The Wooden Granary Nº 1 which building is 37 feet by 23 in the Clear in which we find there are Three floors.
> Contents of   Lower Floor   2 feet 2 inches   of shelled Maize
> Dº   second floor   2 feet   of Dº
> The Third floor being in Cobbs is reported to be about 388 Bushells[11]

The second, of 24 October, is as follows:

> In Wooden Granary Nº 1, which Building is 37 Feet, by 23, in the clear, we find there are two Floors ~
> The first of which is 9 Feet high, and stowed with Bags of shelled Maize, containing by the Deputy Commissary's Report Three thousand, nine hundred and seventy eight Bushels ~
> And on the second Floor, Two hundred and fifty Bushels of cobbed Corn ~[12]

The discrepancy between King's original dimensions, 40 feet by 24 feet, and his later figure, which is supported by these two returns, 37 feet by 23 feet, may be explained partly by the phrase 'in the clear'. The latter dimensions are, presumably, the internal measurements, the appropriate ones for calculating contents, the others the external figures. If each wall had a thickness of 6 inches, this would account for the discrepancy in width, but leaves a 2-feet difference in length to be explained. The simplest explanation is that 2 feet were lost in the dismemberment of the original hut.

More confusing is the discrepancy caused by the first grain return's insistence on three floors. The clue probably lies in the contents of this third floor, a mere 388 bushels of maize in the cob. Either this floor was being grossly under-employed or it did not extend over the full area of the building: that is, it was a small loft contained largely within the roof and with its floor at about the level of the upper wall plates. If this loft ran the full width of the building, it would need to be only 10 feet deep to accommodate the specified amount of grain, leaving the other 27 feet of the upper floor clear to the ridge-cap. King could well have ignored this small third level in his return.

There remains the grain return of 24 October, which reverts to describing the granary as consisting of two floors. The upper of these, however, like the third floor in the earlier return, contained only a small amount of cobbed corn, and is almost certainly the small loft I have hypothesised. The other floor specified is, with equal probability, the upper of the two complete floors in the building. Only in the rarest of circumstances was grain stored at ground level in England, because of the danger of damp, and infestation by rats, weevils and other vermin. Small granaries could be kept close to the ground if mounted on vermin-resistant saddle stones. Large granaries were placed in the upper level of two-storey buildings, in exactly the way Ross had designed the granary whose frame King had recycled, and in exactly the way King's later stone granary was to be used. The July return presumably reflects a time when there was more grain than secure storage space; the October return shows a situation closer to the ideal.

As an extension of this discussion, it should be noticed that Chapman's drawing shows the seaward end of the building with one window at a level appropriate for the upper floor and the other directly above it and within the gable at a point appropriate to a loft. Its oblong appearance suggests that this upper opening was designed in a way common to warehouses, in the style of a door and with a block and tackle rigged over it to haul goods to the first floor and to the loft level. One function of the loft, therefore, was to act as a working platform for this crane. Whatever the details, Chapman's drawing suggests that the loft was at the seaward end of the building.

On the assumptions made so far the argument may be taken a step further. Considering the weight of grain to be carried by the upper level, it is probable that the beams of its floor were supported from below by one or two rows of posts. This would have made the ground level of the building unsuitable for adaptation into a theatre. The upper level thus becomes the most appropriate. The small loft, if it was already in place, and not purpose-built by the actors, could easily have been converted into a gallery. In front of it, for pit and stage, was a space 23 feet wide by approximately 27 feet deep, with vertical walls of 9 feet to the wall plates and then the void of the roof for up to 17 feet above that. This roof space would have been cut across by tie beams, but in vernacular architecture these were often placed high in the roof-frame, so that the clear space would have been substantial, allowing for a well-proportioned proscenium arch.

A few other inferences can be made about this theatre, but they are based on unrelated scraps of information and constitute nothing resembling a complete picture. Since the vice-regal party sat in the second row of the pit, the theatre must have had no boxes. On the other hand, there are two references to audience in a gallery.[13] These references read a little strangely, and it is possible the word is being used in an unorthodox fashion to refer to the auditorium as a whole. A gallery, however, is what one would expect, and the small loft would be an open invitation to provide one. If this small loft was not employed for the purpose, a gallery space could have been cordoned off at the rear of the pit, or a balcony set up by the players.

At one point in his evidence at the inquiry Crowder directs people away from the front row of the pit 'to sit above it' and 'to move higher'.[14] The usage suggests that the players had gone to the trouble of stepping up the successive pit benches. At another point it is indicated that the front bench in the pit seated 13–14 people.[15] At the normal allowance of 18 inches per person, this would have left room for only one narrow aisle, of 2 feet, probably to the side. Two side aisles could have been secured by making the individual allowance 1 foot 3 inches. This figure was occasionally used in England, but it made for an inordinately tight fit.[16]

There are also three references to a 'Front Door', clearly at the front of the auditorium and close to the place where Crowder was sitting.[17] Since it is spoken of as a 'front' door, it follows that there must also have been a 'back' door, presumably serving the gallery. Chapman's drawing shows only one external door in the eastern wall of the granary. This could have served two inside staircases leading to the upper floor; but there was probably another door out of sight in the illustration.

Virtually nothing can be learned from the documents about the stage beyond references to a stage curtain.[18] There is no reference to proscenium doors, but, since the theatre was 23 feet wide, up to 3 feet could have been sacrificed on either side to allow for them, leaving a proscenium arch of 17 feet in width. A statement that Crowder, having confronted Whittle at the front bench, then 'pushed him across the Stage'[19] might suggest that it was not raised, which would have been highly unusual. But the comment probably refers to nothing more than Crowder pushing Whittle across the front of the pit, the full width of the stage. In view of the extent to which the actors became involved in the altercation between Crowder and Whittle, it is curious that no musicians are mentioned and no orchestra pit. This might indicate that the band was placed to one side of the auditorium or behind the scenes, rather than in the usual place in front of the stage.

The most serious gap in the information is any reliable way of estimating the capacity of the house. If 17 of the 37-foot length of the building was devoted to the stage, this could have left up to 20 feet for the auditorium, partly in the gallery and partly in the pit. At 13 persons per row and the standard 2-foot space for each row, the result would be a packed audience of 130. If the stage was not as deep, or if the pit, unusually for the period, extended under the gallery, then the audience could have been larger. Whatever its size, the impression given in the magistrate's records is that on the night of 18 January 1794 the house was reasonably well attended. Some time before Whittle's arrival, Crowder described the theatre as 'about one Third full', while one of the soldiers, Thomas Baker, who also preceded Whittle, declared there were a 'good many' people in the house on his entry. Whittle himself, on his arrival, 'stood for some time … looking for a Seat', suggesting that few were available.[20] People were still arriving after the altercation, leaving aside the vice-regal party and servants, a group of a dozen or more.[21]

NOTE 9: THE FIRST PERFORMANCES AT EMU PLAINS

The date at which performances first took place at Emu Plains is unknown, but the evidence suggests that the theatre was flourishing as early as 1822, a little over two years after the agricultural station had been established.

Some of the evidence for this is admittedly open to debate. Thus the *Sydney Monitor*, 11 April 1829, contains a long letter describing the setting up of a clearing gang, '*Murdoch's falling party*', in January 1823, and the vicious flogging of some of its members later in the year. One of those flogged was 'a lad of some genius. He had taken a character in a play at Emu Plains, when Sir Thomas Brisbane and Chief Justice Forbes visited the Convict Theatre there.' If this young actor had been with the clearing party since January 1823, the production must have taken place no later than 1822.

There is, however, an immediate difficulty with this story. The writer twice places the events in 1823, and claims that it took place when clearing or felling parties were 'newly projected' – itself a comment pointing to 1822 or 1823.[1] On the other hand, Chief Justice Forbes, before whom the lad allegedly performed, did not arrive in the colony until 5 March 1824. Faced with this contradiction, Colin Roderick, who first drew attention to this newspaper item, assumed that the year given was incorrect and the reference to Forbes was accurate.[2] The decision seemed all the more persuasive because Forbes and Brisbane were elsewhere recorded as visiting the theatre together at an unspecified date. In spite of this, however, it may be the reference to Forbes that is mistaken. Thus, on 23 January 1823 a party of 22 men was discharged from Emu Plains, being sent off as 'Mr Murdochs C¹. Party'.[3] The date, size and name of the group accord with the facts given in the *Sydney Monitor*. Perhaps Brisbane had visited the theatre, not only with Justice Forbes, but also, in 1822, with one of Forbes' predecessors, Judge Field or Judge-Advocate Wylde, and the earlier visitor had been confused with the later. Field had almost certainly visited Emu Plains, since an account attributed to him of a visit to Bathurst makes a brief mention of the establishment.[4]

Another source that points to an early date for the opening of the Emu Plains theatre is the manuscript autobiography of the convict actor James Lawrence, alias Laurent. Lawrence tells how he was convicted in Sydney for escaping the colony, was put in the town gaol gang and became its overseer in 1822 before being transferred:

> A few months after sent to Emu Plane then a place of Punishment. Had a Theatre there. Play'd and sang before his Excellency Sir Thomas Brisbane and other Gentlemen. Was a Great Favorite there … Was sent to Port Macquarie for the remainder of my sentence.[5]

Official documents scattered through the records confirm the general time scheme of Lawrence's narrative. There are references to him as assistant overseer of the Sydney gaol gang in early 1821, and in the September 1822 muster he is recorded as still in Sydney and as overseer of the 'Lightworker[s]' – presumably the gaol gang employed as lightermen, or wharf labourers, as described in the Bigge Report. Though no date can be located for his removal to Emu Plains, his transfer from Emu Plains to Port Macquarie was ordered on 17 September 1823.[6] His reference to being a 'Great Favorite' at Emu Plains undoubtedly refers to his theatrical success there. Since the status of 'Great Favorite' could hardly be derived from one performance only, he must have had in mind several appearances, which were probably in 1823 but could have begun late in 1822. There is, of course, nothing to indicate whether he was in the inaugural production. This could have taken place well before his arrival.

Some of Lawrence's accounts of his theatrical exploits are suspect, so that the Emu Plans story could be a fabrication. However, there is a further piece of evidence that strengthens the case for an early beginning to theatre at Emu Plains. On 13 October 1828 the *Sydney Monitor* reminisced:

> Sir Thomas Brisbane and the impenetrable Major once published a proclamation, in which they forbade the Bakers from baking pies and tarts on Sundays. The

people began to think the days of Puritanism were about to return. But when they heard soon after, that Sir Thomas, and a very grave personage, were both decried seated in a *patent* theatre in the bush, to witness the performance, of 'His Majesty's servants' at a penal station, together with the physician who nurses the illustrious little darling lately come into this mutable world, the people began to take courage, and to think, that … Sir Thomas and his Secretary, &c. &c. were, after all, not quite so violent in their piety as was apprehended.[7]

Governor Brisbane's proclamation of Sunday Observance, which included an interdict against bakers preparing 'Bread, Rolls, or Cakes of any Sort', was printed in the *Sydney Gazette* on 25 January 1822. A visit to the theatre 'soon after' probably meant that the playhouse at Emu Plains was active by the middle of that year, if not earlier. Could the 'very grave personage' with whom Brisbane sat have been, once again, Judge Field or Judge-Advocate Wylde, both of whom remained in the colony until 1824? From May 1822 Governor Brisbane claimed to have visited the establishment 'about once a month' to monitor the unfortunate experiment of adding the complement of women to the establishment,[8] and it was also a possible stopover point on his visits to Bathurst and the West. One such journey occupied him from 15 to 28 October 1822, accompanied by Major Goulburn and H.G. Douglass.[9]

NOTE 10: THE ADVERTISEMENT FOR THE EMU PLAINS PRODUCTION OF 30 NOVEMBER 1830

The letter to the colonial secretary of 9 November 1830 reports a claim by the settlement's superintendent, John Maxwell, that no performance was ever planned for 30 November. The advertisement in the *Sydney Monitor*, in other words, was spurious. This advertisement, in the form of a playbill, has some decidedly odd features. It draws on only a small number of the actors and in restricting itself in this way it is forced into a major doubling of roles in the mainpiece, Toogood playing both Young Norval and Lord Randolph, and William Watt both Glenalvon and Old Norval. The first of these doublings is the more significant, since it involves a major mutilation of the play: Young Norval and Lord Randolph share a scene important to the story line. This might suggest that the playbill-advertisement was the work of a forger unfamiliar with the details of the Home's *Douglas*, and so led into palpable error. On the other hand, small English touring companies notoriously involved themselves in such radical doubling and consequent butchery of the text simply through shortage of actors. By November the harvest was under way at Emu Plains. While this would not have affected Watt, Matthews, Toogood and Northall to any extent, it could have taken a heavy toll of those convict actors employed as labourers, particularly since favoured prisoners were allowed extra employment to help the local farmers with their harvesting. It may be significant that the only productions for which we have reliable dates took place in late autumn and winter; and that the mainpiece chosen for that November performance was a play with an exceptionally small cast.

Another problem with the playbill is that three of the names do not appear in Maxwell's list of performers at Emu Plains. These are Samuel Fenton, J. O'Connor and Joseph Hill. In Fenton's case there is an obvious explanation: Samuel Fenton had his ticket-of-leave granted on 8 November 1830 and, while it would have taken some time for the document to be processed, he was effectively beyond any re-allocation.[1] Maxwell could afford to ignore him. There may be some comparable explanation for O'Connor and Hill. Perhaps they also were in the process of receiving tickets-of-leave or certificates of freedom or had already been assigned to a settler.[2] The records of Emu Plains are so incomplete that these two cannot even be identified with any certainty.

If the playbill is genuine, Maxwell's claim that he had never authorised the production could have been a lie, designed to protect himself. That, however, is improbable. It would have been sufficient to declare that he had never given permission for any public advertising. It is more likely that Watt and Matthews, convinced of their influence over Maxwell, had grown careless of protocol and had not fully informed him that a production was being prepared.

The report of 9 November assumes that publication of the playbill was driven by vanity or spleen, but whose vanity or spleen is not defined. If vanity were the motive then the playbill would need to have been genuine. It is difficult to see how a fraudulent playbill could satisfy anyone's vanity. Spleen could have resulted either in a forged playbill or in the calculated release of a genuine one if sufficiently provocative. Captain Wright, in his letter of 9 November, certainly assumes that the *Sydney Monitor* would make political capital out of it, and this raises the possibility that the whole business was concocted in the offices of that newspaper. However, the paper had so little contact with Emu Plains that as late as 5 January 1831 it was unaware the theatre had been closed, and continued to condemn the governor's toleration of it as inconsistent with his suppression of entertainments in Sydney. With contacts so tenuous it is unlikely, though not impossible, that the paper could have known such details of the company as the names of its actors. The probabilities seem to favour a playbill originating at Emu Plains, or in its vicinity.

If the document did come from the Emu Plains area, various possibilities suggest themselves. One is that Sir John Jamison had passed the information on to the *Sydney Monitor*, with the idea of needling the government. As a matter of course, the convicts would have sent him a manuscript playbill of any forthcoming attraction, in the hope of securing his attendance. In this reading the convict players were the innocent pawns in a game of *Realpolitik*. Another possibility is that the players themselves had a collective bout of *folie de grandeur* and dug their own graves. But the most attractive explanation is that the publication of the playbill was an independent initiative of William Watt. His earlier letter to the *Sydney Monitor* from Wellington Valley was an example of the vanity and recklessness that were his characteristics and were to turn him into one of the most provocative troublemakers in New South Wales in later years, until the government finally brought him down.

Two features of the advertisement point to Watt's involvement in its preparation. One is that, while the names of the other actors are spelled out in full, Watt appears, discreetly, as 'William W'. This might have been a half-hearted attempt to conceal his identity in case the advertisement should cause trouble, but it is more likely to reflect his discomfiture at appearing on stage in such company. Whatever the motivation, it is unlikely that anyone other than Watt, in preparing the announcement, would have shown such concern for his feelings.

The other feature of the advertisement is its description of *Douglas* as 'the celebrated national Tragedy'. The concept of a national drama was current in England at the time, but it rarely appeared in the wording of playbills and advertisements. In Scotland, on the other hand, its use in those contexts was widespread, and it was applied not to classics of the British theatre but to specifically Scottish works.[3] *Douglas* was one of the more renowned of these and, since Watt had a Scottish background, he is the most likely person to have adopted this usage.

If Watt was behind the publication in the *Sydney Monitor*, his motivation could not have been vanity, since his identity was partly concealed. It was more likely to have been pride in the production itself and a desire to publicise the achievement. If provocation of the government was also a motive, Watt might have underestimated the strength of the response and the trouble he was making for the members of the company. As it was, he was one of the luckier, subverting the government's intention of sending him to remote Port Macquarie by making himself indispensable in Sydney, while awaiting transfer. While Matthews pined by the Shoalhaven and Northall rotted on the road to Cassilis, Watt was living the life of a dandified clerk in the capital.[4] It was to be several years before another round of provocation saw him finally sent off to Port Macquarie and to premature death on its treacherous harbour bar.

NOTE 11: THE AFTERLIFE OF JEMMY KING

Jemmy King lived a troubled life after his release from Emu Plains. His ticket-of-leave was for the Parramatta region and in the 1828 census he was recorded as a watchmaker in that town. On 26 February 1829 he was allowed to transfer to Windsor, but there, in December 1830, he was convicted of drunkenness and fraud.[1] Stripped of his ticket, he spent the next six months in an iron gang and thereafter was in government service or on assignment until February 1837. His ticket was then restored for the district of the Vale of Clywd, in the Hartley area, in which he had probably passed his period of servitude.[2] Thereafter things briefly improved for him and he became a constable, but once again alcohol was his ruin. While escorting a group of convicts, on a chain, with a military guard, he became involved in a drunken party at a roadside inn from which he emerged and proceeded to harass a group of draymen bedding down for the night. He abused the head man, Peacock, struck him and drew a pistol:

> The prisoner then deliberately stepped back one pace from the prosecutor [Peacock], and fired. A bullet and a slug perforated the skirts of the prosecutor's shooting jacket; the former struck his person, and lodged in the scrotum. He immediately shouted 'murder'.

The adventure ended on a suitably hallucinatory note with the imprisoned King escorted back to the inn, where 'the soldiers and prisoners were drunk, and singing, "Britons never shall be slaves" in full chorus together'.

King's defence, that he was drunk, had no quarrel with Peacock, and in any case missed his target, cut little ice with the jury. Without a moment's hesitation it returned a verdict of guilty. The death sentence was commuted to life imprisonment and he was sent to Norfolk Island with the note that he was never to be returned to the mainland.[3]

King arrived on Norfolk Island on 5 November 1838. He did not adjust to the island immediately, being recorded (but not punished) on 30 November for malingering. He spent several days in the cells after a conviction on 10 December for attempting to gain admission to the hospital on false pretences (he may, of course, have been genuinely ill on his arrival). He then remained out of trouble until almost a year after his performance in Lawrence's production of *The Castle of Andalusia*. His offence on that next occasion, 16 April 1841, was disrespectful and insolent conduct, which earned him two months at Longridge, presumably in the solitary confinement cells Maconochie had constructed there. Later he had a narrow escape when he was acquitted on a charge of abstracting spirits from the Police Office and telling a gross falsehood to the superintendent. There was a similar escape in June 1842, when a charge of stealing plates from the house of the Anglican minister was likewise dismissed.[4]

In 1844 the government of Van Diemen's Land took control of Norfolk Island, and on 18 November 1845 King arrived at the Derwent on the *Governor Phillip*. By now he was about 53 years of age. Described on his first arrival in New South Wales as having a fair to ruddy complexion and dark flaxen hair, he was now being characterised as sallow-skinned, with grey hair and whiskers and a thin face. The indent for the *Governor Phillip* and King's Tasmanian Conduct Record confirm that he was unable to read or write.[5]

On arrival King was sent to the probation station at Salt Water River on the Tasman Peninsular. His term was to have been a year, but he is recorded as 'Emerged from Gang 24 May 1846' and on 29 December of that year he received a ticket-of-leave, which was taken out for the New Norfolk district. No offences in the colony are recorded on his Conduct Record, either during probation or thereafter, and on 30 July 1850 he received a conditional pardon. On 8 May 1849 the application of James King of the *Governor Phillip* to marry Ann Brown of the *Tory* had been approved, and on 24 December 1850 James King married Mary Ann Brown at Launceston, signing the register with a cross and giving his occupation as sawyer.[6] The lady herself has not been identified among the various Miss and Mrs Browns on *Tory* 1 and *Tory* 3 and there is no further record of James King, though a curious set of figures scrawled on his Conduct Record seems to suggest that he died in 1874. By that time he would have been in the vicinity of 82 years old.

Appendix C

(A) RECORDED PRODUCTIONS AT ROBERT SIDAWAY'S THEATRE

DATE	PROGRAM
Sat. 16 Jan. 1796	*The Revenge*: 5-act tragedy by Edward Young *The Hotel*: 2-act farce by Thomas Vaughan, based on Goldoni's *The Servant of Two Masters* Source of information: Collins, 1.375
Thurs. 4 Feb. 1796	[*A charity benefit for Mrs Eades*] *The Fair Penitent*: 5-act tragedy by Nicholas Rowe An unnamed farce Source of information: Collins, 1.379
Sat. 23 July 1796	[*A benefit for Henry Green*] *The Busy Body*: 5-act comedy by Mrs Centlivre *The Poor Soldier*: 2-act comic opera by John O'Keeffe Source of information: *Oracle*, 13 July 1797
Sat. 1 June 1799	[*A benefit for Mrs Parry*] *Fortune's Fool*: 5-act comedy by Frederick Reynolds An occasional address written by Michael Massey Robinson *Bon Ton; or, High Life Above Stairs*: 2-act comedy by David Garrick Source of information: *Bell's Weekly Messenger*, 18 (Apr. 1801), 40
Sat. 8 Mar. 1800	*The Recruiting Officer*: 5-act comedy by George Farquhar *An Old Man Taught Wisdom; or, The Virgin Unmask'd*: 1-act farce/musical entertainment by Henry Fielding Source of information: Playbill, ML, Safe 1/107
Tues. 8 April 1800	*Henry the Fourth [Part 1]*: 5-act history play by William Shakespeare A 'new dance called "The Drunken Swiss"' *The Irish Widow*: 2-act farce by David Garrick Source of information: Playbill, ML, Safe 1/107
Mon. 23 June 1800	[*A benefit for Mrs Parry*] *She Stoops to Conquer*: 5-act comedy by Oliver Goldsmith *Miss in her Teens*: 2-act farce by David Garrick *The Devil to Pay; or, The Wives Metamorphos'd*: 1-act ballad opera by Charles Coffey Source of information: *Sporting Magazine*, 19 (Jan. 1802), 225–6

Between 24 Dec. 1803   *The Recruiting Officer*: 5-act comedy by George Farquhar
& 20 Apr. 1804   *An Old Man Taught Wisdom; or, The Virgin Unmask'd*: 1-act farce/
                           musical entertainment by Henry Fielding (as on 8 March 1800)
                                               Source of information: Eastwick, p. 196

The *Sydney Gazette*, 25 June 1827, describes a production of Shakespeare's *Romeo and Juliet* as
'one of the earliest performances' in New South Wales. If it is not fictitious, the story could
relate to the Brickfield Hill theatre, under Macquarie, rather than to Sidaway's theatre.

(B) RECORDED PRODUCTIONS AT EMU PLAINS

DATE   PROGRAM

Mon. 16 May 1825   Songs ('*solos* and *duetts*')
                           Barsissa; or, The Hermit Robber: melodrama by Charles Dibdin Jnr
                           The Mock Doctor; or, The Dumb Lady Cur'd: 1-act farce/ballad opera
                                by Henry Fielding, after Molière's *Le Médecin malgré lui*
                           Bombastes Furioso: 1-act burlesque by William Barnes Rhodes
                                               Source of information: *Australian*, 26 May 1825

Mon. 11 July 1825   *The Lying Valet*: 2-act farce by David Garrick
                           Barsissa; or, The Hermit Robber (as on 16 May 1825)
                           Bombastes Furioso (as on 16 May, 13 August 1825 & possibly April–
                                July 1827)
                           The Welder's Wedge-box; or, Vulcan Disappointed [author unknown] 'an
                                entire new performance'
                                Sources of information: *Howe's Weekly Commercial Express*, 25 July 1825;
                                               Sydney Gazette, 21 July 1825

Sat. 13 Aug. 1825   A Prologue in verse
                           The Lying Valet (as on 11 July 1825 and scheduled, but probably not
                                performed, on 3 July 1830)
                           The Village Doctor [i.e. *The Mock Doctor*] (as on 16 May 1825)
                           Bombastes Furioso (as on 16 May, 11 July 1825 & possibly April–July
                                1827)
                                               Source of information: Bougainville, pp.102–3

April–July 1827 ?   Includes *Bombastes Furioso* [?]
                                               Source of information: Tucker[1] , p.98

[Mon. 11?] June 1827   *Raymond and Agnes; or, The Bleeding Nun of Lindenberg*: 2-act melodrama
                                by Matthew Gregory ('Monk') Lewis
                           The Devil to Pay; or, The Wives Metamorphos'd: 1-act ballad opera by
                                Charles Coffey
                           'A respectful valedictory address'
                                Sources of information: *Monitor*, 19 June 1827; Tucker[1], pp.99–102

Sat. 8 May 1830   *Rob Roy Macgregor; or, Auld Lang Syne*: 3-act drama with songs by
                                Isaac Pocock
                           The Mayor of Garret: 2-act farce by Samuel Foote
                           and/or

The Village Lawyer: 2-act farce by William Macready

'An appropriate address'

> Sources of information: *Australian*, 14 May 1830;
> *Sydney Gazette*, 15 May 1830

[Sat. 11?] June 1830   Includes *Rob Roy Macgregor:* (as on 8 May & 3 July 1830)

> Source of information: Letter by Christiana Brooks
> (ML, Z 4661, pp.131–2)

Sat. 3 July 1830   *John Bull; or, The Englishman's Fireside:* 3-act comedy by George Colman
the Younger,

or possibly

The Lying Valet (as on 11 July & 13 August 1825)

Rob Roy Macgregor (as on 8 May & [11?] June 1830)

> Sources of information: *Sydney Gazette*, 8 & 10 July 1830

Sat. 30 November 1830 — performance announced, but cancelled

Douglas: 5-act tragedy by John Home

'Between the Pieces, sundry Amusements'

The Padlock: 2-act comic opera by Isaac Bickerstaffe

> Sources of information: *Sydney Monitor*, 6 & 10 November 1830

The *Sydney Gazette*, 15 May 1830, announced a forthcoming production of George Lillo's 5-act tragedy, *George Barnwell*, 'the catastrophe to be omitted, out of regard for the delicate susceptibility of some of the actors'. This is clearly a joke. The same may be true of Maclehose's claim that the Emu Plains convicts 'beguiled their leisure moments, in getting up *Rob Roy, the Bold Outlaw*, and *Honest Thieves* (appropriate pieces, cartainly)'. While *Rob Roy Macgregor* was indeed produced, Thomas Knight's 2-act farce, *The Honest Thieves*, was frequently proposed, facetiously, in the English press, as one of the works performed in Sidaway's theatre in 1796.

Where the source of information is a playbill, it is possible that the advertised performance never went ahead, for one reason or another. The three productions announced in English newspapers and journals are in the form of reproductions of playbills, and so a similar caveat applies, though less strongly.

$\mathcal{N}otes$

ABBREVIATIONS

ADB	*Australian Dictionary of Biography*, gen. ed. Douglas Pike, vols 1–2 [1788–1850], Melbourne, Melbourne University Press, 1966–67
ANL	Australian National Library, Canberra
BL	British Library, London
HRA	*Historical Records of Australia,* Series 1–3, ed. by Frederick Watson, Sydney, Library Committee of the Commonwealth Parliament, 1914–23
HRNSW	*Historical Records of New South Wales,* ed. by F.M. Bladen, 7 vols, Sydney, Government Printer, 1893–1901
JRAHS	*Journal of the Royal Australian Historical Society*
ML	Mitchell Library, State Library of New South Wales, Sydney
OBSP	[The Old Bailey Session Papers], i.e. *The Whole Proceedings of the Kings Commission of the Peace … held at Justice Hall, in the Old Bailey,* London, 1776–
PRO	Public Record Office, London
RONSW	Registrar's Office of New South Wales, Sydney
SG	*The Sydney Gazette*
SRNSW	State Records of New South Wales, Sydney

Note

In order to limit the number of endnotes to the text, some references have been grouped under the one note. To clarify endnotes the following conventions have been adopted: (i) references all relating to a single point in the text are separated by a semi-colon (;) plus two spaces, and (ii) references which relate to successive points in the text are separated by a long dash (—). Thus, in the following example, three successive points of discussion are referenced, the first with three sources and the others one each:

Statham, p.267; PRO, WO25/624, p.11; PRO, WO25/1342, fol.17^r — PRO, WO12/1900, fols 47^r, 63^v — SRNSW, X905, p.405.

Full publication details of the sources cited below may be found in the Bibliography, pp. 333–50.

CHAPTER I

1 For Britain, see Rosenfeld, *passim.* — For the colonies, see Russell, pp.122–57; Benson, pp.222–4, 370, 388–9, 441; Mukherjee, pp.1–7. — For St Helena, see Anon.[7], pp.200–3. The island's population was 'upwards of 2000', including 600 African slaves (p.211).

2 ANL, MS 737 (letter of 2 May 1804, pp.7, 8, 12 & letter of 13 July 1804, pp.3, 6); ANL, MS 195/3, pp.143–4, 163, 177, 186; Edinburgh University Library, Dc.7.123, pp.38–9, 41; Osborne, p.30.

3 Brewer, p.2 — Keneally, pp.65–7, 76–7, 84, 277–9 — Wertenbaker, pp.2, 7–11, 19–22.

4 Love[2], pp.8–12. The more recent, and fascinating, comments on convict theatre in Atkinson[3], pp.220–5, do not directly address this issue.

5 Linebaugh, pp.101–2.

6 Nicholas, pp.68–9.

7 Clark, pp.2–7.

8 For an example of social pressures hardened into house policy, see Nagle, p.153. Nagle, a First-Fleet sailor, was excluded from the boxes of a London theatre for wearing a sailor's short jacket, not a full coat.

9 For this view of late eighteenth- and early nineteenth-century theatres, see Lynch, pp.201–4; Price, pp.86–93; Pedicord[1], pp.19–20; Nicoll, pp.81–2; Donohue[2], pp.15–7.

10 Booth, pp.4–8; Pedicord[2], pp.251–2; Baer, pp.48–9.

11 Baer, pp.142–3.

12 *Times*, 16 & 17 August 1805; Gilliland, 1.155–8; *Spirit of the Public Journals* (1805), pp.245, 349.

13 *Times*, 20 December 1802; Boaden, 2.333–4.

14 Based on reports and obituaries in *Times*, 4 February 1794; *Star*, 5 February 1794; *Gentleman's Magazine*, 64 (January–June 1794), 187–8; Boaden, 2.112–3. To be fair, this audience might have been as atypical as that at a planned riot, since the king was to attend the theatre on this day.

15 Gilliland, 1.135–54.

16 Pedicord[1], pp.1–43.

17 Pedicord[1], pp.4–5; Leacroft, p.138.

18 Donaldson, pp.117–25; Sheridan[2], 3.116–21. For other examples, the first of which is colonial, see Barnard, pp.295–6; *Morning Chronicle*, 28 & 30 November, 2 December 1807; *Spirit of the Public Journals* (1808), pp.74–8.

19 Weston, p.12; Anon.[14], 2.27; Winston, p.46; Brown, pp.51–71; Lewes, 1.15 — Everard, pp.83–5; *Oracle*, 28 July 1797; *World*, 17–25 October 1792; *Ipswich Journal*, 1 March 1794; Hogan[1], pp.76–80; Hogan[2], pp.721–3.

20 Wontner, pp.307–13; Sheridan[1], p.10.

21 Reynolds, 2.381.

22 Cooke, pp.333–4.

23 Bernard, 2.291–2.

24 Vaux, pp.16, 151.

25 For Greville, see Appendix A: Mrs Greville; *SG*, 2 December 1804 — For Mackie, see *Star*, 21 June 1793; *OBSP*, December 1794, pp.190–1 & January 1796, pp.191–2.

26 Nicol, p.130 — For Sterne, see *World*, 5 June & 13 September 1787, *Public Advertiser*, 8 June 1787, *Times*, 23 June 1787, *Morning Chronicle*, 20 March 1788. — For Ackerman, see *London Packet*, 29 December 1798. See also Moritz, 2.525.

27 The improvidence of sailors is a motif that goes back as far as the Restoration at least

(see Ward, pp.100, 106). For specific examples with an Australian connection, see Kelly[2], pp.25, 78 and Vason, p.208.

28　Arundell, p.21.

29　British Theatre Museum, PN2595.5 K4, p.59 — Nicoll, p.41. The alterations to the Bristol theatre in 1800 would have reduced the proportion of gallery places even further. As a seaport Bristol should have been in the mould of Liverpool. The difference probably arose because Bristol was serviced by the exceptionally genteel Bath company.

30　Pasquin, 1.186, 187.

31　Dibdin[1], 2.296–306 — Cameron, pp.15–7. See also Winston, p.19; Parker, 1.163; Thomson, p.269.

32　Tyne and Wear Archives Office, 155/1/4 (entry for 1786) & 155/1/5 (Committee Book, 1804). See also Oswald, p.17, who gives slightly different pit, box and gallery figures from the latter.

33　Broadbent, p.123.

34　Everard, pp.228–9.

35　Snagg, p.37.

36　Mathews, 1.270.

37　Lewes, 1.43 — *Monthly Mirror*, 8 (1799), 246.

38　Bernard, 2.127.

39　Moritz, 2.513–4 — Kelly[1], pp.150–1.

40　Mathews, 1.275, 270.

41　Mather, p.93. 'The Cutlin Heroes' is in an appendix of local songs not attributed to Mather.

42　Goldsmith, 2.89.

43　*Oracle*, 14 March 1796; *Bell's Weekly Messenger*, 8 May 1796; *Star*, 25 June 1800; *Oracle*, 1 July 1800.

44　Marinetti, pp.116–22. See also the analysis by Levine of early nineteenth-century American audiences.

45　Colman, pp.48–52; Donohue[1], pp.29–51.

46　For Astley's, see BL, Theatre Cuttings no.36, 17 June & 19 July 1790, 5 July & 26 August 1791, 12 April 1792, 23 July 1793. — For the Royal Circus, see *World*, 3 & 18 September 1798, 6 October 1798.

47　Arundell, pp.14, 22, 33, 40, 48, 62.

48　*Daily Universal Register*, 22 December 1786. See also Byng, 1.49, 2.215, 2.411 & 3.149.

49　Everard, p.52 — Dibdin[2], p.80 — Bernard, 1.47, 125 — Brown, pp.59, 66. See also Ryley, 1.255.

50　Malcolm, 2.408. See also Wendenborn, 2.248 and Goede, 2.251–2.

51　Everard, pp.104, 105. See also Bernard, 2.128–30.

52　Goldsmith, 2.89.

53　Suttor, pp.12–3.

54　Brown, p.51.

55　Speckman, pp.31, 33; Cameron, pp.15–7; Anon.[5], pp.20–1.

56　Anon.[8], p.8.

57　Snagg, p.55 — Hare, p.xi — *Monthly Mirror*, n.s. 3 (1808), 340–1, 405–6 (but see also p.67) — Wilkinson, 2.236.

58　From the review of Jackman's *All the World's a Stage* in *London Chronicle*, 61 (1777), 336.

59　Anon.[15], p.59.

60   Dunlap, 1.13–4 — Bernard, 1.15.

61   *Times*, 23 November 1790; Cutspear, pp.35–6, 22. See also Anon.[9], p.41.

62   *European Magazine*, 53 (1808), 328 — Robson, p.41 — Thomson, pp.177–82. See also Dyer, pp.4–5 and, for a later date, Teasdale, pp.32–5.

63   Wilkinson, 3.176–88 — Fremantle, 3.211 — Halloran, pp.19–20 — Love[1], p.61.

64   Tilke, pp.45–8 — Teasdale, p.26 — Bond, pp.469–71 — Hone, pp.35–7, 538.

65   Grose[1], p.323.

66   For example, *Town and Country Magazine*, 2 (1779), 14; Barrington[1], p.134; Malcolm, 1.202–13; Ryley, 1.69; Weston, pp.3–4. For modern accounts, see Colby and Thieme.

67   Pasquin, 1.5 –11; Hall[3], p.8.

68   Snagg, p.26 — Anon.[14], 1.235–8.

69   Anon.[16], p.48; *Bonner and Middleton's Bristol Journal*, 25 June 1796; Barker, p.21.

70   Anon.[14], 2.19; Bernard, 1.41; Pasquin, 1.7.

71   Pasquin, 1.8–10.

72   Wagner, p.88.

73   Bee, p.164.

74   Tilke, p.66.

CHAPTER 2

1   Johnson[2], 1.24.

2   Easty, p.79.

3   Tench, p.152.

4   See, for example, SRNSW, SZ765, pp.133–6, 183–6. The second of these, nine days after *The Recruiting Officer*, included the comic actor William Hogg, and a fiddler.

5   Maclehose, pp.128–9.

6   Fowles, p.33.

7   Tench, p.60; Collins, 1.25; Bradley, 1.112–3; ML, MS6544 (Waterhouse letter of 11 July 1788); Fowell, pp.84, 112; Clark, pp.139, 202; King, pp.85, 247–8; Knopwood, p.84.

8   Tench, p.60.

9   Collins, 1.57–8.

10   Tench, p.152.

11   Clark, pp.25–6, 75–7.

12   Captain Hyndman. See Chapter 7.

13   Irving, p.296.

14   Anon.[4], p.xi. How some of them replenished their finery is suggested by the fatal dispute between Mary Pool and the sailor, John Smith (see Paine, pp.24, 26).

15   SRNSW, 5/1147A, p.151. See also Elliot.

16   Flinders, 1.229 — *SG*, 5 June 1803 & 22 January 1804. For the 46 officers on 4 June 1802, see PRO, WO12/9901, pp.119–37; PRO, ADM36/15885, pp.108–15; ML, MS508, item 8; ML, MS509, item 4; *HRNSW*, 4.933, 935. By 1800 there were a few officers' wives and respectable civilians who could have been used to build up the numbers and in 1802 there were also 3 scientists with Flinders. Five British whaling and sealing vessels were in port at the time. Their captains might have been considered eligible to attend.

17   Lambeth Palace Library, ARCH/P/Moore 22, item 1, pp.9–10. A tile shed was also used as a church in the early days of Hobart (see Knopwood, p.97).

18   Dobson, 2.55–7.

19 Brick-making had been established there by March 1788 (Collins, 1.17). For references to tile-making, see Tench, pp.192–3; Collins, 1.277–8.

20 Collins, 1.63.

21 On the other hand, in a return of labour in Sydney for 1797, curiously mixed up with boat-builders' work, appears 'made sheds ... for the brickmakers, the former ones having been suffered to go to decay' (*HRNSW*, 3.337). Boatsheds and tile sheds are similar in construction.

22 Johnson, 1.42.

23 ANL, MS 164, fol.80ʳ. See also *HRNSW*, 5.209.

24 See, for example, Waterhouse's draft reply on the verso of Sir Joseph Banks' letter of 7 June 1806 (ML, MS6544) and Lambeth Palace Library, ARCH/P/Moore 22, item 2, p.55.

25 Collins, 1.408.

26 Vaux, pp.105–6.

27 Cumpston, p.30.

28 Collins, 1.375. Later references to this account of the theatre's opening are not footnoted.

29 *Aris's Birmingham Gazette*, 24 September 1798.

30 Bernard, 1.160. Bloseville, p.300, describes similar transactions in a Spanish village.

31 Ryley, 1.101.

32 Jordan¹, pp.48–9, note 18.

33 Lee, 1.125–6.

34 *Daily Universal Register*, 18 February 1785; *Dramatic Censor* (1800), 149; *Oracle*, 4 July 1800 & 29 August 1801.

35 PRO, ADM51/4023, 52/3468; PRO, ADM 51/1169, 52/3352; National Maritime Museum, ADM/L/R/73. The logs are in nautical time, with pm on 16 January entered as the first part of 17 January.

36 Watts, pp.vii, 84. This collection contains two authentic prologues for the opening of new English provincial theatres, both attributed to Carter.

37 As published in *European Magazine*, 40 (October 1801), 289–90. This is the earliest publication of the prologue that I have discovered. *The Annual Register ... for the Year 1801*, often cited as the earliest publication, would not have appeared before September or October 1802.

38 Davoren, pp.13-6.

39 Gentleman, 2.331–3; Boaden, 2.305. Kalman Burnim, in a private letter, has observed that 'it was seldom acted in London in the last half of the eighteenth century, and Zanga seems to have been a favourite role for newcomers who didn't last very long'. John Philip Kemble had added the part to his repertoire on 19 January 1789, but had performed it only another 4 times before the Sydney opening seven years later, and so is unlikely to have been the inspiration for the antipodean production (Van Lennep, 5.2.1124–5, 1152, 1411, 1595). The play had a further revival in fortunes in the early nineteenth century, with Edmund Kean attempting the part of the Moor (Foster², p.73).

40 *Gazeteer*, 23 & 25 November 1776; *Morning Chronicle*, 22 November 1776. For a more favourable response see *Morning Post*, 22 November 1776. For London performances, see Van Lennep, 5.3.9, 38–42, 55. Fitzsimmons records 5 performances in York in 1777 and 3 in 1778. Hare records only 3 at Bath, in December 1776–January 1777.

41 Wilkinson, 1.255, 2.81–2, 4.20.

42 For further details, see Appendix A: William Richards. A respectably connected servant

of the York manager, Tate Wilkinson, had also made the voyage to Australia as a convict, bringing several boxes with him. While he seems to have had a senior post in Wilkinson's household, he had little or no contact with the theatre, his thefts being from shops and including two volumes of the plays of Otway. In addition, he had died in the colony in 1793, well before the theatre's opening. See Anon.[18] and Wilkinson, 3.157–65, 191, 212–4.

43   Collins, 1.379;   India Office Records, L/MAR/B/215I.
44   *HRNSW*, 3.15–22, 64–7; Collins, 1.379–80; PRO, CO201/13, fols 188ʳ–90ʳ.
45   *Oracle*, 13 July 1797; *Monthly Mirror*, 4 (July 1797), 56–7; *Sporting Magazine*, 10 (July 1797), 208; *Felix Farley's Bristol Journal*, 22 July 1797.
46   SRNSW, SZ765, pp.390–1.
47   The emergence of this idea is traced in Thorne, 1.3–4.
48   Mann, p.54.
49   Wallis, p.33 — Therry, p.61— Heaton, p.87.
50   Ferguson[1], p.19.
51   Noah, p.70.
52   See Appendix A: John William Lancashire.
53   Wilkinson, 2.191.
54   SRNSW, SZ767, p.70.
55   Irving, pp.319–20.
56   SRNSW, SZ766, p.84; SRNSW, SZ767, pp.84, 102, 139; *SG*, 7 August & 6 November 1803; PRO, CO201/10, p.194. Hennings was also a writer of doggerel verse (see *SG*, 17 February 1805).
57   SRNSW, SZ767, p.111.
58   SRNSW, SZ767, pp.124–5.
59   ML, Safe 1/107; *Sporting Magazine*, 19 (1801), 225–6.
60   Harriott, 1.181; Knight, 1.46; Neville, p.11; *Bell's Weekly Messenger*, 10 February 1805; *Oracle*, 21 July 1801.
61   Janson, p.247.
62   ML, A2019, p.171.
63   ML, A3609, p.22.
64   Cumpston, p.46.
65   Eastwick, p.196.
66   Eastwick, p.307; *Asiatic Mirror*, 30 October & 12 November 1816.
67   *HRNSW*, 7.477.
68   Fitzgerald, pp.92–4; Atkinson[3], pp.264–91 — *HRNSW*, 6.155–6, 175.
69   Mann, p.54.
70   *HRNSW*, 6.275–6.
71   Vaux, p.18.
72   Vaux, pp.29, 32, 42, 48–9, 151.
73   Vaux, pp.101, 105–6.

CHAPTER 3

1   For Richmond, see Southern, pp.46–51; Leacroft, pp.156–60.
2   Winston, p.11.
3   Winston, p.12. For another eccentric arrangement, see London's Olympic Theatre of 1807 (Mander, p.113). This, however, was designed for equestrian performances.

4 Jordan[1], 30–52. The next few pages rearrange elements from this article. Accordingly, footnotes are limited chiefly to direct quotations, changes to the original, and new material.

5 Harriott, 1.176–83.

6 Winston, p.12.

7 *HRNSW*, 2.65, 201.

8 Collins, 1.403.

9 *HRA*, 1.2.560; *HRNSW*, 3.139, 2.65–6; Macintosh, pp.68–71.

10 Winston, p.22; British Theatre Museum, PN2595.5 K4, p.50.

11 *HRNSW*, 4.152(*bis*), 3.340. For completion of the Sydney building, see *HRNSW*, 3.505.

12 I am indebted to Richard Fotheringham for this reference.

13 *HRA*, 1.4.319.

14 See Parsons, p.529.

15 Winston, facing p.46. For a reproduction, see Jordan[1], p.40.

16 Winston, pp.46, 22.

17 Noah, p.70 — BL, Add. MS 13880, fol.80[v].

18 McCormick, plate 79.

19 BL, Add. MS 13880, fol.79[v].

20 McGuire, p.7 — Anon.[2], p.37.

21 Collins, 2.93 — McCormick, plate 54.

22 For more details of the case just outlined, see Jordan[2], pp.136–9.

23 Quoted, unsourced, in Shaw, p.67.

24 Wentworth, p.7 — Bigge[1], p.30; Bigge[2], pp.62, 70.

25 *SG*, 14 August 1803.

26 The surveyor's field book of 1815 still reveals many of the rougher dwellings in place (SRNSW, 2/4745, no.108).

27 Meehan's 1808 map marks this track as Church Street and shows Nathaniel Lucas' house at the end of it closest to Windmill Row. In the *Sydney Gazette*, 21 September 1816, what is almost certainly the same dwelling is described as '28 Prince street, at the back of the Church'.

28 Isaac Peyton's stone-built house was said by the *Sydney Gazette*, 28 June 1807, to be 'at the corner of Windmill Row, Rocks' and could be the house listed as No. 1, Windmill Row, in the surveyor's notebook of 1815 (SRNSW, 2/4745, no.108).

29 McCormick, plates 53, 64. Lesueur's original 1802 drawing (plate 64) is too faint to allow interpretation.

30 Notably *SG*, 19 June 1813, but also 20 June 1812, 23 August 1817 & 22 December 1821.

31 SRNSW, SZ767, pp.114–5.

32 For the 'Leaping Bar', see *SG*, 21 August 1808. — For Taber, see Johnson[1], p.4; *SG*, 10 November 1805; SRNSW, 4/1822, no.303; SRNSW, 4/1778, p.88.

33 From its first number, 5 March 1803, the *Sydney Gazette* notes the Saturday arrival of produce boats from Kissing Point, sometimes specifically identifying them as market boats (*SG*, 24 August 1806).

34 Baer, p.88; Fremantle, 3.171–2.

35 Marsden, pp.7,8,35 — Paine, p.34 — ANL, MS 0439, pp.175–6.

36 *Sydney Monitor*, 15 November 1828; ML, A291, p.343; ML, A851, pp.126–7.

37 ML, A3609, p.22.

38 Jordan[2], note 46.

39 Jordan[2], notes 47, 48.

40   West², p.12.

41   Holcroft², 1.163; Sumbel, 1.29. Pasquin, 1.192, refers to a band of two fiddlers in a barn theatre.

42   Hodgson, p.78; Mathews, p.191. See also Everard, p.100.

43   Turner, 2.14–5; Kappey, pp.87–8 — Péron, p.273. In the quarterly pay lists from 25 October 1808 to 24 March 1810 several regular soldiers, varying in number between four and seven, are noted as members of the band (PRO, WO12/9904, fol.299ʳ–12/9905, fol.9ᵛ). The record may be incomplete and there may also have been civilians involved who were funded separately and did not appear in the pay lists. Military bands commonly included (or were completely composed of) civilians. For a special showing the band could also have been augmented by the drummers and fifers, who were regular soldiers with specific military functions, one of each to a company.

44   Trendall, p.9; Farmer, p.56.

45   SRNSW, SZ768, pp.19, 21. For non-military fiddlers, see also *SG*, 15 May 1803, James Strong in Gillen¹, p.348, and possibly the obituary of Michael Robinson (*Australian*, 25 November 1826).

46   Holcroft², 1.153–4; Moore², pp.186, 94; Parker, 1.xi, 27–9, 51–5, 59–60; Dibdin², p.80; Snagg, p.106.

47   The York figures are 1s. for a scene-shifter and 2s. for a cash-handler (York Public Library, Y792/S/R). I have inflated these figures in line with my later comments on wage rates in Sydney.

48   Tucker¹, pp.102, 117.

49   *HRNSW*, 3.197.

50   *HRNSW*, 4.31.

51   *Star*, 18 January 1800; *HRNSW*, 4.109.

52   Troubridge, *passim*.

53   Van Lennep, 5.3.1909–45. In the interval between the premiere of *Fortune's Fool* and Mrs Parry's arrest two other new comedies had been staged successfully.

54   Boaden, 1.343.

55   Straub, pp.131–5; *Daily Universal Register*, 13 September 1785, 15 February & 6 July 1786 and *Times*, 22 March 1790.

56   Hazlitt, p.145.

57   Hunt¹, p.263.

58   SRNSW, SZ767, p.111; SRNSW, 5/1149, p.258; SRNSW, 1147B, p.353. The William Miller who escaped the murder conviction may have been another person of the same name, but Miller the entrepreneur had interests at Kissing Point, where the crime took place. In 1805 a William Miller was charged with threatening behaviour towards James Wood at Kissing Point (see SRNSW, SZ768, p.572).

CHAPTER 4

1   Footnotes have not been provided for information about individual convicts and others, where it is to be found in biographical sketches of them in Appendix A.

2   Respectively, John Sparrow, Henry Green, William Chapman, William Foulkes (or Fowkes), George Henry Hughes.

3   Respectively, William Richards, Philip Parry, Daniel Parnell, Beckwith Smith and Henry Parsons.

4   ANL, MS 737 (letter of 13 July 1804); ML, Safe 1/45, p.618. Campbell, of course, fell

into that category shortly to be described, the son of a gentleman obliged to go into trade. Eastwick, pp.183–4, provides an interesting example of Commissary Palmer endangering his genteel status by acting too much the merchant.

5   Caley, pp.81–2 — PRO, CO201/10, fol.262^v; ML, A2015, pp.227, 230; PRO, CO201/31, fol.114^r. For a much more detailed analysis than I have attempted of the relationship between social status and occupation among the lower orders, see Tracey McAskill's article on the New South Wales Corps.

6   Dunlop, pp.134–42, 248–60; Howe, pp.110–33.

7   Michael Massey Robinson, whose gentility is confirmed by the records of the Inns of Court (Foster^3, p.389; Carr, p.290), had mastered this art of self-presentation to perfection. On the voyage out 'from the superiority of his manners and behaviour, [he] ingratiated himself so happily with the captain and officers as to be allowed a situation entirely remote and detached from the convicts, where … he was indulged every day with a bottle of wine and a cover from the captain's table' (HRNSW, 3.728).

8   Times, 28 April 1790 (but cp. 16 January 1786); Observer, 9 March 1800 — Star, 2 June 1800.

9   Neuberg, pp.57–89; Laqueur, pp.43–57; Schofield, pp.437–54 — ML, MS6544 (letter of 7 June 1806).

10 Holcroft^2, 1.142, 156; Pasquin, 1.213–4 — Lackington, p.87.

11 Blagden, p.248.

12 HRNSW, 4.65. See also Eastwick, pp.199–200; Smith^4, p.213.

13 For Barrington and Robertson, see ADB. — For Stogdell, see pp. 100 above. — For J.J. Grant, see Scottish Record Office, GD243/351/7; GD248/693/2; GD248/701/3; ANL, MS 737 (letter of 22 May 1804), p.19; Palmer, pp.14–5; Flynn^2, pp.58–61 — For Davoren, see SRNSW, 5/1147B, pp.228–9; Davoren, p.32. — For John Grant, see Hill-Reid and Cramer, passim.

14 Collins, 1.327; HRA, 1.3.657, 660.

15 Scottish Record Office, GD248/351/7.

16 Vaux, pp.101–2.

17 Griffin, pp.272–3. The attribution to Delaforce is conjectural.

18 Nicol, pp.132, 134. For an even more romantic version, see Wynn, pp.5–10. See also Eastwick, pp.184–7.

19 Times, 29 & 30 November 1790 and 2, 4 & 6 December 1790; Observer, 25 July 1802; Aris's Birmingham Gazette, 2 August 1802; Oracle, 14 June 1800; ANL, MS 115, p.13.

20 Nicol, pp.136–7, 131–2.

21 For some of the more immediately relevant examples from the extensive literature on women convicts, see Summers, passim, Sturma, passim, and Hughes, pp.244–64. Apart from Oxley's vigorous article in Duffield, pp.88–105, the more recent studies of female convicts (Damousi, Daniels) are not greatly concerned with the ideology and psychopathology of the male commentators of the period.

22 Maclehose, p.129.

23 Collins, 1.375 — BL, Add. MS 13880, fol.80^v — Eastwick, p.196.

24 Eastwick, pp.307–8 — ML, ZB190^2, p.60; ML, Dixson, ZQ181, pp.259–60; Anon.^{12}, p.295; Sydney Herald, 19 October 1841.

25 Mann, p.54.

26 Population return, 12 June 1795 (HRNSW, 2.310). The next available return, for 31 August 1796 (HRNSW, 3.92–3), includes over 200 convicts and reinforcements for the New South Wales Corps, who had arrived on 11 February 1796.

27   BL, Add. MS 13880, fol.80ᵛ.

28   ANL, MS 737 (letter of 2 May 1804), p.15.

29   SRNSW, SZ768, pp.621–2. Presumably, within the society of unmarried officers, there was a more relaxed attitude to fellow officers' *de facto*s. See Whitaker², pp.41–2, 50–1; Currey, pp.241–4.

30   Harris, pp.73, 137.

31   ML, Safe 1/48, p.251.

32   Paine, p.32.

33   ML, A2019, p.171.

34   Mann, p.vi.

35   *OBSP*, 20 October 1784, p.1356.

36   For Stogdell's household possessions, see ML, A2019, pp.113–20. These included pictures in black and gilt frames, a view of Port Jackson, a fiddle, two flutes, '1 pʳ Prints Tragedy &c' and 22 books, including several volumes of poetry and philosophy as well as music scores. For his marriage, see RONSW, Marriages.4.187; for his curricle BL, Add. MS 13880, fol.82ʳ. — For Waterhouse's comment, see his draft reply on the verso of Sir Joseph Banks' letter of 7 June 1806 (ML, MS6544). — On Stogdell's death, see Anon.¹⁰, p.29.

37   Lambeth Palace Library, ARCH/P/Moore, part 2, p.55 — ML, MS6544 (Waterhouse's draft reply on verso of Sir Joseph Banks' letter of 7 June 1806).

38   Whitaker¹, p.47.

39   O'Farrell, pp.25–6. See also Troy, pp.160–70.

40   Reid¹, p.557 — Mathews, p.110.

41   *HRA*, 1.4.83; Kiernan, p.13. For disputes about the number of political prisoners, see Kiernan, *passim*; Rudé¹, p.24 and Whitaker¹, pp.23–32.

42   Perkins, p.86.

43   *Sydney Morning Herald*, 24 September 1994, p.5 — *SG*, 23 May 1812.

44   Smith², pp.26–64.

45   For example, 'The Drunken Peasant', 'The Drunken Sailor Reclaim'd' and 'The Drunken German'. See Van Lennep, 5.2.182, 867 etc.; *Times*, 26 January 1807; BL, Playbills 252 (Theatre Royal, Manchester: 5 January 1804).

46   For West and 'The Drunken Swiss', see Highfill, 16.1–2; Van Lennep, 5.2.1090, 1152 & 5.3.1590, 1597, 1599.

47   Odell, 2.116, 148.

48   PRO, CO201/10, fol.135ᵛ (see also fol.323ᵛ), fol.8ᵛ (see also fol.344ʳ).

49   Eastwick, p.196.

50   Waterhouse², pp.22–5 — *Monitor*, 18 August & 17 November 1826, 15 June 1827; *Sydney Monitor*, 13 October 1828.

51   *Bell's Weekly Messenger*, 8 May 1796; *Oracle*, 1 July 1800; BL, Theatre Cuttings no. 44, 9 November 1794.

52   ANL, MS 737, p.136.

53   *HRNSW*, 3.348, 3.359–60, 4.765.

54   *HRNSW*, 3.495, 3.669, 4.15.

55   *HRNSW*, 5.419.

56   Russell, p.16 — *Dramatic Censor*, 1.15, 46–7, 171 — Reynolds, 2.198–9.

57   *SG*, 7 March 1828 — Anon.¹⁷, p.44 — ANL, MS 737 (letter of 1 January 1805), p.5. Even before this personal experience had sharpened his perceptions, Grant had regarded the

paper as so much under King's control as to write of the governor as its 'Editor' (letter of 2 May 1804, p.12).

58 Schultz, pp.226–69; *Sporting Magazine,* 19 (1801), 226. Boaden ,1.201–2, referred to the play as a 'systematic ... denigration of the higher orders', which worked on the principle that 'if you can destroy the traditional and voluntary, or involuntary, RESPECT, paid to rank and station, those distinctions themselves may be speedily swept away'. On 13 May 1805 the *Morning Chronicle* reported a disturbance during a production of the work at Drury Lane, where Gay's version of 'Greensleeves' (Air 67) 'produced a torrent of applause of an extraordinary kind' and was encored three times:

> Since Laws were made for ev'ry Degree,
> To curb Vice in others, as well as me,
> I wonder we ha'nt better Company,
>> Upon Tyburn Tree!
> But Gold from Law can take out the Sting;
> And if rich Men like us were to swing,
> 'Twou'd thin the Land, such Numbers to string
>> Upon Tyburn Tree!

It is almost impossible to imagine the Botany Bay authorities welcoming sentiments such as those on the Sydney convict stage.

59 PRO, CO201/15, fol.106ʳ.
60 PRO, CO201/15, fols 104ᵛ, 106ʳ.
61 Collins, 1.379.
62 *Oracle,* 14 July 1797 — *Morning Chronicle,* 18 July 1797 — *True Briton,* 20 July 1797 — *Star,* 27 July 1797 — *Craftsman,* 26 August 1797.
63 Chisholm, 1.438–9; Ferguson², 1.133.
64 Anon.¹, p.19.
65 Blosseville, p.300. For the key position of this volume in the French debates about penal settlements, see Forster, pp.72–91.

CHAPTER 5

1   *HRNSW,* 2.747.
2   *HRNSW,* 2.777.
3   Nobbs¹, p. 213.
4   *HRNSW,* 2.32–3 (cp. 2.71).
5   Collins, 1.200.
6   See pp.1–3 of George Caley's account of a visit to the island in late 1806 (ML, FM4/2568).
7   *HRNSW,* 2.32–3.
8   PRO, CO201/9, fols 247ʳ–56ᵛ; ML, A2015, p.169; *HRA,* 1.2.158–60.
9   *HRA,* 1.2.114, 158, 519.
10 Ryan¹, p.227. See also ML, A256, p.667.
11 *HRNSW,* 2. 125, 303.
12 PRO, CO201/10, fol.8ᵛ.
13 PRO, CO201/10, fol.323ᵛ; *HRNSW,* 2.303–4.
14 Wilson¹, 1.18–20 — PRO, CO201/10, fols 323ᵛ, 324ʳ.
15 Key documents such as King's reports to Grose and Dundas and Grose's response, are reproduced in *HRNSW,* 2.103–10, 135–90.
16 *ADB,* 1.2.

17   PRO, CO201/10, fol.5^v.

18   PRO, CO201/10, fol.104^r.

19   PRO, CO201/10, fol.54^r.

20   PRO, CO201/10, fols 11^v, 95^r.

21   *HRNSW*, 5.101–2 — Ritchie[1], pp.26, 114–6, 405.

22   PRO, CO201/10, fol.95^v.

23   PRO, CO201/10, fols 92^v, 102^r.

24   PRO, CO201/10, fol.9^r.

25   PRO, CO201/10, fol.102^{r-v}.

26   PRO, CO201/10, fol.344^r — ML, A81, p.275.

27   PRO, CO201/10, fol.180^{r-v}, quoted below in Appendix A: Thomas Restell Crowder.

28   PRO, CO201/10, fol.344^{r-v}; Appendix B, Note 8.

29   An engraving by James Wright, after a painting by W.R. Pyne, it is reproduced in Mackintosh, plate 312.

30   PRO, CO201/10, fol.323^v. This comment is omitted from the ANL version of the journal, MS 70, pp.88–9.

31   PRO, CO201/10, fol.97^r.

32   PRO, CO201/10, fol.97^r.

33   PRO, CO201/10, fol.95^v.

34   Collins, 1.358.

35   Hill-Reid, p.132.

36   I owe a debt of gratitude to Richard Waterhouse and Grace Karskens for bringing this manuscript to my attention. I am assuming the Sydney of its title relates to the place of discovery and has nothing to do with the fact that the main settlement on Norfolk Island was also called Sydney.

37   The abbreviation 'D^r' is 'debtor' and 'p^r' is *'per'*, indicating the person who made or collected the purchase on behalf of the theatre. Latin dates, for example 'Die Lund' (Monday), 'Die Martis' (Tuesday), 'Die Saturni' (Saturday), are employed consistently throughout the book, but are not a feature of any other Botany Bay merchant's records with which I am familiar.

38   Entries for 16 & 20 December 1805.

39   Whitaker[1], pp.67, 70; ML, B437, 7 January & 6 March 1806.

40   For Robinson and Redfern, see *ADB*.

41   *OBSP*, February 1797, pp.213–5; *Oracle*, 7 & 10 February 1797; *St James Chronicle*, 4–7 & 9–11 February 1797; *Star*, 7 & 10 February 1797; SRNSW, 4/4486, p.51; *Launceston Examiner*, 20 June 1849; Launceston Reference Library, Richard White File. I have been unable to inspect the Allport Library MS by H.B. Holmes, 'The Claytons of Wickford', which contains information on him.

42   *OBSP*, January 1790, pp.198–9 — PRO, CO201/18, fol.167^r; PRO, CO201/55, fol.45^r; PRO, CO201/71, fols 17^r, 74^r; ML, BT Box 49, p.5 — ML, B437, 26 December 1805, 8 February & 8 March 1806 (as an actor), 26 June 1806 (as a company administrator).

43   ML, A1677, p.118.

44   *World*, 11 January 1790.

45   Gillen[1], pp.39-40.

46   Baxter[2], p.185 (D0074).

47   ML, B437, 31 December 1806, 8 March 1806 and, possibly, 16 & 20 January 1806 & 20 February 1806.

48   Collins, 2.75; Schaffer², pp.109–12.

49   PRO, CO201/10, fol.102ᵛ.

50   PRO, CO201/10, fols 98ᵛ, 102ʳ⁻ᵛ, 95ᵛ.

51   The ex-convicts were Thomas Spencer, John Cohn Walsh (or Welsh), John Best and
      James Dodding, Walsh being seated with his wife and child. The ex-marine was John
      McCarthy and the constable John Herbert.

52   PRO, CO201/10, fol.92ʳ.

53   PRO, CO201/10, fol.12ᵛ.

54   The four convict theatregoers identified in the affidavits were John Jones, James Cham,
      Sarah Gregg and Thomas Glaves. Glaves may have been in the front row, since Flynn¹,
      p.291, describes him as Balmain's servant, though the court records (PRO, CO201/10,
      fol.103ᵛ) suggest he was the Commissary's. Peter Hopley, recently free by servitude, and
      Charles Rogers, a serving convict, were identified as playgoers in the records of the
      post-performance riot. The four other civilians mentioned in the riot were convicts
      Charles Cooper, John Malcolm, Joseph Hall and William Fawcett. Malcolm, a watchman,
      had probably arrived after the show, in the line of duty, but the others could well have
      been at the performance.

55   See Colley, pp.232–6, for the use of this imagery in late eighteenth-century England.
      The brief comments on its colonial application in Nichol², pp.10–1, include an example
      of King applying it directly to himself.

56   Tindall and William Green. Neither appears in the 1805–06 Norfolk Island victualling
      books (SRNSW, 4/1167A–B) or the 1805 muster in Baxter².

57   John Barry, John Best, William Fisher, Edward Kimberley, Robert Nash and Joseph
      Simmonds, of whom the last named was still a convict. Their positions are as recorded
      in the 1805 muster in Baxter².

58   The ex-convicts were John Boyle, James Dodding, Andrew Goodwin, James Morrisby
      and George Whittaker. Whittaker's career is slightly confused, and at this stage he seems
      to have been not only a long-term resident of the island and a farmer, but also a private
      in the New South Wales Corps (see Gillen¹, pp.378–9 and Statham, p.355). For Beresford's
      land-holdings, see ML, C191, fols 2ʳ, 4ᵛ; Nobbs¹, pp.123–4.

59   Schaffer², pp.206–7.

60   Schaffer², p.220; West¹, 1.50 — ML, B437, 8 February 1806; von Stieglitz, pp.34–6;
      Skemp, pp.16–30; Hall¹, pp.138–41.

61   For prior trades, see PRO, CO201/9, fols 265ʳ and for Morrisby as guardsman and
      watchman, see OBSP, July 1784, pp.927–8. Evidence of their illiteracy can be found, for
      Dodding, in PRO, CO201/55, fol.34ʳ and, for the others, in PRO, CO201/9, fols 137ʳ,
      180ᵛ; PRO, CO201/30, fols 232ᵛ, 233ᵛ, 107ᵛ, 111ʳ and PRO, CO201/42, fols 7ʳ, 86ʳ⁻7ᵛ.

62   For Barry and Fisher's illiteracy, see PRO, CO201/42, fols 7ᵛ, 86ʳ; PRO, CO201/55,
      fol.72ʳ. — For signatures of the others, see PRO, CO201/10, fols 180ʳ, 182ᵛ; PRO,
      CO201/30, fols 19ᵛ–20ʳ, 42ʳ, 227ʳ; PRO, CO201/42, fols 7ʳ⁻ᵛ, 14ʳ, 86ᵛ, 87ʳ. — Kimberley's
      earlier illiteracy is revealed in RONSW, Marriages.4.128; PRO, CO201/9, fol.182ʳ (the
      last of these dating from 1793).— For trades and backgrounds, see PRO, CO201/9, fols
      265ʳ–7ᵛ. — For Fisher in the boat crew, see Clark, p.132. — For Nash, see Wright¹,
      pp.128–9.

63   PRO, CO201/21, fols 339ᵛ, 345ʳ.

64   ML, Safe 1/2d, p.26. — For doubts concerning the authenticity of the Jones MS, see Wright².

65   SRNSW, 4/1168B, p.58; PRO, CO201/29, fol.233ʳ; PRO, WO25/2170, p.74.

66   For the convict servant, William Haley, see Baxter[2], p.193 (DO426). — For Sutton, see
      Whitaker[1], p.213; ML, A1980, fol.306[r–v]; ML, A2015, p.504.
67   PRO, CO201/42, fol.310[v].

CHAPTER 6

1   Daniels, pp.136–7; Ignatieff, pp.40–1.
2   Foster[4], pp.35–7, 75. Between 1834 and 1839, for example, over 65% convicts were in
      private hands, the bulk of them outside Sydney and Parramatta, with 1838 the peak year
      for convict assignment. Landholders with large estates often had over 50 assignees, a
      sufficient number to generate play performances, as Emu Plains demonstrated in 1830,
      but no evidence of any such activity has been found.
3   HRNSW, 7.477.
4   ML, BT Box 12, p.56.
5   Maclehose, p.129.
6   West[3], p.17.
7   SRNSW, SZ916, Field Book 106. See also SRNSW, Map 5403; SRNSW, 4/1219, Part 5.
8   OBSP, December 1805, pp.65–72; HRA, 1.20.757–8, 1.25.517–8 and 1.26.11–2.
9   Bigge[2], p.70; Mellish, p.54; SRNSW, SZ770, 10 February 1810.
10   Allen, p.48.
11   ANL, MS 195/3, pp.47–8, 53, 54, 58.
12   Cowper, p.72.
13   SRNSW, 4/1752, p.30.
14   SG, 4 February 1815, 17 January 1818, 14 October 1820, 27 January, 18 August 1821,
      and 18 January 1822.
15   SRNSW, 4/1752, p.31.
16   SRNSW, 4/1759, p.71.
17   SRNSW, 4/1219, Part 5 — SRNSW, 4/4520, p.19 — Baxter[5], p.314 (A13796), p.423
      (A18671). By 16 September McKeen had moved to Elizabeth Street, with his wife-to-be
      assigned to him as a servant. Saunders had moved to Pitt Street by 1 November, when he
      was assigned a male servant (SRNSW, 4/4570D, pp.56, 29).
18   Bigge[1], p.30.
19   For Brown, see Chelmsford Chronicle 7, 21 & 28 March 1794; PRO, ASS1 35/234/1 and
      31/17 — Ganges indent — SRNSW, 4/4430, p.19 — Baxter[5], p.57 (AO2374); SRNSW,
      SZ 759, p.411. For Saunders, see OBSP, May 1814, p.287. — SRNSW, 4/5781, p.82 —
      Baxter[5], p.423 (A18671) and note 20, below. For McKeen, see Lady Castlereagh indent. —
      SRNSW, 4/4520, p.19. For Tyson, see OBSP, January 1817, pp.104–5. — Almorah indent
      — ML, Dixson, Spencer 54, pp.334–5; PRO, CO201/121, fol.574[r]; SRNSW, 4/6360, 8
      May 1820 — SRNSW, 4/1868, p.28 — Baxter[5], p.486 (A21480).
20   SRNSW, 4/3864, no.57–5 — SRNSW, 4/6281, p.55. He had been convicted on 4
      November 1823 for obtaining goods under false pretenses from various shops. On 12
      May 1821 he had been sentenced to 2 years at Newcastle on a similar charge, though
      evidently he managed to secure a ticket-of-leave for the Sydney area by early 1822 (SRNSW,
      4/6360, 12 May 1821 & 4 November 1823). On 27 June 1828 he received a 12-month
      sentence at Windsor for theft, being sent to Moreton Bay (Queensland State Archives,
      Film 0078, p.30).
21   Maclehose, pp.129–30.
22   Bigge[2], p.86.

23   *SG*, 28 June 1826. The *Sydney Gazette*, 29 December 1825, gives a figure of 12, while the
     paper of 9 June 1825 has it as low as 7.
24   *SG*, 9 June 1825, 28 June 1826.
25   *ADB*, 1.506–7; Grose², pp.85–111 — *SG*, 5 April 1826; *Australian*, 24 May 1826. The
     affairs of the Sydney Grammar School are reported extensively in all the newspapers in
     1826 with the suspension of operations in the *Monitor*, 27 October 1826.
26   Halloran, pp.19–20 — *Spirit of the Public Journals* (1806), p.117.
27   Irvin¹, pp.1–76.
28   The sections of the novel about Rashleigh and his fellow-convicts' theatrical adventures
     are in Chapters XII and XIV, Tucker¹, pp. 97–102 & 116–22.
29   *HRA*, 1.10.693, 279, 533, 680.
30   Havard, p.248; Anon.¹³, p.113; *HRA*, 1.10.681 & 693, 1.11.79 & 549, 1.14.637 & 1.15.386.
     These figures represent general trends. There were also short-term fluctuations due to
     the dispatch of clearing parties, or to the drafting of men from Hyde Park Barracks to
     help with the harvest.
31   *ADB*, 2.10–2; Fletcher, pp.1–29; Murray, pp.187–97, 275–87. For his assigned servants,
     see Ryan¹, p.7, but cp. SRNSW, 4/1239. For his tenant farmers, see ML, A2012, p.53.
32   ML, A2012, p.43.
33   ML, Dixson, Q168, item 1, p.57. For Lawrence in England and America, see pp. 7–8, 11,
     12. — PRO, CO201/119, fol.363ʳ — SRNSW, 4/4525, p.17 — SRNSW, 2/8283, pp.170,
     173.
34   The other reports are in *Australian*, 26 May 1825 and *SG*, 21 July 1825.
35   His arrest will have post-dated 18 September 1823, when the *Sydney Gazette* recorded
     him receiving a duplicate of his certificate of freedom. On 16 September his wife-to-be
     had been assigned to him as a servant (SRNSW, 4/4570D, p.56). His performances must
     have been in the not-too-distant past for them to be remembered as they were in July
     1826. Of course, the phrase 'the company of comedians at Emu Plains' could be a
     mocking way of referring to the entire establishment, not a specific pointer to McKeen's
     involvement as a player, even further reducing its significance, though it is difficult to
     imagine him being at the settlement without being involved in any productions that took
     place during his residence.
36   Bougainville, pp.89–90, 95, 102–3.
37   *SG*, 29 September 1825.
38   SRNSW, 4/3665, p.277.
39   ML, Z4661, pp.131–2.
40   Tucker¹, pp.99, 118.
41   O'Connell, p.65 — SRNSW, 4/2088, no.30/8715 (enclosed with 31/3856).
42   Tucker¹, p.97.
43   SRNSW, Maps 2660 (see Fig. 14) and 2669 — Tucker¹, p.78.
44   Tucker¹, pp.78–9.
45   Tucker¹, p.97.
46   Tucker¹, pp.98, 102. The text on p.98 is mangled. The reconstruction includes a few
     words from the 1962 edition (pp.92–3) used to fill out lacunae in the original.
47   Tucker², pp.116, 97, 119. Painted drop or traverse curtains were probably used to close
     the back of the scene. The most likely means of changing scenery was the conventional
     English groove system, and, since even the temporary theatre at the inn (in the novel)
     had a raised stage, Emu Plains would certainly have had one, making the installation of

grooves a relatively simple task. A raised stage could also have accommodated a rudimentary stage trap.

48   Lewis, p. 34. There is another version of *Raymond and Agnes*, by Henry William Grosette, which has much less spectacle, but was relatively unknown. The 'Monk' Lewis version was much more readily available.

49   *SG*, 21 July 1825.

50   This discussion of settings and machinery owes much to John Golder, who, incidentally, pointed out that there is a character in *Rob Roy Macgregor* called Rashleigh Osbaldistone. Is this the source of the name James Tucker gave to the eponymous hero of his novel?

51   ML, Z4661, pp.131–2.

52   Maclehose, p.129 — O'Connell, pp.95–6. For Hunt, see Watson, *passim*; White[1], p.465; Therry, pp.99–100; Ryan[1], pp.129–30.

53   Evidence that 'The Exile of Erin' was written by Rev. John McGarvie makes this suggestion extremely doubtful. See Butterss, p.7.

54   SRNSW, 4/3665, p.277.

55   Tucker[1], p.100. In the early years the recorded productions took place on Mondays. This could have permitted preparatory work on the Sunday, thus easing the burden. The violation of the Sabbath that this involved could have been the reason for the later move to Saturday performances, though even these had their problems. See Tucker[1], pp.100, 118.

56   The John Cook recorded as baker in the weekly return of August 1826 (SRNSW, 4/1917.3) had only arrived in late 1825 or early 1826 (SRNSW, 4/2055.1, no.29/9603). Though still there in 1830 he was not included in the list of players and is again recorded as the baker in 1831 (SRNSW, 4/2106, no.31/3528).

57   SRNSW, 4/6428, p.131 — Tucker[1], p.122.

58   Toogood appears on the August 1826 list of convicts at Emu Plains along with King (SRNSW, 4/1917.3). Matthews was transferred there with Tucker (SRNSW, 4/3665, p.277). King's ticket-of-leave is at SRNSW, 4/4063, no.27/100.

59   Tucker[1], p.119.

60   Tucker[1], p.102.

61   SRNSW, 4/2055.1, no.28/5595 (enclosed with 29/9686).

62   Tucker[1], p.101.

63   Tucker[1], p.118. This could well have been the John Matthews who arrived at Emu Plains with Tucker (SRNSW, 4/3665, p.277).

64   Tucker[1], p.78.

65   Tucker[1], p.97.

66   SRNSW, 4/1917.3 — SRNSW, 4/3499, p.260 — PRO, CO201/119, fol.363[r] — SRNSW, 4/1866, p.36.

67   PRO, ASSI25/15/4.

68   ML, Dixson, Q168, item 1, pp.1, 11.

69   SRNSW, 4/2088, no.30/8996 (enclosed with 31/385) — SRNSW, 4/2055.1, no.29/9604.

70   *News*, 4 May 1828, p.143.

71   SRNSW, 4/2103, no.31/2882.

72   *Sydney Monitor*, 27 June 1829. Watt's authorship is revealed in Maxwell, pp.138–43, 200.

73   *Times*, 6 January & 7 March 1825.

74   Maxwell, pp.183–4, 193, 196–7. For Wright's reputation, see the admittedly hostile pages of the *Sydney Monitor*, 12 February 1831 & 28 February 1834.

75   PRO, HO17/122. Yh39 — SRNSW, 4/4570D, p.125 — SRNSW, 4/4521, p.102; SRNSW, 4/6671, p.57 — SRNSW, 4/1917.3 — SRNSW, 4/1922, no.27/1651; SRNSW, 4/1924, no.27/2201. His ticket-of-leave is at SRNSW, 4/4081, no.31/873. For his career as a restauranteur and publican, and his association with free-and-easies, see *Australian*, 29 May 1835, 7 August 1838 & 31 October 1840 and J.M. Forde's 'Old Chum' columns, the *Truth*, 30 April 1911, 29 December 1918 & 27 July 1919. For the first recorded theatrical licensing of his hotel, see the *Sydney Herald*, 28 August 1843. His brother Alfred was also the subject of a petition (PRO, HO19/5, Ar30) and earned a brief reference in Rudé[2], p.128, as well as bulking large in the 'Old Chum' columns.

76   PRO, ASSI25/19/16; *Taunton Courier*, 29 March & 5 April 1826 — *SG*, 19 May 1828, SRNSW, 4/4164, no.42/1607.

77   *OBSP*, September 1825, p.510 — SRNSW, 4/2088, no.31/385.

78   *OBSP*, April 1813, pp.268–9; *Morning Chronicle*, 16 April 1813 — *SG*, 1 October 1815 — SRNSW, 4/1856, p.201 — SRNSW, 4/1747, p.13; ML, Dixson, Spencer 54, p.185 — SRNSW, 4/3502, p.406 — SRNSW, X820, p.67; SRNSW, 4/1868, p.44 — SRNSW, 4/2057, no.29/10186.

79   In 1848 a fellow doctor claimed White had gained his professional knowledge 'as a servant to a Surgeon and was a quack'. White sued for defamation, but lost the case (Bowd, p.89).

80   SRNSW, 4/4094, no.34/545 — SRNSW, 4/440, no.42/208.

81   SRNSW, 4/2088, no.31/385. Stiles appears as a butcher on the *Agamemnon* indent, but was employed as a wheelwright at Emu Plains (SRNSW, 4/2118, no.31/7827).

82   For Matthews, see SRNSW, 4/2165, no.32/5991. — 'Old Chum', *Truth*, 1 November 1908, 2 April 1911 & 26 May 1917. For Watt, see Walker, pp.21–2. For Toogood, see SRNSW, 4/4437, no.39/288; SRNSW, 4/4488, no.43/37, and the card index 'Hotel Licences' in SRNSW. For his death notice, see *Empire*, 8 December 1853. He left a will (Supreme Court, Probate Division 1.2786).

83   The plays scheduled for 3 July 1830 were *John Bull* and *The Lying Valet*, but the *Sydney Gazette*, 8 July, reports that *Rob Roy* was substituted for the latter. If so, the program would have consisted of two mainpieces, resulting in a very long evening and, presumably, violation of the Sabbath, as the spectators would have been travelling home after midnight (Tucker[1], p.100). Perhaps the paper was confused, and *Rob Roy* was substituted for *John Bull*, the logical change to make.

84   Tucker[1], pp.99–100.

85   Tucker[1], p.101 — *SG*, 15 May 1830 — *Howe's Weekly Commercial Express*, 25 July 1825.

86   *HRA*, 1.15.105–16, 1.16.788–9 & 1.17.336–41.

87   SRNSW, 4/2055.1, no.29.9686.

88   SRNSW, 4/2088, no.30/8715 (enclosed with 31/385).

89   SRNSW, 4/3719, pp.123–4.

90   SRNSW, 4/2088, no.30/8996 (enclosed with 31/385).

91   SRNSW, 4/2088, no.31/385 — SRNSW, 4/3670, pp.165–6.

92   SRNSW, 4/2101, no.31/2250.

93   The following account is based on SRNSW, 4/2103, no.31/2610 and its numerous enclosures, and SRNSW, 4/3719, pp.261–4.

94   SRNSW, 4/2103, no.31/1511 (enclosed with 31/2610).

95   SRNSW, 4/2103, no.31/1512, pp.4–5 (enclosed with 31/2610). Wright had been in the audience on 3 July 1830 (*SG*, 8 July 1830).

96 SRNSW, 4/2103, no.31/1430, items 1 & 3 (enclosed with 31/2610).

97 SRNSW, 4/2103, no.31/1512, p.6 (enclosed with 31/2610).

98 SRNSW, 4/2103, no.31/1512, pp.1, 6 (enclosed with 31/2610).

99 SRNSW, 4/2101, nos 31/2248 (and enclosures), 31/2013 & 31/2342.

100 SRNSW, 4/3719, pp.248–9 — SRNSW, 4/3670, pp.297–8.

101 SRNSW, 4/2101, no.31/2250 — SRNSW, 4/3719, pp.261–4.

102 SRNSW, 4/2103, no.31/1877, p.31; SRNSW, 4/2102, no.31/2362.

103 SRNSW, 4/2106, no.31/3528.

104 SRNSW, 4/2101, no.31/2342, p.3.

105 The *locus classicus* for the study of modes of convict protest is Atkinson[1]. Nichol[1] provides an excellent analysis of malingering. More recent articles often take the form of studies of particular institutions or individual convict experiences (see, e.g., Duffield[1], Daniels[1], Reed[2], Duffield[2], Ihde).

106 SRNSW, 4/2101, no.31/2342, p.3.

107 SRNSW, 4/2101, no.31/2342, pp.4–7 — SRNSW, 4/3670, pp.333, 450 — SRNSW, 4/2105, no.31/3112 (and enclosures) — SRNSW, 4/3671, pp.124, 438–9 — SRNSW, 4/2166.1, no.32/1990 — SRNSW, 4/3674, pp.76–7.

108 SRNSW, 4/2103, no.31/1511, p.9 (enclosed with 31/2610), and a private, unnumbered, letter enclosed with SRNSW, 4/2101, no.31/2342.

109 SRNSW, 4/2103, no.31/1430 (enclosed with 31/2610).

110 Mudie, p.104.

CHAPTER 7

1 SRNSW, 4/2196.1, no.33/5954 — SRNSW, 4/1710, pp.290–1, 296–7.

2 O'Connell, pp.64–5. Palmer, the actor, chose the part of Richard III for his benefit in September 1834.

3 For Buckingham, see Parsons, p.113; for White, see the convict indent to the *England* (1826); for Lawrence, see ML, Dixson, Q168, item 1, pp.66–7. For Denis Fitzgerald I am indebted to Brian Siversen.

4 SRNSW, 4/2196.1, no.28/8420 (enclosed with 33/5954): 'Your Petitioner always intended to exclude the Prison Population from the Theatre by giving Tickets to Subscribers only, and making those Tickets not transferable' (Petition of 21 October 1828).

5 Caley, p.162 — Mayhew, 3.73–7. Certain types of peep-show (Mayhew, 3.88–90) might also have warranted the term.

6 SRNSW, 7/2691, p.104.

7 *Monitor*, 25 August 1826.

8 SRNSW, 4/1710, p.422 — For Croft, see SRNSW, 4/1710, p.480 and Parsons, p.508.

9 Ryan[1], pp.7, 114–5, 117. For doubts about Ryan's accuracy, see Waterhouse[1], p.31, note 36. The newspaper reports of Sydney race meetings 1810–25 mention 'cordial booths and gingerbread stalls', temporary taverns, dance halls and (apparently) music rooms, but nothing of a more theatrical nature.

10 SRNSW, 4/1710, pp.295, 375, 405, 418, 420, 428.

11 Von Hügel, p.258 — Ryan[1], pp.10–2 — Govett, pp.47–50.

12 For Windsor, see SRNSW, 4/1710, pp.374, 416, 436 and *Commercial Journal and Advertiser*, 6 April & 15 May 1839. For Norfolk Island, see Best, pp.190, 210; Anderson, pp.168-70. For Melbourne, see SRNSW, 4/1710, pp.469, 473, 482.

13 Tucker[2], pp.25–7; *ADB*, 2.539–40 — SRNSW, 4/4211, no.47/86.

14   *HRA*, 1.20.152–3, 155.

15   *HRA*, 1.20.536–7.

16   *HRA*, 1.20.802. For overviews of Maconochie's time at Norfolk Island, see Barry and McCulloch.

17   *Australian*, 4 June 1840.

18   Maconochie, pp.10–12.

19   PRO, CO201/199, p.108.

20   Maconochie, p.11 & note.

21   Anderson, pp.168–9.

22   Maconochie, p.9.

23   Anon.[11], p.601.

24   *SG*, 25 June 1840. The *Australian Chronicle*'s article of 23 June 1840 also raises the issue of morality.

25   SRNSW, 4/2502, no.40/6205.

26   ML, B218, pp.154–5.

27   ML, Dixson, Q168, item 1, p.78.

28   ML, Dixson, Q168, item 1, pp.12, 16.

29   O'Keeffe, p.9.

30   *Colonial Magazine*, 5 (1841), 295.

31   SRNSW, 4/2502, no.40/6205, pp.8–9. See also Maconochie, pp.11, 13 and the report in *Sydney Herald*, 24 June 1840, of his address to the convicts before the celebrations. See also *HRA*, 1.20.536.

32   Anon.[6], p.24.

33   Anon.[6], p.24.

34   ML, Dixson, Add. 552/6, pp.239–44; SRNSW, 4/2698, lists 22 November 1843, 23 February 1844 and one, undated, 'Men specially recommended for good service to be removed to Sydney'. The description of Whitton comes from the indent to the *Gilmore*.

35   SRNSW, 4/6280, p.60. An 1819 record had described him as blind in the left eye (PRO, CO207/1, fols 107[v]–108[r]).

36   For Monds, see convict indent, *Exmouth*. The others are James Cranston, *John* 2, boatbuilder (SRNSW, 4/2620, no.42/5757; SRNSW, 4/3691, no.44/246; SRNSW, 4/4208, no.46/830) — James Porter, *Marian Watson* (see Porter, introduction and notes) — John Rae, *America* 1, labourer (Archives Office of Tasmania, CON148; SRNSW, 4/2698, lists 22 November 1843 and 20 January 1844) — George Rolfe, *Bussorah Merchant* 1, labourer (SRNSW, 4/4174, no.43/770) — Andrew Sanderson (not R. Sanderson, as in the playbill), *Lady Kennaway*, boatman (Archives Office of Tasmania, CON148; SRNSW, 4/2658, no.44/3815) — William Yelverton, labourer (SRNSW, T50, case 49; *Sydney Monitor*, 29 December 1837).

37   *HRA*, 1.20.714, 690.

38   Maconochie, p.12; *Sydney Herald*, 31 July 1841; *Free Press*, 20 January 1842.

39   Anon.[6], p.9.

40   ML, Dixson, Q247, 1.173.

APPENDIX A

MARY BARNES

1   Flynn[1], p.149.
2   RONSW, Marriages.4.312.
3   SRNSW, 5/1113, no.30/52. See also ML, A3609, p.108 — SRNSW, SZ773, 4 April 1812.
4   *SG*, 28 April 1821, under the heading 'DEED LOST' — *SG*, 21 April 1820, where the house is described as being in Castlereagh Street.
5   SRNSW, SZ768, p.12 — *OBSP*, October 1798, p.604 (Sarah Wood) & June 1799, p.613 (Sarah Thomas) — SRNSW, SZ770, 7 January 1809.
6   RONSW, Burials.11.285 — Gillen[1], p.44 (entry for James Bradley).

WILLIAM CHAPMAN

1   A second William Chapman, sentenced at York and embarked on the *Admiral Barrington*, died on the voyage, as the indent reveals.
2   *OBSP*, April 1791, pp.304–5.
3   SRNSW, 4/1821, no.58.
4   SRNSW, 5/1147B, p.176 — Chapman is absent from the list of constables, 8 February 1800, in SRNSW, SZ767, pp.142–3.
5   Hunt[2], pp.154–61; Flynn[1], pp.429–30 — HRA,1.4.681; SRNSW, 5/1157, pp.14–5.
6   SRNSW, SZ768, p.95; HRA,1.3.623. See also SRNSW, SZ767, p.54.
7   HRA, 1.3.657–8, 660 — HRA, 1.3.691–2 — SRNSW, 4/1719, p.192.
8   *SG*, 8 April, 28 October & 15 November 1804, 18 & 25 August 1805, 13 April & 22 June 1806, 26 February 1809 (*bis*), 21 January 1810 — SRNSW, SZ758, p.19.
9   In a number of the above advertisements, in the petition of 30 January 1810, and even on his tombstone.
10   ML, BT Box 12, p.52 — Johnson[1], p.8 (no.127).
11   SRNSW, SZ774, 29 May 1813 — Hunt[2], pp.157, 159–60 — Karskens, pp.110, 137–8.
12   SRNSW, X702, p.5; SRNSW, 4/1821, no.58; RONSW, Marriages.4.208.

MRS CHARLETON

1   *OBSP*, September 1788, p.655. See also Flynn[1], pp.290-1.
2   ML, A1958, p.57 (as Gaters) — Flynn[1], pp.199–200; Statham, pp.262–3 — PRO, CO201/10, fol.93ᵛ.
3   ML, A1958, pp.6, 57; RONSW, Burials.4.978. Charleton was briefly on detachment at the time of the 1799 production, but was in Sydney for all three of the recorded productions of 1800. See PRO, WO12/9899, fol.213ʳ & PRO, WO12/9900, fols 46ʳ, 62ʳ, 92ʳ.
4   Baxter[1], p.139 (CA133) — SRNSW, 4/1167A, p.299 — RONSW, Marriages.3.998; Flynn[1], pp.290–1.
5   *OBSP*, December 1789, p.26 — Baxter[1], p.48 (AE206).

I. OR J. COX

1   John Cox (*Neptune*) and John Cox (*Albemarle*) died on the voyage, and James Cox (*Charlotte*) while escaping. John Massey Cox was on Norfolk Island. For the last two, see Gillen[1], pp.84–5.
2   PRO, ASSI23/8 — Baxter[1], pp.40 (AD270), 94 (AJ120) — Baxter[5], pp.122 (AO4832),

547 (BOO497); ML, BT Box 24, p.5760d — RONSW, Burials.23.668.

3   PRO, T1/749, *Lion* (25 March–20 June 1795) — RONSW, Marriages.7.189 — SRNSW, 4/4493, p.143 — SRNSW, 4/1857, p.82.

4   Baxter[4], p.103 (no.4576); Baxter[5], p.112 (AO4823) — RONSW, Burials.37.50 — Baxter[2], p.21 (AO690); Baxter[1], p.124 (BG197); *HRNSW*, 3.598, 624–5.

5   PRO, ASSI31/17 & 35/237/3 — RONSW, Marriages.7.10.

6   RONSW, Marriages.4.220 — SRNSW, 4/1823, no.55.

7   Statham, p.267; PRO, WO25/642, p.11; PRO, WO25/1342, fols 17[r]–18[v] — PRO, WO12/9900, fols 47[r], 63[r], 93[r] — SRNSW, X905, p.405.

8   PRO, WO25/642, p.11.

9   Statham, p.267 — PRO, WO12/9900, fols 43[v], 59[v], 89[v] — RONSW, Baptisms.1.863.

10   Cumpston, pp.36–7; PRO, WO12/9900, fol.109[r] — PRO, CO201/29, fols 104[r], 186[r] — Launceston Reference Library, William Ellis Cox, 'The Cox Family of Norfolk Plains', pp4–6.

11   ML, B437, 16, 17, 25 & 26 December 1805, 6 February 1806 for Cox, and 22 February 1806 for Mrs Cox. On the other hand, an entry for non-theatrical purposes on 22 June 1805 is specifically to 'Cox the Soldier', who may be being distinguished from the Cox associated with the theatre.

MRS DAVIS

1   This account of the robbery, capture and trial is compiled from the Chronicle section of *Annual Register*, 27 (1784–85), 239; *Chelmsford Chronicle*, 17 March 1786; *London Chronicle*, 9–11 March 1786 and *Morning Chronicle*, 11 March 1796, supported by PRO, ASSI31/14 & 35/226/1.

2   Thompson; Anon.[3]; Anon.[20]

3   Smyth, p.4.

4   SRNSW, SZ765, p.228; Gillen[1], pp.6, 97.

5   Clark, pp.119–20 — ML, A1958, p.54.

6   SRNSW, 4/4486, p.2.

7   Johnson[1], p.53 (no.965).

8   Baxter[1], p.118 (BF027).

9   BL, Add. MS 13880, fol.31[v].

10   SRNSW, 2/8147, p.435; SRNSW, 2/8132, pp.39, 43.

11   RONSW, Marriages.5.195.

12   Statham, p.320; Ryan[2], p.158 — ML, A3609, p.171 — ML, A3611, pp.24, 44.

13   *SG*, 17 February 1810. That the licence was for the Hawkesbury is suggested by the other names on the list.

14   ML, A3611, p.246; ML, A4420, Misc.1978; SRNSW, 5/1166, 23 October 1813 — *SG*, 31 July 1813.

15   SRNSW, SZ758, p.406 — SRNSW, 5/1166, 23 October 1813.

16   SRNSW, 4/1713, p.81 — Baxter[6], p.143 (no.18224).

17   RONSW, Burials.127.139; Foster[1], p.161; Johnson[1], p.53 (no.965).

J. DAVISON

1   Hall, pp.91–3; Collins, 1.399, 2.24.

2   Baxter[1], p.62 (AF179).

3   PRO, ASSI23/8. Sentenced to 7 years at Southampton, March 1791. Arrived in the *Pitt*.

4   Gillen[1], p.100 — PRO, ASSI45/36/2, nos. 34–37. Sentenced to 7 years, Northumberland, July 1788.

5   Flynn[1], pp.239–40 — PRO, T1/691, *Stanislaus*, 12 October–12 January 1791.

6   The other James Davison (alias Tanner) was 19 when sentenced to 7 years at Hertford (*Admiral Barrington* indent; PRO, T1/631, *Dunkirk*, 26 June–25 October 1789). This would have made him a plausible 30-year-old Hotspur in 1800. However, the discrepancy between his age and that of the survivor, as recorded in 1808, must be added to the weight of evidence against him. The one thing in his favour is that an annotation on the *Neptune* indent identifies the Old Bailey convict as a printer, whereas in 1808 the survivor was listed as a silk-dyer by trade. The annotation, however, is in a different hand from the rest of the indent, and is the only note regarding occupation in the entire indent.

7   Statham, p.271; Baxter[1], p.122 (BG022); SRNSW, 4/4430, p.4 — ML, A1958, p.9 — PRO, WO12/9900, fol.60[v].

8   PRO, WO25/1342, p.23[v] — PRO, WO25/642, p.22.

R. EVANS

1   SRNSW, 4/1821, no.103; Statham, p.277; Baxter[2], p.36 (A1375); RONSW, Marriages.4.214.

2   *OBSP*, September 1790, pp.869–70.

3   PRO, HO47/13.

4   SRNSW, SZ766, pp.10, 19, 22–4 — SRNSW, SZ767, p.13 & 2/8147, p.241 — SRNSW, SZ766, p.92 — SRNSW, X905, p.363.

5   RONSW, Marriages.4.278 — SRNSW, 2/8147, p.109.

6   SRNSW, 2/8148, p.776 — SRNSW, 2/8149, p.959 — ML, BT Box 12, p.53.

W. FOWKES

1   PRO, HO26/1, p.8.

2   *OBSP*, September 1791, pp.484–5.

3   RONSW, Burials.4.817.

H. GREEN

1   *OBSP*, February 1791, pp.186–9.

2   PRO, HO47/15.

3   SRNSW, 2/8147, p.179.

4   Baxter[1], p.118 (BFO4O).

MRS GREVILLE

1   *OBSP*, January 1790, pp.158–9.

2   SRNSW, SZ766, p.40 — SRNSW, SZ767, p.7.

3   SRNSW, SZ766, p.43.

4   *OBSP*, February 1805, pp.244–5.

5   SRNSW, 4/1219 shows them as living in Upper Pitt Street in 1822 with a 16-year-old son, born in the colony. — RONSW, Marriages.3.917 — Baxter[5], p.200 (AO8728).

MASTER HADDOCKS

1   *ADB*, 2.373–5; Irvine, pp.35–52.

2   Statham, p.288 — Baxter[1], p.47 (AE140) — Baxter[2], p.54 (A2169).

3   PRO, WO25/643, fol.62[r].

G. H. HUGHES

1   Collins, 1.364, 375.
2   Baxter[1], p.55 (AE534).
3   SRNSW, SZ766, p.173 — SRNSW, SZ767, p.124.
4   SRNSW, 5/1149, p.110.

L. JONES

1   *OBSP*, April 1788, pp.354–5.
2   ANL, MS 96, p.15.
3   Flynn[1], pp.370–1.
4   SRNSW, 4/4003, p.255 — Archives Office of Tasmania, RGD34, no.106; Baxter[3], p.70 (no.3198); PRO, HO11/1, p.392 — PRO, HO26/11, pp.70–1.
5   Registers of St John's Church, Parramatta, Marriages. pp.15–26 (copy at ML, FM4/3700) — Lambeth Palace Library, ARCH/P/Moore 22, item 3, p.39.
6   Lambeth Palace Library, ARCH/P/Moore 22, item 2, p.38 & item 3, pp.13, 15.
7   Flynn[1], p.369 — Statham, p.302. The other pre-1794 arrivals of that name were all young: *per Salamander*, 12 on conviction (*OBSP*, May 1788, p.445), *per Albemarle*, 17 (PRO, T1/692, *Stanislaus*, 12 October–12 January 1791) and *per Admiral Barrington*, 21 (PRO, T1/692, *Ceres*, 12 January–13 March 1791).

W. KNIGHT

1   SRNSW, SZ767, pp.9, 72 — Flynn[1], pp.388–9 — Collins, 1.356, 382–3, 598–9.
2   Flynn[1], pp. 388–9 — *OBSP*, July 1786, p.863 & January 1787, p.329 — PRO, T1/672, *Lion*, 12 January–12 April 1789 — ML, A1958, p.25 — PRO, CO201/9, fol.197[r] — Ryan[2], p.97 — PRO, CO201/9, fol.137[r].
3   PRO, CO201/9, fol.199[r] — ML, A1958, pp.25, 55.
4   SRNSW, 5/1147B, p.52 — Ryan[2], p.65 — ML, BT Box 88, p.3463.
5   ML, BT Box 12, p.80 — Ryan[2], p.30; Baxter[1], p.18 (AB009) — Ritchie[2], p.81.
6   The *Sydney Gazette*, 25 March 1804, reports William Knight's appointment as a supervisor at Newcastle. However, other sources reveal the appointee was Isaac Knight, an ex-sergeant of marines (see Gillen[1], pp.209–10).
7   Flynn[1], pp.387–8 — *OBSP*, September 1787, pp.991–2 — PRO, T1/672, *Stanislaus*, 12 July–12 October 1789.
8   SRNSW, 4/4430, p.2; Baxter[1], p.122 (BG021); Statham p.306 — PRO, WO25/1342, fol.45[r].
9   Ryan[2], p.168 — Baxter[2], p.61 (A2466) — ML, BT Box 24, p.5166.
10   *SG*, 23 June 1805, 3 September 1809, 12 May 1810, 21 December 1811 — ML, A3609, pp.114, 170; ML, A3610, pp.29, 11; ML, A3611, p.317; ML, A3613, p.73.
11   SRNSW, 4/1736, p.5; SRNSW, 2/8130, p.377; SRNSW, 4/1847, p.151; SRNSW, 4/1819, pp.193, 198, 434 — Baxter[2], p.67 (A2717) — RONSW, Marriages. 3.1623 — RONSW, Burials. 2.3670.
12   PRO, WO12/9899, fol.230[v]; PRO, WO12/9900, fols 90[v], 113[v], 395[v], 413[v].

JOHN WILLIAM LANCASHIRE

1   *OBSP*, April 1796, pp.420–2. For a biographical account, see Kerr, pp. 445–6.
2   PRO, HO26/5, p.50 — Anon.[19], 2.204.
3   PRO, CO201/15, fol.104[r].

4   *HRNSW*, 3.464.
5   SRNSW, SZ766, pp.44–5 — *HRNSW*, 3.464.
6   SRNSW, SZ766, pp.87, 89, 128, 133.
7   *HRNSW*, 3.601, 621.
8   PRO, CO201/15, fols 101^r–3^r.
9   *HRNSW*, 3.616–22, 579–84.
10 ML, A1980^2, p.138.
11 PRO, CO201/16, fols 30^r–35^r — SRNSW, SZ767, p.150.
12 ML, A1980, 2.138 — SRNSW, SZ768, p.22.
13 SRNSW, SZ768, p.113 — SRNSW, 5/1149, pp.115–20.
14 ML, A1980, 2.138–49, 304–8 — SRNSW, SZ768, pp.357–9, 556–8 — SRNSW, 5/1149, pp.251–66. See also *SG*, 17, 24 & 31 July 1803, 29 September, 24 December 1805, 12 January 1806.
15 ML, A1980, 2.138,143.
16 *SG*, 11 September & 18 December 1803 — ML, A3609, p.94.
17 *SG*, 13 October 1805.
18 ML, A2015, p.523 — *SG*, 20 July 1806.
19 BL, Add. MS 13880, fol.80^v.
20 Kerr, p.445.
21 PRO, CO201/15, fols 104^v, 106^v.

H. LAVELL

1   Greater London Record Office, Depositions, Old Bailey, 1782 September/24 — *OBSP*, September 1782, pp.604–6.
2   Gillen^1, pp.214–5, 435–6 — PRO, T1/613, *Dunkirk*, 1 December 1784 — PRO, T1/641, *Dunkirk*, 25 September–25 December 1786. For details of the *Mercury* affair, see Gillen^2.
3   Clark, pp.49, 81.
4   Clark, pp.102–3; White^2, pp.116–7, 140–1.
5   ML, A1958, p.22 — Clark, p.184 — PRO, CO201/9, fols 40^{r-v}, 27^r, 39^v.
6   SRNSW, 5/1147A, pp.341–9.
7   SRNSW, SZ766, pp.40, 46, 48, 67, 115.
8   SRNSW, 4/4486, p.4 — Baxter^1, p.118 (BF054).
9   Parke, p.27.
10 For example, *HRNSW*, 3.728; ANL, MS 737 (letter of 2 May 1804, p.1).

MRS McCANN

1   PRO, HO26/6, p.65 — *OBSP*, September 1797, p.549; *London Chronicle*, 23–26 September 1797.
2   PRO, HO77/4, 20 September 1797, Indictment 69.
3   *Bell's Weekly Messenger*, 6 July 1800. The following account of Sarah's crime and trial is based on OBSP, September 1797, pp.546–50, the *London Chronicle*, 23–26 September, the *Oracle*, 26 September, and the *Morning Chronicle*, 27 September. Accounts also appeared in *The Times*, 27 September, *Bell's Weekly Messenger*, 1797, p.599, the *Evening Mail*, 25–7 September, the *Observer*, 1 October, the *Star*, 26 September and *Johnson's British Gazette*, 1 October 1797.
4   SRNSW, SZ767, p.111 — SRNSW, SZ768, p.57.

5   Baxter[1], p.27 (AC058) — Flynn[1], pp.494–5 — Baxter[2], p.76 (A1325) — Baxter[4], p.149
    (no.6617) — Baxter[5], p.304 (A13368).
6   Baxter[6], p.354 (no.30469).
7   Statham, p.343.
8   SRNSW, 4/1739, pp.121–4. Baxter[6], reproduces a conflation of musters of 1823–25. If
    its information about McCann comes from 1823 or 1824, she may well have had time
    for a relationship with James Elgin.

MRS MILLER

1   *OBSP*, September 1795, pp.1066–7.
2   *OBSP*, December 1789, pp.4–7, December 1790, p.90.
3   Collins, 1.402 — SRNSW, 5/1147B, pp.103–10; SRNSW, SZ766, p.91.
4   RONSW, Baptisms.2.501; SRNSW, 5/1147B, p.103–10.
5   SRNSW, 2/8150, part 1, pp.54 — SRNSW, SZ767, p.71 — SRNSW, 2/8150, part 1,
    pp.8,77.
6   SRNSW, SZ767, p.111.
7   SRNSW, X905, p.258.
8   SRNSW, 2/8150, part 2, pp.6, 61 — Cumpston, p.68; SRNSW, X905, pp.481–4.
9   *SG*, 26 June 1803 and *passim* — SRNSW, 5/1149, p.508.
10 SRNSW, 4/4486, p.8; Baxter[1], p.119 (BF105) — *SG*, 15 October 1809; SRNSW, 4/
    1822, no.223.
11 Thus a Mrs Mary Miller almost drowned in a boating accident, while *en route* from Sydney
    to Lane Cove (*SG*, 6 January 1816). She is presumably the wife of the William Miller,
    who held a 60-acre farm there (SRNSW, X702, pp.105–7; *SG*, 12 October 1816). He
    may be the man who announced his intention of departing the colony on the *Harriet*
    (*SG*, 7 June 1817), since within a year the Lane Cove farm is described as formerly
    Miller's (*SG*, 21 February 1818).

J. PAINE OR PAYNE

1   *Aris's Birmingham Gazette*, 26 July 1790.
2   PRO, ASSI31/16 & ASSI35/230/2; *Chelmsford Chronicle*, 23 July 1790.
3   Baxter[1], p.122 (BG027); SRNSW, 4/4430, p.2 — Statham, p.328, where he is recorded
    as two separate men, one for each enlistment.
4   PRO, WO25/642, p.121 — Ryan[2], p.308; Statham, p.328.
5   PRO, WO12/9900, p.57[v].
6   PRO, WO25/642, p.121 — PRO, WO25/1342, fol.67[v] — SRNSW, 4/1819, pp.164–5
    — PRO, WO12/9907, *passim*.
7   SRNSW, 4/7015.2, p.17; SRNSW, 4/3509, p.484 — PRO, WO12/11229, fols 49[r]–162[r]
    — RONSW, Burials.24.432.

D. PARNELL

1   *Felix Farley's Bristol Journal*, 8 April & 15 April 1797; *Bonner and Middleton's Bristol Journal*, 8
    April 1797 — PRO, HO47/21.
2   Noah, p.68; Baxter[1], pp.92 (AJ036), 124 (BG198) — SRNSW, 4/1821, no.75 — SRNSW,
    4/4493, p.15 — SRNSW, SZ76, p.85.
3   *HRA*, 1.3.624.
4   SRNSW, SZ768, p.97.

5   PRO, CO201/30, fols 89^r, 214^v. Parnell probably arrived on Norfolk Island, along with William Richards, on HMS *Buffalo*, on 9 May, and was disembarked on 14 May (Nobbs[1], p.217).

6   SRNSW, 2/8148, pp.713, 715, 770, 783. The cases date from 16 September 1805 to 2 May 1806.

7   *HRNSW*, 7.477.

8   ML, BT Box 12, p.56. In the 1828 census Parnell is recorded as having an absolute pardon, but none is listed in SRNSW, 4/4486.

9   SRNSW, 4/6360, 12 March 1822 — SRNSW, 4/3505, p.45 — Baxter[5], p.372 (A16386).

10   Baxter[6], p.444 (no.35661).

11   *SG*, 25 April & 16 July, 18 July 1827; *Australian*, 25 April & 13 July 1827; SRNSW, 4/8447, April 1827, no.17 & July 1827, no.8.

12   SRNSW, 4/8435, no.21, p.177 — SRNSW, 4/6437, no.1516.

P. PARRY AND MRS PARRY

1   The above account comes from PRO, HO47/21. See also PRO, ASSI35/237/7 and PRO, ASSI31/17, no.13.

2   The above account of Parry's capture and trial comes from *OBSP*, January 1796, pp.136–40. See also *Star*, 16 January 1796.

3   SRNSW, SZ767, p.156; Baxter[1], pp.88 (AH067), 92 (AJ034) — *SG*, 14 April 1805 (Advertisement of L. Daveran), 10 November 1805 (Thomas Taber's advertisement).

4   RONSW, Marriages.4.274.

5   On 1 September 1800, shortly before his departure, he appears as a debtor, being pursued for £8 by Joseph Ward (SRNSW, 2/8147, pp.329–30).

6   SRNSW, 2/8147, p.327.

7   SRNSW, SZ76, pp.48,54; SRNSW, 4/4486, p.6 (*bis*) — PRO, ADM36/14230, p.235 — Baxter, p.118 (BF079, BF081).

H. PARSONS

1   Where not otherwise noted details of Parsons' life are drawn from Gillen[1], p.277 or Evans, pp.109–11.

2   Clark, pp.191–3.

3   Statham, p.327 — RONSW, Marriages. 4.228 — Ryan[2], p.170 — PRO, WO25/642, p.121 & WO25/1342, fols 67^{r–v} — *SG*, 26 June 1809.

4   SRNSW, SZ759, p.375 — Evans, p.110; RONSW, Burials.2.4307.

5   *HRA*,1.4.103.

6   PRO, WO12/9904, fols 299^r,319^r,339^r,359^r & WO12/9905, fol.3^r.

7   SRNSW, SZ759, p.492.

MR AND MRS RADLEY

1   PRO, HO26/56, pp.17–8 — *OBSP*, October 1792, p.440. The following account of their crime and trials is also based on *OBSP*, December 1792, p.181 and newspapers such as the *World*, 19 & 24 September, 5 November 1792, and the *Public Advertiser*, 27 September 1792. See also Flynn[2], pp.50–1, 124–6.

2   *World*, 24 September 1792 — *OBSP*, October 1792, p.440.

3   *Public Advertiser*, 27 December 1792, *Star*, 27 December 1792, *York Herald*, 29 December 1792.

4   PRO, HO47/15.

5   *OBSP*, January 1793, p.300; PRO, HO26/56, p.18.

6   Palmer, *passim*; SRNSW, 5/1156.

7   SRNSW, SZ76, p.43; SRNSW, 4/4493, p.12 — SRNSW, 2/8150, part 2, pp.63, 66 — *HRA*, 1.3.692.

8   ML, A3609, p.22 — SRNSW, SZ767, pp.124–5.

9   RONSW, Burials.2.1767.

10   Baxter[2], pp.41 (A1589), 159 (CO439).

11   SRNSW, SZ770, 29 October 1808.

12   Baxter[1], p.27 (AC053).

13   RONSW, Baptisms.6.407, 481 — RONSW, Marriages.3.2060.

14   ML, A2131, pp.30, 95 — Baxter[5], p.393 (A17349) — SRNSW, 4/1219, vol. 2, part 5 — Baxter[6], p.471 (no.37257).

15   RONSW, Burials.116.2002.

W. RICHARDS

1   PRO, ASSI23/8 — T1/693, *Dunkirk*, 26 January–19 March 1791.

2   ML, A1958, p.32 — PRO, CO201/10, fol.197[r] — Baxter[1], p.55 (AE530).

3   PRO, WO12/9900, fol.375[v] — PRO, WO12/9904, fol.220[r] — PRO, WO25/642, p.133 — Statham, p.335.

4   Baxter[3], p.107 (no.4924) — Baxter[4], p.83 (no.3685). He disappears from later musters, but in Baxter[5], p.403 (no. A17760) is replaced as a worker at Liverpool by a William Richards, *per Royal Admiral*, 1800, free by servitude. The same man appears as a landholder in Liverpool in Baxter[6], p.483 (no. 37939). Since no William Richards is recorded elsewhere as arriving on the *Royal Admiral*, the probability is that this is the convict who actually came on the *Salamander*.

5   The assize records relating to the case are PRO, ASSI45/37/1, nos.201–5.

6   SRNSW, 5/1147B, pp.275–9.

7   SRNSW, SZ767, p.93 — Baxter[1], p.48 (AE218).

8   SRNSW, SZ768, pp.117, 151— SRNSW, 5/1149, pp.115–20.

9   PRO, CO201/30, fol.89[r]— Baxter[2], p.187 (no.DO174) — SRNSW, 4/1168A, fol.435[v].

10   ML, B437, 17, 20 (*bis*), 22, 24 & 26 (*bis*) December 1805, 2, 10 (*bis*), 15 January & 7 March 1806.

11   *Felix Farley's Bristol Journal*, 24 April 1819 — *Eliza* indent — SRNSW, 4/4781, p.106 — SRNSW, 4/4520. p.19 — SRNSW, 2/8283, p.100; SRNSW, 4/1800, p.205 — SRNSW, 4/1801, p.68.

R. SIDAWAY

1   For earlier biographical accounts see *ADB*, 2.444 and Gillen[1], pp.329–30.

2   Hackney Archives Department, Shoreditch Land Tax, 1746/7, 1756/7, 1762/3.

3   Society of Genealogists, London, 'Apprentices of Great Britain, 1710–62', no.23/104 (1762) — Grimwade, pp.658, 548; Anon.[19],1.286 — PRO, PCC. PROB.11, 1275 (1796, Middx, May, 274) — Clark, p.4.

4   *Evening Mail*, 29 June–2 July 1792.

5   *OBSP*, June 1778, pp.227–8, April 1782, p.304, September 1782, pp.576–7 & October 1762, pp.684–5.

6   Gillen[1], p.329.

7　　Clark, p.78.

8　　Smyth, p.75 — White[2], p.141.

9　　SRNSW, SZ765, p.247 (old p.257); *Evening Mail*, 29 June–2 July 1792.

10　Though the story appears in several newspapers and journals, it is only in the *Weekly Entertainer*, 20 (1792), p.62 that the baker is identified as Sidaway.

11　SRNSW, SZ765, p.294 (old p.311).

12　SRNSW, 5/1147A, pp.255–9, 287–94.

13　SRNSW, 5/1147A, pp.151–61.

14　SRNSW, 4/4430, p.2 & 4/4486, p.2; Collins.1.327.

15　SRNSW, SZ766, p.90 — SRNSW, 5/1147B, p.224; Ryan[2], p.220 (lease renewed, p.249)— ML, A3609, pp.1, 6 & A3610, p.4; Baxter[1], pp.85 (AG412), 112 (BD278).

16　*London Chronicle*, 31 August–2 September, 1797 (vol. 82, p.223). Also in *True Briton*, 7 September 1797, *Saunders' News-Letter*, 12 September 1797.

17　*Sporting Magazine*, 10 (July 1797), 208. A different version of this account appeared in the *Oracle*, 13 July 1797, the *Monthly Mirror*, 4 (July 1797), pp.56–7 and *Felix Farley's Bristol Journal*, 22 July 1797.

18　*HRNSW*, 3.612–5.

19　*HRNSW*, 4.18–20; SRNSW, 2/8150, part 1, pp.68, 86–90.

20　SRNSW, 2/8148, pp.507–8.

21　SRNSW, 2/8150, part 2, pp.3, 23 — ML, A3609, pp.1, 49 — *SG*, 17 April 1803 — Baxter[2], pp.138–9 (BO538) — *SG*, 8 September 1805, 28 August 1808 & 7 May 1809; *HRA*, 1.6.155, 714 — ML, A1982.

22　*SG*, 27 October 1805, 5 October 1806.

B. SMITH

1　　PRO, ASSI34/1399 — PRO, T1/749, *Fortune*, 21 March–20 June 1795.

2　　SRNSW, SZ767, p.17 — RONSW, Marriages.4.281 — Baxter[4], p.41 (AD338).

3　　PRO, CO201/29, fols 162[r], 218[v] — SRNSW, 4/1167A, p.311 — Baxter[2], p.94 (A3922).

W. SMITH

1　　Smith, pp.127–223; Davies, p.30. Smith was a linen draper by trade. His surviving letters, both in style and handwriting, point to a good education. See Wilson[2], p.6; ML, A859, pp.41–4, 69–72.

2　　For the sailor, see *OBSP*, August 1792, pp.318–9; for the soldier, see PRO, HO47/18; for the militia-man, see *Cambridge Chronicle*, 26 March 1796. For Bingham, see PRO, ASSI23/8 and, in the colony, Baxter[1], pp.34 (AD042), 38 (AD202).

3　　PRO, WO12/9899 and WO12/9900, *passim* — PRO, WO25/1342, fol.84[r]. For his presence at Parramatta, see SRNSW, 5/1147B, p.59. I am assuming the index to the colonial secretary's correspondence, 1788–1825, is wrong in identifying the *Ganges* convict with the William Smith hanged in Hobart in 1822. The Sydney Gaol Register (SRNSW, 4/6360) records the latter as arriving in Australia on the *Prince Regent*, and he and his colleague claimed at their trial (SRNSW, SZ796, p.32) to be 'entire strangers in this part of the colony [i.e. Sydney]'.

4　　PRO, WO25/642, p.143 — PRO, WO12/9899 and WO12/9900, *passim* — Statham, p.344 — PRO, WO25/1342, fol.85[r].

5　　Baxter[2], p.76 (A3125) — Statham, p.343.

6　　Baxter[6], p.540 (no.41226) — SRNSW, 4/1770, p.49 — *SG*, 12 & 19 May 1805.

7   Gillen[1], p.337.

8   One First-Fleet William Smith and a colleague 'had so much the appearance of gentlemen'
     that they almost escaped apprehension for stealing a large amount of silverware from a
     house (Gillen[1], p.337). He would make an attractive candidate for the position as actor,
     particularly if he were the clerk to the commissary praised for meritorious service in
     1789 (SRNSW, 5/1150, p.242). The argument, however, cannot be taken further. By
     1800 the house-breaker would have been about 42.

MRS SPARKS

1   There was a Samuel Sparks on the hulk *Justitia* in 1789–90 (PRO, T1/671 *sqq.*). He had
     been tried at the Old Bailey in May 1786 and sentenced to 7 years for stealing clothes
     from a washing line (*OBSP*, May 1786, pp.764–5).

2   SRNSW, 5/1149, p.31.

3   SRNSW, SZ767, pp.35–6.

4   SRNSW, SZ767, pp.63–4.

5   Flynn[1], p.135.

6   SRNSW, SZ767, p.148.

7   In the court papers the case flows on directly from that of the two men whose hats were
     stolen. Presumably they had been in the gaol as remand prisoners awaiting trial, and it
     was during this period that their hats had been taken.

8   Baxter[2], p.60 (A2409); Gillen[1], p.120.

J. SPARROW

1   Republished by the London Borough of Hackney, Library Services, Archives Department,
     1991.

2   Hackney Archives Department, Shoreditch Land Tax, 1747–48, p.43.

3   Hackney Archives Department, Shoreditch Land Tax, 1762–63 & 1756–57, p.4.

4   Atkins, pp.269, 103.

5   *OBSP*, April 1791, p.313 — *Times*, 5 April 1786.

6   Collins, 1.267–8.

7   Baxter[2], p.93 (A3909) — SRNSW, 4/1727, p.193.

8   For example, SRNSW, 2/8147, pp. 123, 184, 316, 332, 398; SRNSW, 2/8148, pp.707,
     709; ML, A3609, pp.3, 52; ML, A1976, pp.24–5.

9   SRNSW, 2/8148, p.368 — SRNSW, 2/8150, part 1, pp.68, 86–90 — Baxter[1], pp.21, 189
     (AB091). See also SRNSW, 2/8147, p.362.

10   SRNSW, 2/8148, pp.652–3 — SRNSW, 2/8147, pp.173–4.

11   *HRA*, 1.3.691–2; SRNSW, 4/1719, p.192.

12   Baxter[2], p.54 (A2152) — Baxter[1], pp.48 (AE217, AE219), 69 (AF837, AF838) — SRNSW,
     2/8148, pp.652–3.

13   Gillen[1], pp.194–5.

JOSEPH VASCONCELLIS

1   Statham, pp.351–2.

2   Ryan[2], p.306; *HRNSW*, 2.353 — SRNSW, SZ767,p. 70 — PRO, WO12/9900, *passim.*

J. WHITE

1 *OBSP*, June 1796, pp.674–6 — SRNSW, 4/1847, p.237 — *SG*, 12 & 26 November 1809; Baxter[2], p.107 (A4495)— *SG*, 8 September 1810 — SRNSW, SZ768, p.489; SRNSW, SZ770, 2 December 1809 — SRNSW, SZ758, p.73.
2 SRNSW, 4/1847, p.237 — SRNSW, 4/4486, p.27 — Baxter[3], p.134 (no.6199).
3 *SG*, 12 June 1808 — SRNSW, SZ767, pp.130–1.
4 Flynn[1], p.607.
5 Statham, pp.354–5 — PRO, WO12/9989–9990, *passim* — PRO, WO25/642, p.164 and WO 25/1342, fol.110[v] .

H. WYNN

1 *OBSP*, April 1790, pp.429–30 — ML, A1958, p.60 — PRO, CO201/10, fol.200[r].
2 PRO, HO47/12.
3 Van Lennep, 5.2.655 & *passim*.
4 PRO, CO201/10, fol.200[r].
5 *OBSP*, February 1789, p.281.

THOMAS RESTELL CROWDER

1 Westminister City Libraries, Archives Section, St Martin-in-the-Fields Registers of Births, Marriages, Deaths — Armytage, p.200 — Nathaniel's Will (PRO, PCC.PROB.11/1113) proved 11 February 1784.
2 St Martin-in-the-Fields Poor Rates records for 1783, held in the Westminster City Libraries, Archives Section.
3 McKenzie, pp.95–6 — Taylor, 2.403–5.
4 *OBSP*, December 1782, pp.46–50 — PRO, CO201/9, fol.266[v]. For Edward, see *OBSP*, December 1787, pp.52–7, September 1789, pp.888–9; *Times*, 2 November 1789, and the interesting letter from J. Rose, 7 November 1789, in PRO, HO47/9. For confirmation that these two convicts are brothers, see PRO, CO201/10, fol.92[r].
5 Gillen[1], p.88.
6 PRO, HO47/3 (letter of 22 April 1785).
7 *Felix Farley's Bristol Journal*, 29 May 1794. The following account of his Bristol adventures draws, not only on this newspaper for 26 March & 9 April 1785, but also on *Bonner and Middleton's Bristol Journal*, 9 April 1785 and on the *Western Flying Post*, 31 May 1784. Crowder was charged with robbing the premises of James Cunning, auctioneer; Philip George, brewer; John Thomas, grocer; and Edward Stock. For reports of the first three robberies, see *Felix Farley's Bristol Journal*, 24 April, 15 & 22 May 1784.
8 PRO, T1/641, *Justitia*, 12 October 1786–12 January 1787.
9 RONSW, Marriages.4.59 — SRNSW, 2/1147A, pp.61–4 — SRNSW, SZ765, p.113.
10 Gillen[1], p.88 — ML, A1958, p.20 — PRO, CO201/9, fols 247[r]–52[v].
11 ML, C187, pp.102, 128 — SRNSW, 4/4493, p.2 — SRNSW, 4/4486, p.3 — PRO, CO201/10, fol.251[v].
12 PRO, CO201/9, fol.63[r]— PRO, CO201/10, fols 54[r], 71[r], 111[r].
13 PRO, CO201/10, fols 57[v], 353[v].
14 PRO, CO201/10, fols 180[r–v].
15 PRO, CO201/10, fol.158[v] — ML, A1958, p.37 — Wright[1], p.124— ANL, MS 0439, p.168 — PRO, CO201/10, fol.145[r].
16 PRO, CO201/10, fol.365[v], — ML, A1958, p.38.

17   PRO, CO201/18, fol.151[r].

18   For example, PRO, CO201/29, fols 29[v], 66[r], 72[r], 98[v], 171[r], 266[r]; PRO, CO201/30, fols 88[v], 109[v]; PRO, CO201/42, fols 86[v], 93[r]; Ryan[2], pp.88, 89; Gillen[1], p.89.

19   ML, A254[1], pp.88–9.

20   Gillen[1], p.89; Flynn[1], p.224.

21   ANL, MS 737 (letter of 19 May 1810).

22   Schaffer[2], p.217 — Wright[1], pp.123–5 — PRO, CO201/64, fols 220–1.

23   *HRA*, 3.3.332 — *HRA*, 3.3.324 — Gillen[1], p.89 — Schaffer[1], p.134 — *Hobart Town Gazette*, 22 June 1816 & *passim*.

24   Bigge, 1.20, 44, 54, 55.

25   *HRA*, 3.3.52, 64 & 3.2.565 — Gillen[1], p.89.

26   *Hobart Town Gazette*, 3 December 1824; Archives Office of Tasmania, RGD34, no. 872 — Knopwood, p.317; *Hobart Town Gazette*, 20 September 1817 — Schaffer[2], pp.55–7.

WILLIAM DORAN

1   Flynn[1], p.248.

2   ML, A1958, p.37 — PRO, CO201/10, fol.353[v].

3   PRO, CO201/10, fols 94[v], 95[v].

4   PRO, CO201/10, fol.353[v] — ML, A1958, p.38.

5   ML, A1958, p.38

EDWARD FLYNN

1   Gillen[1], pp.129–30 — *OBSP*, January 1784, p.191 — PRO, T1/613, *Dunkirk*, 25 September–25 December 1786 and receipt dated 1 December 1784.

2   Clark, p.2 — RONSW, Marriages.4.72 — ML, A1958, p.22 — PRO, CO201/9, fol.36[r].

3   PRO, CO201/10, fols 98[v], 101[v], 138[v]–9[r], 184[r].

4   ML, A1958, pp.22, 54 — Baxter[1], p.45 (AEO81) — SRNSW, 4/4486, p.6 — SRNSW, 5/1112, no.18/30 — SRNSW, SZ766, pp.69, 177; SRNSW, 2/8147, p.197. For comments on the Dore address, see *HRNSW*, 3.550,554.

5   Baxter[2], pp.124–5 (BO112) — *SG*, 19 May, 2 June & 30 June 1810 — Baxter[4], p.115 (no.5101) — Baxter[5], p.169 (AO7350) — Baxter[6], p.192 (no.21034).

6   Gillen[1], p.130.

7   PRO, CO201/9, fols 222[r], 259[v].

ROBERT HIGGINS

1   Statham, p.293; PRO, W025/642, p.55.

2   ML, A1958, p.5 — PRO, CO201/10, fols 70[r], 172[r].

3   PRO, CO201/10, fols 8[v], 99[v], 100[r–v], 172[r].

4   ML, A1958, p.5 — Statham, p.293 — Baxter[1], p.88 (AH051); *SG*, 19 January 1804; PRO, WO12/9899–9901, *passim*.

5   Ryan[2], p.264 — PRO, WO25/1342, fol.35[v] — PRO, WO12/9904, p.8; PRO, WO12/9905, p.364; *SG*, 24 September & 8 October 1809.

6   PRO, WO12/800 — RONSW, Marriages.5.153.

7   SRNSW, 9/2652, p.10 — Baxter[4], pp.80 (no.3553), 91 (no.4033) — SRNSW, 4/1728, p.134 — SRNSW, 4/1819, p.581.

8   Baxter[5], p.228 (AO9983); Baxter[6], p.261 (no.25028) — Atkinson[2], p.205 — RONSW, Burials.27.624.

WILLIAM HOGG

1 *OBSP*, April 1784, pp.644–5 — PRO, T1/618, *Censor*, 11 July–12 October 1784 & T1/619, *Censor*, 12 January–12 April 1785.
2 Collins, 1.358 — Grimwade, p.548.
3 SRNSW, SZ765, pp.183–6 — RONSW, Marriages.4.61.
4 ML, A1958, p.24 — PRO, CO201/9, fols 35^r, 28^r— PRO, CO201/10, fol.95^r.
5 Collins, 1.358.

MICHAEL LEE

1 *OBSP*, February 1789, pp.318–22 — PRO, HO47/12 (20 August 1790) — SRNSW, 4/3998, p.86. The cutting away of portmanteaux was a practice going back at least to the beginning of the eighteenth century (Smith[1], p.107).
2 ML, A1958, p.35 — PRO, CO201/9, fol.137^r — PRO, CO201/10, fols 184^r, 225^r — PRO, CO201/9, fol.184^r.
3 Ryan[2], pp.91, 145.
4 For example, PRO, CO201/29, fols 29^r, 33^r, 63^v, 65^v, 67^r, 174^v, 184^r, 186^r.
5 Baxter[2], p.189 (DO236) — PRO, CO201/55, fol.32^r —Schaffer[2], p.222.
6 Wright[1], p.77 — Ryan[2], p.227 — ML, A2563, p.667.
7 PRO, CO201/42, fol.309^v.
8 PRO, CO201/10, fol.99^v.
9 Wright[1], pp.119–24 — ML, CY1092, p.412.
10 *Hobart Town Gazette*, 12 June 1819 — Archives Office of Tasmania, LSD1/6, pp.293–9; Archives Office of Tasmania, LSD1/83, pp.304–5.
11 Levi, p.70.

JOSEPH MORRELL

1 *OBSP*, May 1784, pp.790–1.
2 PRO, HO47/3.
3 PRO, T1/616, *Censor*, 11 July–12 October 1784.
4 *OBSP*, December 1786, pp.65–6.
5 *OBSP*, September 1787, p.890 — Flynn[1], p.453.
6 ML, A1958, p.24 — Nobbs[1], p.115 — Clark, p.185 — PRO, CO201/9, fols 28^v, 37^v.
7 Clark, p.189 — PRO, CO201/9, fol.28^v.
8 PRO, CO201/9, fol.127^r.
9 PRO, CO201/10, fol.97^v.
10 PRO, CO201/10, fol.192^r.
11 SRNSW, SZ76, p.60 — Baxter[1], p.123 (BG164).
12 *SG*, 2 April, 28 (*bis*) August, 4, 18 September & 4, 11, 18 (*bis*) December 1803.
13 *SG*, 22 April 1804; PRO, CO201/33, fol.171^r.
14 Delano, pp.639–40.
15 PRO, CO201/33, fols 170^r–1^v — SRNSW, SZ768, p.529.
16 *SG*, 27 January, 10 February & 19 May 1805 — Provis, p.81.
17 SRNSW, 2/8148, p.705.
18 *SG*, 27 October & 3 December 1805, 16 April 1809.
19 *SG*, 6 June, 30 July & 1 October 1809, 5 May & 10 November 1810 — Cumpston, pp.80, 90.
20 *SG*, 6 July 1816, 17 October 1818.

STEPHEN SHORE

1   PRO, ASSI35/227/3; PRO, T1/671, *Lion*, 12 July–12 October 1789.

2   ML, A1958, p.28; PRO, CO201/10, fol.95[r].

3   ML, A1958, p.28 — RONSW, Marriages.4.246 — Baxter[1], pp.49 (AE254), 79 (AG188) — Ryan[2], p.167; Baxter[2], pp.94 (A3942), 122–3 (B0048) — *SG*, 17 December 1809; ML, A3614, p.330. In view of his later activities, it may be significant that Shore's Bankstown property included a half-acre of garden.

4   SRNSW, 4/1725, p.15; *HRNSW*, 4.131 — ML, FM4/3700, p.93 — Baxter [4], p.50 (no.2188); Baxter[5], p.433 (A19092) — SRNSW, 4/1819, p.141 — ML, A3614, p.330 — Baxter[6], p.518 (no.39957) — Baxter[5], p.429 (A18925).

5   Baxter[4], p.67 (no.2957) — RONSW, Burials.10.295 — Baxter[6], pp.518 (no.39957), 587 (no.43967).

LONGER NOTES TO CHAPTERS 1–7

NOTE 1: THE MAN WITH THE SILVER NOSE

1   Brewer, pp.2–3.

2   I am currently preparing an article on Herring's career.

3   A tangled passage in James Lawrence's autobiography suggests he and James Bushelle provided musical entertainment for the officers at Moreton Bay. Bushelle's biography shows him having a pleasant life there teaching music, languages and fencing. See ML, Dixson, Q168, item 1, p.160 & item 4, p.5.

NOTE 2: THE VENUE FOR *THE RECRUITING OFFICER*, 4 JUNE 1789

1   Collins, 1.16–7. On the previous page he writes of some of the marines erecting 'temporary clay huts' for themselves. The convict hut was almost certainly thatched, though some buildings had begun to use shingles by July 1788. See *HRA*, 1.1.48.

2   Tench, p.57.

3   Collins, 1.19 — Tench, p.195.

4   Collins, 1.172.

5   *HRA*, 1.1.48, 74, 194; Collins, 1.82. Irving, p.296, makes a similar argument for the existence of barracks at Sydney large enough for performance, though he does not address the issue of their division into two rooms or explore the subject of women's barracks.

6   Parker, 1.164; Ryley, 1.69; Holcroft, 1.120.

NOTE 3: DINERS AND PLAYGOERS, 4 JUNE 1789

1   Moore[1], pp.294–302 — Gillen[1], pp.65, 314.

2   I have some doubts about James Smith, the commissariat officer at Parramatta (Gillen[1], p.335). Waterhouse has described the provost-marshal's position in 1797 as equivalent to a lieutenancy. In any case, the incumbent in 1789, Henry Brewer, was a midshipman from HMS *Sirius*, on secondment (ML, 6544 (letter of March 1797) — Gillen[1], p.48).

3   Gillen[1], pp.50–1 — *ADB*, 1.311–2 — Fowell, p.112.

4   Rodger, pp.20, 22, 65–7, 96–7, 268. Rodger, pp.65–7, implies others could sometimes be included, but when the *True Briton*, 17 October 1797, listed naval officers killed at the Battle of Cape St Vincent, it went no lower than captain's clerk. A list of 1791 (PRO,

ADM 1/3824, p.137) gives HMS *Supply* a complement of six officers. That number can only be reached by including the master, the surgeon and the clerk as well as the commanding lieutenant and the two midshipmen (there were no master's or surgeon's mates on this tiny vessel).

5   See, for example, the promotions of officers recorded in the pay lists of HMS *Sirius*.
6   *HRNSW*, 4.524.
7   Hunter, pp.225, 228.
8   As per pay lists, PRO, ADM 36/10978, pp.320–33 & ADM 36/10981, pp.213–20.
9   Clark, p.111; Tench, p.39.
10   In 1788 all 4 commissioned officers on HMS *Sirius* (the captain and 3 lieutenants) attended the dinner, but only 3 of the 6 midshipmen (see ML, 5544 (letter of 11 July 1788)). The number of HMS *Sirius'* warrant officers present (surgeons, pursers, masters etc.) is not recorded.

NOTE 4: SEASONAL BRICK-MAKING AND THE BRICKFIELDS THEATRE

1   See the article on bricks in Abraham Rees' expanded version of Chambers' *Cyclopaedia*. The relevant Acts of Parliament are 12 Geo.I.c.35 and 10 Geo.III.c.49.
2   Collins, 1.30.

NOTE 5: THE STORY OF THE OFFICER'S DOG

1   Collins, 1.354.
2   Bennett, p.213. For later examples, see Heaton, p.87, McMahon, p.130, Brodsky[2], p.45 and Hall[2], p.10.

NOTE 6: DRUNKEN ACTORS

1   Oxberry[2], 4.160, 265; Parke, pp.97–8.
2   Oxberry[1], pp.133–5.

NOTE 7: THE OPENING DATE OF THE NORFOLK ISLAND THEATRE

1   ANL, MS 70, p.88.
2   PRO, CO201/10, fol.4[r].
3   PRO, CO201/10, fol.344[r].
4   PRO, CO201/10, fols 8[v]–9[r].

NOTE 8: THOMAS CROWDER'S NORFOLK ISLAND PLAYHOUSE, 1793/94

1   PRO, CO201/10, fol.95[v].
2   PRO, CO201/10, fol.91[v].
3   PRO, CO201/10, fol.9[v].
4   PRO, CO201/10, fol.9[v].
5   Wilson[1], 1.20–1.
6   PRO, CO700 NSW6 — PRO, MPG299. There plans are reproduced in Wilson[1], pl.4 & 5.
7   PRO, CO201/9, fol.104[r].
8   PRO, CO201/9, fol.104[v].
9   For Eyre, see ML, Z SV8/NORFI/1. — For Dayes, see ANL, Petherick 490/1. — For King, see ML, SPF.

10 PRO, CO201/18, fol.172^r.

11 PRO, CO201/10, fol.218^r.

12 PRO, CO201/10, fol.253^v.

13 PRO, CO201/10, fols 94^r, 97 ^{r}.

14 PRO, CO201/10, fols 95 $^{r-v}$.

15 PRO, CO201/10, fol. 95^r. Soldiers occupying 'nearly the half of it' left room for the six or seven servants of Balmain and Mrs King.

16 Jordan[1], p.45.

17 PRO, CO201/10, fols 92^v, 98^{r-v}, 95^v.

18 PRO, CO201/10, fols 92^v, 97^r.

19 PRO, CO201/10, fol.93^r.

20 PRO, CO201/10, fols 95^v, 94^r, 91^v.

21 Apart from the six or seven servants, Governor King, Mrs King, Chapman, Balmain, and one of the military officers are specified in the records or are certain to have been present. At least one overseer may have been attached to the group. A second military officer (but not Abbott), Bain the clergyman, and other civil officials could also have been of the party.

NOTE 9: THE FIRST PERFORMANCES AT EMU PLAINS

1 *HRA*, 1.11.79. The earliest recorded clearing party from Emu Plains was assembled at the beginning of February 1822. See SRNSW, 4/3504A, pp.380–2.

2 Introduction to Tucker[2], p.3.

3 SRNSW, 2/8283, pp.113–208.

4 He is said to be the author of the 'Journal of an Excursion across the Blue Mountains' published in the November issue of the *London Magazine*, 8 (1823), where Emu Plains is mentioned on p.462.

5 ML, Dixson, Q168, item 1, p.57. Lawrence, 'as great a Scamp as any in the Colony', fails to mention that he was sent to Emu Plains for stealing a leg of mutton from a butcher's window, and was sent to Port Macquarie to complete his sentence because he had escaped from Emu Plains (SRNSW, 4/1900, no.26/5235 — SRNSW, 4/6428, p.131).

6 ML, Dixson, Spencer 154, pp.403–4, 485 — Baxter[5], p.286 (A12562) — Bigge, 1.27 — SRNSW, 2/8283, p.156.

7 The 'impenetrable Major' is Brisbane's powerful colonial secretary, Frederick Goulburn, and the physician Sir John Jamison.

8 *HRA*, 1.11.819.

9 *SG*, 18 & 25 October 1822.

NOTE 10: THE ADVERTISEMENT FOR THE EMU PLAINS PRODUCTION OF 30 NOVEMBER 1830

1 SRNSW, 4/4075, no.30/728.

2 For example, James Johnston O'Connor (*per Prince Regent* 3) would have served his seven years by late 1830. There is no certain evidence he was at Emu Plains, but on 6 March 1827 he received a local sentence from the Penrith bench, most of whose customers were Plainsmen (SRNSW, 4/4009, p.225).

3 Bell, pp.96–108.

4 SRNSW, 4/2166.1, no.32/1990.

NOTE 11: THE AFTERLIFE OF JEMMY KING

1   SRNSW, 4/4063, no.27/100 — SRNSW, 4/4069, no.29/21 — *Australian*, 17 December 1830.
2   Archives Office of Tasmania, CON33/68, p.17001 — SRNSW, 4/4110, no.37/436.
3   *Sydney Monitor and Commercial Advertiser*, 8 August 1838 — SRNSW, T50 (August 1838), court case 69.
4   Archives Office of Tasmania, CON33/68, p.17001.
5   Archives Office of Tasmania, CON33/68, p.17001; CON16/3, p.180–1 & CON21/1.
6   Archives Office of Tasmania, CON33/68, p.17001 — Archives Office of Tasmania, CON52/3, p.260 & RGD37/9, no.654.

Bibliography

(1) MANUSCRIPTS

AUSTRALIA

Brisbane, Queensland State Archives
Film 0078	Moreton Bay: Register of Monthly Returns, 1829–37

Canberra, Australian National Library (ANL)
MS 70	Philip Gidley King: Journal
MS 115	Newspaper Clippings
MS 164	James Colnett, 'Voyage to New South Wales in HMS *Glatton*'
MS 195	Ellis Bent: Journal and Letterbook, 1809–11
MS 737	John Grant: Papers
MS 0349	Richard Atkins: Journal

Hobart, Archives Office of Tasmania
CON 16	Convict Indents
CON 33	Convict Conduct Records
CON 52	Convict Applications to Marry
CON 148	Register of Convicts Secondarily Transported from New South Wales to Norfolk Island and Remaining There in August 1844
LSD 1	Land Survey Department: General Correspondence, c.1822–c.1970
RGD 34	Office of the Registrar General: Register of Burials in Tasmania, 1803–38
RGD 37	Office of the Registrar General: Register of Marriages, all Districts, 1838–99

Launceston (Tasmania), Launceston Reference Library
William Ellis Cox, Richard White File	'The Cox Family of Norfolk Plains' (typescript)

Sydney, Mitchell Library, State Library of New South Wales (ML)
Safe 1/2d	Robert Jones, 'Recollections of Thirteen Years Residence at Norfolk Island'
Safe 1/45	William Bligh: Correspondence
Safe 1/48	William Bligh: Papers
Safe 1/107	Playbills: Sydney Theatre, 1800
MS 27	Stenhouse Papers, 1810–74

MS 508	Commissariat: Accounts, Receipts and Returns, etc., 1803–23
MS 509	Commissariat: Accounts … Pay Lists, 1803–06
MS 681	Papers Concerning Norfolk Island
MS 3266	Helene Oppenheim, 'Colonial Theatre: The Rise of the Legitimate Stage in Australia' (typescript)
MS 6544	Henry Waterhouse: Letters
A 254–6	Piper Papers, 1791–1871
A 291	Sir Thomas Mitchell: Papers
A 859	Rowland Hassall: Correspondence
A 1677	Hassall Family Correspondence
A 1958	Norfolk Island Victualling Book, 1792–4
A 1976	Philip Gidley King: Papers
A 1980	King Family Papers: Further Papers, 1775–1806
A 1982	Arrest of Governor Bligh: Various Papers
A 2012	William Edward Riley: Journal
A 2015	Philip Gidley King: Letterbook, 1787–1806
A 2019	Philip Gidley King: Legal Papers
A 2131	John Thomas Bigge: Appendix to Report, 1822. New South Wales Returns, 1819–20
A 3609–3614	Judge-Advocate's Office: Register of Assignments, 1794–1819
A 4420	Supreme Court: Probate Papers
B 217–218	Thomas Sharpe, 'Journal of Norfolk Island, 1837–1839'
B 437	Daybook of a Sydney Merchant, 1805–06
C 187	Philip Gidley King: Letterbook, Norfolk Island, 1788–99
C 191	Norfolk Island: Survey of the Different Lots of Land [1811?]
Z 4661	Christiana Brooks: Diary and Letters
ZB 189	David Burn, 'Australia, Parts 1–3, New South Wales'
ZB 190^2	David Burn: Journal, 1844–45
BT Box 12	Bonwick Transcripts: Bigge, John T. – Appendix
BT Box 24	Bonwick Transcripts: Bigge, John T. – Appendix
BT Box 49	Bonwick Transcripts: Missionary
BT Box 88	Bonwick Transcripts: Records Located in London
CY 1092	Supreme Court: Court of Civil Jurisdiction Proceedings, 1788–1809
FM 4/2568	George Caley: Papers
FM 4/3700	Registers of St John's Church, Parramatta
Dixson, Add. 552/6	Chief Justice's Reports: Supreme Court Sessions, Hobart and Launceston, 1823–39
Dixson, Q168, item 1	James Lawrence, 'The Historical Account of the Life of James Laurence'
Dixson, Q168, item 4	Biography of James Bushelle
Dixson, Q247–249	Aaron Price, 'History of Norfolk Island'
Dixson, ZQ181	Annie Maria Dawbin: Journals
Dixson, Spencer 54	Sydney Bench of Magistrates, 1820–21
Dixson, Spencer 154	Sydney Bench of Magistrates, 1815–16

Sydney, Registrar's Office of New South Wales (RONSW)

Register of Births, Marriages, Deaths, 1788–

Sydney, State Records of New South Wales (SRNSW)

2/4745	Surveyor-General's Field Book, March 1815
2/8130	Colonial Secretary: Special Bundles, 1794–1825
2/8147–8149	Court of Civil Jurisdiction: Rough Minutes of Proceedings and Related Case Papers, 1788–1809
2/8150	Court of Civil Jurisdiction: Minutes of Proceedings, 1799–1801
2/8283	Colonial Secretary: Convict Papers and Returns
4/1167A–1168A	Colonial Secretary: Papers Relating to Norfolk Island, 1794–1807
4/1218–1219	Colonial Secretary: District Constables' Notebooks for Sydney, 1822
4/1239	Colonial Secretary: Census Papers, 1828
4/1710	Colonial Secretary: Commissions and Licences, 1826–48
4/1713	Colonial Secretary: Affidavits Attesting Loss of Certificates of Freedom
4/1719–1778, 1821–1868	Colonial Secretary: Letters and Petitions Received
4/1819	Proceedings of Coroners' Inquests, 1809–22
4/1900–2698	Colonial Secretary: Letters Received
4/3490	Colonial Secretary: Copies of Letters Sent, Local and Overseas, 1809–13
4/3492	Colonial Secretary: Copies of Letters Sent to Van Diemen's Land, Newcastle and Norfolk Island, 1810–13
4/3499–3515	Colonial Secretary: Copies of Letters Sent Within the Colony
4/3665–3691	Colonial Secretary: Copies of Letters Sent re Convicts
4/3719	Colonial Secretary: Copies of Letters Sent to Establishments
4/3864	Colonial Secretary: Copies of Letters Sent to Port Macquarie, 1822–25
4/3998–4003	Principal Superintendent of Convicts: Convict Indents, 1788–1800
4/4009	Principal Superintendent of Convicts: Indents to Convict Vessels, 1823–24
4/4063–4211	Principal Superintendent of Convicts: Ticket-of-Leave Butts, 1827–47
4/4403	Principal Superintendent of Convicts: Butts of Certificates of Freedom, 1846
4/4430	Colonial Secretary: Register of Conditional Pardons, 1791–1825
4/4437–4440	Colonial Secretary: Copies of Conditional Pardons Registered by the Colonial Secretary, 1839–40
4/4486–4488	Colonial Secretary: Registers of Absolute Pardons, 1791–1843
4/4493–4494	Colonial Secretary: Registers of Colonial Pardons, 1788–1867
4/4520–4521	Principal Superintendent of Convicts: Registers of Labourers Assigned, 1821–25
4/4525	Principal Superintendent of Convicts: List of Absconding Convicts and Assigned Servants, 1822–25
4/4570D	Colonial Secretary: Convict Returns, 1822–24
4/5781	Colonial Secretary: Register of Oaths and Licences, 1844–63
4/6280	Hulk *Phoenix*: Description Book, 1833–37
4/6281	Hulk *Phoenix*: Entrance Book, 1825–31
4/6360	Sydney Gaol: Entrance Book, 1819–23
4/6428–6429	Sydney Gaol: Entrance Books, 1822–28
4/6435–6437	Sydney and Darlinghurst Gaols: Entrance Books, 1825–44
4/6671	Colonial Secretary: Returns of Punishments and Fines, 1824, 1832, 1835

4/7015.2	Colonial Secretary: Certificates of Entitlement to Land Grants for Veteran Pensioners, 1823
4/8435	Clerk of the Peace: Quarter Session Depositions, 1824–37
5/1112	Judge-Advocate's Office: Letters Received, 1791, 1798–1811
5/1113	Judge-Advocate's Office: Draft Copies of Miscellaneous Agreements etc., 1796–1815
5/1147A–1150	Court of Criminal Jurisdiction: Minutes of Proceedings, 1788–1815
5/1156	Supreme Court: Miscellaneous Papers, 1787–1800
5/1157	Supreme Court: Oaths and Recognisances
5/1166	Supreme Court: Miscellaneous. Probate Papers, 1790–1814
7/2691	Colonial Trials and Court Records: Benches of Magistrates, 1815– 21
9/2652	Colonial Secretary: Returns of Free Settlers and Other Free Persons to Receive Land, 1810–28
SZ 758–759	Copies of Government and General Orders, 1810–18
SZ 765–774	Bench of Magistrates: Proceedings, 1788–1814
SZ 796	Court of Criminal Jurisdiction: Informations, Depositions and Related Papers, 1822
SZ 916	Surveyor's Field Book 106
T 50	Supreme Court: Criminal Informations, etc., 1838
X 702	Colonial Secretary: Naval Officer, Bonds, 1810–18
X 820	Colonial Secretary: Reports of Prisoners Tried in the Courts of Criminal Jurisdiction, 1820–24
X 905	Court of Criminal Jurisdiction: Minutes of Proceedings, 1798–1800
Map 5403	City of Sydney, Section 12, 12 September 1831

Sydney, Supreme Court

Probate Division 1   Wills

UNITED KINGDOM

Edinburgh University Library

Dc.7.123   James Mitchell: Journals, 1820–22

Edinburgh, Scottish Record Office

GD248   Seafield Muniments

Greenwich, National Maritime Museum

ADM/L   Lieutenants' Logs

London, British Library (BL)

Playbills 252
Theatre Cuttings no. 36
Theatre Cuttings no. 44
Add. MS 13880   John W. Price, 'Journal of a Voyage from Ireland to New South Wales and India on *Minerva*, May 1798–June 1800'
Add. MS 40357   Sir Robert Peel: Papers

London, British Theatre Museum

PN2595.5 K4   Anon., 'Taking the Town' (typescript)

London, Greater London Record Office
Old Bailey   Depositions

London, Hackney Archives Department
Shoreditch Land Tax

London, India Office
L/MAR/BB/2151   Captain's Log: *Minerva*, 1798–1801

London, Lambeth Palace Library
ARCH/P/Moore 22 Richard Johnson: Papers

London, Public Record Office (PRO)
ADM 1	Admiralty and Secretariat: Papers
ADM 36	Admiralty: Accounting Departments. Ships' Musters
ADM 51	Admiralty and Secretariat: Captains' Logs
ADM 101	Admiralty: Medical Departments. Registers, Medical Journals
ASSI 23	Assize Records: Western Circuit. Gaol Books
ASSI 25	Assize Records: Western Circuit. Indictments
ASSI 31	Assize Records: South Eastern Circuit. Agenda Books
ASSI 34	Assize Records: Home Circuit. Various Records
ASSI 35	Assize Records: South Eastern Circuit. Indictments
ASSI 45	Assize Records: Northern Circuit. Depositions
CO 201	Colonial Office: New South Wales. Original Correspondence
CO 207	Colonial Office: Entry Books Relating to Convicts
CO 700	Colonial Office: Maps
HO 11	Home Office: Convict Transportation Records
HO 17	Home Office: Petitions
HO 26	Home Office: Criminal Registers. Middlesex
HO 47	Home Office: Judges' Reports on Criminals
HO 77	Home Office: Newgate Calendars
PCC.PROB.11	Prerogative Court of Canterbury: Registered Copy Wills
T 1	Treasury: In–letters and Files. Treasury Board Papers
WO 12	War Office: Muster Books and Pay Lists
WO 25	War Office: Registers, Various

London, Society of Genealogists
'Apprentices of Great Britain, 1710–62' (typescript)

London, Westminster City Libraries, Archives division
Poor Rates: St Martin-in-the-Fields
Registers of St Martin-in-the-Fields

Newcastle-upon-Tyne, Tyne and Wear Archives Offices
MS155/1   Records of the Newcastle-upon-Tyne Theatre

York, York Public Library
Y792/S/R   Records of the York Theatre

(2) EIGHTEENTH- AND EARLY NINETEENTH-CENTURY NEWSPAPERS AND PERIODICALS

Note: The dates in parentheses following each entry indicate the period referred to in this book.

British and Indian newspapers

Aris's Birmingham Gazette	(1790–1802)
The Asiatic Mirror	(1816)
Bell's Weekly Messenger	(1796–1805)
Bonner and Middleton's Bristol Journal	(1785–97)
The Bristol Gazette	(1792)
The Cambridge Chronicle	(1796)
The Chelmsford Chronicle	(1786–94)
The Craftsman	(1797)
The Daily Universal Register	(1785–87)
as *The Times*	(1788–1825)
The English Chronicle	(1789)
The Evening Mail	(1792–97)
Felix Farley's Bristol Journal	(1784–1819)
The Gazeteer	(1776)
The Ipswich Journal	(1794)
Johnson's British Gazette	(1797)
The London Chronicle	(1777–97)
The London Packet	(1798)
The Morning Chronicle	(1776–1815)
The Morning Post	(1776–84)
The Newcastle Courant	(1790)
The News	(1828)
The Observer	(1800–02)
The Oracle	(1796–1801)
The Public Advertiser	(1787–92)
The St James Chronicle	(1797)
Saunders' News-Letter	(1797)
The Star	(1791–1800)
The Taunton Courier	(1826)
The Times (see *Daily Universal Register*)	
The True Briton	(1791–97)
The Weekly Entertainer	(1792)
The Western Flying Post	(1784)
The World	(1787–98)
The York Herald	(1792)

Australian newspapers

The Australian	(1825–41)
The Australian Chronicle	(1840)
The Colonial Times	(1840)
The Colonist	(1840)
The Commercial Journal and Advertiser	(1839)

The Empire	(1853)
The Free Press	(1842)
The Hobart Town Gazette	(1816–24)
Howe's Weekly Commercial Express	(1825)
The Launceston Examiner	(1849)
The Monitor	(1826–28)
as *The Sydney Monitor*	(1829–37)
as *The Sydney Monitor and*	
Commercial Advertiser	(1838)
The Sydney Gazette [SG]	(1803–40)
The Sydney Herald	(1840–43)
The Truth	(1908–19)

British journals and periodicals

The Annual Register	(1784/5)
The Colonial Magazine	(1841)
The Dramatic Censor	(1784–1800)
The European Magazine	(1801–08)
The Gentleman's Magazine	(1794)
The London Magazine	(1823–25)
The Monthly Mirror	(1797)
The Spirit of the Public Journals	(1805–08)
The Sporting Magazine	(1797–1801)
The Town and Country Magazine	(1779)
The Weekly Entertainer	(1792)

(3) BOOKS, ARTICLES AND THESES

Anon.[1], *An Account of the English Colony at Botany Bay*, London, 1808

Anon.[2], 'Australia's Oldest Theatres', *The Triad*, November 1924, p.37

Anon.[3], *An Authentic Narrative of the most Remarkable Adventures ... of Miss Fanny Davies*, London, 1786

Anon.[4], *A Concise History of the English Colony in New South Wales*, London [n.d.]

Anon.[5], *Confessions of a Gentleman Convict, Written during a Residence at Botany Bay*, London [n.d.]

Anon.[6], *Convict System, Norfolk Island, Copies or Extracts of any Correspondence ... respecting the Convict System Administered in Norfolk Island*, London, 1846

Anon.[7], *A Description of the Island of St Helena*, London, 1805

Anon.[8], *The Life of George Barrington*, Liverpool, 1791

Anon.[9], *The New London Spy*, London [n.d.]

Anon.[10], *New South Wales Pocket Almanack and Colonial Remembrancer*, Sydney, 1806

Anon.[11], 'Norfolk Island by an Officer on the Spot', *Colburn's United Service Magazine* (1848), 594–606

Anon.[12], 'Present State of Sydney, New South Wales', *Colonial Magazine*, 5 (1841), 291–8

Anon.[13], *Report from the Select Committee on Transportation, Together with Minutes of the Evidence, Appendix and Index* [The Molesworth Report], London, 1838

Anon.[14], *The Secret History of the Green Rooms*, 2 vols, London, 1790

Anon.[15], *Senilities; or, Solitary Amusements*, London, 1801

Anon.[16], *The Spouter's Companion*, London [1770]

Anon.[17], *The Trial of John Macarthur, Esq.*, London, 1808

Anon.[18], *The Trials of Edward Robinson (Late Servant to Tate Wilkinson, Esq.; of the Theatre-Royal, York) ... on Tuesday, July 28, 1789*, York, 1789

Anon.[19], *The Universal British Directory*, 5 vols, London [1792]–1798

Anon.[20], *The Whole Life and Adventures of Miss Davis, commonly called the Beauty in Disguise*, London, 1785

Allen, George W.D., *Early Georgian: Extracts from the Journal of George Allen (1800–1877)*, Sydney, Angus & Robertson, 1958

Anderson, Joseph, *Recollections of a Peninsular Veteran*, London, Edward Arnold, 1913

Armytage, George J. (ed.), *The Register of Baptisms and Marriages at St George's Chapel, May Fair*, Publications of the Harleian Society: Registers, vol. 15, London, 1889

Arundell, Dennis, *The Story of Sadler's Wells, 1683–1964*, London, Hamish Hamilton, 1965

Atkins, Charles Edward, *Register of Apprentices of the Worshipful Company of Clockmakers ... 1631–1931*, London, for the Company, 1931

Atkinson[1], Alan, 'Four Patterns of Convict Protest', *Labour History*, no. 37 (1979), 28–51

Atkinson[2], Alan, *Camden: Farm and Village Life in Early New South Wales*, Melbourne, Oxford University Press, 1988

Atkinson[3], Alan, *Europeans in Australia: 1. The Beginning*, Melbourne, Oxford University Press, 1997

Baer, Mark, *Theatre and Disorder in Late Georgian London*, Oxford, Clarendon Press, 1992

Barker, Kathleen, *Bristol at Play*, Bradford-on-Avon, Moonraker Press, 1976

Barnard, Lady Anne, *South Africa a Century Ago*, London, Smith, Elder, 1901

'Barrington[1], George', *Barrington's New London Spy for 1807*, 5th edn, London, 1807

'Barrington[2], George', *The History of New South Wales*, 2nd edn, London, 1802

Barry, John, *Alexander Maconochie of Norfolk Island*, Melbourne, Melbourne University Press, 1956

Baxter[1], Carol J.(ed.), *Musters and Lists: New South Wales and Norfolk Island, 1800–1802*, Sydney, ABGR, 1988

Baxter[2], Carol J. (ed.), *Musters of New South Wales and Norfolk Island, 1805–1806*, Sydney, ABGR, 1989

Baxter[3], Carol J. (ed.), *General Musters of New South Wales, Norfolk Island and Van Diemen's Land, 1811*, Sydney, ABGR, 1987

Baxter[4], Carol J. (ed.), *General Muster of New South Wales, 1814*, Sydney, ABGR, 1987

Baxter[5], Carol J. (ed.), *General Muster and Land and Stock Muster of New South Wales, 1822*, Sydney, ABGR, 1988

Baxter[6], Carol J. (ed.), *General Muster List of New South Wales, 1823, 1824, 1825*, Sydney, ABGR, 1999

Bee, Jon [i.e. John Badcock], *Slang*, London, 1825

Bell, Barbara, 'The National Drama', *Theatre Research International*, 17 (1992), 96–108

Bennett, Samuel, *The History of Australian Discovery and Colonisation*, Sydney, 1865

Benson, Eugene and L.W. Conolly (eds), *The Oxford Companion to Canadian Theatre*, Toronto, Oxford University Press, 1989

Bernard, John, *Retrospections of the Stage*, 2 vols, London, 1830

Best, Abel Dottin William, *The Journal of Ensign Best, 1837–1843*, ed. by N.M. Taylor, Wellington, Govt Printer, 1966

Bigge[1], John Thomas, *Report of the Commissioner of Inquiry, into the State of the Colony of New South Wales*, London, 1822

Bigge[2], John Thomas, *Report of the Commissioner of Inquiry, on the Judicial Establishments of New South Wales and Van Diemen's Land*, London, 1823

Blagden, Cyprian, *The Stationer's Company: A History, 1403–1959*, London, Allen & Unwin, 1960

Blosseville, Ernest de, *Histoire des colonies pénales dans l'Australie*, Paris, 1831

Boaden, James, *Memoirs of the Life of John Philip Kemble, Esq.*, 2 vols, London, 1825

Booth, Michael R., 'The Social and Literary Context', in *The Revels History of Drama in English*, ed. by Clifford Leech and T.W. Craik, 8 vols, London, Methuen, 1975, 6.3–55

Bond, David, 'On Playing Musidors', *Notes and Queries*, n.s. 33 (1986), 469–71

Bougainville, Hyacinthe de, *The Governor's Noble Guest: Hyacinthe de Bougainville's Account of Port Jackson, 1825*, trans. and ed. by M.S. Rivière, Melbourne, Melbourne University Press, 1999

Bowd, Douglas., *Hawkesburg Journey*, Sydney, Library of Australian History, 1986

Bradley, William, *A Voyage to New South Wales*, 2 vols, Sydney, Ure Smith, 1969

Brewer, Francis Campbell, *The Drama and Music in New South Wales*, Sydney, 1892

Broadbent, R.J., *Annals of the Liverpool Stage*, New York, Benjamin Blom, 1969

Brodsky[1], Isadore, *The Streets of Sydney*, Sydney, Old Sydney Free Press, 1962

Brodsky[2], Isadore, *Sydney Takes the Stage*, Sydney, Old Sydney Free Press, 1963

Brown, John, *Sixty Years' Gleanings from Life's Harvest*, Cambridge and London, 1858

Butterss, Philip, 'What has the Presbyterian Church got to do with The Exile of Erin, on the Plains of Emu?', *The Cornstalk Gazette*, no. 183 (December 1988), 7

Byng, John, Viscount Torrington, *The Torrington Diaries*, ed. by C. Bruyn Andrews, 4 vols, London, Eyre & Spottiswoode, 1934–38

Caley, George, *Reflections on the Colony of New South Wales*, ed. by J.E.B. Currey, Melbourne, Lansdowne Press, 1966

Cameron, William, *Hawkie: The Autobiography of a Gangrel*, ed. by J. Strathesk, Glasgow, 1888

Carr, Sir Cecil (ed.), *The Pension Book of Clement's Inn*, Publications of the Selden Society, vol. 78, London, Quaritch, 1960

[Carter, Henry], 'Botany Bay Theatrical Prologue, Spoken on Opening the Theatre at Sydney, Botany Bay', *The European Magazine*, 40 (October 1801), 289–90

Chambers, E., *Cyclopaedia; or, An Universal Directory of Arts and Sciences*, expanded ed. by Abraham Rees, 4 vols, London, 1786–88

Chisholm, Alec H., *The Australian Encyclopaedia*, 10 vols, Sydney, Grolier Society [1963]

Clark, Ralph, *The Journal and Letters of Lieutenant Ralph Clark, 1787–1792*, ed. by P.G. Fidlon and R.J. Ryan, Sydney, Australian Documents Library, 1981

Colby, Elbridge, 'A Defence of Spouting Clubs', *The Nation*, 106 (1918), 124–5

Colley, Linda, *Britons: Forging the Nation, 1707–1827*, New Haven, Yale University Press, 1992

Collins, David, *An Account of the English Colony in New South Wales*, ed. by B. Fletcher, 2 vols, Sydney, A.H. & A.W. Reed, 1975

Colman, George, *Random Records*, London, 1830

Cooke, William, *Memoirs of Charles Macklin*, London, 1804

Cowper, William Macquarie, *The Autobiography and Reminiscences of William Macquarie Cowper, Dean of Sydney*, Sydney, Angus & Robertson, 1902

Cramer, Yvonne, *This Beauteous Wicked Place*, Canberra, National Library of Australia, 2000

Cumpston, John Stanley, *Shipping Arrivals and Departures: Sydney, 1788–1825*, Canberra, Roebuck, 1977

Currey, John, *David Collins: A Colonial Life*, Carlton South, Melbourne University Press, 2000

'Cutspear, W.', *Dramatic Rights*, London, 1802

Damousi, Joy, *Depraved and Disorderly*, Cambridge, Cambridge University Press, 1997

Daniels, Kay, '"The Flash Mob": Rebellion, Rough Culture and Sexuality in the Female Factories of Van Diemen's Land', *Australian Feminist Studies*, no. 18 (1993), 133–50

Davies, John, *The History of the Tahitian Mission, 1799–1830*, ed. by C.W. Newbury, Cambridge, Cambridge University Press, 1961

Davoren, Lawrence, *A New Song Made in New South Wales on the Rebellion*, ed. by G. Mackaness, Australian Historical Monographs, n.s., vol. 33, Dubbo, Review Publications, 1979

Delano, Amasa, *A Narrative of Voyages and Travels*, Boston, 1817

Dibdin[1], Charles, *Observations on a Tour through England and Scotland*, 2 vols, London [1801–02]

Dibdin[2], Thomas, *The Reminiscences of Thomas Dibdin*, London, 1827

Dobson, Edward, *A Rudimentary Treatise on the Manufacture of Bricks and Tiles*, 2 vols, London, 1850

Donaldson, Ian, 'New Papers of Henry Holland and R.B. Sheridan', *Theatre Notebook*, 16 (1962), 117–25

Donohue[1], Joseph, 'Burletta and the Early Nineteenth-Century English Theatre', *Nineteenth-Century Theatre Research*, 1 (1973), 29–51

Donohue[2], Joseph, *Theatre in the Age of Kean*, Oxford, Basil Blackwood, 1975

Duffield[1], Ian, 'The Life and Death of 'Black' John Goff: Aspects of the Black Convict Contribution to Resistance Patterns during the Transportation Era in Eastern Australia', *Australian Journal of Politics and History*, 33 (1987), 30–44

Duffield[2], Ian, 'Daylight on Convict Lived Experience: The History of a Pious Negro Servant', *Tasmanian Historical Studies*, 6 (1999), 29–62

Dunlap, William, *The Life of George Fred. Cooke*, 2 vols, London, 1815

Dunlop, O. Jocelyn and Richard D. Denman, *English Apprenticeship and Child Labour*, London, T. Fisher Unwin, 1912

Dyer, Robert, *Nine Years of an Actor's Life*, London, 1833

Eastwick, Robert William, *A Master Mariner*, ed. by H. Compton, London, 1891

Easty, John, *Memorandum of the Transactions of a Voyage from England to Botany Bay, 1787–1793*, Sydney, Angus & Robertson, 1965

Egan, Pierce, *The Life of an Actor*, London, 1825

Elliot, Jane, 'Was there a convict dandy? Convict consumer interests in Sydney 1788–1815', *Australian Historical Studies*, 26 (1995), 373–92

Evans, Claire C., 'Harry Parsons – Early Sydney Musician', *Descent*, 4 (1967), 109–11

Everard, Edward Cape, *Memoirs of an Unfortunate Son of Thespis*, Edinburgh, 1818

Farmer, Henry George, *The Rise and Development of Military Music*, London, William Reeves, 1912

Ferguson[1], John Alexander, A.G. Foster and H.M. Green, *The Howes and their Press*, Sydney, Sunnybrook Press, 1936

Ferguson[2], John Alexander, *Bibliography of Australia: 1. 1784–1830*, Canberra, National Library of Australia, 1975

[Field, Barron], 'Journal of an Excursion across the Blue Mountains', *The London Magazine*, 8 (1823), 461–75

Fitzgerald, Ross and Mark Hearn, *Bligh, Macarthur and the Rum Rebellion*, Kenthurst, NSW, Kangaroo Press, 1988

Fitzsimmons, Linda and Arthur W. McDonald, *The Yorkshire Stage, 1766–1803*, Metuchen, NJ, Scarecrow Press, 1989

Fletcher, Brian, 'Sir John Jamison in New South Wales, 1814–1844', *JRAHS*, 65 (1979), 1–29

Flinders, Matthew, *A Voyage to Terra Australis*, 3 vols, London, 1814

Flynn[1], Michael, *The Second Fleet*, Sydney, Library of Australian History, 1993

Flynn[2], Michael, *Settlers and Seditionists: The People of the Convict Ship 'Surprize', 1794*, Sydney, Angela Lind, 1994

Forster, Colin, *France and Botany Bay*, Melbourne, Melbourne University Press, 1996

Foster[1], Arthur G., 'The Sandhills. An Historic Cemetery', *JRAHS*, 5 (1919), 153–95

Foster[2], Harold, *Edward Young: The Poet of the Night Thoughts, 1683–1765*, Aldburgh, Erskine Press, 1986

Foster[3], Joseph, *The Register of Admissions to Gray's Inn, 1521–1889*, London, 1889

Foster[4], Stephen G., 'Convict Assignment in New South Wales in the 1830s', *The Push from the Bush*, no. 15 (1983), 35–80

Fowell, Newton, *The Sirius Letters*, Sydney, The Fairfax Library, 1988

Fowles, Joseph, *Sydney in 1848*, Sydney [1848]

Fremantle, Anne (ed.), *The Wynne Diaries*, 3 vols, Oxford, Oxford University Press, 1940

Gentleman, Francis, *The Dramatic Censor*, 2 vols, London, 1770

Gillen[1], Mollie, *The Founders of Australia*, Sydney, Library of Australian History, 1989

Gillen[2], Mollie, 'His Majesty's Mercy: The Circumstances of the First Fleet', *The Push*, no. 29 (1991), 47–109

Gilliland, Thomas, *The Dramatic Mirror*, 2 vols, London, 1808

Goede, Christian August Gottlieb, *The Stranger in England*, 3 vols, London, 1807

Goldsmith, Oliver, *The Collected Works*, ed. by Arthur Friedman, 5 vols, Oxford, Clarendon Press, 1966

Govett, William Romaine, *Sketches of New South Wales*, Melbourne, Gaston Renard, 1977

Grant, John, *Struggles for Just Principles*, Margate [1828]

Griffin, Gwendoline and Ronald Howell, *Port Macquarie: The Winding Sheet*, Port Macquarie, Port Macquarie Historical Society, 1996

Grimwade, Arthur G., *London Goldsmiths, 1697–1837*, London, Faber, 1976

Grose[1], Francis, *A Classical Dictionary of the Vulgar Tongue*, ed. by E. Partridge, London, Routledge, 1963

Grose[2], Kelvin, '"A Strange Compound of Good and Ill": Laurence Hynes Halloran', in *Exiles from Erin*, ed. by Bob Reece, London, Macmillan, 1991, pp.85–111

Hall[1], Barbara, *A Desperate Set of Villains: The Convicts of the 'Marquis Cornwallis', Ireland to Botany Bay, 1796*, Sydney, The Author, 2000

Hall[2], Humphrey and Alfred John Cripps ['Osric'], *The Romance of the Sydney Stage*, Sydney, Currency Press, 1996

Hall[3], John Vine, *The Author of 'The Sinner's Friend': An Autobiography*, London, 1865

Halloran, Laurence, *Rescued Fragments of Cabin Memorandums and Other Writings by and about L. Boutcher Halloran*, Sydney, Laurence Halloran, 1979

Hare, Arnold (ed.), *Theatre Royal, Bath: A Calendar of Performances ...1750–1805*, Bath, Kingsmead Press, 1977

Harriott, John, *Struggles through Life*, 3 vols, London, 1815

Harris, George Prideaux, *Letters and Papers of G.P. Harris, 1803–1812*, ed. by B. Hamilton-Arnold, Sorrento, Vic., Arden Press, 1994

Havard, Olive and L. Ward, 'Some Early French Visitors to the Blue Mountains and Bathurst', *JRAHS*, 24 (1938), 245–90

Hazlitt, William, *Hazlitt on Theatre*, ed. by William Archer and Robert Lowe, New York, Hill & Wang, 1957

Hazzard, Margaret, *Punishment Short of Death*, Melbourne, Hyland House, 1984

Heaton, John Henniker, *Australian Dictionary of Dates and Men of the Time*, Sydney, 1879

Highfill, Philip H. and others, *A Biographical Dictionary of Actors, Actresses, Musicians, Dancers, Managers and Other Stage Personnel in London, 1660–1800*, 16 vols, Carbondale, Southern Illinois University Press, 1973–93

Hill, Errol, *The Jamaican Stage, 1655–1900*, Amherst, University of Massachusetts Press, 1992

Hill-Reid, William Scott, *John Grant's Journey*, London, Heinemann, 1957

Hodgson, Norma, 'Sarah Baker (1736/7–1816): Governess-General of the Kentish Drama', in *Studies in English Theatre History in Memory of Gabrielle Enthoven, OBE*, London, Society for Theatre Research, 1952, pp. 65–83

Hogan[1], Charles Beecher, 'The China Hall Theatre, Rotherhithe', *Theatre Notebook*, 38 (1954), 76–80

Hogan[2], Charles Beecher, *Shakespeare in the Theatre: 1701–1800*, Oxford, Clarendon Press, 1957

Holcroft[1], Thomas, *The Theatrical Recorder*, 2 vols, London, 1805–06

Holcroft[2], Thomas, *The Life of Thomas Holcroft*, ed. by E. Colby, 2 vols, New York, Benjamin Blom, 1968

Holt, Joseph, *A Rum Story: The Adventures of Joseph Holt, Thirteen Years in New South Wales (1800–12)*, ed. by Peter O'Shaughnessy, Kenthurst, NSW, Kangaroo Press, 1988

Hone, William, *The Table Book*, London, 1878

Howe, Ellic (ed.), *The London Compositor*, London, The Bibliographical Society, 1947

Hügel, Baron Charles von, *New Holland Journal*, ed. by D. Clark, Melbourne, Melbourne University Press, 1994

Hughes, Robert, *The Fatal Shore*, London, Pan Books, 1988

Hunt[1], Leigh, *Essays and Sketches of Leigh Hunt*, ed. by A. Symons, London, Dent, 1903

Hunt[2], Levitt W., 'Ann Mash (Marsh?) in Sydney, 1790–1823', *Descent*, 16 (1986), 154–60

Hunter, John, *An Historical Journal of Events at Sydney and at Sea, 1787–1792*, ed. by J. Bach, Sydney, Angus & Robertson, 1968

Ignatieff, Michael, *A Just Measure of Pain: The Penitentiary in the Industrial Revolution*, New York, Columbia University Press, 1978

Ihde, Erin, 'Monitoring the situation: the 'convict journal', convict protest and convicts' rights', *JRAHS*, 85 (1999), 20–35

Irvin[1], Eric, *Theatre Comes to Australia*, St Lucia, University of Queensland Press, 1971

Irvin[2], Eric, *Dictionary of the Australian Theatre, 1788–1914*, Sydney, Hale & Iremonger, 1985

Irvine, Nancy, *Mary Reibey – Molly Incognita*, North Sydney, Library of Australian History, 1987

Irving, Robert, 'The First Australian Architecture', unpublished M.Arch. thesis, University of New South Wales, 1975

Janson, Charles William, *The Stranger in America*, London, 1807

Johnson[1], Keith Arthur and M.R. Sainty, *Gravestone Inscriptions of New South Wales: 1. Sydney Burial Ground*, North Sydney, Genealogical Publications of Australia, 1973

Johnson[2], Richard, *Some Letters of Rev. Richard Johnson BA First Chaplain of New South Wales*, ed. by G. Mackaness, 2 vols, Australian Historical Monographs, n.s., vol. 20, Dubbo, Review Publications, 1978

Jordan[1], Robert John, 'Visualising the Sydney Theatre, 1796', *Australasian Drama Studies*, no. 28 (1996), 30–52

Jordan[2], Robert John, 'The Georgian Theatre in Sydney: Some Facts and Problems', *Theatre Notebook*, 51 (1997), 128–46

Kappey, Jacob Adam, *Military Music*, London, Boosey & Co. [n.d.]

Karskens, Grace, *The Rocks: Life in Early Sydney*, Carlton, Melbourne University Press, 1997

Kelly[1], John Alexander, *German Visitors to the English Theatres in the Eighteenth Century*, New York, Octagon, 1978

Kelly[2], Ebenezer Beriah, *Ebenezer Beriah Kelly: An Autobiography*, Norwich, 1856

Keneally, Thomas, *The Playmaker*, London, Hodder & Stoughton, 1988

Kerr, Joan (ed.), *Dictionary of Australian Artists … to 1870*, Melbourne, Oxford University Press, 1992

Kiernan, Thomas Joseph, *Transportation from Ireland to Sydney: 1791–1816*, Canberra [n. pub.], 1954

King, Philip Gidley, *The Journal of Lt Philip Gidley King*, ed. by P.G. Fidlon and R.J. Ryan, Sydney, Australian Documents Library, 1980

Knight, Charles, *Passages of a Working Life*, 3 vols, London, 1873

Knopwood, Robert, *The Diary of the Reverend Robert Knopwood, 1803–1838*, ed. by M. Nicholls, Hobart, Tasmanian Historical Research Association, 1977

Lackington, James, *Memoirs of the First Forty-five Years of James Lackington*, London, 1794

Laqueur, Thomas W., 'Towards a Cultural Ecology of Literacy in England, 1600–1850', in *Literacy in Historical Perspective*, ed. by Daniel P. Resnick, Washington, Library of Congress, 1983, pp.43–57

Leacroft, Richard, *The Development of the English Playhouse*, London, Eyre Methuen, 1973

Lee, Henry, *Memoirs of a Manager*, 2 vols, Taunton, 1830

Levi, John Simon, *The Forefathers: A Dictionary of Biography of the Jews of Australia, 1788–1830*, Sydney, Australian Jewish Historical Society, 1976

Levine, Lawrence W., *Highbrow/Lowbrow: The Emergence of Cultural Hierarchy in America*, Cambridge, Mass., Harvard University Press, 1988

Lewes, Charles Lee, *Memoirs*, 4 vols, London, 1805

Lewis, Matthew Gregory, *Raymond and Agnes; The Travellers Benighted; or, The Bleeding Nun of Lindenberg*, Cumberland's British Theatre, 38, London [n.d.]

Linebaugh, Peter, *The London Hanged*, London, Penguin, 1993

Love[1], David, *The Life, Adventures and Experience of David Love*, 3rd edn, Nottingham, 1823

Love[2], Harold (ed.), *The Australian Stage: A Documentary History*, Kensington, University of New South Wales Press, 1984

Lynch, James J., *Pit, Box and Gallery*, Berkeley, California University Press, 1953

McAskill, Tracey, 'An Asset to the Colony: The Social and Economic Contribution of Corpsmen to Early New South Wales', *JRAHS*, 82 (1996), 40–59

McCormick, Tim, *First Views of Australia*, Chippendale, David Ell Press, 1987

McCulloch, S.C., 'Sir George Gipps and Captain Alexander Maconochie: The Attempted Penal Reforms at Norfolk Island, 1840–44', *Historical Studies Australia and New Zealand*, 7 (1957), 387–405

McGuire, Paul, *The Australian Theatre*, Melbourne, Oxford University Press, 1948

Mackaness, George (ed.), *Fourteen Journeys over the Blue Mountains of New South Wales, 1813–1841*, Sydney, Horwitz-Grahame, 1965

McKenzie, Donald F., *Stationers' Company Apprentices, 1701–1800*, Oxford Bibliographical Society Publications, n.s. 19, Oxford, for the Society, 1978

Macintosh, Neil K., *Richard Johnson*, Sydney, Library of Australian History, 1978

Mackintosh, Iain, *The Georgian Playhouse*, London, Arts Council, 1975

Maclehose, James, *Maclehose's Picture of Sydney*, Sydney, 1839

McMahon, John, *Fragments of the Early History of Australia*, Melbourne, W. & J. Barr, 1913

Maconochie, Alexander, *Norfolk Island*, Hobart, Sullivan's Cove Publisher, 1973

Malcolm, James Peller, *Anecdotes of the Manners and Customs of London during the Eighteenth Century*, 2 vols, London, 1810

Mander, Raymond and Joe Mitchenson, *Lost Theatres of London*, London, New English Library, 1976

Mann, David Dickinson, *The Present Picture of New South Wales*, London, 1811

Marinetti, Filippo Tommaso, *Selected Writings*, ed. by R.W. Flint, London, Secker & Warburg, 1972

Marsden, Samuel, *Some Private Correspondence of the Rev. Samuel Marsden and Family, 1794–1824*, compiled by G. Mackaness, Australian Historical Monographs, n.s., vol. 12, Dubbo, Review Publications, 1976

Mather, Joseph, *The Songs of Joseph Mather*, Sheffield, 1862

Mathews, Anne, *Memoirs of Charles Mathews, Comedian*, 4 vols, London, 1838–39

Maxwell, John, *Letters of John Maxwell, 1823–1831*, ed. by Bertha Mac Smith and B. Lloyd, Wangaratta, Shoestring Press, 1982

Mayhew, Henry, *London Labour and the London Poor*, 4 vols, London, Cass, 1967

'Mellish, –', 'A Convict's Recollections of New South Wales', *The London Magazine*, n.s. 2 (1825), 49–67

Moore[1], John, *The First Fleet Marines: 1786–1792*, St Lucia, University of Queensland Press, 1987

Moore[2], Mark, *The Memoirs and Adventures of Mark Moore*, London, 1795.

Moritz, Carl Philipp, 'Travels … through Several Parts of England, in 1782', in *A General Collection of the Best and Most Interesting Voyages and Travel*, ed. by John Pinkerton, 13 vols, London, 1808–14, 2.489–573

Mortlock, John Frederick, *Experiences of a Convict*, ed. by G.A. Wilkes and A.G. Mitchell, Sydney, Sydney University Press, 1965

Mudie, James, *The Felonry of New South Wales*, ed. by W. Stone, London, Angus & Robertson, 1965

Mukherjee, S.K., *The Story of Calcutta Theatres, 1753–1980*, Calcutta, K.P. Bagchi & Co., 1982

Mullaney, Steven, *The Place of the Stage*, Chicago, University of Chicago Press, 1988

Murray, Robert and Kate White, *Dharug and Dungaree*, Melbourne, Hargreen, 1988

Nagle, Jacob, *The Nagle Journal*, ed. by J.C. Dann, New York, Weidenfeld & Nicolson, 1988

Neuberg, Victor E., *Popular Education in Eighteenth-Century England*, London, Woburn Press, 1971

Neville, Sylas, *The Diary of Sylas Neville*, ed. by B. Cozens-Hardy, London, Oxford University Press, 1950

Nichol[1], W., '"Malingering" and Convict Protest', *Labour History*, no. 47 (1984), 18–27

Nichol[2], W., 'Ideology and the Convict System, 1788–1820', *Historical Studies*, 22 (1986), 1–20

Nicholas, Stephen (ed.), *Convict Workers*, Melbourne, Cambridge University Press, 1988

Nicoll, Allardyce, *The Garrick Stage*, Manchester, Manchester University Press, 1980

Nicol, John, *The Life and Adventures of John Nicol, Mariner*, London, Cassell, 1937

Noah, William, *Voyage to Sydney in the Ship 'Hillsborough', 1798–1799, and a Description of the Colony*, Sydney, Library of Australian History, 1978

Nobbs[1], Raymond (ed.), *Norfolk Island and its First Settlement, 1788–1814*, North Sydney, Library of Australian History, 1988

Nobbs[2], Raymond (ed.), *Norfolk Island and its Second Settlement, 1825–1855*, Sydney, Library of Australian History, 1991

O'Connell, James F., *A Residence of Eleven Years in New Holland and the Caroline Islands*, Canberra, Australian National University, 1972

Odell, George Clinton Densmore, *Annals of the New York Stage*, 15 vols, New York, Columbia University Press, 1927–49

O'Farrell, Patrick, *The Irish in Australia*, Kensington, University of New South Wales Press, 1987

O'Keeffe, John, *The Castle of Andalusia*, London, 1794

Osborne, Alick, *Notes on the Present State and Prospects of Society in New South Wales*, London, 1833

Oswald, Harold, *The Theatre Royal in Newcastle-upon-Tyne*, Newcastle-upon-Tyne, Northumberland Press Ltd, 1936

Oxley, Deborah, 'Representing Convict Women', in *Representing Convicts,* ed. by Ian Duffield and J. Bradley, London, Leicester University Press, 1997, pp.88–105

Oxberry[1], William, *The Theatrical Banquet*, London, 1809

Oxberry[2], William and Catherine, *Oxberry's Dramatic Biography*, 4 vols, London, 1825–26

Paine, Daniel, *The Journal of Daniel Paine, 1794–1797*, ed. by R.J.B. Knight and A. Frost, Sydney, Library of Australian History, 1983

Palmer, Thomas Fyshe, *Narrative of the Sufferings of T.F. Palmer and W. Skirving*, Cambridge, 1797

Parke, William Thomas, *Musical Memoirs*, 2 vols, London, 1830

Parker, George, *A View of Society and Manners in High and Low Life*, 2 vols, London, 1781

Parsons, Philip (ed.), with Victoria Chance, *Companion to Theatre in Australia*, Sydney, Currency Press, 1995

Pasquin, Anthony [i.e. John Williams], *The Eccentricities of John Edwin*, 2 vols, London, 1791

Pedicord[1], Harry W., *The Theatrical Public in the Time of Garrick*, New York, Columbia University Press, 1954

Pedicord[2], Harry W., 'The Changing Audience', in *The London Theatre,* ed. by Robert Hume, Carbondale, Southern Illinois University Press, 1980, pp. 236–52

Perkins, Harold, *The Convict Priests*, Melbourne, H. Perkins, 1984

Péron, M. François, *A Voyage of Discovery to the Southern Hemisphere*, London, 1809

Pike, Douglas (gen. ed.), *The Australian Dictionary of Biography*, vols 1–2 [1788–1850], Melbourne, Melbourne University Press, 1966–67

Phillip, Arthur, *The Voyage ...to Botany Bay*, London, 1789

Porter, James, *The Capture of the Frederick*, Adelaide, Sullivan's Cove, 1981

Price, Cecil, *Theatre in the Age of Garrick*, Oxford, Basil Blackwell, 1973

Provis, J. Selkirk, 'Joseph Murrell-Sealer', *Descent*, 7 (1975), 75–87

Reid[1], – Mrs, 'Cursory Remarks on Board the *Friendship*', *The Asiatic Journal*, 8 (1819), 237–9, 344–7, 452–6, 555–8 and 9 (1820), 37–40, 130–4 etc.

Reid[2], Kirsty, '"Contumacious, Ungovernable and Incorrigible": Convict Women and Workplace Resistance in Van Diemen's Land, 1820–1839', in *Representing Convicts*, ed. by Ian Duffield and J. Bradley, London, Leicester University Press, 1997, pp. 106–23

Ritchie[1], John (ed.), *A Charge of Mutiny*, Canberra, National Library of Australia, 1988

Ritchie[2], John, *The Wentworths: Father and Son*, Melbourne, Melbourne University Press, 1997

Reynolds, Frederick, *The Life and Times of Frederick Reynolds*, 2 vols, London, 1826

Robson, Joseph Philip, *The Life and Adventures of the Far-Famed Billy Purvis*, Newcastle-upon-Tyne, 1849

Rodger, N.A.M., *The Wooden World*, London, Fontana Press, 1988

Rosenfeld, Sybil, *Temples of Thespis*, London, Society for Theatre Research, 1978

Rudé[1], George, 'Early Irish Rebels in Australia', *Historical Studies*, 16 (1974), 17–35

Rudé[2], George, *Protest and Punishment*, Oxford, Clarendon Press, 1978

Russell, Gillian, *The Theatres of War*, Oxford, Clarendon Press, 1995

Ryan[1], James T., *Reminiscences of Australia*, Sydney, Robertson [n.d.]

Ryan[2], R.J., *Land Grants, 1788–1809*, Sydney, Australian Documents Library, 1981

Ryley, Samuel William, *The Itinerant*, 6 vols, London, 1808–17

Schaffer[1], Irene (ed.), *Land Musters, Stock Returns and Lists: Van Diemen's Land, 1803–1822*, Hobart, St David's Park Publishing, 1991

Schaffer[2], Irene and Thelma McKay, *Exiled! Three Times Over*, Hobart, St David's Park Publishing, 1992

Schofield, Roger S., 'Dimensions of Illiteracy, 1750–1850', *Explorations in Economic History*, 10 (1972–3), 437–54

Schultz, William Eben, *Gay's 'Beggar's Opera': Its Content, History and Influence*, New Haven, Yale University Press, 1923

Shaw, John, *The Rocks: Sydney's Original Village*, The Rocks, Sydney, Sydney Cove Authority, 1990

Sheridan[1], Paul, *Penny Theatres of Victorian London*, London, Dennis Dobson, 1981

Sheridan[2], Richard Brinsley, *The Letters of Richard Brinsley Sheridan*, ed. by Cecil Price, 3 vols, Oxford, Clarendon Press, 1966

Skemp, John Rowland, *Letters to Anne*, Melbourne, Melbourne University Press, 1956

Smith[1], Alexander, *A Complete History of the Lives and Robberies of the Most Notorious Highwaymen*, ed. by A.L. Hayward, London, Routledge, 1926

Smith[2], Keith Vincent, *King Bungaree*, Kenthurst, NSW, Kangaroo Press, 1992

Smith[3], Nan, *Convict Kingston – a Guide*, Norfolk Island, Photopress International, 1997

Smith[4], William, *Journal of a Voyage on the Missionary Ship 'Duff'*, New York, 1813

Smyth, Arthur Bowes, *The Journal of Arthur Bowes Smyth: Surgeon, 'Lady Penrhyn', 1787–1789*, ed. by P.G. Fidlon and R.J. Ryan, Sydney, Australian Documents Library, 1979

Snagg, Thomas, *Recollections of Occurrences* [London], Dropmore Press, 1951

Southern, Richard, *The Georgian Playhouse*, London, Pleiades Books, 1948

Speckman, Charles, *The Life, Travels, Exploits, Frauds and Robberies, of Charles Speckman, alias Brown*, London, 1763

Statham, Pamela (ed.), *A Colonial Regiment: New Sources Relating to the New South Wales Corps, 1789–1810*, Canberra, Australian National University, 1992

Straub, Kristina, *Sexual Suspects: Eighteenth-Century Players and Sexual Ideology*, Princeton, Princeton University Press, 1992

Stieglitz, Karl Rawdon von, *Richmond: The Story of its People and its Places*, Launceston, Telegraph
    Printery [1953]

Sturma, Michael, 'Eye of the Beholder: the Stereotype of Women Convicts, 1788–1852',
    Labour History, no. 34 (1978), 3–10

Sumbel, Mary Leah, *Memoirs of the Life of Mrs. Sumbel*, 3 vols, London, 1811

Summers, Anne, *Damned Whores and God's Police*, Melbourne, Penguin, 1975

Suttor, George, *The Memoirs of George Suttor, F.L.S. Banksian Collector (1774–1859)*, ed. by G.
    Mackaness, Australian Historical Monographs, n.s., vol. 13, Dubbo, Review Publications,
    1977

Taylor, John, *Records of My Life*, 2 vols, London, 1832

Teasdale, Harvey, *The Life and Adventures of Harvey Teasdale, the Converted Clown*, Sheffield, 1867

Tench, Watkin, *Sydney's First Four Years: being a reprint of A Narrative of the Expedition to Botany
    Bay and A Complete Account of the Settlement at Port Jackson*, with an introduction and
    annotations by L.F. Fitzhardinge, Sydney, Library of Australian History, 1979

Therry, Roger, *Reminiscences of Thirty Years' Residence in New South Wales and Victoria*, 2nd edn,
    London, 1863

Thieme, John A., 'Spouting, Spouting-clubs and Spouting Companions', *Theatre Notebook*, 29
    (1975), 9–16

Thompson, – , *The Female Amazon … the Celebrated and Notorious Miss Fanny Davies*, London,
    1786

Thomson, Christopher, *The Autobiography of an Artisan*, London, 1847

Thorne, Ross, *Theatre Buildings in Australia to 1905*, 2 vols, Sydney, Architectural Research
    Foundation, University of Sydney, 1971

Tilke, Samuel Westcott, *An Autobiographical Memoir*, London, 1840

Trendall, John, *Operation Music Maker*, Southampton, Privately Published, 1978

Troubridge, St Vincent, *The Benefit System in the British Theatre*, London, Society for Theatre
    Research, 1967

Troy, Jakelin, '"Der mary this is fine country is there in the world": Irish-English and Irish in
    Late Eighteenth-Century Australia', in *The Irish Emigrant Experience in Australia* , ed. by
    John O'Brien and Pauric Travers, Dublin, Swords, 1991, pp.148–80

Tucker[1], James, *Ralph Rashleigh; or, The Life of an Exile by 'Giacomo di Rosenberg' (James Tucker)*, ed.
    (from the original manuscript) with intro. and notes by Colin Roderick, Sydney, Angus
    & Robertson, 1952

Tucker[2], James, *Jemmy Green in Australia*, ed. Colin Roderick, Sydney, Angus & Robertson,
    1955

Turner, Gordon and Alwyn Turner, *The History of British Military Bands*, 2 vols, Staplehurst,
    Spellmount, 1996

Van Lennep, William and others, *The London Stage, 1660–1800*, 11 vols, Carbondale, Ill., Southern
    Illinois University Press, 1965–68

Vason, George, *Life of the Late George Vason of Nottingham*, intro. by J. Orange, London, 1840

Vaux, James Hardy, *The Memoirs of James Hardy Vaux*, ed. by N. McLachlan, London, Heinemann,
    1964

Wagner, Leopold, *London Inns and Taverns*, London, G. Allen & Unwin, 1924

Walker, Robin Berwick, *The Newspaper Press in New South Wales, 1803–1920*, Sydney, Sydney
    University Press, 1976

Wallis, James, *An Historical Account of the Colony of New South Wales*, London, 1821

Ward, Ned, *The Wooden World Dissected*, 2nd edn, London, 1708

Waterhouse[1], Richard, *From Minstrel Show to Vaudeville: The Australian Popular Stage, 1788–1914*, Kensington, University of New South Wales Press, 1990

Waterhouse[2], Richard, *Private Pleasures, Public Leisure: A History of Australian Popular Culture since 1788*, South Melbourne, Longman, 1995

Watts, Susanna, *Original Poems and Translations … chiefly by Susanna Watts*, London, 1802

Watson, Eric R., *The Trial of Thurtell and Hunt*, Sydney, Butterworth [1920]

Wendenborn, Gebhard Friedrich August, *A View of England towards the Close of the Eighteenth Century*, 2 vols, London, 1791

Wentworth, William Charles, *A Statistical, Historical and Political Description of the Colony of New South Wales*, London, 1819

Wertenbaker, Timberlake, *Our Country's Good*, London, Methuen/Royal Court, 1988

West[1], John, *The History of Tasmania*, 2 vols, Launceston, 1852

West[2], John, *Theatre in Australia*, Stanmore, NSW, Cassell Australia, 1978

West[3], Obed, *The Memoirs of Obed West*, ed. by E.W. Marriott, Bowral, Barcom Press, 1988

Weston, Thomas, *Memoirs of that Celebrated Comedian … Thomas Weston*, London, 1776

Whitaker[1], Anne-Maree, *Unfinished Revolution: United Irishmen in New South Wales, 1800–1810*, Sydney, Crossing Press, 1994

Whitaker[2], Anne-Maree, *Joseph Foveaux: Power and Patronage in Early New South Wales*, Kensington, University of New South Wales Press, 2000

White[1], Charles, *Early Australian History: Convict Life in New South Wales and Van Diemen's Land*, Bathurst, 1889

White[2], John, *Journal of a Voyage to New South Wales*, ed. by A.H. Chisholm, Sydney, Angus & Robertson, 1962

Wilkinson, Tate, *The Wandering Patentee*, 4 vols, York, 1795

Wilson[1], Graham and Martin Davies, *Norfolk Island: Archaeological Survey, Kingston – Arthur's Vale Region*, 2 vols, Dickson, ACT, Department of Housing and Construction, 1980

Wilson[2], James, *A Missionary Voyage to the Southern Pacific Ocean*, London, 1799

Winston, James, *The Theatric Tourist*, London, 1805

[Wontner, Thomas], *Old Bailey Experience*, London, 1833

Wright[1], Reg, *The Forgotten Generation of Norfolk Island and Van Diemen's Land*, Sydney, Library of Australian History, 1986

Wright[2], Reg, 'Who was 'Buckey' Jones?', *Descent*, 28 (1998), 122–5

Wynn, Frances W., *Diaries of a Lady of Quality*, ed. by A. Hayward, London, 1864

Index

Page numbers in bold type, e.g. **21–6**, refer to detailed discussion of the topic.
Page numbers in italic type, e.g. *48*, refer to illustrations.
Names beginning with Mc are filed as if spelled Mac.

A

Abbott, Edward (military officer), 115–6, 118, 275, 281, 331n.21

Abbott, Thomas (business partner of Sidaway), 253

Aborigines, 83, 102–3, 225–6, 276

Abrahams, Esther, 99

Ackerman, James (alias My Lord), 13

acting: Britain, **21–6**, 78–9, 81–2, 146, 153, 289; Emu Plains, 155, 160; New South Wales, 40, 78, 96; Norfolk Island, 114, 188

actors
  Britain, 82–3, 91, 167–8, 263, 283, 301n.39; income, 21–2
  New South Wales, 21–2, 26, 201–3 (*See also* theatrical experience)
  Emu Plains, 144, 150, 153, **160–70**, 201–2, 204, 288–90, 310n.2, 312n.58, 312n.63, 313n.81; later careers, 174–6, 190, 195, 291–2, 312n.56
  Norfolk Island, 122–4, 127–32, 134, 190–2, 194–5, 267–78, 287, 291
  Port Macquarie, 182–3
  Sydney (1789), 29–30, 201, 300n.4
  Sydney theatre (1796–1800), 30, 40, 43, 49, 54, **85–97**, 102, 131, 140, 147, 165, 170, 201, 269; biographical notes, 207–27, 229, 232–50, 253–62; income, 78–84; playbills, *44, 48, 50–2*
  Sydney (after 1807), 139–40, 144, 179–82

actors' benefits, 60, 81, **81–4**, 86–7, 102, 108, 128. *See also* charity performances

actresses
  Emu Plains, 164
  fictional, 6
  Norfolk Island, 122, 132, 211
  Sydney theatre, 47–*52*, 80–1, 85–6, 93–6, 102; biographical notes, 213–7, 222, 233–7, 241, 244–7, 255, 261–2

Acts of Parliament, 13, 18, 73–4

Adams, Mary, 47

addresses. *See* prologues, epilogues & addresses

administrative terms, **x–xi**

advertising: Emu Plains theatre, 154, 156, *157*, 173, 205, **289–91**; Norfolk Island theatre, *126*; Sydney theatre, 72, 79. *See also* playbills

afterpieces & interludes: Britain, 19, 26; Emu Plains, 170–1, 294–5; Norfolk Island, 129, 193–4; Port Macquarie, 183; Sydney, 38, 40, 42–4, 54, 74, 84, 103, 149, 293–4

Airds district, NSW, 162, 169, 269

alcohol
  banned from theatres, 49, *52*–3
  drinking & drunkenness, 13, 27, 104, 115, 174, 197, 225, 241, 251, 264, 291; actors on stage, 95, 283; audiences, 16, 21, 49, 53, 117
  gift of wine to performers, 163
  selling, 125, 127, 130, 209–10, 216–7, 219, 229, 258, 260 (*See also* taverns)

Aldis, Henry, 170, 174

All the World's a Stage (Isaac Jackman), 130

Allen, George, 140–1

Allen, Susannah, 214

Alt, Augustus (Surveyor-General), 258, 281

Alt (or Ault), Sarah (Mrs Flynn), 267–8

amateur theatricals. *See also* spouting
  Britain, 5, 11, 23–6, 128, 130, 149, 263, 280
  Calcutta, 96
  New South Wales, 142, 180–3; Emu Plains, 155, 172–3; Norfolk Island, 128–30; Port Macquarie, 279

Anderson, Joseph (Colonel), 188

Anderson, Mary, 256

Anglicans, 141, 148, 195, 291

'The Antipodean Whirligig' (Robinson), 103

Appin (Airds district), 162, 169, 269

The Apprentice (Arthur Murphy), 24

Arndell, Thomas (surgeon), 281

Arnott, Thomas, 181

assignment of convicts: Emu Plains theatre, 162,

351

Subscribers

Australian Drama Studies Centre, University of Queensland
Humanities Research Program, University of New South Wales
National Institute of Dramatic Art
School of English, Media Studies and Art History, University of Queensland
The Conservatorium, University of Newcastle
School of Theatre, Film and Dance, University of New South Wales

Eric Alexander
Don Batchelor
Philip Bell
Frederick Blackwood
Katharine Brisbane
Jill Brown
Kalman A. Burnim
Mark Carpenter
Dennis Carroll
Terence Clarke
Mimi Colligan
Bill and Linda Condon
Bluey Considine
Peter R. Cooke
Professor Roger Covell
Jim Davis
William Dean
Bill Dunstone
Kim Durban
Richard Fotheringham
Jeremy Gadd
Peter Gerdes
Hilary and John Golder
Ray Goodlass
Professor Warwick Gould
Wayne Harrison

Ken Healey
Robert D. Hume
Alexander Hyslop
G. Hyslop and G. Borny
Charles and Donna Jordan
Harriet Jordan
Jin Hee Jordan
Grace Karskens
Veronica Kelly
Clive Kessler
Diane Kirkby
Adrian Kiernander
Margaret Leask
Living Dodo Puppets
Harold Love
Jenny Lovett
Louise and Richard Madelaine
Ian Maxwell
Dr Gay McAuley
John McCallum
Douglas McDermott
Dr Ian McGrath
Rob McMurdo
Ailsa McPherson
Judith Milhous
Geoffrey Milne

Jessica Milner-Davis
Tara Moss
Katherine Newey
Derek Nicholson
Louis Nowra
Pamela O'Brien
Paul Orenstein
Kathy Robson
Camilla Rountree
Dr Rodney Seaborn, AO OBE
David Spurgeon
Lesley Stern
Jayne Symon
Henri Szeps, OAM
Peta Tait
G.M. and J.M. Tallis
Ross Thorne
Greig Tillotson
John Tulloch
Frank Van Straten, OAM
Richard Waterhouse
David Watt
Elizabeth Webby
Ian Wilkie
Don Wilkie
Chris Worth

Bell Shakespeare Company
Company B Belvoir
Department of Performance Studies, University of Sydney
International Federation for Theatre Research
Io Myers Studio Production Unit
University of New South Wales Library
Swiss Theatre Collection, Berne

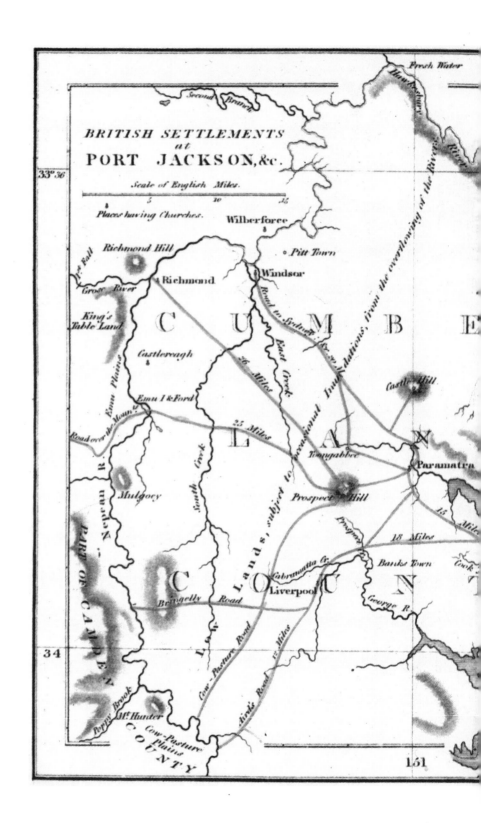

BRITISH SETTLEMENTS
at
PORT JACKSON, &c.

Scale of English Miles.

Places having Churches.

151